THE

KINGFISHER
SCIENCE
ENCYCLOPEDIA

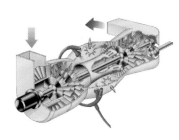

KINGFISHER
Larousse Kingfisher Chambers Inc.
95 Madison Avenue
New York, New York 10016

First published in 2000
2 4 6 8 10 9 7 5 3 1

1TR/0600/CC/UNIV/128JWADMA

LIBRARY OF CONGRESS CATALOGING-IN-PUBLICATION DATA
The Kingfisher science encyclopedia / edited by Professor Charles Taylor.—1st ed.
p. cm.
Includes index.
Summary: An illustrated science encyclopedia arranged in such catagories as "Planet
Earth," "Living Things," "Chemistry and the Elements," "Materials and Technology,"
"Space and Time," and "Conservation and the Environment."
ISBN 0-7534-5269-3
1. Science—Encyclopedias, Juvenile. [1. Science—Encyclopedias.] I. Taylor, Charles
(Charles A.)

Q121 .K55 2000
503—dc21   00-024556

Printed in Hong Kong

GENERAL EDITOR
Professor Charles Taylor, D. Sc., F.Inst.P.,
Emeritus Professor of Physics at the University of Wales,
former Professor of Experimental Physics at the
Royal Institution of Britain

CONTRIBUTORS
Clive Gifford, Elizabeth Longley, Peter Mellett, Martin Redfern, Tom Schiele,
Carole Stott, Richard Walker, Brian Williams

PROJECT TEAM
Project Director and Art Editor Julian Holland
Editorial Team Martin Clowes, Leon Gray, Julian Holland,
Rachel Hutchings, Mike McGuire
Designers Julian Holland, Jeffrey Farrow, Nigel White
Commissioned Artwork Julian Baker
Picture Research Wendy Brown

FOR KINGFISHER
Managing Editor Miranda Smith
Senior Editor Terry Moore
Art Director Mike Davis
DTP Coordinator Nicky Studdart
DTP Operator Primrose Burton
Editorial Team Julie Ferris, Denise Heal,
Laura Marshall, Sheila Clewley
Artwork Research Wendy Allison, Steve Robinson,
Christopher Cowlin
Production Manager Caroline Jackson

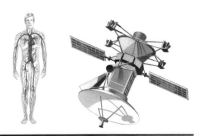

THE
KINGFISHER
SCIENCE
ENCYCLOPEDIA

KINGfisher

NEW YORK

CONTENTS

CHAPTER 5
MATERIALS AND TECHNOLOGY

CHAPTER 6
LIGHT AND ENERGY

CHAPTER 7
FORCES AND MOVEMENT

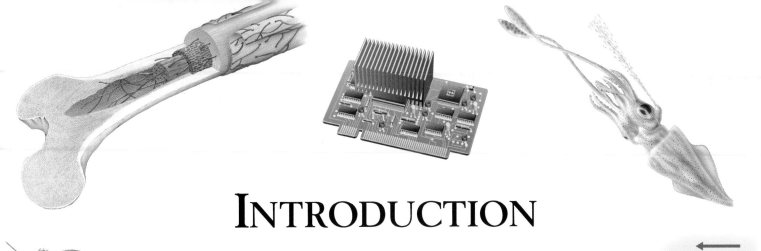

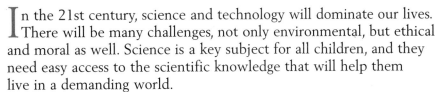

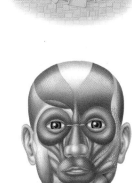

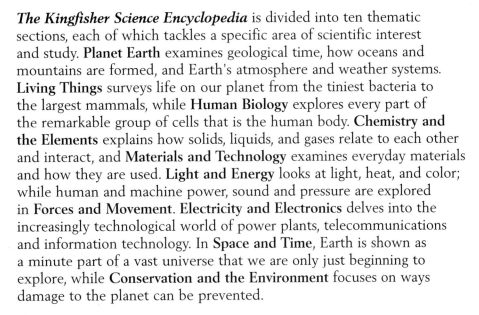

INTRODUCTION

In the 21st century, science and technology will dominate our lives. There will be many challenges, not only environmental, but ethical and moral as well. Science is a key subject for all children, and they need easy access to the scientific knowledge that will help them live in a demanding world.

The Kingfisher Science Encyclopedia is divided into ten thematic sections, each of which tackles a specific area of scientific interest and study. **Planet Earth** examines geological time, how oceans and mountains are formed, and Earth's atmosphere and weather systems. **Living Things** surveys life on our planet from the tiniest bacteria to the largest mammals, while **Human Biology** explores every part of the remarkable group of cells that is the human body. **Chemistry and the Elements** explains how solids, liquids, and gases relate to each other and interact, and **Materials and Technology** examines everyday materials and how they are used. **Light and Energy** looks at light, heat, and color; while human and machine power, sound and pressure are explored in **Forces and Movement**. **Electricity and Electronics** delves into the increasingly technological world of power plants, telecommunications and information technology. In **Space and Time**, Earth is shown as a minute part of a vast universe that we are only just beginning to explore, while **Conservation and the Environment** focuses on ways damage to the planet can be prevented.

The encyclopedia has been written by a team of specialist science authors and consultants led by the eminent Professor Charles Taylor, the first holder of the Royal Society's Michael Faraday Award for contributions to the Understanding of Science in 1986. Whether *The Kingfisher Science Encyclopedia* is used for school work, or simply dipped into at random, it will add to knowledge, stimulate natural curiosity and creativity, and prepare the inquiring mind for an exciting future world.

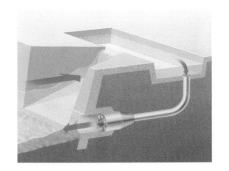

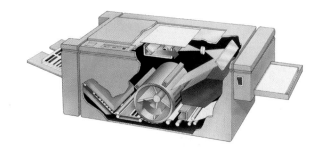

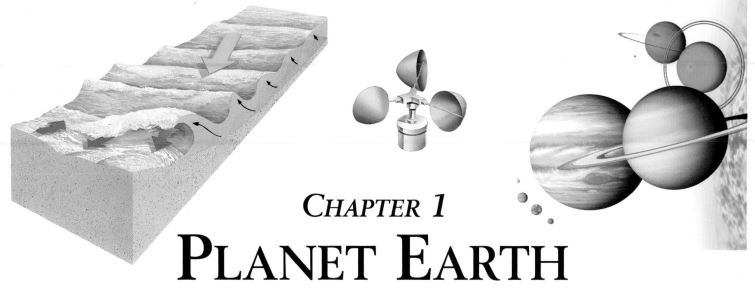

CHAPTER 1
PLANET EARTH

The ground beneath our feet seems to be the most solid and unchanging thing we know. It forms foundations for our cities and an environment in which we can live. Yet, in reality, the Earth is spinning on its axis and hurtling through hostile space, as it orbits the nuclear furnace of our sun. The Earth is an active, dynamic, living planet.

The rock-solid surface is not as solid as it appears. Rather, it is cracked into many irregular, slow-moving slabs. Earthquakes shake our cities and volcanoes erupt, giving clues to the fiery movements beneath the ground. From above, the planet is buffeted by radiation and particles streaming at it through space. But between these extremes is an atmosphere, oceans, and temperatures that are just right for life.

Viewed from space, the Earth would immediately stand out as something special. The composition of the atmosphere, with free oxygen and traces of gases like methane, can only be sustained by life. One could detect the characteristic green of chlorophyll, the pigment used by plants on land and algae in the sea to trap sunlight. Even the cacophony of our radio broadcasts reveals that life here is at least moderately intelligent.

Life has transformed the Earth, and the Earth continues to support life. Buried in the rocks are minerals, gems, and precious metals. Using energy from the Earth in the form of coal and oil, we have transformed them into the artifacts of civilization, from books and buildings to cars and computers.

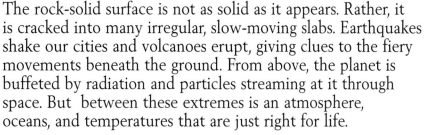

EARTH AND THE SOLAR SYSTEM

A solar system consists of a star and the planets and other bodies that orbit around it. The Earth is the third planet from the sun in our solar system.

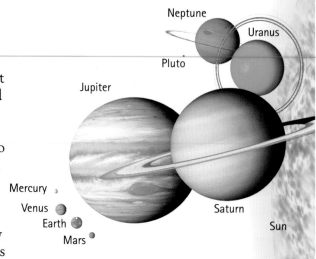

The sun (right) dwarfs everything else in the solar system, even the gas giants Jupiter and Saturn. The Earth and its closest neighbors (left) are minute in comparison.

When the universe began, around twelve billion years ago, the first elements to form were hydrogen and helium. Nuclear reactions in early generations of stars produced the other elements and spat them into space as clouds of dust and gases.

Five billion years ago, one of these clouds began to contract. A spinning ball of dust and gas formed at its center, and gravity compressed this ball until it was hot enough to form a star—the sun.

THE ORIGINS OF EARTH

Radiation from the young sun blew away much of the remaining dust cloud. What was left formed a disk of dust around the sun. Over time, the dust grains clumped together to form rocky lumps. These lumps bumped into each other, sometimes joining together in a process called accretion. Slowly, the dust disk was transformed into a few planets, one of which was to become the Earth.

As the Earth gathered mass, its gravitational field increased. The force of gravity pulled the dust into a ball and

The Earth formed from a disk of dust that surrounded the sun when it was only a few hundred million years old. The dust clumped together in a process called accretion.

compressed it until it started to melt. A dense core of molten iron formed, surrounded by a solid mantle of silicate rock. Volcanoes and colliding debris helped to form the surface features of the new planet. When the Earth was almost complete, an object the size of Mars crashed into it. This threw a cloud of material into orbit. This dust condensed and formed the moon.

OTHER PLANETS

Mercury is closest to the sun. It has a barren, rocky surface and practically no atmosphere. Next are Venus, Earth, and Mars. Venus is about the same size as the Earth; Mars is slightly smaller. Carbon dioxide in Venus's atmosphere led to a greenhouse effect that boiled away any water. On Mars, water froze or escaped into space and left a cold desert. If life began on Mars or Venus, it did not thrive. On Earth, algae consumed carbon dioxide from the atmosphere. This kept the climate balanced and produced oxygen. Beyond Mars are Jupiter, Saturn, Uranus, and Neptune—giant planets consisting of gas. Beyond these is tiny Pluto, a ball of frozen rock.

This satellite image of the Earth was taken by a camera on a Meteosat weather satellite 22,250 mi. (35,800km) above the equator as it crossed the Western Hemisphere. It shows the rich blues of the oceans and the swirling cloud patterns in the atmosphere of a planet where conditions are just right for life.

SEE ALSO PAGES:

244–5 Radiation, 398–9 The solar system, 400–1 Earth and the moon

EARTH'S ROTATION

The Earth spins like a top as it orbits the sun. These rotations cause daily, annual, and seasonal variations in sunlight and temperature on the Earth's surface.

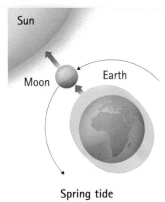

Sun

Moon

Earth

Spring tide

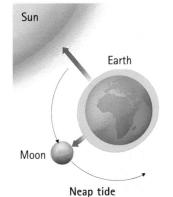

Sun

Earth

Moon

Neap tide

Viewed from the Earth's surface, the sun seems to rise in the east, cross the sky, and set in the west. Stars do the same by night. Until the 1500s, people believed that the Earth was fixed, and the sun and stars moved around it. We now know that the sun and stars seem to cross the sky because the Earth rotates around its axis every day. The Earth also orbits the sun in 365¼ days; this gives us our year.

THE LUNAR MONTH
The moon orbits Earth in around 27 days. It takes about 29 days—a lunar month—to pass through all its phases. After each new moon, the moon is completely dark. It then appears as a thin crescent, lit from one side. The lit area then grows, or waxes, until it becomes full. Finally, the moon wanes until it becomes a thin crescent again.

TIDES AND ECLIPSES
As the moon orbits the Earth, its gravity pulls water in the oceans toward it. The changes in water level that result are called tides. The sun also affects tides. The greatest tidal variations, called spring tides, occur when the sun and moon pull in the same direction.

Occasionally, the Earth comes between the sun and the moon and casts a shadow on the moon. This event is called a lunar eclipse. A solar eclipse is when the moon comes between the Earth and the sun. While the radius of the moon is only ¼₄₀₀ the radius of the sun, the moon is ¼₄₀₀ as far away, so total eclipses can happen.

OTHER CYCLES
Sometimes, the Earth's orbit around the sun is less circular and more elliptical. Also, the Earth's rotation axis slowly wobbles like an off-kilter spinning top. The cumulative effects of these changes in the Earth's cycles can be striking. They can even dramatically affect the planet's climate balance.

▲ Spring tides result when the sun and moon pull the waters of the oceans in the same direction. The much weaker neap tides happen when the moon pulls at right angles to the sun.

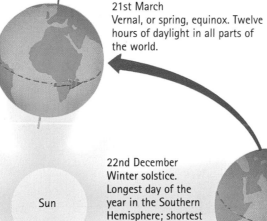

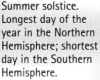

21st March
Vernal, or spring, equinox. Twelve hours of daylight in all parts of the world.

21st June
Summer solstice. Longest day of the year in the Northern Hemisphere; shortest day in the Southern Hemisphere.

Sun

22nd December
Winter solstice. Longest day of the year in the Southern Hemisphere; shortest day in the Northern Hemisphere.

23rd September
Autumnal equinox. Twelve hours of daylight in all parts of the world.

The Earth rotates around an axis inclined at 23 degrees to the planet's orbit around the sun. This tilt causes seasonal variations of daylight hours and climate. In March and September, the sun is directly over the equator. In June, the Northern Hemisphere is angled toward the sun and becomes warmer. In December, the Southern Hemisphere is angled toward the sun and experiences summer. The Northern Hemisphere has winter at this time. Near the poles, there are weeks in the summer when the sun does not set and weeks in the winter when it does not rise.

SEE ALSO PAGES:

394–5 The sun, 400–1 Earth and the moon, 402 Eclipses

FOSSILS AND GEOLOGICAL TIME

Fossils are the preserved remains of once-living organisms. Some are 3.5 billion years old, and all provide vital clues about the Earth's distant past.

The Upper Carboniferous, or Pennsylvanian, period (323–290 m.y.a.), is the source for much of our coal. Fern leaves like this one would gradually have sunk and been compacted, eventually forming deposits of coal. The hard coal would have preserved impressions of the organic matter from which it was formed—in this case a delicate leaf.

The origins of life have long posed a dilemma. Most cultures have stories that relate to the creation of life on Earth—humans are usually seen as the pinnacle of the process, but their creation often coincides with the beginning of time. In 1650, for example, with biblical events as his historical guide, Archbishop Ussher, of the Church of Ireland, decided that all life was created in 4004 B.C. But it is hard to see how the planet could have changed so much in such a short space of time. The discovery of the remains of once-living organisms in the form of fossils remained a mystery.

In the 1800s, geologists realized that slow changes still taking place could account for the rise and fall of the mountains and the discovery of fossils. At the time, scientists dated the Earth at over 20 million years. Today, however, rocks can be dated with some precision by calculating the amounts of radioactive elements within them. Carbon 14, a radioactive form of carbon, for example, is known to decay at a fixed rate, and this

This fossil of a marine reptile called an ichthyosaurus was preserved in shale that dates from the lower Jurassic period. The specimen was found near Lyme Regis, in southern England. Ichthyosaurus was a fast swimmer. It fed on fish, and used its sharp teeth to tear its prey apart.

is used to date charcoal that is up to 50,000 years old. Other elements can date far older rocks and show that the history of the Earth began over 4.5 billion years ago.

CHARTING THE EVIDENCE

Careful study of fossils has revealed that similar life forms existed at the same time in different parts of the world. As a result, fossils have become useful for dating rock. The different types of fossils found in rocks change with time, providing an evolutionary history of life. Sometimes the changes were slow and gradual. Sometimes they seem very sudden, and entire groups of plant or animal species disappear from one layer to the next. A few successful species seem to continue almost unchanged for millions of years, while others perish. Sometimes a sudden

FORMATION OF A FOSSIL

When an organism dies, the remains of its body become buried and will slowly fossilize. Usually only the hard parts, such as shells or bones, survive. Sometimes the remains gradually become stone—the original molecules are replaced by minerals such as calcite or iron pyrites. Often, however, the fossil contains many of the original molecules. A new science called molecular paleontology compares the chemicals or even the genes of extinct species with species that continue to live on the Earth.

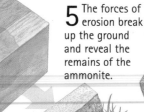

5 The forces of erosion break up the ground and reveal the remains of the ammonite.

1 In the Jurassic period, around 150 million years ago, a type of mollusk called an ammonite dies and falls to the bottom of the ocean.

2 The soft body parts of the ammonite decay or are eaten by predators.

3 The empty shell is then covered by sand and mud.

4 The sand and mud layers are compressed, turn to stone, and lift up and tilt into land above sea level.

6 A fossil hunter cracks open the stone to reveal the fossil and the mold it has left in the rock.

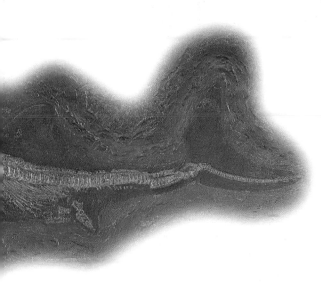

Mya			
21	Quaternary		Cenozoic
	Pliocene		
	Miocene		
	Oligocene		
65	Paleocene and Eocene		
	Cretaceous		Mesozoic
135			
	Jurassic		
195			
	Triassic		
225			
	Permian		Paleozoic
280			
	Carboniferous		
345			
	Devonian		
395			
	Silurian		
430			
	Ordovician		
500			
	Cambrian		
570			
	Precambrian		

◄ Geological time is divided into a series of periods. Each period is characterized by a different range of fossil creatures. The Precambrian period represents 85 percent of the history of the Earth. However, rocks dating from this period are poorly preserved, and there were few large creatures to leave fossils.

In special circumstances, the remains of soft-bodied creatures turn into fossils. Over 40 million years ago, tree resin trapped this fly. The resin turned into amber, and the fly and some of its genetic material have been preserved within it.

diversification populated the world with a whole new range of creatures. The changes define the boundaries between geological periods. The intervals are thought to have occurred as a result of major catastrophes. Some of them may have been triggered by large asteroids or comets hitting our planet and disrupting the climate. At the end of the Cretaceous period, 65 million years ago, thousands of species, including the dinosaurs, are known to have become extinct. This boundary also coincides with an enormous impact crater in the Gulf of Mexico. An asteroid, perhaps over half a mile across, hit the Earth and vaporized, spreading a cloud of dust around the planet, blocking out energy from the sun, and starting global forest fires. Even more species had become extinct at the end of the Permian period 225 million years ago. Indeed, mass extinctions of various degrees mark the boundaries of most of the geological periods.

LIFE ON EARTH

The last 65 million years of the story of life are marked by the rise of the mammals, along with broad-leaved trees and flowering plants. About 200 million years prior to this period, dinosaurs and their relatives ruled the land, and a rich variety of marine life populated the warm seas. In the Carboniferous period, about 300 million years ago, extensive swamps supported a lush growth of primitive plants such as tree ferns and cycads. The remains of these plants have resulted in deposits of coal. Before then, there is not much evidence

for life on land. However, the oceans were teeming with life. Fossils from the Precambrian period, 600 million years ago, are scarce. During this time, there were few large plants and animals on the Earth.

A COMMON ANCESTOR

Life on the Earth began more than 3.6 billion years ago, its component chemicals seeded from space soon after the new planet cooled. But for three billion years, microscopic bacteria and algae dominated. Then, possibly because of a change in climate and the release of nutrients as a supercontinent broke apart, a host of larger, multicellular plants and animals appeared. By 600 million years ago, the ancestors of most of the groups of organisms that exist today had emerged. Among them was what may be our own distant ancestor.

Mounds of cyanobacteria (bacterial blue-green algae), known as stromatolites, are found in the warm tidal waters of Shark Bay in western Australia. Stromatolites are the fossilized remains of some of the earliest-known living organisms on the planet. The Australian stromatolites are more than 3.5 billion years old.

SEE ALSO PAGES:

6–7 Human origins, human change, 50–1 Life: origins and development

HUMAN ORIGINS, HUMAN CHANGE

One mammal appeared late in the history of the Earth, but it is the most successful of all creatures. The species is *Homo sapiens,* or the human being.

Among the rarest of all fossils are those of human ancestors and their relatives. Dinosaurs still roamed the Earth when the first primate-like animal appeared—the tree shrew. By 55 million years ago the ancestors of present-day lemurs had also developed, with their grasping hands and feet, binocular vision, and relatively large brains. The first monkeys date to around 30 million years ago, and apes go back eight to ten million years.

THE FIRST HUMAN ANCESTORS

Molecular evidence suggests that the first human ancestors diverged from those of chimpanzees about five million years ago. The best candidates for fossils of human ancestors come from eastern and southern Africa. In 1974, the three-million-year-old skeleton of a possible ancestor called *Australopithecus* was uncovered near Hadar in Ethiopia. Anthropologists worked out that the specimen was female and nicknamed her "Lucy." Lucy had an apelike skull and a small brain, but her arms were short, and she could walk upright on her long legs. A similar species may have been responsible for the fossilized footprints found at Laetoli in Tanzania, which are 3.6 million years old.

It is not clear which, if any, of the *Australopithecus* species was directly related to present-day humans. However, a new species that appeared about 1.8 million years ago almost certainly was. In 1984, a team of anthropologists headed by Richard Leakey unearthed the bones of a 12-year-old boy near Lake Turkana in Kenya. The bones were 1.5 million years old and belonged to a species called *Homo erectus,* which means upright human. The appearance of this species is characterized by a dramatic change in the quality of stone tools, from roughly chipped stones to carefully crafted hand axes and scrapers. *Homo erectus* was also a traveler and explorer, and spread from Africa into Europe and as far afield as China and Java.

A COMMON ANCESTOR

Evidence suggests that the final chapter in our evolution began in Africa about 500,000 years ago. Similarities in the genetic material of all modern humans suggests they had a common ancestor at that time. Climate change and inquiring

Richard Leakey (1944–) is a member of a family of anthropologists famous for their work in eastern Africa. Here he holds the skull of an *Australopithecus.* This genus of animals is not a direct human ancestor, but is thought to be a close relative.

This well-preserved fossil hand was found in 1999 in limestone in caves near Sterkfontein in South Africa. The fossil has been dated at around three million years old. It also belonged to an *Australopithecus.*

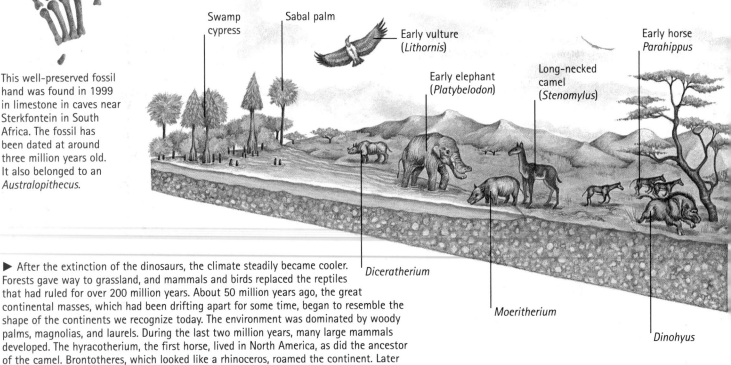

Swamp cypress — Sabal palm — Early vulture (*Lithornis*) — Early elephant (*Platybelodon*) — Long-necked camel (*Stenomylus*) — Early horse *Parahippus* — *Diceratherium* — *Moeritherium* — *Dinohyus*

▶ After the extinction of the dinosaurs, the climate steadily became cooler. Forests gave way to grassland, and mammals and birds replaced the reptiles that had ruled for over 200 million years. About 50 million years ago, the great continental masses, which had been drifting apart for some time, began to resemble the shape of the continents we recognize today. The environment was dominated by woody palms, magnolias, and laurels. During the last two million years, many large mammals developed. The hyracotherium, the first horse, lived in North America, as did the ancestor of the camel. Brontotheres, which looked like a rhinoceros, roamed the continent. Later there were saber-toothed tigers, followed by the ancestors of pigs, sheep, and cattle.

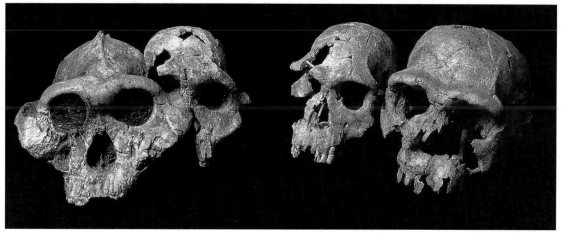

These are some of the skulls of human ancestors or their relations. Many species and subspecies have been discovered. At some points, different species must have lived alongside one another, perhaps in competition. Evolution, however, drove toward species with larger brains. In the end, this trend gave rise to our own species, *Homo sapiens*, the best adapted to survive in the changing world.

The deep brow ridges and powerful jaws of a male *Australopithecus robustus*. He was well adapted to chewing coarse vegetation.

A female *Australopithecus robustus* also had muscular jaws, but they were slightly less powerful.

The more lightweight skull of *Australopithecus afarensis*, the species to which the famous specimen "Lucy" belongs.

Homo erectus, with an enlarged skull, became the dominant African primate around 1.6 million years ago.

minds led these people into northern Europe, rich in large game animals but still coping with the effects of the ice age. By this time, an adaptable *Homo sapiens* had almost certainly learned how to make fire. About 200,000 years ago, a subspecies, commonly called the Neanderthals, moved into Germany and western Europe. But, by about 35,000 years ago, they were being replaced by truly modern humans.

People have changed the face of the Earth. With their large brains, they were able to develop tools and to communicate by using language. Their control of fire is recorded in ocean sediments and marks the mass burning of the African savannas. By about 10,000 years ago, the last ice age was coming to an end. This climate change meant that people no longer had to rely on herds of wild animals and natural grasslands. Instead, they started to clear the land, plant seeds, and herd livestock. This period was the dawn of agriculture, and the more reliable sources of food it brought freed some of the population to build temples and palaces, found the first cities, and develop the art and culture that today we call civilization.

The first modern humans appeared 35,000 years ago. By this time, they could make efficient tools. These delicate flint arrowheads required great skill to make, and would have been excellent tools for hunting large animals.

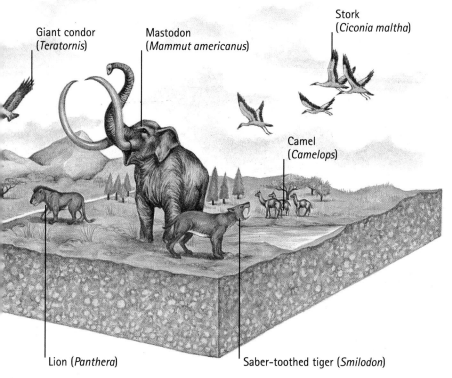

Giant condor (*Teratornis*)

Mastodon (*Mammut americanus*)

Stork (*Ciconia maltha*)

Camel (*Camelops*)

Lion (*Panthera*)

Saber-toothed tiger (*Smilodon*)

This footprint was preserved in hardened volcanic ash. A line of them was left in Tanzania 3.6 million years ago, perhaps by a family of human ancestors. By examining such fossil evidence, scientists can work out the behavior of our ancestors. For example, it is clear that these ancestors were bipedal (could walk on two feet). This is seen as a major turning point in human evolution.

SEE ALSO PAGES:

4–5 Fossils and geological time, 50–1 Life: origins and development

EARTH'S STRUCTURE

The Earth's layered structure consists of a central core, a mantle, and a crust. The planet is constantly changing because of its inner dynamic forces.

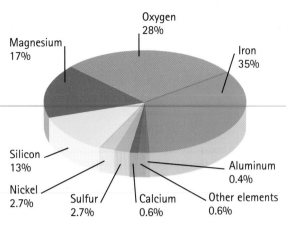

Iron is the largest component of the Earth. This metal is concentrated in the molten core. Compounds called magnesium silicates, which contain magnesium, silicon, and oxygen, form the bulk of the mantle. Most of these elements were formed in space millions of years ago.

Geological processes such as volcanic eruptions, often reveal clues about the Earth's interior. This dense rock originated in the Earth's mantle and contains a green mineral known as olivine. It was brought to the surface during an eruption in the Canary Islands.

⇨ Transverse (S) waves

⇨ Primary (P) waves

⇨ Surface waves

Unlike the rocks at the Earth's surface, the rocks deep within its center are squeezed at such tremendous pressures and temperatures that, even though they are solid, they can flow slowly like ice in a glacier. Early in the planet's history, the densest material, mostly metallic iron and nickel, settled to form a molten core. This core is the densest part of the Earth, with a radius over 1,800 mi. (2,900km). Above the molten outer core is the mantle. This is made up of dense silicate rocks. The ocean crust and continents float on these layers like a film of oil on the surface of water.

INSIDE THE CORE

Conditions in the Earth's core are hard to imagine. Pressures are enormous and the temperature exceeds 5,432°F. Geologists can measure the temperature of the boundary between the inner and outer core. The Earth's core is made up of iron mixed with certain impurities. Scientists have recreated the pressures within the Earth's core and discovered the temperature there to be nearly 7,232°F.

The molten iron in the outer core is slowly circulating. Electrical currents within it generate the Earth's magnetic field. This reaches far into space, and forms a magnetic envelope around the planet's surface. This deflects electrically charged particles from the sun and shields us from harmful radiation. The magnetic field generated in the core probably varies enormously, but most of the variations are dampened by the mantle. However, every 100,000 years or so, they become so great that the magnetic field of the planet reverses entirely.

LOOKING INSIDE THE PLANET

The heat generated by the formation of our planet is still cooling, and it is being released from the interior as the inner core freezes and as radioactive elements decay. This heat has to escape, but rock is a good insulator. To let the heat out, the mantle rocks surrounding the inner core have to circulate. Heat is carried up as hot mantle rock rises. At the surface, where the rock is brittle, the movement causes earthquakes. Seismologists, scientists who study

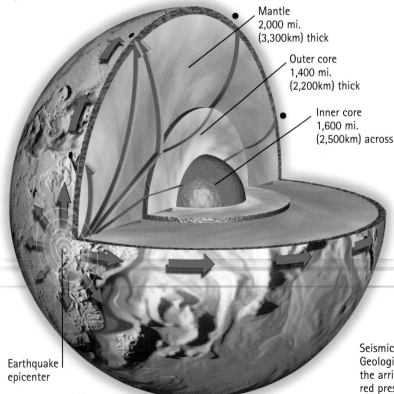

Mantle
2,000 mi.
(3,300km) thick

Outer core
1,400 mi.
(2,200km) thick

Inner core
1,600 mi.
(2,500km) across

Earthquake epicenter

Seismic waves reverberate from an earthquake in eastern Africa. Geologists can work out features of the planet's structure by timing the arrival of the waves at monitoring stations around the world. The red pressure waves can pass through the molten outer core. The blue transverse waves can pass through only the solid mantle and crust.

earthquakes and vibrations, operate a network of monitoring stations. By timing the arrivals of the earthquake (seismic) waves at different stations, powerful computers can build up a picture of the Earth's interior.

ACTIVITY WITHIN

Scans of the Earth reveal plumes of hot mantle material rising toward the surface, often topped by volcanic activity. The seismic waves pass more slowly through this hot, soft material. It contrasts with cold, hard rock that descends into the mantle where cold ocean crust disappears beneath continents. By analyzing the seismic data, geologists have found a barrier about 420 mi. (670km) down into the mantle. Descending rock seems to accumulate there. This leads some geologists to speculate that the entire mantle is not mixing in a single circulation, but that there are two layers of circulating rock.

Recent analysis of seismic data suggests that there is another thin layer at the base of the mantle, many miles thick. This layer is not continuous, but is more like a series of giant continents on the underside of

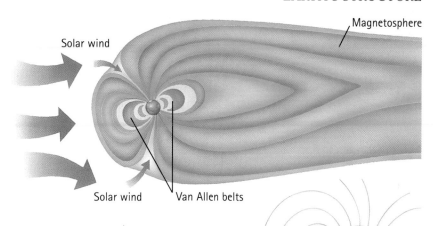

▲ The magnetic field created by the Earth forms an envelope called the magnetosphere. This stretches far above the planet's surface into space. The wind of charged particles streaming out from the sun pushes on the magnetosphere so that it streams out downwind like the tail of a comet.

▶ The shape of the magnetic field makes it look as if there were a huge bar magnet inside the Earth. The strong lines of magnetic force are actually created by electric currents circulating within the molten outer core.

the mantle. The slabs could have formed by the mixing of silicate rocks in the mantle with iron-rich material from the core. Another explanation, however, is that this region is where ancient oceans came to rest. After descending to the base of the upper mantle, the cold ocean crust compressed into an extremely dense rock layer. Then this layer could break through the 415-mile (670-km) layer and sink further. This layer continues to spread out at the base of the mantle. As the core slowly heats the dense rock layer, it will rise once more to form new ocean crust.

WORKING OUT THE CLUES

Land compressed by ice during the last ice age, together with the pull of the moon on the tides, is gradually slowing down our spinning planet. As a result, the lengths of the days and nights are increasing by tiny amounts. However, there are other even smaller variations of a few billionths of a second. These may be the result of atmospheric pressure on mountain ranges. More importantly, the circulation in the outer core pushes on ridges and valleys, similar to upside-down mountains, in the base of the mantle. The changes in day length are a measure of the core's circulation, and provide another clue to the geological processes inside the Earth.

The aurora borealis fills the night sky above the Arctic Circle. Where the Earth's magnetic field converges on the poles, charged particles from the sun hit atoms in the atmosphere, creating the spectacular display. The aurora australis occurs in regions surrounding the South Pole.

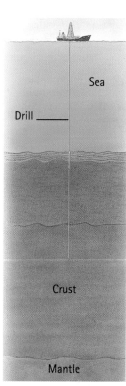

Drill cores can reveal the layers of rock in the Earth's crust. It has not yet been possible to drill through to the mantle.

SEE ALSO PAGES:

10–11 Earth's atmosphere, 20–1 Earthquakes, 400–1 Earth and the moon

EARTH'S ATMOSPHERE

A gaseous envelope called the atmosphere surrounds the Earth. It protects us from the extremes of space, keeps us warm, and causes our weather systems.

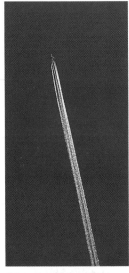

A jet aircraft accelerates through the atmosphere, leaving a visible record of its passage, called a vapor trail, behind it. The trail is supercold air caused by the deposition of water vapor in the engine exhaust as tiny crystals of ice.

Without the atmosphere, living organisms would not be able to survive the constant barrage of solar and cosmic radiation, bombardment by meteors, and exposure to extremes of temperature. The atmosphere protects living things from these potentially lethal threats by surrounding the Earth with a layer of gases, liquids, and other particles, 190 mi. (300km) thick. The force of gravity holds the atmosphere in place. Near the Earth's surface, the atmosphere is highly compressed, but it gets thinner with increasing altitude. In the lower levels of the atmosphere, winds and storms distribute the heat from the sun. In the upper levels, the molecules that make up the atmosphere collide with incoming meteors and radiation.

A BRIEF HISTORY

For the first billion years of the Earth's life, the atmosphere was very different from ours today. Originally, it was a mixture of nitrogen, carbon dioxide, and water vapor. Carbon dioxide is known as

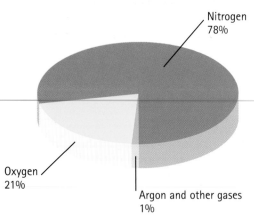

This pie chart reveals the composition of the Earth's atmosphere. Nitrogen and oxygen make up most of the atmosphere. Other gases include argon, carbon dioxide, and methane. Human activities have increased the levels of these gases, warming the climate considerably.

a greenhouse gas. This means that it lets sunlight through to warm the planet, but prevents heat from escaping. As a result, carbon dioxide acted like a blanket to keep the young Earth warm. When the first living things evolved, they began to use up the carbon dioxide in the atmosphere. Because the sun was growing stronger, a balance was struck. In addition, the organisms released a new gas—oxygen. This meant that other animals could survive by breathing oxygen, first through gills and eventually through lungs. In the last billion years or so, oxygen concentrations have stayed constant.

LAYERS OF THE ATMOSPHERE

The atmosphere does not have a definite boundary. Space satellites orbit more than 190 mi. (300km) above the Earth's surface—here an atmosphere exists, but it is so thin it is almost a vacuum. This region is called the thermosphere. Atoms are very hot up there (up to 3,632°F), but so sparse they would not burn you.

This is a section through the atmosphere from sea level up to the beginnings of space. The troposphere makes up the first 9.5 mi. (15km) of the atmosphere and contains the world's weather systems and major aircraft routes. About 12.5 mi. (20km) up is the protective ozone layer, within the stratosphere, which is thin and cold. Weather balloons can rise through the stratosphere, and supersonic aircraft and clouds of volcanic ash reach it. Above it lies the mesosphere, which includes the radio-reflective layer of the ionosphere. The thermosphere stretches up into space and contains the exosphere, where gas molecules escape into space. Aurorae occur toward the base of the thermosphere at each pole.

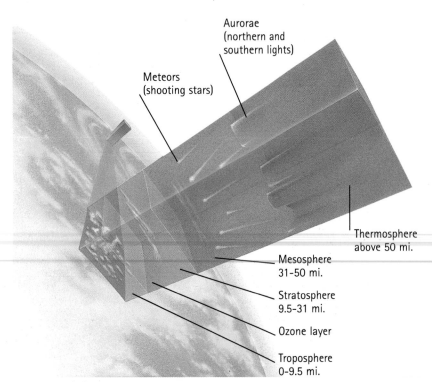

Aurorae (northern and southern lights)

Meteors (shooting stars)

Thermosphere above 50 mi.

Mesosphere 31-50 mi.

Stratosphere 9.5-31 mi.

Ozone layer

Troposphere 0-9.5 mi.

The thermosphere reaches down to about 50 mi. (80km) above the Earth's surface. Here a region called the mesosphere begins. Atoms within the mesosphere are ionized. This means that they have lost electrons and can reflect shortwave radio waves. This area is commonly called the ionosphere and is extremely important for global radio communications. The stratosphere is the next layer, reaching down to about 9.5 mi. (15km) above the Earth's surface. This colder layer contains the ozone layer, a protective screen that blocks out potentially harmful ultraviolet radiation from the sun, but it has been damaged by chemicals released by human activities. Powerful volcanic eruptions can inject dust and acidic gases into the stratosphere. The troposphere makes up the last 9.5 mi. (15km) of the atmosphere and contains 80 percent of its mass. In this part of the atmosphere, the world's weather runs its course.

A DELICATE BALANCE

The atmosphere hangs in a precarious dynamic balance. In the process known as photosynthesis, plants constantly absorb carbon dioxide and produce oxygen. Conversely, animals absorb oxygen in a process called respiration, and return carbon dioxide and other gases, such as methane, to the atmosphere. Today, human activities have transferred much of the carbon stored in rocks back into the atmosphere. This process is causing the world's climate to get warmer.

Similarly, the ozone layer is rapidly depleting as a result of human activities, allowing harmful solar radiation to reach the surface. If we continue to disrupt the atmosphere, our planet may not be such a comfortable place to live in the future.

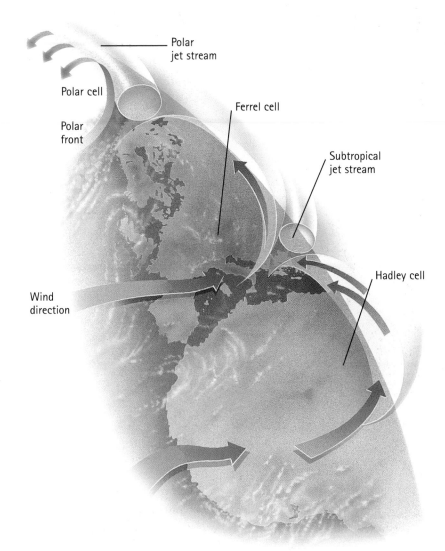

Polar jet stream

Polar cell

Ferrel cell

Polar front

Subtropical jet stream

Hadley cell

Wind direction

▲ Atmospheric circulation transfers heat to and from the equator by a series of convection cells. The first cell, called a Hadley cell, transfers warm air north over the tropics. The temperate latitudes are under the control of the Ferrel cell. Lastly, polar cells, as their name suggests, cover both poles.

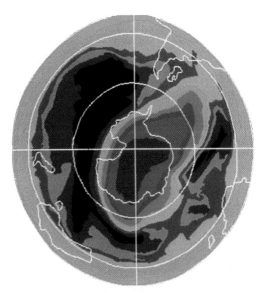

◄ For more than 20 years a hole has appeared in the stratospheric ozone above Antarctica every October. In the cold, still air of the Antarctic winter, chlorine-containing chemicals, called chlorofluorocarbons, break down the ozone. The hole is observed here in satellite data from space.

A scientist studies data at the observatory high on Mauna Loa in Hawaii. Pulses of laser light are used to measure the amount of dust, volcanic gas, and ozone in the stratosphere above.

SEE ALSO PAGES:

36–7 Climate, 56–7
Plant anatomy, 460
Climate change

THE OCEANS

More than 70 percent of the Earth's surface is covered by water. Around two percent of that water is ice; less than one percent is freshwater and water vapor.

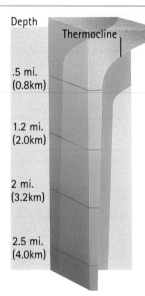

Depth
Thermocline
.5 mi. (0.8km)
1.2 mi. (2.0km)
2 mi. (3.2km)
2.5 mi. (4.0km)

Water at the surface of the ocean is warmed by the sun. Waves mix this warm water with cooler water to a depth of about 328 feet. Beneath this, there is little mixing, and the temperature falls rapidly. The boundary between the warm (pink) and cool (blue) layers is called the thermocline. This boundary prevents nutrients in deep water from moving up.

→ Cold currents
→ Warm currents

Four billion years ago, the Earth's surface was too hot for water to exist as liquid. Water that was erupted as steam in volcanic gases boiled away to be lost in space. Around 3.85 billion years ago, the Earth had cooled to form an atmosphere of volcanic gases, including steam. Water began to condense and form oceans in dips in the Earth's surface.

Since the oceans formed, rain has been falling on land and washing salt from rocks into the sea. This is why seawater tastes salty. On average, 2.9 percent of an ocean is salt. Seas such as the Baltic, with plenty of freshwater from rivers and little evaporation, are less salty. The Dead Sea, where evaporation is rapid, is six times more saline (salty) than average.

UNDER THE SURFACE

When we look out across the ocean we are only aware of its surface. But the average depth of the oceans is around 36,080 feet, and the deepest ocean trenches reach down 16,400 feet. Mount Everest is more than 6,000 feet shorter than these trenches are deep.

The top few feet of the oceans can be as warm as 79°F in the tropics. They take in heat from sunlight during the day and warm the atmosphere at night. This layer of the oceans contains more heat than the entire atmosphere. Where there are

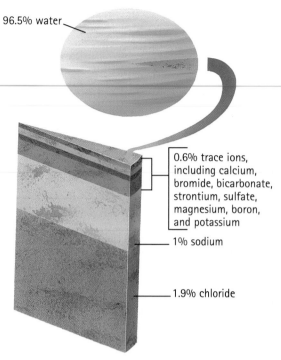

96.5% water

0.6% trace ions, including calcium, bromide, bicarbonate, strontium, sulfate, magnesium, boron, and potassium

1% sodium

1.9% chloride

Average seawater contains 96.5 percent water. Almost three percent is sodium chloride, which gives seawater its salty taste. There are traces of many other salts.

dissolved nutrients in the sunlit waters, extensive blooms of tiny marine algae or phytoplankton flourish. But the warm water floats on the top of the ocean, and very often nutrients are scarce unless they are washed down in rivers or stirred up from deeper water. Beneath the sunlit or photic zone lies a very different world of cold, dark water. Yet it supports a rich diversity of life. The oceans provide food for millions of people. They also conceal rich deposits of oil, gas, and minerals.

OCEAN CURRENTS

Heat circulates in the oceans in a series of large circular currents or gyres. Blown by the winds, they tend to flow clockwise in the Northern Hemisphere and counterclockwise in the Southern Hemisphere. This pattern is disrupted by the continents.

The currents of water at the surfaces of oceans are driven by prevailing winds. These currents move in swirls, called gyres. Most warm currents start near the equator, and most cool currents start near the poles. The Gulf Stream and North Atlantic Drift carry warm water from the Straits of Florida toward western Europe and Scandinavia. The Antarctic gyre is a circular current of cold water that flows clockwise around the South Pole.

THE POWER OF WAVES

Waves begin in the open sea as simple up-and-down oscillations, driven by the wind. As the wave advances, the water moves in a circular motion. As the wave enters shallow water near the shore, the lower part of that motion is slowed down and the crests of the waves break or topple over, and pound onto the shore. The forward motion, or swash, drives sand and gravel up the beach, the backwash pulls it back down. Where waves meet the shore at an angle, material drifts along the beach.

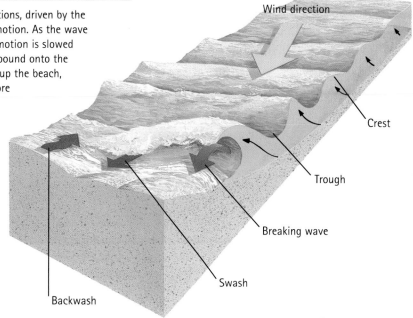

Wind direction
Crest
Trough
Breaking wave
Swash
Backwash

Where large waves from the open sea meet the shore, spectacular breakers can build up. They offer an exciting and sometimes dangerous challenge to surfers.

A map of the main ocean currents at the surface does not reveal the deep circulation that also takes place. The Gulf Stream and the North Atlantic Drift bring warm waters from the Gulf of Mexico northeast across the Atlantic. This keeps western Europe and the British Isles warm. As the warm water flows along, some of it evaporates, and the water gradually becomes cooler and more salty. This makes the water more dense. Eventually, it becomes too dense to stay on the surface. The water then dives down and turns south to complete the circulation like a conveyor belt. If this conveyor belt stopped, western Europe would have winters as cold as those in northeastern Canada.

EXPLORING THE DEPTHS

The deep oceans are the least explored parts of our planet. Going there in a submarine or even sending robot craft can be as complex as mounting a space mission. The crushing pressure on the ocean floor is far greater than that encountered by any spacecraft.

Strange worms, blind shrimp, and giant squid have been found in deep oceans, as well as hydrothermal vents, which eject water as hot as 662°F. Living bacteria that have been found in deep-sea sediments suggest that more than one tenth of life on the Earth lies in the mud and rock beneath the seabed. It is possible that these life-forms are relatives of the first species to colonize the planet.

The Dead Sea lies on the border between Israel and Jordan. Its water comes mainly from the Jordan River. The sea has no exit, so water can only escape by evaporation. This process concentrates salts in the sea, making it a hostile environment for marine species. The salt makes the water so dense that the human body floats easily on its surface.

◀ This satellite image shows the green plant pigment, chlorophyll, in phytoplankton in the oceans. The concentration of plankton in the oceans (shown as yellow and green here) is highest where warm water and plentiful nutrients mix and produce blooms of plankton.

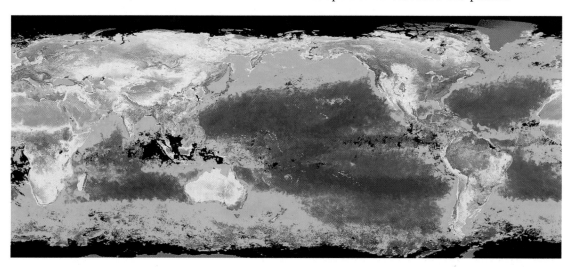

SEE ALSO PAGES:

10–11 Earth's atmosphere,
14–15 The ocean floor,
440–1 Ocean life

THE OCEAN FLOOR

Under the sea there are volcanoes, mountain ridges 43,500 mi. (70,000km) long, and chasms that dwarf the Grand Canyon. They are all clues to the Earth's interior.

Photographed from a submersible, this black smoker lies 10,168 feet beneath the surface of the Atlantic Ocean. Mineral-rich water leaves its rocky vents at 662°F, but soon cools to provide a habitat for primitive bacteria and other forms of life.

The most striking features of the oceans are the mid-ocean ridges that cross the planet's surface like the seam of a tennis ball. Volcanic vents are peppered along the ridges. Sometimes these vents erupt slowly underwater and lava oozes from them like toothpaste from a tube. When the lava comes into contact with the cold seawater, it solidifies, producing pillow-shaped lumps of dense black basalt.

Some vents produce so much lava that they rise through the surface of the sea and form volcanic islands. This happens when a vent sits above a rising plume of hot material in the Earth's mantle. In these zones, new ocean crust forms as the seabed cracks open and spreads.

HYDROTHERMAL VENTS

In areas where the seabed is spreading, water percolates through cracks in the ocean floor. When it meets hot rock, it is heated and dissolves minerals. The water then rises through cracks in the rocks and gushes out of hydrothermal vents at temperatures as high as 662°F. The pressure at the seabed prevents water from boiling at this temperature. As the water starts to cool, the salts that are dissolved in it come out of solution as fine particles. This makes the dark, mineral-rich water resemble a plume of smoke, which is why hydrothermal vents are also called black smokers.

Hydrothermal vents release heat and minerals, particularly metal sulfides. This combination supports colonies of bacteria, tube worms, blind shrimp, and giant clams. These are among the few organisms on the Earth that do not depend on sunlight for energy. Instead, they derive energy for life from sulfide minerals from hydrothermal vents.

THE OCEAN FLOOR

New ocean floor is formed when molten magma rises from the Earth's mantle at a mid-ocean ridge. It cools and hardens as the crust spreads out from the ridge in both directions. Faults cross ridges along their length, and break them into sections. At the center of the ridge is a depression, or rift valley. Where the ocean crust meets a continent, it sinks down into a subduction zone, often forming an ocean trench. As the wet rock enters the mantle, part of it melts and, mixed with steam, rises through the overlying continent to produce violent volcanic eruptions. The ocean floor is not so much being pushed open as pulling itself apart, causing rifting and lowering the pressure at the ridge so more magma can rise.

Descending plate

Moving plate

Continental crust

Subduction zone

Central rift valley

Oceanic crust

Upper mantle

Rising magma

SUBDUCTION

Scientists found evidence of sea-floor spreading in the 1960s, when they discovered stripes of magnetization in the rocks on either side of ridges. These stripes record the reversals of the Earth's magnetic field that occur about every half-million years. The magnetization of crust rock is frozen in the direction that Earth's magnetic field had when it first surfaced at the ridge and solidified.

Hardly any ocean crust is more than a hundred million years old, however, which is a tiny fraction of the Earth's age. Where does old ocean crust go? The process that consumes ocean crust is called subduction. When a slab of ocean crust runs into a continent, the crust sometimes slips under the continent. Seabed sediments are scraped off the surface of the descending crust and pile up as ridges of silt. The ocean crust starts to melt when it enters the hot mantle. Water in the crust forms high-pressure steam, which can force hot, molten rock up to the surface through volcanoes. This effect is responsible for an arc of volcanic activity, called the Ring of Fire, which surrounds the Pacific Ocean.

CONTINENTAL DRIFT

The Atlantic Ocean is widening at a rate of 1–1.5 inches a year. The ocean floor in parts of the Pacific is spreading at up to 4 inches a year. This might seem slow, but it can result in spreads of several thousand miles over hundreds of millions of years. For example, the Atlantic Ocean did not exist until 80 million years ago, but because of sea-floor spreading over millions of years, the Atlantic is now thousands of miles wide.

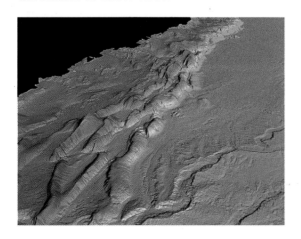

This map of the floor of the Atlantic Ocean shows the mid-Atlantic ridge snaking from Iceland in the north to the southernmost part of the South Atlantic. The Atlantic Ocean began to form around 80,000,000 years ago, after the supercontinent of Gondwanaland broke up. Before then, South America and Africa were joined. This is why the shape of the Brazilian Peninsular matches the shape of the western coast of Africa.

Around 250 million years ago, all the Earth's continents were joined together as a single supercontinent, called Pangaea. Around 200 million years ago, Pangaea broke up to form Gondwanaland in the south and Laurasia in the north. These two continents split again and their fragments were driven apart by sea-floor spread in the gaps between them.

Oceans can expand from mid-ocean ridges, and they can also vanish as land masses move together. In this way, India became linked to Asia and Africa, and Italy joined Europe. Sediments that once covered the ocean floor piled up to form the Tibetan plateau and the Jura mountains north of Geneva. The basalt slab of the ocean floor has sunk back down into the mantle.

This picture of the bed of the Pacific Ocean was made using sonar pulses. It shows the continental shelf off the coast of Oregon. Artificial coloration reveals the depth of the ocean: from white at sea level, orange to 3,280 feet, yellow to 6,560 feet, and blue to 9,840 feet. The long ridges are seabed sediments that piled up where the ocean crust slipped under the edge of the North American continent.

A volcano rises through the surface of the sea.

A fringe of coral grows as the volcano wears away.

A ring of coral stays after the volcano has gone.

▲ A string of volcanic islands forms where one slab of ocean floor sinks under another. In tropical waters, coral reefs form around the islands. Over time, the soft volcanic rock erodes, leaving a circular reef, or atoll.

Mount Everest 29,021 ft.

Mauna Kea 33,465 ft.

Mauna Kea, Hawaii, rises 33,465 feet from the floor of the Pacific Ocean. Mount Everest is around 4,428 feet lower.

SEE ALSO PAGES:

8–9 Earth's structure, 12–13 The oceans, 16–17 Continental drift

CONTINENTAL DRIFT

The Earth's land masses move around the surface of the planet. Over millions of years, they have broken up and joined together to form the present continents.

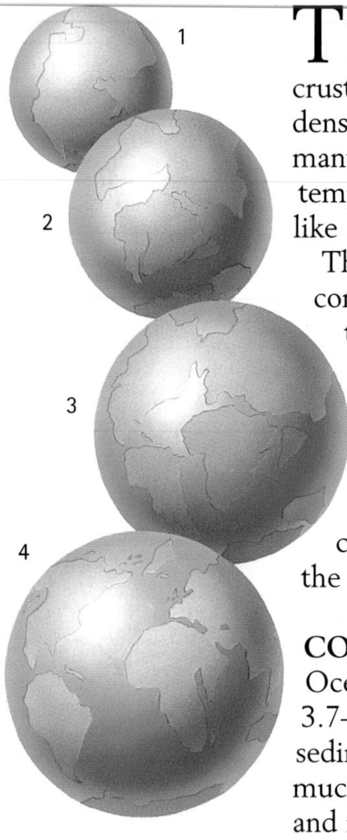
1
2
3
4

▲ 200 million years ago, there was only Panagaea, a supercontinent (1). 100 million years ago, North America was splitting away from Europe. South America was separating from Africa (2). By around 80 million years ago, Africa was about to collide with Europe, and India was joining Asia (3).
Fifty million years from now, Africa is likely to have joined Europe, and North America will have separated from South America, and become joined with Asia (4).

The Earth's solid surface consists of slabs of ocean crust and continental crust. Both types of crust float on the denser rock of the mantle. Although the mantle rock is solid, the pressure and temperature in the mantle make it flow like a thick paste.

The transfer of heat from the Earth's core makes the mantle rock rise from the core toward the surface and sink back again, just as water swirls around a pan when it is placed on a hot stove. This process is called convection. As the surface of the mantle rock moves, it causes the continents to drift slowly around the Earth's crust.

CONTINENTAL CRUST

Ocean crust is a layer of dense basalt just 3.7–4.3 mi. (6–7km) thick, perhaps with sediments on top. Continental crust is much thicker, averaging 18.6 mi. (30km) and reaching 37.3 mi. (60km) in mountain ranges. Because it is mostly silica-rich granite and sediment, it is less dense than ocean crust, and it floats like a scum on the Earth's surface. Like a floating iceberg, the higher the mountains, the deeper the continent's roots sink into the mantle.

Ocean crust is continually being created and destroyed, so its sediment is relatively new. But continental material has been accumulating ever since the Earth's surface solidified. The material at the center of some continents, including Australia and North America, is up to four billion years old. A continent grows thicker as sediment piles up around its edges, volcanoes erupt new rocks onto it, and molten rock is injected into its base.

Where the base pushes lowest into the mantle, it heats up and can begin to melt. Granite is the result of this melting. Lubricated by moisture in the rocks that formed it, vast areas of granite can rise through a continent like giant bubbles of liquid. The granite bakes the rock around it as it solidifies to form great masses of crystalline rock. Rocks exposed by surface erosion produce stark landscapes.

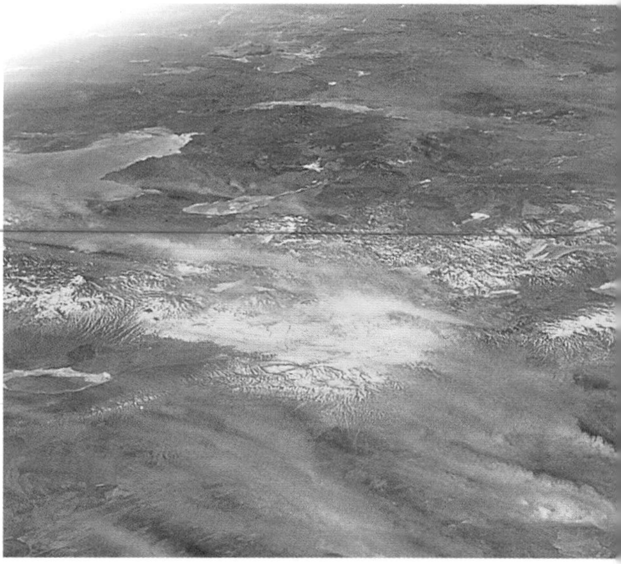

This view of the Andes was taken from a NASA space shuttle. The mountain range runs 5,530 mi. (8,900km) along the western coast of South America. It formed when the edge of the continental plate buckled under pressure from the Pacific plate, which lies to its west.

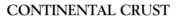

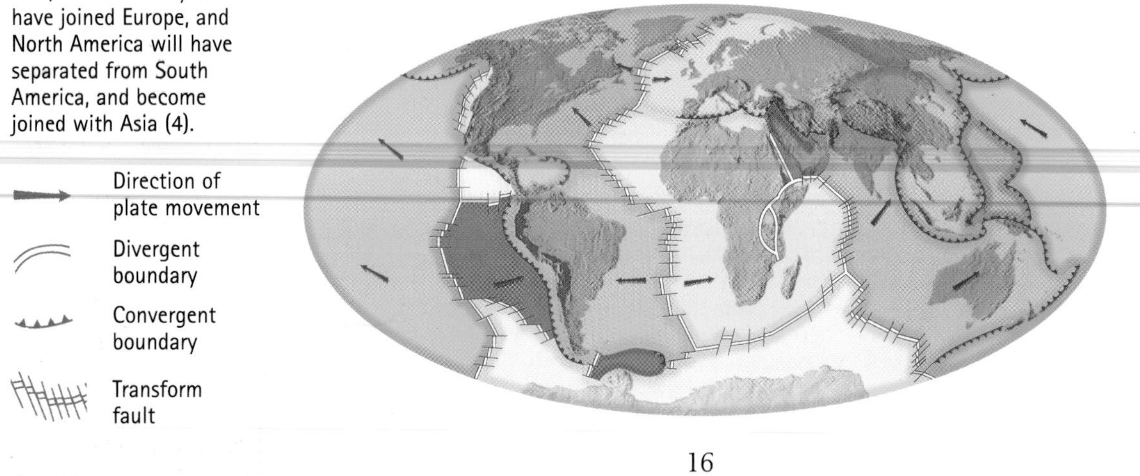
Direction of plate movement
Divergent boundary
Convergent boundary
Transform fault

The tectonic plates of the Earth's crust are shown here in different colors. The red arrows on this map show in which direction each plate is moving. Some plates are drifting apart, some are moving together, and others are grinding past one another. Most volcanic activity and earthquakes happen at the edges of tectonic plates.

◄ This photograph looks southeast along the San Andreas fault in California. The Pacific plate, right, is gradually moving northwest relative to the North-American plate.

Fault line

▲ The stars on this map show the epicenters of past earthquakes along the San Andreas fault. It is difficult to forecast where or when the next earthquake will happen.

PLATE TECTONICS

The slabs of continental and ocean crust that drift around the Earth are called plates. Plate tectonics is the theory of how these plates have split, moved, and collided to form the Earth's surface.

Tectonic plates do not move rigidly across the Earth's surface. Continents can stretch as they move. When this happens, the crust becomes thinner and the surface level drops. The Great Rift Valley, which runs from Syria to Mozambique, formed when the African continent stretched at a weak point. The North Sea formed when the European continent stretched. If a continental plate stretches too much, it can break up. New ocean crust then forms between the fragments.

When tectonic plates collide, they buckle at the edges and form mountain chains. The Alps formed when Africa collided with Europe. The Himalayas, which formed when India crashed into Asia, are still rising as the plates push together.

FAULT LINES

A boundary between two tectonic plates is called a fault. When neighboring plates move in different directions, they grate against each other. This happens at the San Andreas fault, close to the coast of California. If the movement at the fault sticks for months or years, enormous stress can build up in the surrounding rocks. An earthquake results when the fault finally gives and releases stress.

Although continents drift only an inch or so a year, they can be tracked by lasers that measure movement at fault lines, or by satellite monitoring. Geologists can trace the history of continental drift using the magnetism of volcanic rocks, which record the magnetic field at the time and place where they solidified.

This pile of granite is on a hill in southwest England. Granite solidified from molten rock that had bubbled up from the Earth's mantle. With time, wind and rain wore away the hill and left the hard granite exposed.

◄ The North American continental plate. Pressure from neighboring plates has buckled the edges of the continent, and formed vast mountain ranges. There are volcanoes in the west, where the Pacific plate dives under the continental plate.

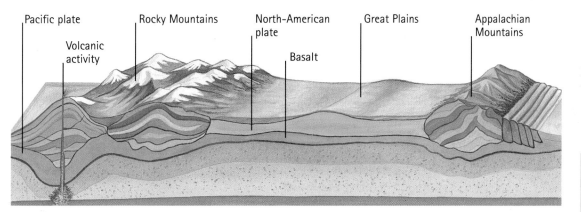

Pacific plate

Volcanic activity

Rocky Mountains

North-American plate

Basalt

Great Plains

Appalachian Mountains

SEE ALSO PAGES:

VOLCANOES

A volcano is an opening in the Earth's crust through which molten lava, ash, and gases erupt. In many cases, lava and ash form a mountain around the opening.

Fissure volcanoes erupt through narrow slits.

Shield volcanoes ooze runny lava over wide areas.

Dome volcanoes are formed by sticky lava.

Conical volcanos form from volcanic ash.

Composite volcanoes may have several side vents.

Calderas are formed by explosive eruptions.

▲ The shape of a volcano depends on the type of lava and how it erupts. Cone-shaped volcanoes are formed from layers of ash and cinders that have sprayed from a central crater. Broad calderas are formed when a volcano first bulges then erupts in a violent explosion.

It used to be thought that volcanoes leaked molten rock and gases directly from the Earth's core. That is not the case. As hot, solid rock rises in the mantle, the pressure drops and a small part of the rock begins to melt. This liquefied rock, called magma, is less dense than solid rock. It squeezes out from the solid like water from a sponge. The rising magma creates wide channels in the crust as it forces its way to the surface. When it breaks through the surface, the pressure drops. Gases dissolved in the magma force it to erupt through the opening as lava.

TYPES OF VOLCANOES

The behavior of a volcano depends on the type of magma that fuels it. Volcanoes such as those near Hawaii and Iceland are sitting on top of a rising plume of hot mantle rock, called a hot spot. The lava that erupts from these volcanoes comes from great depths, sometimes more than 90 mi. (150km) into the mantle. Its composition is not the same as the mantle, because only a tiny fraction of the mantle rock melts. This lava is runny when molten and sets as dense, black basalt. Because the lava is so runny, it can pour out through fissures at vast rates and flow across the land at speeds of up to 31 mph (50kph). Where this type of volcano erupts underwater, the lava cools quickly and

This photograph shows Mount Etna, in Sicily, erupting at night. Gas eruptions spray lumps of molten rock from a crater, and result in a spectacular fiery fountain.

builds volcanic islands as it sets. Where gas bubbles through it, the runny lava erupts in spectacular fountains. Because this type of lava flows freely, eruptions are smooth rather than explosive.

A different type of volcano is found where ocean crust dives under the edge of a continent. The ocean crust partly melts to form a sticky lava that is rich in silica and contains some water. During an eruption, the sudden drop in pressure causes the water to turn to steam. This results in an explosion of fine ash and hot gases. This mixture, which can race down the sides of a volcano at 125 mph (200kph), is called a *nuée ardente*, French for "glowing avalanche."

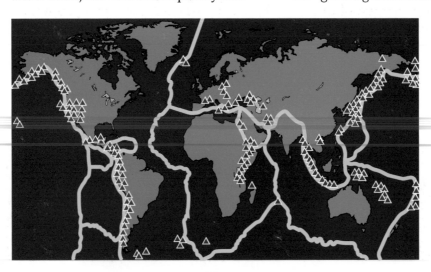

◄ This map shows the sites of active volcanoes as pink triangles. Most volcanoes are located near plate boundaries (yellow). Some are located over hot spots in the Earth's mantle.

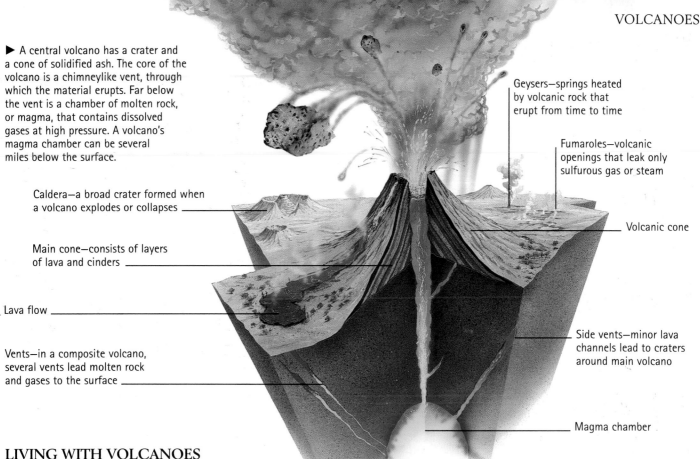

▶ A central volcano has a crater and a cone of solidified ash. The core of the volcano is a chimneylike vent, through which the material erupts. Far below the vent is a chamber of molten rock, or magma, that contains dissolved gases at high pressure. A volcano's magma chamber can be several miles below the surface.

Geysers—springs heated by volcanic rock that erupt from time to time

Fumaroles—volcanic openings that leak only sulfurous gas or steam

Caldera—a broad crater formed when a volcano explodes or collapses

Volcanic cone

Main cone—consists of layers of lava and cinders

Lava flow

Side vents—minor lava channels lead to craters around main volcano

Vents—in a composite volcano, several vents lead molten rock and gases to the surface

Magma chamber

LIVING WITH VOLCANOES

With their combinations of red-hot lava, toxic gases, and suffocating ash, volcanic eruptions can be deadly phenomena. But people continue to live on the sides of volcanoes despite the danger. This is because volcanic soil is often fertile, and eruptions can be few and far between, giving a false sense of security. The consequences can be disastrous. In 1902, when Mount Pelée on the Caribbean island of Martinique erupted, a *nuée ardente* raced down the mountain and engulfed the port of San Pierre. More than 29,000 people were killed. The only survivor was a prisoner in an underground cell. In A.D. 79, a similar eruption from Mount Vesuvius smothered the Roman towns of Boscoreale, Herculaneum, Pompeii, and Stabiae with mud and ash.

It is possible to predict at least some eruptions by monitoring volcanic gases and measuring changes in gravity as molten lava rises inside a volcano. Sometimes, the whole mountain bulges. When Mount St. Helens, in Washington, started to bulge in 1980, most people were evacuated before the mountain blew its top. A huge landslide removed part of the volcano, exposing the pressurized molten lava. The lava then exploded sideways and upward. The blast hurled about half a cubic mile of rock into the air and flattened trees up to 19 mi. (30km) away.

On May 18, 1980, Mount St. Helens, in Washington, erupted with enormous force. The blast of fast-moving dust and hot gases devastated the landscape, killing all forms of life and snapping great pine trees like matchsticks.

These photographs show Mount St. Helens weeks before the 1980 eruption (far left) and during the eruption (left). About half of a cubic mile of rock was pulverized and blasted into the air.

SEE ALSO PAGES:

8-9 Earth's structure,
14-15 The ocean floor,
22-3 Building mountains

EARTHQUAKES

Earthquakes are caused by the sudden release of stress in rocks deep below the Earth's surface. This happens mostly at the borders between tectonic plates.

In a seismometer, a roll of paper turns slowly under a weight. If the ground shakes, a pen attached to the weight records the intensity of the motion.

The San Andreas fault in California is a typical earthquake zone. It is where the Pacific crust and the North American plate meet. The Pacific crust is moving north at an average of 1.36 inches a year, but the motion at the San Andreas fault is not that smooth. It can get stuck for months or years. When this happens, stresses build up along the fault. The longer the wait, the greater the stress. When the fault gives, the ground on either side of the fault can shift by up to 39 feet in a short time, and send shock waves through the surrounding ground.

The shock waves of an earthquake can shake buildings until they collapse. The ground movements can destroy roads, railroad lines, and underground pipes. The gas and water that leak from these pipes add fire and flooding to the side effects of an earthquake.

When an earthquake happens at sea, the rapid shift in water level forms tidal waves, tsunamis, which travel quickly over great distances. As they enter shallow water, they slow down and can rise 30 or more feet above normal sea level. A tsunami can destroy any building in its path and cause terrible flooding.

MAJOR EARTHQUAKES

Location	Year	Magnitude	Deaths
Taiwan	1999	7.7	2,400
Turkey	1999	7.8	17,118
Afghanistan	1998	6.1	4,000
North Iran	1997	7.1	1,560
Russia	1995	7.5	2,000
Japan (Kobe)	1995	7.2	6,310
South India	1993	6.4	9,748
Philippines	1990	7.7	1,653
Northwest Iran	1990	7.5	36,000
San Francisco	1989	7.1	275
Armenia	1988	7.0	25,000
Mexico City	1985	8.1	7,200
North Yemen	1982	6.0	2,800
South Italy	1980	7.2	4,500
Northeast Iran	1978	7.7	25,000
Tangshan, China	1976	8.2	242,000
Guatemala City	1976	7.5	22,778
Peru	1970	7.7	66,000
Northeast Iran	1968	7.4	11,600
Nanshan, China	1927	8.3	200,000
Japan	1923	8.3	143,000
Gansu, China	1920	8.6	180,000

PREPARING FOR EARTHQUAKES

Tiny variations in roughness in a fault or the presence of lubricating water are enough to set off an earthquake. It is almost impossible to predict exactly when and where a major earthquake will strike, but it is possible to deal in probabilities. The regions of the world most at risk of earthquakes are concentrated in thin bands along the major faults between the tectonic plates of the Earth's crust. In these areas, seismologists can predict with near certainty that there will be a major earthquake at some time in the future.

If an area is known to be earthquake-prone, shelters can be built for protection in the event of an earthquake. Buildings can be designed to sway rather than shatter, and rubber in their foundations can absorb some of an earthquake's force. But these precautions are expensive, and many buildings—particularly in poorer countries—are built without them. This is why earthquakes of similar magnitudes can kill tens of thousands in one part of the world, but very few in another.

The only way to completely avoid the risk of death in an earthquake is to evacuate the area before it strikes. However, the inconvenience and cost of evacuating a city are enormous. This is why scientists search for ways to predict earthquakes. Sometimes, but not always, slight tremors on the Earth can indicate

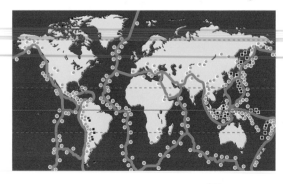

The blue dots show the sites of past earthquakes. Most earthquakes occur along the fault lines at the boundaries between tectonic plates, shown here as green lines.

► The Richter and Mercalli scales record earthquake magnitudes. The Richter scale measures the energy of a quake, and the Mercalli scale charts destructive effects.

◄ Destruction caused by the 1989 earthquake at Loma Prieta, near San Francisco. This photograph shows the collapsed two-tier Nimitz Freeway on the east side of San Francisco Bay. A total of 275 people died in this quake. Over 25,000 people died in Armenia when a quake of a similar magnitude hit poorly constructed buildings in 1988.

 Richter below 3; Mercalli I. Detected by seismographic instruments, but too weak to be felt by people.

 Richter 3–3.4; Mercalli II. Detected by instruments and a few people. Delicate objects may shake.

 Richter 3.5–4; Mercalli III–IV. Obvious shaking felt indoors. Walls crack, hanging objects swing.

 Richter 4.1–4.8; Mercalli V. Felt by most people. Some windows may crack, and loose objects fall over.

 Richter 4.9–6; Mercalli VI–VII. Felt by all. Furniture moves. Some chimneys topple.

 Richter 6.1–7; Mercalli VII–IX. Some houses collapse, roads crack, and pipes rupture.

 Richter 7.1–8.1; Mercalli X–XI. Large cracks form in the ground. Few buildings remain standing.

 Richter more than 8.1; Mercalli XII. Total destruction. The ground rises and falls in waves.

that a major earthquake is due. Attempts have been made to record other warnings such as the level of water in wells, releases of gas, and animal behavior. In 1975, the city of Haicheng, China, was evacuated hours before a massive earthquake on the basis of such warnings. But a year later, in Tangshan, 240,000 people died in a quake for which there had been no warning.

It is now possible to give warnings of a few tens of seconds. Earthquake detectors along a fault zone can sense the start of a major earthquake and send radio messages to control centers in nearby cities. The warning time is not enough to evacuate a city, but a 30-second warning can allow time for computers to save their data, for elevators to open their doors to release people, and for fire engines to move into the open where they will not be damaged. It also helps operators make industrial processes safe before the shock hits.

In January 1995, over 6,000 people died in an earthquake and the resulting fires in Kobe, in Japan. Poorly enforced building regulations and poor-quality concrete construction were largely responsible for the death toll being so high.

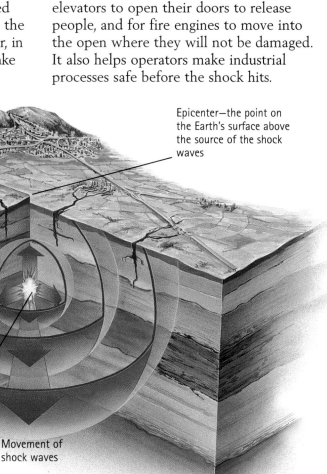

Epicenter—the point on the Earth's surface above the source of the shock waves

Fault line

Shock waves radiate in all directions from the hypocenter when a rock fractures in the lithosphere

Movement of shock waves

◄ When an earthquake strikes, shock waves radiate from a point beneath the ground, called the hypocenter. The point on the Earth's surface directly above the hypocenter is called the epicenter. Both pressure waves and shock waves can radiate from the hypocenter. This can cause cracks in the ground and destroy buildings.

SEE ALSO PAGES:

BUILDING MOUNTAINS

In the Earth's history, mountain ranges have formed and disappeared, all due to the action of volcanoes and earthquakes, continental collisions, and the weather.

The Scottish geologist James Hutton (1726–1797) believed that mountains were built as hot rock erupted from volcanoes. He failed to recognize the effects of continental drift.

These rocks at Stair Hole in Dorset, England, date from the Jurassic period, around 180 million years ago. The fold occurred as the result of a collision of Africa with Europe.

▼ When soft, or incompetent, rocks are compressed horizontally, they will bend or fold. Harder, competent, rocks will fault or fracture. Where the rock is under tension, rifts will form. Under compression, blocks, called horsts, lift up.

The continents are in constant collision. As one continent plows into the next, the impact area continues to buckle and lift up in a process that will last for millions of years. Continental crust is made of hard rock, but the ever-present force of gravity and the pressure of the rocks above make the crust seem softer. As a result, the rock folds up and then the folds sink down, piling up like a crumpled blanket. The resulting mountain range consists of a sequence of repeating folds, each overlapping the next.

AN ONGOING PROCESS

The most recent mountain ranges are still rising. Where Africa collided with Europe, the Alps resulted. Similarly, the Himalayas are the result of a collision between Eurasia and the Indian subcontinent. The process began 65 million years ago, with the huge volcanic eruptions that split India away from the other southern continents. India headed toward the north, pushing the great Tethys Ocean ahead of it. The dense ocean crust subducted beneath Asia, but the sediment on the ocean floor was not so dense. This sediment was scooped up and squeezed between the continents to form a layered cake. It has taken 45 million years for Asia to slow the advance of India, lifting the Tibetan plateau in the process and opening cracks thousands of miles to the north. One of these cracks is a vast rift, more than 29,520 feet deep, occupied by Lake Baikal. Parts of the

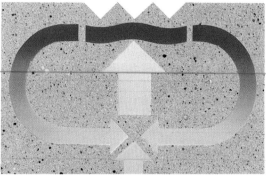

In a process called the rock cycle, rock is thrust up or erupted from the Earth's interior, builds mountains, erodes, and washes away to form new rocks in the sea. Theserocks are scooped up and the cycle is repeated.

Himalayas are still rising. The Nanga Parbat massif in northwestern Pakistan rises 0.2 inches each year. As it rises, however, the rock cannot support its own weight and the region is prone to devastating landslides.

MOUNTAINS IN HISTORY

The most spectacular mountain peaks and the highest ranges are the result of the most recent mountain-building activities. There is, however, also plenty of evidence of more ancient continental collisions. The Appalachian chain that runs along the entire eastern coast of North America, the highlands of northern Scandinavia, eastern Greenland, and parts of Scotland are all about 250 million years old. At one time, before the Atlantic Ocean opened up, they were joined together in a great mountain range, the result of an even older continental collision. Even in the most ancient rocks on the Earth, in Canada, Greenland, southern Africa, and Australia, there is evidence of mountain ranges dating back to when the first continents probably formed.

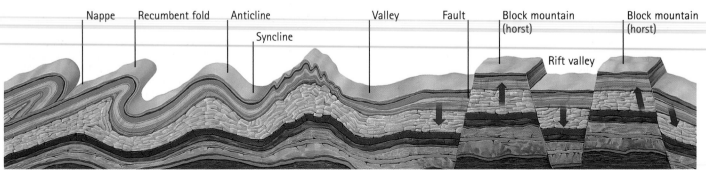

Nappe   Recumbent fold   Anticline   Valley   Fault   Block mountain (horst)   Block mountain (horst)

Syncline   Rift valley

A CONSTANT CYCLE

The Earth's crust records the history of a constant battle between the uplift of the mountains, erosional forces, and gravity. Where steep, jagged mountains rise, at first they will wear away rapidly, with cliffs and valleys cutting across the geology. As the erosion continues, valleys widen and hills become smooth. Layers of hard, resistant rock will appear. Soon the whole landscape will take on the grain of the geology beneath it, with parallel ridges picking out the lines of folds and harder layers of rock. Sometimes the whole area of a continent is lifted, rather than simply being buckled into mountains, forming what is known as a high plateau. Over time, rivers begin to cut gorges and valleys into the plateau, such as the Grand Canyon in Arizona, leaving flat land in between. Eventually, as the valleys widen, the land undulates until it finds a new and lower level, perhaps with just a few isolated ridges of harder rock. The taller a mountain is and the steeper its sides, the more prone it is to landslides and erosion. Snowcapped peaks are shattered by wedges of ice that expand in cracks in the rock. Rivers and glaciers wash the debris down toward the sea. The rivers that drain any mountain area run red with suspended sediment and carry it away into the ocean. There, it settles on the ocean floor, only to be scooped up again several hundred million years later to form a new mountain range. And so the rock cycle continues.

HIGHEST MOUNTAINS	
ASIA	
Mt. Everest	29,021 ft.
K2	28,244 ft.
Kanchenjunga	28,198 ft.
Makalu	27,814 ft.
SOUTH AMERICA	
Aconcagua	22,826 ft.
NORTH AMERICA	
McKinley	20,316 ft.
AFRICA	
Kilimanjaro	19,336 ft.
EUROPE	
Elbrus	18,476 ft.
ANTARCTICA	
Vinson Massif	16,856 ft.
OCEANIA	
Mt. Wilhelm	14,790 ft.

FORMATION OF THE HIMALAYAS

About 45 million years ago, India and Eurasia collided with one another. Continental crust is relatively light, so it was thrust up and folded into a chain of mountains known as the Himalayas. These mountains mark a region of the crust where two tectonic plates are still colliding. The Indo–Australian plate is pushing north into the Eurasian plate. Eventually, the two continental land masses will become locked together.

At 29,021 feet above sea level, Mount Everest is the highest mountain on the Earth. Precise measurements of its height have recently been calculated with the help of satellite data.

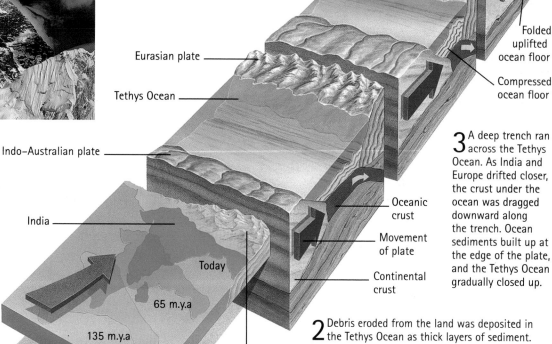

Himalayas

Ocean closes over

Eurasian plate

Tethys Ocean

Indo–Australian plate

India

Today

65 m.y.a

135 m.y.a

Himalayas

Folded, uplifted ocean floor

Compressed ocean floor

Oceanic crust

Movement of plate

Continental crust

1 After Pangaea broke up, some 200 million years ago, the Indo–Australian plate began to move north. About 45 million years ago, the plate smashed into the larger, heavier Eurasian plate and pushed up rock and formed the Himalayas.

2 Debris eroded from the land was deposited in the Tethys Ocean as thick layers of sediment. The northerly movement of the plate pushed the ocean floor forward, and then up and over the scrunched-up edge of the Eurasian plate.

3 A deep trench ran across the Tethys Ocean. As India and Europe drifted closer, the crust under the ocean was dragged downward along the trench. Ocean sediments built up at the edge of the plate, and the Tethys Ocean gradually closed up.

SEE ALSO PAGES:

8–9 Earth's structure,
16–17 Continental drift,
24–5 Building rocks

BUILDING ROCKS

Rocks are natural masses of mineral matter. They range from the hardest granite to the softest clay. Within every rock lie clues to its formation.

1 Talc

2 Gypsum

3 Calcite

4 Fluorite

5 Apatite

6 Orthoclase feldspar

7 Quartz

8 Topaz

9 Corundum

10 Diamond

Rocks exist in three basic types. Igneous rock forms from the solidified magma that has risen from deep within the Earth's crust. Sedimentary rock is material deposited on sea- or riverbeds that, over time, solidifies into rock. Metamorphic rock starts as either of the others, but it is subsequently transformed by heat and pressure inside the Earth.

STUDYING ROCKS

Rocks consist of chemical compounds called minerals. These can form anything from fine grains to vast crystals within the rock. Petrologists, people who study rocks, have a whole battery of techniques at their disposal that help them to identify minerals by simply looking at them. Instruments are also used, both in the field and in the laboratory.

These methods include crystallography, the study of a mineral's crystal system. Many minerals cleave, or break, more easily in one direction than another, and the direction in which they break is called the cleavage plane. Rocks that do not cleave may fracture. Fractures can be conchoidal (shell-like), hackly (jagged), or splintery.

The optical properties of rock are also investigated, not only their color, but also their transparency (how much light they let through), refractive index (how much they bend light), luster (the way in which light is reflected from the surface), and streak (the color left when the mineral

This picture shows crystals of a type of orthoclase feldspar known as microcline. It has a hardness of six on Mohs scale and forms triclinic crystals. Microcline is made up of potassium aluminum silicate.

is scratched across an unglazed tile). The density, or the specific gravity, of a rock is recorded along with the hardness. Often, thin slices of the mineral are examined under a light microscope. Polarized light will reveal a mineral's optical properties.

Electron microscopes can perform microscopic chemical analysis on each grain. The most powerful tool of all is the mass spectrometer, which effectively weighs individual atoms in a sample and compares the ratios of different forms, or isotopes, of the same elements. This is especially useful for measuring the age of a rock from radioactive elements that decay at a known rate. In this way, it is sometimes possible to build up a history of an individual mineral grain, layer by layer during its formation.

FORMATION OF ROCK

Petrologists also study the conditions under which rocks form. Igneous rocks, for example, cool at different rates. A volcanic

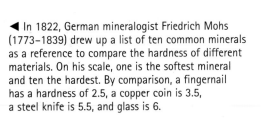

▶ Granite is the most common example of an intrusive igneous rock. This piece of Shap granite contains large pink crystals of orthoclase feldspar, white plagioclase and orthoclase feldspars, black biotite mica, and glassy quartz.

◀ In 1822, German mineralogist Friedrich Mohs (1773–1839) drew up a list of ten common minerals as a reference to compare the hardness of different materials. On his scale, one is the softest mineral and ten the hardest. By comparison, a fingernail has a hardness of 2.5, a copper coin is 3.5, a steel knife is 5.5, and glass is 6.

CRYSTAL SYSTEMS

The Earth contains thousands of individual minerals, each with a precise chemical composition. If the minerals form slowly, precipitating out of solution or slowly cooling from molten rock, they can grow into beautiful crystals.

▼ The main crystal systems are shown in the diagram below. They are: cubic, tetragonal, hexagonal, trigonal, orthorhombic, monoclinic, and triclinic.

▶ Quartz, or rock crystal, is one of the most common minerals and frequently forms beautiful hexagonal crystals in cavities within rocks. This example was found in Switzerland.

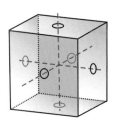 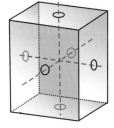 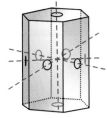 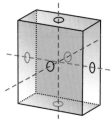 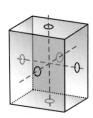 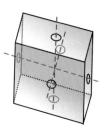

Cubic: 3 equal axes at 90°. Examples: rock salt, pyrite, galena

Tetragonal: 3 axes at 90°, one of different length. Example: cassiterite

Hexagonal and trigonal: 3 equal axes at 120°, one at 90° to their plane. Example: quartz

Orthorhombic: 3 unequal axes at 90°. Examples: olivine, pyrites

Monoclinic: 3 unequal axes, 2 at 90°, 1 at 90° to their plane. Example: pyroxene

Triclinic: 3 unequal axes, none at 90°. Example: plagioclase

eruption under the sea will be quenched quickly by the cold water. As a result, the lava solidifies before any large crystals can grow. A large mass of granite injected into a continent will take a much longer time to cool and can grow crystals many inches long. Even a sand grain has a story to tell. Sand usually consists of quartz or silica. For example, the individual grains of sand from a desert may have been rounded by the grains smashing into each other in the wind. Finer grains will travel farther both by wind and water, so the sand grades itself. Ocean deposits from the edges of continents are sometimes graded with coarse sand at the bottom and finer sand farther up. These are often the result of underwater landslides from which the coarse material has settled first.

ROCK FAMILIES

The bulk of the rocks found in the Earth's crust consist of chemical compounds called silicates. The most important are members of a few simple families.

Quartz is a spiraling chain of silicate

(SiO_4) tetrahedrons (four-sided shapes). It is the most common mineral on the Earth's surface. Feldspars consist of a framework of aluminum silicate tetrahedrons with amounts of potassium, sodium, and calcium. They make up 50 to 60 percent of the mass of all igneous rocks. Olivine has densely packed silicate tetrahedrons with magnesium and iron. Olivines are common in the Earth's mantle and in igneous rocks. Pyroxenes are a family of chain silicates containing magnesium (enstatite), calcium, and magnesium (diopside) or iron and aluminum (augite). Amphibole is a double-chained pyroxene. Micas are layered silicates that split easily into flakes or sheets. They include muscovite (white mica) and biotite (dark mica).

A thin section of olivine basalt shows its structure magnified 25 times. The elongated crystals are plagioclase feldspar. The olivine appears as rounded pink or orange crystals.

This crystal of muscovite mica splits very easily into thin layers. Because the mineral is heat-resistant, it is often used to make windows for furnaces.

Quartz monzonite is a coarse-grained igneous rock that contains a large proportion of feldspar. The forces of erosion slowly produce large rounded boulders similar to this one in Joshua Tree National Park, California.

SEE ALSO PAGES:
8–9 Earth's structure, 194–5 Properties of solids, 264–5 Refraction

ORES AND GEMS

Many of the elements on the Earth are rare, but natural processes have concentrated them, allowing humans to mine them as valuable ores and precious gems.

Bauxite is the main ore of aluminum. It consists of a mixture of hydrated aluminum oxides.

Malachite is one of the main ores of copper, made from copper carbonate. Polished, it is often used for making jewelry.

Iron, copper, gold, and all the other metals that people value exist in trace quantities worldwide. However, the ores of metals have been concentrated by natural processes, and therefore people are able to mine and use them.

SOURCES OF MINERALS

Minerals can be concentrated in a number of ways. In molten rock, crystals will begin to form, and the ones that are most dense will sink to the bottom. This process led to the formation of the Earth's molten iron core, but it happens on a smaller scale in intrusions of molten rock, such as granite. As well as concentrating minerals within it, a mass of molten rock rising through other rocks will drive superheated water and steam ahead of it. Under enormous pressure, these forces can dissolve many of the minerals in the rock, and drive them through cracks

Valuable minerals can be formed in or around hot igneous intrusions, by evaporation or weathering near the Earth's surface, and in or around hydrothermal vents on the seabed.

Stibnite is the main ore of an element called antimony. It is a sulfide mineral and often forms elongated crystals. Stibnite forms around hydrothermal vents in the ocean, often replacing other rocks that have dissolved.

and fissures, where they are deposited as veins of minerals. Other minerals become concentrated near the Earth's surface when water evaporates or when other components in a rock are eroded. In the deep ocean, holes in the ocean floor, called hydrothermal vents, spout mineral-rich water that crystallizes around the vents or precipitates out into the surrounding ocean. Large areas of the deep ocean floor are littered with manganese nodules that are rich in other valuable metals, such as cobalt. The richest mines of all may one

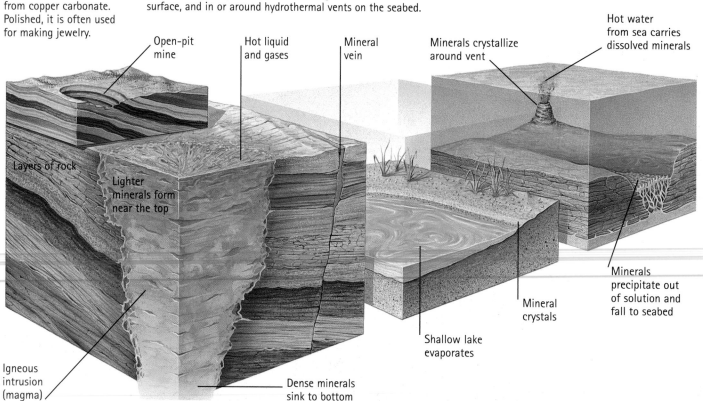

Open-pit mine

Hot liquid and gases

Mineral vein

Minerals crystallize around vent

Hot water from sea carries dissolved minerals

Layers of rock

Lighter minerals form near the top

Igneous intrusion (magma)

Dense minerals sink to bottom

Shallow lake evaporates

Mineral crystals

Minerals precipitate out of solution and fall to seabed

day be not on the Earth but in space. If we could capture and mine a metal-rich asteroid, it could contain platinum and related metals worth trillions of dollars.

PROCESSING THE ORE

Mining techniques depend on the level of concentration of the ore, its depth, and its value to people. Where an ore lies in a thick vein underground, shafts can be sunk to reach it. Sometimes there is a large body of less-concentrated ore near the surface that is worth digging out by open-cast mining techniques. Sometimes nature has already done the digging. For example, gold dust and nuggets can be found concentrated in the gravel of riverbeds.

Most metallic minerals are chemical compounds with properties that are very different to the metals that they contain. The process of smelting is used to extract the metal from the ore. Both heat and a reducing agent such as carbon are used to pull the metal's chemical companions away from it.

GEMSTONES

Some minerals are prized for their natural beauty rather than for any practical use. Any mineral worn as jewelry can be regarded as a gem. Some minerals are organic in origin and include amber (fossilized tree resin) and jet (hard, black coal). Many other semi-precious stones are silicate minerals such as quartz, amethyst, jade, garnet, and topaz. The most precious

stones are also the most rare and the most durable. These include ruby, sapphire, emerald, and diamond, most of which are formed under high temperatures and pressures deep in the Earth.

Although it is the hardest mineral known, diamond—like charcoal—is made of pure carbon. Unlike charcoal, however, diamonds are formed when carbon is placed under enormous pressure, around 375 mi. (600km) beneath the Earth's surface. The famous diamond mines of South Africa are in a volcanic rock called kimberlite, which erupted incredibly violently over a billion years ago.

Natural diamond crystals have eight sides, but for jewelry they are cut carefully with many facets—the brilliant cut has up to 58 facets. Diamonds are so hard that they are used to make industrial drills and saws.

A section through a fossilized tree trunk reveals both the structure of the tree and the opal mineral that has replaced it. Opal is a form of silicon dioxide. Its many colors make it a desirable gem.

Galena is the principal ore of lead. It forms metallic, gray, cubic crystals. It often contains silver, which forms a valuable by-product from the lead-mining industry.

Topaz is a silicate of aluminum and fluorine. It exists in many different colors, including yellow, blue, green, violet, pink, and reddish brown. This is a cut and polished crystal.

▼ The prized green gem emerald is a rare form of beryl (beryllium aluminum silicate). It gets its color from traces of chromium.

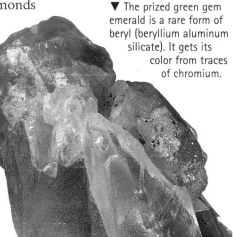

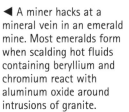

◄ A miner hacks at a mineral vein in an emerald mine. Most emeralds form when scalding hot fluids containing beryllium and chromium react with aluminum oxide around intrusions of granite.

SEE ALSO PAGES:

8–9 Earth's structure, 164–5 Chemical compounds, 201 Precious metals, 213 Coal

IGNEOUS ROCK

Igneous rocks are born from fire, and most originate deep within the Earth. Slowly, igneous rocks rise toward the surface in a molten or semimolten state.

This cliff face contains layers of pumice and obsidian, both of which are extrusive igneous rocks.

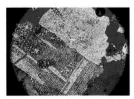

A microscope reveals the mineral crystals in this thin section of magnified porphyritic granite.

Obsidian is a natural glass of volcanic origin. The white areas, or snowflakes, are where the glass has changed to a crystalline state.

Igneous rocks all form from molten magma. They are classified by their texture, composition, and origin. Acidic igneous rocks tend to be light in color and low in density. They contain plenty of silica or quartz, often with various minerals of the feldspar group. Basic igneous rocks are more dark and dense and contain combinations of olivine, pyroxene, and hornblende or amphibole. Ultrabasic rocks are very dense and are close in composition to the upper mantle.

DIFFERENT IGNEOUS ROCKS

Igneous rocks are either intrusive or extrusive. Intrusive rocks are pushed up beneath overlying rocks as large masses that have already solidified. Extrusive rocks erupt from volcanoes or into the dikes and sills associated with them.

The texture of igneous rocks depends on how fast they cool. If they cool slowly as intrusions, large crystals may grow. Sometimes these settle out to form coarse, crystalline pegmatite or get caught up as large phenocrysts in finer-grained material.

If the magma cools rapidly, the grains will be fine or even glassy. They may trap bubbles of gas or large fragments of surrounding rock (xenoliths).

Basic igneous rocks may be formed by the melting or partial melting of the upper mantle, specifically when a mantle plume rises under a hot spot. When this magma erupts from a volcano and cools rapidly, it forms finely grained basalts, which contain feldspar, mica, and hornblende, and is very dark in color. The same mixture injected underground, between rock layers, cools more slowly, and forms larger crystals called dolerite (even slower cooling, over millions of years and at greater depths, makes a granular form called gabbro). This still has the same overall composition.

When the ocean crust sinks under a continent, parts of both melt to make a magma that is more acidic and richer in silica. Water and carbon dioxide make the magma flow more easily, but silica makes it thick. Eruptions of this material form andesite, a paler form of basalt that is rich in silica. Millions of years later, when the continent has been thickened by volcanic eruptions, the base of the continent may begin to melt. This produces intrusions of silica-rich granite.

▶ A section through an intrusion of granite, showing a batholith with dikes and sills around it. Sometimes the intrusion takes the shape of a dome and the surrounding sedimentary rocks produce a laccolith. As the rocks wear away, the granite is exposed.

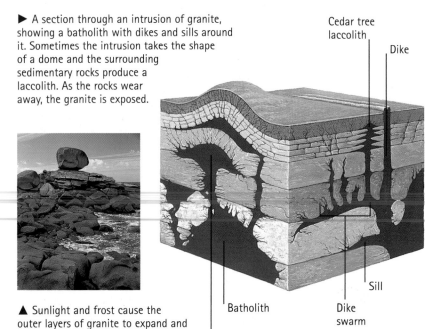

Cedar tree laccolith

Dike

Batholith

Dike swarm

Sill

Laccolith

Devil's Tower, in Wyoming, is the plug or vent of a basalt volcano.

▲ Sunlight and frost cause the outer layers of granite to expand and contract to make rounded boulders.

SEE ALSO PAGES:

8–9 Earth's structure, 18–19 Volcanoes, 24–5 Building rocks

METAMORPHIC ROCK

Metamorphic rocks have been transformed from other rocks by enormous pressures and temperatures thousands of feet below the Earth's surface.

Slate is metamorphosed from shale largely by pressure. The mineral grains are aligned, making it possible to split slate into thin sheets. This quarry in Wales, in Great Britain, once produced slates used in the roofing industry.

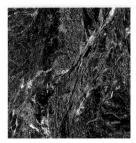

Marble is metamorphosed limestone. It makes a popular, decorative building stone.

When igneous and sedimentary rocks are subjected to enormous pressures and high temperatures, their structure and sometimes their chemical makeup can be changed. Hot, percolating fluids may add or remove different minerals. These conditions can make existing minerals take on different forms. Metamorphic forces can exceed 100 atmospheres and 752°F. Under these conditions, layered minerals may become distorted, stretched, or destroyed. Accordingly, metamorphic rocks are classified according to their texture, composition, and source.

CLASSIFYING THE ROCK

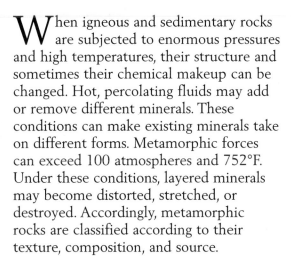

This sample of gneiss contains coarse crystals and resembles granite. The texture of this sample is because of the alignment of grains under pressure.

There are two types of metamorphism: contact and regional. The first, contact, or thermal, metamorphism is where hot intrusions of igneous rock bake the surrounding rocks. The second, regional, or dynamic, metamorphism is where much larger volumes of rock become squeezed, buried, and heated, as in continental collision zones.

Metamorphism will bind the grains of sandstone together to make quartzite. It will also turn limestone into marble. As the calcium carbonate recrystallizes in a marble, impurities get forced out of the crystals. This often forms bands and makes the marble highly decorative. Marble, like the fine white variety from Carrara, in Italy, has been a favorite sculpting material since ancient times.

Schist is formed by regional metamorphism. Crystals of mica are aligned by high pressure. Some of the mica in this piece of schist from the Austrian Alps has turned into garnet.

Regional metamorphism can take a sedimentary rock, such as shale, through a series of changes. A regional compression re-forms many of the clay minerals into thin, flat grains of mica. These tend to align at a perpendicular angle to the direction of compression.

This process can form slate, which can be split into flat sheets along the grain, in a direction that may bear no relationship to the original sedimentary bedding. If the compression continues, the slate changes to phyllite, with more micas and other higher-pressure minerals such as garnet. As the pressure and temperature increase, the mineral layer becomes more distorted, and this produces foliated schist. As the temperature rises further, the minerals become coarser-grained gneiss. Gneiss may melt at the base of continents, rising to produce granite and completing the cycle.

This diagram shows the two different forms of metamorphism. The fold mountains to the left of the fault have piled up a thick layer of rock, squeezing them so that their mineral grains have realigned and turned shale into slate. The deepest, hottest layers of shale and slate have turned into schist and gneiss. On the right, an igneous intrusion has baked the surrounding rocks, causing contact metamorphism and turning limestone into marble.

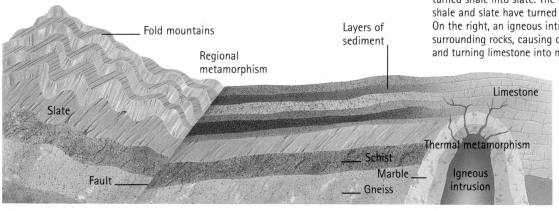

Fold mountains

Regional metamorphism

Layers of sediment

Slate

Limestone

Thermal metamorphism

Schist

Marble

Gneiss

Igneous intrusion

Fault

SEE ALSO PAGES:
8–9 Earth's structure, 24–5 Building rocks, 28 Igneous rock, 30–1 Sedimentary rock

SEDIMENTARY ROCK

The Earth is carpeted by layers of sedimentary rocks. These consist of chemical and biological precipitates, fossils, and the weathered fragments of other rocks.

Rocks are forming all the time, and not just in the eruptions deep beneath the Earth's surface. Some rocks, called sedimentary rocks, are the result of the consolidation of tiny particles, that have accumulated in layers.

These blocks of calcareous mudstone, also known as marl, were deposited deep beneath the sea millions of years ago.

Soft clay is formed when rocks are broken down into particles and deposited as sediment by the wind, water, or glaciers.

▼ This imaginary landscape depicts some of the conditions in which layers of sedimentary rocks form in the Earth.

DIFFERENT SEDIMENTS

There are three main types of sedimentary rock. Clastic rocks form when preexisting rocks are broken down into small particles that are redistributed by the wind, water, or glaciers. These rocks are classified on the basis of their grain size, from large rocks to the finest clays. The grains can be rounded and worn, or angular and broken. They can be loose or unconsolidated, compressed together, or cemented with materials dissolved in groundwater such as calcite, silica, or iron oxide. Another type of clastic sedimentary rock is called pyroclastic, and forms as a result of volcanic activity. Over 75 percent of all sedimentary rocks are clastic.

Chemical sediments form as a result of physical and chemical processes. They can be precipitated from solution in sea water, as happens with flint and chert. They can also form when salty lakes or shallow seas evaporate leaving, for example, gypsum

The chalk cliffs of southern England are fine-grained deposits of limestone formed from the shells of tiny marine organisms that lived nearly 70 million years ago.

and rock salt. They can also be formed by leaching, when groundwater dissolves and re-deposits bauxite, for example.

Limestone can form from the chemical precipitation of calcium carbonate, or it may be biogenic, that is made up of the skeletons of millions of microscopic organisms, such as chalk. Biogenic sediments include fossil fuels such as coal, which is the compressed remains of plants, and oil, made by bacteria from buried organic material.

THE WEATHERING PROCESS

Weathering is a complex process whereby rocks are broken down into sediments. Chemical weathering occurs when rocks are affected by water, carbon dioxide, and organic acids. It is accelerated by warm temperatures. Physical weathering

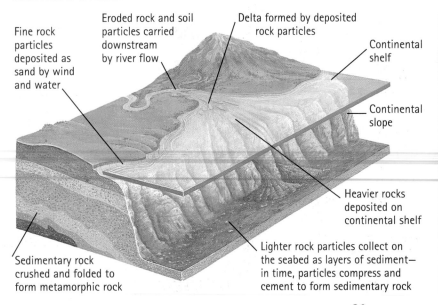

Fine rock particles deposited as sand by wind and water

Eroded rock and soil particles carried downstream by river flow

Delta formed by deposited rock particles

Continental shelf

Continental slope

Heavier rocks deposited on continental shelf

Lighter rock particles collect on the seabed as layers of sediment—in time, particles compress and cement to form sedimentary rock

Sedimentary rock crushed and folded to form metamorphic rock

occurs when rocks are fractured and broken apart, for example, by a freeze-and-thaw action. Water that seeps into the cracks of the rock during the warmer daytime temperatures expands as it freezes at night. This shatters the rock.

CARRYING SEDIMENT

Most of the sediments that form rock are carried by rivers. The Mississippi River, for example, delivers around 180 million tons of sediment each year to the Gulf of Mexico. Some sediment settles on the river bed, and some is deposited at the mouth of a river, forming what is known as a river delta. Yet more sediment is carried to the ocean floor.

Sediment can also be carried by wind and glaciers. In every carrying process, the sediment gets graded by size in a process called sedimentary differentiation. Coarse sediment is difficult to move and is found only in rapid high-energy flows. Very fine-grained muds, however, can be shifted many hundreds of miles or deposited in quiet water, such as shallow lakes and deep seas.

RECORDING EARTH'S HISTORY

More than a billion years of the Earth's history is recorded in layers of sedimentary rock. In the Grand Canyon, in Arizona, there is a spectacular sequence of horizontal sedimentary rock layers, or strata, nearly 5,000 feet deep and many millions of years old. Fossils within the strata record the development

of different forms of life, from the first corals and worms to fish and dinosaurs and mammals. The rock types reveal the conditions at the time they were formed. Coarse conglomerates of rounded pebbles record high-energy and fast-moving rivers. Sandstones indicate ocean shore and deltas. Mudstones indicate sluggish waters, and limestones must have been laid down in warm shallow seas teeming with life.

Linking present-day deposits from different places involves painstaking research, comparing the fossils in rocks and getting date estimates for convenient markers such as lava flows. However, this research has allowed geologists to piece together the history of the development of the land, seas, and life itself.

Different colors of sandstone, worn smooth by glacial erosion, have formed an attractive pattern of lines in the smooth sides of hills in Paria Wilderness Area, in Arizona. The curves in the rock are the result of the actions of wind and water.

Sandstone is often found in brown, pink, or red layers. The color comes from the varying amounts of iron oxides that bind the sediments together.

◄ The mineral content of the sandstone determines its red or yellow color. The gray sedimentary rock at the front of this picture is called graywacke, and dates from the late Triassic period—approximately 210 million years ago.

◄ Limestone consists of calcium carbonate and generally originates as a deposit of marine animal skeletons on the seabed. Acid rain dissolves limestone and produces an effect similar to the one shown here.

► Layers of sedimentary rocks in a cliff face in Utah's Zion National Park date from the Triassic period. The red and yellow layers are deposits of sandstone. The gray layer is called graywacke, a deposit formed as the result of underwater landslides.

SEE ALSO PAGES:

4–5 Fossils and geological time, 32–33 Erosion and weathering, 36–7 Climate

EROSION AND WEATHERING

Erosion and weathering are vital to the rock cycle. Many processes break down rocks, reducing them to dust and leaving spectacular features in the landscape.

This sandstone arch in Utah formed as the result of erosion by windblown sand.

Sea arches are formed by coastal erosion. The action of pounding waves first formed a cave in the headland and eventually carved out the softer, more porous rock to produce the arch.

The surface of the Earth's moon retains features that result from being bombarded by asteroids nearly four billion years ago. Most of the Earth's landscape contains features that are less than a million years old, and the rocks are less than a billion years old. The difference is produced by weathering, caused by the Earth's thick atmosphere and abundant water.

THE WATER CYCLE

The Earth is unique among the planets because it contains water in all three phases—liquid, vapor, and ice. Water is continually changing from one state to another. Solar energy evaporates water from oceans and lakes into the atmosphere where it forms vapor and clouds. This is deposited back onto the Earth as rain or snow. This cycle of change drives the forces of erosion that weather the land.

Water breaks down rock in many ways. Slightly acidic rainwater can dissolve some rocks. Water can also penetrate the tiniest cracks in rocks. If it freezes, it expands, and splits the rock apart. Running water can wash away sand and soil. A fast-flowing mountain stream can tear out

rocks and boulders and pound them against one another, reducing them to gravel, sand, and clay. Similarly, floods can devastate huge areas of land with terrible consequences.

WEATHERING BY WIND

Other agents can weather the land, and the wind is an extremely powerful force. Desert winds often pick up sand and blast it against large rocks. This carves them into mushroom-shaped rocks and spectacular arches. When the wind slackens, it drops some of its load of sand, creating great crescent-shaped dunes that slowly move downwind toward previously fertile land. In this way, desert regions continue to expand.

THE FORMATION OF SOIL

Soil is essential to all life on land, because plants depend on it to grow. Slow and complex interactions, such as the physical breakdown of rocks, chemical weathering, and the action of plant roots and microorganisms, produce soil. Different rocks and different climates produce different soils. In temperate regions, year-long rainfall can wash chemicals, such as iron hydroxide, out of the topsoil, leaving gray or brown podzol. In the tropics, high precipitation, along with high levels of evaporation and the way that the plants

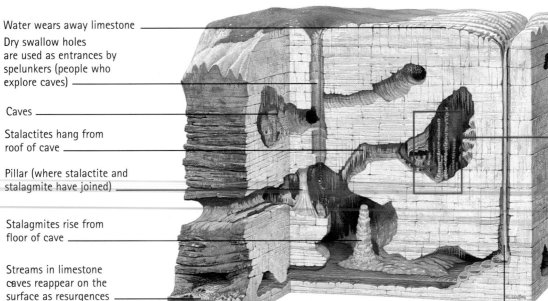

Water wears away limestone

Dry swallow holes are used as entrances by spelunkers (people who explore caves)

Caves

Stalactites hang from roof of cave

Pillar (where stalactite and stalagmite have joined)

Stalagmites rise from floor of cave

Streams in limestone caves reappear on the surface as resurgences

Streams plunge down some swallow holes into caves

▲ When the mineral-rich water in caves evaporates, it deposits calcite as stalactites, stalagmites, and pillars.

◄ Acidic rainwater dissolves limestone, and produces spectacular features in cave systems.

A river running over the lip of a hard rock layer creates a waterfall, the most famous example of which is Niagara Falls (above). Instead of gradually eroding to create a valley, the rock layer breaks off in chunks. As a result, the waterfall remains and advances up a gorge.

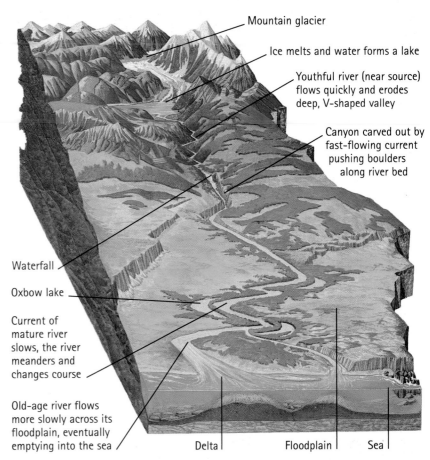

Mountain glacier

Ice melts and water forms a lake

Youthful river (near source) flows quickly and erodes deep, V-shaped valley

Canyon carved out by fast-flowing current pushing boulders along river bed

Waterfall

Oxbow lake

Current of mature river slows, the river meanders and changes course

Old-age river flows more slowly across its floodplain, eventually emptying into the sea

Delta   Floodplain   Sea

draw water into their roots, concentrates iron and aluminum at the surface, producing red laterite. In temperate grassland the grass takes in nutrients from the land, leaving a black soil called chernozem. In all cases, if the vegetation is removed, the soils can wash or blow away and leave the land infertile.

THE EFFECTS OF EROSION

A river running through hills or mountains cuts through rock to form a characteristic winding, V-shaped valley with many tributaries. Where the river meets a hard rock layer, water may flow alongside the layer until it finds a way through, sometimes as a waterfall or through a gorge. Where a hillside is steep and a rocky cliff is exposed, falling rock builds up at its base to form a heap of rock fragments known as a talus. This makes the slope less steep and protects the cliff from further erosion. If a steep slope is made of soft rock or soil, landslides often occur. If there is an impervious clay layer, the water from a heavy rainfall may build above it, lubricating the rocks above so that they slip down the slope. This type of erosion is common along sea cliffs. Gravity, rainfall, and even trampling by animals all add to the effects of erosion.

The amount of eroded material that a river can carry depends on its speed. As the slope becomes less steep and the

valley opens out onto a flood plain, the speed of the river slows and it cannot hold as much sediment. The larger particles settle out as sand and gravel. When the river slows further, it leaves mud behind. A sluggish river will deposit more sediment along its banks, and consequently the river banks slowly rise. If sediment also accumulates on the bottom of the river, thousands of years of deposition will cause the whole river system to rise above its floodplain. If floodwaters break through, the entire plain can flood, disrupting the environment and destroying the landscape. In the long term, however, flooding is a valuable process, because it builds up a new layer of fertile soil.

Different parts of a river move at different speeds. Around a bend, water on the inside of a bend flows more slowly than on the outside of a bend. As a result, sediment is deposited on the inside, and the outside is eroded. This increases the bend of the river so that it meanders back and forth across the floodplain. Sometimes the bends are so great that a neck of land is cut off. The river takes a new course, and leaves an oxbow lake of still water.

▼ This diagram shows a typical river-catchment system. In the mountains, streams and rivers are fast-flowing, so erosion of the rock occurs rapidly. As the watercourses slow onto a floodplain, they deposit the sediments.

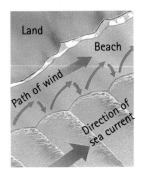

Land

Beach

Path of wind

Direction of sea current

Seas and oceans are continually pounding coastal regions. Where waves hit a beach at an angle, a longshore current is produced. This process carries sand along the shore in the direction of the sea current.

SEE ALSO PAGES:

56-7 Plant anatomy,
400-1 Earth and moon,
436-7 Action zones

GLACIERS AND ICE SHEETS

About ten percent of the Earth's surface is covered by ice. In the form of glaciers, ice can carve out valleys and carry the debris hundreds of miles.

Extent of ice sheets in Northern Hemisphere during last ice age

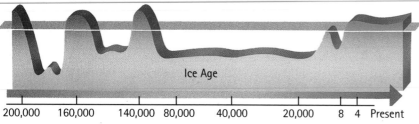

	°F
	59°F
	50°F
	41°F
	32°F

Ice Age

200,000   160,000   140,000 80,000   40,000   20,000   8   4   Present

A plot of the average worldwide temperatures in July over the past 200,000 years shows that it is particularly warm at the present time.

Although ice once covered huge areas of our planet, today it has retreated toward the poles and the highest mountain areas. However, the landscape it carved remains. Although ice is a solid, under pressure it can flow in the same way that rocks flow in the Earth's mantle. The structure is very similar. As snow compacts, air is squeezed out and the white crumbly snow changes into a blue crystalline substance, containing ice crystals rather than minerals. The crystals are

During the last ice age, the ice cap over Scandinavia was nearly 10,000 feet thick. The most recent series of ice ages began about 3.5 million years ago. Scientists are uncertain as to whether the effects are continuing.

lubricated by a microscopic film of water, kept liquid by dissolved salts. The ice can literally transform the landscape.

MOVING ACROSS THE LAND
Ice occupies more volume than water. As water seeps into crevices and freezes, it shatters rocks and boulders. Meanwhile, the snow around the mountains blankets the ground, triggering avalanches or packing into ice. Eventually, this ice begins to move. In extremely cold regions, the ice covers the landscape in a sheet that may

Pyramidal peak

Cirque

Crevasses

LANDSCAPING BY ICE
High in the mountains compact snow begins to move, leaving a cirque (a steep-sided basin) at the head of a valley. Back-to-back cirques leave jagged pyramidlike peaks. As the glacier pulls away, or the surface bends, and crevasses open in the ice, rock debris builds up lateral moraines on the ice. As the glacier moves downhill, the base of the ice can over-deepen a valley and appear to travel uphill. Where a glacier falls down a steep slope it forms jagged, crevassed ice falls. The snout is the end of the glacier where the ice eventually melts.

Movement of glacier

Lakes sometimes form in cirques, or steep-sided basins, made by glaciers

Lateral moraine

◀ Masses of moving ice, called glaciers, leave characteristic U-shaped valleys in their path. These are very different from V-shaped river valleys. This valley in Switzerland was V-shaped until the last ice age, when a glacier deepened it into a U-shaped valley.

Snout of glacier

Meltwater

be thousands of feet thick. Within it, there may be faster-flowing streams of ice caused by the ground beneath falling away, being lubricated by mud, or even being warmed by volcanic activity (as in part of Antarctica). As the ice sheet thins, it can part around rocky peaks, or nunataks, to form valley glaciers and then reunite with the other side into what are called Piedmont glaciers.

The flow rate of a glacier can be very slow—between a few yards and a few hundred yards each year. To maintain the same flow as even a small mountain stream, a glacier has to fill the whole valley. As the glacier moves, it grinds small rocks into powder. Embedded boulders leave deep marks, called striations, in the sides of the U-shaped valleys. In some glacial valleys the ice cuts deep into the ground below, leaving lakes when the ice retreats.

As the ice progresses, a thick layer of fine clay builds up underneath the glacier. The pressure may be enough to keep water liquid here, lubricating the base of the glacier and leaving oval mounds of clay known as drumlins. At the snout of the glacier, the rest of the sediment and rock is deposited as a terminal moraine. Often a block of ice is left behind. This will melt and form a deep pond, or kettle.

ICE AGES

Geologists are uncertain as to what causes an ice age. However, the long-term cycles in the inclination of the Earth's axis, called the Milankovitch cycles, appear to be involved. Fluctuations in the levels of atmospheric

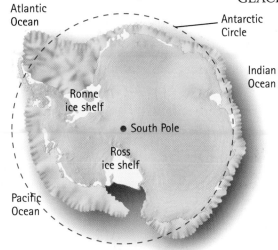

Ice sheet   Ice shelf   Minimum sea ice

carbon dioxide may also play a role. But once the ice starts to advance, the change is rapid. White ice and snow reflect more of the sun's radiation back into space and the planet cools further. Scientists have worked out that global temperatures appear to fluctuate between two relatively stable states. This has occurred about 35 times in the Earth's history. The first clear evidence of an ice age comes from the Precambrian period, dating back some four billion years. The most recent ice age began about 3.25 million years ago. This may still be in progress despite the present mild climate. Until about 14,000 years ago, there was a huge amount of ice locked up in the polar ice caps, and sea levels were about 262 feet lower than present-day levels. But the ice also depressed the land, which is still slowly rising in northern latitudes.

Most of Antarctica is covered by a thick ice sheet. The ice flows from regions of high snowfall in the center of the continent, and streams out toward the coast. In the winter, the sheet extends into the sea. Some thick ice shelves remain all year round, occasionally releasing enormous icebergs. Many scientists fear that global warming could cause the ice sheet in western Antarctica to collapse, and raise global sea levels dramatically.

These giant icebergs have broken away from the ice sheets of Antarctica and clearly show the effects of waves undercutting their edges. About 90 percent of icebergs' volume is invisible beneath the water, which means that they can be extremely dangerous to passing ships. Icebergs can carry clay and rock that it has gouged from the land far out to sea, where it is found in ocean sediments.

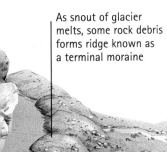

As snout of glacier melts, some rock debris forms ridge known as a terminal moraine

An aerial view shows the large Kahiltna glacier in Alaska. Human activities have given rise to a phenomenon called global warming that has caused many glaciers around the world to shrink. If the Kahiltna glacier melted, it would reveal a deep U-shaped valley that it has gouged in the mountains beneath.

SEE ALSO PAGES:

22–3 Building mountains, 36–7 Climate, 460 Climate change

CLIMATE

The Earth's climate depends on energy from the sun and the ability of the oceans and atmosphere to circulate the heat efficiently around the planet.

Cold air →
Cool air →
Warm air →

Warm air rises at the equator where sunlight is strongest. From there, it moves toward the poles, drawing cool air behind it.

The rain forest vegetation helps keep global warming under control by absorbing carbon dioxide from the air as it grows.

▼ The eight main climate zones have different mean temperatures and rainfall rates. These differences influence the type of vegetation found in them.

The heat that drives the Earth's weather systems comes from the sun. Some of the sunlight that shines onto the Earth is reflected back into space by bright white clouds and ice caps. The rest is absorbed by the land and sea, which get warmer and radiate heat as infrared light. While visible light shines freely through clear air, gases, such as carbon dioxide, reflect infrared back to the Earth. This is called the greenhouse effect. Carbon dioxide in the atmosphere traps heat in the same way that glass in a greenhouse does. Without this effect, the average temperature on the Earth's surface would be about 5°F. Ice would cover the planet, and human life would not exist.

The amount of sunlight that reaches the Earth's surface varies with latitude. Sunlight is most intense at the equator and weakest at the poles. Winds tend to even this out, carrying warm air to higher latitudes. The climate is also affected by the ocean currents. The top six feet of the sea store more heat than the entire atmosphere. Ocean currents carry some of this heat toward the poles, in the form of the Gulf Stream and North Atlantic Drift. Away from the oceanic heat stores, the interiors of continents have more extreme weather, with cold winters and hot, dry summers.

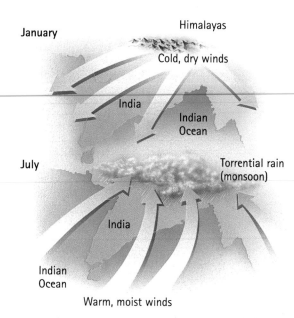

January
Himalayas
Cold, dry winds
India
Indian Ocean
July
Torrential rain (monsoon)
India
Indian Ocean
Warm, moist winds

In the winter, the sea is warmer than the land and the air over it rises, drawing cold, dry air south from the Himalayas. In the summer, the air over northern India becomes very hot and rises. This causes warm, moist air to move north from the ocean, and brings heavy rain to southern Asia—the monsoon season.

CLIMATE CHANGE

For all the variations of weather from day to day and year to year, average world temperatures have not changed by more than half a degree in the last century.

Some climate changes have natural causes. During the 1600s, for example, there were no reported sunspots. Overall, the sun was cooler and this resulted in what has been called the Little Ice Age. At that time, rivers in Europe froze in winter and frost fairs were held on the ice.

Further back in time there were much greater variations in temperature. There is evidence of this in many forms. Tree rings record good and bad growing seasons, including a series of bad winters around 1450 B.C. They may have been caused by the effects of a volcanic eruption that blocked out sunlight. The record goes back even further in ice cores from Greenland and Antarctica, and in layers of lake sediments. Sediment cores from the oceans provide the longest history. Variations in the ratios of oxygen isotopes can reveal the ocean temperature and the amount of polar ice. Carbon isotopes in shells reveal how much carbon dioxide was being drawn from the atmosphere.

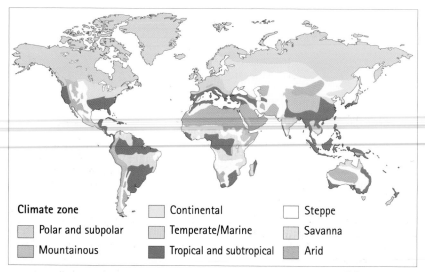

Climate zone

- Polar and subpolar
- Mountainous
- Continental
- Temperate/Marine
- Tropical and subtropical
- Steppe
- Savanna
- Arid

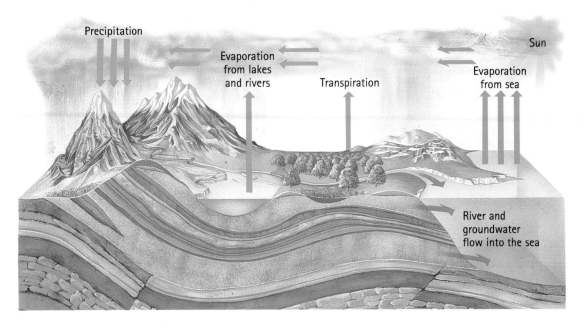

Precipitation

Sun

Evaporation from lakes and rivers

Transpiration

Evaporation from sea

River and groundwater flow into the sea

Heat from the sun drives water in a cycle around the planet. It causes water to evaporate from lakes, rivers, and seas. The sun's heat also causes plants to transpire, or release, water into the atmosphere.

Warm, moist air cools as it rises over hills and mountains, or when it meets cold air. The cooled air can no longer hold all of its water as vapor, so droplets of water form as clouds and rain. Rain feeds streams and rivers and soaks into the soil as groundwater. In these forms, water returns to lakes, forests, and the sea, completing the cycle.

Around 50 million years ago there was probably no ice on the Earth, except on the highest mountains. Antarctica was covered with vegetation. Before that, for over 100 million years, the Earth's climate was much warmer than today, and dinosaurs populated the planet.

GLOBAL WARMING

Not all climate changes are natural. Since 1958, scientists have been monitoring the concentration of carbon dioxide in the atmosphere high on a mountain in Hawaii. Every year, the concentration has been getting higher. The additional carbon dioxide comes mainly from the burning of fossil fuels, such as coal, natural gas, and fuels from oil. Burning releases into the atmosphere carbon that was stored in the tissues of organisms that lived many millions of years ago. Also, the burning

of forests in the Amazon releases carbon dioxide and destroys trees and vegetation that would otherwise consume carbon dioxide. Each year, human activity adds about eight billion tons of carbon to the atmosphere in the form of carbon dioxide. During the 1900s, the additional carbon dioxide increased the greenhouse effect enough to raise the average global temperature by 1°F.

Meteorologists use supercomputers to model the climate and make predictions of future climate changes. The results suggest that the climate is likely to warm by a further 4.5°F over the next century—more than the change from the ice age to the present day. Locally, the changes could be even more dramatic. As polar ice melts, sea levels could rise and cause flooding, deserts would become drier, and coastal regions would get more stormy.

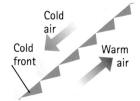

Cold air

Cold front

Cold

Warm air

Frontal systems are where cold and warm air meet. A cold front is where cool, often dry air drives warm air out of its way.

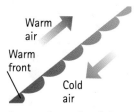

Warm air

Warm front

Cold air

A warm front often brings cloud and rain. Cold air pushes beneath the warm air and lifts it.

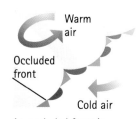

Warm air

Occluded front

Cold air

An occluded front is where cold and warm air mix. As they do, the front weakens and disappears.

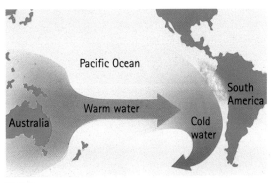

Pacific Ocean

Australia

South America

Warm water

Cold water

Normal conditions

Pacific Ocean

Australia

Warm water

South America

Cold water

El Niño

El Niño denotes an occasional reversal in the currents of the Pacific. Normally, surface currents move west across the South Pacific. This provides moist air for the humid climate of Southeast Asia and allows nutrient-rich water

to well up along the coast of Peru. During El Niño, the current flows east. This causes floods in North and South America and droughts in Southeast Asia. Fish off the Peruvian coast starve.

SEE ALSO PAGES:

12–13 The oceans, 394–5 The sun, 453 Air pollution, 460 Climate change

RAIN AND SNOW

Rain and snow are two forms in which water falls to the Earth from the sky. The water they supply is vital for the survival and growth of plants and animals.

When water freezes, it forms flat, six-sided crystals. Under certain weather conditions, these crystals can join together. This results in complex and beautiful snowflakes.

Water that falls from clouds is called precipitation. In one form of precipitation, raindrops form in clouds when air currents cause tiny droplets of water to collide. These droplets join together to form larger drops that fall as rain. The air must be humid for rain to reach the ground without evaporating, so this type of formation happens mainly in the tropical regions.

Most rain starts as crystals of ice that form high in the atmosphere in clouds where the temperature is low. The ice crystals grow as water freezes onto them. Whether these crystals reach the ground as rain or snow depends on the height of the freezing level—the minimum height at which the temperature and pressure cause water to freeze.

If the freezing level is less than 984 feet above ground, ice crystals do not have time to melt before reaching the ground, so they fall as snow. In warmer conditions, the freezing level is higher and the crystals turn to rain before they reach the ground.

HAILSTORMS

Inside a storm cloud, falling ice crystals or raindrops may be carried upward by currents of warm air called updrafts. At the top of the cloud, they freeze and attract more water. As the developing hailstones then fall to warmer levels, their outside layers melt, but are refrozen as a clear layer of ice when the hailstones are carried to the top of the cloud.

RAIN AND SNOW

If the base of a stratus cloud is low, small droplets of rain may fall as a fine drizzle. Dry snow falls when the temperature near the ground is below 32˚F (0˚C), the freezing point of water. If snow falls into air that is just above 32˚F, some of it will melt. The resulting mixture of snow and rain is called sleet. Wet snow falls when the temperature is exactly 32˚F.

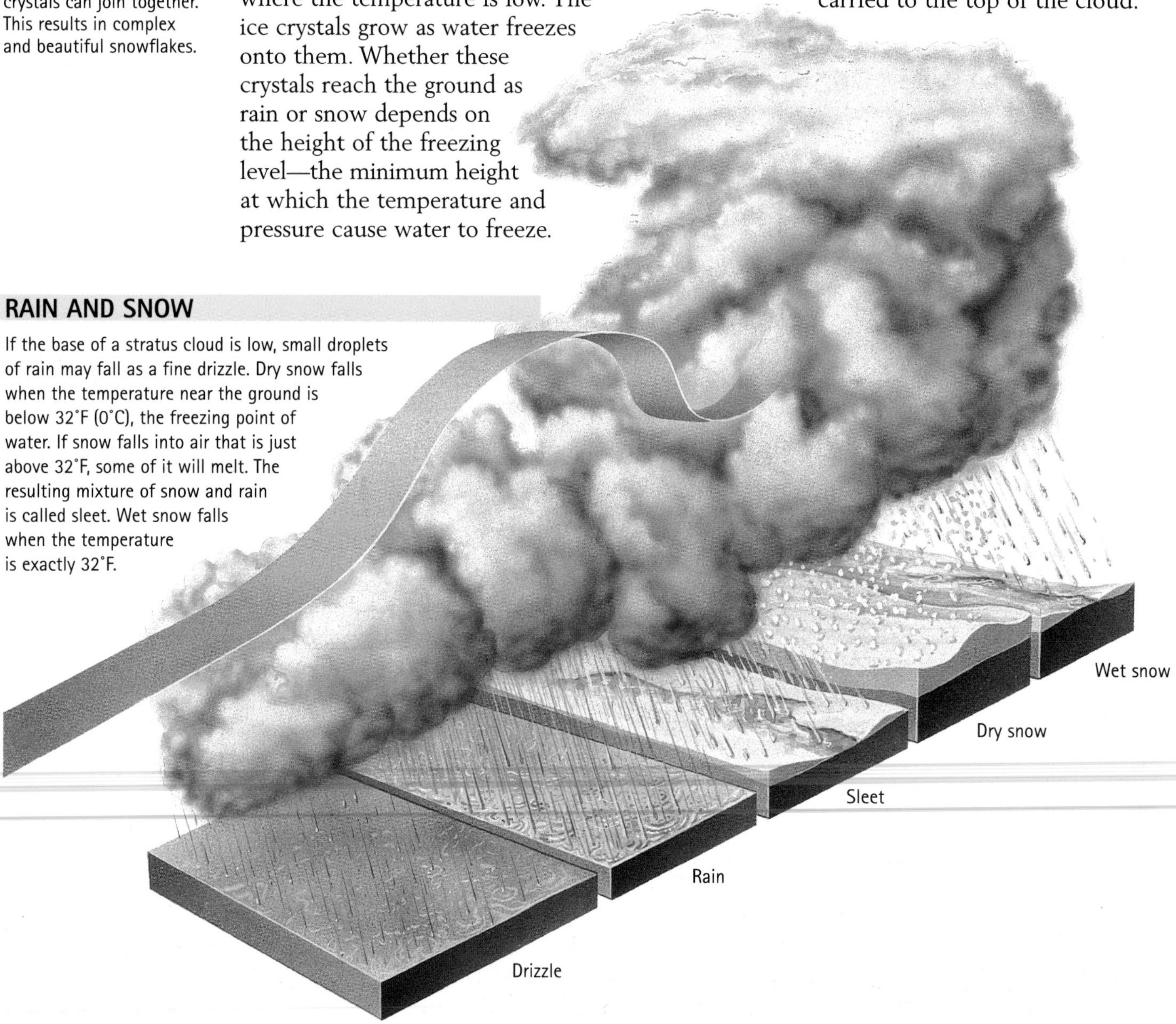

Wet snow

Dry snow

Sleet

Rain

Drizzle

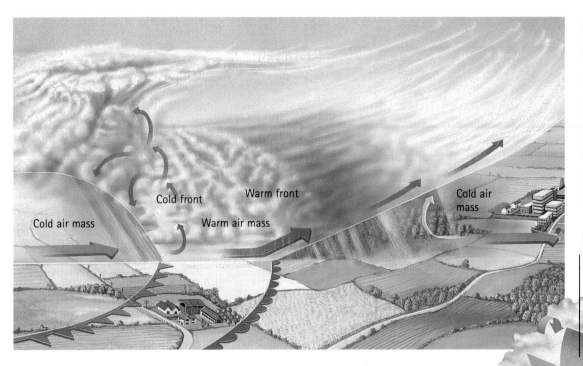

Cold front

Warm front

Cold air mass

Warm air mass

Cold air mass

Clouds form and produce rain when warm, moist air rises. This can happen when a warm air front meets a mass of cold air. The warm air cools as it rises over the cold air, forming clouds, light rain, and drizzle. When a cold front pushes under warm air, the moist air rises rapidly, forming storm clouds and often giving heavy rain. Clear, cooler weather usually follows.

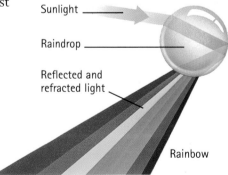

Path of hailstones

Warm updraft

Cold downdraft

Freezing level

Rain

Hail

The hailstones continue to rise and fall, getting larger with each cycle, until they are too heavy for the updraft and fall to the ground. Typical hailstones can be half an inch or more in diameter. The heaviest on record weighed over 1.5 lbs.

RAINFALL LEVELS

Annual rainfalls of 23–59 inches are normal for temperate regions such as northern Europe, but there are desert regions where there has been no rain for years. In part of the Atacama Desert, in Chile, no rainfall was recorded for over 400 years. At the other extreme, Waialeale peak, in Hawaii, receives more than 36 feet of rain in an average year. The greatest snowfall in 12 months was 102 feet,

which fell in the winter of 1971–1972 on Mount Rainer, in Washington.

On March 16, 1952, the town of Cilaos, on an island in the Indian Ocean, received over six feet of rain. Torrential rain of this type can loosen tree roots and destabilize slopes, causing catastrophic landslides and washing away homes. Prolonged heavy rain and suddenthaws can raise the water levels of rivers, making them burst their banks.

Hailstones start off as tiny seeds of ice at the top of a storm cloud. They fall to the bottom of the cloud, but are then swept back to the top by a warm updraft of air. More water freezes onto the seed before it drops and is swept up again. Each hailstone goes through several cycles, building up many layers of ice before it finally falls to the ground.

Sunlight

Raindrop

Reflected and refracted light

Rainbow

Sunlight is a mixture of wavelengths of light. When it is reflected by a raindrop, each wavelength is refracted, or bent, through a different angle. As a result, the different wavelengths are seen as separate colors in a rainbow.

◄ Rainbows can be seen when sunlight is refracted and reflected by millions of droplets of rain.

SEE ALSO PAGES:

36–7 Climate, 50–1 Life: origins and development, 460 Climate change

CLOUDS AND FOG

Heat from sunlight makes water evaporate from the ground. When the air temperature drops, water vapor in the air condenses to form clouds and fog.

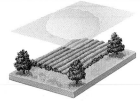

1 Sunshine warms bare soil faster than grass. On sunny days, humid air rises from these areas.

2 As humid air rises and cools, the water vapor in it starts to condense and form clouds.

3 The clouds grow as further pockets of rising warm air feed them with droplets of water.

The amount of water that air can hold as invisible vapor depends on its temperature. If moist air cools below a certain temperature, minute droplets of water start to form around tiny grains of dust or smoke in the air. Clouds and fog are made of these droplets. Fog is cloud that has formed at ground level. At high altitude, where the air is cold, the water in clouds forms ice crystals.

CLOUD FORMATION

In sunny weather, warmth and moisture from the ground produce rising currents of warm, moist air. When this rises into cooler air, the vapor begins to condense and form cloud. But the inside of the cloud is still warm and continues to rise, forming tall, fluffy clouds.

A different type of cloud forms when a warm, moist air front meets a body of cold air. The warm air rises over the cool air and starts to cool. Sheets of unbroken cloud can form at the boundary between warm and cool air. Cloud can also form when moist air rises and cools as it passes over hills or mountains.

TYPES OF CLOUDS

Clouds are usually classified by their appearance and height. The height of a cloud is measured to the cloud's base, but some types of clouds can tower many thousands of feet above their bases. Low-level clouds have bases at altitudes of less than 6,600 feet. Medium-level clouds have bases at 6,600-16,400 feet and high-level clouds have bases around 16,400-46,000 feet.

Examples of low-level clouds include stratus clouds, which form in unbroken sheets, and fluffy white cumulus clouds that resemble small balls of cotton. Cumulonimbus clouds also have low-level bases, but they can reach 42,600 feet into the atmosphere. These clouds are usually anvil-shaped, and they can bring heavy showers and thunderstorms.

Medium-level clouds include altostratus, which form as fine sheets; and darker nimbostratus clouds, which often bring persistent rain or snow. Altocumulus are spectacular bands of medium-level clouds that resemble ripple marks on a seashore.

High-level clouds are types of cirrus, which take their name from the Latin word meaning "tuft." This is because of their wispy appearance. Cirrus clouds are made of minute crystals of ice.

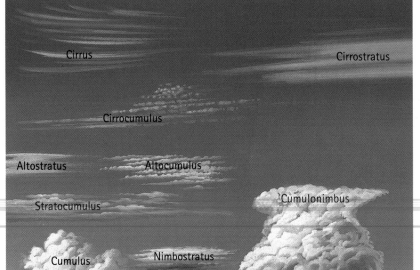

Cirrus · Cirrostratus · Cirrocumulus · Altostratus · Altocumulus · Stratocumulus · Cumulonimbus · Cumulus · Nimbostratus · Stratus

Cirrus clouds are high-altitude strands of cloud. Cirrostratus clouds form a veil. Cirrocumulus clouds are tufts of high-level cloud that can make a regular rippled pattern called mackerel sky. Altostratus is a thin layer of medium-level cloud. Nimbostratus is a thicker sheet of gray cloud that can bring rain or snow. Cloudlets at medium level are called altocumulus. Low-level cloud includes stratus, a layer that often shrouds the tops of hills, and fluffy cumulus clouds. Stratocumulus is a layer of joined cumulus clouds. Strong updrafts of warm air can form anvil-shaped cumulonimbus clouds, and bring the threat of thunderstorms.

Storm clouds produce lightning discharges of 100,000 volts or more. These huge sparks heat air to over 54,000°F. The rapid expansion of air that results causes a thunderclap.

FEATURES OF CLOUDS

A trained meteorologist can often predict the weather by looking at the shapes of clouds and watching how they change. Clouds can form amazing and sometimes beautiful features in the sky. Unstable bulges can hang down below altocumulus clouds to form udderlike fingers of cloud. Air currents descending from mountains sometimes produce series of vertical waves, which form clouds that resemble a pile of plates. These are the clouds that have been mistaken for flying saucers.

When sunlight passes through holes in a cloud, but the sun itself is hidden, beautiful rays of light can be seen as the sunlight catches on particles of dust in the atmosphere. Droplets of very cold water in thin clouds can act as prisms, splitting sunlight into its component wavelengths and making the clouds shine with a variety of colors. At sunset and sunrise, when the sun is low in the sky, its light is scattered by the atmosphere, so that the undersides of high clouds are illuminated with beautiful pink, orange, and red colors. This effect can be particularly spectacular in polluted areas, where dust in the atmosphere adds to the natural scattering effect. High-altitude cirrus clouds can produce the effect of a halo around the sun or the moon as light is refracted through the ice crystals.

FOG AND SMOG

When a cloud forms at ground level, it is called fog. Because fog reduces visibility, it is particularly dangerous for drivers and mountaineers. In extreme cases, visibility can be less than three feet.

Smog is a mixture of smoke and fog that occurs in polluted areas. Until the mid-1950s, smoke from coal fires in cities in England caused such severe smogs that many people died of respiratory illnesses. Pollution control has reduced the severity of smogs, but occurrences of smog still increase death rates, as well as causing eye irritation and asthma attacks.

Sea mist is a common sight in San Francisco Bay. Here, the center of the Golden Gate Bridge is hidden by mist.

Sea mist is a type of advection fog that forms when warm moist air meets a cold ocean current, in this case off the California coast.

FOG FORMATION

Advection fog forms when moist, warm air travels over a cool surface on land or at sea. Frontal fog forms where two air masses of different temperatures meet. Radiation fog forms at night when the ground rapidly loses heat by radiation and cools damp air above it. Radiation fog forms in hollows in the ground. Upslope fog can form when moist air cools as it travels up a slope.

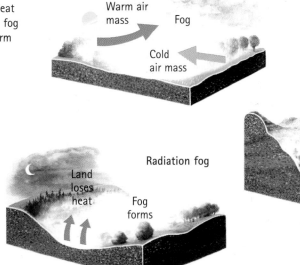

Frontal fog

Warm air mass   Fog

Cold air mass

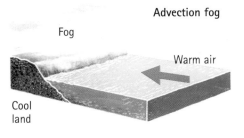

Advection fog

Fog

Warm air

Cool land

Radiation fog

Land loses heat   Fog forms

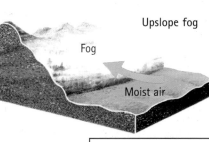

Upslope fog

Fog

Moist air

SEE ALSO PAGES:

36–7 Climate, 42–3 Weather forecasting, 264–5 Refraction

WEATHER FORECASTING

Weather systems are complex and hard to predict. Modern weather forecasters make their predictions using worldwide weather data and computer models.

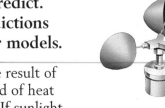

◄ An anemometer measures wind speed as the wind makes its cups rotate around a central shaft.

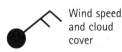

Weather map

Warm front

Cold front

Isobar

Wind speed and cloud cover

These symbols are used to plot data on weather maps. The semicircles and triangles show the type and direction of the front. Isobars plot air pressure.

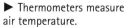

▲ This meteorologist is using a portable computer to collect data from a weather-monitoring station. Some weather stations send their data to a central office by radio, satellite, or telephone links.

Weather systems are the result of sunshine driving a kind of heat engine in the atmosphere. If sunlight fell constantly on a uniform planet, the weather would never change. But sunshine varies with clouds, day and night, seasons, and latitude, and the Earth is not uniform. Oceans hold more heat than dry land, so they act as night storage and warm rapidly in the sunshine. During the day, warm air rises inland and draws in moist air from the sea. As the moist air cools, clouds form, and the moisture falls as rain, sleet, hail, or snow. As the air warms, it expands, creating high pressure systems and winds that drive the weather systems around the globe.

MAKING PREDICTIONS

Anyone can make a weather forecast by simply looking at the weather today and predicting exactly the same for tomorrow. Between the tropics and the poles, this forecast would be correct for about seven days out of ten. But it is more useful, and more difficult, to predict the times when the weather changes. There are many traditional ways of predicting weather changes, and some of them are very reliable. A bright red sunset is a good predictor of improving weather.

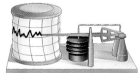

► A barograph uses a pen to record changes in air pressure on a rotating drum.

◄ A wet-and-dry bulb thermometer is used to measure air humidity.

► Thermometers measure air temperature.

All these instruments are used to measure wind speed, atmospheric pressure, humidity, and temperature. These are the four major indicators of weather conditions.

This is because weather systems usually arrive from the west. The red sky is caused by sunlight passing through dry, dusty air beyond the western horizon, an indication of fine weather to come. A red sky in the morning happens when sunshine from the east falls on clouds and bad weather is approaching from the west.

The way that animals behave can also be a good indicator of changing weather. Cattle tend to lie down as rain approaches, for example, and seabirds are often driven inland by storms at sea.

A meteorological office uses information from weather-monitoring devices to plot current conditions and to forecast how they might change. Computer programs help make these predictions as accurate as possible. Televised weather reports use simplified weather maps that are easy to understand. Weather forecasts on television and radio are particularly useful for farmers, gardeners, and sailors, all of whom need to be prepared for sudden weather changes.

A weather-monitoring aircraft takes air samples. A radar device in a pod under the fuselage detects raindrops and hailstones as they form inside clouds.

The National Lightning Detection Network provides valuable information that is used to divert aircraft and warn power-supply companies.

SCIENTIFIC FORECASTING

Modern weather forecasters observe the weather in thousands of different places and calculate the changes that are likely to happen. They get their data from an international network of weather stations, high-altitude balloons, and satellites. The data is fed into computers that predict weather patterns. Such forecasts can be reasonably accurate for up to a week ahead. Longer-range forecasts tend to be inaccurate because of the complex development of weather systems. A small, unpredictable event can affect all the steps in the development of a weather system, so the outcome is completely different from the prediction. This is often compared to a butterfly flapping its wings on one continent and causing a storm on another.

Some forecasters try to predict weather months in advance by looking at variations in the sun's activity, but these predictions frequently are wrong.

Weather is dominated by regions of high and low atmospheric pressure. Winds blow from high to low pressure. Because of the Earth's rotation, wind spirals into areas of low pressure like water down a drain.

Fronts are regions where cold and warm air meet. Since hot air rises, warm air in a warm front rises up over cold air. Its moisture forms clouds and rain. At a cold front, cold air pushes beneath warm air. This makes it rise steeply and often causes heavy showers that soon give way to finer weather. When a cold front meets a warm front, the warm air lifts, and the frontal system dies away.

This helium-filled balloon carries instruments that measure temperature and humidity. Its spiky surface makes it stable in flight.

Hurricane Frederic struck the Gulf of Mexico in September 1979. The New York Stock Exchange used this combination of satellite images and wind speed values to forecast where the most damage was likely to happen. This type of information is of interest because hurricane damage to crops and property can severely reduce the value of agricultural businesses.

HURRICANE FREDERIC CLOUD WINDS (M/S) AND STEREO HEIGHTS.
1922-1945 GMT 12 SEPTEMBER 1979

▲ This Meteosat craft is one of a series of weather satellites that send back images of cloud patterns from fixed positions above the Earth's surface.

SEE ALSO PAGES:

WINDS, STORMS, AND FLOODS

Gentle winds can be refreshing and pleasant. Strong winds, storms, and floods can range from being a simple inconvenience to a threat to life and property.

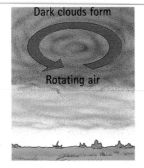

Cloud rotation becomes visible in the dark sky.

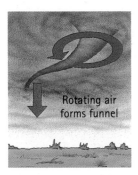

A rotating funnel snakes down from the cloud.

The funnel touches down and sucks up debris.

▲ A tornado can result from a clash between two wind systems that are traveling in different directions. The first sign of a tornado forming is when a patch of dark cloud starts to rotate. Then, a rotating funnel of warm air descends to the ground. The spiraling updraft sucks up dust and debris, which it hurls around at high speed.

Wind patterns on the Earth's surface are part of the three-dimensional pattern of air circulation in the Earth's atmosphere. Around the equator, where sunshine is strongest, warm air rises and horizontal wind speeds can be low. Sailors know these regions as the doldrums. The updraft of air at the equator draws in air over the tropics, causing reliable trade winds from the northeast in the Tropic of Cancer and from the southeast in the Tropic of Capricorn. Higher latitudes are dominated by winds from the west.

In some places, seasonal winds are so well known that they are given names. The mistral, in France, is a cold northerly wind that funnels down the river valleys. The sirocco is a hot, oppressive wind from Libya that affects the northern Mediterranean. The dry, easterly harmattan, in western Africa, brings relief from humid conditions.

TORNADOES

As pockets of air become warm, they expand and rise, swirling around and drawing more air in beneath them. A tornado usually begins inside thunderclouds, where currents of warm and cold air meet in a rotating system called a supercell. As the supercell sucks air more and more rapidly from underneath, a funnel reaches down from the base of the cloud until it meets the ground. The suction inside the funnel is immense, and wind speeds of more than 300 mph (480kph), or 436 feet per second (133mps), are not unusual.

Some tornadoes last for hours, others blow out in a few seconds. The base of a twister can be anything from a few feet to over half a mile wide.

The midwestern United States is sometimes called Tornado Alley. Hundreds of tornadoes strike the area each year as hot, humid air from the Gulf of Mexico meets cold, dry air from Canada.

Force	Speed (mph)	Effects
0	<1	Calm. Smoke rises vertically.
1	1–3	Light air. Smoke drifts, but flags do not move.
2	4–7	Light breeze. Smoke shows the direction of the wind.
3	8–12	Gentle breeze. Flags move gently, leaves rustle.
4	13–17	Moderate breeze. Loose paper blows around.
5	18–24	Fresh breeze. Small trees sway.
6	25–30	Strong breeze. Umbrellas blow inside out.
7	31–38	Moderate gale. Resistance felt when walking into wind.
8	39–46	Fresh gale. Twigs and branches break.
9	47–55	Strong gale. Chimneys topple, roofs damaged.
10	56–63	Whole gale. Trees blown over, but not moved.
11	64–74	Storm. Trees uprooted and moved. Vehicles blown over.
12	>74	Hurricane. Buildings destroyed, widespread devastation.

The Beaufort wind scale was devised in 1805. In the United States a storm technically becomes a hurricane when winds reach 74 mph (119kph).

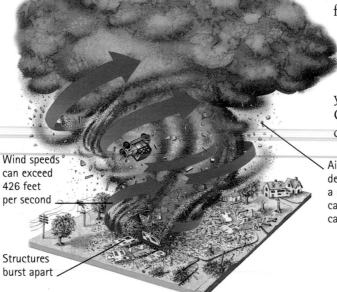

Wind speeds can exceed 426 feet per second

Structures burst apart

Airborne debris is a major cause of casualties

The high-speed wind around a tornado can cause damage in its own right. The damage is worsened by fast-moving debris sucked up through the funnel of the tornado. Added to this is the explosion risk caused by trapped air when a sealed building is caught in the low-pressure funnel.

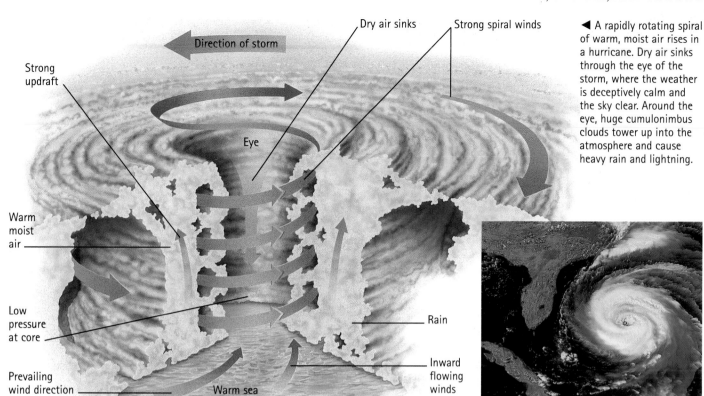

Direction of storm

Dry air sinks   Strong spiral winds

Strong updraft

Eye

Warm moist air

Low pressure at core

Prevailing wind direction

Warm sea

Rain

Inward flowing winds

◀ A rapidly rotating spiral of warm, moist air rises in a hurricane. Dry air sinks through the eye of the storm, where the weather is deceptively calm and the sky clear. Around the eye, huge cumulonimbus clouds tower up into the atmosphere and cause heavy rain and lightning.

This satellite photograph shows Hurricane Fran approaching the North American mainland from the Caribbean Sea in 1996. The eye of the hurricane is clearly visible as a clear area in the center of the spiral of clouds. This hurricane, with wind speeds of 118 mph (190kph), killed 34 people.

TROPICAL CYCLONES

Tropical cyclones cause more widespread destruction than tornadoes. Most tropical cyclones form in late summer. This is when sea temperatures are at their highest, and hundreds of storm systems can come together and rotate as a single great low pressure system, sometimes hundreds of miles across. As the wind speed increases, tropical cyclones tend to move away from the equator. They gather force over warm seas until they hit land.

When they occur in the Gulf of Mexico and the western Atlantic, tropical cyclones are called hurricanes. Hurricanes rotate counterclockwise and most often occur between August and October.

In the Southern Hemisphere, tropical cyclones rotate clockwise and mostly occur between January and April. When they occur off the coast of Southeast Asia, they are called typhoons.

In all cases, tropical cyclones bring heavy rain and wind speeds of up to 125 mph (200kph) or more as warm air spirals around the storm system. Since they are regions of low pressure, tropical cyclones raise the sea level beneath them and can cause devastating floods, called storm surges, if they run into coastlines that do not have strong defenses.

FLOODS

Storm surges are not the only cause of flooding. In mountainous areas, flash floods can surge down steep valleys after heavy rain, or when snow melts quickly. Rivers can burst their banks and flood wide plains. Also, a combination of low pressure, a high tide, and strong onshore winds can flood coastlines. In 1953, storm winds and high tides drove a wedge of water down the North Sea onto the coast of eastern England, the Netherlands, and Belgium. Sea defenses failed and the sea swept 37 mi. (60km) inland. If global warming causes sea levels to rise, such floods could become more frequent. Low-lying coral islands, such as the Maldives, and parts of countries like Bangladesh and Holland could be lost to the seas.

Disastrous floods are an almost yearly event in Bangladesh and the many other countries that suffer from tropical cyclones. Tragically, many of these countries are too poor to be able to fund adequate defenses against flooding.

SEE ALSO PAGES:

10–11 Earth's atmosphere, 36–7 Climate, 42–3 Weather forecasting

MAPS AND MAPPING

Maps are graphical representations of the surface of the Earth. The quality of maps has improved with the use of new technologies, such as satellite imagery.

This map, by Venetian cartographer Battista Agnese dates from 1540. Although the proportions are distorted, the African coast is still recognizable. Very little of the Americas had been charted in the 1500s.

Maps are used to depict almost any kind of geographical information. Since the Earth is a three-dimensional object, the whole surface of the planet cannot be displayed without being distorted in some way. As a result, most maps present a limited area for a specific purpose. World maps can be drawn, but they require the selection of a projection that best represents the portions of the world important to the theme of the map.

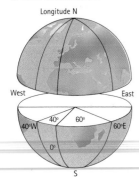

Flemish cartographer Gerhard Mercator (1512–1594) devised the first fairly accurate way to represent the surface of the Earth.

A Mercator projection shows equatorial regions very accurately. However, the continents become more distorted farther from the equator— Greenland appears larger in area than Africa.

ACCUMULATING MAP DATA

New technologies, such as satellite imaging and aerial photography, have made even the most complex map a reality. However, traditional mapping techniques, such as land surveying, are still an essential part of the process. To make any map a useful reference, there must be a grid of fixed points from which every region on the Earth's surface can be located. Before mapmakers could use tools such as aerial photography, the grid was plotted by triangulation, a process that allows the measurement of angles between landmarks such as hilltops. In this way, distances between different reference points can be calculated without the need to take measurements on the ground. Heights are normally shown as contours. These are lines that link points of similar elevation.

LATITUDE AND LONGITUDE

The most obvious reference point on the Earth is the equator. Lines of latitude are measured at angles north or south of the equator. Lines of longitude divide the Earth through each pole in the same way as the segments of an orange. Since there was no obvious reference point for longitude, English navigators used the position of their home port Greenwich, in London, as a reference. Seafarers used to measure latitude by calculating the heights of stars in the sky or the position of the sun as it rose, set, or reached its zenith. It was only after the perfection of the marine chronometer by John Harrison (1693–1776) that accurate longitude measurements, and hence accurate mapmaking, became possible.

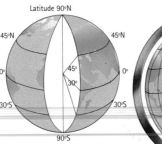

Lines of longitude are imaginary lines that encircle the Earth from pole to pole. They measure the angular distance east or west of the Greenwich Meridian, which is defined as 0° longitude.

Lines of latitude measure the angular distance north or south of the equator, which is defined as 0° latitude. Lines of latitude are parallel and get shorter and shorter toward the poles.

Any point on the Earth can be defined using a combination of latitude and longitude.

Today, mapping data from land surveys and satellite imagery is stored and manipulated using computer software known as Geographic Information Systems (GIS).

DRAWING TO SCALE

All maps must be drawn to a defined scale. With a large scale, objects such as roads and buildings can be depicted as the shape they are in real life, but smaller. As a scale gets smaller, detailed information cannot be drawn accurately, and most objects are shown as symbols. Scales are normally expressed as a ratio between the size of the map and the size of what it represents. Maps of all scales are used. A traveler planning a long-distance trip, for example, might use a scale of 1:250,000.

MAP PROJECTIONS

Representing the surface of a three-dimensional object, such as the Earth, on a two-dimensional surface, such as paper, will never be accurate. So mapmakers, or cartographers, have devised various projections. Imagine a light at the center of a transparent planet Earth. The shining light will project shadows of the continents onto a piece of paper wrapped around the planet. One way to do this is to wrap the paper around the equator to form a cylinder. In this way, Flemish geographer Gerhard Mercator drew the first accurate map in 1569. Today, Goode's projection is the best way to map the Earth. The map looks like a whole orange skin if it is removed and rolled flat. The continents are shown accurately, but the oceans are opened up to stretch out the segments.

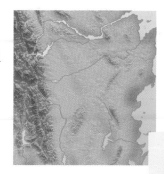

▲ Relief maps show the physical features of the Earth's surface. Most modern relief maps include features such as rivers, plains, hills, and mountains.

MODERN MAPMAKING

Today, satellite images provide the framework for all map data. Information is stored on computer so that it can be quickly updated and with no need to redraw each map. Today, a network of satellites in low Earth-orbit map the planet's surface every few days. Their sensors can record earthquake movements, forest clearance, the health of crops, and even the underlying geology of a region. However, ground-based scientists are always needed to interpret this satellite data and continually monitor the changing face of our planet.

UNDERSTANDING MAPS

Maps can summarize almost any type of geographical information. For example, shading or contour lines can represent different elevations. Other information, such as the distribution of crops or the underlying geology of a region, are often depicted on maps. Roads, railroads, and population density can all be shown.

◄ Here, population density is shown by colors. Dark colors are the areas with the greatest density of human habitation.

▲ Route maps and street maps may show buildings, roads, and railroads. Such maps are useful guides to help travelers find their way around large cities.

▲ The LANDSAT craft is one of a fleet of international remote-sensing satellites that are continually taking images of the surface of the Earth and relaying them back. The data has considerably improved the accuracy of geographical measurements in recent years.

◄ This satellite image shows San Francisco Bay in California. The San Andreas fault, a potential earthquake threat, runs through the hills of the bay and is closely monitored from space.

SEE ALSO PAGES:

20–1 Earthquakes, 424–5
Artificial satellites, 436–7
Action zones

FACTS AND FIGURES

PLANETARY DATA

Equatorial diameter	12,756 km
Polar diameter	12,714 km
Equatorial circumference	40,077 km
Volume	1.083×10^{12} km³
Mass	5.98×10^{24} kg
Density (average)	5.52 (water = 1.0)
Surface gravity	9.78 ms⁻²
Escape velocity	11.18 kms⁻¹
Day length	23 hr 56 min 4.1 sec
Year length	365.24 days
Axial inclination	23.44 degrees
Axial speed at the equator	1,600 km/h
Average temperature	14°C (57°F)
Age	4.6 billion years (approximately)
Distance from the Sun	149,503,000 km (average) 147,000,000 km (minimum) 152,000,000 km (maximum)
Length of orbit	938,900,000 km
Orbital speed	106,000 km/h
Surface area	510 million km²
Land surface	148 million km²
Oceans cover	71% of surface
Mass of water	1.35×10^{21} kg
Ocean depth	3.8 km
Atmospheric composition	N₂ 78%, O₂ 21%
Atmospheric thickness	1,100 km
Atmospheric pressure	101,325 Pa (Nm⁻²) (sea level) 33,440 Pa (Everest summit)

EARTH'S STRUCTURE

Continental crust	35 km thick (av.)
Oceanic crust	7 km thick (av.)
Lithosphere	100 km thick
density	2.7–3
composition	O 46.6%, Si 27.7%, Al 8.1%, Fe 5.0%, Ca 3.6%, K 2.6%, Na 2.8%, Mg 2.1%.
Mantle	2,900 km thick
temperature	3,000°C at base
density	3.3–6.0
composition	silicates of iron and magnesium
Outer core	2,200 km thick
temperature	4,000°C at base
density	10
composition	molten iron, traces of nickel
Inner core	1,300 km radius
temperature	6,500°C at center
density	13
composition	solid iron, traces of nickel

BRANCHES OF EARTH SCIENCES

Climatologists study the climate—the seasonal and longer-term variations in temperature and moisture in the lower atmosphere across the world.

Geochemists study the chemical composition of the Earth's crust, its oceans, and its atmosphere.

Geologists study the Earth's origin and the structure and composition of its layers.

Geomorphologists study the forms and formation of land features such as ocean basins and mountain ranges.

Meteorologists study and attempt to predict day-to-day variations in the weather. They measure and forecast conditions in the lower atmosphere, such as temperature, rainfall, and wind speed.

Mineralogists are geologists who study crystalline minerals and ores.

Oceanographers study marine life and the physical and chemical conditions in the oceans and on the seabed.

Paleontologists study the structure, evolution, environment, and distribution of ancient organisms by examining their fossilized remains. Paleobiologists study animal fossils, paleobotanists study plant fossils, and paleoclimatologists study the climate of the past.

Petrologists study the origins and structures of rocks.

Planetologists examine and make comparisons between planets.

Sedimentologists are geologists who study rocks formed from silt and sandy deposits.

Stratigraphers study layers of rock and how they relate to one another.

KEY DATES

B.C.

*c.*235 — Eratosthenes—a Greek astronomer, geographer, and mathematician—calculates the Earth's circumference from shadows cast at different latitudes at midday.

*c.*5 — Greek geographer Strabo proposes frigid, temperate, and tropical climate zones.

A.D.

*c.*30 — Strabo suggests that there might be unknown continents.

79 — Roman writer Pliny the Younger describes the eruption of Vesuvius that caused the destruction of Pompeii.

132 — Chinese invent first seismograph—finely balanced metal balls that fall if the ground shakes.

1086 — Chinese engineer Shen Kua outlines the principles of erosion, sedimentation, and uplift processes.

1517 — Italian scholar Girolamo Fracastoro suggests that fossils are the remains of creatures left by the biblical flood in the story of Noah's ark.

1546 — German metallurgist Georgius Agricola first uses the term "fossil" for the rocklike remains of plants and animals.

1600 — British physician William Gilbert proposes that the Earth is like a giant magnet.

1735 — British meteorologist George Hadley uses mathematics and physics to explain how the Earth's spin affects trade winds.

1785 — British geologist James Hutton proposes that the Earth's features form through processes, such as sedimentation and volcanic activity, that take place over long periods of time.

1795 — French anatomist Georges Cuvier identifies a set of fossilized bones as belonging to a giant marine reptile.

1811 — British teenager Mary Anning and her family discover and collect fossils of the first known *Ichthyosaurus* sample.

1822 — *Iguanodon* is identified.

1825 — Cuvier proposes that species become extinct as a result of catastrophic events.

1830 — British geologist Charles Lyell suggests that the Earth is hundreds of millions of years old.

1840 — Swiss-born naturalist Louis Agassiz proposes that most of the Earth was once covered by ice.

1859 — British scientist Charles Darwin publishes theory of evolution.

1896 — Swedish chemist Svante Arrhenius shows that carbon dioxide in air helps trap heat in the Earth's atmosphere.

1906 — Irish geologist Richard Oldham finds evidence of the Earth's core in records of seismic waves.

1915 — German meteorologist Alfred Wegener publishes a theory that continents are in motion.

1925 — Echo soundings reveal the Mid-Atlantic Ridge.

1935 — U.S. seismologist Charles Richter devises a scale for reporting the strengths of earthquakes.

1952 — Live coelocanth, a fish thought to have been extinct for 50 million years, found off Madagascar.

1965 — Canadian geophysicist Tuzo Wilson explains how the plates on the ocean floor move.

1981 — Luis Alvarez and his son Walter propose that a giant meteorite impact killed the dinosaurs.

CHAPTER 2
LIVING THINGS

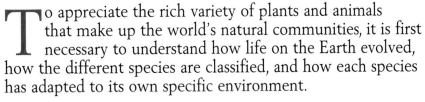

To appreciate the rich variety of plants and animals that make up the world's natural communities, it is first necessary to understand how life on the Earth evolved, how the different species are classified, and how each species has adapted to its own specific environment.

The story of life on the Earth began many millions of years before the appearance of the first human beings. Life began in the oceans over 3.5 billion years ago. Today, there are more than 2 million living species on the Earth. Many are so tiny that they can be seen only with the aid of microscopes. Others live in remote and alien habitats, such as the cold and sunless depths of the ocean. Humans know little about them.

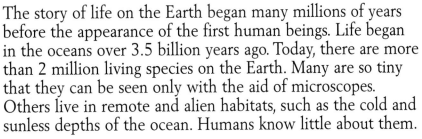

All the species of plants and animals have evolved by gradually adapting to the many different types of environments that the Earth offers its inhabitants. Some plants and animals have had their evolution guided by human intervention. Many garden plants, agricultural crops, farm animals, and domestic pets are examples of species that arose through selective breeding.

Each wild plant and animal species lives in harmony with its surroundings. The living world is a marvelously intricate system that has taken millions of years to develop, and one which exists in a delicate and constantly changing balance.

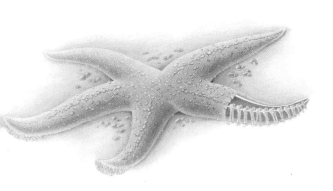

LIFE: ORIGINS AND DEVELOPMENT

Life began on the Earth over three billion years ago. Since then, an astonishing variety of plants and animals has evolved from single-celled organisms.

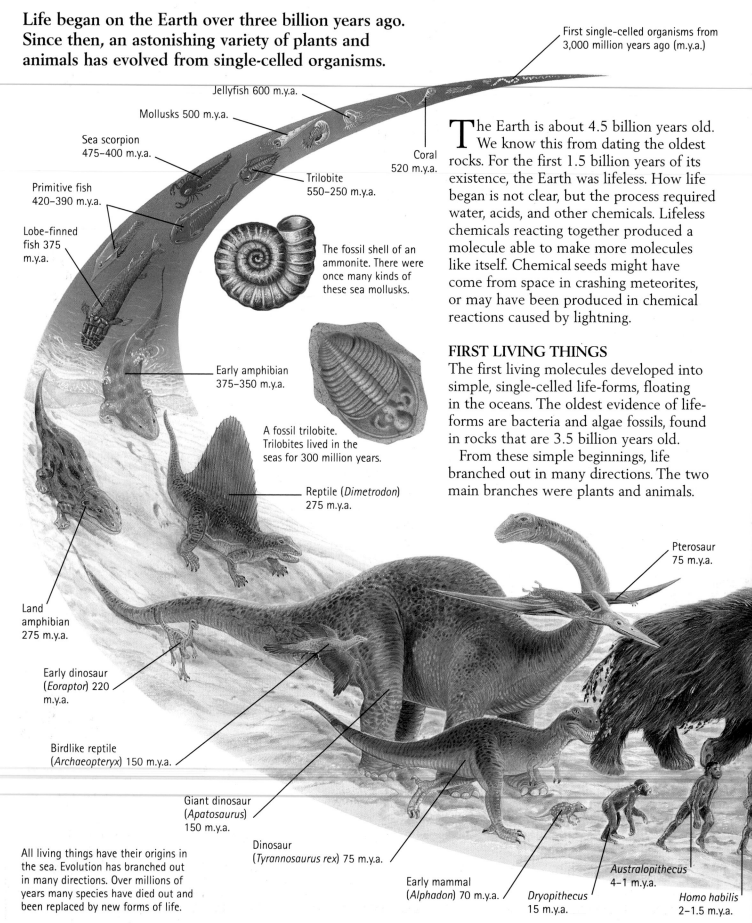

First single-celled organisms from 3,000 million years ago (m.y.a.)

Jellyfish 600 m.y.a.

Mollusks 500 m.y.a.

Sea scorpion 475–400 m.y.a.

Primitive fish 420–390 m.y.a.

Lobe-finned fish 375 m.y.a.

Coral 520 m.y.a.

Trilobite 550–250 m.y.a.

The fossil shell of an ammonite. There were once many kinds of these sea mollusks.

Early amphibian 375–350 m.y.a.

A fossil trilobite. Trilobites lived in the seas for 300 million years.

Reptile (*Dimetrodon*) 275 m.y.a.

Land amphibian 275 m.y.a.

Early dinosaur (*Eoraptor*) 220 m.y.a.

Birdlike reptile (*Archaeopteryx*) 150 m.y.a.

Giant dinosaur (*Apatosaurus*) 150 m.y.a.

Dinosaur (*Tyrannosaurus rex*) 75 m.y.a.

Early mammal (*Alphadon*) 70 m.y.a.

Pterosaur 75 m.y.a.

Dryopithecus 15 m.y.a.

Australopithecus 4–1 m.y.a.

Homo habilis 2–1.5 m.y.a.

All living things have their origins in the sea. Evolution has branched out in many directions. Over millions of years many species have died out and been replaced by new forms of life.

The Earth is about 4.5 billion years old. We know this from dating the oldest rocks. For the first 1.5 billion years of its existence, the Earth was lifeless. How life began is not clear, but the process required water, acids, and other chemicals. Lifeless chemicals reacting together produced a molecule able to make more molecules like itself. Chemical seeds might have come from space in crashing meteorites, or may have been produced in chemical reactions caused by lightning.

FIRST LIVING THINGS

The first living molecules developed into simple, single-celled life-forms, floating in the oceans. The oldest evidence of life-forms are bacteria and algae fossils, found in rocks that are 3.5 billion years old.

From these simple beginnings, life branched out in many directions. The two main branches were plants and animals.

The land dinosaurs and giant sea reptiles died out 65 million years ago. Why? One theory holds that the Earth may have been hit by a gigantic meteorite. This would have caused a long winter as the sun was blotted out by the resulting dust clouds. Plants died. So did most plant-eating reptiles and the carnivores that preyed on them.

The ginkgo tree has lived on the Earth for more than 300 million years. It is the only survivor of a once-common group of plants.

EVOLUTION

All plants and animals have developed through a process of gradual change known as evolution. The species (kinds) of plants and animals alive today have evolved from much earlier kinds, which are now extinct. Trilobites and ammonites swarmed in the seas millions of years ago. Now only their petrified fossils remain.

Plants and animals died out because the conditions where they lived changed. They were replaced by other species that were better able to adapt to these changes.

ADAPTATION

Dinosaurs ruled planet Earth for over 160 million years. There were more than 500 species. Yet they all died out, and today, fossils are all that remain of these remarkable animals.

Living things are constantly evolving through adaptation. They can adapt because every individual life-form is slightly different, even from members of its own species. This means that when conditions change—for example, the climate growing colder—some life-forms may be better at surviving than others.

Plants and animals have colonized almost every environment on the Earth—freezing polar regions, hot and dry deserts, even the dark ocean depths.

The DNA molecules in the cells of all living things contain coded instructions (genes). These control the way the cells behave.

Mammals (Woolly mammoth, tiger, elk) 10,000 years ago

Homo sapiens
100,000 years ago

Homo erectus
1.5–0.5 m.y.a.

Neanderthal man
100,000–35,000 years ago

Berry-feeding

Seed-feeding

Cactus-feeding

Insect-feeding

On the Galapagos Islands, in the Pacific Ocean, Darwin found finches that were descended from one species, but that now had differently shaped beaks. Evolution had adapted each kind's beak to eat a different type of food.

Charles Darwin (1809–1882) was a British scientist. His studies of living animals and fossils led him to his theory of natural selection, published in 1859.

SEE ALSO PAGES:

4–5 Fossils and geological time, 135 Genes and chromosomes

51

CLASSIFICATION OF LIVING THINGS

Classification is the method by which living things are grouped into categories. It is based on the appearance of, and the natural relationships between, organisms.

No one knows exactly how many living things there are on the Earth today. Scientists have discovered over two million, but there may be four times as many, mostly microscopic, organisms that have yet to be discovered.

HOW THINGS ARE NAMED

The scientific study of the diversity of living things and the relationships between them is called systematics. Taxonomy, which is part of systematics, is the study of the rules and procedures of classifying plants and animals. When classifying an organism, it is given a scientific name. This is written in Latin so that it can be identified by scientists all over the world. Classification helps us to study and understand the natural world. It also shows how living species are related to species that died out long ago.

The classification system scientists use today is based on a system developed by Swedish naturalist Carolus Linnaeus (1707–1778) in 1758. Individual organisms, called species, are classed in different levels. The highest level is called a kingdom. All animals belong to the kingdom Animalia. There are four other kingdoms, but the animal kingdom is by far the largest. The differences in the structure of an organism's cells partly determines to which kingdom the organism belongs.

The level below the kingdom is called the phylum (plural: phyla). There are more than 20 different phyla within the animal kingdom. All vertebrates (animals with backbones) belong to the phylum Chordata.

The fossil fish shown above, called *Priscacaria*, is extinct today. However, the species still fits into the classification of living things. Taxonomists compare certain features, such as the arrangement of fins, with some of the 22,000 kinds of fish that live on the Earth today. The fossil fish is then grouped with living fish that have similar attributes.

THE FAMILY TREE OF LIFE

The prehistory of the Earth is marked by periods of time called eras, each lasting many millions of years. There are four eras: the Precambrian, Paleozoic, Mesozoic, and Cenozoic. During the Paleozoic era, there was an enormous increase in the number of different species that lived on the Earth. Some organisms left the warm, shallow seas and lived on dry land. The gradual change in the characteristics of living things over time is called evolution. It has created the many branches of the family tree of life. As species have become extinct (died out), others have developed. Evolution has created the amazing diversity of organisms that are alive today.

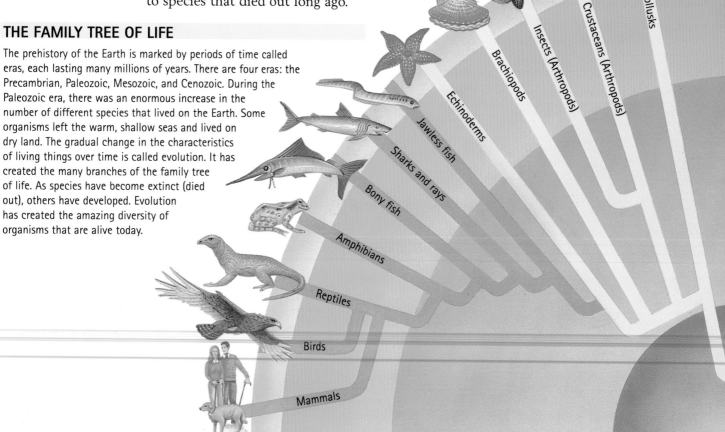

Mollusks

Crustaceans (Arthropods)

Insects (Arthropods)

Brachiopods

Echinoderms

Jawless fish

Sharks and rays

Bony fish

Amphibians

Reptiles

Birds

Mammals

Eras	Cenozoic	Mesozoic	Paleozoic	Precambrian
Millions of years ago	0–65	65–245	245–570	570–3,000

CLASS, FAMILY, AND SPECIES

Organisms are further divided into smaller levels. Below the phylum comes a level called the class. All mammals belong to the class Mammalia. Below the class is the order. All meat-eating mammals, such as foxes, leopards, and otters, belong to the order Carnivora.

Then comes a level called the family. Foxes, hyenas, and wolves all belong to the family called Canidae. Within the family are subgroups of animals that cannot breed with one another—they can mate, but do not have offspring. Each group is a genus. The genus name is written in italics, so the fox genus is *Vulpes*.

Within a genus are one or more species. Each species has a name, which is also written in italics. The little fennec fox from North Africa is *Vulpes zerda*.

EXTINCTION AND CHANGE

Scientists think that the number of organisms today is only a tiny fraction of all the living things that have existed. Over 99 percent of all the species that have ever existed are now extinct.

Animals, plants, and other organisms gradually change as the conditions around them change. In this way, species may evolve into new species. This preserves the diversity of the family tree of life.

The graph below shows the relative numbers of living species. Insects far outnumber all other life-forms. Next come plants and mollusks. Fish are the most numerous vertebrate species (animals with a backbone). There are comparatively few species of mammals in the world.

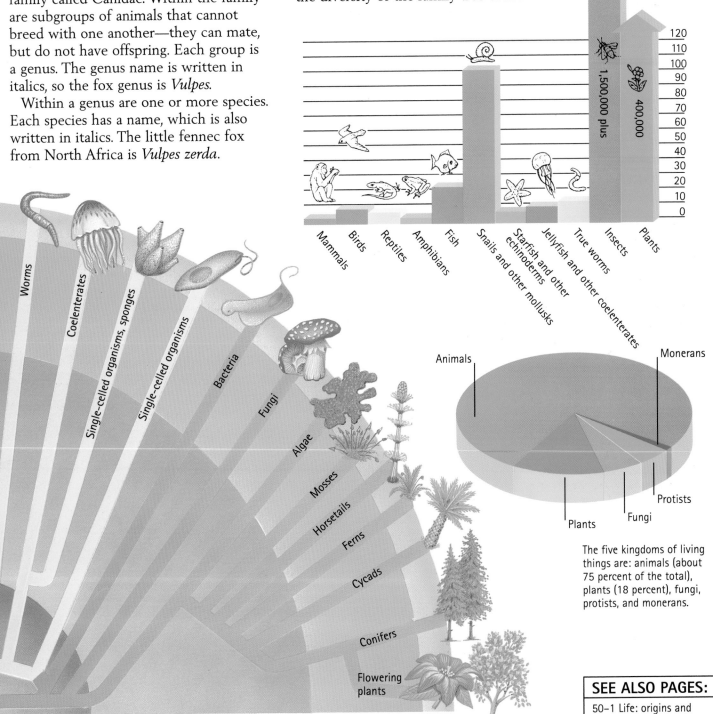

000's

120
110
100
90
80
70
60
50
40
30
20
10
0

1,500,000 plus

400,000

Mammals
Birds
Reptiles
Amphibians
Fish
Snails and other mollusks
Starfish and other echinoderms
Jellyfish and other coelenterates
True worms
Insects
Plants

Worms
Coelenterates
Single-celled organisms, sponges
Single-celled organisms
Bacteria
Fungi
Algae
Mosses
Horsetails
Ferns
Cycads
Conifers
Flowering plants

Animals

Monerans

Protists

Fungi

Plants

The five kingdoms of living things are: animals (about 75 percent of the total), plants (18 percent), fungi, protists, and monerans.

Precambrian	Paleozoic	Mesozoic	Cenozoic
3,000–570	570–245	245–65	65–0

SEE ALSO PAGES:

50-1 Life: origins and development, 442–3 Why species die out, 462–3 Conservation action

SINGLE-CELLED ORGANISMS

The simplest living things are tiny, single-celled organisms. They were the first living things on the planet, and are still the most common.

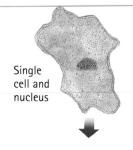

Single cell and nucleus

Nucleus divides

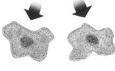

Two new organisms

Cells multiply by splitting in two. Some bacteria can do this once every 15 minutes. A single-celled protist like this amoeba becomes two by a complex process of cell division known as mitosis.

Algae include single-celled diatoms and giant seaweeds. This picture, taken with a powerful electron microscope, shows epiphytic (living on the surface of another plant) green algae cells.

Cells are the smallest units capable of life. The simplest living things have just one cell, which contains all the information and processes needed to keep that organism alive and allow it to reproduce.

INSIDE THE CELL
A cell has a thin outer wall that lets chemicals in and waste out. Within the cell wall is a jellylike fluid called cytoplasm. This contains tiny structures, each of which has a function. The central structure is the nucleus. This contains the genes, which determine the cell's shape and function. Other structures release energy from food, deal with waste, or protect the cell against attack from other organisms.

FIRST LIFE
More than three billion years ago, the first single-celled organisms appeared in the Earth's seas. What kind of chemistry went on to create life is not known. It may have involved the seeding of spores from space. But it is more likely to have been the result of chemical reactions in the oceans and atmosphere, which produced complex molecules able to organize themselves into living organisms.

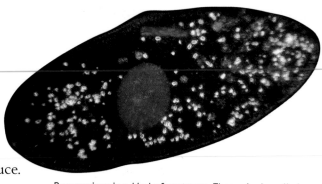

Paramecium is a kind of protozoa. These single-celled organisms have tiny, hairlike filaments called cilia, which they wave in order to move and to catch food.

Today, these simplest of all creatures are classified as monerans. There are two main groups, bacteria and plantlike blue-green algae (cyanobacteria). They are so tiny that they can be seen only through a powerful microscope.

Protists are single-celled organisms and include not only amoebas and tiny algae, but also a number of organisms made up of many cells. Some feed like animals; others trap the sun's energy, like plants. Others feed in both ways. Many protists have one or two taillike structures called flagella, which they flick to propel themselves. Other protists are tiny hunters that can engulf their prey. Most protists reproduce by mitosis.

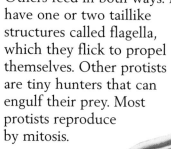

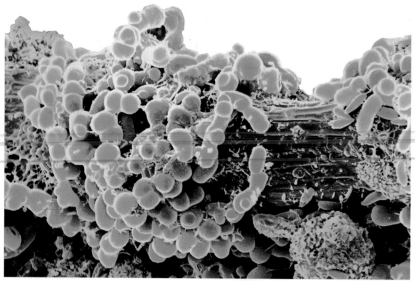

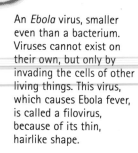

An *Ebola* virus, smaller even than a bacterium. Viruses cannot exist on their own, but only by invading the cells of other living things. This virus, which causes Ebola fever, is called a filovirus, because of its thin, hairlike shape.

SEE ALSO PAGES:
66–7 Plants and people,
136 Bacteria and viruses,
138 Disease

FUNGI AND LICHENS

Fungi and lichens are simple forms of life. They depend upon partnerships with plants and with one another for food and survival.

Amanita muscaria is one of the toadstools to avoid. It is poisonous and may kill animals and people if eaten.

All fungi make sure that they can spread spores. The earthstar hoists its fruiting body above the soil on starlike jacks.

In lichen, a fungus provides the body for single-celled algae. The algae's function is to make food, and so keep the partnership alive.

Fungi have no chlorophyll and so, unlike plants, cannot make their own food. They feed by making chemicals that rot the bodies of other living things (such as plants) and their dead remains. The fungus absorbs nourishment as the bodies decay. Mushrooms, toadstools, yeasts, and slime molds are fungi.

The toadstool or mushroom seen above ground is the fruiting body of the fungus. Beneath the soil or within the rotting wood of trees is the hidden part of the fungus. This is a mass of threadlike cells, called the mycelium. The fruiting body appears when the fungus is ready to reproduce. It contains spores, which it releases into the wind.

LICHENS

A lichen is actually two living things in partnership or symbiosis. The partners are single-celled algae and fungus. The algae use photosynthesis to turn the energy in sunlight into food, and this food supports both the algae and the fungus. The fungus surrounds and protects the algae. Some have hard, chalky skin.

Lichens are often found on rocks, walls, and the bark of trees. They are hardy and are able to withstand even the freezing cold of polar regions and the snow of high mountain peaks. Some types of lichen can live for as long as 4,000 years.

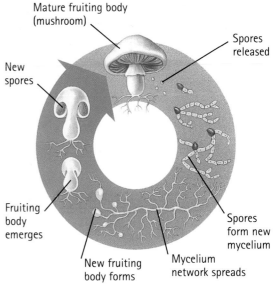

Life cycle of a fungus. A fruiting body releases spores, which form a network of filaments. New fruiting bodies push up to the air and scatter spores of their own.

HARMFUL AND HELPFUL

Lichens are eaten by animals such as caribou. Fungi too can be eaten, by animals and people. But it is wise to know your fungus before you eat it. Some kinds are poisonous and can cause stomachaches and even death.

Fungi are also found in sea- and freshwater, where they can sometimes be seen as foam on the surface. Some fungi live on the skin of animals. A number of skin diseases and mouth and ear infections are caused by fungi. Fungi can be beneficial too. The antibiotic penicillin is made from a mold. Yeast, used to make bread, is a fungus.

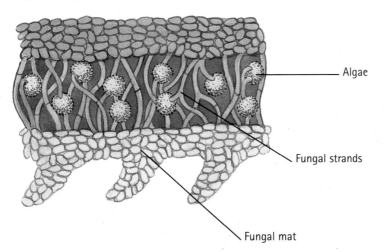

Algae

Fungal strands

Fungal mat

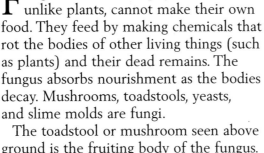

Lichen (*Rhizacarpon geographicum*) growing in Norway. Lichens can put up with extremes of heat, cold, and dryness.

SEE ALSO PAGES:
52–3 Classification of living things, 68–9 Biomes and habitats

PLANT ANATOMY

Apart from some bacteria, plants are the only living things able to make their own food. Tiny grasses and huge trees share the same anatomy, or structure.

There are two main classes of plants. Nonvascular plants, such as mosses and liverworts, do not have tissues to carry food and water from one part of the plant to another. Vascular plants do. They are the larger of the two classes and include trees and flowers.

WHAT PLANTS NEED

All plants need light, because they use energy from sunlight to make their food. They need water and minerals, which most plants obtain through leaves and roots. To reproduce, many plants have flowers that make seeds. But plants have other means of reproducing too—the strawberry, for example, sends out runners. All plants are made of cells. Plant cells differ from animal cells in that they absorb water and grow larger and stiffer as the plant ages. This is why young vegetables are more tender to chew than old ones. Plant cells build thick walls made of cellulose. Each cell is stuck firmly to the walls of neighboring cells.

GREEN MAGIC

Plants also differ from animal cells in that they contain a green pigment called chlorophyll. This allows the plants to make their own food with the aid of sunlight. Only plants and some bacteria can perform this chemical trick.

There are many cells in each plant, and each group of cells has its own tasks. The main body parts of a plant are the roots, stem, leaves, and flowers.

Vacuole (liquid energy store)

Cell wall

Chloroplast (traps sun's energy)

Plant cells are rigid. This is because they have walls of tough cellulose. The vacuoles store water. The chloroplasts trap energy from sunlight.

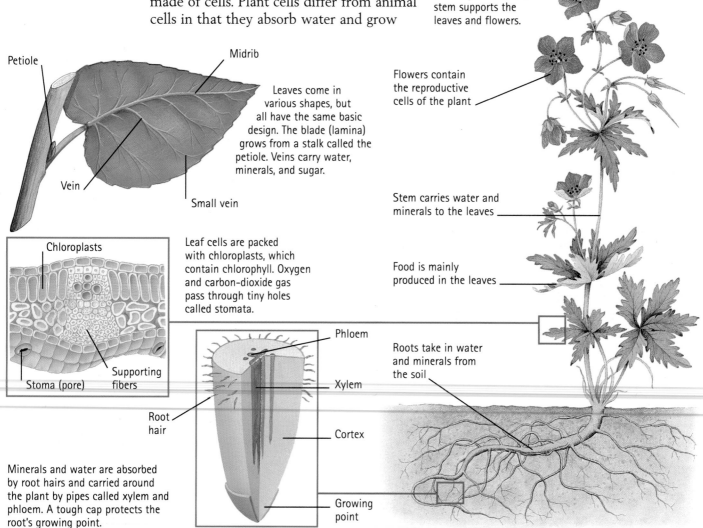

Petiole

Midrib

Leaves come in various shapes, but all have the same basic design. The blade (lamina) grows from a stalk called the petiole. Veins carry water, minerals, and sugar.

Vein

Small vein

Chloroplasts

Leaf cells are packed with chloroplasts, which contain chlorophyll. Oxygen and carbon-dioxide gas pass through tiny holes called stomata.

Stoma (pore)

Supporting fibers

Root hair

Phloem

Xylem

Cortex

Growing point

Minerals and water are absorbed by root hairs and carried around the plant by pipes called xylem and phloem. A tough cap protects the root's growing point.

A plant is anchored in the soil by its roots. A strong but flexible stem supports the leaves and flowers.

Flowers contain the reproductive cells of the plant

Stem carries water and minerals to the leaves

Food is mainly produced in the leaves

Roots take in water and minerals from the soil

ROOTS

Roots hold the plant firmly in the ground, like anchors. They absorb water and mineral salts from the soil through fine hairs. A cap protects the root as it pushes down through the soil in search of water.

STEM

The stem supports the leaves and flowers. Inside are tubes that carry and store water and food. When these tubes are filled with water, they are very strong; when they are dry, they become weak and the plant wilts. Tree wood is really a mass of stiffened tubes.

LEAVES

Leaves are the plant's food-making factories. Their cells contain chlorophyll, which uses the sun's energy to make food from carbon-dioxide gas in the air and in water. Veins carry water from the roots and carry food made in the leaves to the rest of the plant.

FLOWERS

In many plants, flowers are the reproductive parts. Most flowers have male and female organs. The male part makes pollen, which pollinates the female part (usually on another flower). This pollination produces a seed, from which a new plant can grow. Some plants spread their pollen from plant to plant using the wind. Others use insects and other animals to carry it for them. Some flowers grow singly, others form clusters. Many have dazzling colors and strong scents, but some are drab and have no smell.

Light energy

Carbon dioxide

Oxygen out

In photosynthesis, the plants take in small molecules and build them into large ones, storing the sun's energy. As part of the process, they give off oxygen gas.

Chlorophyll in leaves

Chloroplast

Grana

Inside a granum

Chlorophyll

Membrane systems

Inside a plant cell's chloroplasts are tiny grana. Each granum contains chlorophyll, which absorbs light rays.

INS AND OUTS OF PLANT LIFE

The food-making process is called photosynthesis. Water from the roots and carbon-dioxide gas from the air combine to make glucose (a sugar) and oxygen gas. The plant uses glucose as fuel to make energy, in a process called respiration.

Glucose molecules are joined together into long chains. One chain is called cellulose, which is used for growth and developing strength; the other is starch, which is used as a reserve food store. Plants also make amino acids for protein, enzymes, and hormones.

The leaves of *Mimosa pudica*, the sensitive plant, recoil when touched. Changes in pressure within some cells cause this defensive movement.

These time-lapse photographs show a lily flower opening. Many flowers are pollinated by insects, which are attracted by brightly colored petals, tasty nectar, and scent. The center of the flower, where the reproductive organs are, is the target area for visiting insects.

The sharp thorns of a rose are modified leaves. Thorns prevent hungry animals from eating plant leaves, fruit, and flowers.

SEE ALSO PAGES:

NONFLOWERING PLANTS

About 400 million years ago, plants began to grow on the Earth. They were the ancestors of present-day ferns, horsetails, mosses, and liverworts.

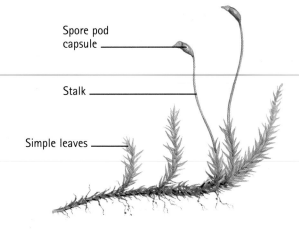

Spore pod capsule ———

Stalk ———

Simple leaves ———

Mosses have rhizoids instead of true roots. Their leaves have no veins. Instead of a flower, mosses grow reproductive structures called spore pods.

In prehistoric times, the Earth was covered with a dense mat of giant ferns, horsetails, liverworts, and club mosses. Today, these plants are still common, and they are some of the most primitive species in the plant world. Unlike the more familiar flowering plants, nonflowering plants have no flowers or seeds. They reproduce by dispersing tiny reproductive units, called spores, in air currents.

▲ Mosses clump together, often forming thick mats where no other plants can survive. This moss is called *Leucobryum glaucum*.

MOSSES AND LIVERWORTS
Mosses and liverworts are known as bryophytes. Unlike flowering plants, they have no real roots. Instead they have shallow rhizoids that look like roots and hold the plant to the ground. Unlike roots, rhizoids cannot take in food or water. Bryophytes have no veins in their leaves, and most species are fairly small. Mosses and liverworts like damp, shady places, but mosses also cling to exposed areas, like rocks and walls. Sphagnum mosses form thick mats in swamps and bogs. The squashed remains of these dead plants eventually turn into peat.

Horsetails prefer to live in wet places like bogs. The marsh horsetail has a hollow, jointed stem and looks like a miniature tree.

HORSETAILS
There are 29 species of horsetails, which all belong to one genus, *Equisetum*. They are jointed, rushlike plants that grow in wet, swampy soil. Their stems contain small amounts of minerals, including gold.

Maidenhair spleenwort is one of the 10,000 kinds of ferns growing on the Earth. Along with mosses, horsetails, and liverworts, ferns are the most primitive species of plants.

FERNS
Most ferns grow in damp, shady places. At first, the leaves, or fronds, are curled in a structure known as a fiddlehead, but the leaves uncurl as the plant grows. Beneath each frond are spore cases (sporangia). Spores are dispersed by the wind and fall to earth—some grow into a prothallus, with male and female cells. A new fern, a sporophyte, feeds on the prothallus until it grows roots and can live on its own.

Tropical tree ferns can grow up to 80 ft. tall. Tree ferns have woody trunks without branches, topped with clusters of feathery leaves, or fronds.

The diagram below shows the stages of growth of a typical fern. Spores from the spore cases are wind-dispersed. Some land many miles away from the parent plant. The spore grows into a prothallus, from which a young sporophyte develops into a mature fern. The fern develops the typical curly fiddlehead at its tip.

Tree ferns

Fern

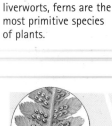

Sporangia

Prothallus

Young sporophyte

New fern grows

SEE ALSO PAGES:
50–1 Life: origins and development, 56–7 Plant anatomy, 68–9 Biomes and habitats, 438–9 Saving the rain forests

FLOWERING PLANTS

Flowering plants, or angiosperms, are the most successful of all the plants. Angiosperms reproduce using seeds that develop in the ovaries of their flowers.

Parts of a flower

Stigma

Petal

Stamen

Style

Sepal

Ovary with ovules

The cotyledon is the leafy part of a plant embryo. It provides the embryo with nutrients during germination and growth.

Flowering plants are among the most successful group of organisms on the Earth. Flowering plants include most of our garden plants, farm crops, and the flowers that are often grown for decoration. They range in size from tiny pondweeds to trees like birches and oaks. The name angiosperm is Greek for "enclosed seed." The developing embryos of angiosperms are enclosed in special structures, called seeds, within the flower. After fertilization, the seeds are protected inside a fruit. Flowering plants, therefore, have a lower-risk survival strategy than other plant species, which probably accounts for their success.

A RICHER WORLD

Flowering plants are believed to have evolved from a now-extinct group of conifers that lived around 250 million years ago, a period of time known as the Permian period. As they evolved, flowering plants came to have a huge influence on other living organisms. Many animals ate the plants or feasted on the nectar they produced. Others used plants for shelter. Put simply, the world would be less rich and much less beautiful without flowers.

Angiosperms advertise their reproductive organs to potential insect pollinators using their flowers, which also serve to protect the organs. The stamens produce male sex cells, called pollen. These are transferred to the female sex cells, called ovules, through the stigma.

TWO MAIN GROUPS

There are two groups of flowering plants, each separated by the way their leaves form as the seed grows. The first group, monocotyledons, have only one seed leaf; the second group, dicotyledons, have two. Monocots and dicots (for short) differ in many ways. For example, dicot leaves are usually broad and grow from the tip. They can be many different shapes, with smooth or irregular edges. Monocot leaves are long and narrow, like a blade of grass, and usually grow from the base, not the tip. As a result, grasses do not die when animals nibble their tips. Once a dicot leaf is nibbled, however, it usually dies.

▲ Monocotyledons have smooth leaves that grow from the base of the plant. These plants are also characterized by parallel leaf veins and flowers with parts usually in multiples of three.

▶ Gardeners choose specific characteristics when breeding ornamental garden flowers.

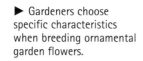

Composite flower

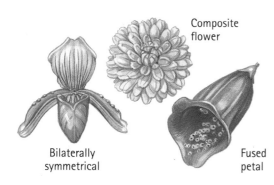

Bilaterally symmetrical

Fused petal

▲ Flowers have many different designs, reflecting their enormous diversity. The daisy is an example of a composite flower; foxgloves have fused petals; and lilies are bilaterally symmetrical (its two halves are alike).

Dicots have complex stems that are either woody or herbaceous. Inside the stem, bundles of tubes are arranged in a ring around a central core. These tubes are important structures that transport water, mineral salts, and other nutrients around the plant. As a woody dicot plant grows, the stem adds new rings and gets thicker. As a monocot grows, the stem gets longer, without getting thicker and without adding new growth rings.

HOW PLANTS GROW

Unlike animals, plants continue to grow throughout their lives. In favorable conditions, some plants grow extremely quickly. In the humid tropical rain forests, for example, bamboos can shoot up one foot in just one day.

Many plants are annuals. This means that they grow, flower, produce seeds, and die within a year. Other plants are biennials—they follow a two-year life cycle. Biennials grow their stem and a few leaves during their first summer. These will die after the first hard frost, but the roots survive. During the second growing season, the plant develops a new stem and more leaves, as well as colorful, seed-bearing flowers. Biennials die after the second year. Other plants are perennial. Their stems and leaves die in winter; but the roots survive, and the plant flowers for successive seasons.

REPRODUCTIVE STRATEGIES

Mushroom spores (reproductive units) are dispersed by the wind in their millions.

Some plants have evolved flowers that mimic insects to attract potential pollinators. The flower of the bee orchid is shaped like a bee. Passing bees try to mate with the flower, collect pollen, and pollinate the next plant they visit.

Flowering plants such as the prickly pear, above, live in hot deserts. They flower quickly after the seasonal rains, and set seeds that may not germinate until the next rainy season.

The Venus flytrap is a carnivorous plant that feeds on insects. The bright red color of the modified leaves attracts insects; they are trapped as the leaves snap shut.

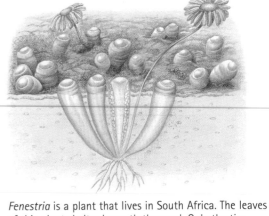

Fenestria is a plant that lives in South Africa. The leaves of this plant shelter beneath the sand. Only the tips emerge above the ground to absorb sunlight.

However, only a few spores fall in places that are suitable for them to grow. Flowering plants have a less risky strategy, which does not rely on being fertilized by accident. Male cells, called pollen, join with female cells, called ovules, to make an embryo contained within a protective structure called a seed. Seeds are then dispersed by a variety of means—they can be carried by the wind or by animals brushing against the plant, or the plants can be eaten by animals that later disperse the seeds in their droppings.

INSIDE A FLOWER

Although an enormous variety of flowers exist, they all flower in a similar way. There are usually four main sets of organs: sepals, petals, stamens (with anthers and filaments), and pistils (stigma, style, and ovary). The four organs are collectively called the whorl, and they can be arranged in a spiral pattern or on a single level.

▶ Many flowering plants are cultivated by farmers. Typical examples are the tea and coffee plants. Other flowering plants are harvested for their medicinal value. For example, foxgloves are harvested for their leaves, which contain a chemical called digitalis. This is used to treat certain heart conditions. These sunflowers, in Italy, are harvested for their seeds, which are used in cooking and to make sunflower oil.

Like all grasses, meadow foxtail and false oat grass (at left) are monocotyledons. The meadowcranes bill (at right), a wild geranium, is a dicotyledon.

The sepals are the outermost parts of the flower and are green and leaflike. Their main function is to protect the flower bud and support the delicate petals. The brightly colored, fragrant petals make up the second layer. The essential function of the petals is to attract insects, which are drawn to flowers by their colors and scents, and by the sweet-tasting nectar that they produce.

At the heart of the flower are the stamens and pistil. The stamens lie inside the petals. Each consists of a head—the anther—which makes the male sex cells, or pollen, and a filament that attaches the anther to the flower.

During pollination, grains of pollen are carried from the anther to the stigma. Once there, the pollen grain forms a tube that grows down through the style and ovary, so that male cells can fertilize the female eggs, or ovules. Following fertilization, the ovules develop into seeds, and the flower dies. The plant then puts all its energy into the production of fruits to protect the developing seeds.

SINGLES AND COMPOSITES

Some plants have single flowers, each on its own stem. Composite flowers, such as sunflowers and daisies, are really many small flowers (florets) that are in a group called an inflorescence. Some flower petals fuse, forming a tubelike shape. Others are not circular but bilaterally symmetrical, with their structures arranged equally on both sides of a line. Some flowers have no petals—the catkins of the hazel tree, for example. Many, but not all, flowers close at night or in cold weather. Some even close when the sun goes behind a cloud.

The world's largest flower belongs to a genus called *Rafflesia*, found in the rain forests of Southeast Asia. Also called the monster plant, the flowers of *Rafflesia* species can reach a diameter of 3 ft. The flower smells of rotting flesh, which attracts flies.

Wetland plants such as this giant water lily are specially adapted for floating on the surface of lakes and ponds. The roots of this plant cling to the soil at the bottom of the lake or pond, and the white flower blooms at the side of the giant leaf.

THE REPRODUCTIVE CYCLE

Flowering plants, such as the poppy, protect their flowers within tough buds until the pollen grains are ripe. When the flowers open, the anther releases the pollen (male sex cells). Pollen is transferred from plant to plant by insects (cross-fertilization), or it can be deposited on the stigma of the same plant (self-fertilization). The pollen caught by the stigma triggers the growth of a tiny pollen tube. This grows from the style down to the ovary and the egg cells. When the tube touches an ovule (female sex cell), it fuses with it. This process is called fertilization. It results in the development of an embryo contained within a protective structure called a seed capsule.

1 Flower buds stay closed until pollen grains inside are ripe.

2 Buds begin to open, revealing brightly colored petals and other flower parts.

3 Flowers attract insects looking for nectar. Pollen from carpels is carried by insects to other flowers.

4 After pollen is released, the flower petals fall off, leaving the seed capsule.

5 Wind shakes ripened seeds out through holes in seed capsule.

6 Most poppies are annuals and live for only one year.

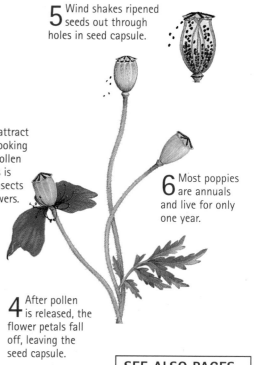

SEE ALSO PAGES:

56–7 Plant anatomy,
58 Nonflowering plants,
62–3 Fruits and seeds

FRUITS AND SEEDS

The seeds of flowering plants are protected inside fruits. All fruits have a way of dispersing themselves that gives the seeds more chance of survival.

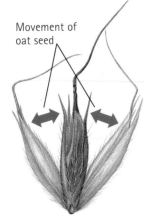

Movement of oat seed

Oat seeds plant themselves by drilling into the soil. Each seed has a long, bristlelike structure called an awn. As it dries out, the awn coils and uncoils, twisting the seed into the soil until it reaches the correct depth for germinating.

Seeds are embryos, or potential plants. The seed is self-contained, with a food supply and a tough coat for protection. It needs to get away from its parent, to find room to grow in a suitable site. But it can survive for months or even years, waiting for the right conditions.

When the conditions of temperature, light, and moisture are right, the seed germinates—it sprouts a tiny root and stem and begins to grow into a new plant.

DRY AND JUICY FRUITS

Seeds are contained inside fruits. Some are   fruits, such as a poppy capsule and a pea pod. These split open to release the seeds inside. An acorn is another dry fruit. Its seed simply forces its way out through the skin.

Others are juicy fruits, like berries, which contain more than one seed. The cherry is a drupe or stone fruit. Its inner layer forms a woody pit or stone. The

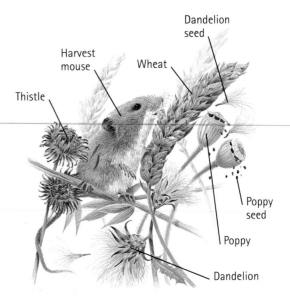

Many seeds are spread by the wind. Others are eaten by animals and pass out with the animal's droppings. Some seeds have hooks that catch on a passing animal's fur.

blackberry is a cluster of small drupes. Its seeds are inside the tiny pips.

Apples and pears are called pomes. They have a fleshy outer layer (the false fruit). This surrounds a core (the true fruit) that contains seeds. Pomes are often sweet. This encourages animals to eat them and so help in their dispersal.

The squirting cucumber is a member of the gourd family. It shoots out its seeds in a jet of liquid. Water pressure builds up inside the fruit until it parts from the stalk and fires its water-jet of seeds.

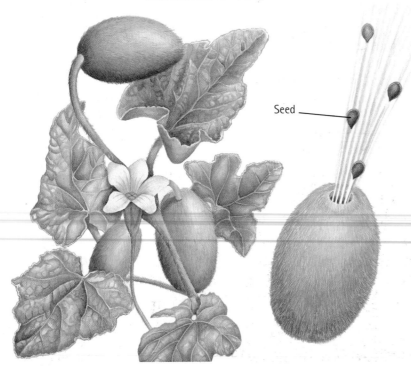

Seed

Banana buds open into small flowers that form a hand of bananas. At first, the bananas are green. New banana plants can be grown from cuttings, or suckers.

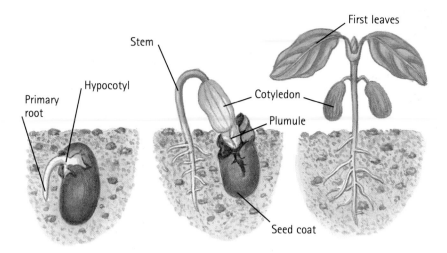

First leaves
Stem
Hypocotyl
Primary root
Cotyledon
Plumule
Seed coat

When a seed starts to germinate, it splits, and a primary root is formed and pushes downward. All other roots grow out from this main root. The stem grows up from the hypocotyl through the soil, and the cotyledons break out of the seed coat. Roots begin to grow, and the first leaves form as the stem grows up toward the sunlight.

Acorns

Blackberry

Peas

Date

Pear

Samara (Ash key)

Tomato

Squash

MALE AND FEMALE

Some plants—squashes, for instance—produce separate male and female flowers on the same plant. Others, such as willow and holly trees, produce them on separate plants. Holly trees that have only male flowers never have berries. Only female date palms produce dates.

SEEDS BUT NO FRUITS

There are other plants, apart from ferns and mosses, that do not have seeds in fruits—conifers are just one example.

Conifers are mainly trees or shrubs, and many of them, like pine trees, have very thin, pointed leaves called needles. Almost all conifers have tough cones. Male cones make pollen, and female cones contain ovules (eggs). Wind carries pollen from male to female to make seeds.

Two small, and ancient, plant groups are the ginkgoes and cycads. Ginkgoes have fan-shaped leaves and fleshy seeds that are not hidden inside cones. Cycads look like large ferns but, unlike ferns, produce seed cones. The Welwitschia, a strange, droopy-looking plant that has adapted to live in the desert, has seeds surrounded by modified leaves, called bracts.

SEED DISPERSAL

Many plants rely on the wind to scatter their seeds. The poppy has a capsule like a saltshaker to scatter its seeds. Dandelion seeds parachute on the breeze. Some squashes shoot out their seeds.

Winged seeds, like those of the sycamore and ash trees, are really fruits. Seeds eaten by animals have tough coats to protect them as they pass through the animal's digestive system. Some of these coats are so thick that the seeds cannot germinate unless their coat has been weakened by an animal's digestive juices. The droppings of the animal, within which the seeds fall to the ground, can act as a fertilizer to help the young plant to grow.

NEW GROWTH

When a seed germinates, it absorbs water and swells. Its skin splits, and the embryo root (radicle) pushes down to find water and anchor the plant firmly in the ground. Now the embryo shoot (plumule) can uncoil and grow upward. When it reaches daylight, the first leaves grow, and the plant starts making its own food. It no longer needs the food store (cotyledon) in the seed from which it grew.

The seeds of some plants grow quickly and produce a fully grown plant in a matter of weeks. Plants like these live only for a few months, in which time they flower and make their own seeds for the next year's growing season. Longer-living plants, like trees, take a long time to grow from their seeds and do not make their own seeds for several years.

Fruits may not look alike, but they all have the same function. Many of what we call vegetables, including tomatoes and scarlet runner beans, are in fact fruits because they contain seeds.

A coconut palm produces huge fruits. Palm nuts may drift across the sea and take root on islands that are thousands of miles away.

SEE ALSO PAGES:

56–7 Plant anatomy,
59–61 Flowering plants,
88–9 Animal reproduction

TREES

There are two main groups of trees: conifers and broad-leaved trees. Trees are among the largest and longest-living of all the life-forms on the Earth.

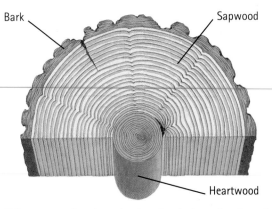

Bark   Sapwood

Heartwood

This cross-section through a tree trunk shows heartwood surrounded by lighter sapwood. A new growth ring is added every year, so this section shows the tree's age. The tree grows more slowly during the winter, leaving a dark ring. The fast summer growth causes a light-colored ring.

Of the two main types of trees, conifers have been around the longest. Coniferous trees are also known as softwoods. They include the pines, spruces, cedars, firs, junipers, cypresses, and (largest of all) redwoods. Common broad-leaved trees include the oak, ash, and willow.

CONIFER LEAVES

Most conifers have small, needlelike leaves. All except the larch are evergreen. They shed old leaves and grow new ones all year round, not all at once in the fall, like many broad-leaved trees. The stiff needles of conifers lose much less water than the leaves of other trees. This allows conifers to grow in cold regions, on mountains, and on the fringes of deserts. In Canada, northern Europe, and Russia, they form vast evergreen forests. Many conifers have a triangular shape; this stops snow from settling on their branches.

BROAD LEAVES

In cool climates with long, dark winters, broad-leaved trees lose their leaves in the fall. Tropical broad-leaved trees keep their leaves all year because the day length does not change much between seasons.

Losing leaves in the fall is an energy-saving trick because there is not enough sunlight in winter for the leaves to make food for the tree. The food and water pipes in the stem are sealed off, starving and drying out the unwanted leaves.

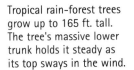

Tropical rain-forest trees grow up to 165 ft. tall. The tree's massive lower trunk holds it steady as its top sways in the wind.

DECIDUOUS TREES

Deciduous trees are broad-leaved, with spreading crowns and roots that spread deep into the soil to find water. These trees have flowers in the spring. The flowers develop into fruits. The horse chestnut (shown here) has pinkish-white flowers. Its seed is cased inside a spiky shell. In the fall, the tree sheds its leaves and the bare branches are exposed, with new buds ready to burst into leaf when the spring comes. In the fall, the leaves glide to the ground because there is not enough light during the winter for efficient photosynthesis.

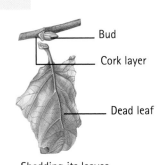

Bud

Cork layer

Dead leaf

Shedding its leaves means that a deciduous tree needs less water in the winter. The food supply is cut off near the bud, and the leaf dies.

Horse chestnut (summer)

Horse chestnut (winter)

Blossom and leaf

Seed (conker)

Roots take in water and minerals, and anchor the tree to the ground. Some trees have long roots, with as much growth below the ground as above it. Other trees, like conifers, have massive trunks, but shallow roots that collect water from a wide area.

Fig tree

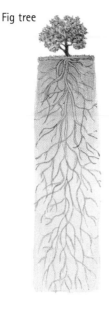

The banyan tree of India has hundreds of air roots, which hang down from the branches.

A giant sequoia in Sequoia National Park, California. Sequoias are shorter than redwoods, but thicker. These conifers can live for over 4,000 years.

The cycad looks like a palm tree with cones. Cycads first grew 225 million years ago.

Some bristlecone pines in the western United States are 4,000 years old and still growing strong.

The tree has already stored enough food to allow the next year's buds to grow, and without its food supply, the leaf dies. The chlorophyll that made the living leaf green is broken down and reabsorbed by the tree for use in next year's leaves. The colored chemicals that remain in the leaf produce the brilliant red, yellow, and brown colors of fall.

INSIDE A TREE

When a tree is cut, you can see the annual growth rings in the slice of trunk. The outer bark, or cork, is a layer of dead tissue. This is hard and protects the softer living parts inside of the tree. Bark can stretch, to let the trunk and branches grow more thickly underneath.

Beneath the bark of most trees is the phloem carrying food through tiny tubes. The inner wood, or xylem, is stiffened with waxy substances for extra strength. Some of the younger xylem acts as a network of tubes to carry water, or sap, from the roots to the leaves. Other plants move water through xylem, but cannot stiffen it to make wood. It is the stiffness of the woody xylem that gives trees their rigidity, and allows them to grow so much taller than other plants.

TREES AND THE ENVIRONMENT

The leaves of a tree, like the leaves of any green plant, make food through a process called photosynthesis. The waste product of this process is oxygen, and it is passed back into the air through tiny pores in the leaves called stomata. By absorbing carbon dioxide and releasing oxygen, trees keep the atmosphere healthy. Forests can be thought of as the Earth's lungs.

Trees also protect the land from erosion. Their leaves and branches absorb heavy rains. Their roots bind the soil and stop it from being washed or blown away. Trees also suck up water and prevent flooding.

CONIFEROUS TREES

Coniferous trees, like this monkey puzzle tree, rarely drop their leaves (needles). They have shallow roots and make their seeds inside cones. Cones may take three years to ripen and release their seeds, which then flutter to the ground. The monkey puzzle is unusual because its male and female cones grow on separate trees. Many conifers produce both male and female cones on the same tree. The male cones release pollen and fertilize the eggs in the female cones.

Bark

Female cone

Monkey puzzle tree

SEE ALSO PAGES:

32–3 Erosion and weathering, 56–7 Plant anatomy, 206 Wood and paper

PLANTS AND PEOPLE

Plants have long been cultivated to eat and to make medicines. Plant materials are also used in the manufacture of clothes, fuels, and other products.

The cultivation of plants as part of worldwide agriculture is the single most important and widespread human activity. Plants provide food for animals and people. People also depend on the cultivation of plants for clothing and shelter. In addition, many plant by-products provide the basic materials needed for chemicals and medicines used to improve our lives.

The earliest farmers probably lived in the Near East about 11,000 years ago. They cultivated plants, rather than just gathering them from the wild, and used crude tools, such as wooden sickles, as farming implements. Over the generations, the methods and tools have gradually improved, leading to the diverse agriculture that we see today.

CHANGING PLANTS

The first farmers developed basic food crops, such as rice and wheat, by selective breeding from wild plants. Today's cultivated plants probably look very different from their wild ancestors. Genetic modification has produced crops that grow more plentifully, resist pests and diseases, and even grow in unfavorable conditions. However, our new ability to genetically "engineer" plants poses some serious environmental, political, and health issues for politicians, scientists, and consumers.

FOOD AND DRINK

There are hundreds of food crops that are cultivated as nutritious food. These include beans, cassava, corn, fruit, potatoes, rice, vegetables, and wheat. Cereal crops, like barley, millet, oats, rice, and wheat, are rich in carbohydrates, as are cassava and potatoes. Beans, peanuts, and soybeans are rich in protein.

Coffee is made from the dried beans (seeds) of the coffee plant. It is grown on plantations in tropical countries such as Brazil, Costa Rica, and Kenya.

Pears and apples are grown commercially in orchards. Fruits like these grow best in cooler (temperate) climates.

The fruits of the grapevine are cultivated and crushed to make juice. This juice may be fermented to make wine. Black and white grape varieties are grown.

Sugar beet and sugarcane are the two sources of sugar. The roots of the beet and the stem of the cane are the sugar-containing parts of the plants.

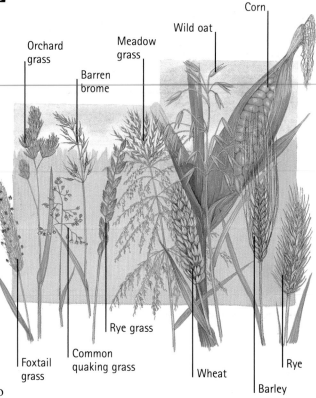

Corn
Wild oat
Meadow grass
Orchard grass
Barren brome
Rye grass
Foxtail grass
Common quaking grass
Wheat
Barley
Rye

Grasses grow best in open country, and there are many species. The first farmers selected wild grasses and, from them, bred improved varieties. The most important cereal crops today are wheat, rice, corn, oats, barley, and rye.

EDIBLE VEGETABLES

Vegetables used as food come from various parts of plants. The bulbs of onion and garlic, the flowers of broccoli and cauliflower, the leaves of kale and lettuce, the roots of carrots and radishes, the seeds and pods of peas and beans, the stems of celery, and the tubers of potatoes can all be eaten. Chili peppers, squashes, and tomatoes contain seeds—these foods are actually fruits.

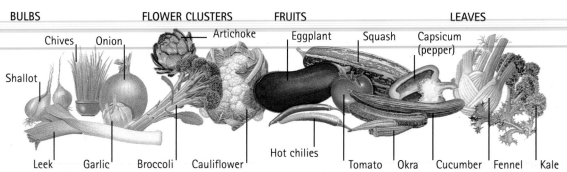

BULBS — Chives, Onion, Shallot, Leek, Garlic

FLOWER CLUSTERS — Artichoke, Broccoli, Cauliflower

FRUITS — Eggplant, Squash, Capsicum (pepper), Hot chilies, Tomato, Okra

LEAVES — Cucumber, Fennel, Kale

Timber is still used all over the world for construction. Most timber used for building is softwood that has been taken from fast-growing coniferous trees. Careful forest management is essential to preserve the world's timber resources.

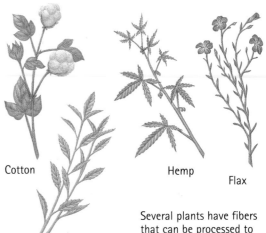

Cotton

Hemp

Flax

Jute

Several plants have fibers that can be processed to make threads used in the manufacture of fabrics. The most important are cotton, jute, hemp, and flax.

Many popular drinks are made from the products of cultivated plants. Beer, cider, cocoa, coffee, fruit juices, soft drinks, whiskey, tea, and wine are all made from various parts of different plants.

MEDICINE PLANTS

The medicinal properties of plants have often been discovered by observing how animals eat them to cure illness. In South America, the bark of the cinchona tree was used to produce quinine, a drug used to fight malaria. Similarly, the leaves of foxgloves contain digitalis, a drug used to treat heart complaints.

Drugs taken from plants can have both good and bad uses. Morphine is a valuable painkilling drug that is made from the opium poppy. However, heroin, derived from morphine, is a very harmful drug that is sold illegally to drug abusers, who can become addicted to it.

RAW MATERIALS

Plants provide many raw materials. The natural fibers from cotton, flax, hemp, and jute plants, for example, are woven into fabrics used for clothing, mats, and ropes.

Trees are harvested for timber. Sometimes this is done responsibly, and new trees are planted as replacements. But some forests are destroyed for quick profit, with no thought of the future.

TREE PRODUCTS

People use timber to build homes and furniture. Softwoods from trees like pine and cedar are easy to cut and shape. Hardwoods, such as oak and tropical mahogany, are stronger and longer-lasting. Other products are also made from trees. Most paper is made from pulped wood, natural rubber comes from the sap of rubber trees, and cork comes from the bark of the cork oak. Even chewing gum comes from a tree.

Wood was the first fuel to be used, and it is still used today. Coal and peat are called fossil fuels because they are formed from the remains of prehistoric plants.

The stem fibers of flax are used to make linen. Hemp, used to make rope and twine, comes from a number of plants.

An ancient Chinese formula using the Artemisia plant is now used to treat malaria.

ROOTS

Beet

Parsnip   Radish   Carrot   Lentil

SEEDS

Soybean

Lima bean

STEMS

Taro   Celeriac

Celery   Asparagus

TUBERS

Yam   Water chestnut

Sweet potato   Jerusalem artichoke

Potato

SEE ALSO PAGES:

58 Nonflowering plants, 59–61 Flowering plants, 140–1 Medicine, 448–9 Food and farming

BIOMES AND HABITATS

A biome is a region of the Earth characterized by climate and containing distinctive plant and animal life. A biome is made up of different habitats.

Deserts are defined as areas in which more water evaporates than falls as precipitation. One fifth of the world's land is desert. Although deserts are harsh, dry habitats, they are far from lifeless. Animals and plants have adapted to these conditions in order to survive.

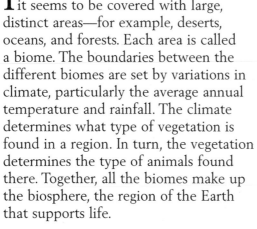

The folds on the stem of the saguaro cactus absorb water and unfold after heavy rains.

If the Earth is viewed from space, it seems to be covered with large, distinct areas—for example, deserts, oceans, and forests. Each area is called a biome. The boundaries between the different biomes are set by variations in climate, particularly the average annual temperature and rainfall. The climate determines what type of vegetation is found in a region. In turn, the vegetation determines the type of animals found there. Together, all the biomes make up the biosphere, the region of the Earth that supports life.

DIFFERENT BIOMES AND HABITATS

There are many different biomes on the Earth, and not all scientists agree on a definitive classification. However, the generally accepted biomes include: tundra, taiga, temperate forest, shrubwood, tropical rain forest, grassland, desert (which includes the polar regions), marine, freshwater, and estuary.

Howler monkeys are commonly found in the Amazon rain forest of South America. Howlers feed mostly on the abundant plant matter surrounding them, but they also eat insects, small mammals, and birds.

A biome is made up of smaller, distinct regions called habitats. A habitat is defined as the area in which an organism lives. For example, a water strider's habitat is a pond or lake; an earthworm's habitat is the soil; and a conifer tree's habitat is the soil, as well as the space above and around the tree. The organisms that live in a particular habitat are called a community.

Honeypot ants act as reservoirs of liquid

Prickly pear cacti store water in fleshy stems

Roadrunner gets water from its prey

Kit fox keeps cool in its burrow by day

Scaly skin stops rattlesnake from drying out

The ocean is a huge biome with many habitats, from the shallow coast to the deep sea. The ocean contains countless invertebrates, fish, reptiles, and mammals.

Key to illustration: 1 Herring **2** Sperm whale **3** Shrimp **4** Rat-tail **5** Anglerfish **6** Grenadier **7** Cod **8** Gulper eel **9** Sea spider, tube worms, clam, white ghost crab **10** Tripod fish **11** Viper fish **12** Swallower **13** Lanternfish **14** Swordfish **15** Yellowfin tuna **16** Giant squid **17** Hammerhead shark **18** Barracuda **19** Portuguese man-of-war **20** Plankton **21** Green turtle **22** Sea lion **23** Common dolphin

Penguins are flightless birds that live in the cold Antarctic. They have layers of fat to insulate their bodies. Adults and chicks huddle together in large groups to keep warm.

Arctic hares change the color of their coats with the changing seasons. In the summer, they have brown fur, but in the winter, they grow a new, white coat to blend in with the snow.

Coral reefs are formed by colonies of tiny coral invertebrates. The reef offers shelter to fish and other sea creatures.

COMMUNITIES

In any habitat, a number of species depend on one another in what are called mutually beneficial relationships. Plants provide food and shelter for animals. In return, animals may help to pollinate the plants. Plant-eating animals, in turn, are eaten by other animals.

WHERE ANIMALS LIVE

Every habitat provides the right conditions for the plants and animals that live in it. Penguins and polar bears are adapted in different ways for life in the bitterly cold polar regions. The kit fox and fennec fox look similar, but are not related. The kit fox lives in the deserts of North America. The fennec is a desert fox of North Africa. If the habitat in which an organism lives changes, some species may be able to change their way of life and adapt to the new conditions. Other species cannot cope, and they have to move or they will die. This adaptation is the driving force behind the process known as evolution.

UNUSUAL HABITATS

Some animals have adapted to live in the harshest habitats. Some polar fish, for example, have evolved a natural form of antifreeze. It prevents ice crystals from forming in their blood and tissues, even below freezing point. The tiniest ice crystals in their blood would kill them. Japanese macaque monkeys keep warm in winter by sitting in thermal pools.

SEE ALSO PAGES:

95 Adaptation and defense, 436–7 Action zones, 438–9 Saving the rain forests, 440–1 Ocean life, 442–3 Why species die out, 450–1 City living

MARINE INVERTEBRATES

The first multicelled animals were invertebrates (creatures without backbones) and lived in the sea. The oceans are still full of invertebrate animals.

The descendants of prehistoric invertebrates still swim and crawl in the oceans. They include worms, corals, clams, snails, starfish, octopuses, and squid.

Sea anemones look more like plants than animals. They cling to rocks and catch their prey in gently waving tentacles.

NO BACKBONE

Being without a backbone is no handicap to these very successful animals. In fact, there are far more invertebrates than vertebrates. In the sea, invertebrates can be very large. The North Sea bootlace worm grows to be up to 80 feet long. The giant clam of the Pacific Ocean can weigh over 660 pounds. Invertebrates can also live to great ages—in the case of the Atlantic quahog clam, as long as 220 years.

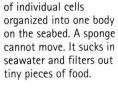

Sponges are a collection of individual cells organized into one body on the seabed. A sponge cannot move. It sucks in seawater and filters out tiny pieces of food.

CORALS

Coral is made of the limestone skeletons of tiny coral polyps. As they grow by budding, each new polyp buries its parent. In this way the mass of coral grows ever larger, to form plantlike shapes and huge reefs.

Corals live in warm, salty, shallow water and have single-celled plants called algae inside them. The algae use sunlight to make sugar, which they share with their coral hosts. The corals protect the algae and provide them with the minerals they need to make proteins and other important chemicals.

A jellyfish catches its prey with stinging tentacles. To swim, it opens and closes its umbrella-shaped body to squeeze out water.

TENTACLES AND SPINES

Jellyfish and anemones have tentacles armed with stinging cells. The Portuguese man-of-war is actually thousands of individual animals acting as one. Its long tentacles paralyze any fish they touch. The outsides of the tentacles are covered in stinging cells that contain tiny, poisonous needles to paralyze the animal's prey. Echinoderms (starfish, sea urchins, sea cucumbers, brittle stars, and feather stars) have spiny skins and tube feet. They pump liquid into their feet to make them expand. If a starfish loses a leg, it will usually grow another one.

Jellyfish can be as small as a pea or as big as a table. The mouth and tentacles dangle beneath the soft body. The tentacles pull food up into the animal's mouth.

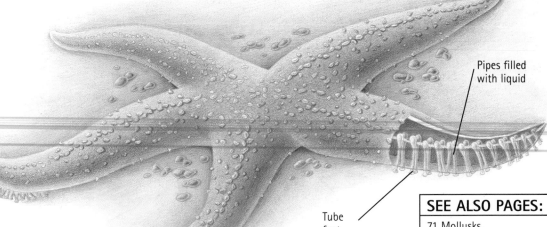

Pipes filled with liquid

Tube feet

Most starfish have five arms, but some have as many as 50. Rows of tube feet along each arm move in rhythm as the starfish hauls itself over the seabed.

SEE ALSO PAGES:

71 Mollusks, 73 Crustaceans, 74 Spiders, centipedes, and scorpions, 75-7 Insects

MOLLUSKS

There are more than 100,000 kinds of mollusks.
They range from tiny snails to enormous giant squid.
Some live on land, but most live in water.

Garden snails move slowly on a trail of moist slime. The snail has sensitive tentacles on its head, which it uses to feel its way around objects.

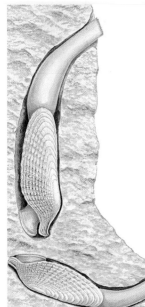

The piddock is a bivalve mollusk. Its paired shells have fine teeth, which grind away like drill bits to make holes in solid rock. The piddock hides inside.

A mollusk has a soft body covered by a mantle. Many mollusks have a chalky shell attached to their mantles, which may be outside the animal's body (as in a limpet or snail), or inside (as in a cuttlefish). The octopus is a mollusk that has no shell at all. Mollusks live on land, and in both fresh- and saltwater.

Some mollusks, like the mussel, hardly ever move. They cling to one place, feeding by opening their shells. Other mollusks have a single foot and can crawl slowly. Limpets move around to feed, but always return to exactly the same spot.

ONE SHELL OR TWO

Snails have one shell, inside which the animal can coil itself to escape danger. Other mollusks have a shell in two halves, hinged so that the halves can be opened. The two-shelled mollusks are known as bivalves, and most are filter feeders. Many live buried in the seabed and seldom move from one spot.

OCTOPUSES AND SQUID

Octopuses and squid are the largest and probably the most intelligent of all mollusks. They have large brains and excellent eyesight, and they move rapidly to escape danger. They can also change the color of their mantle.

An octopus uses long sucker-arms to catch prey, then bites with its beaked mouth. Most octopuses are small, but giant squid can be 50 feet long.

These animals swim by jet propulsion. They suck water under their soft mantles and force it out of a nozzle.

SNAILS AND SLUGS

Snails live on land and in water. Some eat plants others are carnivorous. In dry weather, land snails seal up their shells to keep moist. Slugs are very similar to snails, except that they have either tiny shells inside their mantle or no shells at all.

Snails and slugs have strong teeth made of a substance similar to iron ore. Some types can use their teeth to grind through the shells of other mollusks. Many scientists think snails use their iron teeth like a compass, so that they never get lost.

The squid hunts by stealth, but can make a quick getaway by contracting muscles to squirt a jet of water through a tube. A jet-propelled squid can top 19 mph (30kph) to escape a hungry fish or sperm whale.

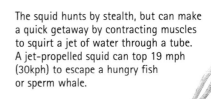

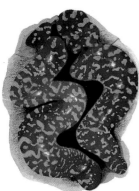

Clams are bivalve mollusks. They open and close their hinged shells with a powerful muscle. Clams filter food out of seawater using hairlike structures called cilia.

Many mollusks burrow into sand to hide from predators. They feed through siphon tubes that protrude from the sand.

SEE ALSO PAGES:

70 Marine invertebrates,
72 Worms, 95 Adaptation
and defense, 440–1
Ocean life

WORMS

Worms are legless invertebrates—animals without backbones. Some live in soil or in water. Others are parasites and live inside other animals.

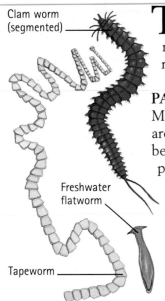

Clam worm (segmented)

Freshwater flatworm

Tapeworm

Leech

Not all worms resemble the familiar segmented earthworms found in the garden. Leeches look like slugs with suckers; the body of the clam worm, a marine worm, is covered with bristly projections.

There are well over 55,000 species of worms. The four main groups are ribbon worms (nemerteans), flatworms, roundworms, and segmented worms.

PARASITES
Most simple worms, such as flatworms, are microscopic organisms, too small to be seen by the naked eye. However, some parasitic tapeworms grow to more than 65 feet in length. Parasitic worms live in or on plants or animals. The larvae (young) of one nematode worm can be ingested by humans and migrate to the lungs. The human host coughs up and swallows the larvae, which are taken to the stomach. Here, they feed off the food eaten by the host and lay eggs that pass out in the host's feces. These eggs may be picked up to infect another person.

EARTHWORMS
The earthworm is a segmented, or annelid, worm. Earthworms swallow soil and digest plant matter in it. Waste soil is then excreted as a wormcast.

The bristle worm is a good swimmer, propelling itself through the water with undulating movements. It has feelers on its head and leglike projections on each body segment.

The worm's body is made up of a series of ringlike segments, covered with tiny bristles that aid movement. Earthworms are hermaphrodite, which means they have both male and female sex organs.

MARINE WORMS
The body structure of marine worms, or polychaetes, is similar to that of annelids, but the bristles on their bodies are longer than on annelids. Some marine worms eat plants, but many are hunters, and shoot out a long tube (proboscis) to grab prey.

The underside of a typical garden earthworm is covered with tiny bristles. The worm uses these to pull itself along. Earthworms breathe through their skins.

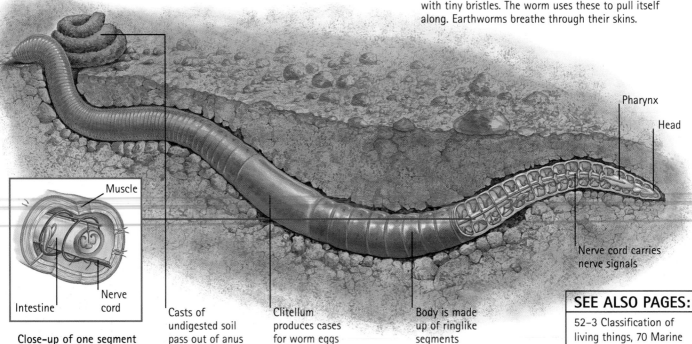

Muscle

Intestine

Nerve cord

Close-up of one segment

Casts of undigested soil pass out of anus

Clitellum produces cases for worm eggs

Body is made up of ringlike segments

Pharynx

Head

Nerve cord carries nerve signals

SEE ALSO PAGES:

52–3 Classification of living things, 70 Marine invertebrates

CRUSTACEANS

Crustaceans form part of a large group of organisms called arthropods. There are more than 38,000 different species, many of which live in the ocean.

A woodlouse has seven pairs of legs. Its body is covered with horny, overlapping plates, which protect it from predators.

Male fiddler crabs have one extra-large claw. They wave this to warn off other males.

Barnacles are small crustaceans that cling to rocks, ships, and piers. They thrust out feathery feet to catch food.

A lobster feasts on a herring. Lobsters are the heaviest crustaceans, and can weigh up to 20 kilograms. Lobsters are important in the fishing industry, because they are extremely popular as food items.

Many crustaceans, including shrimp, lobsters, and crabs, are as familiar in the kitchen as they are in biology books. But there are many more species—woodlice, water fleas, and barnacles all form part of the diverse group of animals called crustaceans. Crustaceans have hard outer shells, called exoskeletons, that protect their soft body tissues; they all have jointed bodies and legs.

A few crustaceans are terrestrial, or land-dwelling, organisms. The woodlouse, for example, inhabits damp, dark places. When alarmed, it rolls itself into an armored ball. Most other crustaceans live in water. But some crabs can live on shore—one kind of crab, the robber crab, even scrambles up trees.

FROM EGG TO ADULT

Crustaceans start life as eggs. These hatch into tiny larvae. Millions of these larvae form the plankton that floats in the sea. Many crustacean larvae look nothing like their parents. Barnacle larvae, for example, are agile swimmers. When the larva becomes an adult, however, it clamps itself tightly to a rock and never moves.

OUTGROWING THEIR SHELLS

As the larva grows, it sheds its shell and grows a new and larger one. This process is called molting. Crustaceans continue to molt all their lives, which poses a problem for the hermit crab. It has no shell, and makes its home in the empty shells of whelks, periwinkles, and other mollusks. When the crab outgrows this shell, it looks for a larger one to move into. While it searches for a new home, this crab is vulnerable to enemies.

Crabs, crayfish, lobsters, and shrimp all have ten legs. The front pair are adapted as pincers that are used for defense, for catching and tearing apart food, and even for signaling to other individuals.

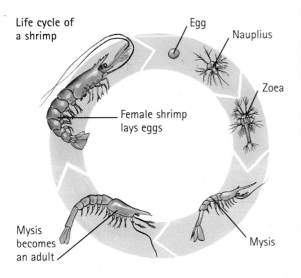

Life cycle of a shrimp

Egg / Nauplius / Zoea / Female shrimp lays eggs / Mysis becomes an adult / Mysis

Shrimp lay eggs that hatch into swimming larvae. The larvae go through several stages of development, eventually becoming mature adult shrimp.

Shrimp (foreground) and lobsters (top right) are among the best-known of the crustaceans. Along with crabs and crayfish, these creatures form a large order of crustaceans called decapods, all of which have five pairs of limbs.

SEE ALSO PAGES:
70 Marine invertebrates, 71 Mollusks, 92 Movement, 93 Migration

SPIDERS, CENTIPEDES, AND SCORPIONS

These animals are arthropods, like crabs and insects. Spiders and scorpions are known as arachnids, and centipedes and millipedes are myriapods.

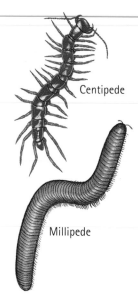

Centipede

Millipede

Not all centipedes have 100 legs. Some have only 14 pairs, others as many as 170 pairs. Millipedes have many more legs—up to 375 pairs. Centipedes are hunters. Millipedes eat decaying vegetation.

Almost all arachnids are hunting animals, armed with poison fangs and an armory of traps. Centipedes are hunters, but millipedes are vegetarians (herbivores). Some millipedes are poisonous, but they use their venom only in self-defense against their predators.

SPIDERS

Spiders are among the most successful hunters in the animal world. Some spin silk webs to trap flying insects. Others swiftly chase their prey or lurk in burrows while they wait to pounce. Crab spiders, which live inside flowers, run sideways. Water spiders, or water spinners, hunt close to or actually in water.

All spiders spin silk, even those that do not make webs. Spiders paralyze their prey with poison fangs. Some kinds, like the black widow, can give people a painful bite, though it is seldom fatal. Spiders can eat only liquid food, so they squirt digestive juices onto their victims to turn them into a liquid that is then sucked up by the spider.

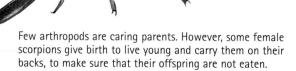

Young are carried on female scorpion's back

Few arthropods are caring parents. However, some female scorpions give birth to live young and carry them on their backs, to make sure that their offspring are not eaten.

SCORPIONS

Scorpions are found mostly in warm, dry climates. They have pincer claws for seizing prey and a poison sting in the tail. The tail curls over the scorpion's head when it is ready to strike. The stings of many types of scorpions can make a person sick, but very rarely kill anyone.

CENTIPEDES AND MILLIPEDES

Like spiders, centipedes have a poisonous bite. The first pair of a centipede's legs are actually modified fangs. Centipedes hunt at night, scuttling at high speed to catch their prey—mollusks, worms, and small insects. Millipedes have twice as many legs as centipedes. They eat the leaves of plants and rotting material.

Trapdoor

Orb weaver

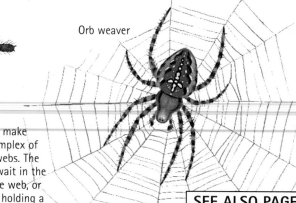

Spider in burrow

Many spiders hunt by lying in wait for unsuspecting passersby. The trap-door spider hides in its burrow. It opens the hinged door and pounces when it senses a passing insect.

Bird-eating spider

The bird spider is a kind of giant tarantula. Its body is almost 3.5 in. long. It is powerful enough to kill nestlings in birds' nests, but insects make up most of its day-to-day diet.

Orb weavers make the most complex of all spiders' webs. The spider may wait in the middle of the web, or hide nearby, holding a signal thread to alert it when the sticky web catches an insect.

SEE ALSO PAGES:
71 Mollusks, 72 Worms, 73 Crustaceans, 95 Adaptation and defense

INSECTS

Insects have only one limitation—size. They can live anywhere in the world and eat any kind of food, but they cannot grow to more than a few inches long.

A human louse, like all sucking lice, feeds on the blood of mammals. Some lice can bite. All lice have mouthparts adapted for their way of feeding.

The male Goliath beetle of Africa is the world's heaviest insect. It is 4 in. long and weighs 4 oz. If a beetle were any heavier, it would collapse under its own weight.

Insects are by far the most numerous of all animal species. More than a million species are known—more than all other animal species added together.

AN INSECT'S BODY

Insects range in size from tiny fleas that can be seen only through a microscope to beetles as large as your hand. Insects have no bones. Instead, their bodies have hard outer coverings, or exoskeletons.

All insects have a similar body plan. The body is in three parts: a head, a thorax, and an abdomen. The head has eyes, jaws, and feelers. The thorax is the middle part, to which the legs and wings are attached. All insects have six legs, and many have one or two pairs of wings. The rear section, the abdomen, contains the stomach, reproductive organs, and breathing tubes called spiracles. These tubes take the place of lungs, but because of them, insects cannot grow to a large size. Any larger and insects would suffocate, because air could not get into their bodies quickly enough through the spiracles.

Many insects have compound eyes made up of hundreds of lenses, each of which gives a tiny image. The insect's brain combines these images into one picture.

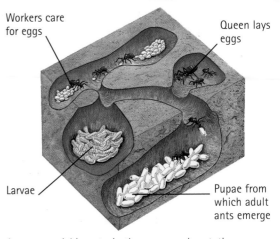

Ants are social insects. In the communal nest, the queen lays eggs. Workers look after the eggs and larvae. Soldiers guard the colony.

SOCIAL INSECTS

Ants, termites, and many wasps and bees are social insects. They function only as members of a colony. The life of the colony centers on a single, egg-laying queen. Males exist solely to fertilize the queen—after mating, the males die. Workers carry out various tasks to keep the colony going. They are divided into castes, each doing a different job. Soldier ants, for example, protect the colony. New queens fly off to form new colonies.

Social insects build complex structures. Wasps make paper nests from chewed-up plant matter. Bees build geometric honeycombs of wax cells. Ants and termites build huge nests out of soil.

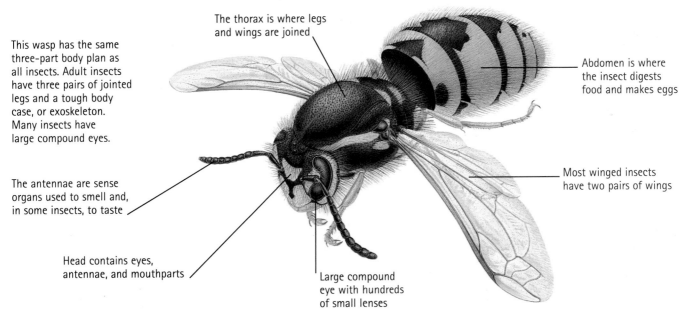

The thorax is where legs and wings are joined

This wasp has the same three-part body plan as all insects. Adult insects have three pairs of jointed legs and a tough body case, or exoskeleton. Many insects have large compound eyes.

The antennae are sense organs used to smell and, in some insects, to taste

Abdomen is where the insect digests food and makes eggs

Most winged insects have two pairs of wings

Head contains eyes, antennae, and mouthparts

Large compound eye with hundreds of small lenses

Flies are one of the largest insect groups, with more than 750,000 kinds. Many flies lay their eggs in dung and rotting food. Some spread diseases, such as cholera and malaria.

Dragonflies are the fastest fliers in the insect world. They can hover and even fly backward as they hunt, catching prey with their long legs. The dragonfly nymphs develop underwater in ponds.

A grasshopper lays eggs that hatch into wingless nymphs. As the nymphs grow wings, they look like smaller versions of their parents. The nymphs can only hop, so they are found near the ground. The adults can fly onto stems.

LIFE CYCLE OF A MONARCH BUTTERFLY

The butterfly lays its eggs on a food plant, the milkweed. Each egg hatches into a larva, or caterpillar. The caterpillar eats and grows rapidly. Hungry birds are warned to keep away by the caterpillar's vivid markings. When full-grown, the caterpillar becomes a pupa, or chrysalis. Inside this apparently lifeless case, many changes take place. The pupa splits open, and the adult crawls out. As soon as its wings are dry, it flies away.

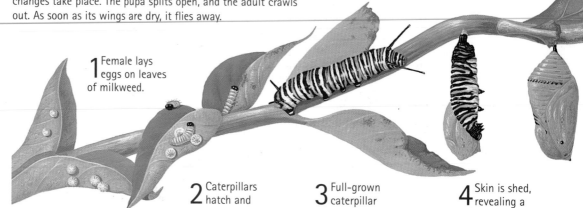

1 Female lays eggs on leaves of milkweed.

2 Caterpillars hatch and start to eat.

3 Full-grown caterpillar spins silken thread.

4 Skin is shed, revealing a chrysalis (pupa).

FLYING

Most insects have two pairs of wings, though worker ants and fleas never have wings. A beetle does not appear to have wings. Its front wings form hard cases that cover the delicate back wings, with which the beetle flies. Faster fliers, like wasps, have two pairs of wings. True flies have one pair of flying wings; their second pair has evolved into flexible rods used for balance.

LIFE CYCLES

All insects lay eggs. The young of most insects go through four stages of growth and development. In butterflies and moths, the stages are: egg, larva, chrysalis, adult. The immature insect is a caterpillar, which looks nothing like the adult. Caterpillars do little else but eat plants. The main role of adult butterflies and moths is to mate.

Other insects, such as grasshoppers and cockroaches, go through a three-stage growing process—from egg to nymph to adult. The nymph looks like a miniature version of the adult insect, although nymphs usually do not have wings, whereas the adult form usually does.

FOOD

Evolution has equipped insects to eat an astonishing variety of foods. Some are carnivorous, hunting by speed (like the dragonfly) or by stealth (like the praying mantis). Others are plant-eaters and chew leaves, suck sap, or bore into wood.

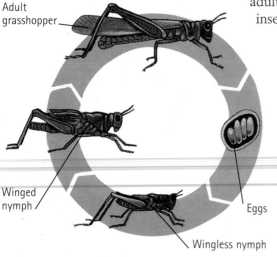

Adult grasshopper

Winged nymph

Wingless nymph

Eggs

► Mating, for some insects, is a dangerous business. A female praying mantis eats anything within reach of her jaws—including the male with which she has just mated.

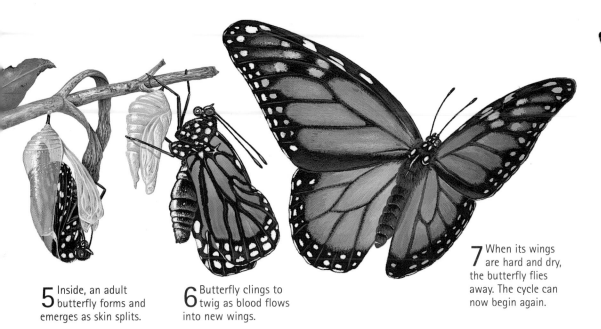

Swallowtails are large butterflies of Africa, Europe, and Asia. Most butterflies fly by day.

5 Inside, an adult butterfly forms and emerges as skin splits.

6 Butterfly clings to twig as blood flows into new wings.

7 When its wings are hard and dry, the butterfly flies away. The cycle can now begin again.

Moths fly mainly at night. They tend to be less colorful than butterflies. The luna moth is about 4 in. across.

PESTS AND HELPERS

A few insects, like the desert locust of Africa, are destructive pests. Swarms of locusts can eat an entire field of crops in a few hours and cause a famine in days. Many other insects, however, are helpful to people. Without bees and other flying insects, flowering plants would not be pollinated, and fruit trees would not bear fruit. Honey, made from the sugary nectar of flowers by bees, has been collected by humans for thousands of years.

Scavenging insects, such as burying beetles, feed on dead matter and help to make the soil fertile. Ladybugs and some wasps are helpful because they eat other insects, such as aphids, that are pests. The silkworm (the larva of the silk moth) is reared by people for the silk that it spins when turning into a pupa.

MINIATURE MARVELS

There are some extraordinary record-breakers in the insect world. A cicada's song can be heard 1,600 feet away. A queen termite may live for 50 years. Many insects can lift or drag objects 20 times their own weight. The largest insect, the Queen Alexandra's birdwing butterfly, measures one foot across.

An emperor moth. Moths hold their wings open when resting. When they flap their wings, the spots can startle enemies.

Locusts, usually solitary, come together to form vast migratory swarms, to lay their eggs. Armies of nymphs march overland, then take wing. Some swarms eat every single leaf in sight.

Large butterflies, like this Rajah Brooke birdwing, flutter in tropical forests. Butterflies fold their wings when at rest.

SEE ALSO PAGES:

74 Spiders, centipedes, and scorpions, 88–9 Animal reproduction

FISH

Fish were the first animals with backbones (vertebrates) and skeletons made of bone. They are the animals best adapted to life in water.

TYPES OF FISH
Fish are grouped by their body structure and skeleton. There are jawless fish, cartilaginous fish, and two kinds of bony fish.

The lamprey (above) and hagfish are primitive fish, with sucker mouths instead of hard teeth and jaws. All existing fish are descended from fish like these.

Sharks have a skeleton of cartilage, not bone. These ferocious hunters swam in prehistoric seas. Many sharks are now threatened with extinction.

The coelacanth is a primitive bony fish of the Indian Ocean. Discovered in the mid-1900s, it is a living fossil, having been around for nearly 400 million years.

The perch is an example of a modern bony fish. It lives in freshwater. There are about 20,000 species of bony fish, many more than other types.

If its pool dries up, the African lungfish survives by burying itself in the mud. Motionless, it keeps alive by breathing air using lungs.

There are three groups of fish, all of which are found in seawater and freshwater. The cartilaginous fish have gristly, rather than bony, skeletons and leathery skins, not scales. They include the sharks and rays. The smallest group are the jawless fish, such as lampreys and hagfish. By far the largest group are the bony fish, which have bony skeletons and bony scales covering their bodies. Bony fish are found in both ancient and modern forms.

LIVING IN WATER
The first fish appeared in the oceans about 540 million years ago. By breathing through gills, fish are fully adapted to life in water. Most fish cannot live out of water. Only the lungfish can breathe air because it has primitive lungs. Lungfish live in stagnant water that has little oxygen in it, so they have to gulp breaths of air at the surface.

SALT OR FRESH?
About 60 percent of fish species live in saltwater. A few kinds can live in either salt or fresh. Sea fish need salt and other chemicals to live. Because seawater is saltier than their own body fluids, they lose water through their skins by a process called osmosis. They drink seawater to prevent their bodies from drying out. The opposite is true for freshwater fish. Their bodies are saltier than the water, so they

The deep-sea anglerfish lives in darkness and uses a luminous lure to attract prey. Many deep-sea fish make their own light, sometimes to attract mates.

absorb water. Freshwater fish get rid of the extra water by passing a lot of urine.

MIGRATION
Some fish make long migrations to their breeding grounds. Salmon begin their lives in freshwater, swimming downriver to the sea. When ready to breed, adult salmon make an astonishing return journey to the same river in which they were spawned. There they mate, breed, and die—their life cycle complete. American and European eels make similar migrations, from freshwater rivers to the salty water of deep oceans.

PARENTAL CARE
All female fish lay eggs—usually a large number of them—which are fertilized by males. When the babies hatch, they must fend for themselves. Only a few fish show any care for their young. Sticklebacks build nests, which the male defends aggressively. Some cichlids shelter their young in their mouths. Baby seahorses hatch and develop in a pouch on their father's body.

Lungfish in water

Lungfish in burrow

PARTS OF A FISH

The body of a typical bony fish is streamlined for swimming, although many fish have round or flat shapes. Fish use tails for swimming, fins for balance and steering. Fish senses include the lateral line system, which detects subtle changes in water pressure.

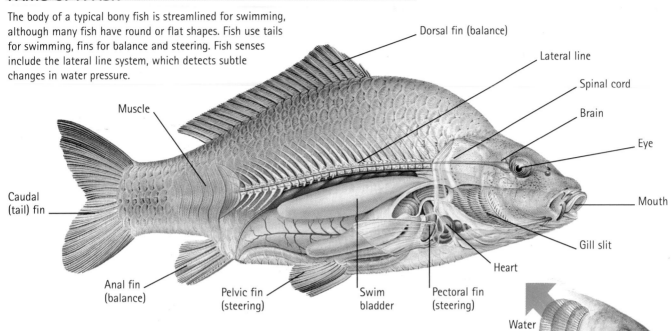

Dorsal fin (balance)
Lateral line
Spinal cord
Brain
Eye
Mouth
Gill slit
Heart
Muscle
Caudal (tail) fin
Anal fin (balance)
Pelvic fin (steering)
Swim bladder
Pectoral fin (steering)

SHAPES AND ADAPTATIONS

Fish come in a variety of body shapes. Eels look more like snakes. Flatfish like flounder begin life the right way up and then lie on their sides. One eye travels across the head as it grows, so that the adult fish can lie hidden on the seabed with two eyes looking up. Porcupine fish have prickly skins and blow themselves up, like balloons, to frighten away or baffle a predator. Some fish, like scorpion fish and stingrays, have poisonous spines, which can even kill humans.

Fish have many unusual adaptations. Deep-sea fish, living in a gloomy world without sunlight, make their own chemical lights. Anglerfish wave a lure to entice prey within snapping reach. Freshwater archerfish catch prey by knocking them out of the air with jets of water.

Some fish can leave the water—temporarily. Mudskippers use leglike fins to crawl over mud. Flying fish use their long, stiffened fins as wings and glide through the air to escape enemies.

Water out
Water in
Gills

Fish breathe through gills on each side of the head. Water passes out through the gill slits.

Blood capillaries
Filaments
Water flow
Blood pumped to gills
Oxygen-rich blood

The gills contain tiny, blood-filled filaments. These remove oxygen from water that the fish gulps in through its mouth.

A school of black-striped salema. Fish swim in groups for protection. One fish is hard to catch among so many.

SEE ALSO PAGES:

12–13 The oceans,
80–1 Amphibians, 82–3
Reptiles, 93 Migration

AMPHIBIANS

Amphibians are the smallest class of vertebrates.
Although they were the first animals to colonize the
land, amphibians must return to the water to breed.

A long-tailed salamander spends most of its life on land.

Like all newts, the smooth newt hunts for food in the water. It uses its long tail to whip through the water as it swims.

Like many frogs, the green treefrog inflates a throat sac to sing during the mating season to attract potential female mates.

Caecilians live in tropical regions. They hunt at night and live in burrows underground. There are only 160 species in this group of amphibians.

Amphibians are the smallest group of vertebrates (animals with a backbone), with around 3,000 species. Like fish and reptiles, amphibians are cold-blooded animals. This means that amphibians cannot regulate their own temperature and rely instead on the sun to warm their bodies. Most amphibians begin their lives in the water and breathe with gills. As they grow, they develop lungs and legs and are able to move on dry land.

WHERE AMPHIBIANS LIVE

Amphibians are found throughout the world, except in the polar regions. They live in a number of different habitats, including rain forests, ponds, woodlands, and lakes, as well as high mountain grassland and even deserts.

Although adult amphibians can survive dry periods, most need to live in a damp environment, such as a river or pond. In humid tropical rain forests, many frogs can survive without a permanent water source—they use tiny droplets of water that accumulate in the leaves of plants.

Since amphibians are cold-blooded creatures, they become inactive in cold conditions. In extreme cold they may hibernate, often in mud at the bottom of a pond or under a log.

THE THREE GROUPS

Frogs and toads make up 80 percent of all amphibian species. Their back legs are long and powerful, allowing the creatures to leap, although many toads prefer to

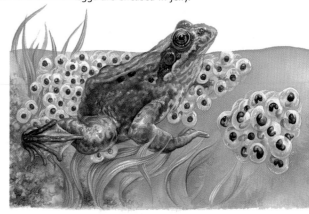

1 Frogs lay eggs, or spawn, in water. The eggs are encased in jelly.

crawl along the ground. Newts and salamanders form the second group; they have short legs and long tails. The third and smallest group are the caecilians, which look like worms and live underground.

FOOD AND FINDING MATES

Many people find it difficult to tell frogs and toads apart. As a general rule, frogs have smoother skins than toads and spend more of their time in water. Most frogs and toads prey on insects and other small animals, staying perfectly still and waiting for their prey to pass. Some use their long, sticky tongues to catch prey.

Some toads and frogs have a long tongue with a sticky tip. They shoot it out to catch unsuspecting insect prey.

▶ The axolotl of Mexico and the western United States is a curious member of the salamander family. Axolotls never grow up. Instead, they remain in the tadpole stage of development—complete with gills—all their lives and even breed as tadpoles.

AMPHIBIAN LIFE CYCLE

The life cycle of the common frog starts when a male and female mate. Male frogs compete vigorously to mate with females. Many males make loud cries to attract females and deter rivals. Females produce masses of eggs, or spawn, which are usually fertilized externally. After about 10 days, the eggs hatch into tadpoles with gills, which live and feed in the water. Eventually, the tadpole grows back legs, then front legs, and its tail shrinks. Finally, after the adult frog has developed lungs, it clambers out to find food on dry land.

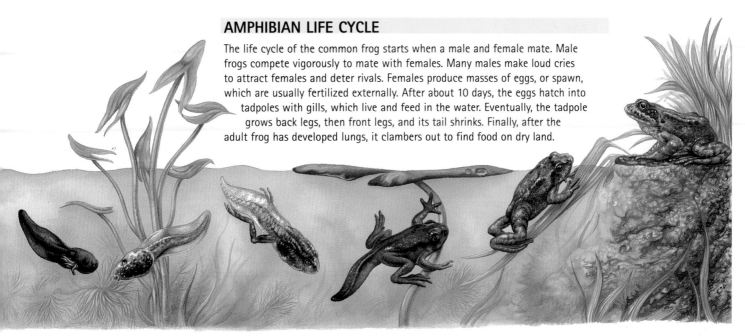

2 After about ten days, spawn hatches into tadpoles with gills.

3 The back legs of the tadpoles grow first.

4 The legs and lungs grow, and the tail shrinks.

5 With fully developed lungs, the adult frog can leave the water.

Male frogs croak to call females during the mating season. They do this by forcing air over their vocal cords. The loudest frogs have an inflatable vocal sac that puffs up with air, like a balloon.

FROM EGG TO ADULT

Amphibian courtship is often a frantic affair, with males and females gathering in large numbers. Once the eggs have been fertilized, most amphibians take no further interest in their young.

However, some take measures to protect the eggs. For example, caecilians coil themselves around their eggs inside their burrows. Baby Surinam toads hatch from eggs encased in tiny pockets on the surface of their mother's skin. The male midwife toad attaches its eggs to its back legs and carries them around for about three weeks until they hatch.

The largest amphibians, such as the six-foot-long Chinese giant salamander and the cane toad, have few enemies. Most of the smaller species rely on camouflage and escape to evade a predator. Others hop around in full and colorful view.

POISON FROGS

The startling colors of the little poison dart frogs of South America serve as danger signals to potential predators. Poison frogs are venomous. The golden poison dart frog of Colombia, for example, contains enough toxin in its body to kill around 1,000 people.

The bullfrog of North America is noted for its loud, croaking mating call.

Gliding frogs stretch folds of skin beneath their toes. The folds act like parachutes when they leap.

A poison dart frog, from South America, is brightly colored to warn off potential predators.

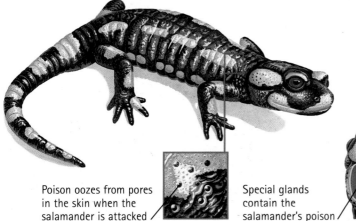

Poison oozes from pores in the skin when the salamander is attacked

Special glands contain the salamander's poison

Like all amphibians, the fire salamander has slime-producing glands that lie just beneath the surface of the skin. The slime made by these glands helps to keep the skin moist and also provides a chemical defense against predators. The striking colors of the fire salamander warn other animals that it is poisonous. In ancient times, some people believed that salamanders could live in fire.

SEE ALSO PAGES:
82–3 Reptiles, 88–9
Animal reproduction, 95
Adaptation and defense

REPTILES

Reptiles are cold-blooded animals, and they prefer to live in warm climates. They are characterized by their dry, scaly skin. Most reptiles lay leathery-shelled eggs.

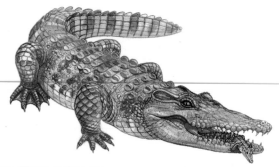

Crocodiles have huge jaws for seizing prey, but can pick up their young with surprising gentleness.

Sea turtles spend most of the year in the ocean. Once a year, however, the females leave their ocean habitat to lay their eggs.

1 The female makes her way to a sandy beach and hauls herself ashore, using her flippers as legs.

2 She digs a shallow hole above the level of high tide, covers her eggs with sand, and returns to the sea.

3 After a short period of development, the hatchlings break out of their shells and dig their way out of the sand.

4 Finally, the newly hatched turtles race for the water. Many are eaten by predators; only about 1% survive into adulthood.

For over 150 million years, reptiles were the dominant life-form on the Earth. The best-known of these animals were the dinosaurs, but there were many others, including the flying pterosaurs and ocean-dwelling plesiosaurs and ichthyosaurs.

Today, there are four main groups of reptiles: alligators and crocodiles (about 25 species), tortoises and turtles (about 250 species), and snakes (about 2,700 species) and lizards (over 3,700 species). The other group contains just one species, the tuatara of New Zealand.

LIVING ON LAND

Most reptiles are excellent swimmers, and some, like turtles and terrapins, spend most of their lives in water. But reptiles can lay their eggs on land, unlike most amphibians. The leathery shells of the eggs keep the embryos from drying out.

Reptiles have dry, scaly skins. Many are agile, fast-moving animals, the fastest being the snakes. All reptiles are considered to be cold-blooded animals, but the term is misleading. Although a reptile's body warms in sunlight and is less active when cold, reptiles have a temperature regulation mechanism. Scientists have yet to discover exactly how this mechanism works.

CROCODILIANS

Crocodiles and their relatives—alligators, caimans, and gavials—are collectively called crocodilians. These reptiles are large carnivores, with strong jaws and powerful tails. They either lie on river banks, basking in the sun, or stay almost submerged in the water, with just their

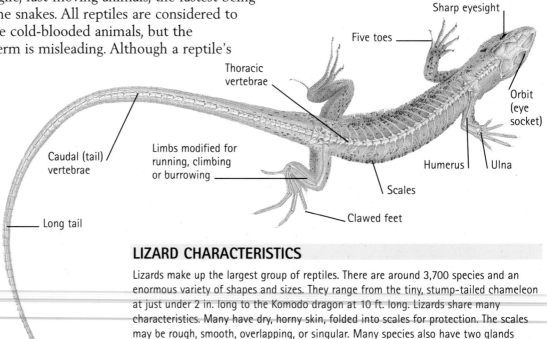

Sharp eyesight

Five toes

Thoracic vertebrae

Orbit (eye socket)

Caudal (tail) vertebrae

Limbs modified for running, climbing or burrowing

Humerus

Ulna

Long tail

Scales

Clawed feet

LIZARD CHARACTERISTICS

Lizards make up the largest group of reptiles. There are around 3,700 species and an enormous variety of shapes and sizes. They range from the tiny, stump-tailed chameleon at just under 2 in. long to the Komodo dragon at 10 ft. long. Lizards share many characteristics. Many have dry, horny skin, folded into scales for protection. The scales may be rough, smooth, overlapping, or singular. Many species also have two glands called Jacobson's organs, which detect odors. Most species have four limbs (two front legs and two hind legs). As a result, they are active runners and climbers, and are also known to burrow. Lizards have large heads, with well-developed eyes and eyelids. Food, either plants or other animals, is seized in the jaws. Many lizards have long tails— a tempting target for a predator. This is often all the hunter ends up with, however, since the tail snaps off. The lizard makes its getaway and grows a new tail.

The largest snakes, like the 30-foot-long anaconda from South America, are constrictors. They grab their prey with their fangs and tightly coil themselves around it. As the victim's major blood vessels rupture, it suffocates.

eyes and nostrils showing. Crocodilians are caring parents. Females lay their eggs in sand or in nests of vegetation and fiercely guard their newly hatched young.

TURTLES AND TORTOISES

Turtles and tortoises are covered in a hard shell—only the head, legs, and tail are exposed. When alarmed, the tortoise hides its head inside the shell. Marine turtles are fast swimmers, but are almost helpless when they come ashore to lay their eggs.

SNAKES AND LIZARDS

Snakes move by wriggling their bodies. Most species are found in deserts and tropical forests, but some live in the ocean.

Snakes are carnivorous animals, which means they feed only on meat. They sense their prey by smell, using their flicking tongues to taste the air, or with special heat-sensing organs. Poisonous snakes can bite as soon as they hatch. Vipers and rattlesnakes have long fangs; cobras and sea snakes have shorter fangs.

Many snakes are not poisonous. They kill with a bite alone or, like boas and anacondas, by crushing prey to death in powerful coils.

Most lizards have legs, with the exception of slowworms. Some, like the Australian thorny devil, have spines; some, like the Gila monster of the southwestern United States, are poisonous. A few lizards and snakes give birth to live young, but most lay eggs.

CATCHING FOOD

Many reptiles prey on insects and small mammals. Some snakes pursue mice into their burrows or climb trees to take young birds from nests. A small lizard called a gecko has sucker pads on its feet, allowing this animal to run across flat ceilings of houses to catch insects. The chameleon moves slowly and whips out a long, sticky tongue to catch its next meal.

The largest lizard of all is the Komodo dragon from Komodo Island in Indonesia. Up to 10 feet long, it will eat small deer or wild pigs.

Venom canal

Venom sac

Fangs

Hinged jaw

Poisonous snakes bite their victims with fangs that spring down from the roof of the mouth. The venom is injected from a sac at the back of the head.

The giant tortoise of Aldabra is a slow-moving herbivore. Other giant tortoises live on the Galapagos Islands in the Pacific Ocean.

A Galapagos iguana can dive up to 50 ft. underwater to feed on algae, kelp, and other marine plants that grow near the rocky shore where it lives.

The chameleon changes color to blend in with its surroundings. This is triggered by anger, fear, or by variations in light intensity or temperature.

SEE ALSO PAGES:

90–1 Animal behavior, 92 Movement, 95 Adaptation and defense

BIRDS

Birds make up the largest group of warm-blooded vertebrates. All birds have feathers, beaks, and two front limbs that have been modified into wings.

Birds of prey have hooked claws, or talons, that can grasp and crush prey.

Perching birds have one backward-pointing toe that provides a firm grip.

Swimming birds have webbed feet that they use like paddles.

▲ Most birds have four clawed toes. The feet and claws of different species are adapted to suit their different ways of life.

A hummingbird hovers in front of a flower, sipping at the sugary nectar inside with its long tongue.

Birds are one of nature's finest examples of adaptation. They are found throughout the world, from the coldest polar ice cap to the hottest desert. They live in the air, on land, and in water. The ability to fly is found in many insects and some vertebrates, but it is most developed in birds. It has allowed them to occupy every land environment and to travel great distances in search of food.

Several unique features have helped birds to become masters of the sky. They are the only animals with feathers, hollow bones for lightness in the air, and strong breast muscles to work their wings.

FEATHERED FINERY

Feathers are perfectly designed for flight. They provide not only a lightweight, aerodynamic surface, but also an excellent insulation for the bird's body. Feathers are made from a protein called keratin and come in various designs. For example, the soft down feathers are closest to the skin and provide insulation. Flight feathers are larger and stiffer. Depending on the species, a bird has between 900 and 25,000 feathers on its body.

Male birds often have more colorful feathers, or plumage, than females. In the breeding season, males use their distinctive plumage as a courtship display to attract females as mates.

Since a bird depends on its feathers to fly, it needs to keep them in good condition. It does this by preening—cleaning and combing its feathers.

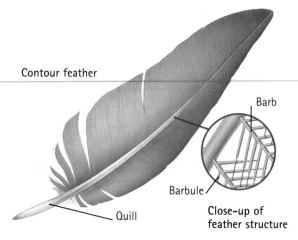

Contour feather

Barb

Barbule

Quill

Close-up of feather structure

▲ A flight feather has a central rod called a quill. In close-up, the threadlike barbs can be seen. The barbs are held in place by hooked structures called barbules.

BIRDSONG

Birds call or sing as part of their mating behavior. Specific calls are used to attract a mate or to warn other males about territorial limits. The sounds are produced by the syrinx, a structure unique to birds, which is located at the base of their trachea, or windpipe. The syrinx contains elastic membranes that vibrate when air is expelled from the lungs. Changes in the tension of the membranes alter the pitch of the call or song.

NESTS AND EGGS

All birds hatch from eggs. The egg has a hard shell, which protects the embryo inside. Most birds lay their eggs in nests, but some just lay them on the ground. The materials from which nests

At nearly 10 ft. tall, the flightless ostrich is the largest of all birds. The ostrich also lays the largest egg, weighing 3.75 lb.

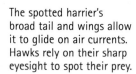

The spotted harrier's broad tail and wings allow it to glide on air currents. Hawks rely on their sharp eyesight to spot their prey.

Woodpecker (drill) Crossbill (nutcracker) Kestrel (tearing) Spoonbill (detector/strainer) Oystercatcher (probe)

◄ The size and shape of a bill determines the type of food a bird eats. A kestrel's hooked bill, for example, is used for tearing flesh, but the probing bill of the oystercatcher is used to find and open shellfish.

The plover lays its eggs in a scrape on the ground.

are built usually blend in with the surroundings, so that the chicks that hatch in them remain safe. The eggs themselves are often colored for camouflage to avoid the attention of predators.

Some birds lay one or two eggs, others as many as ten. They are incubated by one or both parents sitting on them until the hatchlings emerge.

TAKING FLIGHT

To fly, birds need to generate muscle power to beat their wings. The breast muscles are the source of propulsion for powered flight. A well-oxygenated blood supply is essential for the muscles to work efficiently. As a result, birds have evolved a well-developed pair of lungs and, like mammals, a four-chambered heart to make

sure that muscles get the maximum oxygen from the blood. Large birds, such as albatrosses and vultures, can flap their wings slowly or hover in the air on rising air currents. Smaller birds need to flap their wings faster to stay in the air.

Some birds have lost the ability to fly. The ostrich runs and turns quickly to escape its enemies, and penguins have become masterful swimmers and divers.

FINDING FOOD

Birds eat high-energy foods, including seeds, fruits, insects, worms, fish, and other animals. These provide birds with the energy to maintain their body temperature and to fly. Birds avoid low-energy foods like grasses.

Birds of prey are determined and ferocious predators. The fastest is the peregrine falcon, which dives vertically through the air at speeds of up to 185 mph (300kph). Vultures are scavengers, flying high to spot dead animals. They glide down to pick the bones clean.

Waterbirds, such as grebes, nest on or beside the water.

Swallows make mud nests, stuck to the walls and rafters of buildings.

The robin uses twigs and grasses to make a cup-shaped nest.

▲ Birds' nests can be little more than a scrape in the ground or a delicate structure of plant material, mud, and saliva.

► The Australian lyrebird shows off its long tail feathers to attract a potential mate. Many male birds perform courtship displays during the breeding season.

◄ A North American bald eagle catches a fish, snatching it from the water with its feet. Eagles are one of the largest birds of prey. They seize prey in their talons, tearing the flesh into chunks with their hooked bills.

SEE ALSO PAGES:

90–1 Animal behavior, 92 Movement, 93 Migration, 95 Adaptation and defense

MAMMALS

Mammals are warm-blooded animals that feed their young from milk-producing glands. Some species are the most intelligent creatures on the Earth.

Like humans, the adult male pygmy chimpanzee of Zaire is a primate. Primates are considered to be the most intelligent of all the animals.

Mammals are an extremely diverse group of organisms, and they occupy almost every type of habitat on the planet. They live on land, in hot or cold climates, in the sea, and even in the air.

Mammals are warm-blooded animals, often with leathery or furry skin. This means that all species control their body temperature by sweating or panting when it is hot and shivering when it is cold.

GROUPS OF MAMMALS

Mammals appeared relatively late in the evolutionary timescale. There were mammals during the age of the dinosaurs, but they were small animals, rather like the shrews, squirrels, and badgers of today.

Mammals belong to the class Mammalia. This class consists of three main groups.

All the animals that belong to the class Mammalia are warm-blooded creatures with hair. Among them are the smartest, fastest, and largest animals on the Earth.

The most primitive lay eggs, as reptiles and birds do. These animals are called monotremes, and only two species survive today—the platypus and the echidna.

MARSUPIALS

Although marsupials give birth to live young, the offspring are only partially developed. As a result, the offspring stay in their mother's marsupium (pouch) and feed on her milk until fully developed. The kangaroo is probably the best-known marsupial. Most species are found in Australia and New Zealand.

THE HIGHER MAMMALS

The placental mammals are the most advanced group. The term placental refers to the fact that this group gestates (develops young) their offspring inside their bodies, providing nutrients through the placenta in the uterus. There are many different species. These include flying mammals (bats), sea mammals (seals, dolphins, and whales), large herbivores or plant-eaters (elephants and giraffes), and powerful carnivores (dogs, cats, and bears). The primates include apes, monkeys, and human beings.

THE LARGEST MAMMALS

Whales are the largest mammals that have ever lived on the Earth. These humpback whales are filter-feeding, scooping up mouthfuls of small krill from the water and straining the food through bristlelike growths in their mouths. The huge size of whales means that they need to consume vast quantities of krill every day. Since mammals need air to breathe, whales must come to the surface regularly to take in air. The blue whale is the largest animal on the planet. This huge marine mammal may reach up to 100 ft. in length and weigh 135 tons.

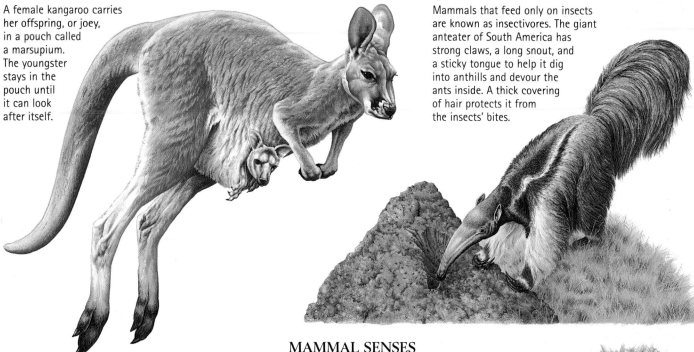

A female kangaroo carries her offspring, or joey, in a pouch called a marsupium. The youngster stays in the pouch until it can look after itself.

Mammals that feed only on insects are known as insectivores. The giant anteater of South America has strong claws, a long snout, and a sticky tongue to help it dig into anthills and devour the ants inside. A thick covering of hair protects it from the insects' bites.

LOOKING AFTER THE YOUNG

Mammals owe much of their success to parenting. They are generally the most caring parents in the natural world. The female feeds her young with milk from her own body and looks after them until they can fend for themselves. During this time, the offspring learn essential survival techniques, such as social behavior and methods of obtaining food. Some mammals are born blind and helpless and require an intensive period of parental care—mice, for example. Others, like deer, stand and run within minutes of being born.

MAMMAL SENSES

Mammals have highly developed senses. This has also contributed to their success. Some have two eyes, one on each side of the head. Each eye provides a different view of the surroundings. Others have binocular vision—the eyes are at the front of the head and work together. This type of vision allows the animal to judge distances more accurately.

Some mammals have specialized senses, such as the bat's sonar (echolocation) and the mole's sensitive whiskers. For some mammals, the sense of smell is most important. For example, dogs use scent-messages to mark their territory.

In cold climates, some mammals, such as the European dormouse, hibernate. They do not eat during this period—they live on the fat stored in their bodies.

The duck-billed platypus of Australia is one of the few mammals that lay eggs. The female cares for the helpless young in a burrow, feeding them with milk from special glands on her body.

Instead of teats, the female platypus has milk pores.

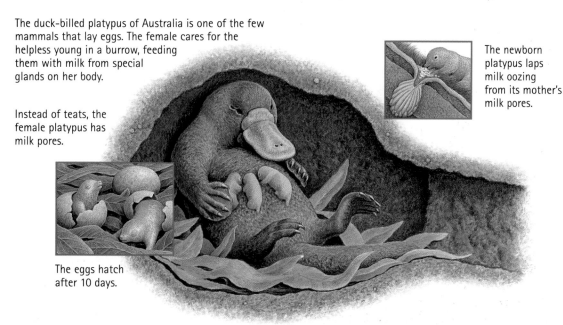

The newborn platypus laps milk oozing from its mother's milk pores.

The eggs hatch after 10 days.

Bats eat insects and feed from flowers. Bats are the only true flying mammals. The wing of a bat consists of a thin membrane that stretches between the fingers, body, and leg.

SEE ALSO PAGES:

88–9 Animal reproduction, 92 Movement, 95 Adaptation and defense

ANIMAL REPRODUCTION

The longer an animal takes to reproduce, the larger it is and the longer it lives. Some animals can breed in hours; others take many years.

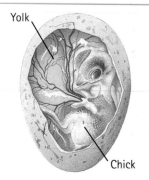

Inside a bird's egg, the chick is fed from the yolk. The chick of a hen starts to hatch about 21 days after the egg is laid. By this stage, its feathers and claws are fully formed.

Yolk

Chick

Although there is a great variety of life on the Earth, there are only a few basic methods of reproduction. An animal's life span is determined chiefly by the time it needs to reach adulthood, mate, and reproduce. Animal reproduction takes two forms: asexual (only one parent produces the young, as in sponges and corals) and sexual (male and female cells combine to form a new animal).

PLACENTAL MAMMALS

Mammals need the most time to reproduce, because most baby mammals take months or even years to develop. In the higher mammals—the placentals—the unborn baby develops inside its mother's body, to which it is joined by a two-way filter called the placenta. The placenta provides the baby with food and oxygen from the mother's blood and takes away the growing infant's waste.

After birth, a baby mammal suckles milk from its mother. The milk is produced in breasts, or mammary glands. These glands are unique to mammals and give them their name.

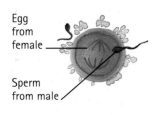

Egg from female

Sperm from male

In sexual reproduction, a sperm from the male fertilizes the larger egg cell of the female. In fertilization, chromosomes from the male and female sex cells come together.

Mating involves pairing of males and females. Courtship rituals often involve elaborate behavior, like the dancing of these egrets. Some mated pairs stay together for life.

REARING YOUNG

Birds that lay a clutch of eggs every year produce far more young in a lifetime than an elephant, which, every five years, gives birth to a baby that has taken nearly two years to develop inside its body.

Rearing young takes up most of a parent's (usually the mother's) energy. Bears are by nature solitary animals. After giving birth, the female bear guards her young with care. She teaches them to find food, so that they will be able to look after themselves. Cubs will usually stay with their mother for one or two years.

The offspring of hydra reproduce by budding off from their parent.

The fertilized egg is the start of a new life. The first cell divides, and subsequent cells divide many times in a process called mitosis. Eventually, cells specialize to form organs.

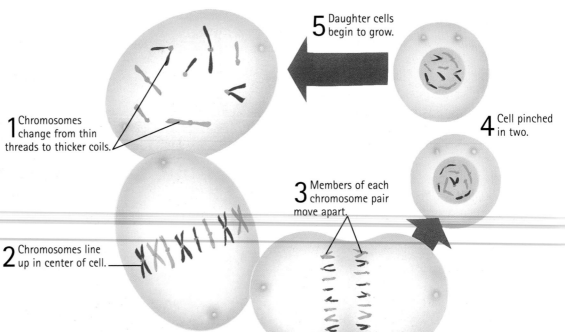

5 Daughter cells begin to grow.

1 Chromosomes change from thin threads to thicker coils.

4 Cell pinched in two.

3 Members of each chromosome pair move apart.

2 Chromosomes line up in center of cell.

GESTATION PERIODS

Scale shown in months

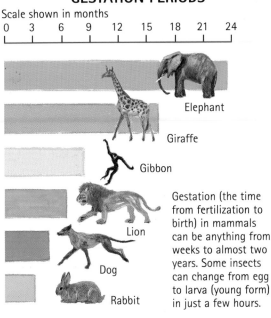

Gestation (the time from fertilization to birth) in mammals can be anything from weeks to almost two years. Some insects can change from egg to larva (young form) in just a few hours.

Elephant

Giraffe

Gibbon

Lion

Dog

Rabbit

Mammals form bonds between mates and within larger groups. Male lions father cubs, but do little else. Females rear the young and do most of the hunting for the group, or pride, working together as a team.

PARENTING AND LEARNING

Animal parents show various levels of concern for their young. A male king penguin keeps its egg and, later, the chick warm beneath a flap of skin on his feet all winter, until the comparatively warm weather of a polar spring arrives.

Parents teach by example, and the more complex an animal's way of life is, the more there is for young animals to learn. After all, it takes humans many years to learn how to look after themselves without their parents' help.

Bird chicks can recognize their parents' voices. However, most of what a bird does is instinctive. Fox cubs, on the other hand, must learn to hunt by imitating their parents and through play. Monkeys and other animals that live in groups also learn by watching and copying. Even adults may pick up new behavior in this way, by copying the food-gathering techniques of a more ambitious or daring individual.

LIFE SPANS

No animal lives as long as the oldest plants. A mayfly emerges from its larval stage, breeds, and dies in a few hours. Over 20 years is old for most mammals. Some fish, like carp, can live from 50 to 80 years. Elephants live to be over 60; tortoises and turtles to 100 or more. Humans in developed countries usually live about 70 years, slightly longer than chimpanzees, which average 50–60 years.

CLONES

Clones are genetically identical organisms. They can occur naturally. The offspring of plants and animals that can reproduce asexually—that is, without joining a male and female cell together—are clones of their parents. Most higher animals do not form clones naturally. Identical twins are clones of each other.

However, scientists have learned how to clone living things in the laboratory. The ability to clone animals and plants could be very useful in farming and medicine, but many people fear that the technology could be misused.

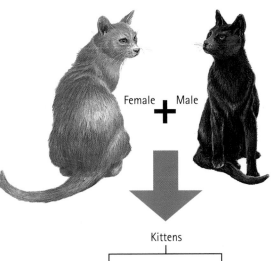

Female + Male

Kittens

Cloning techniques make it possible for scientists to make identical copies of an animal. Dolly the sheep became the first cloned adult mammal in 1997. She was an exact replica of her mother, and had no father.

◀ Pairs of chromosomes carry two genes for the same character. One gene may always be dominant. But sometimes two genes may be equal and mix their effects. So if a black male cat and an orange female cat have kittens, some kittens will be black; some orange; and some tortoiseshell, a mixture of the two.

SEE ALSO PAGES:

62-3 Fruits and seeds,
90-1 Animal behavior,
135 Genes and chromosomes

ANIMAL BEHAVIOR

Animal behavior, as individuals or in groups, is the way in which an animal reacts both to what happens to it internally and to its external environment.

The chimpanzee on the left is using a stick as a tool to extract termites from their nest. The young chimpanzee watches his mother and learns the skill. In time, and with practice, he may improve the technique.

Storing food, as squirrels do by burying nuts in the fall, is an instinctive form of behavior. Instinct controls the lives of insects. Mammals can alter instinctive behavior through learning.

▲ A hibernating chipmunk goes into a deep state of sleep and appears dead. Its metabolism slows, using very little energy from its stored fat supply. Animals hibernate because food is scarce during the winter.

▶ An elephant herd is led by a dominant older female, called the matriarch. A female giving birth is watched over by other females, and the herd protects the newborn elephant from danger.

The way in which an animal behaves is the outcome of millions of years of evolution. Most animal behavior is instinctive. For example, an animal eats to maintain the energy needed to survive, but it does not have to be taught to eat. Some animals with large brains can solve simple problems. Apes and dolphins are two of the most intelligent animal species. Chimpanzees plan searches for food, communicate by gestures, and use simple tools. Dolphins and whales show concern for one another and communicate underwater by a wide range of sounds.

Many animals learn. A rabbit that has eaten a bad-tasting plant or a bird that pecks at a poisonous caterpillar learns to avoid that particular food choice.

SURVIVAL

The main aim of most behavior is to make sure that animals survive and reproduce. Animals have amazing ways of protecting themselves from enemies. There are many examples: the porcupine's quills, the ink cloud squirted by an octopus, and the hognose snake lying on its back and playing dead.

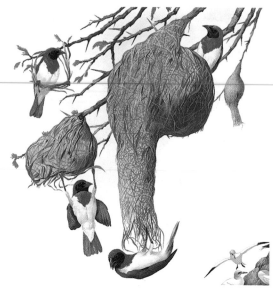

Weaver birds nest in huge colonies, numbering thousands of individuals. Nest-building is instinctive to all birds, but some make much better nests than others.

SOCIAL LIFE

Social insects, like ants, live in colonies of hundreds or thousands of individuals. Each insect functions only as a member of the community; they all exist to defend and feed the queen and her offspring.

In higher animals, group living offers individuals greater safety against predators. For this reason, most grazing animals live in herds. A herd of zebra on the plains of Africa, for example, has many pairs of eyes and nostrils, all of them alert for the sight or smell of a hungry lion or cheetah.

The cheetah's sharp eyesight and sprinting speed make it an effective predator of Thomson's gazelles. The gazelle, however, has also evolved the ability to run and swerve quickly to escape. Most big cats prefer to ambush their prey.

PACK HUNTING

Many predators, like tigers and polar bears, are solitary hunters. Others, such as wolves, hyenas, and lions, hunt in packs. Each member of the pack cooperates to select, pursue, and kill the prey. Hunting in packs gives these predators the chance of killing large, powerful animals that an individual would not be able to tackle on its own. This hunting method also binds the animals into a social group.

RANK AND DOMINANCE

Within a group of animals, size and strength often determine the individual's rank within the community. The strongest male seal on a beach will mate with more females. Weak or young individuals may never mate. One day, a younger rival will challenge and defeat the dominant male and take over his position.

In many animal species, rival males challenge one another during the breeding season. However, these contests rarely end in fights-to-the-death. Most confrontations are just means by which stronger males assert their authority. The inferior male usually gives way and retreats.

An animal cornered by a predator, however, will fight back. In this case, the hungry predator may choose to back away, rather than risk injury.

Within a social group, such as a wolf pack, dominant animals seldom have to fight to keep their position. Weaker animals show by submissive behavior that they are willing to accept their inferior position in the pack's social order.

Superior

Inferior

▲ The inferior wolf in this scene is pressing its body close to the ground, curling up its tail, folding back its ears, and licking the face of the dominant wolf. This is a typical display of submission. The superior wolf stands tall, raises its tail, and ruffles the hair around its neck. In a wolf pack, every member knows its place.

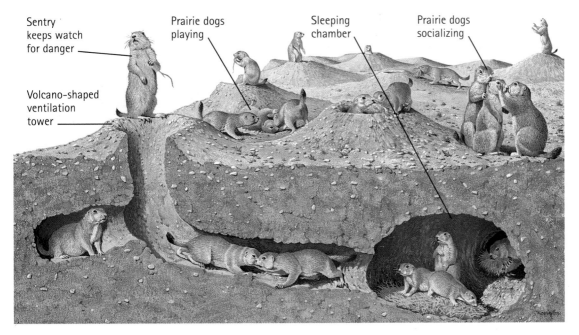

Sentry keeps watch for danger

Prairie dogs playing

Sleeping chamber

Prairie dogs socializing

Volcano-shaped ventilation tower

Prairie dogs and marmots live in underground burrows, or colonies, called towns. Every member of the colony works together to excavate a maze of tunnels, with volcano-shaped air vents. Sentries keep watch for enemies, like circling hawks. In this way, all the animals benefit from living in a community. This type of cooperative behavior is called altruism.

SEE ALSO PAGES:

50–1 Life: origins and development, 94 Animal partnerships

MOVEMENT

Animals move for various reasons—to find food, to find a mate, or to escape predators. Many animals have evolved unusual ways of getting around.

Dolphins swim with up-and-down movements of their tails. They seem to enjoy leaping clear of the water.

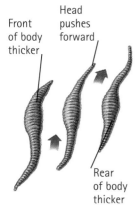

In order to move, a scallop opens its shell to draw in water. When the shell snaps shut, water shoots out, and the scallop jets off in the opposite direction to the water.

There are various reasons why an animal moves. A predator may chase its prey, which also moves to escape being killed. Terrestrial, or land, animals move by using muscle power alone. A giraffe's legs act much like props and levers. The legs push against the ground and propel the animal forward. At top speed, a running antelope has only one foot on the ground and may lift all four legs in the air as it speeds along. The kangaroo's hop is not a unique form of movement, but is not typical of mammals.

LEGLESS MOTION

Legs are not essential to move quickly. For example, the fastest snake, the venomous black mamba, can reach speeds of up to 19 mph (30kph). Many snakes move on land or in water with a wriggling motion. Snails have a single foot and move in muscular waves, extending and then withdrawing the foot.

Head pushes forward

Front of body thicker

Rear of body thicker

An earthworm contracts ring-shaped muscles along the length of its body to push its way through the soil. The muscles squeeze fluid in the body so that the worm's front end gets longer, pushing forward. The worm anchors its head and then draws up its tail.

HYDRAULICS

Some invertebrates (animals without a backbone), like earthworms and starfish, use hydraulic forces to move. They change shape as their muscles force fluid from one part of their body to another.

FLIGHT

Insects, birds, and some mammals can move through the air. Birds are the masters of flapping and soaring flight. Fast fliers, like falcons, have slim, tapered wings. Owls have broad wings that allow them to glide silently as they hunt. Bats are the only mammals that can truly fly.

◄ Hoofed animals, such as these giraffes, run on their toes. Their long legs make giraffes among the fastest animals on the African plains.

These photographs show a little owl in flight. Powerful wingbeats provide lift and thrust as the bird takes off. The primary feathers part on the upstroke. The tail acts as a rudder and as a brake when landing.

SEE ALSO PAGES:
75-7 Insects, 80-1 Amphibians, 82-3 Reptiles, 84-5 Birds, 86-7 Mammals

MIGRATION

Migration is a periodic movement of animals between two regions to breed or find food. They may do this every year, or only twice in a lifetime.

Humpback whales migrate from polar waters to warmer seas to give birth to their young.

Monarch butterflies migrate across North America as far south as Mexico. Few adults survive to make the return trip.

Each year, the Arctic tern makes a journey of 21,750 mi. (35,000km), from the Arctic to Antarctica and back.

Swallows migrate each year. In the winter, they fly south, and return north in the spring to breed.

Reindeer move in herds to southern feeding grounds to escape the harsh Arctic winter.

Migrations are seasonal or lifetime journeys made to the same destination. Animals migrate by instinct, finding their way across land and sea in ways that are still not clearly understood. Animals migrate to find food and to breed. The instinct is most common among animals living in regions with extreme seasonal variations.

MIGRATORY BIRDS
Birds are common migrants. Swallows, for example, fly south from Europe and North America every fall to winter in Africa or South America. They eat insects, a food

A herd of reindeer in Russia start their long migration. As winter freezes the tundra habitat in which they live, reindeer move south, seeking shelter in the forests.

not plentiful during northern winters.

Each year, the Arctic tern migrates from summer in the Arctic to summer in the Antarctic, a return trip of over 21,750 miles (35,000km). To navigate, migrating birds follow geographical features. They may also be guided by the sun, the stars, and the Earth's magnetic field.

OTHER MIGRANTS
Other animal travelers include reindeer (caribou), whales, turtles, eels, salmon, and even butterflies. Monarch butterflies from the United States and Canada fly south in flocks to winter in Mexico. Some travel for over 1,550 miles (2,500km).

KEY TO MAP

←→	Swallow
←→	Reindeer
←→	Monarch butterfly
←→	Arctic tern
←→	Humpback whale

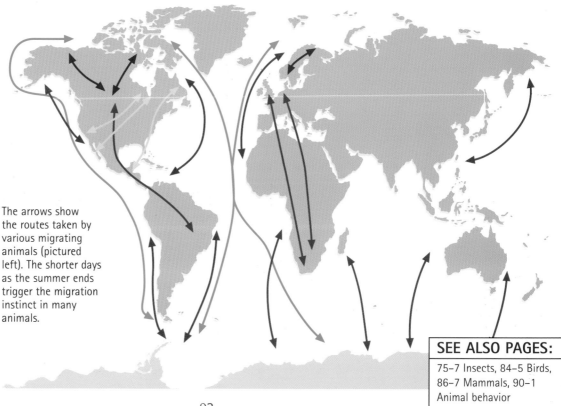

The arrows show the routes taken by various migrating animals (pictured left). The shorter days as the summer ends trigger the migration instinct in many animals.

SEE ALSO PAGES:
75–7 Insects, 84–5 Birds, 86–7 Mammals, 90–1 Animal behavior

ANIMAL PARTNERSHIPS

An intimate partnership between two organisms of different species is called symbiosis. Benefit is always gained by at least one individual in the partnership.

Anemone

Hermit crab

Some hermit crabs have a sea anemone living on top of their shell. The anemone gets a ride and eats up scraps of food left by the crab. The sea anemone's poisonous stings help to defend both animals against predators.

The Portuguese man-of-war lives in the ocean. It consists of a number of organisms of the same species that live together as a colony. It is in effect a corporate animal—each individual has its own job.

There are many examples of animals and plants that live and have evolved together, forming a beneficial association with one another. Symbiosis is a term given to several different relationships between two organisms. If two organisms interact so that one organism benefits, while the other neither benefits nor comes to any harm, the partnership is called commensalism. If both organisms benefit, the relationship is called mutualism. If one of the organisms benefits at the expense of the other, the relationship is called parasitism.

SHARING SHELTER

Some organisms share a home. A good example of such a relationship is that of the hermit crab and the sea anemone. Hermit crabs are crustaceans that occupy empty mollusk shells. Some crabs have sea anemones living on their shells. The anemones fend off predators by shooting poisonous darts. The anemone benefits by feeding on the scraps left by the crab.

FREE MEALS

The lure of a free meal is the basis for many animal partnerships. For example, oxpeckers ride on the backs of antelope, buffaloes, and rhinoceroses, and feed on

The red-billed oxpecker has a symbiotic relationship with impala antelope. The bird perches on the antelope's head, picking off insects. The oxpecker benefits by getting a meal. In turn, the antelope is cleaned of insect pests.

insects and maggots that live in their hosts' skin. In return, the birds hiss or call when they spot the presence of a dangerous predator.

UNDERSEA PARTNERSHIPS

There are many examples of symbiotic relationships in the ocean. The cleaner wrasse, for example, is a small fish that swims into the mouth of a larger fish to remove food scraps and parasites from its jaws. Even the most voracious predatory fish appear to enjoy this cleaning, and both species benefit.

PARASITES

Many animals have parasites living in their bodies, especially in the intestines. Here, the parasites benefit from a safe habitat and feed on digested food or fecal matter. Some parasites do not harm the host. Many others, such as fleas and tapeworms, do cause harm, often in the form of weakening diseases. Parasites enter the host through the mouth, nose, or other body openings.

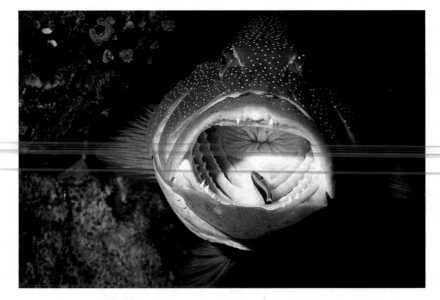

The little cleaner wrasse is safe in the jaws of this coral grouper as it feeds on the fish's parasites.

SEE ALSO PAGES:

50–1 Life: origins and development, 95 Adaptation and defense

ADAPTATION AND DEFENSE

Adaptation is a change that makes an organism better suited to its environment. Defense is the way that organisms protect themselves from harm.

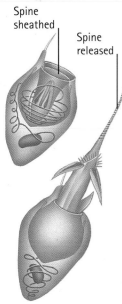

Spine sheathed

Spine released

When a predator touches the tentacle of a sea anemone, cells in the tentacles turn inside out to launch defensive spines.

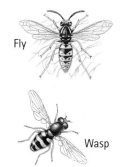

Fly

Wasp

Hoverflies mimic the warning coloration of wasps. This confuses their predators long enough to escape being eaten.

The armadillo has a mechanical defense—its armor of hard, bony plates. To deter a predator, the armadillo curls up into a tight ball.

A ll living creatures must be able to adapt to changes in their environment if they are to continue to survive. For an individual organism, to survive means to grow, to reproduce, and to avoid being eaten or otherwise harmed by another organism equally driven to survive. The need to survive has seen the evolution of some of the most fascinating defensive adaptations in nature.

DEFENSIVE WEAPONS

There are five main types of defensive adaptation. Mechanical defenses include horns, spines, thorns, and armor. The armadillo, for example, is covered in bony armor and curls up when danger threatens. So do prickly hedgehogs. Tortoises withdraw into their bony shells.

Chemical defenses include substances that produce unpleasant tastes and odors, or stings and poisons that harm attackers. Sea anemones, for example, shoot out poisonous darts at potential predators.

Visual defenses include bright coloration, as a warning that the animal is poisonous. Camouflage helps many prey species to escape by blending in with their surroundings. Many animals mimic something inedible or dangerous. Milk snakes are harmless, but have the same

A night-flying bat sends out sound waves to track moths. Some moths detect these waves and take evasive action. They even jam the bat's signals with their own high-pitched calls.

vivid markings as poisonous coral snakes, so they, too, are left alone.

Some fish, such as eels, have special organs that discharge electricity to ward off predators, stun prey, and help them find their way in murky water.

Behavioral defenses cover the full spectrum of defensive tactics, from avoiding danger by hiding or running away, to retaliating against an attacker.

DIFFERENT ADAPTATIONS

Biologists distinguish between two types of adaptation—genotypic and phenotypic. Genotypic adaptations are passed down the generations in the form of genes. They provide the basis for evolutionary change through natural selection. Phenotypic adaptations occur within the lifetime of an individual. Most often, these changes allow the organism to survive sudden changes in its environment.

These Burchell's zebras have evolved a number of defenses to avoid being eaten by lions and other predators of the African savanna. They rely on their sharp senses to detect danger, and on speed to escape. They can also kick and bite. The zebra's stripes break up its outline, making it difficult for the predator to select one individual.

SEE ALSO PAGES:

90–1 Animal behavior, 94 Animal partnerships, 442–3 Why species die out

FACTS AND FIGURES

BRANCHES OF LIFE SCIENCES

Anatomists study the structures of living organisms, often using microscopy.
Biologists study the structure, behavior, and evolution of living things of all kinds.
Botanists are biologists who study plants.
Ecologists study the relationships between living organisms and the environments in which they live.
Embryologists study the formation and development of plants and animals from fertilization until they become independent organisms.
Entomologists study insects.
Ethologists study the inherited behavior of animals in their natural environments.
Ichthyologists are zoologists who study fish.
Marine biologists study life in the oceans.
Mycologists study fungi.
Ornithologists study birds.
Naturalists are people with an interest in nature. They may specialize in particular species, or they may just enjoy watching and recording plants and animals.
Paleontologists study fossils to gather information about forms of life that existed millions of years ago.
Taxonomists classify plants and animals in an ordered system.
Zoologists are biologists who study animals.

TYPES OF BIOMES

A biome is a plant and animal community that covers a large geographical area. The boundaries of a biome are determined mainly by climatic conditions.
Deserts are very dry regions where few plants grow. They may be cold or hot.
Grasslands are most common in temperate regions. In tropical regions with a long dry season, the typical grassland is savanna, grassland with scattered clumps of trees.
Oceans form by far the largest biome in terms of extent. The species that live in a given ocean habitat are determined by the depth, sunlight penetration, temperature, water conditions, and nutrient availability in that particular location.
Scrublands are areas where bushy forms of vegetation dominate. Summers are hot and dry, and fires are frequent.
Taigas, also called **boreal forests**, are regions of subarctic coniferous forests. Winters are cold and long.
Temperate forests are found between the tropical and polar regions. The climate is mild with moderate rainfall. Temperate forest may be coniferous or deciduous.
Tropical rain forests grow where the weather is hot and humid all year. They form the richest biome in terms of its variety of plant and animal species.
Tundras are cold, dry regions where the subsoil is permanently frozen.

CLASSES OF LIVING THINGS

Plants
So far, around 300,000 species of plants have been identified and classified. Plants range in size and complexity from simple algae to massive trees. Scientists predict there could be at least as many species still to be discovered, many of them growing in forests and on mountains where they are difficult to reach. There are far fewer plants than animals.

Fungi
There are approximately 100,000 known species of fungi. A fungus is a single-celled or multicellular organism that absorbs nutrients directly through its cell walls. Many fungi are parasites, taking their nutrients from other organisms.

Animals
Taxonomists group animals into about 30 major classifications, which they call phyla. Some phyla include many thousands of species. The phylum Nematoda, for example, consists of at least 12,000 species of roundworms.

Among the so-called higher animals, the main groups are:
Mollusks: Soft-bodied, boneless marine animals that typically have a protective shell. Snails, bivalves such as cockles, and cephalopods such as squid are all examples of mollusks. There are around 100,000 species in this group.
Arthropods: Animals with jointed legs. About one million arthropods have been identified, most of which are insects. There may be as many as 10 million insects still waiting to be named and described.
Fish: Aquatic animals that fit into three types. Osteichthyes, or bony fish, is a class of about 22,000 known species, including cod, bass, and trout. Sharks and rays are members of a class of about 5,000 known as Chondrichthyes, or cartilaginous fish. Lampreys and hagfish are members of the superclass Agnatha, or jawless fish.
Amphibians: There are about 3,000 known species, including frogs, toads, and newts.
Reptiles: There are about 6,500 species, including snakes, lizards, and crocodiles.
Birds: There are some 9,000 species in the class Aves. All species of Aves lay hard-shelled eggs and have feathers. Of this class, more than 5,700 species are perching birds of the order Passeriformes.
Mammals: Mammals are classified into 18 orders, in two subclasses—the placental mammals and the marsupials. There are 4,500 species of mammals, which include the primates—monkeys, apes, and humans. These animals have body hair and have mechanisms that regulate their body temperature.

KEY DATES

77	Roman naturalist Pliny the Elder completes *Historia Naturalis*, the first encyclopedia about nature.
1665	British scientist Robert Hooke pioneers the use of microscopes to study cells and organisms.
1758	Swedish naturalist Carolus Linnaeus develops a system that is still used for naming animals.
1830s	German scientists Matthias Schleiden and Theodor Schwann show that the cell is the basic unit of all plant and animal life.
1865	Austrian monk Gregor Mendel demonstrates the principles of heredity using pea plants.
1872	Yellowstone National Park is created in the United States. It is the first case of a park being created for the preservation of its natural environment.
1879	What is now the Royal National Park is set up in Australia.
1898	Kruger National Park is created in South Africa.
1909	Sweden opens the first national parks in Europe.
1910	U.S. biologist Thomas Morgan shows that chromosomes carry genetic information.
1953	British biophysicist Francis Crick, U.S. biochemist James Watson, and British chemist Rosalind Franklin discover the structure of DNA.
1982	First cloning of mouse cells, and the creation of "giant mice" in the United States through genetic engineering.
1988	First egg hatched by Californian condors in captivity. This species, of which there were only 27 birds remaining, had been taken into captivity to try to prevent it becoming extinct.
1989	The United States and member countries of the European Union ban ivory imports in an attempt to protect African elephants.
1996	A new squirrellike mammal, the Panay cloudrunner, is found in the Philippines.
1997	First clone of an adult mammal, Dolly the sheep, created at the Roslin Institute in Scotland.
1998	A new species of deer, the Truong Son muntjac, found in Vietnam.
1998	An International Union for the Conservation of Nature and Natural Resources report states that 34,000 plant species are in danger of extinction—around 12 percent, or one in eight, of the Earth's plant species.

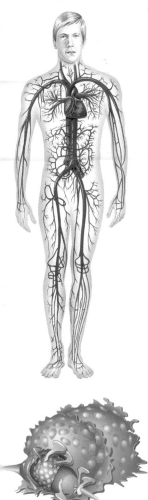
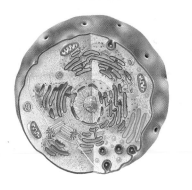
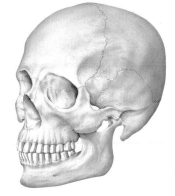

CHAPTER 3
HUMAN BIOLOGY

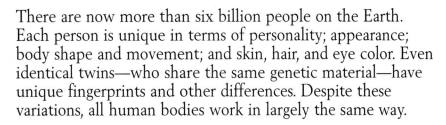

Human beings are the most intelligent and advanced of the millions of living organisms on the Earth. We are self-aware and are capable of studying human biology—how our bodies are built and how they work.

There are now more than six billion people on the Earth. Each person is unique in terms of personality; appearance; body shape and movement; and skin, hair, and eye color. Even identical twins—who share the same genetic material—have unique fingerprints and other differences. Despite these variations, all human bodies work in largely the same way.

For thousands of years, theories about the structure, workings, and diseases of the human body relied more on myth and magic than they did on scientific observation. For example, it was not until the 1500s that the first accurate studies of anatomy were undertaken.

Since the 1600s, biologists and doctors have used increasingly scientific methods to investigate the human body and its diseases. Inventions such as microscopes and X-ray photography quickened the pace of discovery, so that by the end of the 1900s, the workings of the body were well understood, and medicine could treat most diseases. Current research seeks to identify the human genome—the blueprint for human life—and to devise ways to treat diseases encoded in human genetic material.

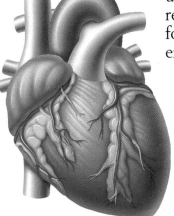

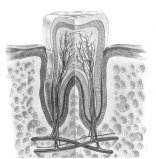
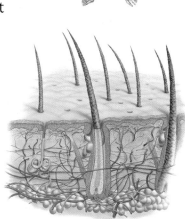

BODY ORGANIZATION

The human body consists of more than 50 trillion microscopic living units, called cells. They perform specific tasks to make the body run smoothly.

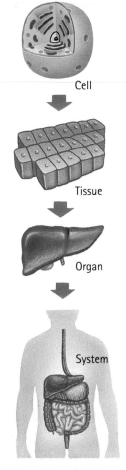

Cell

Tissue

Organ

System

Groups of liver cells form one type of tissue. This tissue, with others makes up the organ called the liver. The liver and other linked organs make up the digestive system.

The human body is organized according to a hierarchy, or sequence, of different levels of complexity, starting from simple molecules right up to the body itself. Molecules such as carbohydrates, lipids, nucleic acids, and proteins form the building blocks from which cells are made. They also take part in the chemical reactions collectively called metabolism. The body's metabolism interacts with the body's building blocks to form tiny living units called cells. To stay alive and give the body energy, each cell needs a constant supply of food and oxygen.

Individual cells that are similar in structure and function join together to form tissues. These perform different roles in the body. Several different types of tissues form structures called organs. Organs include the eyes, kidneys, liver, lungs, and stomach. Each has a specific task or tasks. The role of the stomach, for example, is to store and break down food during digestion. The stomach works with other linked organs to form the digestive system. This not only digests food, but also absorbs useful nutrients from food into the bloodstream and eliminates any waste. The digestive system is one of twelve systems, all of which work together to carry out the functions the body needs to survive.

Each of these young people is unique in terms of looks and genetic makeup, but they all share the same basic body structure, which works in exactly the same way.

TISSUES

The body is made up of four basic types of tissue. Epithelial tissue is made up of tightly packed cells that form leakproof linings for surfaces like the skin and the lining of the digestive system. Connective tissue holds the body together and provides a framework. It includes cartilage and bone. Muscle tissue consists of cells that contract (tighten) to move the body. Nervous tissue, in the brain and nerves, consists of a network of cells that carry electrical signals. Most organs contain all four types of tissue. Within tissues, cells are surrounded by tissue fluid. The fluid provides cells with a stable environment, delivers oxygen and food to the cells, and removes waste products.

BODY SYSTEMS

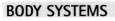

There are 12 major systems in the human body. Seven of these are shown here. The systems not shown here include the respiratory system, integumentary system (skin and nails), male and female reproductive systems, urinary system, and the immune system. Each system carries out one or more processes essential for life. For example, the circulatory system—the heart, blood vessels, and blood—delivers food and oxygen to all body cells and removes their waste products.

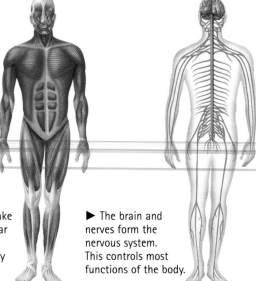

▶ Individual bones make up the skeletal system, which supports the body.

▶ Muscles make up the muscular system, which allows the body to move.

▶ The brain and nerves form the nervous system. This controls most functions of the body.

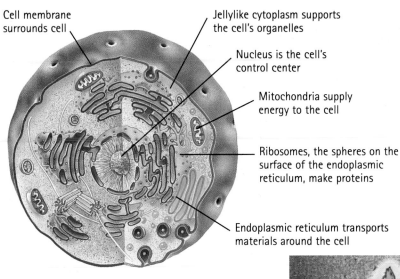

Cell membrane surrounds cell

Jellylike cytoplasm supports the cell's organelles

Nucleus is the cell's control center

Mitochondria supply energy to the cell

Ribosomes, the spheres on the surface of the endoplasmic reticulum, make proteins

Endoplasmic reticulum transports materials around the cell

Although different cells come in various shapes and sizes, they look very similar inside. Organelles ("tiny organs") inside the cell have specific functions. They all work together to produce a living cell.

During the type of cell division known as mitosis, the nucleus (dark area) of the parent cell (1) divides first (2), then the cytoplasm divides (3), and two identical daughter cells are produced (4).

CELLS

Although different cells perform different functions, they all share the same structure. A plasma membrane separates each cell from its surroundings and allows material into and out of the cell. Inside the cell, tiny organelles—microscopic equivalents of the body's organs—float in a watery, jellylike substance called cytoplasm. Organelles do different things, but they all cooperate to produce a living cell. The most important organelle is the nucleus, the cell's control center. The nucleus contains genetic material in the form of deoxyribonucleic acid (DNA). This provides the blueprint for building and running the cell. Other organelles include mitochondria, ribosomes, and endoplasmic reticulum.

Cells reproduce by dividing in one of two ways. Mitosis, which occurs throughout the body, allows the body to grow and repair itself by replacing worn-out cells. Meiosis occurs only in the testes and ovaries. It produces sex cells—sperm and eggs—that take part in reproduction.

▲ This magnified image shows a cell called a lymphocyte. This type of cell is found in the blood. Its nucleus takes up much of the space inside the cell. Lymphocytes play a vital part in defending the body against disease.

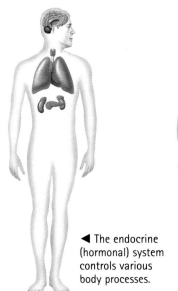

◄ The endocrine (hormonal) system controls various body processes.

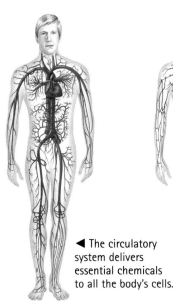

◄ The circulatory system delivers essential chemicals to all the body's cells.

◄ The lymphatic system helps the body to fight infection.

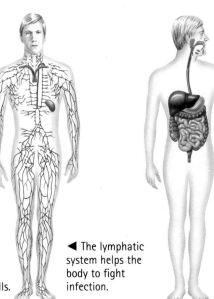

◄ The digestive system digests foods and absorbs nutrients into the body.

SEE ALSO PAGES:

108–9 The brain and nervous system, 120–1 The heart and circulation, 123 Lymphatic system, 137 The immune system

SKIN, HAIR, AND NAILS

A person's skin, hair, and nails are the visible parts of the body. They form a protective barrier between the inside of the body and its surroundings.

Whether hair is curly, wavy, or straight depends on the shape of the hair follicle. Curly hairs have a flat shaft and grow from slotlike hair follicles.

If straight hair is viewed through a microscope, it is seen to have a round shaft. Straight hair grows from hair follicles that have a round opening.

Wavy hair is oval in cross section, as seen when a hair is cut across its shaft. Wavy hair grows from hair follicles that have an oval opening.

The skin is a living, protective organ. It weighs up to 9 pounds and can repair itself if cut or torn. The thinnest skin, on the eyelids, is about 0.04 inches thick. The thickest, on the soles of the feet, is about 0.15 inches thick.

Skin has two main layers: the epidermis and dermis. The epidermis covers the skin's surface. Its upper layers consist of scalelike, dead cells that are filled with a waterproof protein called keratin. These dead cells are continually worn away and replaced by cells that form in the lower epidermis. Cells here also produce melanin, the brown pigment that colors the skin and protects it from the harmful rays in sunlight. Ridges on the skin pads of the fingers mark surfaces with patterns called fingerprints.

The thicker dermis contains blood vessels, sweat glands, hair follicles, and sensors that detect pressure, pain, temperature, and touch. It also contains sebaceous glands, which secrete oily sebum onto skin and hairs to soften and waterproof them.

Skin has many functions. It is waterproof. It helps the body to maintain a temperature of 98.6°F (37°C). Finally, it provides a germproof barrier to protect the body from disease.

Permanent records of fingerprints are kept by the police and the armed forces. Fingerprints are unique to an individual, and if left at the scene of a crime, may be used to identify suspects.

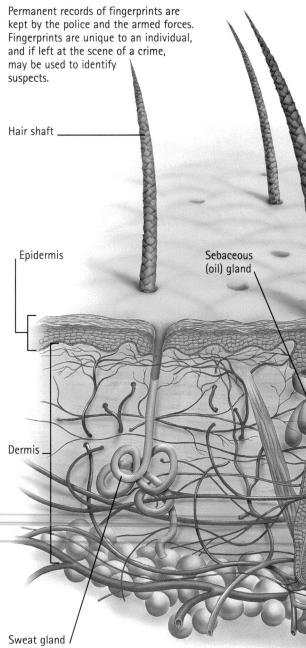

Hair shaft

Epidermis

Dermis

Sebaceous (oil) gland

Sweat gland

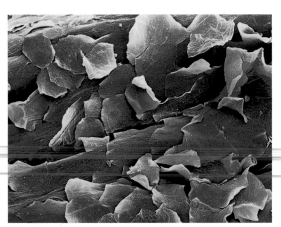

The surface of healthy skin, seen under the microscope, is covered with tiny skin flakes. These are constantly shed from the surface of the epidermis as it is worn away and replaced. Each of us loses about 4 kg of skin flakes a year; these form part of household dust.

HAIR

Millions of hairs cover the body, including over 100,000 on the top of the head. Scalp hairs cut heat loss from the head and protect it from the harmful rays of the sun. The lips, the palms of the hands, and the soles of the feet have no hair.

There are two types of hair. Fine vellus hair covers the bodies of men, women, and children; and coarser hair grows on the scalp and in men's facial hair. Hairs grow from pits in the dermis called follicles. Cells at the base of the follicle divide and push the hair shaft upward. The cells in the hair shaft are dead and filled with the tough protein called keratin. Scalp hairs grow about 0.4 inches each month. The color of hair depends on how much melanin is present.

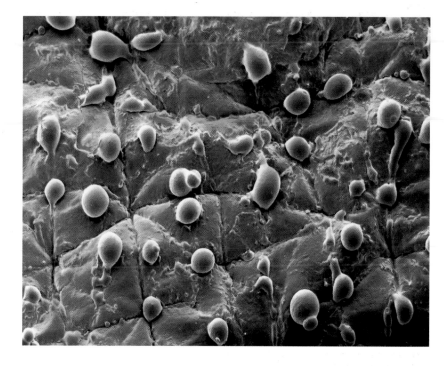

◄ Although most skin is only 0.1 inches thick, it has a complex structure. The epidermis forms a thin, protective surface that is continually worn away and replaced. Beneath it, the thicker dermis contains hair follicles, from which hairs grow; blood vessels, to supply skin cells with food and oxygen; nerve endings, to detect pain, pressure, temperature, and touch; and sweat glands, which release cooling sweat.

▲ Droplets of sweat, magnified 26 times, emerge from sweat gland ducts, through pores, in the furrowed surface of the skin. Sweat is released when the body is hot and evaporates from the skin's surface to cool the body.

NAILS

Nails cover and protect the sensitive tips of the fingers and toes. They are useful for scratching itches and helping to pick up small objects. Cutting nails does not hurt, because they are made of dead cells filled with the protein keratin.

Each nail has three parts, the plate, the bed, and the matrix. The nail is embedded in the skin beneath the cuticle. In the matrix, living cells divide and push forward; this makes the nail grow. Nails grow about 0.2 inches each month, slower in winter than in summer, and faster in the dominant hand—the right hand in right-handed people.

Sweat pore (opening)

Scales on hair shaft

Tough outer layer of epidermis

Nerve ending

Nerve fiber

Muscle that makes hair erect

Hair follicle

Blood vessels

Layer of fat

Hair root

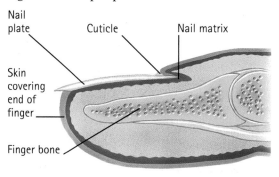

Nail plate — Cuticle — Nail matrix — Skin covering end of finger — Finger bone

The nail grows from the root at the base of the fingertip. Growth of the finger bone and the skin beneath the nail can also cause nail growth.

SEE ALSO PAGES:
112 Touch, 122 Blood, 136 Bacteria and viruses, 138 Disease

THE SKELETON

The skeleton is a flexible framework that shapes and supports the body, protects vital organs like the brain, and anchors the muscles that move the body.

For centuries, bones were regarded as lifeless structures whose main aim was to support the active, softer tissues around them. Gradually, scientists realized that bones are very much alive. Indeed, they have their own blood vessels and are constantly being rebuilt and reshaped.

The skeleton is not just a supportive framework for the body. Flexible joints between different bones allow the bones to move when pulled by muscles. The skeleton also protects vital organs like the brain. Bones themselves act as a supply of calcium. This mineral is essential for muscles and nerves to work. Bones also make different types of blood cells. The skeleton contains cartilage, which covers the ends of bones in joints, and forms part of the skeletal system itself in the ear and nose, and between the sternum (breastbone) and ribs.

There are more than 20 bones in the human skull. Together, they provide a number of clues about the shape of the face and head. Scientists can use these clues to rebuild muscles and skin around the skull using clay. As a result, experts can recreate the faces of people who died long ago.

TYPES OF BONE

The four main kinds of bone are classified according to their shape and size. Long bones, such as the femur (thighbone), are adapted to withstand stress. Short bones include the wrist bones. Flat bones, such as the ribs, are often protective bones. Irregular bones include the vertebrae.

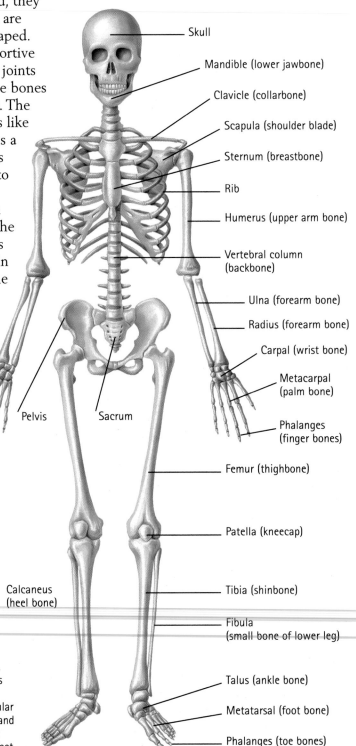

- Skull
- Mandible (lower jawbone)
- Clavicle (collarbone)
- Scapula (shoulder blade)
- Sternum (breastbone)
- Rib
- Humerus (upper arm bone)
- Vertebral column (backbone)
- Ulna (forearm bone)
- Radius (forearm bone)
- Carpal (wrist bone)
- Metacarpal (palm bone)
- Phalanges (finger bones)
- Femur (thighbone)
- Patella (kneecap)
- Tibia (shinbone)
- Fibula (small bone of lower leg)
- Talus (ankle bone)
- Metatarsal (foot bone)
- Phalanges (toe bones)
- Pelvis
- Sacrum
- Calcaneus (heel bone)

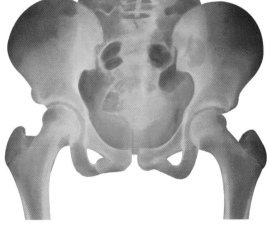

▲ This X ray shows the pelvis of a 13-year-old girl. The image includes the hip bones, femurs (thighbones), and the lower part of the vertebral column. X rays are commonly used to provide images of parts of the skeleton.

▶ An adult skeleton has about 200 bones. It can be divided into two parts. The axial skeleton forms the main axis of the body and consists of 80 bones that make up the skull, vertebral column (backbone), and ribs. This part of the skeleton protects the brain, spinal cord, heart, and lungs. The appendicular skeleton consists of the upper and lower limbs and the pectoral (shoulder) and pelvic girdles that attach them to the axial skeleton. Of the 126 bones that make up the appendicular skeleton, all but 20 are found in the hands and feet.

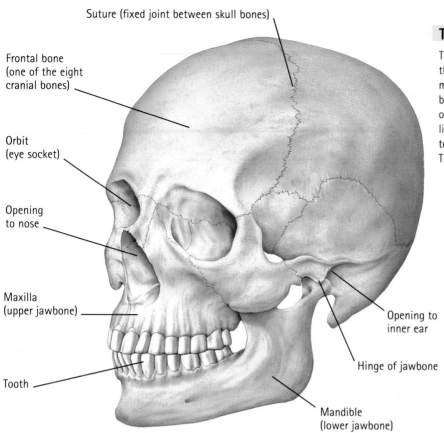

Suture (fixed joint between skull bones)

Frontal bone
(one of the eight
cranial bones)

Orbit
(eye socket)

Opening
to nose

Maxilla
(upper jawbone)

Tooth

Opening to
inner ear

Hinge of jawbone

Mandible
(lower jawbone)

THE HUMAN SKULL

The skull forms the basic shape of the head and protects the brain. It consists of 22 bones. Eight cranial bones make up the cranium, which supports and protects the brain. There are 14 facial bones that form the structure of the face. All but the mandible (lower jawbone) are linked by fixed joints called sutures. The mandible is able to move freely, allowing the mouth to open and close. The skull also houses the ossicles, or ear bones.

Exploded view of skull

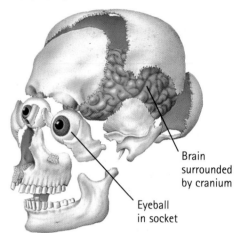

Brain
surrounded
by cranium

Eyeball
in socket

AXIAL SKELETON

The axial skeleton consists of the skull, vertebral column (backbone), ribs, and sternum. The skull houses the brain and major sense organs—the eyes, ears, tongue, and nose. It also contains openings to the digestive and respiratory systems. The flexible, S-shaped spinal column consists of 26 irregular bones called vertebrae. These support the entire body. Muscles and ligaments attached to bony projections on the vertebrae help hold up the spine. Seven cervical vertebrae support the neck and head; twelve thoracic vertebrae form joints with the ribs; and five lumbar vertebrae carry most of the body's weight. The sacrum—five fused vertebrae, with the coccyx at the bottom—connects the spine to the pelvis.

The rib cage protects the thoracic (chest) organs and also aids breathing. It is formed by the sternum (breastbone) and twelve pairs of curved, flattened ribs. The ribs form a joint with the thoracic vertebrae at one end. The upper seven ribs are connected to the sternum by flexible costal (rib) cartilages. The next three, called false ribs, are connected to the true ribs. The lowest two ribs (floating ribs) are attached only to the thoracic vertebrae.

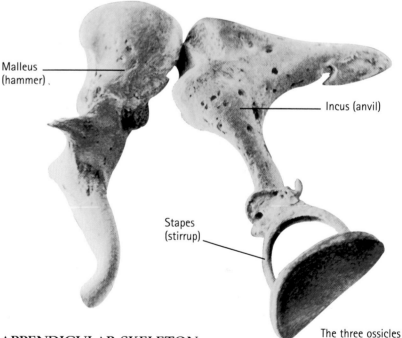

Malleus
(hammer)

Incus (anvil)

Stapes
(stirrup)

The three ossicles (ear bones) are the smallest bones in the body. The ossicles are surrounded by the temporal bone on each side of the skull.

APPENDICULAR SKELETON

The appendicular skeleton consists of the bones in the arms and legs, and the girdles that link them to the body. The pectoral (shoulder) girdle consists of the scapula and clavicle. The pelvic girdle carries the weight of the upper body. The hands and feet contain many small bones. The hands can manipulate objects. The feet help to balance the body.

SEE ALSO PAGES:

104–5 Bones and joints, 106–7 Muscles and movement, 116–7 Ears, hearing, and balance

103

BONES AND JOINTS

Bone is living tissue that is both strong and light. The 200 or so bones that make up the skeletal system are linked at the joints. Most of these move freely.

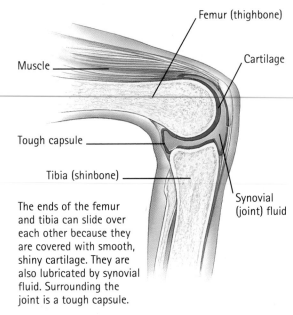

There are few structures that can rival bone in terms of its strength and lightness. All bones consist of a hard material, called matrix, that contains widely spaced bone cells called osteocytes. Bone matrix consists of two main parts—a protein, called collagen, provides flexibility; and mineral salts, in particular calcium phosphate, provide strength. Together, these two components make bone as strong as steel, but five times as light.

Matrix has two forms in bones: hard, compact bone forms the outer layer; lighter, porous bone forms the inner layer. Long bones, such as the femur, contain a central cavity filled with bone marrow. This jellylike material also fills the spaces within porous bone. Red bone marrow, found in the skull, ribs, and pelvis, is responsible for making red and white blood cells. Yellow bone marrow, found in the long bones of adults, stores fat.

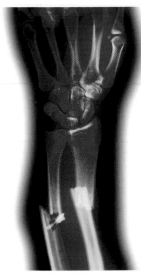

This X ray clearly shows a fracture of the ulna (left) and radius (right). The fractured ends of the bones need to be put back into place by a doctor so that they join correctly as the bones heal. The hand bones are shown at the top of the picture.

The ends of the femur and tibia can slide over each other because they are covered with smooth, shiny cartilage. They are also lubricated by synovial fluid. Surrounding the joint is a tough capsule.

BREAK AND REPAIR

Bones fracture if they are put under stress. If this occurs, a blood clot forms between the broken ends, and bone cells secrete a new matrix. Fractures are compound (open) if the bones project through the skin, or simple (closed) if they do not.

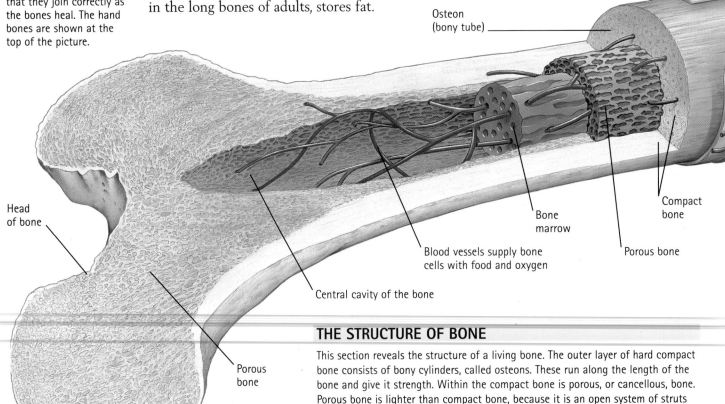

THE STRUCTURE OF BONE

This section reveals the structure of a living bone. The outer layer of hard compact bone consists of bony cylinders, called osteons. These run along the length of the bone and give it strength. Within the compact bone is porous, or cancellous, bone. Porous bone is lighter than compact bone, because it is an open system of struts and spaces, but it is very strong and resists bending. The hollow center of the bone contains bone marrow, which also fills the spaces in porous bone. The bone is protected by a tough membrane called the periosteum. Blood vessels pass through the periosteum and supply osteocytes (bone cells) with food and oxygen.

JOINTS

Joints, or articulations, are the points at which two bones meet. They are classified into three main groups—fixed, slightly movable, and synovial—according to the amount of movement each permits. Fixed joints, as their name suggests, allow no movement. The sutures between the bones of the skull are examples of fixed joints. Their jagged edges are similar to the pieces of a jigsaw, locking the skull bones firmly together. Each tooth is another example of a fixed joint. Teeth are firmly locked in their sockets so that they do not move when food is chewed. Slightly movable joints allow limited movement between adjacent bones. These joints are found between vertebrae. Adjacent vertebra are separated by an intervertebral disk made of fibrocartilage. This allows partial movement between vertebrae. Collectively they give the backbone the flexibility that allows it to bend backward and forward and from side to side.

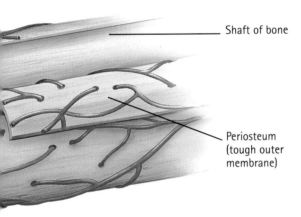

Shaft of bone

Periosteum (tough outer membrane)

SYNOVIAL JOINTS

Most joints—including the knee, elbow, knuckles, hip, and shoulder—are freely movable, or synovial, joints. Synovial joints permit a wide range of movement. All synovial joints share the same basic structure. Bone ends are covered with glassy cartilage. Where the bones meet, they are separated by a synovial cavity, filled with synovial fluid. Together, the cartilage and synovial fluid oil the joint and reduce friction, producing a smooth movement. A joint capsule surrounds each synovial joint. Its inner membrane secretes synovial fluid. The outer part is continuous with tough straps, called ligaments, that hold the joint together.

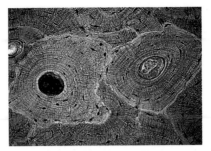

A magnified cross section of compact bone from the femur reveals two osteons. In the middle of each osteon is a central channel that carries blood vessels. Dark spaces in the osteon contain bone cells.

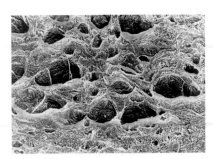

This magnified image of porous bone from a bone in the foot looks very different from compact bone (at left). It consists of hard struts separated by linked spaces filled with bone marrow.

 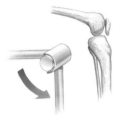 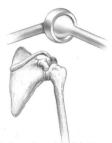

In a pivot joint, the end of one bone rotates within a space formed by another bone. At the top of the backbone, the atlas (first vertebra) rotates around the axis (second vertebra). This allows the head to turn from side to side.

A hinge joint works like a door hinge. The cylindrical end of one bone fits into the curved end of another bone. Hinge joints allow movement up and down, but not side to side. The knee (above) is an example of a hinge joint.

Ball-and-socket joints, such as in the shoulder (above), are the body's most flexible joints. The ball-shaped end of one bone fits into the cup-shaped socket of another. This allows movement in all directions.

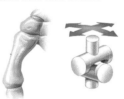  

In the saddle joint at the base of the thumb, the U-shaped ends of wrist and thumb bones fit together. This permits movement backward and forward and from side to side. This joint also allows the thumb to touch the tip of each finger.

Ellipsoidal, or condyloid, joints are found in the knuckles and between the lower arm and wrist bones. The egg-shaped end of one bone fits into the oval cup of another. This allows movement backward and forward and from side to side.

In a gliding, or plane, joint, the surfaces of each bone are level, allowing the bones to make short movements by sliding over each other. Gliding joints are found between carpals (wrist bones) in each hand and tarsals (ankle bones) in each foot.

RANGE OF MOVEMENT

The shape of bone ends, the arrangement of muscles, and the tightness of ligaments holding the joint together all determine the range of movement at a joint. The straightening and bending of the arm at the elbow is an example of extension (straightening) and flexion (bending). The raising and lowering of the lower jaw when chewing food is an example of elevation (lifting) and depression (lowering).

SEE ALSO PAGES:

102–3 The skeleton, 106–7 Muscles and movement, 134 Growth and development

MUSCLES AND MOVEMENT

All movement, from blinking an eye to running in a race, is driven by the body's muscles. Muscles consist of cells that have the unique ability to contract.

Three types of muscle are found in the body: skeletal, smooth, and cardiac. Sprinting uses skeletal muscles; digestion requires smooth muscles; and a heartbeat involves cardiac muscles. As their name suggests, skeletal muscles move the bones of the skeleton and help support the body. The body has over 640 skeletal muscles that cover the skeleton and give the body overall shape. Skeletal muscles make up 40 percent of the body's weight. They range in size from the powerful quadriceps femoris (thigh muscle) to the tiny stapedius in the ear. Tough cords called tendons attach the end of the skeletal muscle to the bone. Muscles extend across joints; when the muscles contract, bones move relative to each other.

All the actions involved in skipping, such as moving the arms and hands, bending the knees, and lifting the feet, are produced by skeletal muscles. Instructed by the brain, these muscles pull the skeleton to produce coordinated movements.

HOW MUSCLES WORK

Skeletal muscle cells, or fibers, are long, thin, and packed with many parallel strands called myofibrils. Myofibrils contain two protein filaments—actin and myosin—which make skeletal muscle fibers look stripy. When a muscle receives a message from the brain along a nerve, the filaments slide past each other, making the fiber shorter, and the muscle contracts. Muscles can only pull, not push; they usually work in pairs. Each pulls bones in opposite directions.

Most muscles work in pairs, each with an action that is antagonistic to (opposes) the other. In the upper arm, for example, the biceps brachii contracts, with the triceps brachii relaxed, to bend the arm. When the triceps brachii contracts, with the biceps brachii relaxed, the arm straightens.

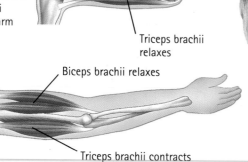

Biceps brachii contracts

Triceps brachii relaxes

Biceps brachii relaxes

Triceps brachii contracts

▶ The body's skeletal muscles are arranged in overlapping layers. The muscles that are just below the skin are called superficial. Beneath these are the deep muscles. This anterior (front) view of the body shows some important superficial muscles and their actions. Muscles are given Latin names for different reasons. These include their action (*flexor* or *extensor*), their shape (*deltoid* means triangular), their relative size (*maximus* means largest), or their location (*frontalis* covers the frontal bone).

Frontalis wrinkles the forehead

Orbicularis oculi closes the eye

Orbicularis oris closes the lips

Deltoid moves the upper arm in many directions

Pectoralis major pulls the arm toward the body, and rotates it

Biceps brachii bends the arm

External oblique tightens the abdomen

Quadriceps femoris straightens the knee during walking and running

Gastrocnemius lifts the heel and bends the knee

Tibialis anterior straightens or lifts the foot

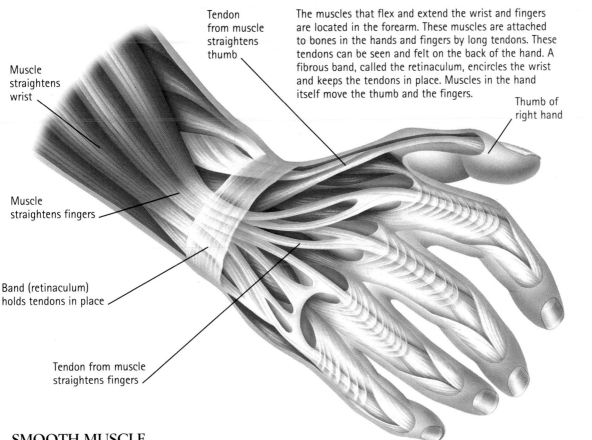

Muscle straightens wrist

Tendon from muscle straightens thumb

The muscles that flex and extend the wrist and fingers are located in the forearm. These muscles are attached to bones in the hands and fingers by long tendons. These tendons can be seen and felt on the back of the hand. A fibrous band, called the retinaculum, encircles the wrist and keeps the tendons in place. Muscles in the hand itself move the thumb and the fingers.

Thumb of right hand

Muscle straightens fingers

Band (retinaculum) holds tendons in place

Tendon from muscle straightens fingers

Skeletal muscle fibers

Smooth muscle fibers

Cardiac muscle fibers

▲ Muscle fibers differ in their appearance. Skeletal muscle fibers are long and striped. Smooth muscle fibers are short and tapered. Cardiac muscle fibers are striped and branched.

SMOOTH MUSCLE

Smooth, or involuntary, muscle is found mainly in the walls of hollow organs such as the esophagus and bladder. Smooth muscle is vital to involuntary processes such as moving food along the alimentary canal during digestion (peristalsis). The short, tapering fibers of smooth muscle are packed into sheets. They contract smoothly and rhythmically under the control of the autonomic nervous system—a person cannot consciously cause them to contract.

CARDIAC MUSCLE

Cardiac muscle is found only in the heart and makes up a large part of its structure. Its branched, striped fibers form an interconnected network. These fibers contract spontaneously without the need for an outside stimulus from the nervous system. Cardiac muscle contracts nonstop over 2.5 billion times in an average lifetime to pump blood around the body.

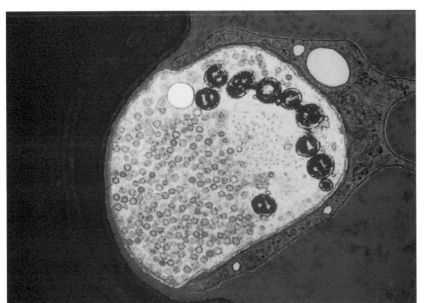

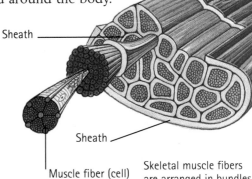

Sheath

Sheath

Muscle fiber (cell)

◄ A neuromuscular junction (magnified 30,800 times) is the point where the end of a nerve fiber (yellow) meets a muscle fiber (red). When a nerve impulse arrives, chemicals are released to make the muscle contract.

Skeletal muscle fibers are arranged in bundles that run along a muscle. Myofibrils inside each fiber consist of filaments that interact to make the muscle contract.

SEE ALSO PAGES:

102–3 The skeleton, 108–9 The brain and nervous system

THE BRAIN AND NERVOUS SYSTEM

Billions of nerve cells, called neurons, link up to form the body's communication network—the nervous system. This complex system is controlled by the brain.

Spinal cord

Spinal nerve

Vertebra (bony segment of spinal column)

▲ The spinal cord extends from the base of the brain to the lower back. It is protected by the vertebrae. Spinal nerves branch off the spinal cord and carry nerve impulses to and from parts of the body.

Nerves consist of bundles of both sensory neurons, which carry nerve impulses from sensors to the brain and spinal cord; and motor neurons, which carry nerve impulses from the brain and spinal cord to the muscles.

The neuron is the basic unit of the nervous system. It is long, thin, and transmits electrical signals, called nerve impulses, along its length. The cell body of the neuron is much like any other cell. It has many branched endings, called dendrites, which receive impulses from other neurons. It also has a long axon, or nerve fiber, which carries nerve impulses to another neuron or a muscle. Neighboring neurons do not touch. They are separated by a tiny gap called a synapse. When an impulse arrives at the end of an axon it releases chemicals that generate an impulse in the dendrites of the next neuron. Sensory and motor neurons carry nerve impulses to and from the brain and spinal cord respectively. Association neurons, which make up 90 percent of all neurons, are found only in the brain and spinal cord.

SPINAL CORD

The spinal cord is essentially an extension of the brain. It extends from the brain to the lower back, protected by the spinal column. Spinal nerves along its length relay information between the brain and body. It also plays a vital role in reflexes. If a person touches a sharp object, for example, nerve impulses pass from the fingertip, through the spinal cord, directly to the upper arm muscles, and instantly pull the finger away from danger.

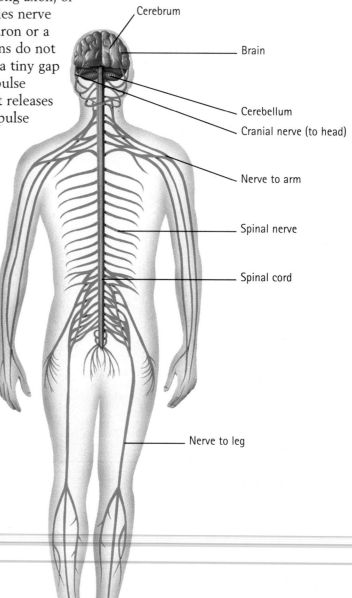

Cerebrum

Brain

Cerebellum

Cranial nerve (to head)

Nerve to arm

Spinal nerve

Spinal cord

Nerve to leg

Nerve fiber

Outer covering of nerve

Bundle of nerve fibers

Blood vessels

▶ The brain controls the entire nervous system. It constantly receives information and sends out instructions, most of which are relayed by the spinal cord. Together, the brain and spinal cord form the central nervous system (CNS); this communicates with the body through nerves. There are 12 pairs of cranial nerves that arise from the brain. Most relay nerve impulses from sense organs, such as the eyes, or carry instructions to muscles in the head. There are 31 pairs of spinal nerves that branch off the spinal cord. These relay nerve impulses to and from the rest of the body.

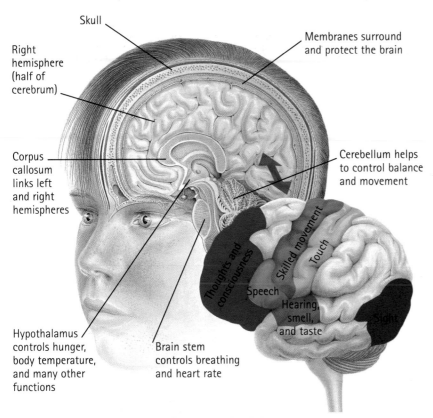

Skull

Right hemisphere (half of cerebrum)

Membranes surround and protect the brain

Corpus callosum links left and right hemispheres

Cerebellum helps to control balance and movement

Thoughts and consciousness

Skilled movement

Touch

Speech

Hearing, smell, and taste

Sight

Hypothalamus controls hunger, body temperature, and many other functions

Brain stem controls breathing and heart rate

INSIDE THE BRAIN

The brain is made up of three main regions. The brain stem automatically controls essential functions such as breathing and heartbeat. The cerebellum coordinates balance, posture, and movement. The cerebrum is divided into two halves called hemispheres, linked by the corpus callosum. Different parts of each hemisphere have different functions. Sensory areas process nerve impulses from sense organs such as the eyes. Motor areas relay instructions to muscles, producing movement and speech. Association areas, such as the front of the cerebrum, make people conscious and able to think. Beneath the cerebrum, the hypothalamus regulates conditions inside the body through the autonomic nervous system.

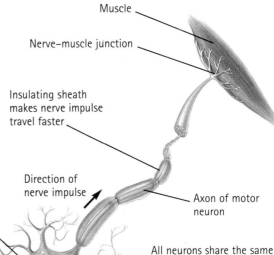

Muscle

Nerve–muscle junction

Insulating sheath makes nerve impulse travel faster

Nucleus of motor neuron nerve cell

Direction of nerve impulse

Axon of motor neuron

Synapse between neurons

Axon of preceding neuron

Cell body

Dendrite

All neurons share the same basic structure. They have a cell body containing a nucleus. Fine processes, called dendrites, receive nerve impulses, via synapses, from other neurons. A long axon, or nerve fiber, carries nerve impulses away from the cell body. The cell body of this motor neuron is located in the central nervous system (CNS). It transmits nerve impulses that instruct parts of the body to do something. For example, a nerve impulse to a muscle may cause it to contract. In the same way, a nerve impulse to a gland may cause it to release a secretion.

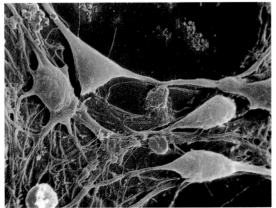

This magnified image shows association neurons from the cerebral cortex, the thin outer part of the cerebrum (the thinking part of the brain). Each neuron is linked to thousands of other neurons.

BRAIN

The brain is made up of over 100 billion neurons. Each one communicates with thousands of other neurons to produce a complex communication and control network. The brain receives information about conditions both inside and outside the body, processes and stores this information, and issues instructions based on what it has learned. The hypothalamus and brain stem control automatic processes such as breathing. The cerebellum regulates smooth body movements. The cerebral hemispheres control thought, imagination, memory, speech, emotion, sight, hearing, smell, taste, and touch.

PARTS OF THE NERVOUS SYSTEM

The nervous system has two main parts: the brain and spinal cord form the central nervous system (CNS), and the nerves form the peripheral nervous system (PNS). Within the PNS, sensory neurons transmit nerve impulses from sense organs to the brain. Motor neurons transmit instructions from the brain and are of two types. Those of the somatic nervous system are under voluntary control and stimulate skeletal muscles to contract. Those of the autonomic nervous system (ANS) regulate processes inside the body, including breathing and digestion. The ANS has two divisions: sympathetic and parasympathetic. These have opposite effects and keep the body in a stable state.

SEE ALSO PAGES:

106-7 Muscles and movement, 110 Sleep and dreams, 142-3 Medical technology

SLEEP AND DREAMS

Sleep takes up about one third of a person's life. It allows the body to rest and the brain to process information taken in during the previous day.

This picture, called *Lena's Dream*, is an artist's attempt to convey the strange mixture of images that people see in their dreams. Here a child is asleep in bed, but in the middle of a field. Dreams occur while the brain is dealing with the experiences of the previous day. In the altered consciousness of sleep, these memories are distorted into dreams.

Sleep occurs naturally as part of a 24-hour cycle of wakefulness and sleep. It is a state of altered consciousness from which a person can be easily aroused. Sleep is important—people deprived of sleep become tired, confused, and experience hallucinations.

Evidence for events that occur during sleep comes from scientists who observe the behavior of sleeping subjects and use an electroencephalograph (EEG) to measure their brainwaves.

Whether we are awake or sleeping, brainwaves are produced constantly by the electrical traffic that passes between the billions of neurons in the brain. Brainwaves are affected by whether someone is awake, mentally alert, falling asleep, or in a deep sleep. Dreams are the events that someone experiences during sleep. They are probably a side effect of the brain organizing the previous day's experiences and storing them in the memory.

DEEP SLEEP AND DREAMING SLEEP

Sleep follows a pattern of events that occur in a certain order and repeat themselves. When people fall asleep, they experience four stages of sleep from nearly awake to deep, or NREM (nonrapid–eye-movement), sleep. The heart and breathing rates decrease, and the brain activity slows. After 90 minutes, they go from deep sleep to light, or REM (rapid-eye-movement), sleep. The eyes move under the eyelids and dreaming takes place. Breathing and heart rate increase, and brain activity also increases. The body does not move, and the muscles are paralyzed, probably to stop the sleeper from acting out his or her dreams. After five to ten minutes, a sleeper will return to deep sleep.

During the night this pattern is repeated up to five times. REM sleep begins about every 90 minutes. Deep sleep decreases during the night, and periods of REM sleep become longer—the final one lasts up to 50 minutes.

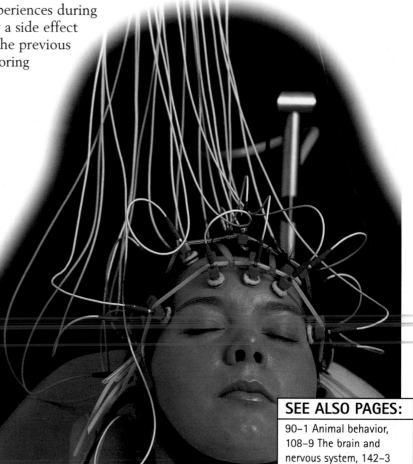

PATTERNS OF SLEEP

A number of electrodes are attached to the head of this sleeping woman. They detect electrical waves, called brainwaves, produced by nerves in the brain. Wires from the electrodes go to an electroencephalograph (EEG); this produces a trace of the waves. Brainwaves change during sleep, showing that a person passes through different stages of sleep. As shown in the graph below, the sleeper first goes into deep sleep (stage 4 or NREM), and then returns to light sleep (stage 1 or REM). This pattern is repeated through the night.

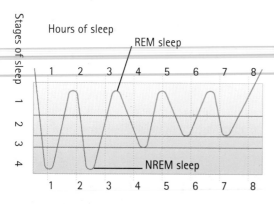

Stages of sleep

Hours of sleep

REM sleep

NREM sleep

SEE ALSO PAGES:

90–1 Animal behavior, 108–9 The brain and nervous system, 142–3 Medical technology

COMMUNICATION

Communication plays an essential role in the lives of all animals. Humans are unique in being able to use language to communicate with one another.

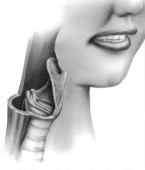

Vocal cord

Larynx

Trachea

During breathing, the vocal cords stay open to allow air in and out of the lungs.

Humans communicate to exchange thoughts, ideas, or knowledge; to show friendship, aggression, or indifference to others; or to reveal pleasure, anger, or anxiety.

Communication is achieved in a variety of ways. Body language involves the, often unconscious, positioning of body parts to convey a message. Facing someone and mimicking their body language, for example, usually indicates interest. Facial expressions, like smiling, frowning, grimacing, or pouting, are indicators of a person's mood and emotions.

LANGUAGE

Spoken language is unique to humans. Speech is controlled by an area on the left side of the brain. When a person wants to speak, nerve impulses are sent from here to muscles in the throat, mouth, and jaw. Two flaps called vocal cords cross the larynx (voice box) and can open and close. Nerve messages from the brain cause larynx muscles to close and stretch the cords. Air from the lungs is then forced through the cords. The cords vibrate and produce sounds that pass into the throat, mouth, and nose. Loose vocal cords produce low-pitched sounds; tight ones produce high-pitched sounds. Sounds are turned into speech by the position of the tongue and the shape of the lips.

Air is forced through closed vocal cords to produce sounds during speech.

▲ At the top of the trachea is the larynx or voice box. Stretched across the larynx are two membranes called vocal cords. Normally these are open, but during speech they close. Air breathed out between closed cords makes them vibrate and produce sounds.

▶ Over 30 small muscles in the face produce a wide range of expressions. Most facial muscles are attached to a skull bone at one end and to the skin on the face at the other. When a facial muscle contracts, it pulls the skin to alter the appearance of the face. Facial expressions convey moods and emotions, and express a wide range of feelings from pleasure to anger.

▲ This frown is produced by the corrugator supercilii muscles.

Corrugator supercilii (pulls eyebrow down during frowning)

Masseter (closes jaw during eating)

Risorius (stretches mouth wide during laughing)

▼ To smile, the corners of the mouth are pulled up and out by the zygomaticus muscles.

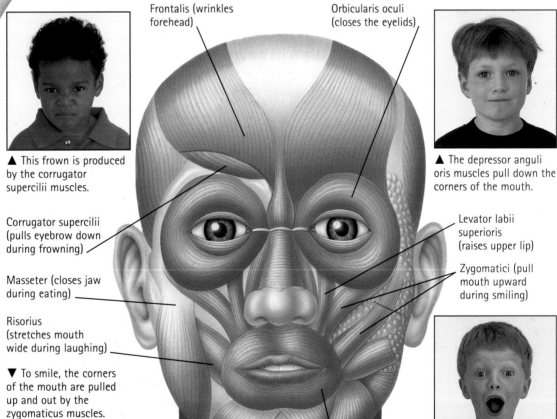

Frontalis (wrinkles forehead)

Orbicularis oculi (closes the eyelids)

▲ The depressor anguli oris muscles pull down the corners of the mouth.

Levator labii superioris (raises upper lip)

Zygomatici (pull mouth upward during smiling)

▲ The frontalis muscle wrinkles the forehead and raises the eyebrows.

Orbicularis orisi (closes lips)

Depressor labii inferioris (pulls lower lip down)

Depressor anguli oris (turns corner of mouth downward)

SEE ALSO PAGES:

106–7 Muscles and movement, 108–9 The brain and nervous system

TOUCH

The sense of touch provides the brain with information about the body's surroundings. Touch sensors are scattered all over the surface of the body.

This person is blind, but is able to read by running her fingertips across the page. The words are written using Braille; the patterns of raised dots correspond to letters or numbers.

Sensors in the skin detect touch, pain, vibration, pressure, heat, and cold. The softness of fur, the vibrations made by running the fingers over sandpaper, the pressure produced by holding a heavy weight, the pain of standing on a pin, the heat from a flame, and the cold felt by plunging a hand into icy water—all of these are experienced when the skin's sensors are stimulated.

Sensors for light touch and pressure are in the upper part of the dermis. Those for heavy touch and pressure are larger and are found deeper in the dermis. Capsules enclose most of these sensors. The sensors that detect heat, cold, and pain are branched nerve endings near the junction between the epidermis and the dermis. These sensors are not in capsules. Information from all the sensors travels as electrical impulses along nerves that lead to the sensory area of the cerebrum (the largest and most highly developed part of the brain). The brain interprets these impulses and provides a "touch picture" of the person's surroundings, including, for example, information about pressure and warmth. The feeling of pain warns the body about possible danger.

This boy looks strange because the size of his body parts are drawn according to how sensitive to touch they are. Some parts of the body, such as fingers and lips, are more sensitive than others because they have many more touch sensors.

HABITUATION

When a person dresses in the morning, the clothes can be felt as they are pulled over the skin. After a short while, the clothes can no longer be felt. This loss of feeling is called habituation. The skin gets used to the stimulation of the clothes, and nerve impulses are no longer sent to the brain. Habituation is important because without it clothes would irritate the skin all day.

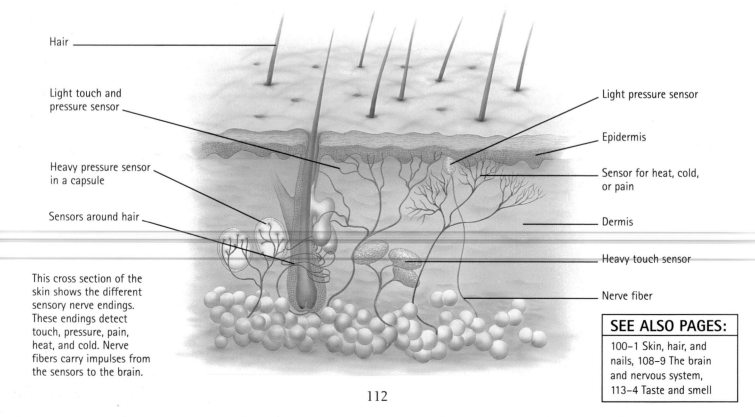

Hair

Light touch and pressure sensor

Heavy pressure sensor in a capsule

Sensors around hair

Light pressure sensor

Epidermis

Sensor for heat, cold, or pain

Dermis

Heavy touch sensor

Nerve fiber

This cross section of the skin shows the different sensory nerve endings. These endings detect touch, pressure, pain, heat, and cold. Nerve fibers carry impulses from the sensors to the brain.

SEE ALSO PAGES:

100–1 Skin, hair, and nails, 108–9 The brain and nervous system, 113–4 Taste and smell

TASTE AND SMELL

Taste and smell are linked senses. Both detect chemicals, either in food or in the air. Together, they enable people to appreciate a wide range of flavors.

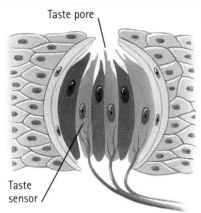

Taste pore

Taste sensor

A mixture of taste sensors and packing cells are clustered together in this taste bud, similar to the segments of an orange. The taste bud detects chemicals dissolved in saliva that enter through the taste pore, which is the opening onto the tongue's surface.

The organ of taste is the tongue. Scattered over its upper surface are about 10,000 taste buds. Taste buds detect four basic tastes—sweet, sour, salty, and bitter. Bitter-tasting foods may be poisonous and can be spat out.

Taste buds are found on the sides of tiny projections, called papillae, that cover the tongue. Fungiform papillae resemble mushrooms; there are seven or eight large ridged papillae at the back of the tongue. Threadlike filiform papillae have no taste buds and help to grip food during chewing. When dissolved food chemicals reach a taste bud, sensory cells send nerve impulses to the brain.

Taste buds occur in zones on the tongue: sweet at the front, bitter at the back, and salty and sour along the sides. The tongue also has receptors for heat and cold, and pain receptors for spicy foods.

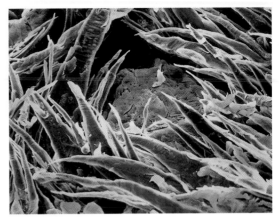

A magnified view of the tongue's upper surface shows pointed filiform papillae surrounding a fungiform papilla (yellow-orange) on the sides of which are taste buds.

SMELL

The sense of smell allows people to enjoy food and avoid dangerous substances in the air and in food. Humans can detect over 10,000 different odors. About 10 million olfactory (smell) receptors are located in the upper part of the nasal cavity in two patches of epithelium (lining), each the size of a postage stamp. Each receptor contains up to 20 hairlike cilia. When air is breathed in, molecules dissolve in a watery mucus and bind to the cilia. Smell dominates taste; a cold can make food taste flavorless.

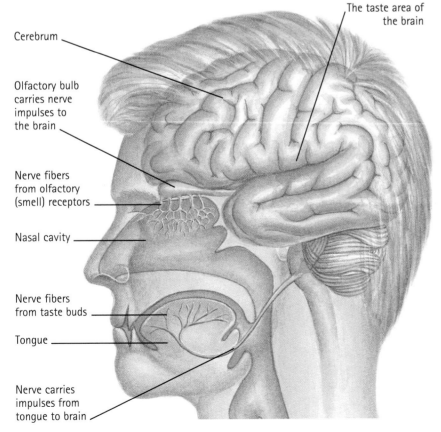

The taste area of the brain

Cerebrum

Olfactory bulb carries nerve impulses to the brain

Nerve fibers from olfactory (smell) receptors

Nasal cavity

Nerve fibers from taste buds

Tongue

Nerve carries impulses from tongue to brain

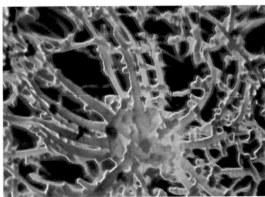

◀ Taste buds are found in the upper surface of the tongue. Impulses from taste buds travel along nerves to the taste area of the brain. Smell receptors are found in the upper part of each side of the nasal cavity. Nerve impulses from these receptors are sent to the part of the brain where smells are identified.

▲ Hair-like cilia radiate from an olfactory (smell) receptor in the upper nasal cavity. When smelly molecules touch these cilia, the receptor sends nerve impulses to the brain.

SEE ALSO PAGES:

108–9 The brain and nervous system, 114–5 Eyes and seeing, 116–7 Ears, hearing, and balance

EYES AND SEEING

Vision is an extremely important sense. The eyes detect light from the body's surroundings and send messages to the brain, allowing a person to see.

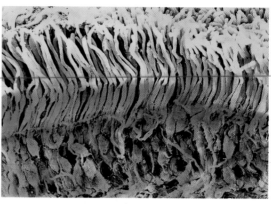

The pupil is the hole that allows light into the eye. In dim light the colored iris makes the pupil larger.

In bright light the iris makes the pupil smaller to prevent too much light entering the eye and damaging the retina.

Eyes are important because they provide the brain with information about the body's surroundings. The retina, which lines the inside of the eye, contains photoreceptors, sensory cells that are stimulated by light. Photoreceptors make up 70 percent of the sensory receptors in the human body, an indication of how important they are.

The eyeballs, each about 1 inch in diameter, are found in orbits in the skull. Only a small part of the eye is visible from the front. Each eyeball moves by using six extrinsic (external) muscles, which enable people to look from side to side and up and down. They cause tiny movements, called saccades, of the eyeballs, which allow the eyes to scan the surroundings.

This is a cross section through the retina, the eye's light-sensitive layer. Rods and cones (yellow) respond to light and send messages to the brain along nerve fibers (pink).

BLIND SPOT

One region of the retina, known as the blind spot, does not contain any light sensors. This is where the optic nerve leaves the eyeball. The blind spot does not interfere with vision because the brain chooses to "ignore" it. Most of the time people do not notice any effect.

THE EYE

The internal and external parts of the eye are revealed by this cutaway. Light enters through the clear cornea. The iris controls the amount of light that enters the eye so that a person can see in dim as well as bright light. The lens focuses light on the retina from both near and far objects. The retina is packed with photoreceptors (light sensors).

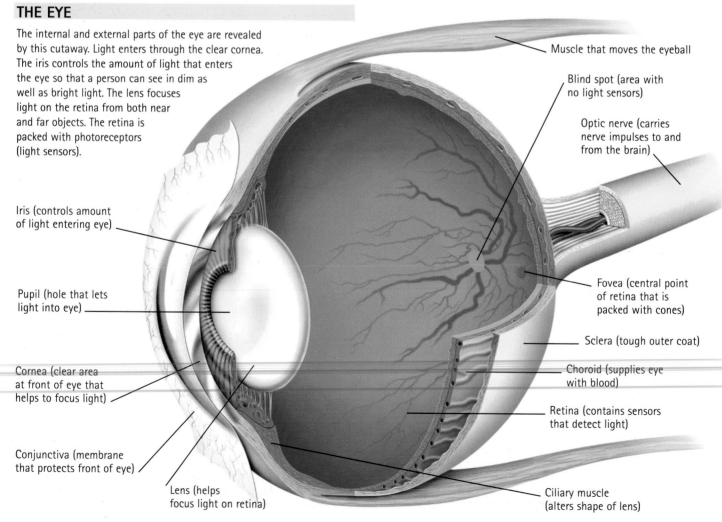

Muscle that moves the eyeball

Blind spot (area with no light sensors)

Optic nerve (carries nerve impulses to and from the brain)

Iris (controls amount of light entering eye)

Pupil (hole that lets light into eye)

Cornea (clear area at front of eye that helps to focus light)

Conjunctiva (membrane that protects front of eye)

Lens (helps focus light on retina)

Fovea (central point of retina that is packed with cones)

Sclera (tough outer coat)

Choroid (supplies eye with blood)

Retina (contains sensors that detect light)

Ciliary muscle (alters shape of lens)

HOW SIGHT WORKS

Light rays that enter the eye are refracted (bent) by the cornea and the lens to focus them on the retina. The ciliary muscle alters the thickness of the lens to focus light from close or faraway objects. The iris controls the amount of light entering the eye. Its muscles continually alter the size of the pupil, making it larger to admit more light or smaller to prevent excessive light from damaging the retina.

The retina is a thin layer of light sensors called rods and cones. The rods (about 120 million) work best in dim light and are sensitive to black and white. The cones (about six million) work best in bright light and detect color. Most of the cones are found in the fovea, which generates the most detailed images. Three types of cone detect green, red, and blue light. When they detect light, rods and cones generate nerve impulses that travel along the optic nerve to the visual areas at the back of the cerebrum, the largest part of the brain. The brain reconstructs the images. Each eye detects a slightly different view. The brain uses these differences to produce a three-dimensional picture of the world, which allows people to judge distances.

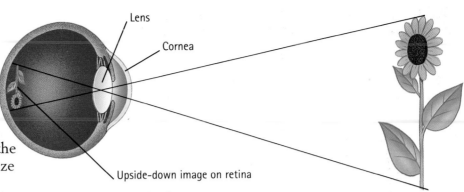

Lens
Cornea
Upside-down image on retina

VISION DEFECTS

Myopia, or nearsightedness, is an inability to see distant objects clearly because light from them is focused before it reaches the retina, producing a blurred image. This can be corrected by contact lenses or glasses. Hyperopia, or farsightedness, is an inability to see close objects clearly because light from them is focused behind the retina, again producing a blurred image. This can be corrected by the use of glasses. Presbyopia may occur as part of aging after the age of 45. Here, the ability to focus on near objects is lost, and glasses are needed for reading and other close-up work. Color blindness, or color deficiency, is the inability to distinguish between certain colors.

When light from an object enters the eye, the cornea and lens focus it to produce a clear, but upside-down, image on the retina. When hit by this light, sensors in the retina send nerve messages to the brain. There the image is seen the right way up.

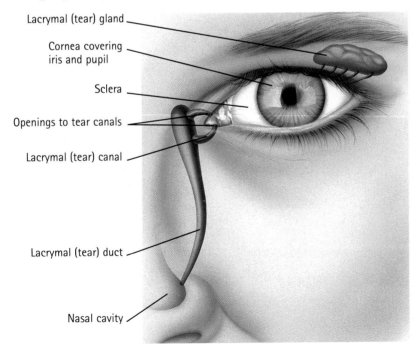

Lacrymal (tear) gland
Cornea covering iris and pupil
Sclera
Openings to tear canals
Lacrymal (tear) canal
Lacrymal (tear) duct
Nasal cavity

▲ Tears are produced by lacrymal (tear) glands. Tears spread over the eye's surface when a person blinks to wash away dirt and dust; they also contain the chemical lysozyme that kills bacteria. Tears then drain through two holes in the corner of the eye and empty into the nose.

▲ This pattern of dots is a test for color blindness, an inability to tell certain colors apart. A color-blind person lacks one of the types of cone (color sensors) that detect red, green, or blue light. Most common is red-green color blindness, an inability to distinguish between those two colors. If you can see the number eight in this pattern, you are not color-blind. Color blindness is more common in males than in females.

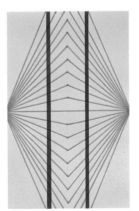
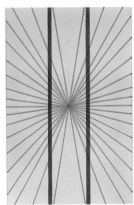

▲ Optical illusions are images that trick the brain. Here both sets of red lines are straight, but they seem to curve inward (left) or outward (right).

SEE ALSO PAGES:

108–9 The brain and nervous system, 112 Touch, 113 Taste and smell

EARS, HEARING, AND BALANCE

Humans can detect over 400,000 different sounds. As well as detecting sound, the ears play an important role in balance and posture.

Sound is created by alternating waves of low and high pressure that pass through the air, similar to the ripples that spread across a pond when a stone is dropped into the water. These pressure waves pass into the ear where they are detected by sensors. These send messages to the brain, which interprets them as sounds.

Most of the ear lies hidden within the temporal bones of the skull. The part we can see, the pinna, channels sound waves into the auditory canal, a tube that secretes cleansing wax. The air-filled middle ear is bordered by the eardrum on one side and the oval window on the other. Its only opening is through the eustachian, or auditory, tube that runs to the throat. The middle ear equalizes the air pressure on both sides of the eardrum. If it is unequal, the eardrum cannot vibrate properly, and hearing is impaired. Sudden pressure changes—such as when an aircraft takes off—can make the pressures unequal. Yawning or chewing forces air into, or out of, the eustachian tube, and the ears pop as the pressures equalize and normal hearing returns. The inner ear contains sound receptors linked to the brain. It is filled with fluid and sealed in a bony structure.

HOW HEARING WORKS

Sound waves arrive from the source that is making them, such as a radio, and enter the ear through the auditory canal. At the end of this canal, a taut piece of skin called the eardrum vibrates as the sound waves hit it. The eardrum passes the vibrations to the three ossicles—the hammer, anvil, and stirrup—in the middle ear. When these bones vibrate, the stirrup bone pushes and pulls the membrane that covers the oval window. This movement sets up vibrations in the fluid in the inner ear; these are detected by the sensors in the cochlea. The sensors send nerve impulses to the brain, which processes them. The person hears the sound. Loud sounds cause larger vibrations in the fluid. The part of the cochlea near the oval window detects high-pitched sounds; and the tip of the cochlea's coil detects low-pitched sounds.

Sound waves usually arrive in one ear a split second before the other. The brain uses this tiny time difference to work out from which direction the sound came.

INSIDE THE EAR

The outer ear channels sounds into the ear. The middle ear is crossed by three tiny bones, called ossicles, that transmit sounds from the eardrum to the inner ear. The inner ear is filled with fluid and a series of channels. The cochlea contains sound sensors. The semicircular canals, the saccule, and the utricle detect movement and position.

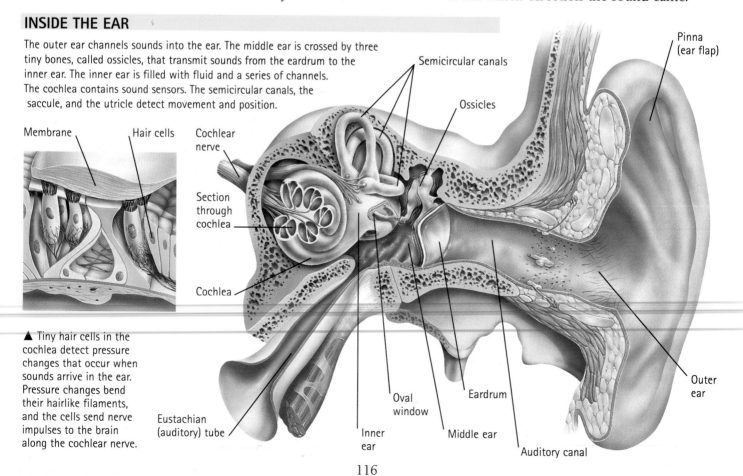

Membrane

Hair cells

Cochlear nerve

Section through cochlea

Cochlea

Semicircular canals

Ossicles

Pinna (ear flap)

Oval window

Inner ear

Eardrum

Middle ear

Auditory canal

Outer ear

Eustachian (auditory) tube

▲ Tiny hair cells in the cochlea detect pressure changes that occur when sounds arrive in the ear. Pressure changes bend their hairlike filaments, and the cells send nerve impulses to the brain along the cochlear nerve.

116

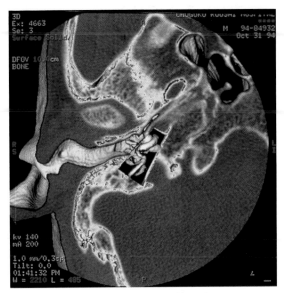

This CT scan shows a section through a living ear. The ear canal (white) runs from the left to the center. The ear bones—ossicles—are highlighted in the center. The larger grey, mottled areas are the bones of the skull.

This view of the inner ear (magnified 2074 times) shows the region of the cochlea that detects sounds. When sounds arrive in the ear and cause vibrations in the fluid, the filaments of the hair cells (yellow) bend, and the hair cells send messages to the brain.

THE EARS AND BALANCE

Balance sensors are found within the inner ear inside two linked structures—the semicircular canals and the vestibule. These lie next to the cochlea and are also filled with fluid. The three semicircular canals are set at right angles to each other and detect movements of the head. At the base of each canal, sensory hair cells are embedded in a jellylike cupule (cup-shaped structure). When the head moves, the fluid in one or more of the canals moves and bends both the cupule and its hairs. The hair cells then send nerve impulses to the brain. By analyzing which semicircular canals sent nerve messages, the brain can tell which way the head and body are moving at any moment.

The vestibule contains two balance sensors, the utricle and the saccule. Both contain sensory hairs embedded in otoliths (ear parts made of calcium carbonate crystals). The utricle detects rapid acceleration and deceleration, while the saccule detects changes in the head's position. This information, combined with messages from the eyes, pressure sensors in the feet, and receptors in muscles and joints, provide the brain with a complete picture of the body's position. The brain can then send out instructions to muscles to alter the body's position to maintain its posture and balance.

HEARING RANGES

Humans can hear a wide range of sounds, from low-pitched hums to high-pitched squeaks. Pitch is determined by a sound's frequency; that is, how rapidly one crest of the wave follows the previous one. Sound frequency is measured in hertz (Hz), or sound waves per second.

Young people can usually hear sounds between 20 Hz and 20,000 Hz. However, the range of sounds people can hear decreases with their age, so older people are unable to hear higher-pitched sounds. Some mammals hear high-pitched sounds that are inaudible to humans. Bats can hear sounds in the range 1,000 to 120,000 Hz, and cats from 60 to 65,000 Hz.

▲ The semicircular canals, the utricle, and the saccule all play an important part in balance. They send information to the brain about the position and movement of the head. The brain instructs muscles to move and position the body so that it does not fall over.

◄ Inside each fluid-filled semicircular canal is a jellylike knob called a cupule. Hair cells are embedded in the cupule. If the head moves, the fluid also moves and bends the cupule. Hair cells send messages to the brain so that a person is aware of their movement.

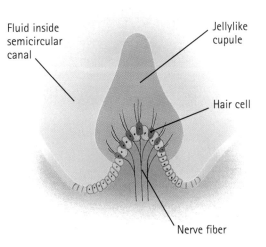

Fluid inside semicircular canal

Jellylike cupule

Hair cell

Nerve fiber

SEE ALSO PAGES:

106–7 Muscles and movement, 108–9 The brain and nervous system

HORMONES

The endocrine system releases chemical messengers called hormones into the body. Different hormones control processes such as reproduction and growth.

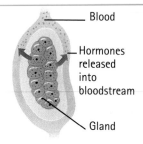

A gland is a group of cells that releases chemicals either into or onto the body. Endocrine, or ductless, glands (above) release hormones into the bloodstream, which carries them to all parts of the body.

Blood
Hormones released into bloodstream
Gland

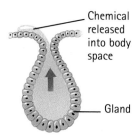

Chemical released into body space
Gland

Exocrine glands include the salivary glands and sweat glands. Also called ducted glands, exocrine glands release their secretions, such as saliva or sweat, through a duct that opens into a space inside the body or onto the surface of the body.

The endocrine, or hormonal, system is made up of a number of endocrine (hormone-releasing) glands. Along with the nervous system, the endocrine system controls and coordinates the workings of the body. The endocrine system plays a key role in reproduction and growth and controls many other processes. The endocrine and nervous systems work in very different ways. In the nervous system, messages are carried in the form of electrical impulses. The endocrine system releases chemical messengers, called hormones, into the bloodstream. Carried by the blood to its target, the hormone alters the activities of cells by increasing or decreasing the speed of processes taking place inside them. Unlike the nervous system, hormones work slowly and have long-term effects. The pituitary gland controls most of the other endocrine glands. In turn, the pituitary gland is controlled by the hypothalamus in the brain. This provides a direct link between the endocrine and nervous systems.

THE ENDOCRINE SYSTEM

The glands that make up the endocrine system are scattered through the head, thorax, and abdomen. The major endocrine glands are the pituitary, thyroid, parathyroid, and adrenal glands. The pituitary gland releases more than nine hormones, controls the activities of most other endocrine glands, and is itself controlled by part of the brain called the hypothalamus. The thyroid gland regulates the body's metabolic rate (the speed of chemical reactions inside body cells). Along with the parathyroid glands, it controls calcium levels in the blood. The adrenal glands also affect metabolic rate and help the body withstand stress. Other organs also have endocrine sections. The pancreas controls glucose levels in the blood, but it also acts as an exocrine gland that releases digestive enzymes into the intestine. The testes in males and the ovaries in females produce sex hormones as well as making sperm and eggs.

REGULATING HORMONES

Hormone levels in the blood are regulated by negative feedback systems. These reverse unwanted changes, making sure that hormones do not have too great or too little an effect. For example, thyroxine speeds up the body's metabolism. Too much thyroxine, and the body works too fast. Too little, and the body slows right down. Low thyroxine levels cause the pituitary gland to release thyroid stimulating hormone (TSH), and the thyroid gland produces thyroxine. High thyroxine levels have the opposite effect.

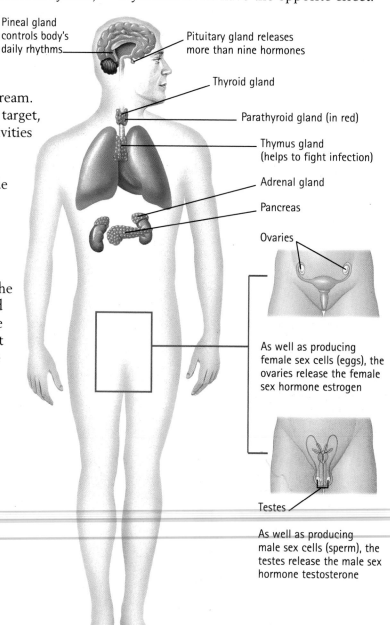

Pineal gland controls body's daily rhythms

Pituitary gland releases more than nine hormones

Thyroid gland

Parathyroid gland (in red)

Thymus gland (helps to fight infection)

Adrenal gland

Pancreas

Ovaries

As well as producing female sex cells (eggs), the ovaries release the female sex hormone estrogen

Testes

As well as producing male sex cells (sperm), the testes release the male sex hormone testosterone

The passengers on this roller coaster are experiencing the effects of the hormone adrenaline, or epinephrine. Adrenaline is released by the adrenal glands. It helps the body to deal with dangerous situations. Adrenaline makes both the heartbeat and breathing speed up. It also diverts blood to the muscles. Following the release of adrenaline, the body is prepared either to confront dangerous situations or to run away from them. This reaction is known as fight-or-flight.

PITUITARY GLAND

The pea-sized pituitary gland at the base of the brain helps to control the endocrine system. The pituitary gland releases more than nine hormones. Some of these hormones control body functions directly, such as a growth hormone that stimulates growth. Others target other endocrine glands, like follicle stimulating hormone (fsh), which stimulates the ovaries to release the female sex hormone estrogen.

The pituitary gland is made up of two parts called lobes. The larger anterior (front) lobe makes and releases most pituitary hormones. Their release is triggered by hormones secreted by the hypothalamus in the base of the brain. The smaller posterior (back) lobe stores and releases two hormones made by the hypothalamus.

ADRENAL GLANDS

An adrenal gland sits at the top of each kidney. The outer cortex of these two glands releases hormones called corticosteroids. They help to control metabolism and regulate the concentration of substances in the blood. The inner medulla secretes adrenaline. If the brain perceives danger or stress, it sends nerve messages to the adrenal glands, causing them to secrete adrenaline. This prepares the body to confront the threat or run away from it.

PANCREAS

The pancreas is located below the stomach. It releases the hormones insulin and glucagon, which control blood glucose levels. Cells need a constant supply of glucose. If glucose levels are too high or too low, cells cannot take in glucose. Insulin and glucagon naturally balance each other to maintain a steady glucose level whether a person is hungry or has just eaten.

Every day this boy uses a special automatic syringe to inject insulin into his body. He suffers from diabetes, which means his pancreas does not produce insulin. Without the injections, the boy's body could not control glucose levels in the blood and he would become very sick.

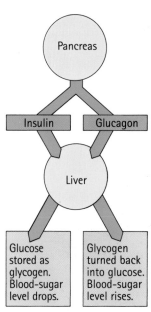

The pancreas releases insulin and glucagon. These hormones work in opposite ways to regulate levels of glucose in the bloodstream. If glucose levels rise, the insulin stimulates cells to take up glucose and the liver to store it as glycogen. If glucose levels fall, glucagon stimulates the liver to turn glycogen back into glucose.

SEE ALSO PAGES:

108–9 The brain and nervous system, 122 Blood, 130 Metabolism, 132-3 Reproduction

THE HEART AND CIRCULATION

The circulatory system supplies the body's cells with vital substances. It also carries away their waste products, and is part of the body's defense system.

English doctor William Harvey (1578–1657) was the first person to show that blood circulates in one direction around the body, pumped by the heart.

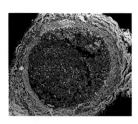

The magnified cross section above shows the thick walls of an artery.

The heart pumps blood through a network of blood vessels, which extend 93,210 miles around the human body. There are three main types of blood vessels. Thick-walled arteries carry blood away from the heart. Thinner-walled veins carry blood back to the heart. Microscopic capillaries link veins and arteries. Formed as branches of arterioles (the smallest arteries), capillaries pass through tissues and supply groups of cells with essential substances. Waste products flow back into the capillaries. Capillaries link up to form venules, which unite to form veins. The human circulatory system is a double circulation with two loops. One loop carries blood to the lungs. The other carries blood to the body. It takes blood about 60 seconds to complete a full circuit of the body.

ANATOMY OF THE HEART

The heart is a powerful, muscular pump, which maintains a continuous flow of blood around the body. The heart is divided into two halves by the septum. Each half has a smaller upper chamber, called the atrium, and a larger lower chamber, called the ventricle. The right atrium receives oxygen-poor blood from the body through large veins called the superior (upper) vena cava and inferior (lower) vena cava. The pulmonary arteries carry blood pumped from the right ventricle to the lungs. The left atrium receives oxygen-rich blood from the lungs through the pulmonary veins. The left ventricle pumps the oxygen-rich blood to the body's cells along the large artery called the aorta.

Arteriole

Venule

◄ Blood flows from the arteries along tiny capillaries, which supply cells, to the veins

Capillary

Artery

Vein

Carotid artery carries blood to head

Superior (upper) vena cava carries oxygen-poor blood to heart

Subclavian artery carries blood to arms

Pulmonary vein carries oxygen-rich blood to heart

Inferior (lower) vena cava carries oxygen-poor blood to heart

Femoral artery carries blood to legs

Jugular vein carries blood from head

Subclavian vein carries blood from arms

Aorta carries oxygen-rich blood to the body

Pulmonary artery carries oxygen-poor blood to the lungs

Heart

Aorta

Femoral vein carries blood from legs

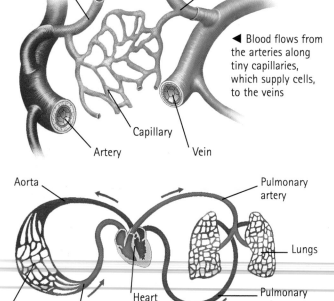

Aorta

Pulmonary artery

Lungs

Heart

Pulmonary vein

Rest of body

Vena cava

▲ The circulatory system is made up of two loops. One carries oxygen-poor blood from the heart to the lungs (where it picks up oxygen) and back to the heart. The other carries oxygen-rich blood from the heart to the rest of the body (where it supplies oxygen to all body tissues) and then back to the heart.

◄ The blood vessels in this map of the circulatory system are color-coded. Those carrying oxygen-rich blood—mostly arteries—are red. Those carrying oxygen-poor blood—mostly veins—are blue. Exceptions are the pulmonary arteries that carry oxygen-poor blood to the lungs, and the pulmonary veins that carry oxygen-rich blood from the lungs.

THE HEART

The front view of the heart (below) shows the main blood vessels carrying blood to and from the heart and the coronary artery that supplies the heart wall. A section through the heart (below right) shows the septum that divides the heart into left and right halves, the atria and the larger ventricles. Heart valves prevent blood flowing backward.

Superior vena cava

Aorta

Pulmonary artery

Pulmonary veins

Left atrium

Right atrium

Left ventricle

Inferior vena cava

Right ventricle

Coronary artery

Aorta

Semilunar valve guarding exit into pulmonary artery

Right atrium

Left atrium

Bicuspid valve between left atrium and left ventricle

Left ventricle

Tricuspid valve between right atrium and right ventricle

Septum

Right ventricle

Thick muscular wall

CORONARY CIRCULATION

Blood passes through the heart too quickly to supply the muscle cells in the heart wall with the oxygen and food they need. The heart has its own blood supply called the coronary circulation. Two coronary arteries branch from the aorta and supply all parts of the heart wall. Blood that has passed through heart muscle empties into the right atrium. If a coronary artery becomes blocked, the part of the heart it supplies may die and cause a heart attack.

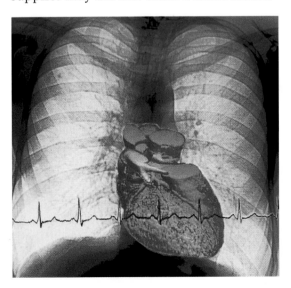

HEARTBEAT

During a single heartbeat, both ventricles fill with blood and then contract to pump blood out of the heart. As the heart fills with blood, semilunar valves close to prevent backflow into the heart from the aorta and pulmonary artery. As the heart empties, valves between the atria and ventricles close to prevent blood flowing back into the atria. As the valves between atria and ventricles close, they produce a long "lubb" sound. As the semilunar valves close, they produce a shorter "dupp" sound. Together, these sounds make up the heartbeat, which can be heard using a stethoscope. The timing of each heartbeat is regulated by a pacemaker in the wall of the right atrium.

▶ On average, the heart beats about 75 times a minute. Each heartbeat is a cycle of three stages—diastole, atrial systole, and ventricular systole. These stages follow each other in a precisely timed sequence. Over the course of the three stages, blood enters the atria, passes into the ventricles, and is then pumped out of the heart.

◀ This X ray shows the heart located inside the thorax (chest) between the two lungs (yellow). The ribs, also visible, surround and protect both heart and lungs. Also shown is an electrocardiograph (ECG), a record of the electrical changes taking place in the heart.

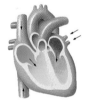

During diastole, the atria and ventricles are relaxed. Both atria fill with blood.

During atrial systole, the atria contract and squeeze blood into the ventricles.

During ventricular systole, the ventricles contract and push blood from the heart.

SEE ALSO PAGES:

122 Blood, 123 Lymphatic system, 124–5 Lungs and breathing, 130 Metabolism

BLOOD

Blood provides the body's trillions of cells with a delivery and removal system. It also helps to defend the body against infection and repairs damaged blood cells.

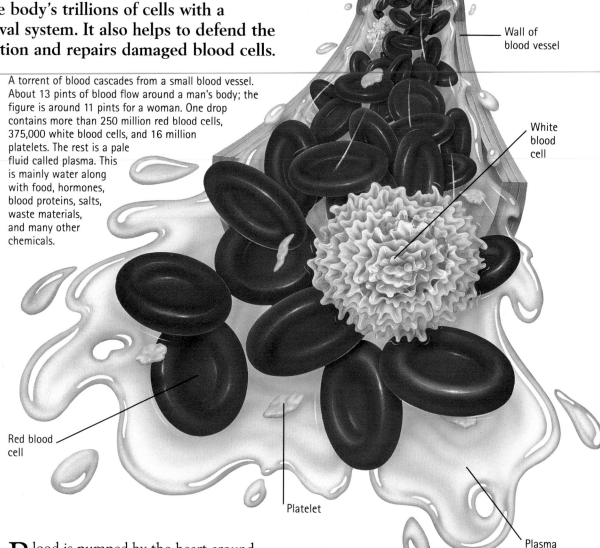

Wall of blood vessel

White blood cell

Red blood cell

Platelet

Plasma

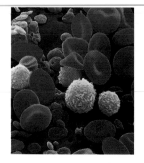

A torrent of blood cascades from a small blood vessel. About 13 pints of blood flow around a man's body; the figure is around 11 pints for a woman. One drop contains more than 250 million red blood cells, 375,000 white blood cells, and 16 million platelets. The rest is a pale fluid called plasma. This is mainly water along with food, hormones, blood proteins, salts, waste materials, and many other chemicals.

▲ Red blood cells, white blood cells (yellow), and platelets (pink), are made in bone marrow. About two million red blood cells are produced every second.

Red blood cells caught in platelet net

Damage to a blood vessel causes the platelets to form a net of fibers that traps red blood cells.

Scab forms

Fibers and red blood cells form a clot to seal off the wound. The surface of the clot hardens into a scab.

Healed tissue under old scab

Underneath the scab, the blood vessel and skin repair themselves. Once this is done, the old, dried-up scab falls off.

Blood is pumped by the heart around the body through arteries, veins, and capillaries. It supplies food and oxygen to the body's cells and removes waste. Blood also maintains the body's temperature, fights disease, and plays a role in repairing damaged blood vessels.

BLOOD AS TRANSPORTATION

Oxygen is carried to cells by the doughnut-shaped red blood cells. These are packed with hemoglobin, a substance that picks up oxygen as blood passes through the lungs and releases it into the body's cells. Plasma is a watery liquid that makes up about 55 percent of blood. It is responsible for carrying food, waste products, chemical messengers called hormones, and many other substances around the body. It also helps the body to maintain a temperature of 98.6°F (37°C).

DEFENSE AND PROTECTION

Tiny disease-causing microorganisms (pathogens) are constantly trying to infect the body. White blood cells called phagocytes and lymphocytes destroy these invaders. Phagocytes hunt down and engulf any pathogens. Lymphocytes release killer chemicals called antibodies. These disable pathogens so that phagocytes can engulf them. Lymphocytes remember pathogens so that they can react even faster if the same pathogens invade again.

Platelets seal leaks in damaged blood vessels. Their action stops pathogens from getting into the body and also prevents the loss of blood from the damaged area.

SEE ALSO PAGES:

120–1 The heart and circulation, 137 The immune system

LYMPHATIC SYSTEM

The lymphatic system drains the excess fluid called lymph from the tissues into the blood. It also contains cells that defend the body against disease.

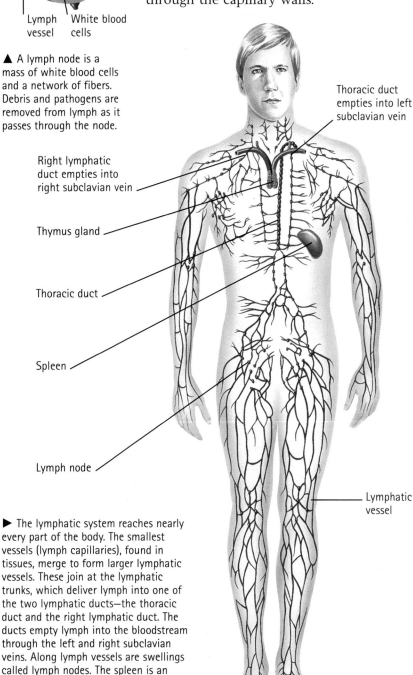

Blood vessels

Lymph vessel

White blood cells

▲ A lymph node is a mass of white blood cells and a network of fibers. Debris and pathogens are removed from lymph as it passes through the node.

As blood flows around the body, a substance called tissue fluid passes out through the capillary walls. This fluid delivers oxygen and essential nutrients to tissue cells. Tissue fluid then removes waste and passes back into the bloodstream through the capillary walls.

Thoracic duct empties into left subclavian vein

Right lymphatic duct empties into right subclavian vein

Thymus gland

Thoracic duct

Spleen

Lymph node

Lymphatic vessel

▶ The lymphatic system reaches nearly every part of the body. The smallest vessels (lymph capillaries), found in tissues, merge to form larger lymphatic vessels. These join at the lymphatic trunks, which deliver lymph into one of the two lymphatic ducts—the thoracic duct and the right lymphatic duct. The ducts empty lymph into the bloodstream through the left and right subclavian veins. Along lymph vessels are swellings called lymph nodes. The spleen is an important part of the lymphatic system and is a primary filter for the blood. It also makes antibodies.

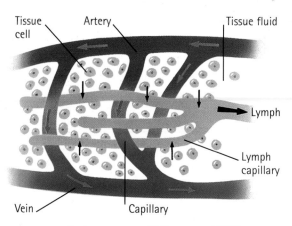

Tissue cell

Artery

Tissue fluid

Lymph

Lymph capillary

Vein

Capillary

Cells in the body's tissues are bathed in a fluid derived from nearby blood capillaries. Excess tissue fluid passes into blind lymph capillaries and becomes lymph.

DRAINAGE

Every day, about 50 pints of fluid leave the capillaries to pass through the tissues. Most passes directly back into the bloodstream, but about 8 pints, now called lymph, are drained into the lymphatic system, which empties back into the blood vessels in the upper chest.

Lymph is a colorless fluid, which contains dissolved substances, debris, and pathogens such as bacteria and viruses. It only flows in one direction—away from the tissues. Unlike blood, which has a heart to pump it, lymph moves through the lymphatic system with the help of skeletal muscles that push the fluid along when they contract. Valves in the lymph vessels stop the fluid flowing backward.

DEFENSE

As lymph flows through lymph vessels, it passes through lymph nodes. Here, white blood cells called macrophages trap and engulf cell debris and pathogens. Other white blood cells, called lymphocytes, produce antibodies which are chemicals that mark pathogens for destruction. Other lymphatic organs have a similar role. The tonsils intercept pathogens that enter the mouth. Together, lymphocytes and macrophages form the immune system, the body's most powerful defense against disease.

SEE ALSO PAGES:

98-9 Body organization, 120-1 The heart and circulation, 137 The immune system

LUNGS AND BREATHING

The oxygen people need to live comes from air breathed into the lungs. In the lungs, oxygen passes into the bloodstream and is then carried to the body's cells.

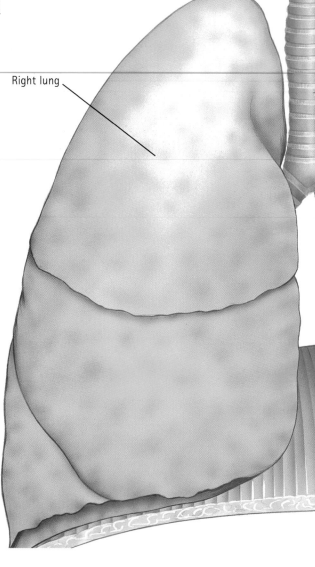

Right lung

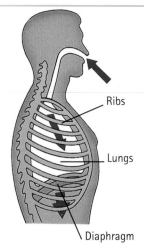

Ribs

Lungs

Diaphragm

During inhalation, or breathing in, the diaphragm contracts and flattens. The intercostal muscles also contract and pull the ribs upward and outward. This makes the lungs larger and decreases the pressure inside them, so that air is sucked into them through the mouth and trachea.

Cells need a constant supply of energy to power their activities. Cells use oxygen to release energy from foods in a process called respiration. Respiration releases carbon dioxide, a poisonous waste product that has to be removed from the body. Delivering oxygen and removing carbon dioxide is done by the respiratory system. This consists of a system of tubes that carry air in and out of the body, and a pair of lungs into which oxygen enters and from which carbon dioxide leaves the blood. Blood carries oxygen from the lungs to the cells, and carries waste carbon dioxide from the cells back to the lungs.

A SYSTEM OF TUBES

Air first passes through the nose. Hairs in the nostrils and sticky mucus that lines the nasal cavity trap particles that would damage the lungs. Air then passes into the pharynx, through the larynx (voice box), into the trachea. This is reinforced by C-shaped pieces of cartilage. Mucus in the trachea also traps dirt. Fine hairlike cilia carry dirt up to the throat. The trachea branches into two bronchi, which themselves branch inside the lungs.

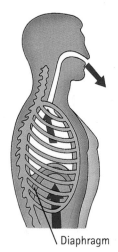

Diaphragm

During exhalation, or breathing out, the diaphragm relaxes and is pushed up by the abdominal organs beneath it. The intercostal muscles relax, so the ribs move downward and inward. This decreases volume inside the thorax. The lungs get smaller. Pressure inside them increases so that air is pushed out.

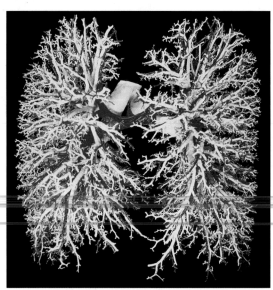

A cast of the lungs shows the bronchi and bronchioles (white), and the pulmonary artery (red). This network is called the bronchial tree—it resembles an upside-down tree with the trachea as trunk and bronchi as branches.

LUNGS

The lungs lie in the thorax (chest) and sit on each side of the heart, protected by the spine and rib cage. They rest on the diaphragm, a muscular sheet that separates the thorax from the abdomen. Healthy lungs are pink because they are full of blood. They also feel spongy, because they consist of a branching network of airways. These end in millions of microscopic air sacs called alveoli, through which oxygen enters the bloodstream. Squeezed into the chest, all the alveoli provide a surface area—two thirds the size of a tennis court—for absorbing oxygen. A thin pleural membrane covers the lungs; another lines the inside of the chest wall. Fluid between the membranes decreases friction and prevents pain during breathing.

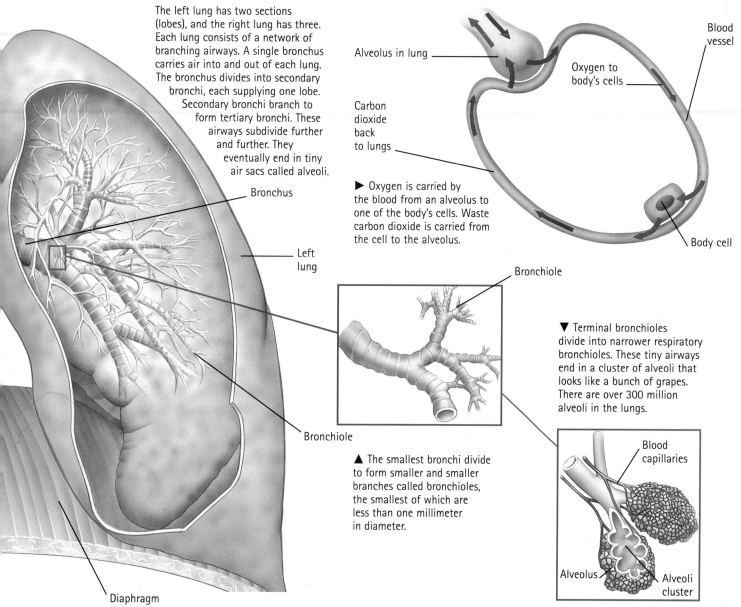

The left lung has two sections (lobes), and the right lung has three. Each lung consists of a network of branching airways. A single bronchus carries air into and out of each lung. The bronchus divides into secondary bronchi, each supplying one lobe. Secondary bronchi branch to form tertiary bronchi. These airways subdivide further and further. They eventually end in tiny air sacs called alveoli.

Bronchus

Left lung

Bronchiole

Diaphragm

Alveolus in lung

Oxygen to body's cells

Blood vessel

Carbon dioxide back to lungs

Body cell

▶ Oxygen is carried by the blood from an alveolus to one of the body's cells. Waste carbon dioxide is carried from the cell to the alveolus.

Bronchiole

▼ Terminal bronchioles divide into narrower respiratory bronchioles. These tiny airways end in a cluster of alveoli that looks like a bunch of grapes. There are over 300 million alveoli in the lungs.

Bronchiole

▲ The smallest bronchi divide to form smaller and smaller branches called bronchioles, the smallest of which are less than one millimeter in diameter.

Blood capillaries

Alveolus

Alveoli cluster

GAS EXCHANGE

Gas exchange takes place continuously in the alveoli. This process makes sure that the body's cells receive a constant supply of oxygen and are not poisoned by an accumulation of carbon dioxide. Oxygen dissolves in a thin layer of liquid that lines each alveolus, then moves by diffusion—the movement of molecules from a high concentration to a low concentration—across the thin wall of the alveolus into the blood capillary and into red blood cells. Carbon dioxide diffuses in the reverse direction from the blood, into the air inside the alveolus, and is exhaled. Inhaled air contains about 21 percent oxygen and 0.04 percent carbon dioxide. Exhaled air contains 16 percent oxygen and about 4 percent carbon dioxide.

BREATHING

Breathing, or ventilation, moves fresh air into the lungs to replenish supplies of oxygen. It also forces stale air out of the lungs to remove carbon dioxide. The elastic lungs depend on the diaphragm and rib muscles to change the shape of the thorax. Pleural membranes cover the lungs' surfaces and line the chest wall. They act like an "adhesive pad," making sure that the lungs follow the movement of the thorax. During inhalation, the diaphragm and intercostal muscles between the ribs contract. This makes the thorax and the lungs larger—and the pressure inside them lower—so that air is sucked in. During exhalation, the reverse occurs. The lungs never completely fill or empty; a reservoir of air remains and is refreshed.

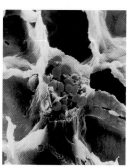

A view inside the lung (magnified 410 times) reveals a capillary (center) filled with red blood cells. These cells pick up oxygen from the surrounding network of alveoli.

SEE ALSO PAGES:

120-1 The heart and circulation, 122 Blood, 131 Waste disposal

FOOD AND NUTRITION

Food provides the body with vital substances called nutrients. Good nutrition means that the body has an adequate, balanced supply of nutrients.

The process by which people obtain a regular supply of food to survive is called nutrition. Most food contains a variety of nutrients, which are released during digestion. Macronutrients—carbohydrates, proteins, and fats—are needed in large amounts each day. Carbohydrates provide energy. They include complex starches found in potatoes, pasta, and rice; and simple sugars in fruit and candy. Proteins provide building blocks called amino acids for growth and repair. Fats provide energy and help insulate the body. Micronutrients—vitamins and minerals—are also needed daily, and are essential for cells to function. They include vitamins A and C, and minerals like calcium. Water is also essential to maintain the body's fluid balance, as is fiber, undigested plant material that keeps the intestinal muscles working properly.

A person who regularly eats fast food is not likely to be receiving a balanced diet. Although the meal shown above contains some carbohydrate in the buns and French fries, it is also very rich in protein and animal fats. It contains no fruit or fresh vegetables to provide vitamins or minerals.

Meals should be well balanced. Pasta and bread provide carbohydrate; beans and fish supply protein and vitamins; and salad contains vitamins, minerals, and fiber.

BALANCED DIET

The word *diet* refers to the type and amount of food a person eats each day. To maintain good health and avoid weight gain, a person's diet should be balanced, and contain a range of nutrients in the right amounts. A balanced diet consists of about 55 percent carbohydrates (mostly complex starches), about 15 percent protein, and 30 percent or less fat (unsaturated fats from plant oils and oily fish are healthier than saturated fats from meat or dairy products). It should also include plenty of fresh fruit and vegetables.

THE FOOD PYRAMID

The food pyramid provides an easy way to plan a balanced diet. The bulk of a balanced diet should be made up of starchy, carbohydrate-rich foods, along with smaller amounts of proteins and fats (preferably not animal fats). It should also provide plenty of vitamins, minerals, and fiber. The food pyramid provides a simple way of getting the balance right by showing the proportions in which the main types of food should be eaten. Starchy foods, such as rice and bread, and vitamin-, mineral-, and fiber-rich foods, such as vegetables and fruits, are found toward the base of the pyramid. Those that should be eaten in smaller amounts, such as meat and dairy products, are farther up the pyramid. Those that should be eaten sparingly or not at all, such as cake and candy, are located at the narrow top of the food pyramid.

Foods rich in fat and sugar should only be eaten in small amounts.

Foods rich in protein such as beans, fish, chicken, meat, and cheese. Protein is essential for growth and tissue repair. However, meat and cheese also contain a lot of fat.

Fresh fruit and vegetables provide not only vitamins and minerals that are essential for good health, but also fiber (roughage), which keeps the digestive system working properly.

Foods rich in starchy carbohydrates such as rice, bread, potatoes, and pasta. They release energy slowly throughout the day.

SEE ALSO PAGES:

128–9 Digestion, 130 Metabolism, 131 Waste disposal, 188–9 Chemistry of food

TEETH

Teeth perform an important role at the start of digestion. They grip food, chop it into small pieces, and crush it so that it can be swallowed with saliva.

A close-up view of bacteria (magnified 4858 times) living on a human tooth. Unless teeth are cleaned regularly, these bacteria form a hard coating called plaque. The bacteria in plaque feed on sugars and release acids that eat into the tooth and cause tooth decay.

Teeth are hard structures that emerge from soft gums and are firmly set in the upper and lower jaws. Each tooth consists of an upper, visible crown and a lower, hidden root. The 32 teeth in an adult's mouth vary in shape and function. In each jaw four chisel-shaped incisors grip and chop food; two pointed canines pierce and tear food; and four flattened premolars, along with six large molars, crush and grind food.

Humans have two sets of teeth during their lifetime. The first set of 20 baby, or deciduous, teeth erupt (appear) between the ages of 6 and 30 months. The second set of 32 adult, or permanent, teeth are already in place in the gums. From the age of six, the permanent teeth gradually erupt, replacing the baby teeth, which fall out. The last permanent teeth to appear, the back molars, or wisdom teeth, usually do so during the teenage years.

CHEWING AND SWALLOWING

The lips and front teeth pull food inside the mouth. Powerful muscles move the lower jaw up and down to crush food between the premolars and molars. Three pairs of salivary glands squirt saliva into the mouth, and the tongue mixes the ground-up food with the saliva. The tongue pushes the slippery package of food, called a bolus, into the throat. The bolus sets off an automatic reflex action of muscular contraction, called peristalsis. This pushes chewed food toward the stomach for the next stage of digestion.

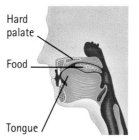
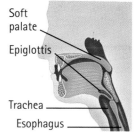

Hard palate

Food

Tongue

Soft palate

Epiglottis

Trachea

Esophagus

▲ The tongue pushes food into the throat. The reflex action of peristalsis squeezes food down the esophagus. The epiglottis closes off the opening to the windpipe to prevent food from entering the lungs.

STRUCTURE OF TEETH

Teeth are made up of several layers. The outer layer covers the crown and is made of enamel, the hardest material in the body. Dentine is a bonelike material that forms roots in the jawbone. The soft pulp cavity contains blood vessels to keep the tooth alive and nerve fibers that allow people to feel when they are chewing.

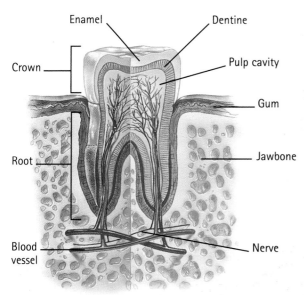

Enamel

Dentine

Crown

Pulp cavity

Gum

Jawbone

Root

Blood vessel

Nerve

▶ Baby teeth are pushed out and replaced by adult teeth from the jaw below the gums.

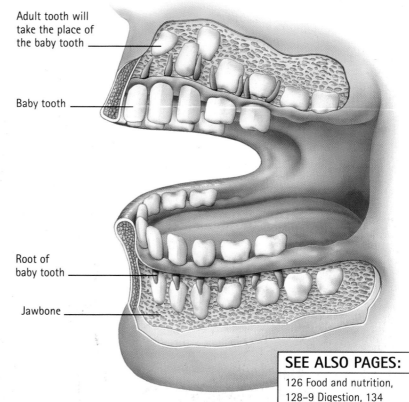

Adult tooth will take the place of the baby tooth

Baby tooth

Root of baby tooth

Jawbone

SEE ALSO PAGES:

126 Food and nutrition, 128–9 Digestion, 134 Growth and development

DIGESTION

The digestion of food releases simple nutrients in a form that can be used by the body's cells. This process takes place in the digestive system.

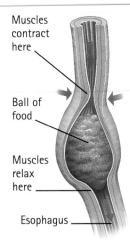

Muscles contract here

Ball of food

Muscles relax here

Esophagus

Swallowed food is pushed down the esophagus by wavelike muscular contractions called peristalsis. The muscles contract behind the food to push it downward.

The nutrients essential for life are "locked" inside the large molecules that make up food. The job of the digestive system is to break down these large molecules—such as carbohydrates, proteins, and fats—to release simple nutrients like sugars, amino acids, and fatty acids.

The digestive process has four stages: ingestion, digestion, absorption, and egestion. During ingestion, food is taken into the mouth, chewed, and swallowed. During digestion, food is broken down either by muscular crushing or by chemicals called enzymes. Absorption involves moving nutrients from the alimentary canal into the bloodstream. Finally, egestion ejects waste through the anus.

THE STOMACH

The stomach plays three roles in digestion. First, its muscular walls contract to churn and crush food. Second, glands in the stomach wall release acidic gastric (stomach) juice. This contains an enzyme—pepsin—that digests proteins in food. The crushing action and the pepsin combined turn swallowed food into a thick liquid called chyme. Third, the stomach expands to store food for up to four hours. Its exit into the duodenum is guarded by a ring of muscle called the pyloric sphincter. This opens from time to time to release chyme into the duodenum.

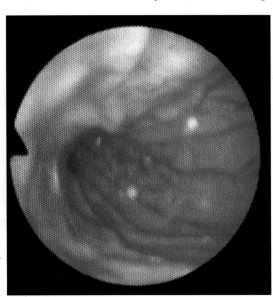

▲ An image of the stomach, as seen through an endoscope, clearly shows the slippery mucus that lines and protects the wall of the digestive system.

▶ The digestive system extends for about 30 feet from the mouth to the anus. Food enters through the mouth. Here the teeth and tongue crush it into smaller pieces, and the salivary glands lubricate it with saliva. Peristalsis takes the processed food from the esophagus to the stomach, which partly digests and stores the food. The liver and pancreas release secretions into the small intestine, which completes digestion and absorption. The main function of the large intestine is to process waste.

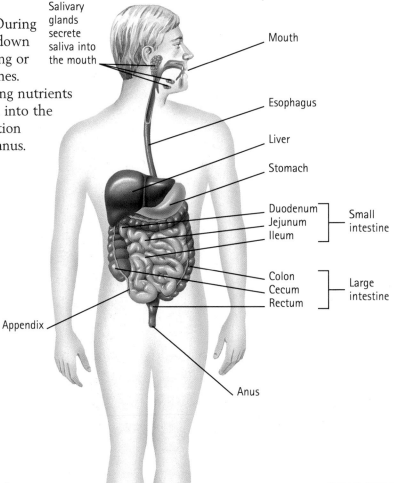

Salivary glands secrete saliva into the mouth

Mouth

Esophagus

Liver

Stomach

Duodenum
Jejunum   Small
Ileum   intestine

Colon
Cecum   Large
Rectum   intestine

Appendix

Anus

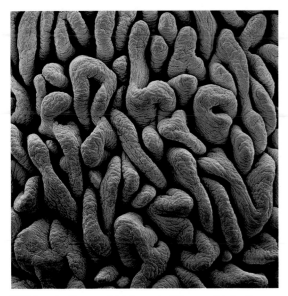

Villi line the ileum, which is part of the small intestine. This view, magnified 18 times, reveals a forest of these tiny flaps, each of which are about 0.04 inches long.

MAKING DIGESTION AN EFFICIENT PROCESS

The small intestine is coiled up in the abdominal cavity. It is between 20 and 23 feet long and holds food long enough for it to be digested and for simple nutrients to be absorbed into the bloodstream. The inner surface of the small intestine has many circular folds, which are covered by tiny projections called villi. Each villus contains a capillary network and a branch of the lymphatic system called a lacteal. Both carry nutrients away from the small intestine. Together, the circular folds and villi provide a massive surface area across which digested food can be absorbed quickly and efficiently.

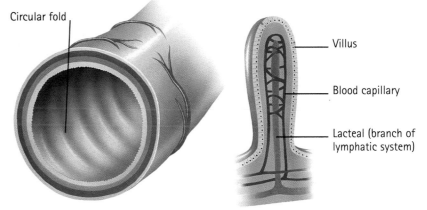

Circular fold

Villus

Blood capillary

Lacteal (branch of lymphatic system)

THE SMALL INTESTINE

The small intestine runs from the pyloric sphincter to the cecum of the large intestine. It is the most important part of the digestive system because most digestion and absorption takes place there. The small intestine is made up of three parts: the duodenum, the jejunum, and the ileum.

The first part, the duodenum, is about 10 inches long. It receives chyme from the stomach. It also receives pancreatic juice from the pancreas which produces enzymes to digest carbohydrates, proteins, and fats. Finally, it receives bile from the liver, which breaks up fats and makes them easier to digest. These secretions, along with intestinal juice secreted by the duodenal wall, make the food less acidic and allow enzymes to work more efficiently.

The jejunum is about 8 feet long. It produces enzymes that complete the digestion of carbohydrates, proteins, and fats. This, in turn, produces amino acids, fatty acids, and simple sugars such as glucose.

The ileum is the last and longest part of the small intestine. The lining of the ileum is covered with fingerlike villi. Sugars and amino acids pass through the villi into the bloodstream. They are then carried to the liver for processing and distributed to the body's cells. Fatty acids pass into lacteals—a part of the lymphatic system.

THE LARGE INTESTINE

The large intestine is 5 feet long and consists of the cecum, colon, and rectum. Water is absorbed from the waste products of digestion as they pass through the colon. The waste forms semisolid feces, consisting of dead cells, fiber, and bacteria. Feces are stored in the rectum and released through the anus.

The lining of the colon (here magnified 747 times) mainly consists of two types of cell. The cells shown in brown absorb water from feces, making them more solid. The rounded depressions shown in gray are cells that produce mucus.

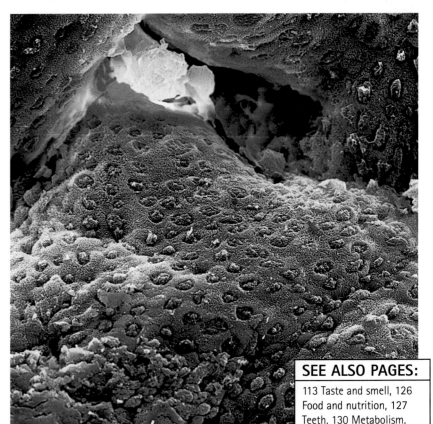

SEE ALSO PAGES:

113 Taste and smell, 126 Food and nutrition, 127 Teeth, 130 Metabolism, 188–9 Chemistry of food

METABOLISM

Metabolism is the combination of all the chemical reactions that take place inside the body's cells to maintain life. The liver plays a vital role in metabolism.

This boy is measuring his body temperature by using a heat-sensitive strip on his forehead. Metabolism releases heat to maintain the body at a constant temperature of about 37°C (98.6°F). An increase, or decrease, in body temperature can mean that someone is sick.

Day and night, thousands of different chemical processes take place inside each body cell. These metabolic reactions occur rapidly because they are catalyzed (sped up) by proteins called enzymes. These enzymes are controlled by DNA (genetic material) in the cell nucleus.

The process of metabolism is split into two functions. Catabolism breaks down substances, such as glucose, to release energy. Anabolism uses raw materials to make complex substances that the body needs; for example, the production of proteins from their building blocks, amino acids. The energy released by catabolic reactions is used to power anabolic reactions. Metabolic rate is controlled by hormones (chemical messengers) like those released by the thyroid gland.

FUNCTIONS OF THE LIVER

The dark red, wedge-shaped liver is the body's largest internal organ and occupies most of the upper right abdomen. Its billions of cells, called hepatocytes, perform more than 500 metabolic functions that control the blood's chemical makeup. The liver plays a major role in processing nutrients. This includes storing vitamins, especially A, D, and B_{12}; and minerals, notably iron and copper—both needed to make hemoglobin (an oxygen-carrying substance in the blood). Hepatocytes produce bile, which helps digest fats in the small intestine. They also break down toxins, such as alcohol, and other poisonous chemicals. Its chemical content adjusted, blood leaves the liver through hepatic veins. Heat released by the liver helps the body maintain a constant temperature of 98.6°F (37°C).

THE LIVER

After digestion, nutrients are absorbed through the small intestine. This causes a rapid rise in levels of nutrients—particularly sugars, amino acids, and lipids (fats)—in the blood. The liver controls blood nutrient levels to prevent this surge disrupting the activities of body cells. The liver has two blood supplies: one through the hepatic portal vein, rich in sugars and amino acids direct from the small intestine; and one through the hepatic artery. This second supply delivers fats absorbed by the lymphatic system and then emptied into the blood. In the liver, excess sugars are stored as glycogen, and excess amino acids are broken down to form urea. Excess fats are processed by liver cells or sent to adipose (fat) tissue for storage.

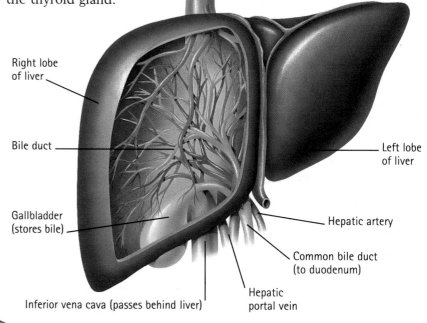

Inferior vena cava (to heart)

Right lobe of liver

Bile duct

Gallbladder (stores bile)

Left lobe of liver

Hepatic artery

Common bile duct (to duodenum)

Hepatic portal vein

Inferior vena cava (passes behind liver)

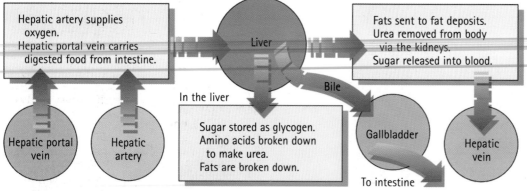

Hepatic artery supplies oxygen.
Hepatic portal vein carries digested food from intestine.

Liver

Fats sent to fat deposits.
Urea removed from body via the kidneys.
Sugar released into blood.

In the liver

Bile

Sugar stored as glycogen.
Amino acids broken down to make urea.
Fats are broken down.

Hepatic portal vein

Hepatic artery

Gallbladder

Hepatic vein

To intestine

SEE ALSO PAGES:

122 Blood, 123 Lymphatic system, 126 Food and nutrition, 128–9 Digestion

WASTE DISPOSAL

The body constantly produces waste products as a result of chemical activity in its cells. Waste must be disposed of or it can build up and poison the body.

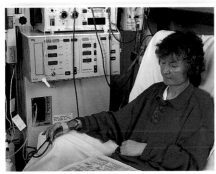

Dialysis machines provide a lifeline for patients with kidney failure. As this patient's blood passes through the machine, poisonous waste is removed from the blood. To stay alive, she must be attached to the machine for four to eight hours, three times a week.

The process of waste disposal, called excretion, is carried out by excretory organs. Without them, waste would accumulate in tissue fluid, poisoning not only the cells but the whole body. Major excretory organs are the lungs, skin, liver, and kidneys. The lungs excrete carbon dioxide, the waste product of energy release in cells, by breathing it out. The skin excretes water, salts, and other wastes in sweat. The liver breaks down many poisonous substances; excretes wastes in the form of bile; and produces urea, a waste made from excess amino acids. The kidneys excrete urea and other wastes in urine.

HOW THE KIDNEYS WORK

Kidneys process blood by excreting wastes like urea and removing excess water. Together, wastes and water make urine. The 2.5 pints of blood received each minute through the renal (kidney) arteries is processed by nephrons. Each one consists of a glomerulus, renal capsule, and renal tubule. In a glomerulus, a liquid called a filtrate is filtered under pressure from the blood into the hollow renal capsule. Filtrate contains waste and excess water, and also useful substances such as glucose and amino acids. As filtrate passes along the renal tubule, useful substances and most water are absorbed back into the blood. The remaining liquid, urine, is stored in the bladder, which empties during urination.

Every day, about 381 pints of filtrate are filtered from the bloodstream, but only 2.5 pints of this is released as urine. The body's whole blood supply is processed by the kidneys about 60 times a day.

THE URINARY SYSTEM

The urinary system consists of two kidneys, two ureters, the bladder, and the urethra. The two bean-shaped kidneys lie on the back wall of the abdomen, one each side of the spine, and behind the stomach. Each consists of three layers: the cortex, medulla, and inner renal pelvis. The cortex and medulla contain microscopic filtering units called nephrons that produce urine. This passes into the renal pelvis and down the ureters to be stored in the bladder until released through the urethra. In males the urethra opens at the tip of the penis; in females it opens internally in front of the vagina.

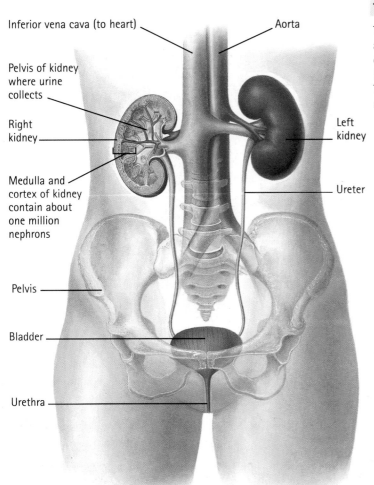

Inferior vena cava (to heart)
Aorta
Pelvis of kidney where urine collects
Right kidney
Left kidney
Medulla and cortex of kidney contain about one million nephrons
Ureter
Pelvis
Bladder
Urethra

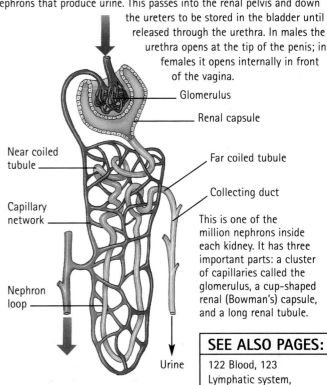

Glomerulus
Renal capsule
Near coiled tubule
Far coiled tubule
Capillary network
Collecting duct
Nephron loop

This is one of the million nephrons inside each kidney. It has three important parts: a cluster of capillaries called the glomerulus, a cup-shaped renal (Bowman's) capsule, and a long renal tubule.

Urine

SEE ALSO PAGES:
122 Blood, 123 Lymphatic system, 128-9 Digestion

REPRODUCTION

Without reproduction, the human species would become extinct. The male and female reproductive systems allow men and women to have children.

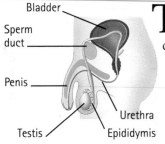

Bladder
Sperm duct
Penis
Testis
Urethra
Epididymis

Testes make millions of sperm every day. During sexual intercourse, the erect penis is put into the female's vagina. Sperm travel along the sperm duct and out of the penis.

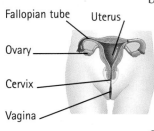

Fallopian tube   Uterus
Ovary
Cervix
Vagina

The ovaries contain a store of eggs, one of which is released each month. If it is fertilized by a sperm cell, it develops into a baby in the uterus. At birth, the baby passes out through the vagina.

The reproductive system does not become active until puberty during the early teens. Male and female reproductive systems differ, although both produce sex cells. Sex cells are made by a type of cell division called meiosis. Sex cells contain only 23 chromosomes (genetic material) in their nucleus, half the number found in other cells. The male sex cells, called sperm, are made in the two testes. More than 250 million sperm are made each day. The female sex cells, called eggs or ova, are produced in the two ovaries before birth. After puberty, one egg is released each month during ovulation and the body prepares for possible pregnancy. Sperm and egg are brought together during sexual intercourse. The man inserts his penis into the woman's vagina and releases millions of sperm. They swim toward the fallopian tubes. If this happens within 24 hours of ovulation, a sperm may penetrate the egg. This is called fertilization. The sperm's nucleus (23 chromosomes) fuses with that of the egg (23 chromosomes); the combined genetic material (46 chromosomes) gives the blueprint for a new human being.

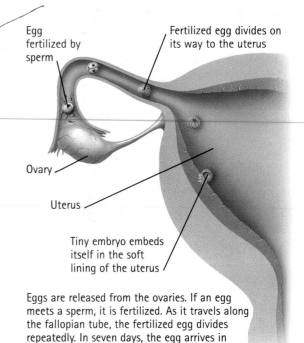

Egg fertilized by sperm
Fertilized egg divides on its way to the uterus
Ovary
Uterus
Tiny embryo embeds itself in the soft lining of the uterus

Eggs are released from the ovaries. If an egg meets a sperm, it is fertilized. As it travels along the fallopian tube, the fertilized egg divides repeatedly. In seven days, the egg arrives in the uterus. It is now a hollow ball of cells.

CONCEPTION

Conception is the time between fertilization and implantation. As the fertilized egg passes along the fallopian tube it divides repeatedly to form a ball of cells called a blastocyst, or conceptus. After seven days, this sinks into the soft lining of the uterus and becomes an embryo. If the cell separates into two parts when the fertilized egg first divides, the two cells will develop independently and result in identical twins. If two eggs are released during ovulation and both are fertilized by sperm, they will produce nonidentical, or fraternal, twins.

HOW A BABY DEVELOPS IN THE WOMB

After fertilization, the fertilized egg travels to the uterus. What started as a single cell becomes a fetus made up of billions of cells. Development occurs within a fluid-filled sac, protected within the uterus. Food and oxygen pass through the umbilical cord from the placenta, where blood from the fetus and mother come into close contact.

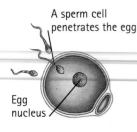

A sperm cell penetrates the egg
Egg nucleus

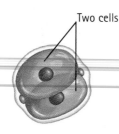

Two cells

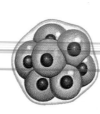

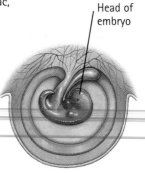

Head of embryo

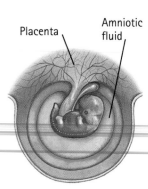

Placenta
Amniotic fluid

1 During fertilization, the nucleus of a sperm cell fuses with the nucleus of the egg to produce a fertilized egg.

2 Approximately 36 hours after the egg is fertilized, the egg has divided once, resulting in two cells.

3 About 72 hours after fertilization there are 16 cells. In a few days, the ball of cells will settle in the uterus.

4 After four weeks, the embryo is floating in a fluid-filled sac. The heart is beating, and the brain has started to develop.

5 After five weeks, the embryo is the size of an apple seed. It has buds that will become arms and legs. The tail is shrinking.

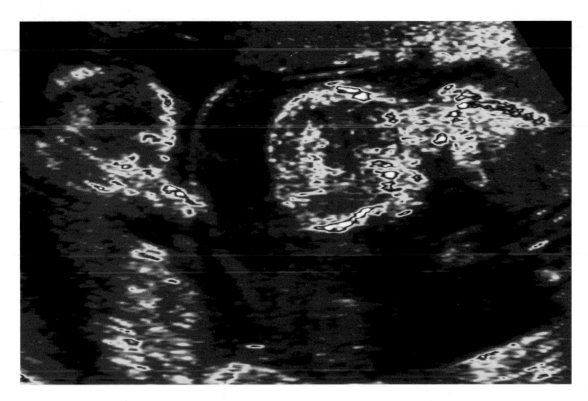

An ultrasound scan of the uterus of a pregnant woman shows that she is carrying twins. The left fetus is seen in side view, with its body directly below its head. The right fetus has its head facing down and its body horizontal. Both heads are at the top of the picture. Ultrasound is a safe, painless way of checking that the fetus is healthy. Sound waves are directed into the uterus. The echoes that bounce back produce an image.

The picture above shows a healthy baby boy. The human body never grows as fast as it did in the uterus. If growth continued at the same rate, a baby would be 5,280 feet tall by its first birthday.

PREGNANCY

Pregnancy is the time between conception and birth. For the first two months the developing baby is called an embryo. After this, when its organs are working, it is called a fetus. Amniotic fluid surrounds and protects the fetus. The growing baby is kept alive by the placenta, which is attached to the uterus. Inside the placenta, food and oxygen pass from the mother's blood to that of the fetus, and waste passes in the opposite direction. The umbilical cord carries blood between placenta and fetus.

BIRTH

About 38 weeks after fertilization, the uterus starts to contract. This process, called labor, usually begins about 12 hours before the birth. Powerful contractions push the baby out through the vagina, and the baby takes its first breath of air.

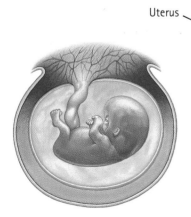

Uterus

6 After eight weeks, the embryo—now called a fetus—is about the same size as a strawberry and has developed tiny fingers and toes.

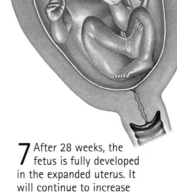

Uterus — Placenta

7 After 28 weeks, the fetus is fully developed in the expanded uterus. It will continue to increase in weight before birth.

Uterus — Umbilical cord — Amnion — Cervix — Vagina

8 At full term, about 38 weeks after fertilization, the fetus has moved its head downward in preparation for birth.

SEE ALSO PAGES:

98–9 Body organization, 134 Growth and development, 135 Genes and chromosomes

GROWTH AND DEVELOPMENT

Growth and development—from birth to adulthood—follow a fixed pattern in the first 20 years of life. By the age of 40, the first signs of aging begin to appear.

Growth and development occur simultaneously. Growth is an increase in size. Development is where cells specialize to perform specific functions. During the first year of their lives, infants are totally dependent on their parents for food and protection. However, the infant is already starting to develop skills such as talking, walking, and interacting with others. These skills become more obvious and develop further as an infant gets older.

▲ Mother and baby make eye contact. This bonding process starts from the very moment a baby is born. Being held makes babies feel secure; they respond by smiling and making noises. Bonding reinforces the natural feelings parents have for their children.

▼ Every person follows the same pattern of growth and development. There are slight differences between the development of the male and female reproductive systems. After rapid growth in the first year, children grow steadily until their early teens. Then, during puberty, the body grows rapidly and takes on an adult appearance. By the age of 20, the body has completed its growth.

PUBERTY AND ADOLESCENCE

Puberty is a time of rapid growth that leads to sexual maturity. It starts around the age of 11 in girls and about 13 in boys. In both sexes, underarm and pubic hair grows. A girl's body becomes more rounded. Breasts develop, and the hips become wider. Her ovaries start to release eggs, and menstruation begins. A boy's body becomes more muscular and hairy. His shoulders widen, his voice deepens, and the testes start to produce sperm. Puberty is part of adolescence, and also involves mental changes. These changes make a young adult become more independent and develop sexual feelings.

Face and skull aged 6

Face and skull aged 16

Two photos of the same person taken at different ages show how the face changes shape between the ages of 6 and 16. The bones of the face—as shown by the shape of the skulls—grow rapidly during late childhood.

AGING

The body ages fairly rapidly after the age of 40. As cells become less efficient, the skin becomes more wrinkled, muscles less powerful, bones more brittle, senses less acute, and the hair thins and turns gray. Eventually, one or more body systems stop working and the person dies.

Age 2   Age 6   Age 10–12   Age 20–22   Age 30–34

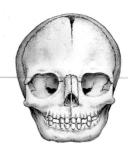

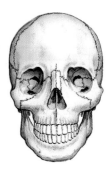

SEE ALSO PAGES:

111 Communication, 118–9 Hormones, 132–3 Reproduction, 135 Genes and chromosomes

GENES AND CHROMOSOMES

Chromosomes are found in the nucleus of nearly every cell. Each chromosome contains sets of instructions called genes.

DNA

Deoxyribonucleic acid, or DNA, stores the information needed to build a cell. Together, cells make up a functioning human body. DNA molecules are coiled up and packaged on threadlike chromosomes. There are 46 chromosomes in the nucleus of most cells. DNA molecules are organized into two linked strands that spiral around one another, forming a structure called a double helix. The strands are held together by four different chemicals called bases. The sequence of bases along a DNA molecule provides coded instructions for cell construction and operation.

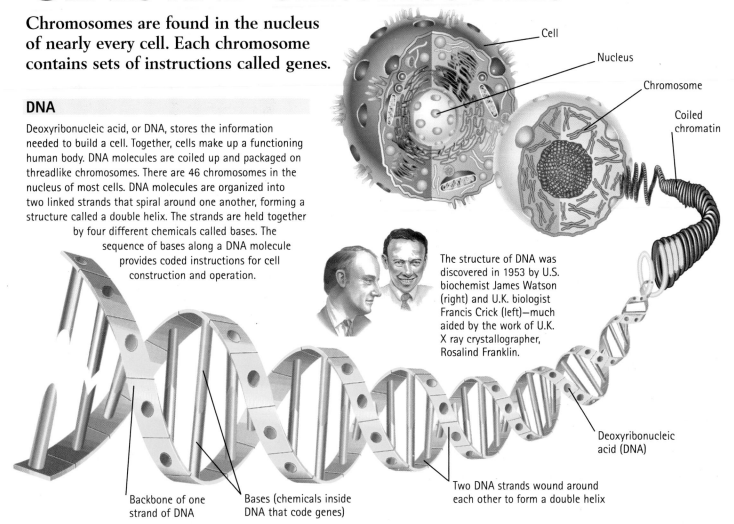

Cell

Nucleus

Chromosome

Coiled chromatin

The structure of DNA was discovered in 1953 by U.S. biochemist James Watson (right) and U.K. biologist Francis Crick (left)—much aided by the work of U.K. X ray crystallographer, Rosalind Franklin.

Deoxyribonucleic acid (DNA)

Two DNA strands wound around each other to form a double helix

Backbone of one strand of DNA

Bases (chemicals inside DNA that code genes)

There are about 100,000 genes in the human body. A single gene consists of a small section of a DNA molecule. Each gene instructs a cell to make a specific protein. Because proteins control cell metabolism, genes shape and operate our bodies. Apart from identical twins, gene combinations vary slightly for each person. Genes are arranged on a pair of matching chromosomes, one maternal (from the mother) and one paternal (from the father). There are two versions of the same gene on each pair of matching chromosomes. For example, a maternal chromosome may carry a gene for brown eyes, and a paternal chromosome a gene for blue eyes. In this case, only the brown gene is expressed and the child has brown eyes. The Human Genome Project, being carried out by scientists worldwide, aims to identify every human gene to find out what it controls.

CHROMOSOMES

Chromosomes contain thousands of genes. Genes are passed on from parents to their offspring. In the ovaries and testes, a process of cell division called meiosis makes sex cells (eggs and sperm) that contain 23 chromosomes. At fertilization, a sperm cell joins the egg to produce the full complement of 46 chromosomes. One pair of chromosomes, the sex chromosomes, differs from the other 22 pairs of chromosomes. While they carry genes, they are not the same in both sexes. Males have a longer (X) chromosome paired with a shorter (Y) chromosome. Females have two X chromosomes. The presence of XY chromosomes in the embryo causes male reproductive organs to be formed.

▼ An electron micrograph reveals 8 of the 46 chromosomes found inside the nucleus of a human cell. This image was taken during mitosis. In this type of cell division, the chromosomes become much shorter and thicker.

SEE ALSO PAGES:

132 Reproduction, 134 Growth and development, 136 Bacteria and viruses

BACTERIA AND VIRUSES

Bacteria are microorganisms, whereas viruses are packages of chemicals. Some bacteria and viruses, called pathogens, can infect the body and cause disease.

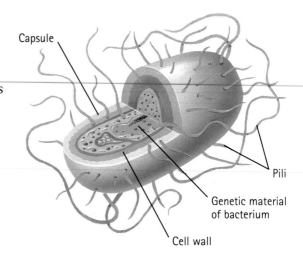

Capsule

Pili

Genetic material of bacterium

Cell wall

Diseases like the common cold are spread from person to person through tiny droplets in the air. If an infected person sneezes, droplets filled with microorganisms are projected out of the nose and into the air at high speed. If other people breathe them in, they may become infected.

▼ A virus reproduces by attaching itself to a cell (1). It injects its genetic material into the cell (2), which interferes with the cell's metabolism (3) and forces it to make new viruses (4). The new viruses then break out of the dying host cell (5).

Bacteria are single-celled microorganisms that are much simpler than the cells that make up plants and animals. Bacteria are everywhere. They thrive in the soil, the air, and even in our digestive systems. Most bacteria are harmless organisms, but some species, called pathogens, are harmful and cause disease. Pathogenic bacteria are divided into three groups according to their shape. Cocci are spherical and cause sore throats, boils, and pneumonia. Bacilli are shaped like rods and cause typhoid and salmonella. Spirochetes are spiral and cause Lyme disease and syphilis.

Bacteria invade the body in various ways: in droplets that are breathed in from the air, through cuts in the skin, in water or food that is swallowed, and through the reproductive system during intercourse. Once inside the body, bacteria feed and divide and release toxins that harm human cells. Usually, the immune system detects bacteria and destroys them. Infections can also be treated by antibiotics. They can be prevented by immunization, proper hygiene, clean drinking water, and by cleaning wounds with an antiseptic.

Bacteria are prokaryotes (simple cells). Unlike eukaryotes (complex cells), prokaryotes do not contain a nucleus or other organelles. They are surrounded by a cell wall and a protective outer capsule. The rod-shaped bacterium, or bacillus, above is covered with fine threads called pili. Pili are used to attach the bacterium to food or other cells.

VIRUSES

Viruses cause many human diseases, including cold sores (herpes), the common cold, measles, and mumps. Viruses are non-living packages of chemicals, consisting of a strand of genetic material—either DNA or RNA—surrounded by a protein coat. In order to reproduce, viruses invade a host cell and copy themselves. They cause disease either by destroying their host cell or through the response of the immune system to them, which may result in fatigue, fever, or even severe tissue damage. Most viruses are dealt with by the immune system without ill effects. Some infections, such as herpes, can hide inside the body, reemerging periodically to cause further outbreaks. Some viral infections can be prevented by immunization, but most are difficult to treat using drugs. Antibiotics are totally ineffective. One viral disease, human immunodeficiency virus (HIV), attacks the immune system itself. In time, opportunistic infections attack the defenseless body, causing acquired immunodeficiency syndrome or AIDS. There is no cure for HIV at present.

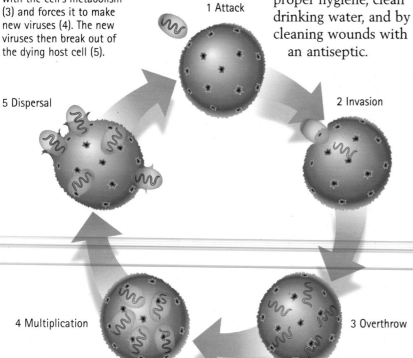

1 Attack

2 Invasion

3 Overthrow

4 Multiplication

5 Dispersal

SEE ALSO PAGES:

137 The immune system, 138 Disease, 452 Water pollution

THE IMMUNE SYSTEM

The human body is under constant threat from pathogens. The immune system provides a formidable defense against these disease-causing microorganisms.

Red blood cell

White blood cell

Bacterium

Blood vessel

There are three ways the body defends itself from invading pathogens. Physical barriers include the skin, and tears and saliva, which contain the bacteria-killing chemical lysozyme. Pathogens that do get through are engulfed by white blood cells called phagocytes, destroyed by natural killer cells in the lymphatic system, or targeted by antimicrobial proteins. Lastly, pathogens are tackled by the most powerful line of defense—the immune system.

1 The immune system is made up of defensive white blood cells found in the lymphatic system and in blood. The white blood cells shown above are called B lymphocytes. They recognize antigens (markers) on the surface of bacteria that have invaded the bloodstream.

English doctor Edward Jenner (1749–1823), shown above, performed the first vaccination. He used the fluid taken from a blister caused by a mild infection called cowpox to vaccinate a boy against a related but often fatal disease called smallpox. When exposed to smallpox, the boy survived.

Magnified 2340 times, a white blood cell—called a macrophage, is engulfing a pathogenic protist (blue). This protist causes a tropical disease called leishmaniasis, resulting in painful ulcers. It is spread to humans by bites from infected sandflies.

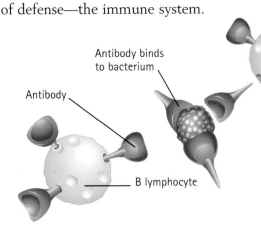

Antibody binds to bacterium

Antibody

B lymphocyte

2 The B lymphocytes multiply rapidly, producing plasma cells. These cells release antibodies, which attack the invading bacteria. Antibodies lock onto the antigens and disable the bacteria.

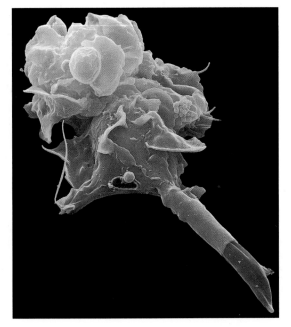

THE IMMUNE RESPONSE

The immune system consists of cells called lymphocytes, which recognize chemicals called antigens on the pathogens' surfaces. B cells, or B lymphocytes release antibodies that lock onto specific antigens, disable pathogens, and mark them for destruction. T cells, or T lymphocytes identify and directly destroy pathogens. Memory cells "memorize" antigens. The immune system takes a few days to respond to a new antigen—the primary response. The person may become ill. The next time, memory cells cause a rapid response by B and T lymphocytes—the secondary response—destroying invaders. The person is now immune to the disease.

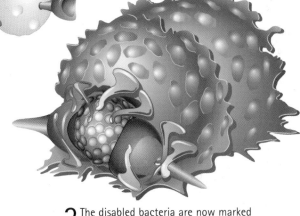

3 The disabled bacteria are now marked for destruction. White blood cells, called macrophages, seek them out and destroy them. Some lymphocytes, called memory cells, can memorize the invader's identity.

IMMUNIZATION (VACCINATION)

Immunization primes the immune system to act rapidly against particularly nasty pathogens. A person is injected with a vaccine containing altered pathogens. These stimulate the immune system to produce antibodies without causing sickness. If the real pathogen later invades the body, the immune system responds immediately. Active immunization has significantly decreased infectious diseases worldwide. In 1975, for example, it eradicated smallpox.

SEE ALSO PAGES:

DISEASE

Disease occurs when there is a breakdown in the body's normal functioning. It may be caused by external agents, such as bacteria, or internal disruption, such as cancer.

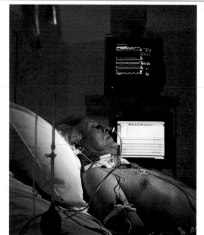

Here a patient in an intensive care unit has his heart rate and blood pressure continuously monitored and is given oxygen. The screen (top) shows his heart rate (green), blood pressure (red and light blue), blood oxygen levels (dark blue), and breathing rate (white).

Many diseases are short-lived; others are more serious and require medicine or surgery to tackle them. Diseases fall into two groups: infectious and noninfectious. Infectious diseases are caused by organisms called pathogens, particularly bacteria and viruses. Some are caused by single-celled protists, such as malaria and sleeping sickness; by fungi, such as athlete's foot; or by parasitic worms, such as tapeworms that live and feed in the small intestine.

Pathogens invade the body through various routes including the mouth or nose and through cuts. Some diseases are spread by insects like mosquitoes, fleas, and and lice. Rabies can be caught from the bite an infected animal.

If these diseases are not immediately challenged by the immune system, pathogens multiply, attack tissues, and cause infection. Infections, such as colds or measles, that are passed on easily, are called contagious; they may result in epidemics and affect many people.

This scolex, or head of the 10-meter–long beef tapeworm, is magnified 22 times. Its suckers grip the wall of the small intestine. Humans become infected by eating raw beef.

NONINFECTIOUS DISEASES

Noninfectious diseases are the most common cause of death in developing countries. People cannot catch these diseases. Instead, they are caused by instructions contained within genes; by hazardous chemicals in the environment; by lifestyle factors such as smoking, poor diet, or lack of exercise; or by a combination of these factors. The most common noninfectious diseases are heart disease and cancer. Some noninfectious diseases are inherited. They include sickle-cell anemia, where red blood cells do not work properly, and cystic fibrosis, where breathing and digestion are affected.

African tsetse flies feed on human blood by pushing their tubular, sucking mouthparts into the skin. These flies also carry a protist parasite that causes trypanosomiasis, or sleeping sickness. As the fly feeds, parasites enter a person's bloodstream and invade the lymphatic system and brain. An infected person suffers confusion and extreme tiredness and eventually dies. Infection is diagnosed through blood samples (far right) and can be treated with drugs.

Parasite that causes sleeping sickness in bloodstream

Human skin

Tsetse fly uses proboscis to bite through skin and into blood vessel

Red blood cell

SEE ALSO PAGES:

136 Bacteria and viruses,
137 The immune system,
140–1 Medicine

EXERCISE AND FITNESS

A fit body is one that is more likely to be, and remain, healthy. Fitness is achieved through regular exercise, reducing stress, and eating a balanced diet.

Fitness is a person's ability to carry out a wide range of everyday activities without any undue stress, tiredness, or gasping for breath. Unfortunately, modern lifestyles tend to make humans less fit. Whereas everyday activities such as hunting would have kept our ancestors fit, modern humans use buses or cars rather than walk, and spend hours sitting in front of the television or computer. This lack of activity makes people more prone to lifestyle problems such as heart disease. Fortunately, regular exercise can improve both fitness and health. Among other benefits, it reduces body fat and weight, makes the heart and lungs more efficient, improves posture and muscle tone, reduces the risk of heart disease, reduces stress, and helps a person to sleep more soundly.

TYPES OF FITNESS

Exercise improves fitness in three areas: stamina, muscle fitness, and flexibility. Stamina, or cardiovascular endurance, is the ability of the heart and blood vessels to deliver oxygen efficiently to the body's cells. It is improved by regular aerobic exercise, such as running or cycling.

Muscle fitness has two parts. Muscle strength—the force a muscle produces—is improved by, for example, weight training. Muscle endurance, the muscle's ability to contract repeatedly in a short time, is improved, for example, by running or cross-country skiing.

Flexibility is the ability of muscles to stretch and the joints to move freely and without discomfort through a full range of movement. Activities such as yoga and swimming improve flexibility.

A varied exercise program will improve all aspects of fitness. Before exercise, it is important to warm up to help prevent damage to muscles and other tissues. Cooling down after exercise, preferably by stretching, is also important.

▲ Stretching forms an important part of an exercise routine, especially during cooling down. This woman is supporting the man as he stretches muscles in his arms, the side of his body, and his legs. Stretching makes muscles and joints more flexible. This increases the body's range of movement as well as preventing muscle stiffness.

▶ During aerobic exercise, muscles need more glucose and oxygen to provide extra energy. The heart speeds up to pump more blood to the muscles. The breathing rate increases to get more oxygen into the blood. Blood is diverted from other body parts, such as the digestive system, to hardworking muscles. Regular exercise improves fitness by increasing the efficiency of heart, lungs, and muscles.

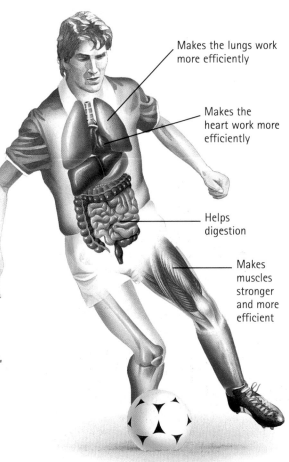

Makes the lungs work more efficiently

Makes the heart work more efficiently

Helps digestion

Makes muscles stronger and more efficient

▲ Aquarobics provides the benefits of aerobic exercise, but reduces strain on the knees because the body is supported in water.

SEE ALSO PAGES:

120–1 The heart and circulation, 124–5 Lungs and breathing

MEDICINE

Medicine is the study, treatment, and prevention of human disease. Modern medicine helps people to live longer and healthier lives.

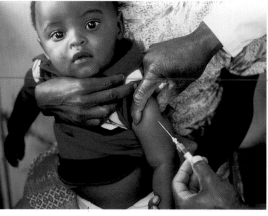

This child is being injected with the DPT vaccine. It will immunize, or protect, him against three diseases: diphtheria, pertussis (whooping cough), and tetanus.

Medicine deals with all aspects of disease, including its causes, prevention, and treatment. It was only in the 1900s that the effective cure and control of disease became possible. For the first time there were skilled, well-trained doctors and nurses. A wide range of drugs, such as bacteria-killing antibiotics, became available, as did immunization to eliminate childhood diseases, such as polio. Doctors had new ways of diagnosing their patients' illnesses. Patients could survive surgery because it was carried out in clean, germ-free conditions, using sterile instruments and with the patient anesthetized. Many new surgical methods, such as transplants, were developed.

Liquid medications, such as syrup, make swallowing medicine easier.

Capsules and pills are commonly used to give drugs to a patient.

Drugs can be injected into the blood or under the skin using hypodermics.

Inhalers and eyedrops send drugs rapidly to their target area.

Sometimes medicine needs to be released into the bloodstream slowly. Slow-release capsules contain hundreds of tiny, hollow balls, or pellets, which contain the drug. Pellets are color-coded according to how thick their outer coat is. Thin-coated pellets release their contents into the stomach soon after swallowing; thick-coated pellets release the drug later in the small intestine.

PREVENTIVE MEDICINE

Preventive medicine deals with the prevention of disease. Clean drinking water and efficient sewage-treatment systems are public health measures that prevent the spread of disease through water. Health education informs people about the health risks of smoking cigarettes or drinking too much alcohol and about the benefits of regular exercise and a balanced diet. Immunization protects children against serious diseases. Screening programs detect diseases such as cancer or high blood pressure (hypertension) before they cause symptoms.

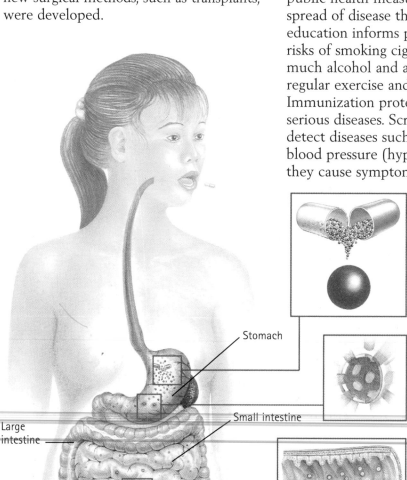

Stomach

Small intestine

Large intestine

1 Within an hour of swallowing, digestive enzymes in the stomach dissolve the outer capsule so that it releases its color-coded pellets.

2 Pellets with the thinnest outer coat dissolve in the stomach. The drug they contain is absorbed through the stomach wall into the bloodstream.

3 A few hours after swallowing, enzymes break open pellets with a thicker coat. Their content is absorbed through the wall of the small intestine.

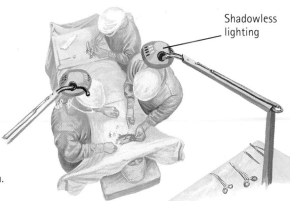

◄ Doctors use different pieces of equipment to look for signs of disease to make a diagnosis. Here a doctor is using an ophthalmoscope to examine a woman's eye. The instrument may reveal problems with vision, or the eye's blood vessels may show whether she has any problems with circulation.

Shadowless lighting

DIAGNOSIS

A doctor makes a diagnosis to determine what is wrong with a patient. To do this, the doctor follows a series of logical steps. First, the doctor listens to the patient talk about the symptoms; that is, those things the patient feels are wrong. The doctor asks for an account of the illness: how long the symptoms have been present and whether the patient has experienced them before. Second, the doctor examines the patient to look for identifiable signs of disease. This may involve pressing affected part of the body or using instruments like a stethoscope to listen to the heart and lungs, or a sphygmomanometer to measure blood pressure. If more information is needed, the doctor may order tests to analyze blood or urine, or body images such as X rays or CAT scans.

TREATMENT

If the doctor can make a diagnosis, the patient can often be treated. If the doctor is still unsure or feels that the disease is too serious to deal with, he or she may refer the patient to a specialist. Treatment often uses drugs, which are chemicals that alter the working of the body to get rid of the cause of the disease. Other forms of treatment are bed rest, physical therapy to aid recovery from muscle or bone injury, radiation therapy to destroy tumors (growths), or a surgical procedure.

ALTERNATIVE THERAPIES

Many alternative therapies are becoming accepted by conventional medicine. Some, such as acupuncture and herbalism, have ancient origins. Others, such as osteopathy and homeopathy, are more recent.

Alternative therapies tend to treat the whole person rather than individual symptoms. Acupuncture uses fine needles to restore health. Herbalism uses traditional plant extracts to treat a person. Yoga involves meditation and posture correction to relieve stress and improve flexibility. Osteopathy uses manipulation and massage. Homeopathy treats disease with drugs that produce the same symptoms as the disease.

This patient is undergoing an operation in an operating room. The patient lies on an operating table. The patient who has been given a general anesthetic, is completely unconscious and does not feel anything. Doctors wear masks and gowns to avoid passing on any infections. They use instruments to open a patient's body in order to diagnose or treat a disease.

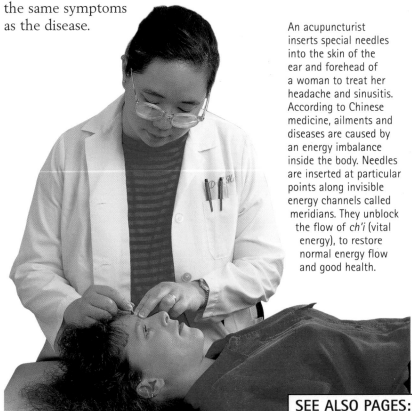

An acupuncturist inserts special needles into the skin of the ear and forehead of a woman to treat her headache and sinusitis. According to Chinese medicine, ailments and diseases are caused by an energy imbalance inside the body. Needles are inserted at particular points along invisible energy channels called meridians. They unblock the flow of ch'i (vital energy), to restore normal energy flow and good health.

SEE ALSO PAGES:
137 The immune system, 138 Disease, 139 Exercise and fitness, 142–3 Medical technology

MEDICAL TECHNOLOGY

Modern medicine owes a lot to advances in technology in the 1900s. New techniques allow doctors to diagnose and treat diseases more effectively.

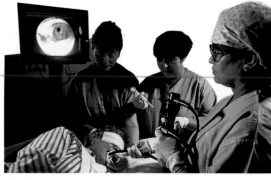

Doctors look inside the body using an endoscope to make a diagnosis or carry out treatment. Here, doctors insert an endoscope through the mouth to examine a patient's stomach. The view inside appears on the screen.

Wilhelm von Röntgen (1845–1923) discovered X rays. X rays reveal the hard parts of the body, like bones. For the first time doctors were able to look inside a living body without cutting it open.

Medical technology allows doctors to treat diseases and to perform complicated surgery under safer conditions. Imaging techniques produce a clear, electronic picture of the inside of the body so doctors can pinpoint problems. Endoscopy allows doctors to look directly through a viewing tube inside the body to see what is wrong.

Together, imaging and endoscopy mean doctors can perform minimally invasive, or keyhole, surgery, entering the body through the smallest of incisions (cuts). This minimizes tissue damage and makes recovery time for the patient shorter. The use of lasers, such as the laser scalpel, to cut through tissue, remove growths, and seal blood vessels is much more effective than standard surgical methods.

Computers are now a major part of medicine. They are used in scanning to generate and store images and to transmit them elsewhere. Virtual-reality systems are used to train doctors in surgical techniques without their having to touch a patient.

ENDOSCOPY

Doctors use endoscopes to look inside the body to diagnose or treat diseases. Modern endoscopes are narrow and flexible and are inserted either through body openings into the digestive, respiratory, urinary, or reproductive systems; or through incisions in the skin into body cavities. Endoscopes use long, thin optical fibers to illuminate and transfer the images onto a monitor screen, which the doctor looks at while conducting the examination. The endoscope may also have, for example, tiny forceps to carry out a biopsy (the taking of a tissue sample) for diagnosis.

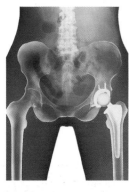

This X ray image shows an artificial hip joint. In the past, a diseased hip joint used to stop a person from walking. Today, it can be removed and replaced by a prosthesis (artificial part) made of stainless steel and plastic.

▶ Lasers produce a concentrated beam of light radiation. They have many uses, including cutting through tissue, and destroying tumors (growths). Here a doctor aims a laser into the eye of a patient using a retinal camera. The laser beam is delivered in a series of short bursts. In eye surgery it can be used to mend a detached retina or to seal blood vessels to stop their bleeding.

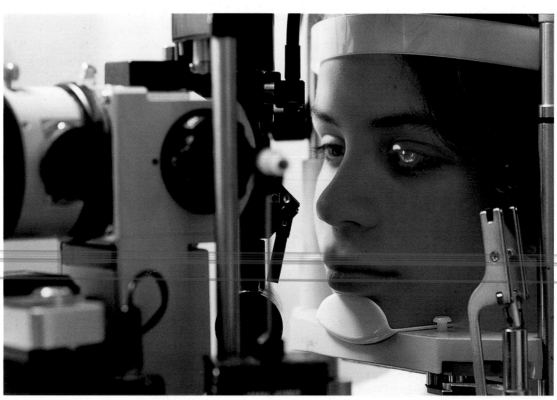

LOOKING INSIDE THE BODY

A computerized axial tomography (CAT) scanner combines X rays and a computer to produce clear "slices" through the body. These reveal far more about the body's tissues than do X rays alone. Here a patient's head is going to be scanned. He lies on the scanner table and remains still while scanning takes place. As the scanner rotates around the patient, bursts of X-ray beams, each lasting a fraction of a second, pass through his head at different angles. The way in which X rays are absorbed by different parts of the head is recorded by detectors.

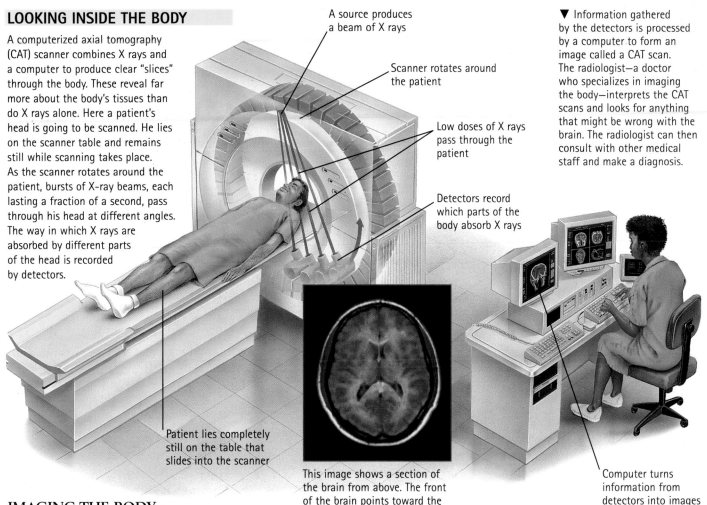

A source produces a beam of X rays

Scanner rotates around the patient

Low doses of X rays pass through the patient

Detectors record which parts of the body absorb X rays

Patient lies completely still on the table that slides into the scanner

This image shows a section of the brain from above. The front of the brain points toward the top of the page.

Computer turns information from detectors into images

▼ Information gathered by the detectors is processed by a computer to form an image called a CAT scan. The radiologist—a doctor who specializes in imaging the body—interprets the CAT scans and looks for anything that might be wrong with the brain. The radiologist can then consult with other medical staff and make a diagnosis.

IMAGING THE BODY

Imaging techniques allow doctors to look inside the body to make diagnoses and plan treatment without having to cut the body open. The pioneer of imaging was Wilhelm von Röntgen, who discovered X rays in 1895. This remained the only useful imaging method until the 1970s. Since then a new generation of imaging techniques has been developed.

Although they work in different ways, all scan a particular body region piece by piece and then use a computer to make two- or three-dimensional images.

Ultrasound is the most common imaging technique. It uses inaudible, high-frequency sound waves that are reflected from body parts. It is a safe method for observing unborn babies and for viewing moving parts, such as blood flow through the heart.

CAT scans use X rays to form images. PET (positron-emission tomography) scans use radioactive substances that, when injected into the body, reveal active cells within the scanned parts of the body.

REPLACEMENT PARTS

Many diseased or damaged body parts can be replaced. The earliest replacement parts were prostheses such as wooden legs. Modern prostheses, plastic arms with moving fingers, for example, are more lifelike. Internal replacement parts are a relatively recent development.

Transplantation takes a living organ from a donor and inserts it into the patient. Kidney transplants, for example, are carried out to treat people with kidney failure. The body's immune system regards transplanted organs as foreign and attempts to reject them. The transplant patient has to take medicine that prevents rejection by reducing the effectiveness of the immune system.

Implants are artificial internal devices that are not rejected by the immune system. They include artificial joints that can replace diseased joints and electronic pacemakers that regulate heart rate.

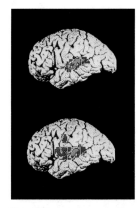

This PET scan shows brain areas at work. The top scan shows a person listening to words: the brain's hearing area (yellow) is working. Below, the person is listening to words and repeating them. Both hearing area and speech area (green) are activated.

SEE ALSO PAGES:

140–1 Medicine, 262–3 Reflection and absorption, 376–7 Computers

FACTS AND FIGURES

BRANCHES OF HUMAN BIOLOGY AND MEDICINE

Anatomists study the structure of the body and how its parts fit together.
Biochemists study the chemical processes that occur in and around the body's cells.
Cardiologists study the heart and blood vessels and diseases that affect them.
Cytologists study cells.
Dermatologists study the skin and its disorders.
Endocrinologists study the hormonal system and its disorders.
Epidemiologists study causes of diseases and their spread through populations.
Geneticists study DNA, chromosomes, genes, and the mechanism of inheritance.
Gynecologists study the female reproductive system and its disorders.
Hematologists study the properties and disorders of blood and bone marrow.
Histologists study body tissues.
Immunologists study the immune system and its disorders.
Neurologists study the nervous system and its disorders.
Oncologists study the causes, mechanisms, and treatment of cancers.
Ophthalmologists study the eye and its disorders.
Pathologists study and determine the causes of disease and death.
Physiologists study how the body's component parts function.
Psychiatrists study mental illness and its prevention and treatment.

BODY SYSTEMS

Circulatory system of heart, blood, and blood vessels carries materials to and from cells throughout the body.
Digestive system breaks down food so its nutrients can be used by the body.
Endocrine system releases hormones that control many body processes.
Immune system defends the body against microorganisms that cause diseases.
Integumentary system of skin, hair, and nails covers and protects the body.
Lymphatic system drains fluid from the tissues and destroys pathogens.
Muscular system moves the body and helps to support it.
Nervous system of brain, nerves, and sense organ, controls the body and allows a person to think and feel.
Skeletal system of bones, cartilage, and ligaments supports the body, protects internal organs, and permits movement.
Reproductive system allows humans to produce offspring.
Respiratory system carries oxygen into the bloodstream to be delivered to cells.
Urinary system removes waste materials.

KEY DATES

B.C.

c.500 Greek physician and philosopher Alcmaeon proposes that the brain, rather than the heart, is the organ of thinking and feeling.

c.420 Greek physician Hippocrates teaches a diagnostic approach to medicine based on observation.

A.D.

129 Birth of Greek anatomist and doctor Galen, who wrote about the workings of the human body. His ideas, many of them false, held back the understanding of human biology and medicine for the next 1,000 years.

1037 Islamic physician and philosopher Avicenna dies. His medical texts continue to dominate European and Middle Eastern medicine for more than 500 years.

1268 British philosopher and scientist Roger Bacon records the use of glasses to correct eye defects.

1288 Syrian physician Ibn An-Nafis dies. He had demonstrated that blood flows through the lungs.

1543 Belgian anatomist Andreas Vesalius publishes an accurate description of human anatomy, correcting many of Galen's errors.

1628 English physician William Harvey publishes a description of how blood circulates around the body.

1661 Italian physiologist Marcello Malpighi discovers capillaries, the links between arteries and veins.

1674 Dutch microscopist Antoni van Leeuwenhoek observes and describes red blood cells.

1796 British physician Edward Jenner performs first vaccination and shows that cowpox fluid protects against smallpox.

1839 German physiologist Theodor Schwann proposes that animals consist of tiny, living cells.

1846 First use of an anesthetic— ether—during surgery in a Boston hospital.

1848 French physiologist Claude Bernard describes liver function and establishes concept of homeostasis.

1858 German biologist Rudolf Virchow shows that diseases occur when normal cells become defective, establishing cell pathology.

1860s French chemist and biologist Louis Pasteur establishes the link between germs and diseases.

1865 British surgeon Joseph Lister uses carbolic acid as an antiseptic during surgery and dramatically reduces deaths from infection.

1880 French surgeon Paul Broca dies. He discovered that parts of the brain control body functions.

1882 German physician Robert Koch discovers *Mycobacterium tuberculosis*, the bacterium that causes tuberculosis.

1895 German physicist Wilhelm Roentgen discovers X rays.

1899 British physician Ronald Ross proves that mosquitoes carry malaria from human to human.

1900 Austrian neurologist Sigmund Freud publishes *The Interpretation of Dreams*, which contains the basic concepts of psychoanalysis.

1900 Austrian-born U.S. pathologist Karl Landsteiner discovers blood groups A, O, B, and AB.

1907 British biochemist Frederick Hopkins discovers vitamins.

1910 U.S. biologist Thomas Morgan discovers how chromosomes carry genetic information.

1922 Canadian physiologists Frederick Banting and Charles Best discover insulin, providing a means to control diabetes.

1928 British microbiologist Alexander Fleming discovers penicillin, the first antibiotic.

1951 British physicist Francis Crick and U.S. biologist James Watson discover the structure of DNA, helped by the X ray evidence provided by British biophysicist Rosalind Franklin.

1952 U.S. physician Jonas Salk develops the first polio vaccine.

1958 First ultrasound scan taken of a fetus in its mother's uterus.

1967 South African surgeon Christiaan Barnard performs the first successful heart transplant.

1972 Computerized axial tomography (CAT) scanning introduced as a means of producing images of the internal organs of the body.

1979 World declared free of the killer disease smallpox as a result of a worldwide vaccination campaign.

1981 The first cases of Acquired Immune Deficiency Syndrome (AIDS) reported. AIDS is recognized as a new disease.

1990 The Human Genome Project is started in the U.S. to analyze human DNA and find the genes in all 46 human chromosomes.

1995 Work starts to develop genetic engineering techniques as a possible means for treating inherited diseases.

1999 Chromosome 22 becomes the first human chromosome to have all its genes identified.

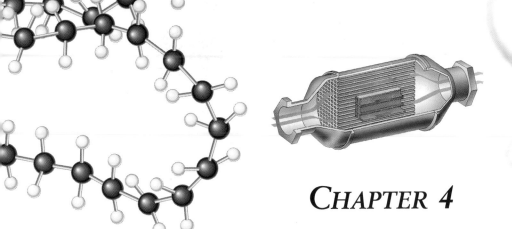

CHAPTER 4

CHEMISTRY AND THE ELEMENTS

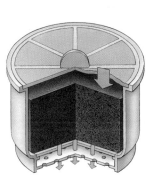

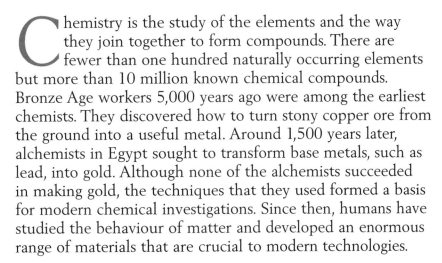

Chemistry is the study of the elements and the way they join together to form compounds. There are fewer than one hundred naturally occurring elements but more than 10 million known chemical compounds. Bronze Age workers 5,000 years ago were among the earliest chemists. They discovered how to turn stony copper ore from the ground into a useful metal. Around 1,500 years later, alchemists in Egypt sought to transform base metals, such as lead, into gold. Although none of the alchemists succeeded in making gold, the techniques that they used formed a basis for modern chemical investigations. Since then, humans have studied the behaviour of matter and developed an enormous range of materials that are crucial to modern technologies.

The chemical industry provides the concrete, metals and plastics to create buildings, machinery, and vehicles; fuels for transportation and heating; synthetic fibers for clothes; and fertilizers and pesticides to improve the yield of food crops. The knowledge of chemistry makes it possible to produce high-quality silicon for microprocessors. Biochemistry helps us to understand the processes that occur in living organisms, and pharmacological chemistry provides drugs and medicines to treat diseases, many of which were once impossible to cure.

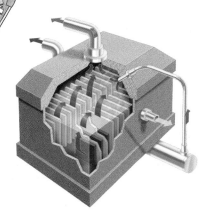

THE ORIGINS OF CHEMISTRY

Modern chemistry started to develop about 200 years ago from the ancient studies made by alchemists during the previous 2,000 years.

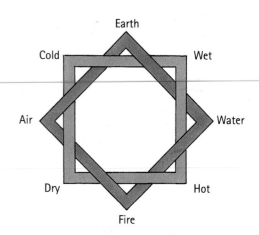

Alchemists thought that there were four elements: air, earth, fire, and water. Each element contained two of four properties: cold, dry, hot, and wet.

Centuries ago, most of the people who studied alchemy had the same goal in mind: they wanted to discover a way to change ordinary metals like iron and lead into gold. Apart from being valuable, gold was thought to cure all diseases and give everlasting life. Alchemy can be traced back thousands of years to a mixture of ideas formed by philosophers, magicians, and stargazers. The earliest writing about alchemy comes from Egypt (1500 B.C.), China (600 B.C.), and Greece (500 B.C.). Some people think the name alchemy comes from the Arabic *al-Khem*, meaning "the art of Egypt."

Like modern chemists, early alchemists spent their time trying to change one substance into another. Unlike modern chemists, they did not carry out scientific experiments to discover how and why changes happened. For centuries, they stirred and heated their strange mixtures and recited their spells. Although they did not discover a way to turn common metals into gold, alchemists invented many useful pieces of apparatus, and developed techniques to make solutions and separate mixtures by filtering and distilling.

ALCHEMICAL THEORIES

One of the main theories of alchemy was the theory of the four elements. This theory claimed that all substances are made from different mixtures of just four elements. These elements are air, earth, fire, and water. Each element is made from a pair of four properties: cold, dry, hot, and wet. Fire is a combination of hot and dry, earth is dry and cold, air is hot and wet, and water is wet and cold. Alchemists would explain a process such as boiling by saying that heat was driving out the cold from cold-wet water, for example, to form the hot-wet air that is steam.

This alembic is 1,000 years old. It was used by Islamic alchemists to distill liquids. Impure liquid would be boiled in the bottom part. Vapors would condense in the dome, and purified liquid would trickle out through the spout.

The English scholar and philosopher Roger Bacon (1214–1292) concentrated his early studies in magic and alchemy. About 1250, he became a Franciscan monk and turned his interest toward science and experimentation. He wrote widely on mathematics, as well as science and philosophy. He encouraged people to learn from their own experience, rather than simply accepting ideas written in ancient books.

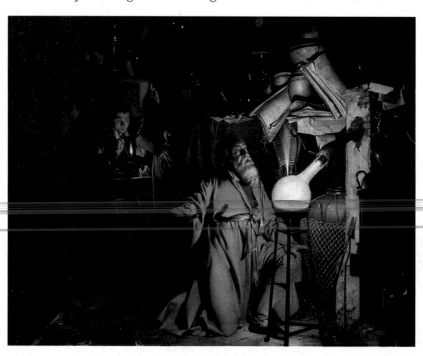

The obsession of alchemy was to change base metals into the highly desirable, noble metal gold. In 1669, the alchemist Hennig Brand of Hamburg was experimenting with mixtures containing urine collected from lions. He thought that the golden liquid made by these noble animals would contain gold. Instead, he discovered a new glowing element that he called phosphorus. In Greek the word means "light-bearing."

THE DECLINE OF ALCHEMY

The study of alchemy reached its peak around A.D. 1400. From then on, people began to doubt the theories of alchemy that had been handed down through the ages. They started to perform experiments and make careful measurements. They tried to explain what they saw without the help of ideas based on magic and superstition. Their studies slowly became more organized and scientific. At the same time, the spread of printed books helped scholars to share their ideas.

THE BIRTH OF CHEMISTRY

Chemistry and alchemy existed together up to the middle of the 1600s. Then, in 1661, the British chemist Robert Boyle (1627–91) published *The Sceptical Chymist*. This book helped to untangle chemistry from alchemy and to set up chemistry as a subject in its own right.

Boyle used the ideas of Roger Bacon, a monk and philosopher, to lay down the rules for careful scientific investigation. He described experiments that proved that the four element system could not explain the behavior of many substances. Instead, Boyle said that each element is a single, pure substance that cannot be split into simpler substances. Interest in alchemy died as chemists concentrated on purifying substances and carefully investigating their properties.

A chemistry laboratory of 1914 used the same basic equipment as a modern laboratory—pure chemicals from bottles to carry out chemical reactions in glass apparatus.

DEVELOPMENTS

In 1766, English scientist Henry Cavendish discovered a way to make hydrogen gas by pouring acid onto metals such as zinc or iron. He called this gas "inflammable air" when he found that a lighted match would make it catch fire.

Around 1772, Swedish chemist Carl Scheele (1742–1786) discovered the presence of oxygen in air. In 1781, English chemist Joseph Priestley (1733–1804) showed that water forms when hydrogen burns in air. Later, Cavendish made water by burning hydrogen in oxygen. All these results were collected over about 15 years, but no one fully understood them. Then, in 1783, the French chemist Antoine-Laurent Lavoisier repeated Cavendish's experiments and used the idea of elements to explain the results. Lavoisier said that hydrogen and oxygen were elements, and that water was a compound of hydrogen and oxygen. He also suggested that metals were elements, and that acids were compounds that contained hydrogen. When metals and acids mixed, the metal was taking the place of hydrogen, which was released as a gas. This idea that elements break apart from each other and join up in different combinations is one of the foundations of modern chemistry.

In 1783, French chemist Antoine-Laurent Lavoisier (1743–1794) used this apparatus to show that hydrogen and oxygen combine to make water. This disproved the 2,000-year-old belief that water was an element.

English scientist Henry Cavendish (1731–1810) performed experiments with gases. He discovered hydrogen and showed that air is a mixture of gases. He also suggested that water was not an element.

SEE ALSO PAGES:

148–9 The elements,
154–5 Chemical analysis,
160–1 Separation and purification

THE ELEMENTS

Elements are substances that cannot be broken down by chemical methods. There are 92 naturally occurring elements and 20 synthetic elements.

Realgar

Pyrite

Malachite

Fluorite

All these substances are minerals found in the ground. Realgar contains the elements arsenic and sulfur, while pyrite contains iron and sulfur. Malachite is a mixture of copper carbonate and copper hydroxide, which together consist of copper, carbon, oxygen, and hydrogen. Fluorite contains calcium and fluorine.

Elements can be classified as metals and nonmetals. Metals are usually shiny solids that conduct electricity. Most metals only melt at high temperatures. Metals are malleable, which means they can be hammered into different shapes. Most are also ductile, which means they can be stretched without breaking. Iron, copper, zinc, and uranium are examples of metals.

With the exception of graphite—a form of carbon—nonmetals do not conduct electricity. Solid nonmetals, like sulfur and phosphorus, are brittle (they break into pieces when hit). Most non-metals melt at much lower temperatures than metals; many are gases at room temperature. Chlorine, hydrogen, and oxygen are nonmetals.

There are 92 natural elements. With the exceptions of helium and neon, all can combine with other elements to form compounds. Chemical reactions can be used to break down compounds and free the elements they contain.

Element	Symbol	Details
Iron	Fe	The Latin name *ferrum* was used for over 4,000 years.
Lead	Pb	The Latin name *plumbum* was used for more than 3,000 years.
Copper	Cu	The Latin name for Cyprus, *cuprum*, was used for more than 5,000 years.
Sodium	Na	First isolated pure in 1807. Latin name *natrium*.
Aluminum	Al	First isolated pure in 1825.
Uranium	U	Discovered 1789; isolated pure 1841. Named after the planet Uranus.
Plutonium	Pu	First made in 1940; named after the planet Pluto.
Phosphorus	P	Discovered in 1669.

About one fifth of the elements are nonmetals; the rest are metals. Most elements exist in nature as compounds that contain two or more elements joined together.

SYMBOLS AND NAMES

Chemists use symbols of one or two letters to represent the elements. The first letter is always a capital letter and the second letter is always a small letter. The symbols for hydrogen and zinc, for example, are H and Zn.

Elements discovered before about 1800 were often given Latin names. The Romans called lead *plumbum*. Since lead is easily bent into shape, the Romans used lead to make pipes for carrying water. The Latin name gives the symbol Pb and also shows the origin of the words plumber and plumbing. Metallic elements discovered more recently usually have names that end in -ium. Plutonium, for example, was discovered and named in 1940.

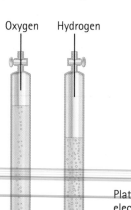

Oxygen   Hydrogen

Platinum electrodes

Anode connection   Cathode connection

An electric current can break down some liquids and solutions. This process, called electrolysis, can be used to decompose water into its elements.

▲▶ Phosphorus is a nonmetallic element. It must be stored underwater. When exposed to air, it catches fire and forms a compound called phosphorus oxide. Phosphorus also reacts violently in a stream of chlorine gas (right).

The airship *Hindenburg* contained 190,000 cubic meters of hydrogen. In 1937, 35 of the 97 people aboard died when the hydrogen exploded.

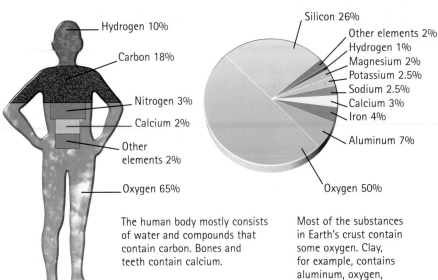

The human body mostly consists of water and compounds that contain carbon. Bones and teeth contain calcium.

Hydrogen 10%
Carbon 18%
Nitrogen 3%
Calcium 2%
Other elements 2%
Oxygen 65%

THE ELEMENTS

Silicon 26%
Other elements 2%
Hydrogen 1%
Magnesium 2%
Potassium 2.5%
Sodium 2.5%
Calcium 3%
Iron 4%
Aluminum 7%
Oxygen 50%

Most of the substances in Earth's crust contain some oxygen. Clay, for example, contains aluminum, oxygen, and silicon; sand is a combination of silicon and oxygen.

EARLY DISCOVERIES: METALS

A few elements are found in Earth's crust as pure substances. Because it does not combine easily with other elements, gold is an element that is found in rocks as tiny flakes or small lumps of pure metal. People first extracted and used gold about 5,500 years ago.

About 3,500 years ago, people discovered how to make iron by heating iron ore—a compound of iron and oxygen—with charcoal. Copper, lead, and zinc were made in similar ways.

EARLY DISCOVERIES: NONMETALS

Carbon and sulfur are the only nonmetals that occur as pure substances in nature. Carbon is found as diamonds and graphite; charcoal (an impure form of carbon) was made for centuries by partly burning wood. It was used to manufacture iron. Sulfur is found as solid, yellow lumps or powder around the craters of some volcanoes. From the early 1200s, it was used to make gunpowder and antiseptics.

LATER DISCOVERIES

Lavoisier founded modern chemistry in 1783 when he fixed the idea of elements at the center of the subject. Just 26 pure elements were known at that time. As their apparatus and techniques improved, chemists discovered new elements with increasing speed. By 1900, all the naturally occurring elements had been identified, purified, and given names.

SYNTHETIC ELEMENTS

The universe consists mainly of hydrogen (90%) and helium (9%). The immense pressures and temperatures inside stars like the sun cause nuclear reactions that turn hydrogen into helium. Further nuclear reactions squeeze hydrogen and helium together to make heavier elements. Earth formed from these elements when parts of the sun broke away. Here on Earth, scientists use nuclear reactions to make heavy, artificial elements from natural elements. These synthetic elements are so unstable that they decay and fall apart, often in minutes or even seconds.

Nuclear reactions convert atoms of one element into atoms of other elements. An enormous amount of energy is released as this happens: the explosive force of an atomic bomb can be equivalent to that of thousands of tons of ordinary explosives.

SEE ALSO PAGES:

146–7 The origins of chemistry, 170 Carbon, 181 Sulfur

ATOMS

The universe is made up of tiny particles called atoms. Atoms are so small that billions of them would fit on the period at the end of this sentence.

The English physicist and chemist John Dalton (1766–1844) produced an atomic theory of matter. Dalton believed that atoms were shaped like tiny spheres.

About 2,500 years ago, Greek philosophers argued about the make-up of matter. One group of thinkers, the atomists, believed that if it were possible to cut matter into smaller and smaller pieces, there would eventually be a piece so small that it could not be divided any more. The word *atom* comes from the Greek *atomos*, meaning "uncuttable."

Between 1803 and 1807, the English scientist John Dalton worked on these ideas in his atomic theory of matter. He said that atoms could not be created or destroyed. A pure sample of an element contains atoms that are all the same.

MODERN ATOMIC THEORY

Dalton's theory said nothing about the structure inside atoms. Then in 1897, the first subatomic particle, called the electron, was discovered. In 1911, the British physicist Ernest Rutherford (1871–1937) discovered that atoms contain dense, positively charged nuclei. In 1932, the neutron was discovered.

Modern atomic theory states that an atom consists of a nucleus of protons and neutrons surrounded by orbiting electrons. Neutrons and protons are more than 1,800 times as heavy as electrons. Protons have a positive charge, electrons have a negative charge, and neutrons are uncharged.

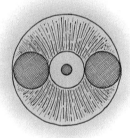

▲ Dalton invented symbols for different atoms. He suggested that atoms joined together to make compounds. This example of Dalton's diagrams shows two oxygen atoms joined to one carbon atom in carbon dioxide.

▶ The nucleus of an atom consists of protons and neutrons. The nucleus makes up most of an atom's mass. Electrons move in fixed orbits around the nucleus, because there is an electrical attraction between the negative charge of the electron and the positive charge of the protons in the nucleus. Neutrons help hold the nucleus together. Without them, the positively charged protons would repel each other.

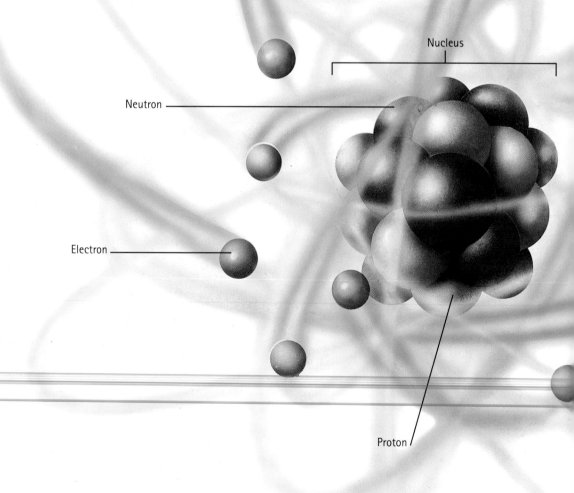

Nucleus

Neutron

Electron

Proton

ATOMS AND ELEMENTS

Atoms have equal numbers of electrons and protons. The negative charges of the electrons cancel out the positive charges of the protons. As a result, atoms have no overall electric charge.

The simplest element is hydrogen. It has one proton and one electron; it is the only element that does not contain a neutron. Other elements contain more electrons, protons, and neutrons, and are heavier than hydrogen. For example, aluminum atoms have 13 protons, 13 electrons, and 14 neutrons. Uranium is the heaviest naturally occurring element: it has 92 protons, 92 electrons, and 146 neutrons. Elements that are heavier than uranium are unstable. Their nuclei burst apart because the forces that draw the protons together are not strong enough to overcome the repulsion between their positive charges.

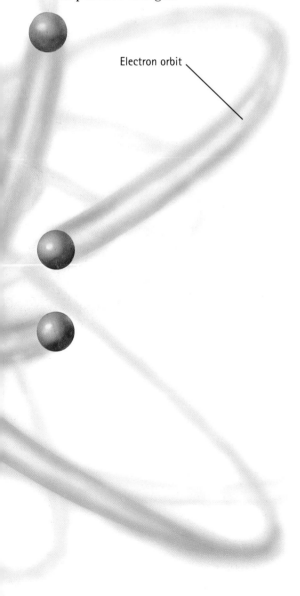

Electron orbit

◀ The atomic-force microscope (AFM) was developed during the 1980s. A computer monitors the forces on a tiny diamond point as it scans across the sample.

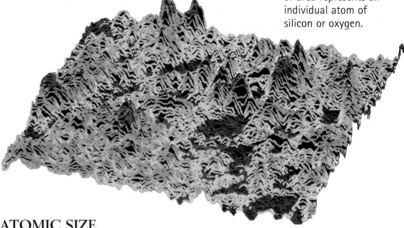

▼ This is a computer-generated AFM image of the surface of a piece of glass. Each raised point or area represents an individual atom of silicon or oxygen.

ATOMIC SIZE

Atomic theories are models that scientists use to explain the results of their experiments. Because atoms are so small, nobody has actually seen one—an atom would have to be magnified 100 million times to see an image just half an inch across. Another problem is that atoms are mostly empty space. A scale model with a tennis ball as the nucleus would use pinheads for the electrons, and the whole model would be about 3000 feet in diameter. Modern atomic theory also states that electrons move too fast to estimate their location in an atom with any certainty. They behave like a cloud of negative charge surrounding the nucleus.

SEEING IS BELIEVING?

Light waves are very large compared to the size of atoms. For this reason, ordinary optical microscopes cannot detect single atoms; they simply blur the images of millions of atoms together.

Atomic-force microscopes (AFMs) do not use light. Instead, a sharp probe moves back and forth across the surface of a sample, sensing the electron cloud around each atom. A computer builds up a picture of the atoms on the surface.

In 1922, Danish physicist Niels Bohr (1885–1962) won the Nobel Prize for physics for his theory of atomic structure.

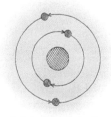

In Bohr's theory, electrons move around the nucleus of an atom in spherical shells called orbits.

SEE ALSO PAGES:

148–9 The elements,
156–7 States of matter,
168–9 Solid structures,
268–9 Microscopes

THE PERIODIC TABLE

The periodic table lists the chemical elements in order of increasing atomic number. Elements with similar properties are grouped together.

Sodium is in Group 1. Although it is a metal, it is so soft that a knife can cut easily through it. Sodium is stored in oil in order to stop air or moisture reacting with it.

Russian chemist Dmitry Mendeleyev (1834–1907) drew up the first periodic table in 1869. He left gaps in the table for elements not then discovered and predicted their properties by comparison with neighboring elements.

The periodic table lists all the elements in eighteen vertical columns, or groups; and seven horizontal rows, or periods. The elements are arranged so that their atomic numbers increase from left to right through a period. An element's atomic number is equal to the number of protons in its nucleus and the number of electrons orbiting the nucleus.

The groups of the periodic table are labeled 1–18 from left to right, although other numbering systems are sometimes used. Elements in the same group have similar properties. The chemical properties of an element depend largely on the number of outermost electrons.

THE STRUCTURE OF THE TABLE

The periodic table consists of four main areas, or blocks, named with the letters s, p, d, and f. Groups 1 and 2 form the s block on the left. The p block on the right contains groups 13 to 18. The d and f blocks form groups 3 to 12.

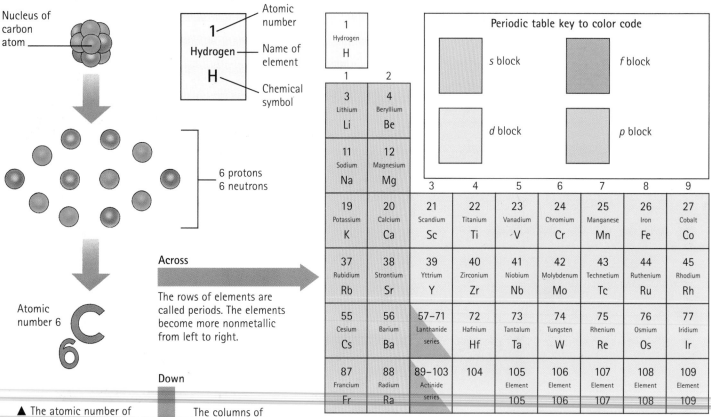

Nucleus of carbon atom

Atomic number
Name of element
Chemical symbol

6 protons
6 neutrons

Across

The rows of elements are called periods. The elements become more nonmetallic from left to right.

Atomic number 6

Down

▲ The atomic number of an element is the number of protons in an atom of that element. For carbon, this number is six. The chemical symbol for an element can be written with the atomic number, written below and to the left of the main symbol.

The columns of elements are the groups. Elements in the same group have similar properties. As atomic number increases down a group, the elements show increasing metallic character.

Periodic table key to color code

s block   f block
d block   p block

152

S-BLOCK ELEMENTS

With the exception of hydrogen, the elements of the s block are all very reactive, soft metals with low densities. Most group 1 metals melt below 212°F (100°C), and most group 2 metals melt below 1,652°F. Compounds of s-block elements are used to color fireworks. Sodium and potassium salts are needed for the nervous system to work properly; magnesium compounds are vital for making chlorophyll in plants.

D-BLOCK ELEMENTS

These elements are all hard, dense metals; most of them melt well above 1,832°F. The d-block metals include elements such as iron, copper, and titanium. They are much less reactive than s-block metals.

All the d-block metals have just one or two outermost electrons, so they have similar chemical properties. Although atomic number increases across all three periods, the extra electrons orbit on an inner shell, closer to the nucleus.

P-BLOCK ELEMENTS

This block is a mixture of metals and nonmetals. The elements above a diagonal line that runs from aluminum to polonium are nonmetals. Elements in the line and below it are metals. Tin and lead are typical p-block metals. They are softer than d-block metals and less reactive.

The gases nitrogen, oxygen, fluorine, and chlorine are at the top right of the p block. The members of group 18 are called the noble, or inert, gases because they are almost completely unreactive.

F-BLOCK ELEMENTS

These elements are all rare metals. The members of the first row are all very reactive. The second row elements are all radioactive; many of them are synthetic elements made in laboratories or in the cores of nuclear reactors.

This motorcycle engine is mostly made from alloys of aluminum and iron. Both metals are mixed with small amounts of other elements to make alloys. These substances are designed to withstand mechanical wear and tear.

▲ One of the fuels used in nuclear power plants is uranium, which is element 92. It has the highest atomic number of all the naturally occurring elements. Energy is released when the nucleus splits to form other elements.

												18
												2 Helium He
					13	14	15	16	17			
					5 Boron B	6 Carbon C	7 Nitrogen N	8 Oxygen O	9 Fluorine F			10 Neon Ne
					13 Aluminum Al	14 Silicon Si	15 Phosphorus P	16 Sulfur S	17 Chlorine Cl			18 Argon Ar
10	11	12										
28 Nickel Ni	29 Copper Cu	30 Zinc Zn	31 Gallium Ga	32 Germanium Ge	33 Arsenic As	34 Selenium Se	35 Bromine Br	36 Krypton Kr				
46 Palladium Pd	47 Silver Ag	48 Cadmium Cd	49 Indium In	50 Tin Sn	51 Antimony Sb	52 Tellurium Te	53 Iodine I	54 Xenon Xe				
78 Platinum Pt	79 Gold Au	80 Mercury Hg	81 Thallium Tl	82 Lead Pb	83 Bismuth Bi	84 Polonium Po	85 Astatine At	86 Radon Rn				

66 Dysprosium Dy	67 Holmium Ho	68 Erbium Er	69 Thulium Tm	70 Ytterbium Yb	71 Lutetium Lu
98 Californium Cf	99 Einsteinium Es	100 Fermium Fm	101 Mendelevium Md	101 Nobelium No	103 Lawrencium Lr

▲ The elements in group 18 are sometimes called the noble, or inert, gases. The lightest, helium, has just two electrons. All the other elements in the group have eight electrons in their outermost orbit. These arrangements are very stable, which explains the lack of reactivity.

Many of the noble gases are used in lighting. The lamp in this lighthouse uses xenon to produce an intense, bluish-white light.

SEE ALSO PAGES:

148–9 The elements,
166–7 Bonding and valency, 196–7 Properties of metals

CHEMICAL ANALYSIS

Chemists use a variety of techniques and equipment, or apparatus, to identify the elements or compounds in a sample, their amounts, and how they are arranged.

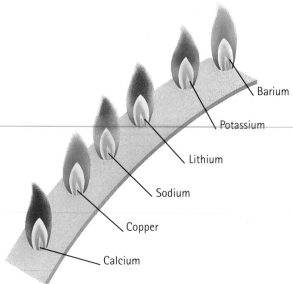

Flame tests help to identify some chemical elements. A speck of the sample on the end of a platinum wire gives a distinctive color to a Bunsen-burner flame.

Chemists use three main types of analysis. Qualitative analysis reveals which elements or compounds are present in a sample. Examples include small-scale reactions in test tubes, chromatography, and electrophoresis. Quantitative analysis measures the amounts of elements or compounds in a sample. A common example is titration, used to measure the concentrations of solutions. Structural analysis uses X rays or other radiation to explore the arrangements of atoms in crystals, or the shapes of molecules.

CHROMATOGRAPHY

Paper chromatography is used to separate mixtures of colored compounds, like ink. A solvent spreads through a piece of absorbent paper and carries with it the dyes in the mixture. The distance moved by each color depends on how strongly it attaches to the paper.

TITRATION

Titration measures the volumes of solutions that react together. A substance called an indicator changes color when the reaction is complete. Chemists can then calculate the amount of the substance dissolved in one of the solutions.

CHEMICAL TESTS

Chemists can often identify elements and compounds from the results of chemical tests using test tubes, chemical reagents, and simple apparatus. For example, carbonate compounds always react with dilute hydrochloric acid to produce bubbles of carbon-dioxide gas. Flame tests are the simplest tests of all. Some of the metals contained in compounds give distinct colors to a Bunsen-burner flame. Carrying out tests in a systematic order can identify most simple substances.

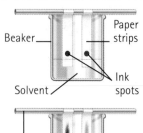

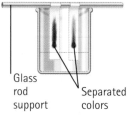

Paper chromatography can be used to separate the dyes in inks. As the solvent rises slowly up the paper, the dyes move at different rates and become separated.

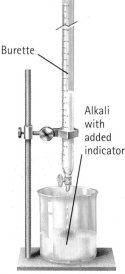

▲ In acid–alkali titrations, a known strength of acid is dripped into a beaker that contains alkali and a small amount of indicator. The amount of alkali in the beaker can be worked out from the amount of acid required to change the color of the indicator.

▶ Has this driver had too much to drink? The breathalyzer measures the concentration of alcohol vapor in his breath.

ELECTROPHORESIS

Electrophoresis is similar to chromatography. It uses an electric current rather than a moving liquid to separate substances in a mixture. An example of its use is in genetic fingerprinting to identify individuals. Enzymes break DNA from body cells into fragments. A solution of these fragments is placed on a special jelly. The fragments move at different speeds in the direction of the electric current. After a while, they separate into different bands. Each person's DNA produces a unique pattern of bands.

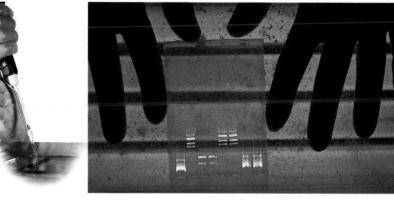

▲ In the final stage of genetic fingerprinting, a pipette dispenses drops containing DNA fragments onto a glass plate covered in a layer of jelly.

▲ Glowing pink in ultraviolet (UV) light, separated bands of DNA help to identify criminals from traces they leave at crime scenes.

X RAY CRYSTALLOGRAPHY

This technique shines a beam of X rays through a crystalline sample of a substance. The atoms inside crystals are arranged in regular patterns. Rows of atoms act as a diffraction grating that scatters the X rays. Interference between different rays alters their intensity, depending on the angle at which they emerge from the crystal. Sensors spaced around the crystal measure the X ray intensities. A computer uses this to show a picture of the crystal structure.

This researcher uses X ray diffraction equipment to find the structure of a protein. The repeating pattern of atoms in a crystal of the protein scatters the X ray beams that pass through the crystal. Sensors around the sample feed information about the scattering pattern to a computer. The computer then analyzes the pattern and calculates the protein's structure.

CARBON DATING

All living things are based on molecules that contain carbon atoms. These atoms come from plants that grow by taking in carbon dioxide from the air. Most carbon atoms are carbon 12, or C^{12}. A small proportion of unstable carbon atoms have two extra neutrons: they are carbon 14.

Although carbon 14 decays, it is constantly being made by cosmic rays hitting nitrogen atoms in the upper atmosphere, so the total amount in the air stays constant. This keeps the ratio of C^{14} to C^{12} constant in organisms during life. After death, the C^{14} in the remains decays and is not replaced. The C^{14} to C^{12} ratio can reveal the age of plants or animals that were alive as long as 40,000 years ago.

Radiocarbon dating can be used to find the age of this ancient Egyptian mummy.

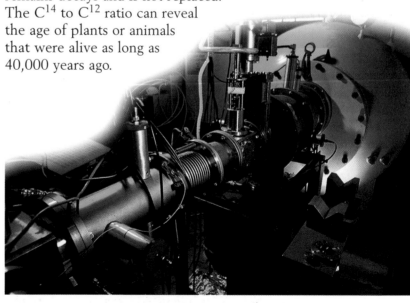

Radiocarbon dating measures the age of a sample by comparing the amount of the radioisotope C^{14} (radiocarbon) to the amount of C^{12} present. The smaller the proportion of C^{14} compared to C^{12}, the older the sample. This accelerator mass spectrometer counts the small number of C^{14} atoms present.

STATES OF MATTER

Solid, liquid, and gas are the three common states
of matter. They have distinctly different structures.
Pure substances melt and boil at fixed temperatures.

Solid

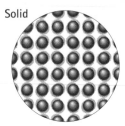

The particles in a solid
are packed tightly. Often,
they form a regular pattern
called a lattice. Particles in
a solid do not move freely;
they vibrate around fixed
points in the lattice.

Gas

The particles in a gas
are spread out much more
than in solids. They move
at great speeds—about
186 mph (300kph)—and
collide with each other
and the walls of
their container.

Liquid

The particles in a liquid can
move around and glide past
each other, as the particles
in a gas do. However, they
are packed much closer,
more like the particles
in a solid.

▶ This graph shows the
spread of the energies of
particles in a solid, liquid,
or gas. The higher the
energy, the faster the
particles move or vibrate.
Few particles have very
high or very low energies.

Matter consists of particles. These
can be separate atoms, molecules,
or ions (see page 166). Although particles
often have complex shapes, chemists
usually use spheres to make models
of solids, liquids, or gases.

In any substance, forces that attract
particles toward each other oppose the
energy of the particles, which makes them
move. This energy, called kinetic energy,
increases with temperature. Whether a
substance is solid, liquid, or gas depends
on the balance between kinetic energy
and forces of attraction.

SOLIDS

Substances are solids when the forces
of attraction between their particles are
strong enough to prevent the particles
from moving freely. Solids have fixed
shapes because the particles are held
together firmly, often in a regular pattern
called a lattice. Crystals are examples of
highly regular lattices.

LIQUIDS

Liquids are fluid—they can change their
shape. In a gravitational field, they collect
at the bottom of a container and have a
flat upper surface. In a liquid, the forces of
attraction between particles are too weak
to hold them in a rigid formation. Instead,
the particles can glide past each other.

White-hot molten iron is poured into molds in a process
called casting. When the temperature falls below 1,535°C,
iron solidifies in the shape of the mold.

GASES

Substances exist as gases when the kinetic
energy of their particles is large enough
to completely overcome the forces that
attract them. Like liquids, gases are
fluid—they change their shape to fit their
containers. Unlike liquids, however, gases
have enough kinetic energy to spread out
and completely fill their containers.

MELTING POINTS

The melting point (or freezing point) of a
substance is the temperature at which the
kinetic energy of the substance's particles
is just great enough to free them from
the rigid lattice structure.

The amount of energy needed to
melt a solid depends on the strength
of the attractive forces in the solid. The
forces in iron, which melts at 2,765°F, are
much greater than the forces in ice, which
forms at 32°F. Oxygen, which freezes at
–362°F, is held together by forces weaker
than both water molecules and iron atoms.

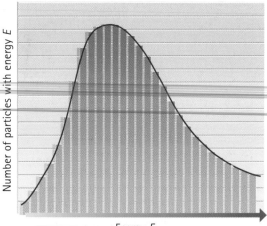

Number of particles with energy E

Energy E

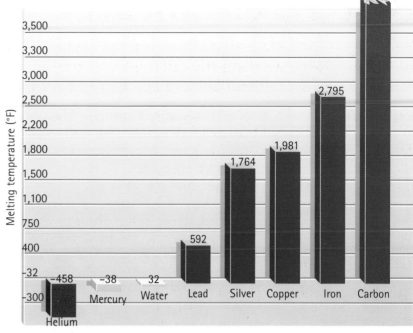

▲ The melting point of a substance depends on the attraction between its particles. This force is so weak for helium that it only solidifies at more than 25 times atmospheric pressure.

▼ Boiling points also depend on pressure and the force of attraction between particles. At the summit of Mount Everest, the boiling point of water is 82°F lower than at sea level.

BOILING POINTS

A liquid boils when bubbles of vapor grow in the liquid, rise to the surface, and burst. The boiling point of a substance is the temperature at which the kinetic energy of the particles of that substance are great enough for them to completely escape the forces that pull the particles together. Just as with melting points, each pure substance has its own particular boiling point. For example, water boils at 212°F to form steam, liquid hydrogen boils at −436°F, and ethanol boils at 174°F.

Not all substances melt before they boil. Some solids turn into gas without passing through a liquid stage. This process is called sublimation. Solid carbon dioxide (dry ice) is a substance that sublimes—it becomes carbon dioxide gas at −173°F.

IMPURITIES AND PRESSURE

Impurities (small quantities of other substances) and pressure both affect boiling and melting temperatures. High pressure forces particles together, so they need more kinetic energy to melt or boil. This means that boiling point and melting point increase at high pressure.

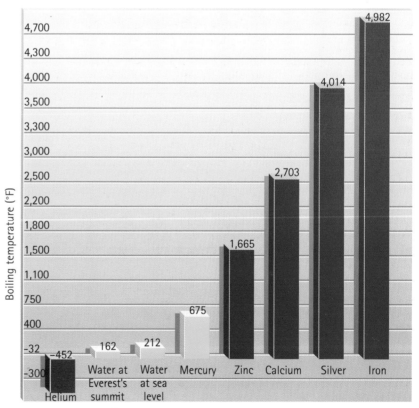

Impurities change boiling and melting points by interfering with the forces between particles. This is why ice melts when salt is sprinkled over it. Salt also increases the boiling point of water.

SEE ALSO PAGES:

166–7 Bonding and valency, 194–5 Properties of solids, 204–5 Shaping materials, 292–3 Potential and kinetic energy

SOLUTIONS

Solutions consist of one or more substances dissolved in another substance. The most common solutions are solids or gases dissolved in liquids.

If you stir salt into a glass of water, the solid salt crystals start to dissolve in the water to form a solution. In all solutions, the substance that dissolves is called the solute. The substance that dissolves the solute is called the solvent. Different solvents dissolve different solutes. For example, salt dissolves in water, but not in pure alcohol or in gasoline. Sugar behaves differently and dissolves in all three of these solvents.

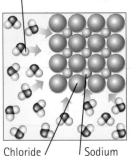

Water molecules (H₂O)

Chloride ion (Cl⁻)   Sodium ion (Na⁺)

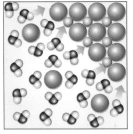

Water molecules pull ions away from the crystal.

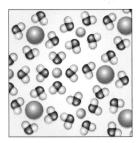

Water molecules surround the ions in solution.

▲ Grains of salt consist of sodium and chloride ions bound together in a formation called a crystal lattice. Water dissolves salt by pulling ions away from the lattice and surrounding them.

▶ Each pint of seawater contains about 2.7 ounces of salt. Cooking salt is produced by trapping seawater in shallow pools. Heat from the sun evaporates the water. The salt crystallizes and is raked into mounds to dry.

DISSOLVING

Solids consist of particles that are tightly packed in a fixed pattern. There are strong forces of attraction between the particles. The particles in a liquid are in constant motion. When a solid comes into contact with a liquid, particles in the liquid strike the surface of the solid. In these collisions, some of the particles in the solid become dislodged. A solution forms if the solid particles are more strongly attracted to the liquid particles than they are to each other. Solvent particles surround solute particles as the solid steadily dissolves. The result is a solution.

SOLUBILITY AND CRYSTALLIZATION

The mass of solute that can dissolve in one liter of solvent is called the solubility of the solute. A solution that contains the maximum possible amount of solute is called a saturated solution. The solubility of most solids increases with temperature.

If a solution is left in an open container, the volume of liquid decreases as the solvent evaporates. The solute does not evaporate. After some time, there is not enough solvent present to dissolve all the solute. The solution becomes saturated, and crystals of solid solute start to form as the solvent continues to evaporate.

Frost crystals form when moist air cools below 0°C. Moisture that is dissolved in the air forms droplets of water that settle on cold surfaces and freeze. These elaborate patterns are crystals of ice.

SOLIDS

Solid solutions are made by allowing a liquid solution to solidify. Alloys form an important class of solid solution. Alloys are solid solutions of one or more metals or nonmetals in another metal that forms the major part of the solution. Alloys usually have very different properties from the original metal. Pure aluminum, for example, is very soft. By dissolving small amounts of copper and other elements into aluminum, a tough, light alloy called duralumin is produced. Duralumin is very light but very strong, so it is used to make the bodies and wings of aircraft.

As with other sorts of solutions, there is a limit to how much solute can dissolve in a solid solution. For example, pure iron is a soft, malleable metal. Dissolving tiny amounts of carbon in molten iron makes steel, which is much harder. The carbon atoms are scattered evenly throughout the solid solution. Iron can dissolve up to 0.4 percent carbon. Adding more carbon results in tiny lumps of undissolved iron carbide, which make the steel brittle.

Bronze is an alloy, or solution, of up to 30 percent tin in copper. It was first made more than 6,000 years ago and was used to produce armor, tools, weapons, helmets, and ornaments.

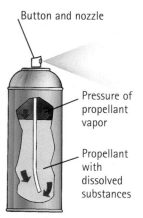

Button and nozzle

Pressure of propellant vapor

Propellant with dissolved substances

▲ Aerosol cans contain pressurized solutions of substances such as deodorants, insecticides, and paints. When pressure is released by pressing the button, the solvent in the aerosol boils and forces the solution through the nozzle. A fine spray of the aerosol's contents comes out whenever the button is pressed.

GASES

Gases can also dissolve in liquids to form solutions. The solubility of gases decreases as the temperature increases. This is why small bubbles of air form in heated water long before it boils. Increasing the pressure of a gas makes more gas dissolve in a liquid. Gas solubility is measured at 32°F and one atmosphere pressure. Oxygen, for example, has a solubility of 49 cm^3 per liter of water under these conditions.

Liquids dissolve in gases, too. For example, water evaporates from the sea and the water vapor mixes with the air. When warm, moist air rises and cools, it can no longer dissolve all the water vapor it contains. Then tiny droplets of liquid water appear as clouds, mist, and rain.

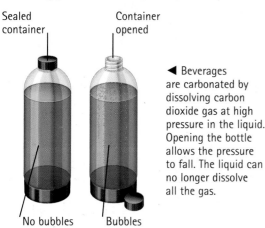

Sealed container

Container opened

No bubbles

Bubbles

◀ Beverages are carbonated by dissolving carbon dioxide gas at high pressure in the liquid. Opening the bottle allows the pressure to fall. The liquid can no longer dissolve all the gas.

▶ A solution is always transparent, even when it is colored. This blue solution is cobalt chloride dissolved in water. A solid can be made to dissolve more quickly in a heated solvent.

SEE ALSO PAGES:

40 Clouds and fog,
156 States of matter,
184 Acids, 185 Bases
and alkalis, 198 Iron,
202–3 Alloys

SEPARATION AND PURIFICATION

Many substances are mixtures of simpler substances. A number of techniques can be used to separate mixtures into their component parts.

This still produces brandy by heating wine and collecting its vapors. The distillate contains 60 percent alcohol compared with 10 percent alcohol in the wine.

Many solutions consist of a soluble solid dissolved in a liquid solvent. An example is a solution of sugar in water. The sugar can be separated by leaving the solution in a warm place until all the water has evaporated. The result is crystals of pure sugar. The evaporated water can be collected by condensing it on a cold surface. Mixtures of insoluble solids and liquids can be separated by filtration or centrifuging. Mixtures of liquids are separated by distillation.

FILTRATION

When chalk dust is mixed with water, it does not dissolve. Instead, it forms a cloudy suspension. Suspensions consist of fine particles of solid spread through a liquid. Filtration is the simplest method for separating a suspension. The top of a funnel holds a hollow cone of filter paper. The paper is made from a tangled mesh of microscopic fibers and acts like a strainer. When the suspension is poured into the funnel, the liquid passes through the paper, but the solid particles do not. The filtered liquid is called the filtrate, and the solid in the filter-paper cone is the residue.

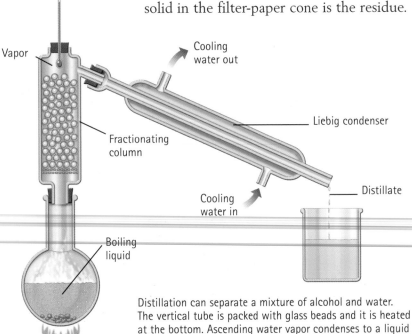

Filtration catches insoluble solids in a filter paper. A clear solution passes into the flask below the funnel.

Distillation can separate a mixture of alcohol and water. The vertical tube is packed with glass beads and it is heated at the bottom. Ascending water vapor condenses to a liquid and falls back into the flask. Alcohol vapor continues upward and over into the condenser.

CENTRIFUGING

Not all suspensions can be separated by filtration. In some cases, the suspended particles are so fine that they would either pass through a filter or clog its pores and prevent the liquid from draining.

Another way to separate a suspension is by leaving it to stand. After a while, the solid particles settle to the bottom and the liquid can be poured off. Unfortunately, many of the suspensions that are too fine to filter also refuse to settle out. This is because the solid particles are constantly being battered by fast-moving liquid molecules, preventing them from settling.

Centrifuges are used to separate suspensions that are difficult to separate by other methods. Tubes containing the suspension are placed in holders around the edge of a rotor inside the centrifuge. A vertical shaft at the center of the rotor, driven by an electric motor, turns the rotor at high speed. The holders swing out from the center of the rotor as the tubes spin around, with their open ends pointed toward the central shaft.

The smallest centrifuges spin the tubes at about 2,000 revolutions per minute (rpm). The result is a force on the solid particles equal to 250 times the force of gravity. A suspension of chalk dust in water will settle in less than 30 seconds; suspensions of finer solids take longer.

Centrifuges can also separate emulsions—suspensions of one liquid within another. An example is milk, which is separated into cream and skimmed milk.

SEPARATING MIXTURES BY CENTRIFUGE

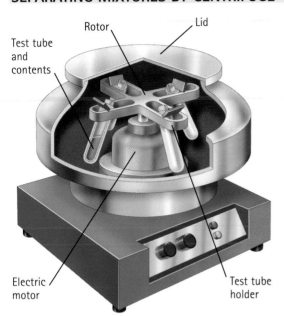

Rotor — Lid
Test tube and contents
Electric motor
Test tube holder

When soil is shaken with water, the result is a suspension. If left undisturbed for some time, the solid particles settle to the bottom of their container. They form layers in their order of density, with dense grains of sand at the bottom and lighter clay particles suspended in the liquid at the top. Centrifuges accelerate settling processes by spinning a sample and creating a downward pull that is typically several hundreds of times more powerful than gravity. This pull can separate mixtures such as blood, which does not separate by the effect of gravity alone.

◀ This centrifuge holds four test tubes. Tubes on opposite sides of the rotor must have exactly the same mass so that the rotor spins evenly without vibration.

▲ Blood contains red and white blood cells in a solution called plasma. A centrifuge is used to separate these cells, because they are all too small to settle naturally. After centrifuging, each layer is carefully suctioned off using a glass pipette with a rubber bulb on the end.

SIMPLE DISTILLATION

Distillation is used to separate liquids from solutions by boiling. When a solution of salt in water boils, the vapor that rises from the boiling mixture is pure water. In a distillation apparatus, the steam passes through a water-cooled pipe called a condenser. As it cools below 212°F, the steam changes into pure liquid water. When all the steam has evaporated, the salt from the solution remains in the base of the flask that contained the solution.

FRACTIONAL DISTILLATION

Simple distillation is useful for separating liquid solvents from solutions and for separating mixtures of liquids that have very different boiling points. However, it does not completely separate mixtures of liquids that have similar boiling points.

Fractional distillation separates mixtures of liquids with similar boiling points by repeating the distillation process many times within a single apparatus. The part of the apparatus where the separation occurs is called a fractionating column. It is a vertical pipe packed with beads. Boiling vapors rise into the fractionating column where they partly condense. The mixture that condenses contains more of the liquid with the higher boiling point. This falls back into the boiling mixture. The vapors that do not condense rise into a cooler part of the column. These vapors,

which contain more of the substance that boils at the lower temperature, partially condense. The part that remains vapor contains even more of the low-boiling substance. This process is repeated until—if the column is long enough— the vapors that emerge at the top of the column contain only the pure, low-boiling substance.

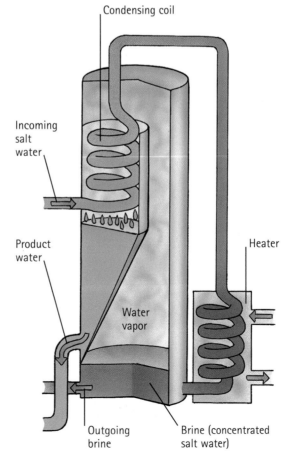

Condensing coil
Incoming salt water
Product water
Water vapor
Heater
Outgoing brine
Brine (concentrated salt water)

This desalination plant produces fresh drinking water from seawater. Cold seawater first passes through a condenser coil. The water becomes warm as pure water vapor condenses on the outside of the coil. The warm seawater is then heated to boiling point and pumped into a chamber where it boils. Water vapor rises and condenses to liquid water on the surface of the coil, warming more incoming seawater.

SEE ALSO PAGES:
142–3 Medical technology, 190–1 Petrochemicals, 210–11 Oil and refining, 456–7 Resources

CHEMICAL REACTIONS

In a chemical reaction one set of substances changes into another set. Reaction speeds vary and depend on temperature.

Methane

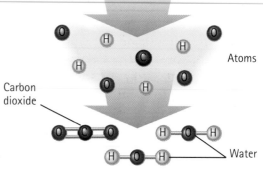
Oxygen molecules

Atoms

Carbon dioxide

Water

When natural gas burns, methane (CH_4) and oxygen (O_2) molecules break into atoms. The atoms recombine to form water (H_2O) and carbon dioxide (CO_2) molecules.

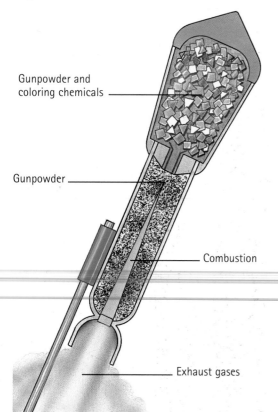

Iron filings and powdered sulfur

Iron attracted

Nonmagnetic iron sulfide

A magnet separates iron from a mixture of iron filings and powdered sulfur. Heating the mixture makes a new substance, a compound called iron sulfide, which is not magnetic.

Chemical reactions change the chemical composition of substances. They can either break complicated substances down into smaller parts, or join together simple substances to make more complex ones.

The substances present at the start of the reaction are called the reactants. The substances present when the reaction has finished are called the products. Chemical reactions change the way the atoms of different elements in the reactants are grouped together.

Some chemical reactions, like rusting, happen very slowly; others, like explosions, happen very fast.

BUILDING UP
Iron and sulfur are elements. When iron filings and powdered sulfur are stirred together, they simply form a mixture. The mixture has all the properties of the two separate ingredients: the iron filings are attracted to a magnet, for example, and the individual substances can be seen with a

magnifying glass. Heating the mixture makes it glow as a chemical reaction occurs. Iron atoms join with sulfur atoms to form iron sulfide. Heat starts the reaction, in the same way a match lights a gas pilot light. This reaction is an example of simple substances joining together to make a more complex one. The product has different properties from the mixture: for example, it is not magnetic.

Gunpowder and coloring chemicals

Gunpowder

Combustion

Exhaust gases

◄ Fireworks contain gunpowder, which is a mixture of potassium nitrate, sulfur, and charcoal (carbon). When heated, potassium nitrate decomposes to form oxygen, which causes the sulfur and carbon to burn rapidly, producing gases. These gases propel the fireworks into the sky and scatter the coloring chemicals that provide the firework's display.

► Chemical explosives decompose in a few thousandths of a second to form large amounts of hot, high-pressure gases. The expansion of these gases produces a blast that can be strong enough to demolish a building.

162

BREAKING DOWN

When baking soda (sodium hydrogen-carbonate, $NaHCO_3$) mixes with vinegar, acid in the vinegar makes the baking soda break down into smaller parts. One of these products is carbon dioxide (CO_2), which makes the mixture bubble.

Gas stoves and heaters use oxygen from the air to burn methane gas. During the reaction, heat breaks down each molecule of methane (CH_4) into one carbon atom and four hydrogen atoms. These atoms then join up with oxygen to form carbon dioxide and water (H_2O).

REACTION RATES

The chemical reaction between iron and sulfur needs heat to make it happen. Heat is not necessary for the reaction between baking soda and vinegar to happen, but raising the temperature will make it happen faster: increasing the temperature increases the reaction rate.

The rate of a reaction is how quickly it changes reactants into products. Chemical reactions happen when molecules and atoms collide. The reaction rate increases when there are more collisions per second. Raising the temperature increases the kinetic energy of particles, so they move faster and collide more often. This is why reactions get faster at high temperatures.

The rate of a reaction also increases if more concentrated reactants are used. The higher concentration means that the

molecules that could react are crowded closer together; so they collide more often, and the reaction happens faster. With gases, high pressure is the equivalent of high concentration. A diesel engine uses a combination of high pressure and high temperature to start an explosive reaction.

Rusting is a slow chemical reaction involving iron, water, and oxygen. In time, the iron in this old car will change completely to crumbly, brown iron oxide.

1 Dilute acid and marble chips
2 Dilute acid and marble powder
3 Marble chips and concentrated acid
4 Marble chips and high temperature

1 Marble chips react with acid to form carbon dioxide gas. Reaction rates increase when: 2 powdering the marble increases contact between the reactants; 3 concentrated acid and 4 higher temperature increase the number of collisions per second.

◄ The stalactites (hanging down) and stalagmites (forming upward) in this limestone cave have taken thousands of years to grow. Carbon dioxide in rainwater seeping down reacts with the rock above the cave to form salts. These salts become insoluble and form solid deposits as the dripping water evaporates in the cave.

SEE ALSO PAGES:
32–33 Erosion and weathering, 176 Catalysts, 178 Oxidation and reduction

CHEMICAL COMPOUNDS

Chemical compounds are substances made from atoms of two or more different elements in fixed proportions. Compounds are held together by chemical bonds.

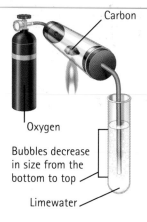

Carbon

Oxygen

Bubbles decrease in size from the bottom to top

Limewater

Some compounds can be made by simply heating elements together. Passing oxygen gas over heated carbon forms carbon dioxide. During the reaction, each carbon atom bonds to two oxygen atoms. As limewater dissolves the carbon dioxide, the limewater becomes milky and the bubbles become smaller.

There are more than 110 known chemical elements. Atoms of these elements join together in different combinations to make countless millions of different compounds. Strong forces of attraction called chemical bonds hold atoms together in these compounds.

Some compounds are very simple. For example, table salt contains just two elements, sodium and chlorine, bonded together. Its chemical name is sodium chloride. Other compounds are extremely complex, particularly those like DNA and proteins that are found in living things.

CHEMICAL BONDS

Substances such as sodium chloride are made up of particles that have negative and positive charges. These particles are called ions. The positive ions are strongly attracted to the charge of the negative ions and vice versa. This attraction, called ionic bonding, holds the ions together like mortar holds bricks in a wall.

Other substances have bonds that join atoms together in groups called molecules. For example, water is a compound of the elements hydrogen and oxygen. Each water molecule consists of one oxygen atom and two hydrogen atoms. The bonds between atoms within a molecule are strong; the forces of attraction between molecules are much weaker.

▼ Carbon dioxide molecules contain just three atoms each. The attraction between the molecules is weak, so carbon dioxide is a gas at room temperature.

Temporary, very weak bonds between moving molecules

▼ There are many different alcohols. All contain an oxygen atom joined to a carbon atom at one end and to a hydrogen atom at the other end. The chemical name for the alcohol with formula C_2H_5OH is ethanol.

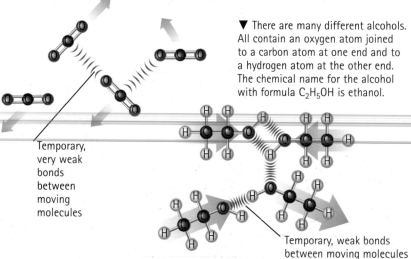

Temporary, weak bonds between moving molecules

POLYETHYLENE MOLECULES

Polyethylene is a compound that contains carbon and hydrogen only. The carbon atoms join together to make long chains. Each carbon atom is also joined to two hydrogen atoms. A single polyethylene molecule contains between 3,500 and 200,000 carbon atoms. The chains tangle together to give a soft, waxy-feeling solid.

▼ Polyethylene items are separated from other trash for recycling as garbage bags and other products.

Carbon atoms form "backbone"

METAL SALTS

Metal salts contain one or more metals bonded to one or more nonmetals. Table salt, or sodium chloride, is a familiar example. The chemical formula of salt is NaCl, which shows that it contains equal numbers of sodium (Na) and chlorine (Cl) atoms. Another example of a salt is calcium carbonate ($CaCO_3$), which is the main component of limestone and chalk. Calcium carbonate has equal numbers of calcium (Ca) and carbon (C) atoms, and three times as many oxygen (O) atoms.

Salts are usually solids that melt at high temperatures. Sodium chloride melts at 1,479°F, for example.

Hydrogen atoms are joined to the carbon "backbone"

NONMETALS

Compounds that contain only nonmetals mostly exist as molecules; many of these compounds are liquids or gases. Water, for example, consists of hydrogen and oxygen, which are both nonmetals. The chemical formula of water is H_2O, which shows that each molecule is made up of two hydrogen atoms and one oxygen atom.

Most of the nonmetal compounds that are solids melt at low temperatures. Candle wax, which is a mixture of compounds of carbon, hydrogen, and oxygen, melts at around 158°F.

Ammonium dichromate ($(NH_4)_2Cr_2O_7$) is an unstable compound of chromium, hydrogen, nitrogen, and oxygen atoms. Heating the orange crystals breaks the bonds between the atoms to form simpler substances—steam, nitrogen gas, and green chromium oxide.

THE NOBLE GASES

Helium, neon, argon, krypton, xenon, and radon are the noble, or inert, gases. They form group 18 of the periodic table. Helium, neon, and argon are completely inert: they never take part in chemical reactions. Krypton, xenon, and radon can react, but only under extreme conditions. The noble gases are so unreactive because their electronic structures are very stable.

STABILITY

When elements take part in chemical reactions, they exchange or share electrons to achieve the same number of electrons as the closest noble gas. As a result, many compounds are more stable than the elements that make them up.

Some compounds, such as sodium chloride, are very stable. Often, highly reactive elements combine to form highly stable compounds. They seldom react with other substances and do not break down when heated because the bonds between their atoms are strong.

▲ The chemical name for polyethylene is poly(ethylene). Chemists use the prefix "poly" to indicate that a compound is made from the same simple part repeated many times. Polyethylene is made from ethylene, a molecule that contains two carbon and four hydrogen atoms.

▶ Gold is found mixed with quartz rock deep underground. Most metals occur in their ores as compounds. Gold is so unreactive that it occurs naturally as pure metal.

SEE ALSO PAGES:

148–9 The elements, 166–7 Bonding and valency, 180–1 Noble gases

BONDING AND VALENCY

Ionic bonds mostly form between metal and nonmetal atoms. Covalent bonds form between nonmetal atoms. Valency is the number of bonds an atom can form.

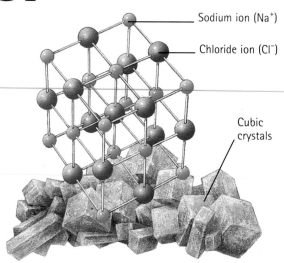

Sodium ion (Na⁺)

Chloride ion (Cl⁻)

Cubic crystals

Each ion in a sodium-chloride crystal is surrounded by ions of opposite charge. The ions are arranged in a cubic lattice so that each salt crystal has a cubic shape.

Sodium atom (Na)

Sodium ion (Na⁺)

A sodium atom has 11 electrons in shells around a nucleus that contains 11 protons. A sodium ion has one negatively charged electron fewer, which gives it an overall charge of +1. Sodium ions are smaller than sodium atoms.

Chlorine atom (Cl)

Chloride ion (Cl⁻)

A chlorine atom has 17 electrons and 17 protons. A chloride ion has one more electron and a charge of –1. Chloride ions are larger than chlorine atoms. Like sodium ions, chloride ions have a full outer shell of electrons.

Each atom of an element contains a number of electrons that is exactly equal to the number of protons in its nucleus. The positive charges of the protons balance the negative charges of the electrons, and the atom has no overall charge. The electrons orbit the nucleus in layers called shells. There is a limit to the number of electrons that each shell can hold. The first shell, which is closest to the nucleus, can hold up to two electrons. The second shell can hold eight electrons, and the third can hold 18.

The rows of the periodic table list elements in order of increasing atomic number, which is the number of protons in an atom of an element. Each row starts with an element that has only one electron in its outermost shell. At the end of each row is a noble gas, which has a full set of electrons in its outermost shell. This arrangement of electrons, which is called a configuration, is unusually stable. This is why noble gases seldom react.

VALENCY

In chemical reactions, bonds form between atoms as they gain, lose, or share electrons. As a result of these changes, each atom in a compound usually has a full outer shell of electrons. This is the stable electron configuration of the noble gas closest to each element in atomic number.

The valency of an element is the number of bonds it must make to have a noble-gas configuration. Metals usually have only one or two electrons in their outer shells. They easily lose these electrons so that the next shell down becomes a complete outer shell. The nonmetals at the far right of the periodic table are only one or two electrons short of a complete shell. For this reason, they easily accept electrons from atoms of other elements. The valencies of these elements are the numbers of electrons that they must gain or lose to form a complete shell.

Elements in the middle of the main block of the periodic table have outer shells that are three or four electrons short of a full shell. Carbon is an example: it has four electrons in an outer shell that can contain eight. It seldom accepts four electrons, however, because the negative charges would repel each other too much. Instead, carbon atoms overlap their outer shells (i.e. bond) with shells of other atoms and share four electrons to make up the full count. The valency of carbon is four.

► This picture shows sodium glowing brightly in chlorine gas. The chemical reaction that bonds the two elements together produces large quantities of heat and forms white crystals of sodium chloride, or common salt.

166

IONS AND IONIC BONDING

Ionic compounds form when atoms of two or more elements trade electrons to form charged particles, or ions, of each element. The ions have noble-gas configurations and their charges balance each other to give the compound no overall charge.

A sodium atom has 11 electrons. Two of these are in the first shell; eight are in the second shell. These two shells are complete. The last (11th) electron is alone in a shell that can hold up to 18 electrons. The outer shell of a chlorine atom is one electron short of being full. On their own, chlorine atoms link up in pairs to form Cl_2 molecules. In these molecules, a shared pair of electrons makes up the outer shell. If sodium is introduced, however, chlorine atoms give up this sharing arrangement to have an electron of their own. Each sodium atom loses its 11th electron and becomes a positively charged sodium ion (Na^+). At the same time, each chlorine atom gains an electron and becomes a chloride ion (Cl^-). The opposite charges of these two types of ions attract each other strongly. The ions bond together in a regular pattern called a crystal lattice.

Magnesium also forms an ionic chloride. Unlike sodium, magnesium has two electrons in its outer shell. Its atoms lose both of these electrons to twice as many chlorine atoms. Magnesium ions (Mg^{2+}) form a salt with the formula $MgCl_2$. Magnesium has a valency of two.

In the five examples of covalently-bonded molecules below, each line represents a single covalent bond, which is a pair of electrons shared between two atoms. The valencies of the elements are: carbon (C) = 4; chlorine (Cl) = 1; hydrogen (H) = 1; oxygen (O) = 2; phosphorus (P) = 3.

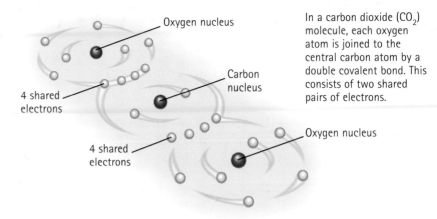

In a carbon dioxide (CO_2) molecule, each oxygen atom is joined to the central carbon atom by a double covalent bond. This consists of two shared pairs of electrons.

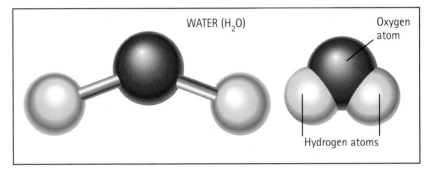

WATER (H_2O)

COVALENT BONDING

Ionic compounds mainly form between metals at the left of the periodic table and nonmetals at the right. Compounds that contain only nonmetals are usually held together in molecules by their atoms sharing pairs of electrons. This type of bonding is called covalent bonding.

Carbon dioxide (CO_2) is an example of a covalent compound. The valencies of carbon and oxygen are four and two, because each carbon atom needs four electrons to fill its outer shell and each oxygen atom needs two. In carbon dioxide, one carbon atom shares one pair of electrons with each of two oxygen atoms. In this way, all three atoms fill their outer shells.

▲ There are two ways to draw molecules. One is the ball-and-stick model (left), which shows the bonds between atoms. The second way is the space-filling model (right), which shows the shape of the space occupied by the electrons in a molecule.

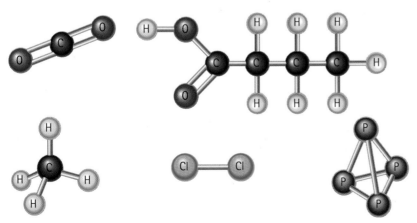

▲ Acetylene (C_2H_2), also called ethyne, burns to produce carbon dioxide (CO_2), water (H_2O), and enough heat to melt steel.

SEE ALSO PAGES:

148–9 The elements, 150–1 Atoms, 152–3 The periodic table

SOLID STRUCTURES

Solids consist of atoms, molecules, or ions bonded together. The properties of a solid depend on the strength of the bonds that hold it together.

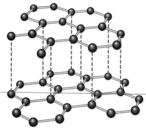

Iodine molecule I₂

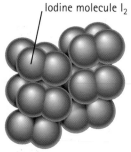

Solid iodine consists of iodine molecules arranged in a regular lattice. Each molecule contains two iodine atoms strongly bonded to each other. Iodine is soft, because the bonds between the molecules are weak.

The structures of many solids are based on regularly repeating patterns of atoms, molecules, or ions. These regular arrangements are called lattices.

There are four main types of lattice structures. Ionic solids, such as sodium chloride, consist of alternating positive and negative ions. Molecular solids, such as the element iodine, consist of simple molecules packed together in a lattice. Macromolecular solids, such as diamond, graphite, and glass, contain huge molecules with millions of atoms each. Metallic solids consist of metal atoms held together by clouds of electrons that freely move from one atom to another.

IONIC SOLIDS

Ionic solids are hard and have high melting points. These properties result from strong forces of attraction between the oppositely charged ions in an ionic lattice. Ionic solids are also brittle. A force applied to the outside of a crystal can slide the layers of ions so that ions with similar charges are beside each other. The like charges repel strongly and the layers then break apart, cracking the lattice.

▼ Sodium chloride crystals consist of sodium and chloride ions. This cage model represents the ions as balls. The balls are spaced so that their 3-dimensional lattice structure is clear.

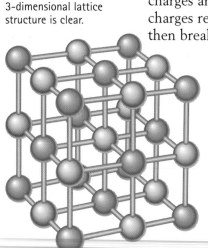

Each ion is surrounded by six ions of opposite charge. The attraction between charges holds the lattice together.

Chloride ion (Cl⁻)   Sodium ion (Na⁺)

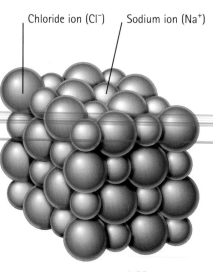

▶ This space-filling model is a scale model of the cubic sodium-chloride lattice. It shows the relative sizes of the two types of ions and how they are arranged in space.

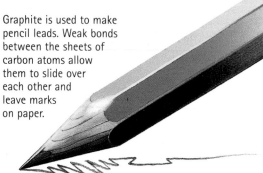

Graphite is used to make pencil leads. Weak bonds between the sheets of carbon atoms allow them to slide over each other and leave marks on paper.

MOLECULAR SOLIDS

Molecules consist of atoms held together by strong covalent bonds. For example, iodine molecules contain just two iodine atoms joined by a single covalent bond. In a molecular solid, the molecules are held together by weak forces of attraction. Molecular solids melt at low temperatures. Melting does not break the covalent bonds between the atoms; it breaks the weak attractive forces between molecules.

MACROMOLECULAR SOLIDS

The element carbon can exist in two forms: diamond and graphite. Both are macromolecular solids that contain only carbon atoms, but they have very different structures. In graphite, each carbon atom is joined to three others by covalent bonds that are short and strong. Hexagonal rings of six atoms join together to make flat sheets. The forces of attraction between the sheets are weak and the sheets can easily slide over each other. This is why graphite feels greasy and is used as a solid lubricant. In diamond, each carbon atom is joined to four others by strong covalent bonds. Billions of carbon atoms join together to make a 3-dimensional lattice of enormous strength. This makes diamond the hardest known solid. Glass has a structure similar to diamond. But it consists of silicon and oxygen atoms instead of carbon atoms. Glass is less hard than diamond because its bonds are easier to break.

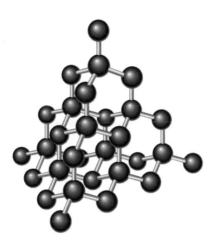

◀ Diamond is much rarer and more valuable than graphite. Like graphite, it consists entirely of carbon atoms. But the structure of diamond (below) is entirely different from that of graphite, which is why the two solids are so different.

▲ At −109˚F, solid carbon dioxide changes to a gas, without melting. Dropped into water, it vaporizes and creates a cloud of ice crystals. This mixture is used to create a dense fog for stage effects.

METALLIC SOLIDS

Solid metals consist of separate atoms in a lattice structure. The atoms pack together in layers that stack on top of each other. Most metals have high melting points because of the strength of the bonds that hold metal atoms in lattices.

Metallic bonds are different from ionic and covalent bonds. Some electrons from each metal atom are free to move from one atom to the next. The metal atoms become positive ions when they give up their electrons. They are held together in a lattice by a sea of free electrons.

If a voltage is applied to a sample of metal, the free electrons start to drift away from the negative terminal to the positive terminal. This is how electrical current flows through metal conductors.

Unlike ionic solids, metals can bend and stretch. This is because the layers of metal ions can slide over each other without the layers of the lattice breaking apart.

OTHER ELECTRICAL CONDUCTORS

An electric current is a flow of electrical charges. The charge can be carried by either electrons or ions that are free to move. In some cases, the ability of a solid material to conduct electricity reveals information about its structure. Graphite, for example, is a rare example of a nonmetallic conductor. This is because each carbon atom in graphite has only three of its outer electrons in bonds that are fixed between pairs of carbon atoms. The fourth bonding electron of each atom takes part in a huge bond that spreads through the whole sheet of carbon atoms. This type of bond, called a delocalized bond, is a pool of electrons that can move freely through the sheet and conduct electricity.

When an ionic salt melts or dissolves in water, its lattice breaks down, and the ions become free to conduct electricity. This effect helped scientists to discover that ionic solids consist of charged particles.

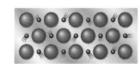

Metal atoms are packed closely together in the solid state. The outermost electrons move freely and randomly between atoms. This sea of electrons holds the metal together.

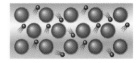

When an electric current flows through a metal, the free electrons continue to move chaotically. But there is an average drift from the negative part of the metal to the positive part.

SEE ALSO PAGES:

150–1 Atoms, 194–5 Properties of solids, 196–7 Properties of metals

Metals and ionic solids have similar structures. Metal atoms or ions pack together to form layers of linked hexagons. These layers fit together to form a 3-dimensional lattice.

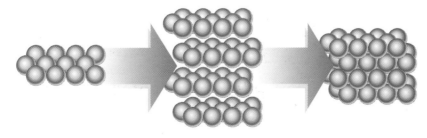

CARBON

The nonmetal carbon is the basis for all life on Earth. It forms more compounds than any other element, but is not particularly plentiful in the Earth's crust.

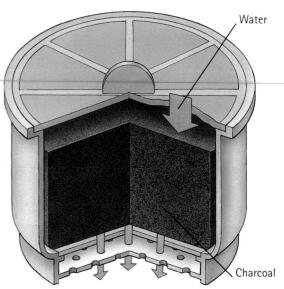

Water

Charcoal

Many household water filters contain charcoal. As water passes through the filter, the charcoal absorbs dissolved substances, such as chlorine, from the water.

Carbon occurs in nature as graphite and diamond. Carbon forms many compounds with other elements and is found in many minerals. Limestone, chalk, and marble are all different forms of calcium carbonate ($CaCO_3$), which formed from tiny marine organisms that died millions of years ago.

Most importantly, carbon is the only element whose atoms can bond with each other to form rings and chains with almost no size limit. Carbon forms more compounds than all the other elements combined. It is the basis of chemicals present in living things, fossil fuels, and petrochemicals. Carbon is constantly being exchanged between carbon dioxide in the atmosphere and compounds in plants and animals. Fossil fuels also produce carbon dioxide.

This baby, like all humans, is about 20 percent carbon. About 4 percent of grass and 40 percent of an insect's shell is also carbon.

A NEW FORM OF CARBON

Buckminsterfullerene is a form of carbon made by heating graphite with an electric arc or a laser beam. It also occurs in soot. It consists of 60 carbon atoms in the shape of a ball. The carbon atoms form 12 pentagons and 20 hexagons on the surface of the ball. The compound was named after U.S. architect Richard Buckminster Fuller (1895–1983), because its molecules resemble the dome-shaped buildings he designed.

Buckminsterfullerene was discovered in 1990. Its molecules are balls that each contain 60 carbon atoms.

CHARCOAL

The carbon atoms in charcoal are randomly arranged. Charcoal is made by burning wood in an oven with little air. It can be used as a smokeless fuel, and glows red-hot as it reacts with oxygen in the air to form carbon dioxide.

Charcoal is very porous. It absorbs many kinds of molecules by forming weak chemical bonds with them. Charcoal filters are used to purify gases and to decolorize liquids. They are used, for example, in gas masks and in water filters. Charcoal is also used in the sugar-refining industry to remove the brown color from sugar solution so that it crystallizes to produce pure white sugar.

Carbon cycle

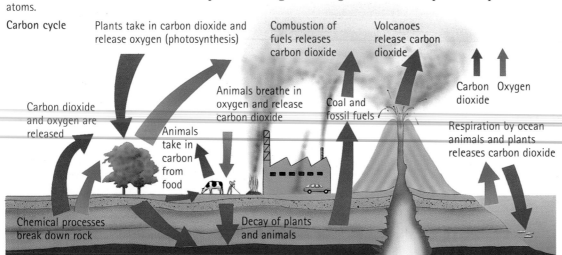

Plants take in carbon dioxide and release oxygen (photosynthesis)

Combustion of fuels releases carbon dioxide

Volcanoes release carbon dioxide

Carbon dioxide and oxygen are released

Animals breathe in oxygen and release carbon dioxide

Animals take in carbon from food

Coal and fossil fuels

Carbon   Oxygen dioxide

Respiration by ocean animals and plants releases carbon dioxide

Chemical processes break down rock

Decay of plants and animals

Plants take in carbon dioxide and release oxygen during photosynthesis. Plants are eaten by animals, which take in oxygen and release carbon dioxide by respiration. The combustion of fossil fuels uses oxygen and releases carbon dioxide.

SEE ALSO

56–7 Plant anatomy,
150–1 Atoms, 162–3
Chemical reactions,
434–5 The natural balance

NITROGEN AND OXYGEN

Air is the mixture of gases that surrounds the Earth and makes up its atmosphere. Ninety-nine percent of air consists of the gases oxygen and nitrogen.

Oxygen molecules have two oxygen atoms joined together by a double covalent bond.

Oxygen and nitrogen are both gaseous elements. Their molecules consist of two atoms joined by covalent bonds. In nitrogen molecules (N_2), three bonds hold the molecule together; in oxygen (O_2), there are only two. Oxygen is a very reactive element. It often releases great amounts of heat when it reacts. Nitrogen has a much lower chemical reactivity.

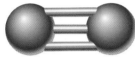

Nitrogen molecules have two nitrogen atoms joined together by a triple covalent bond.

CHEMICAL REACTIONS

Oxygen reacts with most other elements to form compounds called oxides. The most common example is hydrogen oxide, better known as water (H_2O). Iron reacts slowly with oxygen from the atmosphere to form rust, or iron oxide (Fe_2O_3).

When fuels burn and living things respire, they use oxygen to form carbon dioxide (CO_2). Plants use carbon dioxide and water to form oxygen and tissues. This process is called photosynthesis. Nitrogen is a key part of proteins in living things. The element constantly changes between nitrogen molecules in the atmosphere and compounds of nitrogen in the soil and in plant and animal proteins. This is called the nitrogen cycle.

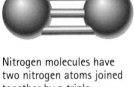

Steel wool burns brightly in pure oxygen. The reaction is faster than with a solid lump because the fine strands of steel have better contact with the oxygen.

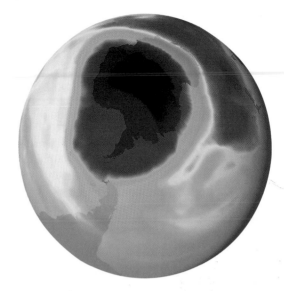

This computer-enhanced picture was taken by satellite over Antarctica. It shows a record-sized hole in the ozone layer of (10,425,000sq mi.) 27 million square kilometers.

OXYGEN AND OZONE

A second form of oxygen, called ozone, has the formula O_3. Its molecules have three oxygen atoms bonded in a triangle. Ozone forms a layer about 15.5 mi. (25km) above the Earth. Ultraviolet (UV) radiation in sunlight splits oxygen molecules into separate atoms. These combine with O_2 molecules to form ozone. Ozone acts as a sunscreen that prevents harmful UV from reaching Earth's surface. Aircraft exhausts, some aerosols, and chemicals used in old refrigerators destroy ozone. Holes in the ozone layer, increase UV radiation, damaging plants and causing skin cancer.

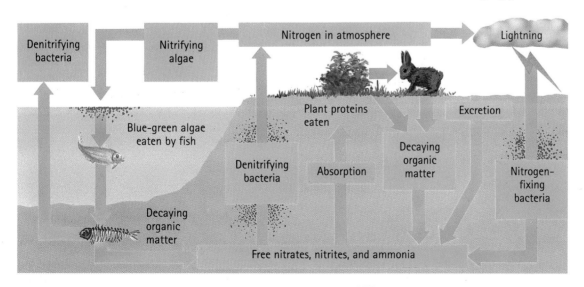

The nitrogen cycle constantly exchanges nitrogen between the air and living things. Lightning and bacteria convert nitrogen gas into nitrates in the soil. Plants use these salts to form proteins, which are eaten by animals. Decay and excretion return salts to the soil, where some bacteria release nitrogen.

SEE ALSO PAGES:

56–7 Plant anatomy,
162–3 Chemical
reactions, 172 Air

AIR

The gases that make up the atmosphere, or air, are vital to survival. These gases continuously interact with living things and can be affected by them.

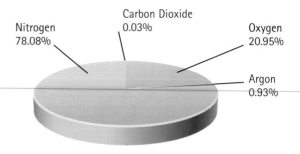

Carbon Dioxide
0.03%

Nitrogen
78.08%

Oxygen
20.95%

Argon
0.93%

The main composition of the atmosphere remains fairly constant from day to day. The amount of pollution in the air varies with time and geographical location.

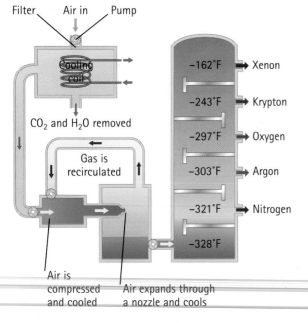

Almost 80 percent of air is nitrogen; just over 20 percent is oxygen; and about one percent is argon. Air also contains small amounts of carbon dioxide and traces of noble gases other than argon. There is enough air to breathe up to 6 mi. (10km) above Earth's surface. If Earth were the size of a basketball, the breathable atmosphere would be less than 0.04 inches thick.

Here acid rain has dissolved part of a statue so badly that its face must be entirely replaced. Acid rain is a dilute mixture of nitric and sulfuric acids. It forms when gases from burning fossil fuels mix with rain.

GASES FROM THE AIR

Many industrial processes use gases from the air. Oxygen is used in the production of steel and for welding. Nitrogen is used to make ammonia; this, in turn, is used to make fertilizers, explosives, medicines, dyes, and plastics. Carbon dioxide gives carbonated beverages their bubbles. Argon is a noble gas with almost no chemical reactivity; it is used to fill lightbulbs. These gases are obtained by fractional distillation.

AIR POLLUTION

Almost all industries depend on fossil fuels for energy. Burning these fuels produces oxides of sulfur and nitrogen that cause lung diseases and acid rain. Acid rain gradually dissolves some types of stone and can kill trees and fish.

Carbon dioxide in the atmosphere traps heat from the sun and prevents the Earth from being too cold to support life. This is the greenhouse effect. The carbon dioxide from burning fossil fuels is increasing the temperature of Earth's atmosphere. This effect, called global warming, could cause long-term environmental damage.

Filter   Air in   Pump

Cooling coil

CO_2 and H_2O removed

Gas is recirculated

Air is compressed and cooled

Air expands through a nozzle and cools

−162°F → Xenon

−243°F → Krypton

−297°F → Oxygen

−303°F → Argon

−321°F → Nitrogen

−328°F

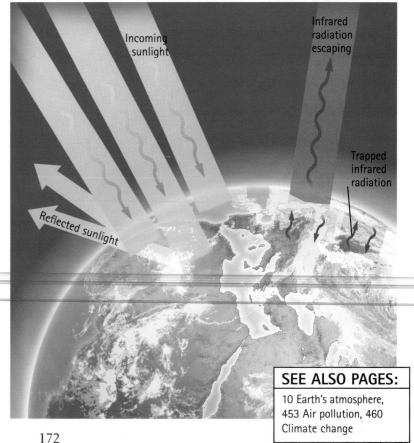

Incoming sunlight

Infrared radiation escaping

Reflected sunlight

Trapped infrared radiation

▲ At −328°F, liquid air can be separated into its component gases by distillation. Chilling removes carbon dioxide (CO_2) and water (H_2O) from the air. Repeated compression, chilling, expansion, and then cooling the air until it becomes liquid.

▶ Earth's surface is heated by the sun. Earth loses heat in the form of infrared radiation. Carbon dioxide in the atmosphere traps some of this radiation, causing the greenhouse effect.

SEE ALSO PAGES:

10 Earth's atmosphere, 453 Air pollution, 460 Climate change

WATER

Water is a colorless liquid that has no odor. Its chemical formula is H_2O. At normal atmospheric pressure, water freezes at 32°F and boils at 212°F.

Most substances become denser when they solidify. But ice is slightly less dense than liquid water. This is why icebergs float in the sea and ice cubes float in a glass of water.

A mature oak tree gives off about 530 pints of water vapor a day during the summer.

Although water is one of the most familiar chemical substances, it has some unusual properties. Ammonia (NH_3) and hydrogen sulfide (H_2S), both similar to water, are both compounds of nonmetals with hydrogen. They are heavier than water molecules, which would normally make their boiling points higher. In fact, both are gases at room temperature, and water is a liquid. The unusually strong attraction between water molecules makes it a liquid at room temperature.

A water molecule consists of an oxygen atom bonded to two hydrogen atoms. The oxygen atom pulls electrons away from the hydrogen atoms. This gives the oxygen atom a small negative charge, while the hydrogen atoms have positive charges. These charges attract water molecules to each other. This makes water an excellent solvent for charged particles, such as the ions that make up salts.

WATER EVERYWHERE

Water covers 70 percent of Earth's surface. Around 97 percent of this water is in the oceans. The remainder is mostly ice or snow. Less than one percent is in lakes and rivers.

Water is essential to life. It makes up about 70 percent of the human body. Animals and plants use water to carry nutrients and waste products around inside them. For example, human blood is around 90 percent water. Sap, which circulates in plants, is also mainly water.

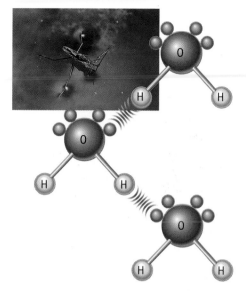

The attractive forces between water molecules give water a surface skin (surface tension). Some insects can walk on this skin without sinking through it.

WATER SUPPLIES

Water is taken from reservoirs, rivers, or underground wells to supply homes and industry. Water from these sources contains substances that are dissolved from rocks in the ground and can contain chemicals used by farmers. Hard water, which forms a scum when mixed with soap, contains dissolved calcium and magnesium salts. Untreated water may also contain solid substances, such as sand or soil particles and, often, harmful germs.

Water treatment plants make water fit for drinking by removing solid matter and by killing harmful organisms. Harmless dissolved salts are usually not removed.

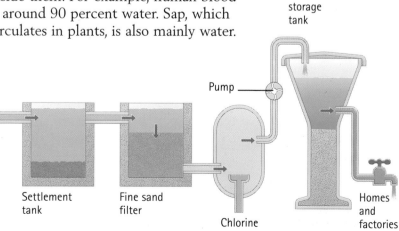

Pump

Screen filter

Coarse sand filter

Settlement tank

Fine sand filter

Pump

Chlorine

Elevated storage tank

Homes and factories

A water treatment plants receives water from a lake, river, or stream. Screens remove large objects, and increasingly fine filters remove all suspended solid particles. Chlorine (Cl_2), kills germs. In some countries, ozone is used to kill germs. Ozone (O_3), affects the water's taste less than chlorine does.

SEE ALSO PAGES:

12 The oceans, 38 Rain and snow, 452 Water pollution, 458 Renewable energy

ORGANIC CHEMISTRY

Organic chemistry is the study of carbon compounds. Many of these substances are formed by living organisms. Others are made artificially.

There are around 3 million organic compounds. Most of these compounds contain carbon atoms linked together in rings and chains.

HYDROCARBONS

Hydrocarbons are organic compounds that contain only carbon and hydrogen atoms. Crude oil is a mixture of about 300 hydrocarbons, depending on the type of oil; natural gas contains up to 99 percent methane (CH_4). Hydrocarbons are used as fuels and include natural gas, bottled gas, gasoline, diesel oil, and kerosene.

Propane (C_3H_8) is an alkane. It can be stored under pressure in steel cylinders. The liquefied gas vaporizes in the burner and burns with a hot, clean flame.

ALKANES

Methane is the first member of a family of hydrocarbons called alkanes. The others are ethane (C_2H_6), propane (C_3H_8), and butane (C_4H_{10}). Each member has one carbon atom and two hydrogen atoms more than the previous member. The *-ane* ending shows that a compound is a member of this group.

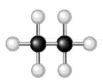

Methane has the molecular formula CH_4, which shows the types and numbers of atoms present. The structural formula shows how the atoms are grouped together.

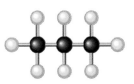

The molecular formula of ethane is C_2H_6. The structural formula CH_3–CH_3 shows that each carbon atom is joined to three hydrogen atoms.

The formula of propane is C_3H_8. The *prop-* in the name shows that it contains three carbon atoms. *Pent-*, *hex-*, *hept-*, and *oct-* indicate five, six, seven, and eight carbons.

ALKENES

Alkene molecules have one or more double bonds between their carbon atoms. They are called unsaturated compounds, because of these multiple bonds. Alkanes contain only single bonds and are saturated. The first members of the family are ethylene (C_2H_4) and propene (C_3H_6). The structural formulae of ethylene (CH_2=CH_2) and propene (CH_3-CH=CH_2) show their double bonds.

Double bonds give alkenes increased reactivity compared to alkanes. One of the pair of bonds can break open and form bonds with other atoms. Polyunsaturated vegetable oils, which contain many double bonds, react with hydrogen to form solid, saturated fats. Their carbon–carbon double bonds open up to form carbon–hydrogen bonds and leave single bonds where their double bonds were.

Simple alkenes can join together to make extremely long molecules called polymers. The polymerization reaction of ethylene makes polyethylene when a double bond in each molecule opens up and connects it to two more ethylene molecules as the polymer chain grows.

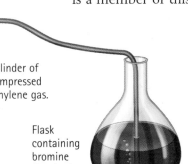
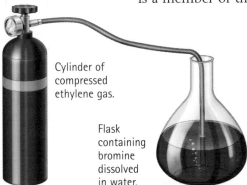

Cylinder of compressed ethylene gas.

Flask containing bromine dissolved in water.

Bromine is a liquid halogen element. It is highly reactive and has a red-brown color. The color fades slowly as bromine replaces the hydrogen atoms in ethane one by one. This type of reaction is called a substitution reaction.

Cylinder of compressed ethene gas.

Flask containing bromine dissolved in water.

The color of bromine disappears rapidly when mixed with an alkene. The carbon–carbon double bond opens up and the bromine atoms add onto the hydrocarbon. This type of reaction is called an addition reaction.

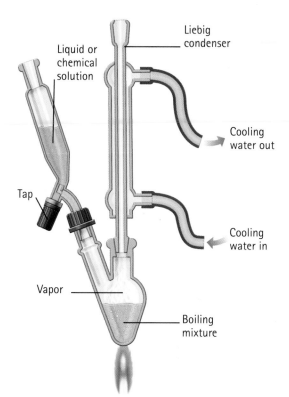

Slow chemical reactions can be made to go faster by heat. This apparatus has three main parts. The reaction takes place in the heated flask at the bottom. The tap controls the addition of liquids to the flask. The vertical condenser cools vapors that rise from the flask. This turns them into liquid that flows back into the flask.

FUNCTIONAL GROUPS

The double bond in alkene molecules gives them their distinctive properties. It is an example of a functional group. New families of compounds result when different elements or groups of atoms replace hydrogen atoms in alkanes and other hydrocarbons.

The alcohols all contain a hydroxyl group (–OH) attached to a carbon atom. Ethanol (C_2H_5OH) is a sharp-smelling liquid present in alcoholic drinks, whereas ethane (C_2H_6) is a gas. A form of propyl alcohol (C_3H_7OH) is a useful cleaning fluid for VCRs and other appliances.

Vinegar contains an acid called acetic acid (CH_3COOH). The functional group in this case is carboxylic acid (–COOH). The smell of rancid butter and sweat is caused by butyric acid (C_3H_7COOH).

There are only about 20 common functional groups. Millions of different organic molecules result from adding different combinations in different places on hydrocarbon molecules that are different lengths and shapes.

DNA molecules are coiled inside cell nuclei. Based on the shape of a twisted ladder, the rungs at the heart of the ladder carry a code that instructs each cell how to make proteins. An uncoiled DNA molecule would be about 3 feet long.

ORGANIC MOLECULES FOR LIFE

The chemistry of living beings is called biochemistry. We eat complex organic molecules in our food and break them down by digestion. Carbohydrates from starchy foods give glucose; proteins from meat and grains provide amino acids. Blood carries these small molecules to the cells in our bodies. Glucose breaks down further into water and carbon dioxide and releases energy that we use to move and to power other chemical reactions. Amino acids join together to make proteins for muscle and skin tissues, as well as other body structures. Some proteins are enzymes that help all these complex reactions to happen. Proteins control the shape of our bodies and the way they work. The reactions that make our proteins are controlled by the DNA coiled inside each cell. We inherit our DNA structure from our parents.

Hemoglobin carries oxygen in red blood cells. It is a protein molecule that consists of four chains of 145 amino acids each, wrapped around an iron atom. The Austrian-born British biochemist Max F. Perutz (1914–) worked out the structure of hemoglobin in 1959, after decades of research. He was joint winner of the 1962 Nobel prize in chemistry for his breakthrough.

SEE ALSO PAGES:

128–9 Digestion, 135 Genes and chromosomes, 162–3 Chemical reactions, 166–7 Bonding and valency, 210–11 Oil and refining

CATALYSTS

Catalysts are substances that speed up chemical reactions. They themselves remain unchanged. Catalysts are used in many industrial processes.

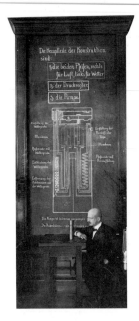

In 1908, German chemist Fritz Haber (1868–1934) discovered that an iron catalyst helps hydrogen and nitrogen to react together. The product, ammonia, is an important raw material for making a wide range of chemicals, including plant fertilizers, dyes, and explosives.

Molecules can only react together when they collide with sufficient force. Some reactions are slow because too few particles collide with sufficient force to react. A catalyst works by breaking down one difficult reaction step into two or more easier steps.

In the first step, one of the molecules combines with the catalyst to produce a substance called an intermediate. The intermediate then reacts with a second molecule to form the product. In this second step, the catalyst is released from the intermediate. The catalyst is then free to react again. In a well-catalyzed reaction, both of these steps require much less energy than the uncatalyzed reaction.

Many catalysts are transition elements such as iron and platinum. This is because these metals form and break bonds easily with reacting atoms, molecules, and ions. The solid metals are also easy to separate from liquids and gases after the reaction.

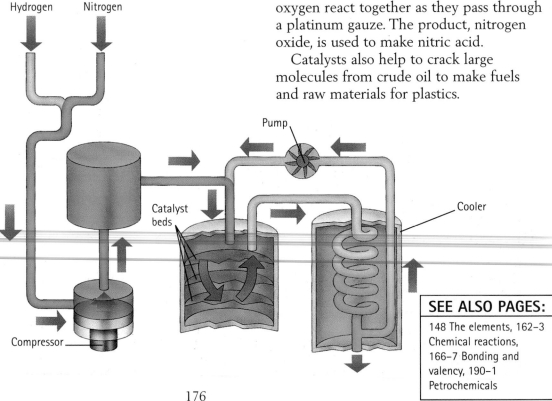

Honeycomb coated with metal catalysts

To exhaust

Metal casing

CO   Carbon monoxide
CO_2 Carbon dioxide
NO_X Nitrous oxides
HC   Hydrocarbons
N_2 Nitrogen
H_2O Water

Vehicle exhaust pollutants include unburned hydrocarbons, oxides of nitrogen, and carbon monoxide. A platinum catalyst converts them to harmless CO_2, H_2O, and N_2.

CATALYSTS IN ACTION

Catalyzts help in the manufacture of a wide range of items. Nickel, for example, catalyzes the reaction between hydrogen and vegetable oils to produce margarine.

Polyethylene was first made more than 60 years ago by compressing ethylene gas to dangerously high pressures. Using a catalyst mixture of titanium and aluminum compounds, the reaction happens at normal pressure and 140°F.

Platinum is an important catalyst for reactions between gases. Ammonia and oxygen react together as they pass through a platinum gauze. The product, nitrogen oxide, is used to make nitric acid.

Catalysts also help to crack large molecules from crude oil to make fuels and raw materials for plastics.

Hydrogen   Nitrogen

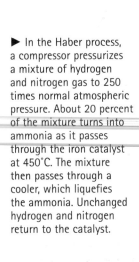

▶ In the Haber process, a compressor pressurizes a mixture of hydrogen and nitrogen gas to 250 times normal atmospheric pressure. About 20 percent of the mixture turns into ammonia as it passes through the iron catalyst at 450°C. The mixture then passes through a cooler, which liquefies the ammonia. Unchanged hydrogen and nitrogen return to the catalyst.

Pump

Catalyst beds

Cooler

Compressor

SEE ALSO PAGES:

148 The elements, 162–3 Chemical reactions, 166–7 Bonding and valency, 190–1 Petrochemicals

ENZYMES

Inside every living cell there are biological catalysts that enable the biochemical reactions that support life to happen. They are called enzymes.

Reacting molecules

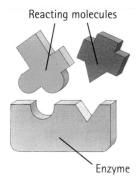

Enzyme

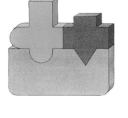

Product

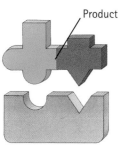

▲ Reacting molecules lock into a part of an enzyme molecule called an active site. When the reaction is complete, the product detaches from the active site.

Enzymes are coiled protein molecules that catalyze biochemical reactions. These reactions can happen several billion times faster with enzymes than without them. Most enzymes catalyze only one specific reaction. Pepsin, for example, is an enzyme in digestive juices. It starts the digestion of proteins by breaking them into smaller pieces. The job of breaking down starch in food is done by enzymes called amylases.

Enzymes work best over a narrow range of temperatures. They work only slowly below 86°F, and they break up above 104°F. Many inherited diseases are caused by the presence of faulty enzymes.

ENZYMES AT WORK

The part of an enzyme molecule that catalyzes reactions is called its active site. When reacting molecules fit into the active site, they are held in the correct position for the reaction to happen. The active site in many enzymes contains a metal atom. Others contain a small molecule called a coenzyme, which is usually a vitamin. Traces of metal atoms and vitamins are present in a balanced diet. Lack of vitamins and trace metals can stop enzymes working properly and even lead to diseases like scurvy.

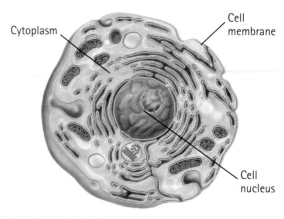

Cytoplasm / Cell membrane / Cell nucleus

A typical animal cell contains up to 100,000 different enzymes. These enzymes catalyze around 1,500 different life-supporting chemical reactions.

Enzymes are now made that can be used outside living cells. Biological detergents contain enzymes that break down grease. These enzymes are extracted from plants. Enzymes that cause color changes can be used to detect tiny amounts of substances. One of these enzymes is used in pregnancy-testing kits.

▲ Exercise uses energy to drive muscles. Triose phosphate isomerase is one of the enzymes that catalyze the release of energy from glucose in the blood.

◄ A spider injects its prey with digestive enzymes. After a few hours, it will suck out the digested insides of the insect.

SEE ALSO PAGES:

74 Spiders, centipedes, and scorpions, 98–9 Body organization, 106–7 Muscles and movement

OXIDATION AND REDUCTION

Oxidation and reduction reactions involve the gain and loss of oxygen or the transfer of electrons between substances in a chemical reaction.

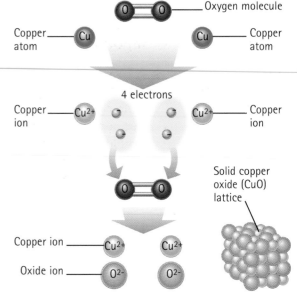

Oxygen is a common and reactive element that combines with most other elements. Heating copper in the air, for example, forms a surface layer of black copper oxide. Hydrogen gas burns in air to form water. The products of both reactions are oxides. Chemists classify these types of reactions as oxidations.

REDOX REACTIONS

When hydrogen gas passes over hot copper oxide, the hydrogen removes oxygen from the copper oxide to form copper metal and water. The equation for the reaction between copper oxide and hydrogen shows what happens:

$$CuO + H_2 \rightarrow Cu + H_2O$$

Hydrogen combines with oxygen from copper oxide to form water, so hydrogen is oxidized in this reaction. At the same time, copper oxide is reduced to copper metal by removing its oxygen.

Reactions of this type are called redox reactions, because they are combined *red*uction and *ox*idation reactions. The substance that causes the oxidation—in this case copper oxide—is called the oxidant. The reductant is the substance that causes the reduction. In this reaction the reductant is hydrogen.

In the reaction between copper and oxygen, copper loses electrons and is oxidized. Oxygen gains electrons and is reduced. Copper oxide is a lattice of copper and oxide ions.

ELECTRON TRANSFER

Chemists describe redox reactions in terms of the transfer of electrons between substances. The reaction between copper and oxygen forms copper oxide (CuO), which contains copper ions (Cu^{2+}) and oxide ions (O^{2-}). Each copper atom loses two electrons as it becomes a copper ion. These electrons are accepted by oxygen molecules, which form two oxide ions each. In general, oxidation is the removal of electrons from a substance, and reduction is the addition of electrons to a substance.

When redox reactions are described as transfers of electrons, many reactions that do not involve oxygen can be classified as oxidation and reduction reactions. For example, the reaction between sodium metal and chlorine gas is a redox reaction. Each sodium atom (Na) loses one electron to form a sodium ion (Na^+). At the same time, each chlorine molecule (Cl_2) gains two electrons to form two chloride ions. The result is the ionic compound sodium chloride (NaCl). In this reaction, chlorine is the oxidant, and sodium is the reductant.

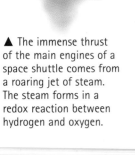

▲ The immense thrust of the main engines of a space shuttle comes from a roaring jet of steam. The steam forms in a redox reaction between hydrogen and oxygen.

► These iron rails are being welded together by the Thermite process. In this process, a mixture of aluminum and iron oxide is ignited to start the redox reaction between the two substances. The heat of the reaction is enough to melt the rails.

SEE ALSO PAGES:

150–1 Atoms, 162–3
Chemical reactions, 420–1
Rockets and space shuttles

HYDROGEN

Hydrogen is the simplest element with the smallest mass of all. It is the most common element in the universe and has important industrial uses.

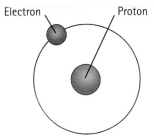

Electron   Proton

The nucleus of ordinary hydrogen is a proton.

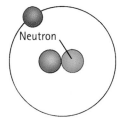

Neutron

The deuterium nucleus has one neutron and a proton.

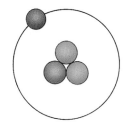

Tritium has two neutrons and a proton in its nucleus.

▲ All three isotopes of hydrogen have a proton and an electron. Nuclei of deuterium (D) and tritium (T) also have neutrons.

Hydrogen is a colorless, odorless gas. It is the lightest element in the periodic table. Hydrogen gas consists of diatomic molecules (H_2). In hydrogen molecules, each atom contributes one electron to the covalent bond that holds the molecule together.

Hydrogen is highly flammable. It burns with oxygen to form water. Hydrogen is found in a range of compounds, including acids, hydroxides, and hydrocarbons.

ISOTOPES

Isotopes are atoms of the same element that have different numbers of neutrons in their nuclei. Almost all hydrogen atoms consist of an electron orbiting a proton. Of every million hydrogen atoms, 150 have a nucleus that contains a neutron as well as a proton. This isotope of hydrogen is called deuterium (D).

Isotopes have the same chemical properties because they have the same number of electrons. Deuterium bonds with oxygen to form heavy water (D_2O). This liquid is used in nuclear reactors and in chemical experiments.

A third isotope of hydrogen is called tritium (T). Tritium is made in nuclear reactors and is radioactive.

The main use of hydrogen is for the manufacture of a wide range of chemicals. It is also used as a propellant for space rockets and as a fuel for welding.

USES OF HYDROGEN

The Haber process reacts hydrogen with nitrogen to make ammonia (NH_3), which is used to manufacture fertilizers, dyes, explosives, and plastics. Hydrogen is also used to change vegetable oils into margarine.

Hydrogen is a good fuel for rockets and welding. It burns in air to produce large amounts of energy and pure water, which does not cause pollution. Hydrogen is being tested as an alternative fuel for cars.

Unfortunately, hydrogen fuel is difficult to store. Hydrogen gas occupies too much space, and liquid hydrogen must be kept at temperatures below −423°F.

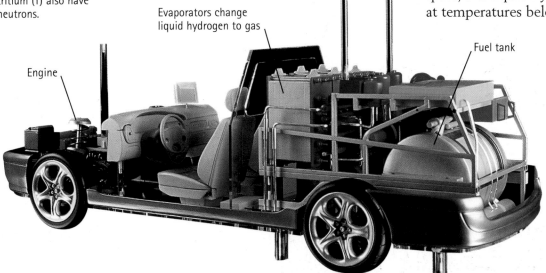

Evaporators change liquid hydrogen to gas

Fuel tank

Engine

This experimental car burns hydrogen fuel in an ordinary piston engine. Its exhaust gases cause no pollution, because they contain only water vapor.

SEE ALSO PAGES:
148–9 The elements,
150–1 Atoms, 164–5
Chemical compounds

NOBLE GASES

The noble gases are the elements that form group 18 of the periodic table. They all have full outer electron shells, which makes them extremely unreactive.

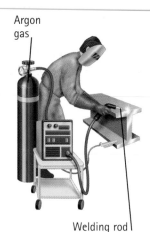

Argon gas

Welding rod

Arc welders use electric currents to melt metals. Argon is often used to surround the electric arc. Argon excludes air from the hot area and prevents oxygen in the air from reacting with the metal and weakening it.

In order of increasing atomic mass, the noble gases are helium, neon, argon, krypton, xenon, and radon. They are all colorless, odorless gases that do not burn.

Helium is the second lightest and second most common element in the universe. Helium is rare on Earth, but small amounts of helium are found in natural gas. Neon, argon, krypton, and xenon are obtained from air by the fractional distillation of liquid air. Radon is a radioactive element. It is produced by the radioactive decay of elements such as radium. Radon gas can seep into houses that are built over naturally radioactive granite rocks. If breathed in, it can damage cells and cause cancers to start growing.

The boiling points of the noble gases, in kelvin, compared to other gases. The boiling points in degrees Celsius are 273° lower. Boiling points increase with atomic mass.

Boiling temperature K

Helium	4K	
Neon	27K	
Argon	87K	
Krypton	120K	
Xenon	165K	
Chlorine	239K	
Oxygen	90K	
Nitrogen	77K	

USES

The only noble gas compounds made so far are the fluorides of krypton, xenon, and radon. They have no practical uses.

Helium is used to fill airships and some party balloons. These balloons float because helium is less dense than air. Helium is mixed with oxygen as a breathing mixture for deep-sea divers. This is because the nitrogen in air becomes poisonous when breathed at high pressure.

The noble gases are mainly used in electric lights. Argon and neon give off brightly colored light when an electric current passes through tubes that contain them at low pressure. The tube can be bent into the shapes of letters and numbers for advertising displays. Small lamps that contain krypton or xenon give out an intense, bluish-white light. Flash attachments on cameras use these gases to produce intense bursts of light.

Helium, neon, and argon are used in lasers that produce continuous beams of light that have a single wavelength.

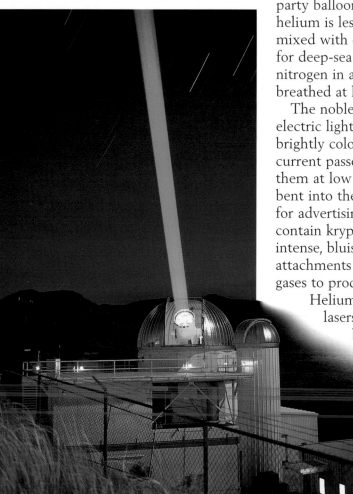

▶ The Starfire noble-gas laser in New Mexico creates an artificial image of a star in the upper atmosphere. An astronomical telescope then detects changes in this image caused by atmospheric conditions. A computer adjusts images of real stars to cancel out distortions caused by atmospheric conditions.

SEE ALSO PAGES:

152–3 The periodic table, 358–9 Electricity through gases, 416–7 Astronomical telescopes

SULFUR

Sulfur is a yellow, solid, nonmetallic, element from group 16 of the periodic table. Its most important use is for the manufacture of sulfuric acid.

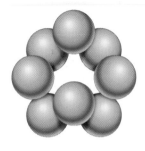

Solid sulfur exists as crown-shaped molecules that contain eight atoms in a ring. The rings stack together in a lattice. When sulfur melts, the rings break open and split into smaller molecules.

Sulfur is a bright yellow element that occurs naturally in volcanic regions and near oil fields. Mechanical diggers can retrieve sulfur from surface deposits, but the main sources are underground deposits in Poland, Mexico, and the United States. Sulfur is mined from deep deposits by pumping air and pressurized water at 338°F into the ground through pipes. A froth of sulfur, air, and water rises to the surface through another pipe. Sulfur is also a by-product of oil refining.

Many minerals are compounds of metals with sulfur. Galena, which is lead sulfide (PbS), is one example. Gypsum, which is hydrated calcium sulfate ($CaSO_4.2H_2O$), is another.

Sulfur is an essential element for living things. It is present in food, notably eggs, mustard, and garlic, and is part of two of the amino acids that form proteins.

SULFURIC ACID

By far the most important use of sulfur is for the manufacture of sulfuric acid (H_2SO_4). Economists have shown that the wealth of an industrial country is directly linked to the amount of sulfuric acid it produces. Sulfuric acid is used to make an enormous variety of items, ranging from fertilizers and fuels to paints, plastics, detergents, and medicines.

OTHER USES

Sulfur is used to vulcanize natural rubber. Vulcanization toughens natural rubber so that it can be used to make tires for cars and other vehicles. Natural rubber is soft and stretchy because it contains long, coiled molecules that slide past each other easily. Heating rubber with powdered sulfur forms links between the molecules. These links harden the rubber and make it more durable.

Sulfur is used as an ingredient in gunpowder, matches, and fireworks. It is also used as medicine for fungal diseases.

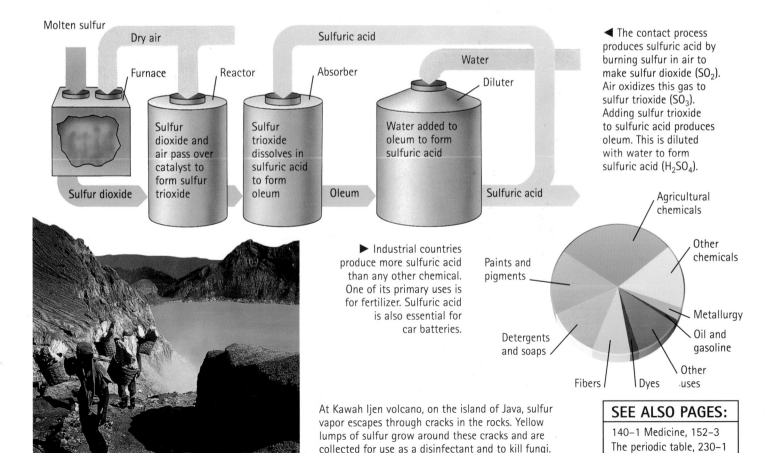

Molten sulfur / Dry air / Sulfuric acid / Water / Furnace / Reactor / Absorber / Diluter

Sulfur dioxide and air pass over catalyst to form sulfur trioxide

Sulfur trioxide dissolves in sulfuric acid to form oleum

Water added to oleum to form sulfuric acid

Sulfur dioxide / Oleum / Sulfuric acid

◀ The contact process produces sulfuric acid by burning sulfur in air to make sulfur dioxide (SO_2). Air oxidizes this gas to sulfur trioxide (SO_3). Adding sulfur trioxide to sulfuric acid produces oleum. This is diluted with water to form sulfuric acid (H_2SO_4).

▶ Industrial countries produce more sulfuric acid than any other chemical. One of its primary uses is for fertilizer. Sulfuric acid is also essential for car batteries.

Agricultural chemicals / Other chemicals / Paints and pigments / Metallurgy / Oil and gasoline / Detergents and soaps / Other uses / Fibers / Dyes

At Kawah Ijen volcano, on the island of Java, sulfur vapor escapes through cracks in the rocks. Yellow lumps of sulfur grow around these cracks and are collected for use as a disinfectant and to kill fungi.

SEE ALSO PAGES:

140–1 Medicine, 152–3 The periodic table, 230–1 Food production

THE HALOGENS

The halogens are the elements that form group 17 of the periodic table. They are reactive nonmetals and include fluorine, chlorine, bromine, and iodine.

Some refrigerators contain chlorofluorocarbons, or CFCs. They can cause holes in Earth's ozone layer. CFCs must be removed before the refrigerators are scrapped.

Dry ski slopes are made with PTFE-coated tiles.

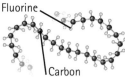

Fluorine

Carbon

PTFE molecules contain only carbon and fluorine.

▲ Polytetrafluoroethene, or PTFE, has a surface that is more slippery than ice. Its many uses include coatings for cooking utensils and ski slopes.

The halogens are five nonmetallic elements that form group 17 of the periodic table. Molecules of these elements have two atoms joined by a single covalent bond. Fluorine (F_2) is a pale yellow gas; chlorine (Cl_2) is a greenish-yellow gas; bromine (Br_2) is a dark red liquid; iodine (I_2) is a purple-black solid. Astatine is a radioactive metallic solid that can only be made in nuclear reactors.

The halogens are all poisonous and will attack skin. Their reactivity decreases in the order F > Cl > Br > I. Fluorine reacts explosively with many substances; iodine reacts only slowly, if at all. The halogens combine with metals to form ionic salts called halides. Examples include sodium chloride (NaCl), which is common salt or table salt. Most halides are soluble in water, and many are found in seawater. The halides of hydrogen are acids and include hydrochloric acid (HCl). Halogens also form compounds with some nonmetals, such as carbon and sulfur.

EXTRACTION AND USES

Fluorine is made by electrolyzing a liquid mixture of hydrogen fluoride and potassium fluoride at 100°C. Fluorine is used to make fluorocarbons, such as the plastic PTFE, and to purify nuclear fuel. Small amounts of sodium fluoride (NaF) in drinking water help prevent tooth decay.

Chlorine is made by the electrolysis of sodium-chloride solution. Chlorine is used to sterilize drinking and bathing water, and for the manufacture of bleach and plastics.

Bromine is made by reacting chlorine with magnesium bromide from seawater. Similarly, chlorine reacts with iodide salts from seaweed. These two halogens are used in the manufacture of photographic film, medicines, and antiseptics.

9	Fluorine
F	Atomic number 9
19.0	

17	Chlorine
Cl	Atomic number 17
35.5	

35	Bromine
Br	Atomic number 35
79.9	

53	Iodine
I	Atomic number 53
126.9	

85	Astatine
At	Atomic number 85
210.0	

Halogen atoms are just one electron short of a complete outer electron shell. They react readily to accept one electron each from other atoms.

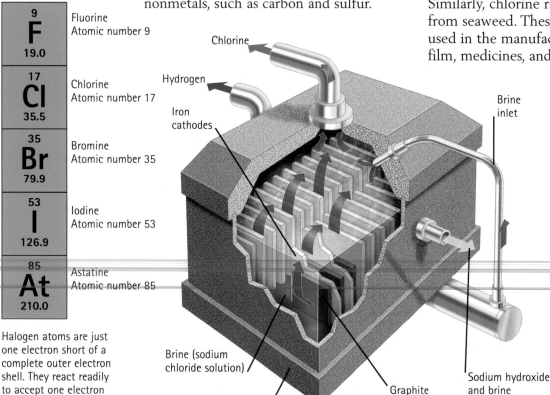

Chlorine

Hydrogen

Iron cathodes

Brine inlet

Brine (sodium chloride solution)

Concrete casing

Graphite anode

Sodium hydroxide and brine

Hooker cells are used to manufacture chlorine and sodium hydroxide by electrolysis. Brine flows past electrodes inside a concrete casing. Bubbles of chlorine form at the graphite anodes and rise up through the brine. Chlorine leaves the cell through a pipe at the top. Hydrogen gas forms at the iron cathodes and leaves the cell through side pipes. The brine leaving the cell contains sodium hydroxide, a useful chemical substance.

SEE ALSO PAGES:

150–1 Atoms, 152–3 The periodic table, 453 Air pollution, 460 Climate change

METALS

Most metals are extracted from ores that are mined from the Earth's crust. The method of extraction depends on the chemical reactivity of each metal.

Every 8 hours, workers wearing protective clothing open the hole at the bottom of a blast furnace. White-hot molten iron runs out at a temperature of about 1,600°C.

REACTIVITY SERIES OF METALS	
Potassium	**K**
Sylvite (KCl)	
Sodium	**Na**
Rock salt (NaCl)	
Calcium	**Ca**
Limestone ($CaCO_3$)	
Magnesium	**Mg**
Dolomite ($MgCO_3.CaCO_3$)	
Aluminum	**Al**
Bauxite (Al_2O_3)	
Carbon	**C**
Zinc	**Zn**
Zinc blende (ZnS)	
Iron	**Fe**
Hematite (Fe_2O_3)	
Tin	**Sn**
Cassiterite (SnO_2)	
Lead	**Pb**
Galena (PbS)	
Copper	**Cu**
Copper pyrites ($CuFeS_2$)	
Mercury	**Hg**
Cinnabar (HgS)	
Silver Metal	**Ag**
Gold Metal	**Au**
Platinum Metal	**Pt**

The reactivity series of metals. The nonmetal carbon occupies the space between aluminum and zinc. Carbon is more reactive than the metals below it, but less reactive than the metals above it.

About 80 of the elements are metals. They are to the left and in the center of the periodic table. All metals are shiny solids at room temperature, except mercury, which is a liquid. Metals are malleable and ductile; this means they can be hammered or stretched into different shapes. They are also good conductors of heat and electricity because their outermost electrons can move from one atom to the next.

METAL REACTIVITY

Gold and platinum are examples of metals that rarely react with other elements to form compounds. Potassium and sodium are extremely reactive metals. They even react violently with relatively unreactive substances, such as water. The reactivities of most metals lie between these two extremes. Iron, for example, rusts slowly in moist air. Copper is almost unaffected under the same conditions.

The reactivity series lists the common metals in order of reactivity. The most reactive metals are normally at the top of the list. Nonmetals carbon and hydrogen are often included in the list to give a comparison of their reactivities.

Aluminum oxide is mixed with cryolite, so that it melts at 850°C. Electrolysis between graphite electrodes produces aluminum metal at the cathode and oxygen gas at the anodes. The electrolyzing current keeps the mixture hot enough to stay liquid. Oxygen gradually oxidizes the anodes, so they have to be replaced from time to time.

ORES AND METAL EXTRACTION

Most metals occur as compounds in Earth's crust. Only the least reactive metals, such as gold and platinum, are found as pure elements. Rocks that contain metal compounds are called ores. Hematite, a type of iron ore, contains iron oxide (Fe_2O_3). The main lead ore is galena, or lead sulfide (PbS).

Many metals are extracted by heating their ore in a furnace with a substance that removes the elements attached to the metal. This process is called smelting. Smelting iron ore with carbon produces iron metal and carbon-dioxide gas. Carbon removes the oxygen from iron oxide.

Carbon can be used to smelt metals that lie below it in the reactivity series. Zinc, iron, tin, and lead are all produced by smelting their ores with carbon.

Carbon cannot smelt metals that are more reactive than itself. As a result, the metals from aluminum to potassium in the reactivity series are produced by electrolysis of their molten compounds.

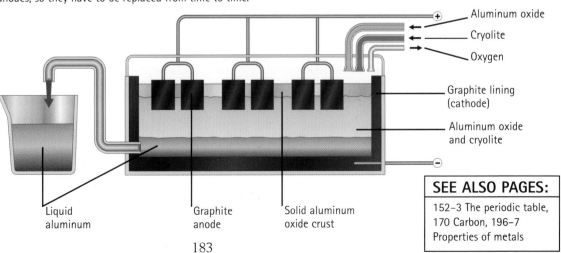

Aluminum oxide
Cryolite
Oxygen
Graphite lining (cathode)
Aluminum oxide and cryolite

Liquid aluminum
Graphite anode
Solid aluminum oxide crust

SEE ALSO PAGES:
152–3 The periodic table, 170 Carbon, 196–7 Properties of metals

ACIDS

Acids are compounds of hydrogen that produce hydrogen ions with water. The hydrogen ions make the solution acidic. Acids turn litmus paper red.

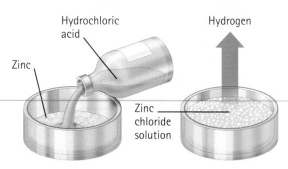

Small pieces of zinc metal dissolve rapidly in hydrochloric acid. Bubbles of hydrogen gas are given off, and the zinc dissolves to form a solution of zinc chloride.

Many everyday things contain acids. Lemons contain citric acid and vinegar contains ethanoic acid, which is also called acetic acid. Different acids give lemons, vinegar, and sour apples their sharp taste. Car batteries contain sulfuric acid, and digestive juices in the stomach contain hydrochloric acid.

Acids are solutions of substances that produce hydrogen ions (H^+) when they dissolve in water. Many acid substances can be obtained as pure solids, liquids, or gases, but they act as acids only when they are dissolved in water.

ACID REACTIONS

Acids can be detected by adding a special dye called an indicator. Litmus paper, for example, contains an indicator dye that changes from purple to red in acidic solutions. Many acids produce hydrogen gas when mixed with reactive metals, such as zinc or magnesium. In another test, acid is mixed with sodium bicarbonate ($NaHCO_3$). Strong acids make the mixture fizz as carbon dioxide gas is produced.

▲ Bottles of laboratory acids carry a warning label that shows they are corrosive and harmful (top). Organic acids in fruit taste sharp and are harmless, but the acid in wasp stings causes a painful reaction. Car batteries (bottom) contain harmful sulfuric acid.

▶ Concentrated sulfuric acid is a dehydrating agent. It removes hydrogen and oxygen from substances to form water. This picture shows sugar being turned into carbon by sulfuric acid. The acid converts sugar ($C_{12}H_{22}O_{11}$) into 11 molecules of water and 12 carbon atoms. The heat of the reaction turns some of the water into steam. This forms a froth of black carbon.

ORGANIC ACIDS

Plants and animals produce a variety of acidic carbon compounds called organic acids. Most are harmless, and many give flavor to fruit and other food. Oils and fats are compounds of organic acids with glycerol. Soaps are salts of organic acids that are made from oils and fats. DNA, deoxyribonucleic acid, is an extremely complex acid that carries genetic code.

A few naturally-occurring organic acids are harmful. Nettles and some ants defend themselves with methanoic acid (HCO_2H), which causes stings. An old name for this acid—formic acid—comes from the Latin word for ant, *formicus*.

The leaves of some plants, such as rhubarb, contain poisonous oxalic acid. Animals soon learn not to eat these plants.

INORGANIC ACIDS

Acids made from minerals and nonmetals are called inorganic acids. The common inorganic acids are sulfuric acid (H_2SO_4), hydrochloric acid (HCl), nitric acid (HNO_3), and phosphoric acid (H_3PO_4).

Industry produces millions of tons of these acids every year. They are used to make plastics, fibers, fertilizers, dyes, and other chemicals. Concentrated inorganic acids are often highly corrosive. They can damage skin and rapidly dissolve most metals. Hydrofluoric acid (HF) can dissolve glass. Other inorganic acids are not at all dangerous. Boric acid (H_3BO_3) is the main ingredient in soothing eye lotions.

SEE ALSO PAGES:

164–5 Chemical compounds, 448–9 Food and farming

BASES AND ALKALIS

A base is a substance that can neutralize an acid by reacting with hydrogen ions. An alkali is a base that dissolves in water. Bases turn litmus paper blue.

Sodium bicarbonate solution with indicator

Vinegar

Indicator changes color

▲ A litmus indicator turns blue in a solution of sodium bicarbonate (top). This is because the solution is alkaline. If drops of vinegar (above center) are added to the solution (above), the acid in the vinegar turns the litmus red for a moment until it is neutralized by the alkali. When all the bicarbonate has been neutralized, the solution becomes purple. If more acid is added, the solution turns red.

▶ Crops do not grow well in acidic soil. Soils that are slightly alkaline are ideal for plant growth and for the spread of beneficial soil organisms. Farmers add powdered lime, calcium hydroxide, to acid soil. The lime neutralizes the acid and makes the soil slightly alkaline.

Most bases are minerals that react with acids to form water and a salt. Bases include the oxides, hydroxides, and carbonates of metals. Examples are sodium hydroxide (NaOH), calcium carbonate ($CaCO_3$), and potassium oxide (K_2O).

Bases react with the hydrogen ions in an acidic solution to make water. Copper oxide (CuO) is a typical base. It neutralizes sulfuric acid (H_2SO_4) to produce copper sulfate ($CuSO_4$) and water. A chemical equation shows this change:

$$CuO + H_2SO_4 \rightarrow CuSO_4 + H_2O.$$

If black copper oxide powder is added to the colorless acid, the powder dissolves and the solution becomes colored with blue copper sulfate. After a while, no more copper oxide dissolves. The acid is no longer present and the solution does not turn indicators to their acid color. This is a neutralization reaction. The salt produced in the reaction consists of a copper ion (Cu^{2+}) and a sulfate ion (SO_4^{2-}). The positive copper ion is from the base and the negative sulfate ion is from the acid. The other product of the reaction is water. The part of an acid that forms salts in neutralization reactions is called the acid radical. The acid radical of sulfuric acid is (SO_4^{2-}).

Acids from rotting vegetation and acid rain harm aquatic organisms. This lime-dosing column adds calcium hydroxide to a flowing river to neutralize acids.

ALKALIS

Alkalis are bases that dissolve in water. A solution of alkali can be detected by adding an indicator. A solution of sodium hydroxide, for example, changes litmus from purple to blue. Alkaline solutions contain hydroxide ions (OH^-). When acidic and alkaline solutions mix, hydroxide ions from the alkali react with hydrogen ions from the acid to form water. A salt is also produced.

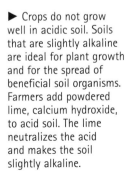

SEE ALSO PAGES:

162–3 Chemical reactions,
230–1 Food production,
453 Air pollution

INDICATORS AND pH

The pH scale shows whether a solution is acidic or alkaline, and how strong it is. Indicators are dyes that change color according to the pH of a solution.

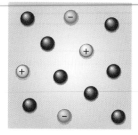

Weak acids ionize only partially in solution.

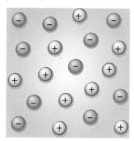

Strong acids ionize completely in solution.

▲ Solutions of strong acids contain hydrogen ions and acid radical ions only. Solutions of weaker acids contain some ions and molecules of acid that have not ionized (red).

When zinc metal is dropped into hydrochloric acid, it reacts rapidly and dissolves. Even when concentrated, a solution of citric acid has almost no effect on this metal. Organic acids, such as citric acid and ethanoic acid, are classed as weak acids. Inorganic acids, such as hydrochloric acid and sulfuric acid, are strong acids.

THE pH SCALE
The pH value of a solution is an indication of its acidity or alkalinity. The normal range of pH runs from pH 1 to pH 14. Neutral solutions, which are neither acidic nor alkaline, have a pH value of seven.

Acidic solutions have pH values less than seven. The lower the pH value, the stronger the acid. Ethanoic acid, which is weak, has a pH value around five. Strong acids have pH values close to zero; some can even have negative pH values.

Alkaline solutions have pH values greater than seven. Solutions of strong alkalis, such as sodium hydroxide (NaOH) can be pH 14 or even greater.

Very slight changes in pH affect the organisms living in water. This biologist is using an electronic pH meter that gives readings to an accuracy of 0.1 of a pH unit.

MEASURING pH
The simplest way to measure the pH value of a solution is by using an indicator. Indicators are dyes that have different colors in different pH ranges. Litmus, for example, is a vegetable dye that is red in acid and blue in alkali. Litmus and litmus paper are used to identify acids and alkalis. Other indicators change color at more specific pH values. Methyl orange, for example, changes color in the range pH 3–4.5. Combinations of indicators give better estimates of pH values.

The best way to measure pH is with a pH meter. A pH meter measures the concentration of hydrogen ions and calculates the precise pH value.

STRENGTH AND IONIZATION
The pH value of a strong acid shows that all of its molecules have split up into hydrogen ions and acid radical ions. Weak acids only partially ionize. This means that only a small fraction of their molecules split up to produce hydrogen ions. This is why their solutions are less acidic than strong acids. In a similar way, weak alkalis form only very few hydroxide ions.

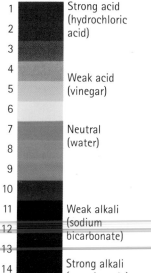

1	Strong acid (hydrochloric acid)
2	
3	
4	Weak acid (vinegar)
5	
6	
7	Neutral (water)
8	
9	
10	
11	Weak alkali (sodium bicarbonate)
12	
13	
14	Strong alkali (caustic soda)

▲ A universal indicator is a dye mixture that has several color changes and gives an indication of the pH value of a solution.

UNIVERSAL INDICATOR

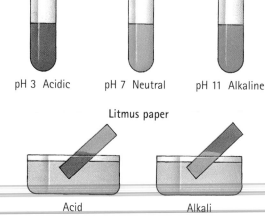

pH 3 Acidic   pH 7 Neutral   pH 11 Alkaline

Litmus paper

Acid   Alkali

Methyl orange

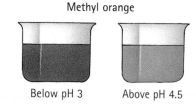

Below pH 3   Above pH 4.5

Litmus paper shows whether a solution is acidic (pH < 7) or alkaline (pH > 7). Methyl orange changes from yellow to red below around pH 4.

SEE ALSO PAGES:
158–9 Solutions, 184 Acids, 185 Bases and alkalis

SOAPS AND DETERGENTS

Soaps and detergents make fats and grease dissolve in water. Soaps are made from natural fats and oils. Detergents are made from petrochemicals.

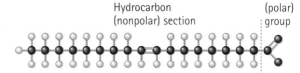

Hydrocarbon (nonpolar) section

Acid (polar) group

A typical detergent molecule has a nonpolar part that is attracted to oils and grease. A polar part, often an acid, enables the molecule to dissolve in water.

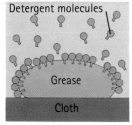

Detergent attacks grease.

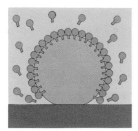

A grease droplet forms.

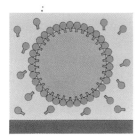

The grease droplet floats away from the fabric.

▲ Detergent molecules have fat-loving tails that attach themselves to grease, and water-loving heads that make grease droplets mix with water.

Bars of hand soap and soap flakes are examples of soapy detergents. They are mostly made from vegetable oils, such as palm oil, olive oil, and coconut oil. Some soaps are made from animal fats and grease.

Soapless detergents are the cleaning agents in dishwashing liquid, shampoo, and laundry powder. Soapless detergents are made from by-products of oil refining.

DISSOLVING GREASE

Grime on clothes and skin is a mixture of dirt and grease. Dirty dinner plates are covered with scraps of greasy food. Since oils and grease repel water, washing with water alone will not dissolve greasy dirt. Detergents help clean clothes, skin, and plates by helping water to dissolve grease.

There are many different kinds of soapy and soapless detergent molecules, but they all have a polar part and a nonpolar part. The polar part has an electrical charge that attracts it to water. The nonpolar part is electrically neutral and dissolves well in grease. When a detergent is mixed with grease, the nonpolar parts of the detergent molecules dissolve in the grease. The polar parts stick out from the surface of the grease. Rubbing and squeezing breaks the grease into droplets that are surrounded by a layer of detergent molecules. The polar groups are on the outside of this layer, so the droplet dissolves in water.

SOAPMAKING

Humans have been making soap for many hundreds of years. They stirred together animal fat, water, and ashes from the fire and left the mixture for several weeks. The water and ashes formed an alkali that broke down the animal fat to make soap. The chemistry of modern soapmaking is very similar to this ancient method, but the process is now very different.

Animal and vegetable fats are chemical compounds of glycerol and fatty acids. Fatty acids are long chains of carbon and hydrogen atoms that are tipped with a carboxylic acid group ($-CO_2H$). An alkali, usually sodium hydroxide, converts fat molecules into glycerol and fatty acids. Then, the alkali reacts with the fatty acid to form a salt. The long hydrocarbon chain of the fatty acid becomes tipped with a polar carboxylate ion ($-CO_2^-$), which attracts water. This is the crude soap. After the other chemicals in the reaction have been washed away, the purified soap is dried. Color and perfume may be added before the soap is molded into bars or made into flakes. The by-product of the reaction, glycerol, is used for making explosives, plastics, and other chemicals.

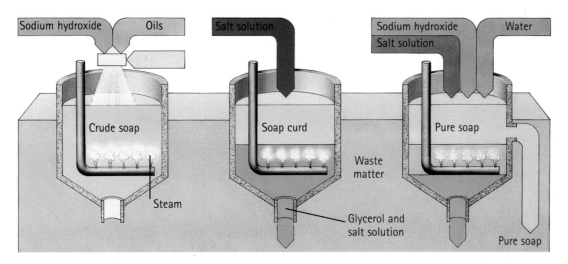

Sodium hydroxide | Oils

Crude soap

Steam

Salt solution

Soap curd

Glycerol and salt solution

Waste matter

Sodium hydroxide | Water
Salt solution

Pure soap

Pure soap

In the first stage of soap manufacturing, sodium hydroxide solution splits oil molecules into soap and glycerol. Steam heats the mixture. Then, salt solution is added to curdle the crude soap. More sodium hydroxide splits up any remaining oil in the soap and salt solution, and water washes the soap to remove impurities.

SEE ALSO PAGES:

CHEMISTRY OF FOOD

Food provides energy and gives nourishment for the growth and repair of tissue. Carbohydrates, fats and oils, proteins, and vitamins are components of food.

Life depends on an enormous number of chemical reactions that involve molecules based on carbon. The sum of all the chemical processes in an organism is called its metabolism. There are two parts to metabolism. Catabolism includes all the reactions that break down large molecules with the release of energy. Anabolism uses simple molecules to synthesize proteins, fats, and other complex substances.

Starch molecule (consists of many glucose molecules)

Glucose molecule

Amylase enzymes break starch into separate glucose molecules

Cells in wall of alimentary canal

Blood vessel

Glucose in the bloodstream

CATABOLISM

The major part of catabolism is the digestion of food. Digestive enzymes break large molecules into simple substances that are absorbed into the bloodstream. Carbohydrates from cereals contain starch, some of which breaks down to form molecules of glucose. The digestion of proteins results in amino acids. Digestion does not break fat into simpler molecules. Bile from the liver acts as a detergent and forms an emulsion of tiny fat droplets. Blood vessels that surround the intestines carry all these substances to the liver.

ANABOLISM

The liver is the body's chemical factory. It stores glucose, and also regulates the amount of glucose in the blood so that the correct amount of energy is available to all cells. The liver also uses glycerol from fats and oils to make extra supplies of glucose. It processes amino acids from digested proteins and makes sure that the correct amounts circulate in the blood. Cells around the body synthesize proteins by joining amino acids together in a sequence controlled by DNA. The liver also breaks down fat and converts the products into oily substances, called lipids, that are needed to form cell membranes. Surplus lipids are stored around the body as fat.

▼ A healthy, balanced diet contains the correct proportions of carbohydrates, fats and oils, fiber, and protein. Dietary fiber is an indigestible form of starch. Although fiber is not digested, it helps healthy digestion by carrying food through the alimentary canal.

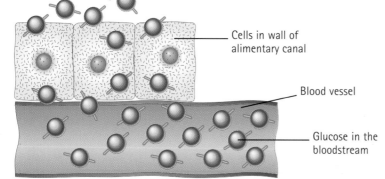

▲ Starch molecules consist of thousands of glucose molecules joined end to end. Enzymes in saliva and digestive juices in the alimentary canal split starch molecules into glucose. This is soluble in water and passes through the canal wall and into the bloodstream. Body cells take glucose from the blood and break it down with the help of oxygen to produce energy.

Carbohydrate 50%

Protein 20%

Fiber 15%

Fats and oils 15%

Amino acids join together to make proteins. The –OH of the acid group combines with a hydrogen atom from the amine group (–NH$_2$) to form water.

H_2N — ☐ — C $\overset{O}{\underset{}{||}}$ — OH + H — N $\overset{H}{\underset{}{|}}$ — ▲ — C $\overset{O}{\underset{}{||}}$ — OH → H_2N — ☐ — C $\overset{O}{\underset{}{||}}$ — H — N $\overset{H}{\underset{}{|}}$ — ▲ — C $\overset{O}{\underset{}{||}}$ — OH + H_2O

◄ The seed grains from cereals such as barley contain all the major food substances. It takes about 10 lbs of grain to make a pig grow by 1 lb. Meat such as pork is mostly protein and fat, so eating too much meat provides an unbalanced diet and is a poor use of farmland.

◄ These root nodules contain bacteria that change nitrogen into nitrates. They live on the roots of legumes, such as peas and beans. The legume provides food for the bacteria and receives nutritious nitrates.

▼ Nitric acid is made by passing air and ammonia (NH_3) over a catalyst. The initial product is nitrogen oxide (NO). Oxygen from the air converts nitrogen oxide into nitrogen dioxide (NO_2). Nitrogen dioxide and water form nitric acid (HNO_3), which is used to make nitrate fertilizers.

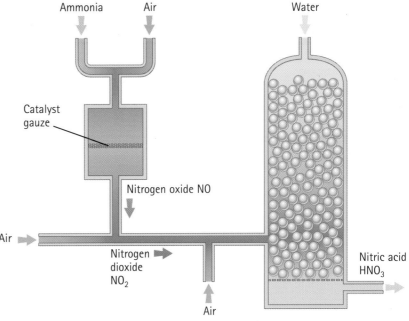

Ammonia Air Water

Catalyst gauze

Nitrogen oxide NO

Air

Nitrogen dioxide NO_2

Air

Nitric acid HNO_3

GROWING FOOD

Most human food comes from plants. Even meat comes from animals that feed on plants. Plants use photosynthesis to build up glucose from water and carbon dioxide. They then join glucose molecules to make starch. They also use glucose as the starting-point for the synthesis of fats and oils. These processes use compounds of carbon, hydrogen, and oxygen from the photosynthesis reaction. To make proteins, plants also need nitrogen.

THE NITROGEN PROBLEM

Plants take in nitrogen in the form of nitrate salts dissolved in groundwater. Bacteria in soil convert nitrogen from the air into nitrates. Other soil bacteria break down dead plant and animal remains to form nitrates. These natural processes produce enough nitrates for normal plant growth. Intensive farming soon drains nitrates from the soil, so farmers must add artificial fertilizers to the soil to provide the nitrates for plants to make proteins.

Ammonium nitrate (NH_4NO_3) is a common fertilizer made from ammonia (NH_3) and nitric acid (HNO_3). Since nitric acid is made from ammonia, both these materials depend on the Haber process for converting nitrogen from air into ammonia (see page 176). Potassium nitrate (KNO_3) and ammonium sulfate (($NH_4)_2SO_4$) are other fertilizers that contain nitrogen in a form that plants can use.

Vitamin	Usual Sources	Action in Body
Vitamin A	Liver, fish oils, dairy products, fruit and vegetables	Needed for healthy eyes, skin, and tissues
Vitamin B (several types)	Meat, dairy products, whole grains (as in wholewheat flour and bread), vegetables	Used by cells in the release of energy, and in red blood cell production
Vitamin C (ascorbic acid)	Oranges, lemons, many other fruits and vegetables	Needed for healthy bones and teeth, and for tissue repair
Vitamin D	Oily fish, dairy products, eggs. Some vitamin D is made in the skin by sunlight.	Needed for bone growth
Vitamin E	Brown flour, wheat germ, liver, green vegetables	No proved function in the human body
Vitamin K	Leafy vegetables. Also made by harmless bacteria in the intestines	Helps with blood clotting

Vitamins are necessary for many enzymes to function properly. If a person's diet lacks vitamins, they may become sick because the enzymes in their body are not functioning. Only a tiny fraction of a gram of each vitamin is needed each day to maintain good health.

SEE ALSO PAGES:

PETROCHEMICALS

Petrochemicals are hydrocarbons that are separated from crude oil. They include a wide range of fuels, lubricants, and raw materials for industrial chemicals.

This child's apron, paints, plastic tubs, and tray are made from petrochemicals.

Petrochemicals come from crude oil, which is also called petroleum. Crude oil formed from marine organisms that existed some 600 million years ago. It is found in spongy rocks deep underground.

Crude oil is a mixture of hundreds of compounds of carbon and hydrogen. Its exact composition varies from one oil field to another. North-Sea crude oil consists mostly of small molecules; Venezuelan crude contains much larger molecules. Crude oil is transported by pipeline or ship from the oil field to the refinery. There it is turned into useful substances.

FRACTIONAL DISTILLATION

The first stage in crude-oil refining is fractional distillation. A furnace heats the crude oil to between 600°F and 752°F. When the oil passes into a fractionating column, most of it vaporizes and rises to the upper part of the column. The mixture of hydrocarbons that do not vaporize is called bitumen. It sinks to the bottom of the fractionating column.

The fractionating column is hotter at the bottom and cooler at the top. It contains a number of trays at different temperatures. These trays contain liquid hydrocarbons through which the vapors pass as they rise through the column. Each hydrocarbon condenses to a liquid when it reaches a tray that is cooler than its boiling point. Large molecules have high boiling points and condense in the lower trays. Small molecules have lower boiling points and so condense in the higher trays. The lightest molecules reach the top of the column without becoming liquid.

SPLITTING CRUDE OIL INTO MANY PRODUCTS

A fractionating column separates crude oil into mixtures called fractions. Each fraction is a mixture of hydrocarbons with similar boiling points. For example, diesel oil contains hydrocarbons that boil between 428°F and 662°F. The gases ethane (C_2H_6) and propane (C_3H_8) come from the top of the column. The highest-boiling fraction is bitumen. Cracking converts high-boiling fractions into chemicals that are used to make fuels and plastics.

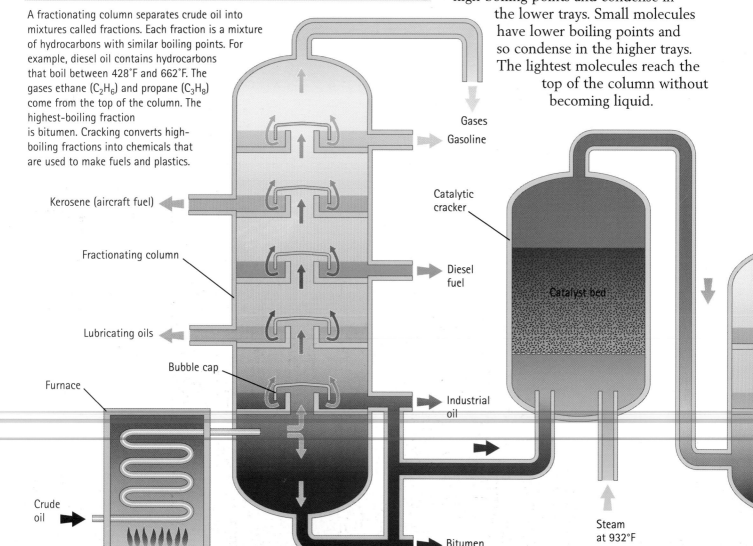

Gases
Gasoline

Catalytic cracker

Kerosene (aircraft fuel)

Fractionating column

Diesel fuel

Catalyst bed

Lubricating oils

Bubble cap

Furnace

Industrial oil

Crude oil

Steam at 932°F

Bitumen

The beaker on the left contains shredded plastic waste. A bed of sand at 752°F converts this waste into a hydrocarbon blend that can be refined in the same way as crude oil.

CRACKING

The greatest demand is for substances that come from the upper part of the fractionating column. These substances include gasoline, kerosene, and diesel oil, as well as propane and butane.

Bitumen, or asphalt, is a tarry substance used to waterproof roofs and pave roads. More bitumen is produced than can be used, so the rest is split into smaller molecules in a cracking plant. First, heat and a catalyst split the large hydrocarbon molecules. A fractionating column then separates the mixture into fuels and a smaller amount of bitumen. Cracking also produces small alkene hydrocarbons that contain double-bonded carbon atoms. Alkenes are used to make plastics.

END PRODUCTS

Many of the products from fractional distillation and cracking can be used immediately after a small amount of extra purification. Compressing propane and butane gases changes them into liquids. Called liquefied petroleum gases, or LPGs, these are sold in steel cylinders as fuel for portable heaters and camping stoves.

Gasoline, kerosene, and diesel oil are sent to storage depots, then to gas stations, airports, and other places where fuels are needed. Some tars and sticky oils are used in ships' boilers and power plants.

Not all the petrochemicals from crude oil are burned as fuel. Some are used as lubricating oils and many are raw materials for other industrial processes. These use chemical reactions to change basic petrochemicals into products such as plastics, fertilizers, explosives, synthetic fibers, dyes, detergents, and drugs. Thousands of carbon-containing chemicals are used in laboratories and in industry.

Ethylene molecules have a double bond between their two carbon atoms. The bond opens out to join ethylene molecules (right) together and make long, chainlike molecules of polyethylene (below).

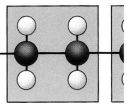

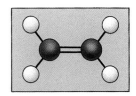

Gases

Fractionating column

Gasoline

Diesel fuel

Bitumen

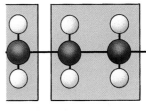

◀ The many towers of a typical oil refinery are mostly fractionating columns, some more than 100 feet tall. The white clouds are steam, which has been used in many of the refining processes. Strict environmental controls keep hydrocarbons from escaping to the atmosphere as pollution.

FACTS AND FIGURES

BRANCHES OF CHEMISTRY

Analytical chemists explore the types and proportions of substances in a sample.
Astrochemists identify substances found in stars and other bodies in space.
Biochemists study the compounds and chemical reactions in living organisms.
Electrochemists investigate the relationship between the flow of electricity and chemical reactions.
Environmental chemists study how changes in the natural environment affect living organisms.
Geochemists analyze the chemical composition of the Earth.
Inorganic chemists study the chemistry of all the elements and their compounds, except for those compounds that contain mainly carbon and hydrogen.
Nuclear chemists investigate changes that happen in atomic nuclei.
Organic chemists study hydrocarbons—compounds of carbon and hydrogen—and other related compounds.
Photochemists investigate the relationship between light and chemical reactions.
Physical chemists use the principles of physics to explain observations about chemical substances and their reactions.
Radiochemists study the radioactive isotopes of the chemical elements.

THE ELEMENTS

Elements are substances that ordinary chemical reactions cannot break down into simpler substances.

An **element** is a substance that consists of atoms that all have the same number of protons. There are 90 naturally occurring elements and 21 artificial elements.
  There are 16 nonmetals, 5 metalloids, and 90 metals. Under normal conditions of room temperature and pressure, 11 elements are gases, and 98 are solids. Only two elements—bromine and mercury—are liquids under normal conditions.
  An **atom** is the smallest part of an element that can exist separately. An atom consists of electrons orbiting around a nucleus. The **nucleus** contains two kinds of nucleons: protons and neutrons. The number of protons equals the number of electrons in a neutral atom.
  The **atomic number** of an element is equal to the number of protons in its nucleus. The atomic number is sometimes called the proton number.
  The **mass number** of an element is the sum of the numbers of protons and neutrons. An atom of iron, for example, consists of 26 protons, 26 electrons, and 30 neutrons. The atomic number of iron is 26, and the mass number is 56.

LAWS AND PRINCIPLES OF CHEMISTRY

Avogadro's Law

At the same temperature and pressure, equal volumes of different gases contain the same number of molecules.
(*Amedeo Avogadro, 1811*)
By this law, a cubic foot of hydrogen contains the same number of molecules as a cubic foot of carbon dioxide.

Law of conservation of mass

During a chemical reaction, matter is neither created nor destroyed.
(*Antoine Lavoisier, 1774*)
According to this law, the total mass of the products of a chemical reaction is equal to the total mass of the substances that react together.

Law of constant composition

No matter how a substance is made, it will always contain the same elements in the same proportions.
(*Joseph Proust, 1779*)
By Proust's law, carbon dioxide exhaled in breath and carbon dioxide from a car exhaust both consist of molecules that contain one atom of carbon and two atoms of oxygen.

Heisenberg's uncertainty principle

It is impossible to specify both the precise position and the momentum of a particle at the same time.
(*Werner Heisenberg, 1927*)
The more accurately the position of a particle is measured, the less accurate the knowledge of its momentum becomes, and vice versa. The effect only becomes noticeable for subatomic particles, such as electrons and protons.

KEY DATES

B.C.
*c.*450 Leucippus of Miletus introduces the idea of atoms. Empedocles of Akraga introduces the four elements: earth, air, water, and fire.
430 Democritus of Abdera develops the idea of atoms and suggests they explain the properties of matter.
340 Greek philosopher Aristotle proposes that substances are all combinations of the four elements.
A.D.
750 Arabian alchemist Geber describes how to prepare acids and their salts.
1473 Democritus's theory of atoms becomes known to alchemists in Europe through its Latin version.

1597 German chemist Andreas Libavius writes *Alchemia*, the first important chemistry textbook.
1610 French chemist Jean Béguin publishes the first chemistry book not based on alchemy.
1661 Irish chemist and physicist Robert Boyle publishes *The Sceptical Chymist*, introducing the concept of chemical elements.
1766 British chemist Henry Cavendish discovers hydrogen, which he names "inflammable air."
1777 French chemist Antoine Lavoisier suggests air consists of two gases.
1781 British chemist and clergyman Joseph Priestley makes water by burning hydrogen in oxygen.
1803 British chemist and physicist John Dalton formulates atomic theory.
1807 British chemist Humphry Davy uses the recently invented electric battery to isolate the elements sodium and potassium.
1811 Italian chemist and physicist Amedeo Avogadro proposes that equal volumes of different gases contain the same number of molecules.
1828 German chemist Friedrich Wöhler makes urea, an organic compound, from inorganic ammonium cyanate.
1833 French chemist Anselme Payen discovers diastase, an enzyme.
1856 British chemist William Perkin makes the first synthetic dye.
1869 Russian chemist Dmitri Mendeleyev publishes the first form of the periodic table.
1893 German chemist Felix Hoffman synthesizes aspirin.
1911 British physicist Ernest Rutherford discovers the proton.
1913 Danish physicist Niels Bohr proposes a theory of atomic structure based on electron orbits.
1926 Austrian physicist Erwin Schrödinger develops a wave equation of atomic structure.
1932 British physicist John Cockcroft and Irish physicist Ernest Walton build the first particle accelerator to change one element into another.
1935 U.S. chemist Wallace Carothers develops nylon, the polymer of the first totally synthetic fiber.
1938 German chemist Otto Hahn splits atoms of uranium.
1942 Italian-born U.S. physicist Enrico Fermi creates the first controlled nuclear chain reaction.
1971 U.S. company DuPont begins production of Kevlar, a polymer that is stronger than steel.
1985 Ball-shaped carbon molecules are discovered and named fullerenes.

CHAPTER 5

MATERIALS AND TECHNOLOGY

E ver since humans started to take an interest in the world around them, they have studied the appearance and feel of objects and materials they encountered. Gradually, they experimented with materials to discover how they could be used. Along the way, much was learned about the properties of the materials—properties such as weight, strength, the ability to conduct heat, and the ability to burn if placed in a fire.

Modern studies of materials use sensitive instruments, computers, and other advanced technologies to measure and calculate the properties of materials in great detail. Materials scientists use this knowledge to develop new materials, and engineers use it to choose materials that are best suited to the construction of buildings, vehicles, machines, and other objects.

Technology—the creation and use of tools and machines to perform tasks—goes hand in hand with the development of materials. Technology is driven by the understanding of materials, and it helps to expand the range and improve the quality of available materials. Technology has also helped to create whole new groups of materials, such as artificial polymers and plastics made from oil, and composite materials that consist of several different materials bonded together to improve their properties.

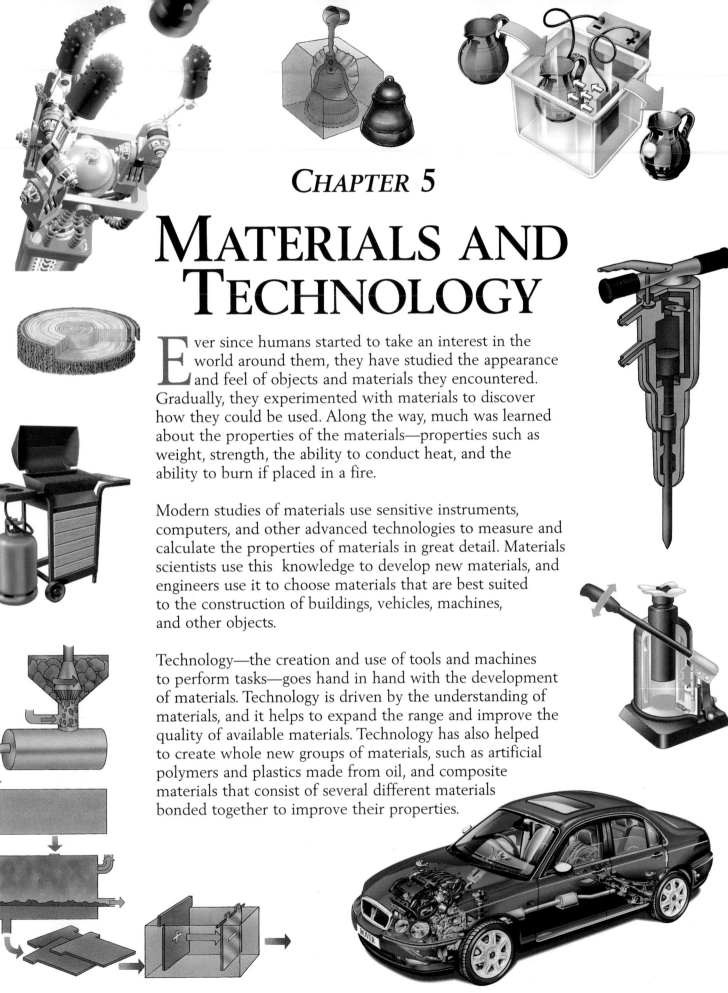

PROPERTIES OF SOLIDS

Materials such as rock, wood, rubber and diamond are all examples of solids. How they can be used depends on their individual properties.

The Mohs scale lists ten minerals in order of their hardness. Talc is the softest mineral on the Mohs scale. It can be scratched by a fingernail and, therefore, has a value of one.

Diamond is the hardest known substance. It has a value of ten on the Mohs scale. Diamond is pure carbon that has formed into crystals.

The first materials used by people were those that grew or lay around them. Rocks and stones were chipped, or knapped to form spearheads and crude tools. Plant fibers were used to make rope, string, and thread. The thread was used to sew clothes from animal skins and furs.

Over many centuries, people have discovered new natural substances and found ways to make new materials. One early discovery was that clay could be hardened by heat to make ceramic pots, vessels, and storage containers.

Materials that are used to make other materials are called raw materials. The products of this processing are called manufactured or synthetic materials. For example, clay is a raw material that can be made into pottery, a manufactured material. Wood can be processed to make manufactured materials such as paper, cardboard, and textiles. Glass is a synthetic material that is made by heating sand with salts and other substances.

Materials such as dry leaves and wood can easily catch fire. In dry conditions, a discarded match can start a major inferno. Forests like this one, near Sydney, on Australia's east coast are especially vulnerable to fires.

PROPERTIES

A material's properties include its hardness, strength, and flexibility. Some materials are combustible, which means they can catch on fire and burn. Others allow heat or electricity to pass through them and are called conductors. The properties of a material determine how it can be used.

▲ Solders melt at lower temperatures than most common metals. They are used to join metal surfaces together. Hot solder melts and then flows around and into the gap between the surfaces. When it cools, it solidifies, forming a strong bond.

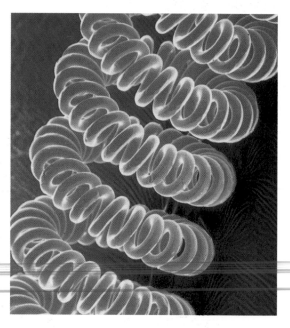

◄ Many metals can be drawn and spun to make thin wire. The device pictured winds niobium metal wire into coils for superconducting magnets.

▲ This photograph shows a lightbulb filament called a coiled coil. This type of filament is made by bending a tightly coiled wire into a looser coil.

Mohs value of 10. Talc, which is soft and crumbly, has a value of 1. Other materials can be given Mohs values by comparing them with the minerals in the Mohs scale. A typical fingernail has a hardness of 2½, and glass has a hardness of 6.

Hardness does not necessarily equal strength. A piece of rubber might feel soft and flexible, but it is extremely strong. Rubber is an example of an elastic material. Elastic materials return to their original shapes, after being stretched. Materials that can be formed into different shapes have the property of plasticity. Materials that stretch easily without cracking or breaking are ductile.

When designers plan how to make an object, one of their first decisions is which materials to use. In addition to choosing materials that have a good combination of hardness, flexibility, and formability, the designer might have to choose materials that can withstand extreme temperatures or corrosive chemicals. Often, cost is the factor that determines which material is used out of a range of possible options.

Clay can be hardened by heat. Bricks and ceramic items are made by firing soft clay objects in a kiln.

Wood is a common material that is light and strong. It can be fashioned into a variety of shapes.

A material's hardness is its ability to resist being scratched or dented. Hardness depends mainly on how tightly the atoms in a material are bound together.

German mineralogist Friedrich Mohs (1773–1839) drew up a scale of hardness using ten natural materials called minerals. He numbered them from one to ten in order of increasing hardness. Diamond is the hardest known material and has a

MATERIALS USED IN A CAR

A variety of materials is used to build a modern car such as this British Rover 75. The engine is made from a metal alloy that can withstand heat and force. The windshield is made from layers of glass and plastic and will not shatter over the passengers if the window breaks. The seat covers are made from leather, which is comfortable and easy to cut, color, and stitch. Soft foam bumpers reduce the severity of injuries in collisions with pedestrians.

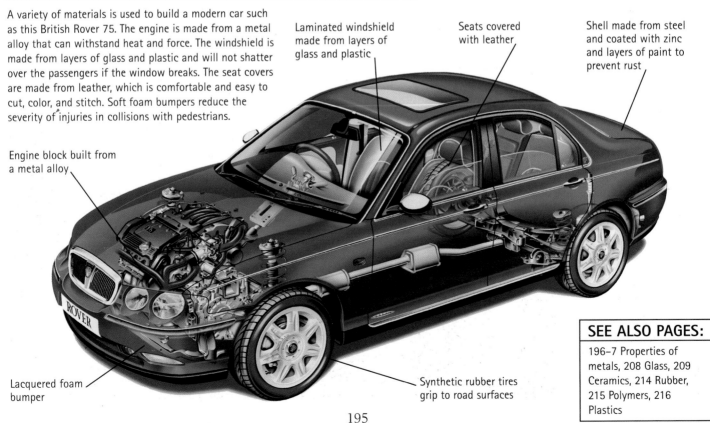

Laminated windshield made from layers of glass and plastic

Seats covered with leather

Shell made from steel and coated with zinc and layers of paint to prevent rust

Engine block built from a metal alloy

Lacquered foam bumper

Synthetic rubber tires grip to road surfaces

SEE ALSO PAGES:

196–7 Properties of metals, 208 Glass, 209 Ceramics, 214 Rubber, 215 Polymers, 216 Plastics

PROPERTIES OF METALS

The metals are a group of chemical elements. They share a number of properties that have made them important materials in the modern world.

Metals can be formed into a variety of shapes, including tubes.

Steel girders are used in construction. Steel is an alloy of iron, carbon, and other chemical elements.

Tin is extracted from its ore by first roasting the ore in air to form tin oxide. Tin oxide is then heated with coke and limestone.

Most metals are hard, shiny solids at room temperature. Many are ductile, which means they can be stretched into long tubes or wires. A large number of metals are also malleable, which means they can be hammered into thin sheets.

Copper, gold, and lead are among the most malleable metals. Gold is the most malleable of all the metals; it can be beaten into sheets that are only two micrometers, or microns, thick.

Metals are generally easy to shape when hot. Most metals can be made liquid by heating them to very high temperatures. The molten, or liquid, metal can then be poured into a cast or mold. Once the metal cools, it becomes solid and hardens in the shape of the mold.

Metals are good conductors of both heat and electricity. This is because electrons in a metal can move around more freely than the electrons in a nonmetal.

A small number of metals, including iron, cobalt, and nickel, can become permanently or temporarily magnetized.

Modern aircraft, such as this Airbus A300 airliner, are built using lightweight metals and alloys. These allow the aircraft to take off while carrying passengers and freight weighing up to about 132,276 pounds.

EXTRACTING METALS

Common metals such as iron and tin are present in large quantities in the Earth's crust. They are normally found in rocks as impure chemical compounds called ores. Ores have to be purified and chemically treated to obtain the pure metal. These processes are known as extraction techniques because they extract pure metals from impure metal compounds.

In the first stage of most extraction processes, mined or quarried ore is treated to separate the ore from rocks that do not contain the desired metal. This is often done by crushing and washing the ore.

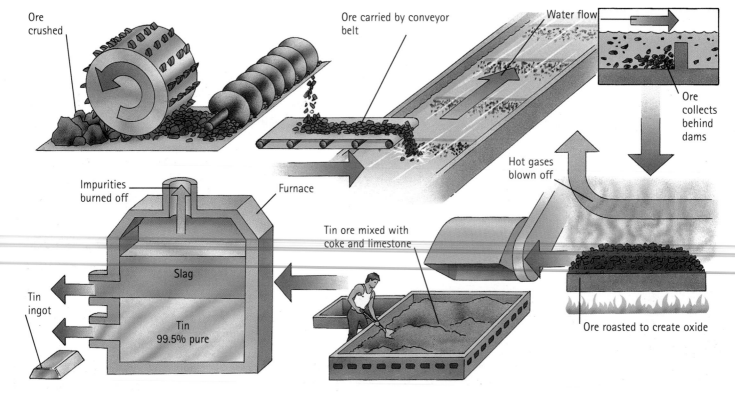

Ore crushed

Ore carried by conveyor belt

Water flow

Ore collects behind dams

Hot gases blown off

Impurities burned off

Furnace

Tin ore mixed with coke and limestone

Slag

Tin ingot

Tin 99.5% pure

Ore roasted to create oxide

Aircraft, like this Boeing 737, are regularly inspected for metal fatigue. These technicians are using bundles of optical fibers to take pictures of parts of the plane that are too difficult to reach with a normal camera.

Once the ore has been separated from impurities, chemical reactions convert it into the pure metal. Iron, for example, is made by heating iron oxide ore with coke. This turns the oxide into pure metal.

Precious metals are normally found as almost pure deposits. Gold and platinum are rare, which is why they are so valuable.

METALLURGY

Metallurgy is the study of metals, their properties, and how they can be recovered from their natural ores. Metallurgists also explore how the properties of metals can be modified by mixing metals to produce substances called alloys.

A key part of metallurgy is the study of metal fatigue, which is the gradual weakening of metal objects. Metal fatigue can be caused by repeated stress (pushing, pulling, and twisting) acting on metal components. If the metal suffers too much stress, small surface cracks may appear. These cracks concentrate any further stresses and may cause more cracks, and sometimes breakages, to occur.

Engineers have to allow for metal fatigue when designing aircraft, cars, bridges, and machinery. Many such objects have to be checked frequently for early signs of metal fatigue.

A thin layer of tin-plating prevents steel food cans from rusting.

The filament inside a lightbulb is made from the metal tungsten.

Metal detectors can find objects, such as ancient coins, buried below the surface of the ground.

▲ This steelworker is one of the many thousands of people who work in industries that extract and purify metals from their natural ores.

SEE ALSO PAGES:

170 Carbon, 178 Oxidation and reduction 194–5 Properties of solids, 198 Iron, 199 Copper, 202–3 Alloys

IRON

Iron is one of the most common metals in the Earth's crust. It has been worked with for thousands of years. Now it is mainly used to make steel.

Hematite is an ore of iron. It often forms kidney-shaped lumps. These give the ore its nickname of kidney ore.

▼ The steamship *Great Eastern* had a 692-foot-long hull made from riveted iron plates. The ship was designed by English engineer Isambard Kingdom Brunel (1806–1859) and was launched in 1858. For over 40 years it was the largest ship ever built.

I ron makes up about 5 percent of the Earth's crust and about 35 percent of the Earth as a whole. Most is in the Earth's core.

Iron is the cheapest, most commonly used metal. In its natural state, iron is normally combined with oxygen as iron-oxide ores. Hematite and magnetite are the two main iron ores.

Since the 1300s, huge ovens called blast furnaces have been used to turn iron ore and coke into pig iron. Pig iron is iron that contains a small amount of carbon left over from the blast furnace coke—a form of carbon. Pig iron was used to make tools, weapons, and many other objects.

Since the 1850s, an increasing amount of pig iron has been converted into steel. Steel contains less carbon than pig iron and is more flexible. Steel is made by blowing air or oxygen into pig iron.

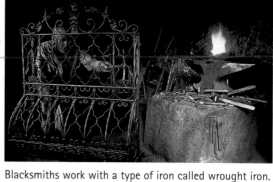

Blacksmiths work with a type of iron called wrought iron. Wrought iron can be beaten and bent into shape when it has been softened in a red-hot furnace.

PROPERTIES OF IRON

Pure iron is a shiny, silver-white metal. It melts at 2,795°F, and it is ductile and malleable. Forms of iron that contain a small amount of carbon, such as steel, are harder than pure iron. This hardness makes steel more useful than pure iron for many uses.

Iron forms compounds with elements such as chlorine, oxygen, and sulfur.

When unprotected iron is exposed to moist air it corrodes. A reddish-brown, flaky oxide forms. This oxide is rust.

BLAST FURNACE

In a blast furnace, measured amounts of iron ore, coke, and limestone are loaded into the main chamber. Iron ore contains iron oxide, coke is a form of carbon made from coal, and limestone is calcium carbonate.

Hot air is blasted into the bottom of the furnace. This causes the coke to burn and form carbon monoxide. The burning coke heats the contents of the bottom of the furnace to more than 2,912°F. At this temperature, oxygen in the iron oxide reacts with carbon monoxide, freeing iron from its ore.

The liquid iron flows to the bottom of the furnace and is drawn off every three or four hours. The limestone reacts with impurities in the iron ore and forms a product called slag. A layer of liquid slag forms on top of the liquid iron and is removed from time to time.

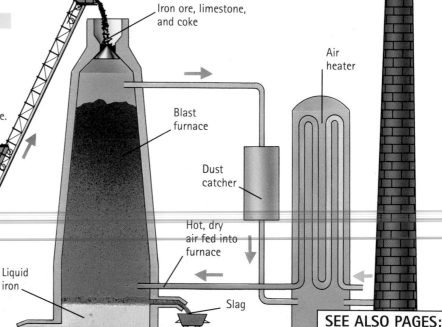

Iron ore, limestone, and coke

Waste gases

Air heater

Blast furnace

Dust catcher

Hot, dry air fed into furnace

Liquid iron

Iron

Slag

SEE ALSO PAGES:
162–3 Chemical reactions, 170 Carbon, 178 Oxidation and reduction, 213 Coal

COPPER

Copper is a soft reddish-brown solid metal that has been widely used since 3000 B.C. for its flexibility and, more recently, for its ability to conduct electricity.

Malachite is an ore of copper. Its brightly dramatic bands of dark green make it desirable for jewelry and decorative objects.

Electric cables often consist of fine strands of copper wire woven together and enclosed in a plastic casing.

In nature, copper occurs both as the free metal and as compounds in copper-bearing ores and minerals.

Pure copper melts at 1,981°F, which makes it easy to cast in molds. Copper is also very malleable; this makes it easy to hammer into shapes. As a result, copper has been used to make a wide range of objects, including coins, cooking utensils, and ornaments.

Although pure copper is too soft for many uses, it forms hard, strong alloys, like brass and bronze, when it is mixed with other metals. Brass is an alloy of copper and tin. Bronze contains zinc.

PROPERTIES AND USES OF COPPER

Copper is widely used in the electrical industry because it is an excellent conductor of electricity and can be extruded and stretched to make wires as fine as 0.001 inches in diameter. Copper wire is used for household electrical circuits and for wiring electric appliances. Electromagnets, generators, and motors also frequently contain coils of copper wire.

This copper statue, believed to be the world's oldest metal sculpture, is an image of Egyptian pharaoh Pepi I. This Old Kingdom monarch reigned from 2289 to 2244 B.C.

The flexibility of copper and brass make them ideal materials for making pipes for plumbing systems.

Copper reacts with other elements less quickly than iron. However, copper will corrode slowly in moist air. Over time, reddish-brown copper statues and roofs become coated in a green patina. This coating is copper carbonate. It forms when copper reacts with moisture and carbon dioxide in the air.

MAKING COPPER

Copper ore is mined and then crushed into granules. The ore is mixed with water and then ground in a ball mill to form a slurry of fine particles. The slurry is heated in a furnace to form crude metallic copper. Electrolysis then purifies and refines the copper to over 99.9 percent purity. The final processing stage consists of melting and casting the copper into cakes, bars, ingots, and billets. Billets are blocks of copper that are used to make copper tubing and piping. The photograph below shows copper piping being bent through a right angle.

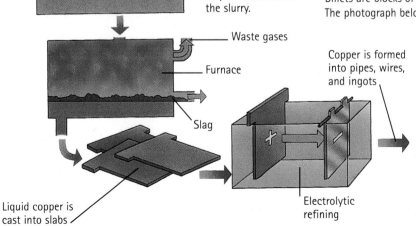

Copper ore is crushed into small pieces

Water is added to make a slurry

A ball mill grinds the copper ore into a fine powder

Air and chemicals are added. These help to concentrate the slurry.

Waste gases

Furnace

Slag

Liquid copper is cast into slabs

Electrolytic refining

Copper is formed into pipes, wires, and ingots

SEE ALSO PAGES:
196–7 Properties of metals, 202–3 Alloys, 356 Electrochemistry

199

ALUMINUM

Aluminum is a flexible, light metal that is a good conductor of electricity and has a good resistance to corrosion. It is the most widely used metal after iron.

Most soft-drink cans are made from aluminum. Recycling aluminum uses only 30 percent of the energy needed to produce new aluminum from bauxite.

Alloys of aluminum are used to make aircraft wings and bodies. Aircraft would be much heavier and would need more powerful engines if they were made from steel.

Aluminum is the most abundant metal in the Earth's crust. It occurs in a number of forms that include clays and emeralds. It is never found as the pure metal.

Aluminum is refined from an ore called bauxite. This ore is first turned into aluminum oxide by treatment with a strong alkali (see page 185). The oxide can then be split into the pure metal by electrolysis. The electrolysis bath becomes very hot as the current passes through it.

Enormous amounts of electrical power are needed, which adds to the cost of aluminum extraction. Many aluminum plants are found near hydroelectric plants. These provide a convenient power source.

PROPERTIES OF ALUMINUM

Aluminum is a silver-white metal that reacts with oxygen in air to form a coating of aluminum oxide, or alumina. This layer is resistant to chemical attack and protects the metal from further corrosion.

Aluminum is a light metal. A block of aluminum weighs less than one third of the weight of a similar-sized block of steel. Alloys of aluminum and other metals are often strong but light, which makes them ideal for use in aircraft construction.

An aluminum wire can conduct electricity just as well as a copper wire, but weighs less. For this reason, aluminum is often used for overhead power lines.

Aluminum's flexibility and resistance to corrosion make it well suited to making beverage cans and foil for cooking.

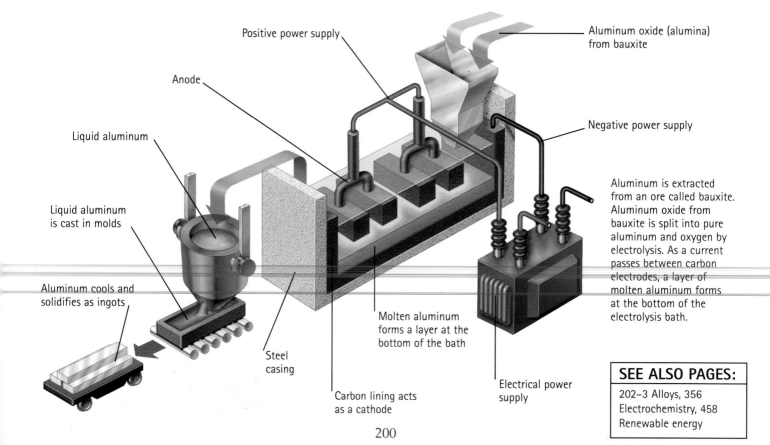

Positive power supply

Anode

Liquid aluminum

Liquid aluminum is cast in molds

Aluminum cools and solidifies as ingots

Steel casing

Carbon lining acts as a cathode

Molten aluminum forms a layer at the bottom of the bath

Electrical power supply

Negative power supply

Aluminum oxide (alumina) from bauxite

Aluminum is extracted from an ore called bauxite. Aluminum oxide from bauxite is split into pure aluminum and oxygen by electrolysis. As a current passes between carbon electrodes, a layer of molten aluminum forms at the bottom of the electrolysis bath.

SEE ALSO PAGES:
202–3 Alloys, 356
Electrochemistry, 458
Renewable energy

PRECIOUS METALS

Precious metals are attractive, rare, and highly prized. They are used to make jewelry and trophies, but also have a wide range of industrial uses.

Unlike most metals, gold is found as pure nuggets or veins within rock.

Gold prospectors panned streams for grains, flakes, or nuggets of gold.

Silver is usually found, combined with other substances, as ores.

Precious metals are so highly prized by people because they are rare and expensive. The most familiar examples are gold, silver, and platinum. One of their most notable properties is that they hardly ever react with other chemicals.

GOLD AND SILVER

Gold and silver have been used for currency, jewelry, and ornamentation for thousands of years. They are attractive, easy to shape, and resistant to tarnishing by air and water.

Gold is one of the least reactive metals. Only a concentrated combination of hydrochloric and nitric acids can dissolve gold to form salts.

Pure gold is extremely soft. It is often mixed with silver or copper to harden it. The purity of gold is measured in carats: 18-carat gold is 75 percent pure, and 24-carat gold is 100 percent pure.

Nearly half the gold in the world is held by governments in gold reserves. It is usually stored in the form of standard-sized bars called ingots.

Of all the metals, silver is the best conductor of heat and electricity and is used in many electronic circuit boards. Almost 40 percent of the world's silver is used in photography. Compounds of silver, called halides, are used to make light-sensitive emulsion for photographic film. Silver is also used as a coating for mirrors and to make surgical equipment.

PLATINUM

Platinum is an excellent conductor of electricity. Its ability to resist corrosion and heat make it useful for high-quality electrical circuits and heat-resistant laboratory equipment.

Platinum is prized for jewelry. It is also used in catalytic converters, which help clean road vehicles' exhaust gases.

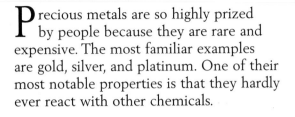

Battery provides electricity

Pitcher made of a base metal such as iron

Pitcher is completely immersed in a bath of water and silver salts

Objects made from metals, such as iron, can be made more attractive by electroplating with silver. The object and a block of silver are placed in a solution of silver salts and connected to a power supply. When the power is switched on, silver ions travel from the silver strip and coat the object with a shiny layer of silver atoms.

Electrical current causes silver ions to travel to the pitcher, forming a fine layer of silver plate

Silver-plated pitcher

Silver strip

SEE ALSO PAGES:

ALLOYS

Alloys are mixtures of metals with other metals and some nonmetals. The properties of alloys are often superior to the properties of their components.

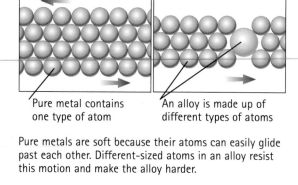

Pure metal contains one type of atom

An alloy is made up of different types of atoms

Pure metals are soft because their atoms can easily glide past each other. Different-sized atoms in an alloy resist this motion and make the alloy harder.

Most alloys are mixtures of two or more metals. Some are mixtures of metals with small amounts of other elements, such as carbon. They resemble metals in many ways: they are lustrous, or shiny, and conduct heat and electricity.

Alloys are normally designed to keep the good properties of a metal while eliminating its bad properties. This has been true since the first alloy, bronze, was made more than 6,000 years ago.

Bronze is an alloy of copper and tin. Like copper, it can be hammered into shape, but it was found to be much harder than either pure copper or pure tin, which made it more useful for armor, tools, and weapons. Bronze is still used to make heavy-duty machinery.

Today, many different alloys are manufactured for specific purposes. Some are designed to withstand extreme temperatures or strong chemicals; others are made to be light but strong. The most widely used alloy is steel.

TYPES OF STEEL

There are numerous types of steel. All are alloys of iron and carbon. Some steel also contains other elements.

More than 90 percent of all the steel that is made is a form of carbon steel. Carbon steel contains amounts of carbon with small traces of manganese, silicon,

and copper. Carbon steels are used to make a variety of objects, including springs, car bodies, and girders for construction.

Alloy steels and tool steels contain larger amounts of manganese, silicon, and copper than carbon steels. They also contain elements like the metals molybdenum, tungsten, and vanadium. Alloy steels are used where a hard-wearing material is needed, such as in truck transmissions and machine tools. They are more expensive than carbon steels because of the higher cost of their ingredients.

High-strength-low-alloy (HSLA) steels are a new class of steel. They are stronger than ordinary carbon steel but more economical to produce than alloy steels. This is because they contain less of the more expensive elements such as vanadium. HSLA steels are used for the same applications as carbon steels.

This Celtic helmet, shield, and sword are made of bronze—an alloy of copper and tin. All are around 2,000 years old.

Brass instruments, such as this trumpet, are made of an alloy of copper and zinc.

▼ This photo shows a cross section of a cylinder made from an alloy of titanium and aluminum. This alloy is widely used in the aerospace industry.

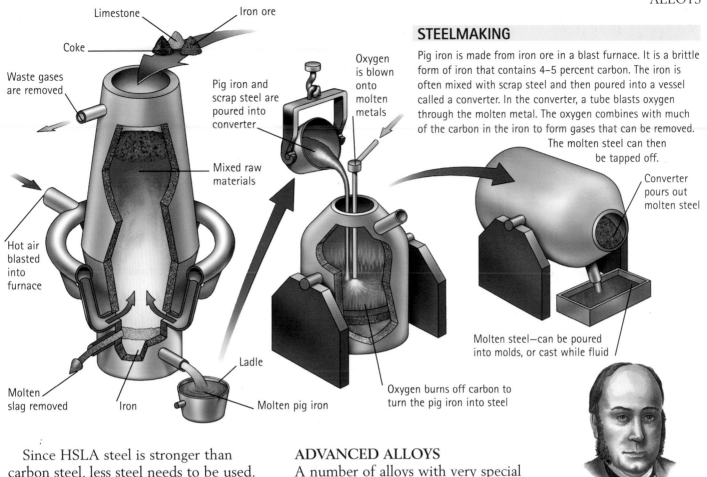

Limestone
Iron ore
Coke
Waste gases are removed
Mixed raw materials
Hot air blasted into furnace
Molten slag removed
Iron
Ladle
Molten pig iron
Pig iron and scrap steel are poured into converter
Oxygen is blown onto molten metals
Oxygen burns off carbon to turn the pig iron into steel
Molten steel—can be poured into molds, or cast while fluid
Converter pours out molten steel

STEELMAKING

Pig iron is made from iron ore in a blast furnace. It is a brittle form of iron that contains 4–5 percent carbon. The iron is often mixed with scrap steel and then poured into a vessel called a converter. In the converter, a tube blasts oxygen through the molten metal. The oxygen combines with much of the carbon in the iron to form gases that can be removed. The molten steel can then be tapped off.

British engineer Henry Bessemer (1813–1898) invented a vessel called a converter for making large quantities of steel.

Since HSLA steel is stronger than carbon steel, less steel needs to be used. An HSLA girder, for example, would be thinner and lighter than a normal girder of the same strength.

Stainless steel contains chromium and nickel, which makes it shiny and resistant to rusting and stains. Stainless steel is used to make a variety of objects from kitchen sinks and cutlery to surgical instruments, such as scalpels.

In industry, stainless steel is shaped into pipes and containers to house corrosive chemicals safely. It is also used to make ball bearings.

ADVANCED ALLOYS

A number of alloys with very special properties have been made. Among them are superconductors and shape-memory alloys, or SMAs.

Superconducting alloys have almost no electrical resistance when cooled to extremely low temperatures. An example is an alloy of tin and niobium metals.

Shape-memory alloys "remember" their shape and return to it. When cold, the alloy can be twisted out of shape. When heated, it returns to its original shape. SMAs are useful for making frames for glasses, and orthodontic wires and braces.

▼ Many different types of stainless steel exist. The type used for cutlery is sometimes called 18-8. This is because it contains 18 percent chromium and 8 percent nickel.

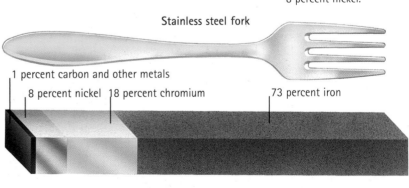

Stainless steel fork

1 percent carbon and other metals
8 percent nickel
18 percent chromium
73 percent iron

◀ Completed in 1889, the Forth Bridge in Scotland was the first cantilever railroad bridge. Around 55,000 tons of steel were used to make the Forth Bridge.

SEE ALSO PAGES:

158–9 Solutions, 170
Carbon, 198 Iron, 199
Copper, 217 New materials

SHAPING MATERIALS

Many materials have to be cut to size, shaped, molded, or joined to each other, before they can be used to their best effect.

Natural materials rarely occur in the ideal shape for human use. At first, people used materials in the shapes that were available to them. Ancient walls were built by carefully fitting together irregular lumps of rock. Over time, humans learned ways of manipulating the shapes of materials for specific needs.

Jagged pieces of flint were the first tools. They were used to scrape animal hides, to cut plants, and to tip spears.

WOOD AND STONE

Wood has been a popular raw material for thousands of years. This is because wood is abundant in many places and because it is easy to shape. Wood can be sawed, planed, drilled, and chiseled into a variety of shapes using the appropriate tools. The same is partly true of stone, although harder tools and more effort are needed.

METALS

Metals can be hard, brittle, and difficult to shape when cold. When they are heated, however, most metals become soft and malleable. Processes where metals are shaped as hot solids are called forging. Blacksmiths use tools such as hammers and tongs to forge iron into horseshoes and other items.

Metal is cast by melting it and then pouring it into a mold. When the molten metal cools, it hardens in the shape of the mold.

Tools such as chisels, planes, and saws have been used for centuries to shape wood.

Hot metal can also be formed in mechanical forges. A drop forge molds blocks of hot, soft metal between two halves of a mold, called dies. The top die drops with great force onto the metal in the bottom die. Forging rollers squeeze blocks of hot metal into long strips as the metal rolls back and forth between them.

If a metal is heated above its melting point, the liquid metal can be poured into a mold. When it cools and solidifies, the metal takes the shape of the cavity inside the mold. This process is called casting. Copper and bronze were the first metals to be cast and are still cast today.

One type of mold is made from a mixture of sand and clay. A model of the object to be cast is placed in a box and the mixture is packed firmly around it.

Machine tools are used to drill holes and to chisel, grind, press, or cut materials. The tools are driven by a motor. The material that is being shaped is called the workpiece.

Borer   Punch press   Grinder   Press brakes

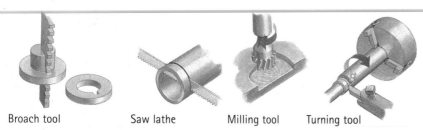

Broach tool   Saw lathe   Milling tool   Turning tool

► This scientist is testing an experimental cutting device. The device has a laser mounted on a robotic arm. Lasers such as this are frequently used to cut through metal plates. The use of robotics helps to produce an accurate cut.

Most metals can be joined together by welding. A heat source melts the edges of the metal surfaces. The surfaces fuse together when the metal cools and hardens.

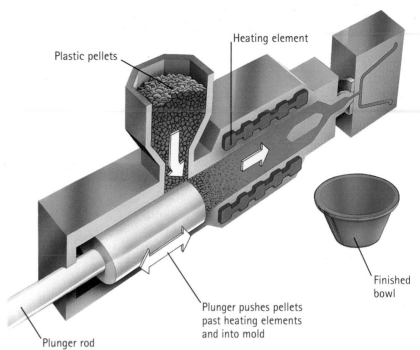

When the mold has hardened, the model is removed, and two holes are made in the top of the mold. Molten metal is poured in through one hole, and air escapes through the other.

Once the basic shape of a metal object has been formed by casting or forging, more detail can be added by machining. Machine tools perform a wide variety of tasks from drilling and bending copper piping to cutting a screw thread on a bolt.

SHAPING PLASTICS

Many plastics soften at much lower temperatures than metals, which makes them easier to mold.

Injection molding is similar to casting, but lower temperatures are used. Hot, softened plastic is squeezed into molds.

Extrusion produces plastic films and tubes by squeezing hot plastics through slots in the form of the finished product.

In blow molding, hollow fingers of plastic, called preforms, are heated and inflated inside a mold.

In an injection-molding machine, a plunger pushes plastic pellets through a heated chamber. The plastic softens and is squeezed into a mold. When the plastic cools, the mold is opened and the finished object removed. In this case, the mold is the shape of a bowl.

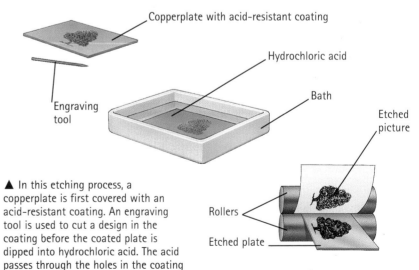

▲ In this etching process, a copperplate is first covered with an acid-resistant coating. An engraving tool is used to cut a design in the coating before the coated plate is dipped into hydrochloric acid. The acid passes through the holes in the coating and etches the engraved pattern into the surface of the plate. The plate can then be used to print the etched design.

SEE ALSO PAGES:

196–7 Properties of metals, 198 Iron, 206 Wood and paper, 216 Plastics, 456–7 Resources

WOOD AND PAPER

Wood is a tough material that forms the trunks and branches of trees. It is used as a building material, as fuel, and as a raw material for making paper.

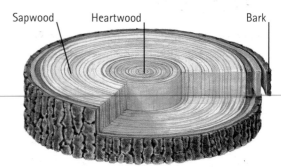

Sapwood   Heartwood   Bark

The layer of wood beneath the bark of a tree carries moisture and is called sapwood. The hard, solid wood in the center of the trunk is called heartwood.

Wood is a versatile material. It is tough, flexible, easy to fashion, and relatively strong. The logging and lumber industries cut down trees, and turn them into planks, beams, and panels. These are used to construct buildings, and furniture, and for making many other goods.

There are many kinds of wood, all of which have unique properties. Balsa, for example, is extremely light; ash is tough and can withstand sudden and repeated bending and stretching.

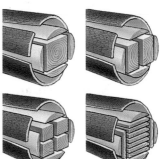

Wood is turned into lumber in a lumber mill. After the bark has been removed, mechanical saws cut the wood into thin planks or thicker beams, depending on what the lumber is to be used for.

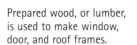

Prepared wood, or lumber, is used to make window, door, and roof frames.

PAPER AND RECYCLING

Paper is made mainly from the cellulose in wood. Paper is used to make books and stationery, waxed cartons for liquids, and filter papers for car engines. Paper can be made using cellulose from sources other than wood. Paper currency and expensive writing paper contain cellulose fibers from cotton plants, which make paper tough and very smooth.

On average, each person in the United States uses about 600 pounds of paper a year. About half that amount is recycled to make newspapers, toilet paper, and other low-quality papers. The rest is incinerated or dumped in landfill sites.

MAKING PAPER

Modern paper is largely made from coniferous trees, such as pine, spruce, and fir. The fibers in wood consist of a strong material called cellulose. This makes the paper very strong, so it does not fall apart easily when pressed, folded, or stretched. In a modern papermaking machine, wood chips are first boiled with sodium hydroxide or another chemical in a tank. This releases the strong fibers of cellulose. Liquid is removed from the fibers to leave a pulp. The cellulose pulp is then spread on a conveyor belt and squeezed between hot rollers to remove moisture. The result is finished paper.

Bark removed

Wood chipped into small pieces

Water and chemicals added and wood chips cooked into pulp

Pulp beaten to break down the fibers

Pulp cleaned and bleached to make it white

Pulp drained on fine mesh belt

Heated rollers dry paper and press fibers firmly together to form a sheet (of paper)

Finished paper is wound onto a reel

Pulp from recycled paper

SEE ALSO PAGES:

204–5 Shaping materials, 207 Fibers, 222–3 Construction, 456–7 Resources

206

FIBERS

Fibers are used to make fabrics for clothing, bedding, and many other products. Some fibers are natural products; others are made by chemical processes.

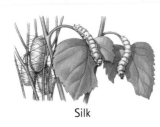
Silk

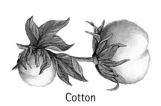
Cotton

Wool

Flax and cotton come from plants. Wool is from the fleece of sheep. Silk is produced by silkworms.

Natural fibers are obtained from animals and plants. These fibers can be spun to make yarn, which can then be woven on a loom to make cloth.

Wool, the most common animal fiber, is made from the fleece of sheep. The quality of wool depends on the breed of sheep.

Silk is made by a type of caterpillar called a silkworm. The silkworm spins a cocoon to prepare for their transformation into moths. In silk farming, the long fibers are collected before the cocoon forms.

Many fibers are obtained from plants. Cotton comes from a clump of fibers that forms around the head of cotton plants. Jute, sisal, and hemp are strong plant fibers used to make rope and canvas. Linen is made from the stem fibers of flax.

SYNTHETIC FIBERS

The first synthetic fibers were made from cellulose early in the 1900s. Rayon is prepared from cellulose by dissolving wood pulp in an alkali. This mixture is then treated with a chemical that turns

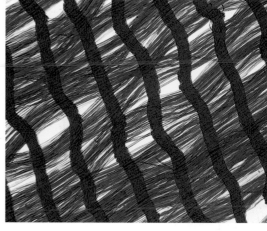
A close up of crepe de Chine. This type of fabric is made by weaving fine silk fibers with thicker silk thread. The thread is made by spinning silk fibers together.

it into a sticky liquid called viscose. The viscose solution is sprayed through tiny holes into a bath of sulfuric acid. The acid makes the viscose solution harden and form fibers that resemble silk. These fibers can be spun to make yarn and then woven to make a silky cloth.

Fibers such as nylon, polyester, and acrylic are produced from oil by chemical processes. They are similar to plastics.

Synthetic fibers are often stronger than natural fibers. They can be woven to form crease-resistant cloth and are also used to make ropes and carpets.

Cotton fibers are formed into fine threads by a process called spinning. Rollers and teasing wires flatten and divide the cotton fibers. The fibers are then gathered into slivers, which are stretched between more sets of rollers before being spun to make yarn.

Pressure rollers flatten cotton fibers

Teasing wires form loose bundles of fibers called slivers

Cotton fiber

Dividers

Rollers that move at different speeds stretch the slivers

Slivers stretched and spun to form cotton yarn

Slivers wound onto bobbins

Yarn bobbin

Weft

Shuttle

Warp

◀ A weaving loom interlaces threads to make cloth. Two sets of warp threads are stretched across the frame of the loom. A shuttle pulls the weft thread between the two sets of warp threads. The loom then reverses the upper and lower warp threads before the shuttle passes back between them.

SEE ALSO PAGES:
66–7 Plants and people,
185 Bases and alkalis,
215 Polymers, 216 Plastics

GLASS

Glass is a transparent material. It is made by melting a mixture of sand and salts at high temperatures. The mixture solidifies as glass when it cools.

Glass has been made from sand, flint, or quartz for more than 4,000 years. Today, glass is made from a mixture that is mostly sand. It is molded, blown, and rolled to make objects such as lenses, windows, and ornaments.

Glass can be stretched to make fiberglass, which can be used for insulation and for reinforcing plastics.

Special types of glass can be stretched to produce optical fibers. Optical fibers can channel light over long distances. They are used to transmit images and data such as telephone signals.

PROPERTIES OF GLASS

The properties of glass can be modified by adding small quantities of chemicals to the basic glass mixture. Borax, for example, makes glass more resistant to heat and is used to make ovenproof glass. Lead oxide improves the sparkle of cut glass and is used to make decorative glassware.

Laminated glass for car windshields is made by sandwiching a layer of plastic between two sheets of glass. The plastic holds the glass together if it shatters.

Stained glass windows are made by joining small pieces of colored glass using strips of lead. The glass is colored by adding metal salts during the glassmaking process.

A glassblower uses shears to cut off a lump of hot molten glass, which he will then shape by blowing air through a pipe.

British glass manufacturer Alistair Pilkington (1920–1995) invented the float-glass process in the 1950s. Liquid glass from a furnace gradually cools and solidifies on a bed of molten tin. The process makes glass that has a very smooth surface.

1 A mixture of 72% sand, 15% soda, 6% lime, 4% magnesia, 2% alumina, and 1% boric oxide is melted in a furnace at about 1,292°F.

2 Rollers spread an even layer of liquid glass onto a bed of molten tin

3 The glass is kept liquid long enough for it to even out over the molten tin. This results in a smooth surface. The glass then starts to solidify

4 The solid glass cools on rollers until its surface is hard enough not to be scratched by handling

5 The glass is cut into sheets for use as windows and mirrors

SEE ALSO PAGES:

194–5 Properties of solids, 216 Plastics, 366–7 Telecommunications

CERAMICS

Ceramics form a group of materials that includes clay, glass, and pottery. Many ceramics are heat resistant and good electrical insulators.

Ceramic cooktops have smooth surfaces that are easy to clean. Those parts of the cooktop that are not directly above a hot element remain cool to the touch.

Common ceramic products include tableware, tiles, ornaments, and pipes for water and sewage. These objects are made from clays that are soft and pliable, but become hard and brittle when they are baked at high temperatures.

The term "ceramics" once applied only to clay and earthenware. It now describes a multitude of earthy substances that can be hardened by baking.

Ceramics are usually resistant to water and most chemicals. They also tend to be good electrical insulators. Many ceramics have extremely high melting points and are not damaged by high temperatures. Such ceramics, called refractories, are used to line kilns and furnaces.

NEW USES FOR CERAMICS

Plastics have advantages over ceramics in many traditional uses. Plastic pipes, for example, are lighter and easier to mold

Ceramic pottery has been used since ancient times to create beautiful vessels, such as this vase.

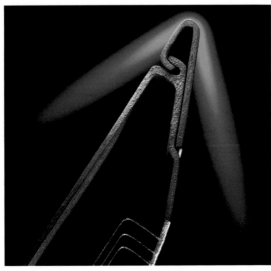

▶ The leading edge of this aircraft wing is made from a ceramic mixed with carbon fibers. The material is capable of withstanding temperatures of up to 2,012°F.

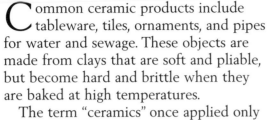

Potters have fashioned clay into tableware, storage jars, and ornaments for thousands of years.

than earthenware pipes. However, scientists have developed new types of ceramics with different properties that make them suitable for new uses.

Ceramics are mixed, pressed, and baked with powdered metals to form heat resistant alloys called cermets. Cermets are used in aerospace, for example, to make nose cones and heat resistant tiles for NASA's space shuttles.

Ceramic car engine casings are also being developed. They are strong, very heat resistant, and more lightweight than the usual cast-iron casings.

Although most ceramics are insulators, some ceramics that contain copper oxide are superconductors at extremely low temperatures (see page 360). Scientists are working to develop superconductors that work at higher temperatures.

▼ Bone china is a type of fine porcelain made from kaolin, the mineral china stone, and roasted oxen bones that have been ground to a fine powder. The powders are mixed with water to make a clay that can be molded. The clay object is fired in a kiln to harden it. It is then painted with a glaze and fired again to harden the glaze.

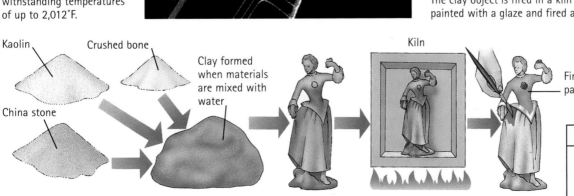

Kaolin   Crushed bone   Clay formed when materials are mixed with water   Kiln   Fired clay figurine is painted and glazed

China stone

SEE ALSO PAGES:

194–5 Properties of solids, 217 New materials, 360–1 Conductors, 362 Insulators

OIL AND REFINING

Oil or petroleum is a liquid that can be refined to make fuels and lubricants, as well as raw materials for the chemical industry.

This pump in Bakersfield, California, is an example of a nodding donkey. It draws oil to the surface as it "nods" up and down.

Oil is the decomposed remains of tiny organisms that lived in the sea many millions of years ago. After they died, they were covered with layer upon layer of sediment. Over time, the weight of those layers turned the organic remains into crude oil. The appearance of crude oil varies from a pale yellow liquid to a black sticky tar. More than half the world's known oil reserves are in the Middle East.

Crude oil, or petroleum, is a complex mixture of chemical compounds that consists mainly of hydrogen and carbon. This mixture is separated and treated in oil refineries to produce materials that are used to make a huge range of materials called petrochemicals or oil derivatives.

The main derivatives of oil are fuels such as diesel, jet fuel, and gasoline. Other derivatives include dyes, lubricants, medicinal drugs, nylon and polyester fabrics, plastics and polymers, solvents, synthetic rubber, and waxes.

Oil rigs are designed to provide a stable platform for the incredibly powerful drill bit to bore deep down into the Earth. It taps into a reserve of oil. Life on oil rigs is dirty and sometimes dangerous, but usually well paid.

FINDING AND PRODUCING OIL

The search for oil is called oil exploration. The extraction of oil from natural reserves is called oil production.

As oil forms underground, it tends to seep up through porous rock toward the Earth's surface. If it hits a "roof" of nonporous rock, it becomes trapped and starts to form a reservoir of oil.

Oil and natural gas collect in domes or ridges of porous rock that lie under solid rock. When the rock above the reserve is punctured by a drill, natural pressure forces the gas and oil to the surface.

Many oil reserves lie out at sea. One type of offshore oil rig floats on large pontoons and is held in place by computer-controlled engines. Huge drills are sunk into the ground in search of deposits of oil.

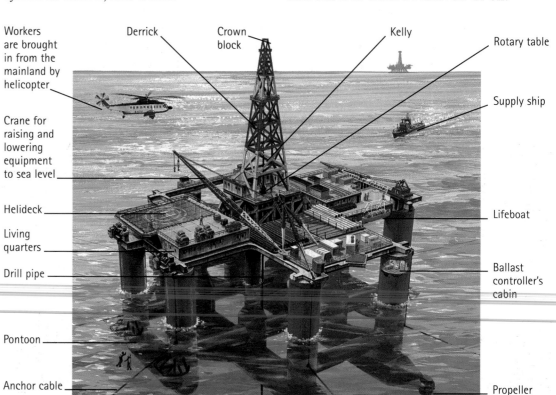

Workers are brought in from the mainland by helicopter

Crane for raising and lowering equipment to sea level

Helideck

Living quarters

Drill pipe

Pontoon

Anchor cable

Derrick

Crown block

Kelly

Rotary table

Supply ship

Lifeboat

Ballast controller's cabin

Propeller

▲ The Trans-Alaska Pipeline carries crude oil 798 mi. (1,284km) through Alaska. The pipeline is 1.2 meters in diameter and can transport 318 million liters of crude oil a day.

▶ Oil is frequently transported by ships called tankers. The larger tankers, such as this Arco Alaska oil transporter, are known as supertankers. They can be hundreds of meters long.

Geologists know the patterns of rock where oil is likely to collect and have developed surveying techniques that help to locate potential oil deposits.

In one method, explosives are set off to send vibrations underground. The echoes of the explosions are then detected and analyzed to form a picture of the rock structure that lies underground. If the rock structure is likely to hold oil, a number of test wells are drilled. If the test wells find oil, production oil wells are built.

Oil production is measured in units called barrels. One barrel is equal to 337 pints. The current world production of crude oil is about 25,000 million barrels a year. Experts believe that there are between 1.5 and 2 billion barrels of oil still remaining in underground reserves and could be extracted in the future.

OIL REFINING
Crude oil is transported to oil refineries by pipelines or by large tanker ships. There, a process called fractional distillation is used to separate it into mixtures of products that have similar boiling points. Those mixtures are then further treated to produce a range of fuels and a multitude of raw materials for the chemical industry.

▲ An enormous number of products are derived from oil, including polymers and solvents for paints, lubricating oils, waxes, and fuels.

◀ Crude oil is processed in large refineries such as this one in Wales. Fractionating columns up to 246 feet tall are used to separate the components of the oil.

SEE ALSO PAGES:

174–5 Organic chemistry, 190–1 Petrochemicals, 215 Polymers, 216 Plastics, 456 Resources

NATURAL GAS

Natural gas is an important energy resource. It is used to provide heat and energy, and is an important raw material for the chemical industry.

Hot-air balloons burn propane or butane from cylinders to warm air inside the balloon. This lifts the balloon into the sky.

The composition of natural gas varies depending on where it is extracted. North-Sea gas contains 92 percent methane, 3.5 percent ethane, 2.5 percent nitrogen, and 1 percent propane.

Bottled gas is a portable source of fuel for appliances like gas barbecues.

Natural gas, like crude oil, formed over millions of years from the remains of marine organisms. Natural gas also collects in the types of rock structures where crude oil is found. For this reason, gas reserves are often found with oil reserves.

The main component of natural gas is methane, the simplest hydrocarbon (compound of carbon and hydrogen). Mixed with the methane are smaller amounts of other hydrocarbon gases such as ethane, butane, and propane.

Natural gas provides almost a fifth of the world's energy supplies. Also, the components of natural gas are important raw materials for chemical processes.

Most of the world's natural gas comes from wells in Canada, Siberia, and the United States.

PRODUCING AND PROCESSING GAS

Natural gas is extracted through wells that are similar to oil wells. Many gas reserves lie offshore, and gas is piped from offshore gas-production platforms to an onshore collection point and then on to a refinery where it is purified.

In the first stage of purification, water and any other liquids are allowed to settle out from the gas under the action of gravity. The dry gas then passes through

Surplus natural gas is sometimes burned off by flares, such as this one on a gas-production platform in the Bruce field in the North Sea.

a cooler, where butane and propane liquefy and are collected. These gases, called liquefied petroleum gases (LPGs), can be sold as raw materials for the manufacture of chemicals or bottled and used as fuel for heaters and stoves.

The remaining natural gas can be piped through a supply network or cooled and pressurized to form liquefied natural gas (LNG). Liquefied natural gas takes up much less space than natural gas and is a convenient way to ship the gas in tankers.

This view along the deck of a liquefied natural gas (LNG) carrier shows the tops of its large, insulated steel tanks. The tanks contain liquefied gas at −260°F.

COAL

Coal is an impure type of carbon that formed from the remains of prehistoric plants. Coal burns very easily, releasing large amounts of heat.

Coal, like oil and gas, is a fossil fuel. Oil and gas formed from the remains of living organisms; coal formed from the remains of decaying plants from prehistoric forests. These remains were compressed and changed by the layers of rock above them.

There are three main types of coal, each containing a different amount of carbon: anthracite, bituminous coal, and lignite. Anthracite contains approximately 95 percent carbon and is the most valuable form of coal. Bituminous coal contains around 70 percent carbon, and lignite, or brown coal, contains less than 50 percent carbon. Most coal is found in underground bands or seams.

The coal-mining industry extracts more than 4 million tons of coal every year. More than half of this total is mined in China and the United States. The amount of coal that could be mined from known reserves is some 1.2 trillion tons.

Anthracite is the hardest form of coal. It releases more heat than any other type of coal when it burns. Anthracite contains about 95 percent carbon. Another form of carbon is the graphite that is used in pencils.

USES OF COAL

Coal was the main fuel for the Industrial Revolution at the end of the 1700s. It powered steam engines and was used for making iron and steel. Today, most coal is burned in power plants to generate electricity. Coal-fired power plants use filters and other devices to trap soot and other pollution that forms when coal burns.

When coal is heated in a chamber called a retort, it releases gas, oil, and tar. The gas can be burned as fuel. The oil and tar contain chemicals that can be used for making products such as dyes, perfumes, and artificial fibers. The solid that is left behind in the retort is coke. It is used as a smokeless fuel and for making iron.

MINING COAL

Different types of mines and mining techniques are used, depending on the land conditions and how deep the coal seam is. Deep deposits are reached through vertical shafts, and horizontal tunnels are dug into the coal seam. Coal deposits near the surface are mined in strip, opencast, and slope mines, which cost less to construct and operate than shaft mines.

Excavator working an opencast mine

Ventilation fans

Shaft mines extract coal from deep seams

Slope mines extract coal from shallow seams

Ventilation shaft

Strip mine built where coal seam reaches surface

Coal seam

Cage travels up and down main shaft

Tunnel

Main shaft

SEE ALSO PAGES:

RUBBER

Natural rubber is made from the sap of rubber trees. Synthetic rubber is made from oil by the chemical industry. Both types are extremely versatile materials.

It is estimated that the energy produced by burning one tire can serve the daily energy needs of a typical household. This power plant in California produces energy by burning more than four million waste tires a year.

For hundreds of years, natural rubber has been made by tapping the sap from rubber trees and letting it dry and harden.

During the 1900s, advances in chemistry allowed an artificial version of rubber to be manufactured using chemicals from oil. About two thirds of the 18 million tons of rubber produced each year is now synthetic.

Rubber can be made into a tough, flexible material for making a range of products, such as clothing, hoses, and tires.

The shock-absorbing properties of rubber make it useful for car suspensions and for reducing the vibrations caused by industrial machinery.

Since rubber is water-resistant, it is used for diving suits, rainwear, and medical tubing. Rubber is a good insulator of electricity and is often used as a covering for electric power lines.

Rubber can be whipped and whisked into a foam containing millions of air bubbles. This foam can be molded and set to create a variety of lightweight products like sponges and cushions.

Natural and synthetic rubber are used for a variety of products. Rubber is an easy-to-grip, flexible, and waterproof material.

VULCANIZED RUBBER

The uses of crude rubber are limited by its softness. Crude rubber can be made harder by heating it with sulfur in a process called vulcanization.

The molecules of rubber have a long, zigzag shape. They straighten when the rubber is stretched but also break easily. Vulcanizing causes the rubber to form bonds that join molecules from side to side. This makes the rubber tougher. It still stretches when pulled but snaps back to its original shape when released.

▲ Three-piece golf balls are made from a solid core or a water-filled ball of latex rubber. A thin rubber band, several miles long, is wound around the core. The golf ball is surrounded by a tough dimpled plastic cover.

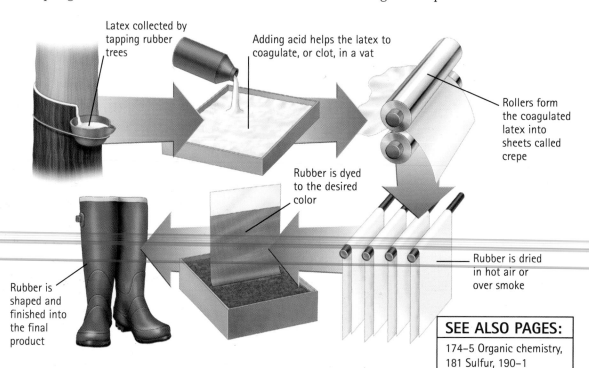

Latex collected by tapping rubber trees

Adding acid helps the latex to coagulate, or clot, in a vat

Rollers form the coagulated latex into sheets called crepe

Rubber is dyed to the desired color

Rubber is dried in hot air or over smoke

Rubber is shaped and finished into the final product

▶ Natural rubber is made from the sap of rubber trees, which grow in tropical countries. The milky sap, called latex, is tapped from the trunk of the tree, coagulated, then rolled, and dried. The raw rubber can be dyed, shaped, or molded to form finished products.

SEE ALSO PAGES:
174–5 Organic chemistry, 181 Sulfur, 190–1 Petrochemicals, 215 Polymers, 216 Plastics

POLYMERS

Polymers are very large molecules that are made up of thousands of smaller molecules, all joined together. Polymers can be natural or synthetic.

This is just a small part of a polymer chain.

Polymers occur frequently in nature. DNA, wood, and protein are all polymers. Natural fibers, such as wool and silk, are also polymers.

Synthetic polymers have been made since the late 1800s. They are the basis of all synthetic plastics and fibers.

Polymers consist of long, chainlike molecules that are made by joining together smaller molecules called monomers. Polyethylene, for example, is made by joining together many thousands of molecules of the monomer ethylene.

Polymers can have one of three types of structure: linear, branched, or cross-linked. Linear polymers consist of long, simple chains of monomers. Nylon and polyvinyl chloride (PVC) are linear polymers. Some linear polymers have kinked chains. The chains straighten out when stretched, but spring back when the force is removed. This makes some polymers elastic.

Branched polymers have shorter chains attached along their main chains, rather like the teeth of a comb.

Cross-linked polymers have links between their chains that form a net; this makes the polymer harder and less flexible.

Raw materials for nylon are heated to form a stream of liquid polymer. This forms a filament of nylon when it cools in a water bath. The filament is dried, chopped, melted, then sprayed through a spinneret, which resembles a showerhead. Cold air turns the spray into fine fibers. These are then stretched and crimped.

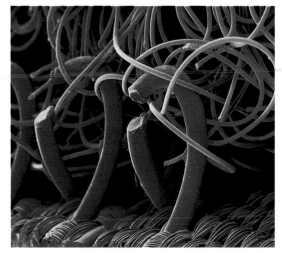

VeVelcro, seen here magnified 24 times, consists of two textures of nylon. The hooks at the bottom catch in the looped whiskers at the top.

NYLON

Nylon was the world's first synthetic fiber. It was developed by U.S. chemist Wallace H. Carothers (1896–1937) in the 1930s.

Nylon was originally designed as a cheap alternative to silk. Nylon polymer makes a fiber that is stronger than cotton and wool. It can be mixed with natural fibers or used on its own to make yarn for weaving textiles.

Different types of nylon can be made by varying the raw materials used for making the polymer. Some nylons are hard enough to make gears and bearings for machines. These types are also resistant to heat and chemical attack.

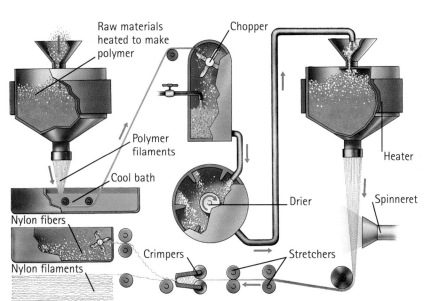

Raw materials heated to make polymer

Chopper

Polymer filaments

Cool bath

Nylon fibers

Nylon filaments

Crimpers

Drier

Stretchers

Heater

Spinneret

▲ This fly-fisherman in the River Dee, in Scotland, uses a nylon line on his rod. The strength of nylon makes it ideal.

SEE ALSO PAGES:

PLASTICS

Plastics are materials that can be easily stretched or molded into shape. Most plastics are made from chemicals that have been derived from oil.

Many familiar objects, from casings for electrical goods to bags, drink containers, and football helmets, are made from different types of plastic.

Articles such as brushes and combs are made by molding plastic. The bristles of toothbrushes are nylon fibers.

Plastics are a form of polymer. The first plastics, such as celluloid, were made from naturally occurring polymers. The first completely synthetic plastic was Bakelite, invented in 1907 by U.S. chemist Leo Baekeland (1863–1944). Since then, hundreds of plastics have been developed. Nearly all are made using chemicals derived from oil.

The wide range of uses for plastics stems from their properties. They can be rigid or flexible and can be colored, shaped, and formed in a number of ways. Plastics are good electrical insulators and many are resistant to chemical attack.

Plastics do not all behave in the same way when they are heated. Some, called thermoplastics, soften when they are heated. Polyethylene is a thermoplastic.

Other plastics, called thermosets, become harder when they are heated. Once they have set during manufacturing, they cannot be reshaped. Electric plugs are made of thermosets, which is why they do not melt if the wires inside them overheat.

The walls of this exhibition squash court are made using Lucite. This material is transparent like glass, but much more resistant to high-speed impacts.

ENVIRONMENTAL ISSUES

The chemical resistance of plastic is a good property for most uses. That same resistance becomes a problem in garbage landfills. The bacteria that cause wood, paper, and natural fibers to biodegrade, or rot, cannot break down most plastics. As a result, plastic materials remain unchanged in landfills.

Scientists are developing plastics that are biodegradable, some of them based on plant materials. However, recycling as much plastic as possible is considered the most practical way to avoid the buildup of plastics in landfill sites.

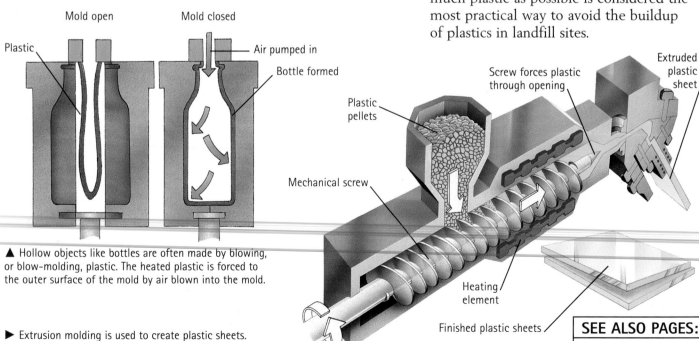

▲ Hollow objects like bottles are often made by blowing, or blow-molding, plastic. The heated plastic is forced to the outer surface of the mold by air blown into the mold.

▶ Extrusion molding is used to create plastic sheets. Pellets of plastic are mixed and softened by heat before being forced through an opening by a mechanical screw.

SEE ALSO PAGES:

170 Carbon, 190–1 Petrochemicals, 215 Polymers

NEW MATERIALS

Traditional materials are increasingly being replaced by newer ones in applications where they offer significant improvement or some other advantage.

Carbon-fiber-based materials are used to make tennis rackets that are light yet strong.

The range of materials available for building and manufacturing goods has increased enormously, particularly since the beginning of the 1900s.

Many new materials are superior to traditional materials like concrete and steel. Frequently, the improvement is in strength, weight, ease of shaping, and resistance to extreme temperatures. In some cases, the new material might be cheaper or better for the environment than the traditional material.

Plastic reinforced with carbon fiber, magnified 923 times in this photomicrograph, is about one-fourth the weight of steel and twice as strong.

COMPOSITES

Many new materials are composites. Such materials are made up of two or more different substances. A composite is designed to combine the useful properties of each substance while minimizing any bad properties. Composites often consist of strong fibers embedded in a material that holds the fibers together.

Fiberglass-reinforced plastic combines the flexibility of a plastic with the strength of the fiberglass that is embedded in the plastic. The brittleness of fiberglass is not a problem when it is combined with plastic in the composite. This tough material is used to make automotive body panels and boat hulls.

Carbon fibers are frequently used in composites with plastic, ceramics, and metal. They are light, very strong, and can withstand extreme strain without breaking, even at high temperatures.

The frame and wheels of this bicycle are made of a carbon-fiber composite.

Kevlar is lightweight but strong. It is used to make body armor and bulletproof vests.

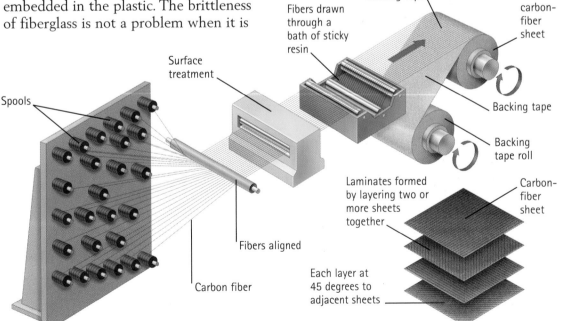

A form of carbon-fiber composite is made by sticking resin-coated carbon fibers to a backing tape. Because the strength of the composite is in the direction of the fibers, a strong laminate is made by stacking sheets with fibers aligned in different directions.

Labels: Spools · Surface treatment · Fibers drawn through a bath of sticky resin · Sticky fibers pressed onto backing tape · Roll of carbon-fiber sheet · Backing tape · Backing tape roll · Fibers aligned · Carbon fiber · Laminates formed by layering two or more sheets together · Carbon-fiber sheet · Each layer at 45 degrees to adjacent sheets

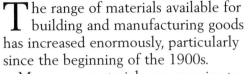

Flexon frames for glasses are made from a material that returns to its original shape after being twisted.

SEE ALSO PAGES:

194–5 Properties of solids, 202–3 Alloys, 208 Glass, 209 Ceramics, 215 Polymers, 216 Plastics

ADHESIVES

Adhesives are natural and synthetic materials that are used to stick objects and surfaces together. Glues, cements, and resins are all adhesives.

Laminated car windshields are made by bonding layers of glass with adhesive resin.

Adhesives attach to surfaces by filling the tiny pits and holes in even the smoothest surface and then setting hard. If a drop of adhesive attaches itself to two surfaces, those surfaces will be bonded together when the adhesive hardens.

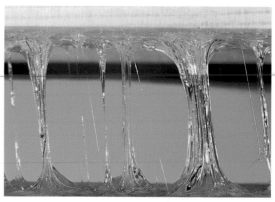

Adhesives bond pieces of wood together by penetrating the two surfaces and then setting hard as the adhesive's solvent evaporates or as the adhesives start to cure.

NATURAL GLUES AND GUMS

One type of glue is made by boiling animal bones in water. Plants that contain a lot of starch, such as corn and potatoes, can also make useful glues. Algin, a gum made from seaweed, is used on the backs of postage stamps and some envelopes. The main disadvantage of natural adhesives is that they can be weakened over time by microorganisms like mold.

An adhesive resin holds together the fibers in the fiberglass used to make canoes and kayaks.

CEMENT

Builders' cement is a type of adhesive made from powdered rocks and chemicals. Cement is a powder that, when mixed with water and sand, forms mortar. Mortar is put in the gaps between bricks and forms a bond when it dries.

SYNTHETIC ADHESIVES

Synthetic adhesives are usually solutions of polymers in solvents. Some harden as the solvents evaporate. Others are packaged as two solutions that are mixed just before use. Mixing the two solutions makes them start to cure (harden).

The strength of adhesives varies greatly. Those used in aircraft construction are incredibly strong; the glue on peel-off price labels is deliberately weak.

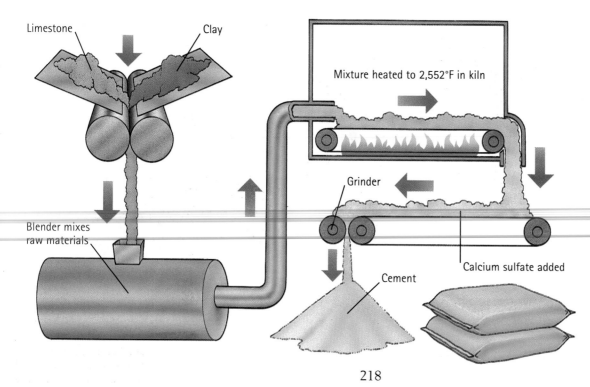

Limestone

Clay

Mixture heated to 2,552°F in kiln

Grinder

Blender mixes raw materials

Calcium sulfate added

Cement

To make cement, water is added to a mixture of limestone rock and clay. The mixture is heated to 2,552°F in a rotating kiln. The material produced, called clinker, is cooled and mixed with calcium sulfate. This mixture is ground to a fine powder and packaged in bags.

SEE ALSO PAGES:

215 Polymers, 216 Plastics, 220–1 Brick, stone, and concrete, 222–3 Construction

PIGMENTS AND DYES

There are many different pigments and dyes. Both natural and artificial dyes and pigments are used to color various objects and materials.

In 1856, English chemist William Perkin (1838–1907) accidentally discovered the world's first artificial dye. It was a mauve dye derived from coal tar.

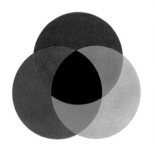

▲ Any color can be produced by mixing three colors: cyan (blue), magenta (red), and yellow.

Objects have color because they absorb certain colors of light and reflect others. The colors that are reflected combine to form the color that is seen by the human eye. The chemical compounds that cause these colors are called dyes and pigments. Dyes dissolve in water and other solvents. Pigments are solids that do not dissolve.

Many dyes and pigments occur naturally in plants. Indigo, for example, is a plant dye that has been used to color fabrics since Roman times. Other pigments are made by grinding rocks into powder. Yellow ocher is obtained by grinding an ore of iron. Ultramarine blue pigment is made by grinding a bright blue semiprecious stone called lapis lazuli.

In addition to natural coloring agents, many dyes and pigments are products of the chemical industry. Some are metal salts; others are derived from oil.

An infinite range of colors can be made by using different combinations of dyes and pigments.

This technician is inspecting machinery used in the manufacture of yellow pigment for paint. The pigment being produced is yellow iron oxide.

INKS, PAINTS, AND DYEING

Dyes and pigments are used to color inks and paints. Printing inks are used to produce books, greeting cards, magazines, and posters. When inks are applied to a surface, they dry and leave the dyes and pigments on the inked surface.

Paints are used to provide decorative and protective coatings for surfaces. Paints are usually applied as liquid and then harden to form a surface covering that contains the dyes and pigments.

In dyeing processes, solutions of dyes soak into the fabric of the object to be colored. Solid pigments are not used for dyeing, since they do not dissolve and would sit on the surface of a material rather than soak into it.

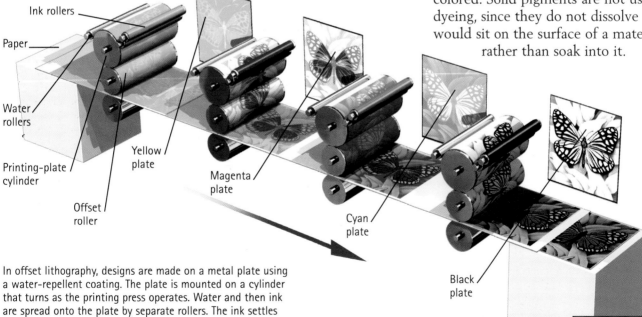

Ink rollers

Paper

Water rollers

Printing-plate cylinder

Offset roller

Yellow plate

Magenta plate

Cyan plate

Black plate

In offset lithography, designs are made on a metal plate using a water-repellent coating. The plate is mounted on a cylinder that turns as the printing press operates. Water and then ink are spread onto the plate by separate rollers. The ink settles over the water-repellent coating to match the design. The ink then transfers first to an offset roller, then to the paper that is being printed. A color image is built up in stages by printing separate yellow, magenta (red), cyan (blue), and black images.

SEE ALSO PAGES:

190–1 Petrochemicals, 207 Fibers, 272–3 Color, 274–5 Color mixing

BRICK, STONE, AND CONCRETE

Brick, stone, and concrete are some of the oldest materials used for building. They are hard, strong, and easily available in many locations.

Brick, stone, and concrete are three of the most versatile materials used in construction. Bricks were used as long ago as 7000 B.C. in Mesopotamia. Stone has been used even longer. Concrete was used by the Romans to build structures like the Pantheon, the Roman temple restored by Hadrian (A.D. 114–128).

BRICKS
Bricks are blocks of clay that have been hardened by heat. Some bricks contain straw and are simply dried in the heat of the sun. Most bricks are baked in kilns.

Bricks have a number of properties that are useful for construction. Their regular shapes fit together easily, and kiln-baked bricks resist damp and heat.

STONE
Common types of stone are limestone, basalt, granite, marble, and sandstone. Stone is extracted from quarries, which are pits in the ground or in hillsides.

In one method of quarrying, called dimension-stone quarrying, blocks of stone are cut from the rock. Hand tools and power saws are used to cut blocks into useful shapes and sizes.

In crushed-stone quarrying, rocks such as granite, limestone, and sandstone are blasted apart using explosives. The rubble is collected and used for making concrete and for road building.

These adobe bricks will be dried in the sun for about two weeks. They are made from a type of clay soil that is easy to mold when wet, but becomes extremely hard when dry. Adobe bricks are used for building in areas such as Mexico, where there is too little rain to soften and destroy the bricks.

▼ Limestone is obtained from quarries, like this one in County Durham, in England. Limestone is used as a raw material for making cement and concrete. Blocks of limestone can be used for building.

Bricklayers arrange bricks in patterns called bonds. The bricks are held in place by a layer of mortar, which sets hard in the gaps between bricks.

CONCRETE
Concrete is made by mixing cement with solids called aggregates, which include sand, gravel, and small stones. When water is added, this mixture forms a heavy paste that gradually hardens to a solid.

Concrete has many advantages. It is cheap and durable, and its raw materials are widely available in many parts of the world. Concrete can be mixed on building

▲ The ornate frontage of the New York Stock Exchange was carved from blocks of stone. This impressive building, designed by George B. Post, was completed in 1903.

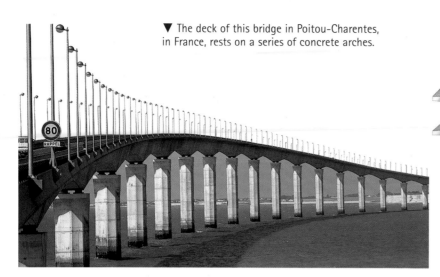

▼ The deck of this bridge in Poitou-Charentes, in France, rests on a series of concrete arches.

Normal concrete

Concrete reinforced with steel bars or wires

Concrete cast around tensioned steel bars

Normal concrete (top) is weak under tension. Reinforced concrete (middle) and post-tensioned concrete (bottom) are both strong under tension.

sites as it is needed or delivered as a paste. Unlike brick and stone, this paste can be molded, poured, or sprayed to form many different shapes. Concrete is used to build bridges, dams, piers, and roads, as well as apartment and office buildings.

Concrete can withstand very strong compressive (crushing) forces. It has less resistance to tensile (stretching) forces, which tend to pull it apart. This weakness can be overcome by combining concrete with steel, which resists tensile forces.

In reinforced concrete, for example, concrete is poured around steel bars or nets.

The tensile strength can be improved by stretching the steel framework before the concrete sets around it. This technique is called prestressing. In another technique, called post-tensioning, nuts on the ends of the reinforcement bars are tightened after the concrete has set. In both cases, the bars increase the strength of the concrete considerably.

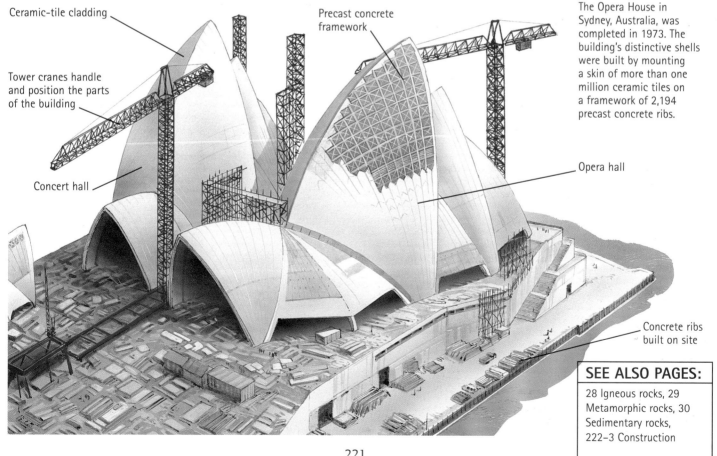

Ceramic-tile cladding

Tower cranes handle and position the parts of the building

Concert hall

Precast concrete framework

Opera hall

Concrete ribs built on site

The Opera House in Sydney, Australia, was completed in 1973. The building's distinctive shells were built by mounting a skin of more than one million ceramic tiles on a framework of 2,194 precast concrete ribs.

SEE ALSO PAGES:

28 Igneous rocks, 29 Metamorphic rocks, 30 Sedimentary rocks, 222–3 Construction

CONSTRUCTION

The construction industry builds all sorts of structures, from factories, houses, offices, and roads to bridges, dams, and docks.

A beam bridge is a simple flat deck that is supported by columns at intervals along its length.

The construction industry employs thousands of people. In the United States, construction accounts for 15 percent of all jobs.

Until the late 1800s, construction was mainly the work of bricklayers, carpenters, and stonemasons. Although most of these specialists still work in construction, new materials and techniques have changed the way many structures are built.

Reinforced concrete and steel are now major materials in the construction industry. Tall buildings are built around frameworks of steel and concrete. Walls and windows are hung on the framework and, unlike in older buildings, do not have to support the walls above them. For this reason, walls can be thinner and lighter.

Concrete and steel are also used to build new designs of bridges, factories, and houses that would not have been possible using brick, stone, and wood.

The shape of an arch carries the weight of the arch and the bridge deck to supports at the two ends of the arch.

The deck of a suspension bridge is hung from cables that are stretched between tall towers.

STRUCTURAL DESIGN

When designing a building, an architect works with a structural engineer who calculates the weight of each part of the building and designs a structure to support that weight. Structures must be able to withstand gusts of wind and sometimes earthquakes, river currents, or waves, depending on where the building is built.

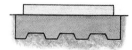

A raft foundation spreads the weight of a building.

Friction piles are clusters of small piles.

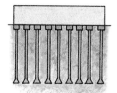

Foundation piers are piles with splayed bases.

Bearing piles.

▲ Rafts, piles, and piers spread the weight of a building to prevent it from sinking into soft ground. Bearing piles rest on solid bedrock.

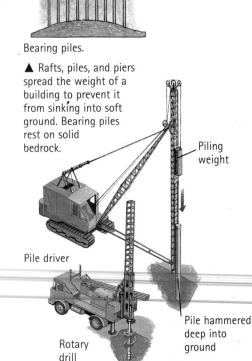

Pile driver

Rotary drill

Piling weight

Pile hammered deep into ground

Foundation piles can be driven up to 328 feet deep by repeatedly hammering the pile with a piling weight. Concrete piles can be cast in holes made by rotary drills.

ROAD CONSTRUCTION

Roads are built on soil that has first been compacted by heavy rollers. A layer of coarse stones, the subbase, spreads the weight of the road over the surface of the compacted soil. A base course of rough concrete strengthens the road. The road surface, called the pavement, is made up of concrete or asphalt and small stones.

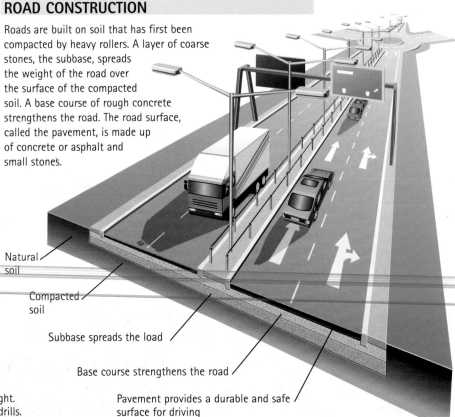

Natural soil

Compacted soil

Subbase spreads the load

Base course strengthens the road

Pavement provides a durable and safe surface for driving

Models of proposed structures are built and fitted with gauges that measure forces and movement. The models can then be tested in wind tunnels, water tanks, and shaking tables to simulate natural conditions. Computer analysis of the test results helps to improve the designs.

Certain shapes are particularly strong. Tubes and triangles are among the strongest. For example, steel structures, such as antennas, metal bridges, and the metal towers that carry power lines, consist of steel struts bolted together in patterns of steel triangles. This is the most efficient way of spreading forces evenly throughout a structure. Tunnels and the legs of oil rigs are tubular because the shape of a tube helps resist bending forces.

Modern high-rise buildings usually have a strong steel frame onto which their floors and wall panels are bolted. The frame supports the weight of the building.

STAGES OF CONSTRUCTION

There are three main stages in the building of a large structure. First, the foundation must be laid below the ground to support the structure. Tough materials like steel columns and concrete are used to help support the building, bridge, or dam. The type of foundation is determined by the properties of the soil in that area.

Second, the part of the structure above the foundation is built. In many cases, components are built somewhere else and then assembled on the building site.

Third and finally, the exterior surfaces are finished, and, in the case of buildings, the infrastructure is installed. This includes electricity, gas, and water fittings, as well as air conditioning.

A rivet gun drives a hot metal pin, called a rivet, through steel plates.

The protruding end of the rivet is flattened, which leaves the plates firmly joined together.

The skyline of Seattle is a showcase paying tribute to the importance and variety of the modern high-rise building.

SEE ALSO PAGES:

198 Iron, 202–3 Alloys, 204–5 Shaping materials, 220–1 Brick, stone, and concrete

GASOLINE AND DIESEL ENGINES

Gasoline and diesel engines burn fuel to create mechanical energy. This is used everyday to drive machinery, including cars, trucks, and boats.

German engineer Nikolaus Otto (1832–1891) built the first practical four-stroke gasoline engine in 1861. In 1876, he invented the four-stroke internal combustion engine.

Gasoline and diesel engines are types of internal combustion engines. They take this name because they combust, or burn, fuel inside their cylinders. Some of the energy is released when the fuel burns and is converted directly into mechanical energy. The rest is lost as heat.

Internal combustion engines are used to power most road vehicles and boats. They also power some aircraft and railroad locomotives. Gasoline or diesel engines are frequently used to operate emergency electricity generators.

The designs of four-stroke diesel and gasoline engines are very similar. In both cases, a mixture of fuel and air burns inside cylinders that are fitted with pistons. As the burning mixture expands inside a cylinder, it forces the piston to slide toward the mouth of the cylinder and push against a crank on a crankshaft, just like a cyclist pushing against a pedal. The exhaust valve then opens and the waste combustion gases start to escape.

FOUR-STROKE GASOLINE ENGINE

German engineer Gottlieb Daimler (1834–1900) worked with Nikolaus Otto to develop the design of Otto's engine. Daimler patented a high-speed version of the four-stroke engine in 1887. Typical gasoline engines have up to eight cylinders. A piston in each cylinder drives the crankshaft around when fuel and air ignite, driving the piston down. Springed valves allow the fuel–air mixture to enter the cylinder and the exhaust gases to leave.

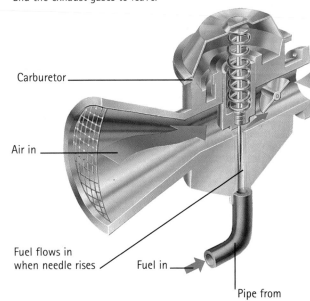

Carburetor

Air in

Fuel flows in when needle rises

Fuel in

Pipe from fuel tank

At the same time, the crankshaft pushes the piston back into the cylinder, driving out the remaining gases.

When the piston reaches the top of the cylinder, the exhaust valve closes and the inlet valve opens. As the crankshaft pulls the piston down, it draws fuel and air into the cylinder. This is called induction.

The inlet valve closes and the piston is pushed into the cylinder by the crank. This compression, or squeezing, causes the mixture of fuel and air to become hot.

In the case of a gasoline engine, a spark from the spark plug then ignites the hot mixture and starts a new power stroke.

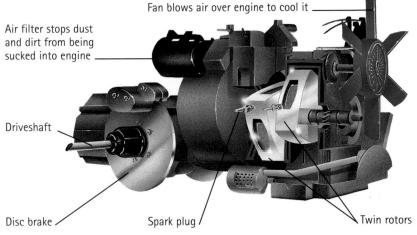

Fan blows air over engine to cool it

Air filter stops dust and dirt from being sucked into engine

Driveshaft

Disc brake

Spark plug

Twin rotors

German engineer Felix Wankel (1902–88) built a rotary engine in 1957. A triangular piston turns inside a chamber through the combustion cycle.

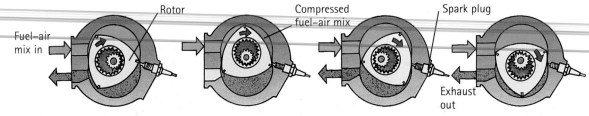

Rotor

Fuel–air mix in

Compressed fuel–air mix

Spark plug

Exhaust out

1 Induction: turning rotor sucks in mixture of gasoline and air.

2 Compression: fuel–air mixture is compressed as rotor carries it around.

3 Ignition: compressed fuel–air mixture is ignited by the spark plug.

4 Exhaust: the rotor continues to turn and pushes out waste gases.

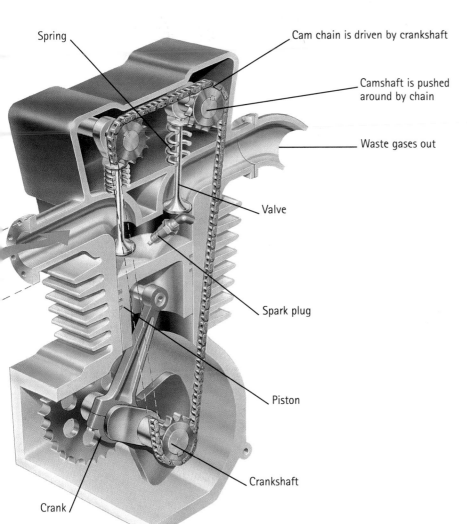

Spring

Cam chain is driven by crankshaft

Camshaft is pushed around by chain

Waste gases out

Valve

Spark plug

Piston

Crankshaft

Crank

1 **Induction:** the piston falls, drawing air and fuel into the cylinder.

2 **Compression:** the rising piston compresses the fuel–air mixture.

3 **Power:** a spark ignites the fuel and air, which forces the piston down.

4 **Exhaust:** the piston rises and forces the exhaust gases out.

▲ The four-stroke cycle is used in most car engines. The four piston strokes, or movements, are called induction, compression, power, and exhaust. Only the power stroke drives the crankshaft around. In a four-cylinder engine, each cylinder will be at a different stage in the sequence at any one time.

DIESEL ENGINES

The diesel engine was invented in 1896 by German mechanical engineer Rudolf Diesel (1858–1913).

A diesel engine compresses the fuel–air mixture to roughly twice the pressure found in a gasoline engine. This makes the fuel–air mixture hot enough to ignite without the need for a spark plug.

Diesel fuel is usually less expensive than gasoline. Also, diesel engines burn fuel more efficiently and so use less fuel.

IMPROVEMENTS

Gasoline and diesel engines can be improved by increasing their fuel efficiency and reducing the pollution that they emit.

In many new engine designs, the carburetor has been replaced by electronic fuel injectors that pump fuel into the cylinder during the induction stroke. A microprocessor controls the amount of fuel that is injected as well as the timing so that the fuel burns efficiently with less pollution.

◄ The diesel engine of a diesel–electric locomotive drives an electricity generator. This powers the locomotive's electric traction motors. The turbocharger pumps air into the engine, which produces more power.

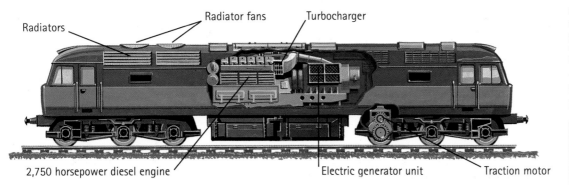

Radiators

Radiator fans

Turbocharger

2,750 horsepower diesel engine

Electric generator unit

Traction motor

SEE ALSO PAGES:

210–11 Oil and refining, 254 Combustion, 294–5 Work and energy

JET ENGINES AND GAS TURBINES

Jet engines drive aircraft forward by forcing gases backward at high speed. Gas turbines convert the force of expanding gases into mechanical energy.

English engineer Frank Whittle (1907–1996) designed the jet engine in 1930. The first successful aircraft to be powered by one of his engines flew in 1941.

The Concorde reaches speeds greater than the speed of sound using the power of jet propulsion.

The rotor blades that keep Chinook helicopters in the air are driven by a form of gas turbine.

In a gas-turbine system, a compressor forces air into a combustion chamber. There, it mixes with fuel. The mixture is ignited by a spark. Hot gases are produced when the fuel burns. They expand and drive a series of fan blades called a turbine. The rotation of the turbine can be used to drive a generator as well as driving the compressor at the turbine's air intake.

Jet engines can power aircraft at greater speeds than propeller engines by burning fuel and compressed air in a combustion chamber and expelling the combustion gases backward.

Gas turbines are similar to jet engines, but the hot gases that they produce are used to make a turbine rotate.

In either case, air enters the engine at the front and is compressed by a series of turbines. It enters the combustion chamber where it is mixed with fuel. The fuel-air mixture is ignited and burns fiercely to produce hot, expanding gases.

The hot gases pass through another turbine as they leave the combustion chamber. This turbine drives the compressor at the front of the engine.

In an aircraft's jet engine, these gases escape from the rear at high speed and drive the aircraft forward.

Simple jet engines are called turbojets. They are capable of driving aircraft at great speeds and are used to power military aircraft. Turbojets, however, have the disadvantages of being noisy and not fuel efficient.

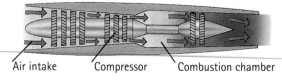

Turbojet

Air intake   Compressor   Combustion chamber

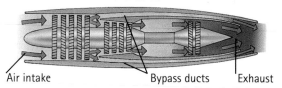

Turbofan

Air intake   Bypass ducts   Exhaust

Turbofan engines are quieter and more efficient than simple turbojet engines. Turbofans circulate air around the combustion engine as well as through it.

Jet airliners are usually powered by jet engines called turbofans. The compressor of a turbofan engine sucks in more air than is needed for the fuel that it burns. The extra air passes around the combustion chamber and is forced out of the rear of the engine. Turbofans are less noisy and more efficient than turbojets.

In a gas turbine, the force of the expanding hot air escaping from the combustion chamber is used to make a turbine shaft rotate. The rotation of the turbine shaft can be used, for example, to drive an electricity generator.

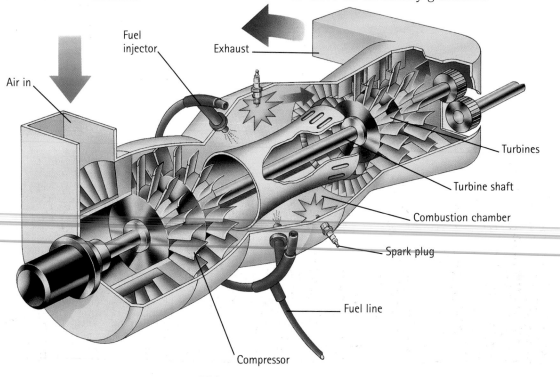

Fuel injector
Exhaust
Air in
Turbines
Turbine shaft
Combustion chamber
Spark plug
Fuel line
Compressor

STEAM ENGINES

Steam engines use pressurized steam from a boiler to drive pistons. They convert heat energy from burning fuel into mechanical energy.

English engineer Thomas Newcomen (1663–1729) built one of the first steam engines in 1705. It was used to pump water from mines.

English inventor James Watt (1736–1819) developed the first practical steam engine. In 1764, he invented a condenser that turned waste steam back into water to be used again.

When water boils in an open pot, it produces about 2,000 times its own volume of steam. If water boils in a sealed tank, the steam cannot expand. Instead, its pressure increases.

Steam engines work by letting pressurized steam from a heated boiler expand in their cylinders. This expansion forces a piston to move along the cylinder. When the piston is close to one end of the cylinder, a valve opens and pressurized steam forces the piston in the opposite direction. While this happens, the steam on the other side of the piston escapes. A connecting rod and crank turn the back-and-forth motion of the piston into the rotation of a shaft.

STEAM ENGINE HISTORY

Some of the first steam engines were built by Thomas Newcomen in the early 1700s. They were used to pump water from mines. In the 1760s, James Watt made improvements on the early designs. By the end of the 1700s, steam engines were widely used to power machinery in factories.

In 1804, British engineer Richard Trevithick (1771–1833) built the first steam locomotive. Steam locomotives were widely used until the 1960s.

STEAM TURBINES

In 1884, Irish engineer Charles Parsons (1854–1931) invented a turbine that used expanding steam to make a shaft rotate. By 1897, Parsons had built a steam-turbine-powered ship called Turbinia. It was the fastest boat of its time.

Steam turbines have an advantage over piston engines because they produce rotational motion directly, rather than needing a connecting rod and crank to turn a shaft. Steam turbines run more smoothly than piston engines, they are more efficient, and they occupy less room than piston engines of equivalent power.

Today, the main uses of steam turbines are in power plants and for the propulsion of nuclear-powered ships.

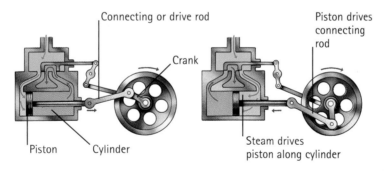

Connecting or drive rod
Crank
Piston   Cylinder

Piston drives connecting rod
Steam drives piston along cylinder

Crank converts motion to turn wheel

▲ Steam from a boiler drives a piston in a cylinder. The piston is connected to a crank that converts its back-and-forth motion into a circular motion.

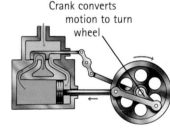

◄ Locomotives such as these were capable of hauling express passenger trains at speeds of around 100 mph (160kph) using steam power.

SEE ALSO PAGES:

213 Coal, 255 Expansion and contraction, 311 Pressure, 348 Power plants

HYDRAULICS AND PNEUMATICS

Hydraulic systems use pressurized liquids to transmit power from one place to another. Pneumatic systems use pressurized gases for the same purpose.

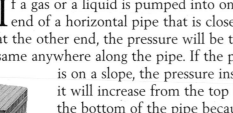

Forklifts use hydraulic systems in order to lift heavy loads, such as packing cases.

If a gas or a liquid is pumped into one end of a horizontal pipe that is closed at the other end, the pressure will be the same anywhere along the pipe. If the pipe is on a slope, the pressure inside it will increase from the top to the bottom of the pipe because of the weight of the gas or liquid above. Nevertheless, if more gas or liquid is pumped in, the pressure will increase by the same amount throughout the pipe.

Hydraulic and pneumatic systems use this effect to transmit pressure through a network of pipes.

PRESSURE AND FORCE

Pressure is defined as force per unit area (see page 311). If a fluid is pumped into a cylinder fitted with a piston, the force on the piston is the pressure of the fluid multiplied by the cross-sectional area of the piston. If fluid is pumped at exactly the same pressure into a cylinder with twice the cross-sectional area, the force on the larger piston will be double the size of the force on the smaller piston.

The flaps on the wing of this Airbus aircraft are operated by hydraulic mechanisms. The lift produced by the wing depends on the positions of these flaps.

HYDRAULICS

Hydraulic systems use liquids, normally oils, to transmit pressure through pipes. Many hydraulic systems are used to lift heavy weights using little force.

A one-ton weight resting on a piston 3-foot-wide produces the same pressure as a fraction (eg, $\frac{1}{100}$) of that weight on the same fraction ($\frac{1}{100}$) of the area.

A hydraulic car jack uses the same principle to raise a car by hand, pumping oil into a large cylinder that carries the weight of the car. Little force is needed, since the piston that pumps the oil is much smaller than the piston that raises

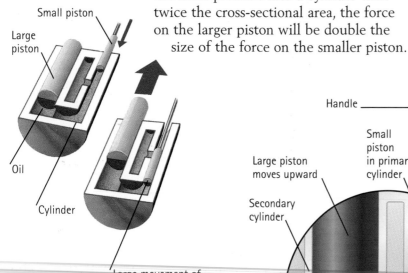

▼ Hydraulic systems with cylinders of different sizes can be used to amplify force. A large movement of the small piston causes a smaller movement of the larger piston, but with greater force.

Small piston

Large piston

Oil

Cylinder

Large movement of the small piston causes a small movement of the large piston

▶ This hand-operated hydraulic jack can lift one side of a car off the ground. Operating the lever forces the liquid in the primary cylinder through a ball-and-spring valve into the secondary cylinder. This makes the piston in the secondary cylinder rise.

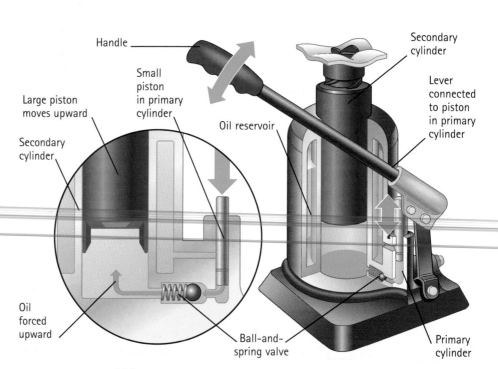

Handle

Small piston in primary cylinder

Large piston moves upward

Secondary cylinder

Oil reservoir

Secondary cylinder

Lever connected to piston in primary cylinder

Oil forced upward

Ball-and-spring valve

Primary cylinder

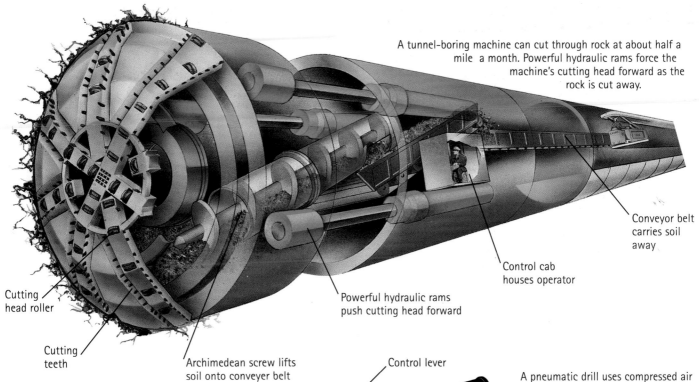

A tunnel-boring machine can cut through rock at about half a mile a month. Powerful hydraulic rams force the machine's cutting head forward as the rock is cut away.

Conveyor belt carries soil away

Control cab houses operator

Powerful hydraulic rams push cutting head forward

Cutting head roller

Cutting teeth

Archimedean screw lifts soil onto conveyer belt

the car. However, several pump strokes are needed to fill the space in the larger cylinder as the car is lifted.

Typical hydraulic systems use pumps to provide pressurized hydraulic fluid. One pump might provide enough pressurized fluid to operate several hydraulic rams (pistons) at the same time. The flow of fluid into each ram is controlled by valves. The pressure is released by closing the fluid inlet valve and draining the fluid back to a tank through a return pipe.

Hydraulics are used to move robotic arms, to drive tunneling machines forward, to control aircraft flaps, and to drive power-assisted braking and steering systems in cars and trucks.

PNEUMATICS

Pneumatic systems are similar to hydraulic systems because they use pipes to transfer pressure from a pump to tools. The main difference is that pneumatic systems use air instead of a hydraulic fluid.

Pneumatic systems are not used for the heavy-duty lifting and pushing jobs done by hydraulic systems. This is because air compresses easily and large volumes of air would have to be compressed to achieve the pressures used in hydraulic systems.

Control lever

A pneumatic drill uses compressed air to move a piston rapidly up and down. The piston strikes an anvil at the top of a drill bit. The repeated blows help the drill to cut through hard surfaces, such as rock and concrete.

Cylinder

Air in

Air out

Piston repeatedly forced up and down by air

Anvil

Diaphragm changes the route of the compressed air several times a second

Drill bit

In most pneumatic systems, the compressed air is used to drive piston engines or turbines. For example, a pneumatic drill uses a type of piston engine to drive its bit back and forth. Dental drills are driven by air turbines. In both cases, the air is released after use.

Pneumatically powered motors are useful where electrical motors would be too unwieldy to use or where a spark from a motor could trigger an explosion.

Pneumatic pressure pushes out the chemical contents of fire extinguishers when they are operated.

SEE ALSO PAGES:

FOOD PRODUCTION

Food is produced by cultivating and harvesting crops; by harvesting fish from seas, rivers, and fish farms; and by rearing and slaughtering animals.

Sugar-cane

Crusher

Sugar juice passes through filter

Lime is added

Sulfur dioxide is added

Evaporation pan

Sugar crystals

Sugar can be made from sugarcane by crushing the stems of the plant to extract its juice. The juice is filtered, purified using lime (calcium carbonate), bleached using sulfur dioxide, and then filtered. Crystals of sugar form as water evaporates from the resulting sugar solution.

In prehistoric times, people lived by hunting animals, by fishing, and by gathering food where it grew naturally. Gradually, people learned how to sow, cultivate, and harvest crops, and to rear animals for food. Archaeological evidence shows that farming began around 10,000 B.C. Since then, inventions and technology have radically changed farming techniques.

FOOD CROPS

The first farmers used hand tools to till soil and reap harvests. Food production was hard work. From the A.D. 400s, the Romans and other peoples started to use ox-drawn plows with iron blades. This let them farm soil that was too hard to till by hand.

From the 1700s, machines were invented that made sowing and harvesting less time-consuming. During the 1900s, motorized machinery allowed larger areas to be farmed in even less time.

Also in the 1900s, the use of synthetic fertilizers and insecticides helped increase the productivity of farms, as did genetic

These green peppers are being harvested in California. Like many other fruits and vegetables, they are picked by hand and then carried on a conveyor belt to a truck.

modification and the breeding of more productive plant species.

Many crops are still picked by hand, including tea leaves and some fruits and vegetables. In the future, it is likely that machines and robots will perform these tasks.

FISH AND OTHER SEAFOOD

Fishing is one of the world's most important food industries. About 100 million tons of fish and other seafood are caught each year. Although the oceans are enormous, most fish live and are caught within 62 miles of the coast.

▶ Combine harvesters collect grain from cereal crops such as wheat, oats, and barley. First, a cutting wheel reaps, or cuts, the growing stalks. The stalks are then threshed in a rotating drum that separates the grain from the rest of the plant, called the chaff. The chaff is ejected from the back of the vehicle while the grain collects in a hopper. From time to time, the grain is loaded onto trucks through a grain boom.

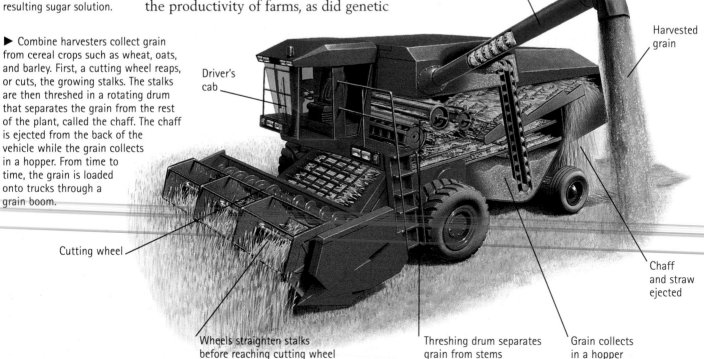

Grain boom

Harvested grain

Driver's cab

Cutting wheel

Wheels straighten stalks before reaching cutting wheel

Threshing drum separates grain from stems

Grain collects in a hopper

Chaff and straw ejected

DAIRY FARMING

Most of the world's milk product is obtained from cows. On modern dairy farms, cows are usually milked by machine twice a day. A sterile tube takes the milk directly from the cow to a room where the milk is cooled and stored before being shipped out. Milk is either treated and bottled at a plant or processed to make dairy products such as butter, cheese, and yogurt. A dairy cow can produce between 6,000 and 9,000 liters of milk a year, depending on the breed of cow.

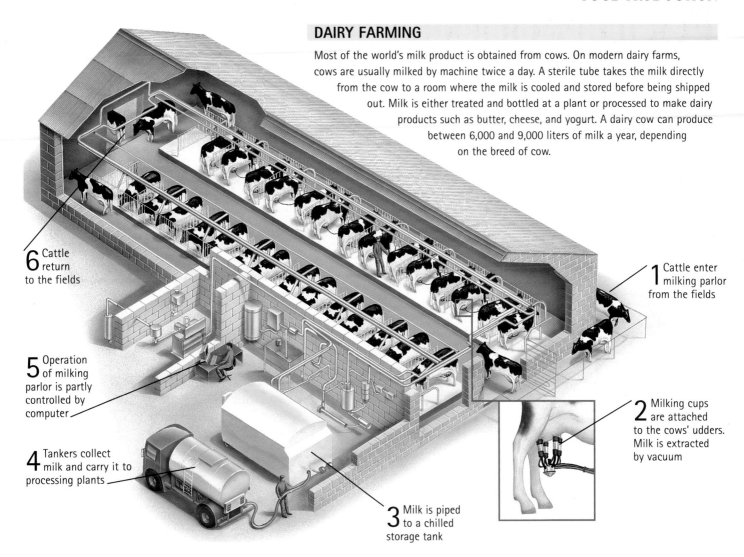

6 Cattle return to the fields

5 Operation of milking parlor is partly controlled by computer

4 Tankers collect milk and carry it to processing plants

1 Cattle enter milking parlor from the fields

2 Milking cups are attached to the cows' udders. Milk is extracted by vacuum

3 Milk is piped to a chilled storage tank

Improvements in fishing technology during the 1900s included the use of echo sounding to locate schools of fish, as well as factory trawlers that catch and freeze huge numbers of fish in a single trip. From the 1940s, concerns over falling fish stocks led to the catch sizes for certain species of fish being limited by treaty. At the same time, increasing numbers of fish have been reared in tanks, ponds, or underwater cages in fish farms.

Salmon, trout, mussels and oysters are commonly farmed. About a tenth of all seafood sold now comes from fish farms.

FOOD FROM ANIMALS

Humans have bred and kept animals for their eggs, meat, and milk since around 9000 B.C. However, animal farming only became industrialized relatively recently.

Most dairies were mechanized in the 1900s, and pigs and poultry were kept in confined areas to cut costs. Farmers started to use new types of nutrition, antibiotics, and other medicines to improve yields. From the 1960s, however, organic farming (without the use of chemicals) started to become popular.

On some large fishing boats, the catch is processed as the boat sails. When the nets are winched in, the haul is first sorted into different types of fish. The fish are gutted (their internal organs are removed) and cleaned before being packed with ice in boxes and stored in freezer compartments below deck. This keeps the fish fresh on the way to the market.

SEE ALSO PAGES:

66–7 Plants and people,
126 Food and nutrition,
232–3 Food processing

FOOD PROCESSING

Many foodstuffs are processed before being sent to stores and supermarkets. Much of this processing is concerned with packaging and preserving the food.

A technician at Lawrence Livermore National Laboratory, in California, lowers a casket of fruit into an irradiation chamber. In many countries, irradiation is being investigated as a way of preserving food.

Some types of food, including certain fruits and vegetables, need little processing. In many cases, they are simply cleaned, inspected, and graded before they are packed into cartons and sent to stores and customers. Many foodstuffs, however, are prepared and packaged in food processing plants, or factories. Such factories are highly automated. Some machines detect and reject irregular or spoiled foodstuffs. Others mix, cook, shape, and bake foods before they are canned, frozen, or packaged, again by machine.

Food is often processed to make it more appetizing or convenient to use. Most fruit and vegetables are washed, peeled, and cut before being sold, and some cheese is packaged as individual slices. Food packaging is also designed to attract customers and increase sales.

Glass and plastic bottles are used to package many juices, sauces, and other liquid foodstuffs. On this production line apple juice is packed into glass bottles.

PRESERVING FOOD

Food decomposes when bacteria and other microorganisms consume it. The decay caused by microorganisms can spoil food and even cause food poisoning. Some bacteria, such as species from the genera Botulism and Salmonella, can cause serious illness and sometimes death. A variety of food-preserving methods are used to prevent bacteria from spoiling food.

SORTING COFFEE

Automatic coffee-bean sorting machines use ultraviolet light to detect decayed beans. A blast of air separates the decayed beans from the good ones, which will then be roasted. A single decayed bean, called a stinker, can ruin a whole batch of beans if it is not removed before roasting.

Coffee beans are the seeds of the cherrylike fruit of the coffee shrub. Coffee cultivation is an important source of income for many tropical countries.

Ultraviolet lamps

Ultraviolet detector

Control box

Control circuits

Unsorted coffee beans

Hopper

Feed chute
conveyor belts

Hopper

Vibrator

Blast of air

Ejector

Accepted beans

Rejected beans

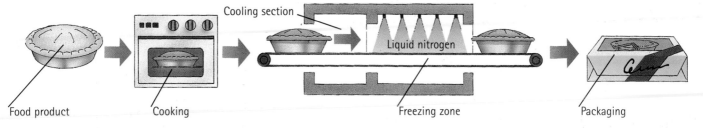

Food product
Some foods, like pies, are cooked in food processing plants.

Cooking
Ovens cook the pies at a precisely controlled temperature for an exact period of time.

Cooling section

The pie cools on a conveyor belt as it moves toward the freezing zone.

Liquid nitrogen

Freezing zone
A spray of liquid nitrogen at –320°F rapidly freezes the pie. Other systems use a blast of air at -40°F to freeze food.

Packaging
The finished pie is packaged by machine and then packed into cartons for distribution to stores and supermarkets.

In many traditional methods, food is preserved by removing the water that microorganisms need for growth or by adding chemicals that limit their growth.

For centuries, certain types of meat and fish have been preserved by drying. In some cases, salt is added to limit the growth of bacteria even further. In another technique, fish is dried over a smoky fire. Chemicals in the smoke help kill bacteria. Brine (salty water), sugar, and vinegar also preserve foods by poisoning bacteria.

Many food-spoiling organisms require air to grow. Some foods are preserved by vacuum-packing or by sealing them in plastic packages that contain nitrogen or carbon dioxide instead of air.

The growth of bacteria can be slowed by chilling food. Ice can be used to keep food at 32°F; ice mixed with salt can keep food as cold as –4°F.

Many types of food are kept chilled at around 39°F in refrigerators. Some foods are frozen using liquid nitrogen or cold air and are kept in freezers at 0°F or lower.

CANNING AND BOTTLING
Food can be prepared by sealing it inside aluminum or tin-plated steel cans. The food is boiled in the can to produce steam that drives out air from the gap between the food and the loosely fitted lid. The lid is then sealed onto the can, and the contents are heated to around 248°F. This kills any microorganisms in the food. No new microorganisms can affect the food until the can is opened.

Liquids for drinking are often kept in bottles. The drink can be pasteurized—heated to between 130–158°F—which kills most of the microorganisms. The liquid is then sealed in sterilized bottles.

IRRADIATION
A new technique called irradiation bombards food with radiation, such as gamma rays. The radiation kills bacteria, eliminates tiny pests in cereal grains, and slows the processes that ripen and soften fruits and vegetables. However, irradiation is yet to be approved in most countries.

▲ Many food products are frozen at the plant or factory. Refrigerated trucks carry the frozen goods from the plant to a warehouse and then to stores and supermarkets. The food is displayed in freezer cabinets and should be kept frozen by the customer until it is cooked.

Waxed containers, or cartons, are used to package many liquid foods, including fruit juices, milk, sauces, and soups.

Cans are used to preserve and package foods as diverse as fruit, baked beans, and cooked meat.

A food packer inspects and sorts red capsicums, or bell peppers, before gently placing them in packing cartons. Delicate fruits and vegetables are packed by hand to avoid damage. In the future, machines will most probably be used for this task.

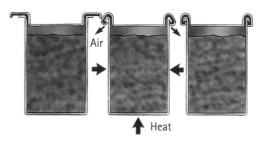

Air

Heat

When food is cooked in an unsealed can, steam from the food expels air through the gap under the lid. The can is then sealed and heated to destroy bacteria.

SEE ALSO PAGES:
126 Food and nutrition, 128–9 Digestion, 136 Bacteria and viruses

AUTOMATION

Automation is the use of machines to perform tasks without human assistance. Automated machines work according to sets of programmed instructions.

Invented in 1793, the hand-turned cotton gin simplified the removal of seeds from cotton. Until then, seeds had to be picked out by hand.

Henry Ford (1863–1947) pioneered automation in the production of his Model T car. About 15 million Model Ts were built between 1908 and 1927.

An automated machine or process is one that works routinely with little or no human supervision. Such machines control sequences of small operations according to computerized instructions.

Modern life depends on automation. Electronic cash registers recognize goods by a pattern of stripes and numbers called a bar code, or Universal Product Code (UPC). Price and sale information is sent to a central computer that controls stocks and orders goods. Traffic lights, heating controls, and aircraft autopilots are all examples of automated systems.

STEPS TOWARD AUTOMATION

The term automation was coined in 1946, by which time telephone exchanges and other equipment were already automatic. Moves toward automation had started almost two centuries before then.

Mechanization is the use of machines to perform tasks that would otherwise have to be done by humans. The first examples of mechanization took place in the textile factories of the late 1700s when machines were first used to spin yarn and weave cloth.

Early machines needed humans to control each step of their operations. Later machines were programmed to perform sequences of tasks.

The first programmable machine was a loom built in 1801 by French inventor Joseph-Marie Jacquard (1752–1834). The Jacquard loom used a system of punched cards to control the pattern of threads woven by the loom.

▲ By 1913, the assembly time for a Model T had decreased from twelve hours to 90 minutes. This significant time saving was mainly the result of using assembly lines.

▶ Automated guided vehicles, or AGVs, operate in many factories. They ferry goods and materials along carefully marked routes. Many AGVs are guided by signals from electrical loops buried under factory floors.

◄ These robots are welding a car body on a Honda production line in Ohio. Robots are ideal for performing simple, repetitive tasks accurately. This welding line can be programmed to weld different models of car.

▲ The movements of this paint-spraying robot are programmed to make sure that paint coverage is even. The use of robots to spray paint protects workers from harmful fumes.

The spread of mechanization was encouraged by the availability of new power sources. Waterwheels and steam engines were used to power machines in factories via systems of belts and drive-shafts. Later, electric motors were used to power machinery.

Throughout the 1900s, the growing car industry was a major influence for automation. In 1913, Ford's Model T car was the first to be built on an assembly line. The line moved car bodies through all the stages of construction, and operators at each stage would repeat a number of tasks on each car as it passed.

The introduction of assembly lines reduced the cost of cars by increasing the efficiency of production. Other industries soon adopted the same approach.

ROBOTS AND AUTOMATION

The first robot started work in a car factory in 1961. The use of robots has grown continuously since then.

Robots are well suited to doing repetitive tasks with a great deal of accuracy. They can be programmed to perform a variety of tasks, often by "learning" the actions of human operators. Robots can also send information about their own rate and quality of production to a central computer.

The use of computer-aided design, or CAD, saves many hours of producing detailed technical drawings. Even more work is saved by combining CAD with computer-aided manufacture, or CAM. CAD/CAM was used to design and build this French submarine.

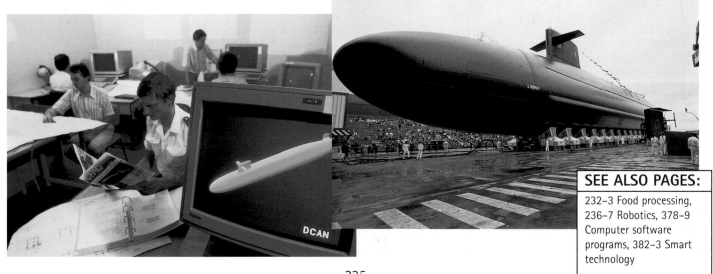

SEE ALSO PAGES:

232–3 Food processing, 236–7 Robotics, 378–9 Computer software programs, 382–3 Smart technology

ROBOTICS

Robotics is the study of robots—machines that can mimic certain human actions. Some robots respond automatically to their surroundings.

German engineer Rudolf Gantenbrink's 14-inch-long *Upuaut 2* robot is fitted with a camera. In March 1993, it was used to explore shafts inside the Great Pyramid of Cheops near Cairo, in Egypt.

The word robot comes from the Czech word *robota,* meaning "forced labor." Most robots do exactly that—they work long hours performing repetitive tasks. Some experimental robots are used by scientists to explore how closely they can simulate human motion.

Robots can be programmed to perform tasks that humans would find tedious or unpleasant. If their circuitry and mechanisms are protected, robots can also operate under hazardous conditions.

Robots can handle radioactive materials, spray paint in booths full of paint fumes, work deep underwater, and explore the hostile environments of planets such as Mars. Robots are also used to detect and defuse bombs and land mines.

TYPES OF ROBOTS

Many industrial robots are types of robotic arms, which have mechanical joints that allow them to move. Some robotic arms can also telescope to change their length. The movements can be powered by motors or hydraulic or pneumatic systems.

The number of directions in which a robotic arm can move are called its degrees of freedom. A joint that can twist, move up and down, and from side to side provides three degrees of freedom.

Wabot-2 of Waseda University, in Japan, can read music and play an electric organ using its hands and feet.

At the end of a robotic arm is a device called an end effector. These include robotic hands or grippers, spray guns, lasers, cutting and welding tools, or machine tools. A microprocessor instructs motors in the robotic arm to position the end effector exactly where it is needed.

ROBOTIC INSECTS

In the future, military robots could be packed with incendiaries, which are materials used to start fires. Antlike robots such as these could have four, six, or eight legs. This keeps them stable and allows them to step over obstacles on the way to their targets.

▼ The wires protruding from the front of this robotic "ant" are touch sensors. When they touch a solid surface, the sensors send signals to a microprocessor that controls the movements of the robot.

On July 5, 1997, the roving vehicle *Sojourner* became the first robot to explore the surface of Mars. Powered by a solar panel, it analyzed soil and rock samples and sent data and images to Earth by high-frequency radio signals.

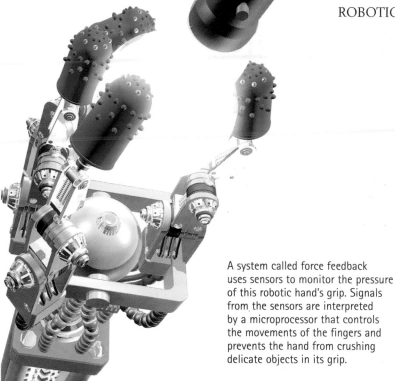

A system called force feedback uses sensors to monitor the pressure of this robotic hand's grip. Signals from the sensors are interpreted by a microprocessor that controls the movements of the fingers and prevents the hand from crushing delicate objects in its grip.

Some robots move on tracked or wheeled platforms. Others move on legs. Instructions can be programmed into a microprocessor in the robot or received from a remote controller. Camera-equipt robots send visual guides back to the remote controller.

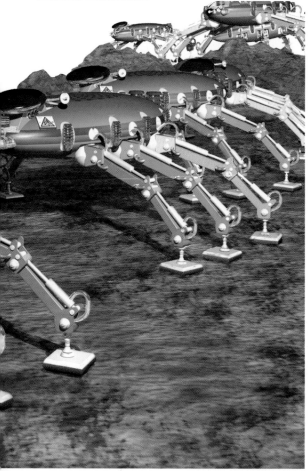

INTELLIGENT ROBOTS

Basic robots perform simple tasks according to a set of instructions. A mobile robot might not know what to do if it bumps into a wall, for example.

More sophisticated robots are fitted with sensors that let them feel their way around. High-powered computers and complex programming define instructions that cater for a variety of circumstances, and intelligent robots can effectively choose actions that fit their surroundings.

▲ Nanobots, whose dimensions are measured in nanometers (billionths of a millimeter), may one day be used to perform delicate eye surgery or repairs to other parts of the human body. The tiny surgical nanotool will be controlled and supplied with power by a larger nanomachine.

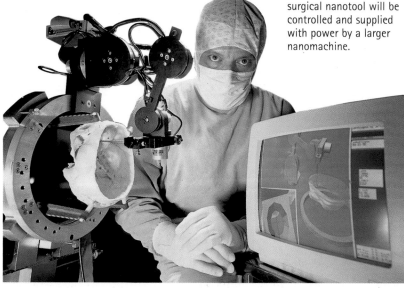

▲ This robotic arm is used as a tool in brain surgery. Under a surgeon's control, it can enter the brain through a tiny hole in the patient's skull and locate diseased areas with great accuracy. The brain is displayed on the screen.

SEE ALSO PAGES:
142–3 Medical technology,
234–5 Automation,
374–5 Microprocessors

237

TECHNOLOGY TIMELINE

4000–3000 B.C.
Bricks invented in Egypt and Assyria.
3000 B.C.
People in Egypt and Mesopotamia invent the plow for breaking up soil and improving farming.
800 B.C.
Assyrians first to equip army with weapons made of iron.
500 B.C.
The abacus invented in China as a device for counting.

200 B.C.
Archimedes's screw, invented by Greek mathematician Archimedes, first used to raise water.

200 B.C.
Paper in use in China.
A.D. 105
Paper first created from pulp.
1550
First spinning wheel believed to be invented in China.
1642
First calculating machine invented by Blaise Pascal.
1650
Air pump invented by Otto von Guericke.
1669
Hennig Brand discovers phosphorous.
1698
First successful steam pump invented by Thomas Savery.

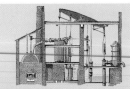

1712
Thomas Newcomen builds first practical steam engine to pump water from mines.
1733
Flying shuttle to speed up weaving invented by John Kay.
1751
Nickel discovered by Axel Cronstedt.
1760s
Massive improvements made to steam engines by James Watt.
1766
Hydrogen discovered by Henry Cavendish.
1769
Water frame developed by Richard Arkwright. This device made continuous spinning of threads possible.
1772–4
Oxygen discovered by Joseph Priestly and Karl Scheele, working separately.

1779
First bridge made of iron completed by Abraham Darby.
1785
First mechanical loom invented by Edmund Cartwright.
1790
Cotton gin—i.e. engine—invented by Eli Whitney.
1796
Lithography—a method of printing by transferring an image—invented by typographer Alois Senefelder.
1797
The precision lathe—a very important machine tool—invented by Henry Maudsley.
1797
Chromium discovered by Louis Vauquelin.

1800
First electric battery developed by Count Alessandro Volta.
1804
Francois Appert develops the first food canning process.

1804
First programmable machine, the Jacquard loom, invented.
1807
First steam-powered passenger boat, the *Clermont*, built by Robert Fulton.
1812
First tin cans manufactured to hold and preserve food.
1815
Invention of the miner's safety lamp by Sir Humphry Davy.
1819
Macadam road paving—used to create smooth roads—developed by John L. McAdam.
1822
First mechanical reaper invented by Jeremiah Bailey.
1827
Invention of the friction match by John Walker.
1827
Aluminum discovered by Hans Christian Oersted.
1834
Cyrus McCormick patents the first sucessful semiautomatic reaping machine.

1835
Early computer developed by Charles Babbage.

1836
Fiberglass invented by Ignace Dubus-Bonnel.
1839
Vulcanized rubber first developed by Charles Goodyear.
1851
Isaac Singer patents the sewing machine.
1852
Elisha G. Otis invents the elevator.

1855
Petroleum isolated from oil by chemist Benjamin Silliman.
1855
Xylonite, a kind of celluloid, invented by Alexander Parkes.
1856
Bessemer converter enables good-quality steel to be produced.
1858
First refrigerator invented by Ferdinand Carre.
1858
First steamroller—built by Louis Lemoine—used in road construction.
1861
The material linoleum first developed by Frederick Walton.

1876
Nikolaus Otto patents the four-stroke engine cycle.
1880
First carbon fibers produced by Thomas Edison.
1885
First skyscraper, the Home Insurance Building, built in Chicago.
1892
Reinforced concrete invented by Francois Hennebique.
1892
The zipper invented by Whitcomb Judson.

1896
Diesel engine invented by Rudolf Diesel.

1897
Charles Parsons demonstrates the first turbine-driven ship, the *Turbinia*.

1897
First offshore oil well built off the California coast.

1901
First vacuum cleaner invented by Cecil Booth.

1902
First lightweight tractor on sale.

1903
Wright brothers' Wright *Flyer 1*, powered by an internal combustion engine, becomes the first successful heavier-than-air craft.

1904
Prestressed concrete invented by civil engineer Eugene Freyssinet.

1904
First artificial silk, eventually known as rayon, created by the British textiles company, Courtaulds.

1908
First synthetic polymer, the material Bakelite, developed by Leo Baekeland.

1908
Cellophane, used as a wrapping seal among other uses, first developed from wood pulp by chemist Jacques Brandenberger.

1908
First Model T Ford car built by Henry Ford. The Model T was the first affordable car powered by an internal-combustion engine.

1909
Laminated glass patented by Edward Benedictus.

1909
Synthetic ammonia first produced by Fritz Haber. It was later used to make fertilizer.

1911
American Benjamin Holt invents the combine harvester.

1912
First oceangoing ships to be powered by diesel engines built.

1913
Introduction of Henry Ford's first factory assembly line.

1913
William Burton develops an improved method of refining oil—thermal cracking. It doubles the yield of petroleum from crude oil.

1913
Stainless steel first created by Harry Brearley.

1914–18
Seismography first used for prospecting for oil.

1917
Albert Einstein proposes the theory behind the laser.

1917
Electric hand drill introduced by inventors S. Duncan Black and Alonso G. Decker.

1920
Electric arc-welding widely used in industry.

1921
First train powered by diesel engines enters service with Tunisian Railways.

1924
Industrial deep-freezing of fruit and vegetables developed by Clarence Birdseye.

1924
First type of fiberboard, weather-resistant Masonite, invented by William Mason.

1933
Two scientists working for ICI invent Polythethylene.

1935
Invention of first fully-synthetic fiber, nylon, by Wallace Carrothers.

1930s
Development of first jet engine by Sir Frank Whittle.

1937
Instant coffee marketed by Swiss company Nestlé.

1939
Powerful electron microscope, capable of investigating the structure of many materials, invented by Vladimir Zworykin and others.

1939
First aircraft to fly using a jet engine—a German Heinkel.

1939
Insecticide DDT is patented by chemist Paul Muller.

1941
First mass-produced modern combine harvester built by Massey-Ferguson.

1944
First automatic digital computer built by a team headed by mathematician Howard Aiken.

1945
First precooked frozen meals produced by U.S. company Maxson.

1948
Invention of velcro by engineer Georges de Mestral.

1949
De Havilland Comet is first airliner powered by jet engines.

1950
Wankel rotary gasoline engine invented.

1952
First commercial passenger service by jet-powered airliners.

1951
Ruben Rausing creates first carton designed to hold liquids.

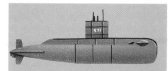

1954
First nuclear-powered submarine, *Nautilus*, goes into service with the United States Navy.

1958
Invention of float glass by Alistair Pilkington.

1960
Invention of the laser by Theodore Maiman.

1961
Unimate—the first industrial robot—deployed in a car factory.

1964
First computers using silicon chips go on sale.

1968
Cutting materials by high-pressure water jet invented.

1970
First industrial application of composite materials.

1970
First computer microprocessor with all the computing features on one chip developed in the United States.

1970
Carbon-dioxide lasers used for high-accuracy cutting of materials.

1980s
Personal computing boom brings computer automation into offices and homes.

1989
First plastics made from natural materials.

1994
Channel Tunnel linking England and France opens.

1997
First mobile robot, *Sojourner*, deployed on another planet as part of NASA's Pathfinder mission to Mars—landed 1997.

1998
Hong Kong airport completed—the largest construction project involving land reclamation.

FACTS AND FIGURES

MAJOR MINERALS

A mineral is a naturally occurring inorganic material. Many minerals are metal salts.

Alabaster Hydrated calcium sulfate—translucent, fine-grained form of gypsum used for making ornaments.

Apatite Calcium fluoride–phosphate—former ingredient of phosphate fertilizers and source of phosphorus, now replaced by rock phosphate.

Asbestos Various magnesium silicates—natural fiber and good thermal insulator. Exposure to asbestos dust can cause lung diseases, so its use has been prohibited.

Azurite Hydrated basic copper carbonate—used as a pigment for its blue color.

Bentonite A type of clay that swells in water—used as a filler in making paper.

Calcite Calcium carbonate—the second most common mineral after quartz.

Clay Fine-grained aluminosilicates—used to make bricks, pottery, and fine ceramics.

Dolomite A mixture of calcium and magnesium carbonates.

Fluorite The mineral form of calcium fluoride—used in making glass and ceramics, and as a source of fluorine.

Graphite A soft form of carbon—used in nuclear reactors and in lead pencils.

Gypsum A soft form of calcium sulfate—used for making cement and plaster.

Kaolin A form of clay, also called china clay—used to make ceramics and in the manufacture of paper, rubber, and paints.

Limestone Rock, consisting mainly of calcium carbonate—used as a building stone and in iron smelting.

Marble A highly crystalline form of calcium carbonate—used in architecture and sculpture.

Mica Various aluminum silicates—used in electrical capacitors and as an electricity insulator. Micas split into thin plates, which makes them useful as pearl-effect pigments for paints.

Oriental alabaster A variety of calcite—harder than true alabaster.

Rock phosphate Calcium phosphate—an ingredient in fertilizers and the main source of phosphorus.

Quartz Silicon dioxide. The most common mineral, quartz occurs in opaque and transparent forms that are sometimes colored by impurities—used for making glass and some ceramics.

Saltpeter Potassium nitrate—used to make gunpowder and fertilizers.

Silica A hard, mineral form of silicon dioxide with a high melting point.

Slate Mixed minerals that naturally split into thin sheets—used for roofing.

Talc A soft, white or greenish material—used in paints, ceramics, and products of the cosmetics and health-care industries.

MOHS HARDNESS SCALE

German mineralogist Friedrich Mohs devised a scale of hardness based on ten minerals. The greater the number, the harder the mineral. A typical fingernail has Mohs hardness 2–3, since it scratches gypsum but is scratched by calcite. Materials up to Mohs hardness 4 can be scratched using a coin.

1 Talc
2 Gypsum
3 Calcite
4 Fluorite
5 Apatite
6 Orthoclase
7 Quartz
8 Topaz
9 Corundum
10 Diamond

Diamond is the hardest of all minerals. It will scratch all other materials. Silicon carbide, or Carborundum, is a synthetic material with Mohs hardness 9.5. It is manufactured for use as an abrasive.

MAJOR ORES

An ore is a mineral source of a metal.

Bauxite An impure form of aluminum oxide from which aluminum is extracted by electrolysis.

Cassiterate An impure tin oxide, this mineral is the chief ore of tin.

Chalcopyrite Gold-colored mixed copper–iron sulfide, also known as copper pyrites. The main ore of copper.

Chromite A mixed chrome–iron oxide, the main source of chromium.

Galena Lead sulfide. The principal source of lead.

Hematite The mineral form of iron oxide and one of the main ores of iron.

Halite Sodium chloride, also known as rock salt. A source of chlorine, sodium hydroxide, and sodium metal.

Ilmenite A mixed iron–titanium oxide. The main ore of titanium.

Malachite Copper hydroxide–carbonate. A bright green mineral used as an ore of copper and as a semiprecious stone for making ornaments.

Pentlandite Iron–nickel sulfide. The main ore of nickel.

Pitchblende Uranium oxide. The main source of uranium for making fuel for the nuclear industry.

Rutile Titanium oxide. A minor source of titanium metal.

Sphalerite Zinc sulfide, also known as zinc blende. The main ore of zinc.

Zincite Zinc oxide. A minor source of zinc, also known as spartalite.

TOP TEN METALS PRODUCED

Iron	973,000,000 tons
Manganese	23,600,000 tons
Aluminum	17,700,000 tons
Chromium	12,500,000 tons
Copper	9,000,000 tons
Lead	3,300,000 tons
Nickel	895,000 tons
Tin	219,000 tons

REACTIVITY SERIES OF METALS

The reactivity series of metals lists metals in order of decreasing ease of reactivity, so potassium is more reactive than platinum. The more reactive metals are less easy to extract from their compounds.

Potassium
Sodium
Calcium
Magnesium
Aluminum
Zinc
Iron
Tin
Lead
Copper
Silver
Gold
Platinum

TEN COMMON ALLOYS

Coinage bronze—copper (95%), tin (4%), zinc (1%)—used for making coins and tokens for vending machines.

Coinage silver—silver (90%), copper (10%)—used for making coins.

Dental gold—gold (58%), silver (14–28%), copper (14–28%)—used for dental repair work.

Duralumin—aluminum (95%), copper (4%), manganese (0.5%), magnesium (0.5%)—used for making structural components for aircraft.

Manganin—copper (82.5%), manganese (16%), nickel (1.5%)—used in the circuits of electrical meters.

Nichrome—nickel (80%), chromium (20%)—used for making electrical resistors and heating elements.

Pewter—tin (65–80%), lead (20–35%)—used for making utensils, decorative drinking vessels, and ornaments.

Solder—lead (20–70%), tin (30–80%)—used to join metal objects, particularly electrical wiring and circuit components.

Stainless steel—iron (60–80%), chromium (10--20%), nickel (8–20%)—used in kitchen utensils, sinks, and machinery fittings.

Tool steel—iron (90–95%), molybdenum (6–7%), chromium (2%–4%)—used in tools such as chisels and saws.

CHAPTER 6
LIGHT AND ENERGY

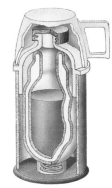

The sun is the Earth's main energy source. Electromagnetic radiation carries its light and heat through 93 million miles (150 million km) of space to the Earth. Without the sun, life on the Earth would not exist. Light helps plants to grow on land and in the sea, providing food for the Earth's animal life. Heat energy keeps the Earth at a suitable temperature for life to exist. It evaporates water to make clouds, makes winds blow, and makes waves move across oceans. Fossil fuels contain energy from sunlight that fell on the Earth millions of years ago. These fuels provide most of the energy for industrial societies.

Many of the machines that we use depend on the flow of heat energy to make them work. Scientists and engineers have formulated laws of thermodynamics that describe the flow of heat in chemical and mechanical systems. These laws help them to design heating and cooling systems, as well as engines and motors. Scientists have developed kinetic theory to explain the influence of heat on the behavior of the particles that make up materials.

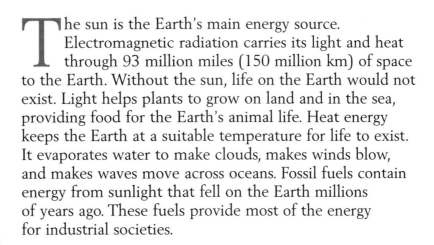

Light is a form of energy. Electric lamps and lasers are two sources of artificial light. Precisely engineered lenses and curved mirrors in microscopes and telescopes bend light rays to form magnified images. Instruments that focus and detect electromagnetic radiation outside the visible spectrum give information about the temperature, composition, and speed of motion of distant objects in space.

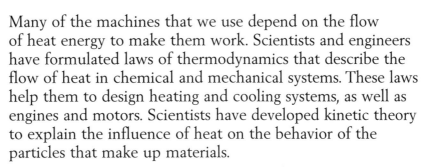

HEAT AND LIGHT FROM THE SUN

The sun is the star at the center of our solar system. It is 93 million miles (150 million kilometers) from the Earth and is its main source of heat and light energy.

▲ Filtered by the Earth's atmosphere, the sun's rays keep the temperature on a sunny day at around 25°C (75°F). If the temperature were 15°C (25°F) lower, the children in this photograph would be shivering; if it were 15°C (25°F) warmer, they would be uncomfortably hot.

During the day, sunlight provides heat and light, which are two types of energy. Life exists on the Earth because the sun provides just the right amount of energy. Planets that are closer to the sun, such as Venus, receive more energy and are too hot for life. Planets that are farther away, such as Mars, are too cold.

Energy is needed to do work and make things happen. Practically everything that happens on the Earth depends on energy that originally came from the sun. Plants depend on energy from sunlight for growth, and part of this energy is passed on to the animals that eat them. Carnivorous animals gain energy from the meat of other animals that thrive as plant-eaters. Also, coal, oil, and natural gas are all formed from the remains of plants and animals that grew thanks to energy from sunlight.

Heat from sunlight evaporates water from the oceans, warms the air, and makes the winds blow. These winds carry heat and water vapor around the world and control its weather patterns.

The leaves of plants absorb energy from sunlight. Plants use this energy to make complex chemicals from simple ones. Plants are the ultimate source of food for most life on the Earth.

NUCLEAR FUSION

The sun consists of about 70 percent hydrogen and 30 percent helium. The sun's energy comes from nuclear fusion reactions in its core, where atoms of hydrogen join together to make helium atoms. The mass of a helium atom is less than the mass of the hydrogen atoms that form it. This lost mass turns into energy: one kilogram (2.2 lbs) of lost matter gives about 100 billion megajoules, or a large power plant's total output over 25 years.

ENERGY FROM THE SUN

The diameter of the sun is 100 times that of the Earth, and its volume is one million times greater. The immense force of gravity produces enormous pressure in the core and raises the temperature to about 27 million°F. At this temperature, hydrogen exists as a soup of electrons and protons, called plasma, that is denser than lead. Four hydrogen nuclei combine to create a helium nucleus and release a large amount of energy.

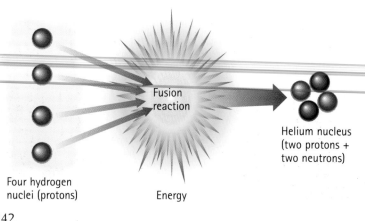

Fusion reaction

Four hydrogen nuclei (protons)

Energy

Helium nucleus (two protons + two neutrons)

Energy for living comes from food. Food comes from plants that use the sun's energy, or from animals that eat plants, so human life is powered by sunshine.

SUNLIGHT AND FOOD

Plants use energy from sunlight to create complex chemicals from water and carbon dioxide. These complex chemicals have energy locked up in the bonds that hold their atoms together. Animals that eat plants are called herbivores. Meat-eating animals, or carnivores, eat the herbivores. In this way, energy from sunlight is trapped by plants and then passes on to different animals. Animals digest their food and release energy by breaking down the chemicals in it. The animals use this energy to move around and carry out all the internal processes needed to maintain their lives.

KEEPING COMFORTABLE

The Earth's atmosphere acts as a filter that absorbs energy from the sun's rays. Temperatures near the equator are as high as 45°C (113°F) because the sun shines from high in the sky. Heat and light pass straight down through the atmosphere. Around the North and South Poles, temperatures can sink to around –40°C (–40°F). For most of the year, the sun is low on the horizon. The sun's rays are spread over a wider area, and much heat and light is absorbed as they travel at a shallow angle through the atmosphere. Humans thrive at 25°C (77°F), the average temperature midway between the poles and the equator.

ENERGY IN THE FUTURE

Most of the energy used for heating and powering transportation comes from fossil fuels that formed millions of years ago. Reserves of these fuels are running out and may be exhausted within 50–100 years. Scientists are working to produce power using nuclear fusion, the process that makes energy in the sun. They hope to build a fusion reactor that uses two isotopes of hydrogen called deuterium and tritium. Experimental Tokamak fusion reactors use powerful electromagnets to compress a plasma of deuterium and tritium. When the temperature reaches 100 million °C (180 million°F), scientists expect the isotopes to fuse together to produce helium—and enormous amounts of energy.

Most deserts are near the equator, where the sun is high in the sky for most of the day. The sun's heat evaporates water and splits rocks into parched grains of sand.

The Arctic sun stays close to the horizon for most of the year. All the surface water is frozen, and plants cannot survive. Most polar animals are carnivores that depend on creatures that live in the sea.

◀ Russian Tokamak fusion reactors such as this are used to research nuclear fusion. Magnetic fields heat and compress hot gases, turning them into plasma and keeping them away from the walls of the container. The reactor has reached the necessary temperature for nuclear fusion, but not at the same time as the other conditions needed to produce energy. Scientists hope to have achieved controlled fusion by 2025.

SEE ALSO PAGES:

10–11 Earth's atmosphere,
282–3 Light energy,
294–5 Work and energy

RADIATION

The sun pours radiation into space. This radiation consists of streams of particles and electromagnetic radiation, which includes heat and light.

The solid core, or nucleus, of the Hale-Bopp comet is about 25 mi. (40km) across. It made its closest approach to the Earth since 2000 B.C. in March 1997. When it is closest to the sun, Hale-Bopp releases 10 tons of particles per second into its coma, or tail. The coma glows visibly as it reflects light from the sun.

The visible light from the sun is a form of electromagnetic radiation. It is similar to radio waves, but has a much shorter wavelength. The sun's rays also include other kinds of electromagnetic radiation. Invisible ultraviolet (UV) rays have frequencies higher than those of visible light. They can cause sunburn, particularly in people with fair skin, and increase the risk of skin cancer. Infrared (IR) rays are also invisible, but their frequencies are lower than the frequencies of visible light. Infrared rays carry heat energy and warm the skin. They are absorbed by water vapor in the air; ultraviolet rays are not. This is how people can get sunburn without feeling hot on an overcast summer's day. The sun's rays also include X rays, gamma rays, and radio-frequency waves, but these are mostly blocked by the Earth's atmosphere.

THE SOLAR WIND

The sun emits a stream of subatomic particles, mostly protons and electrons. They leave the sun's outer atmosphere at 600,000–2 million mph (1–3 million kph). This stream of particles spreads out through the entire solar system and is called the solar wind.

COMET TAILS AND AURORAS

Comets are balls of ice and dust. Close to the sun, heat vaporizes the ice, and the comet produces a trail of vapor and fine dust. This tail, or coma, can be several million miles long. The coma always points away from the sun, even when the comet is moving away from the sun, because it is blown by the solar wind.

Auroras are shimmering curtains of colored light that appear in the skies near the North and South Poles. They are another effect of the solar wind. The Earth's magnetic field traps charged particles in the solar wind and channels them toward the poles, where the magnetic field is strongest. The particles cause gases in the air to emit light. Auroras happen when there are large numbers of particles, usually after a solar storm, when the solar wind is more intense.

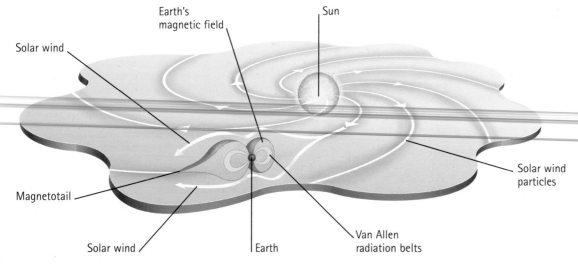

Earth's magnetic field — Sun

Solar wind

Magnetotail

Solar wind

Earth

Van Allen radiation belts

Solar wind particles

The solar wind results from charged particles in the sun's outer layer that have sufficient energy to escape the enormous pull of gravity. The Earth's magnetic field traps some particles to form the doughnut-shaped Van Allen radiation belts. During solar flares, particles dip into the upper atmosphere and cause auroras or interfere with radio communications.

◄ Auroras are patterns of light that sometimes appear in the sky near the poles. Auroras near the North Pole are called aurora borealis, or northern lights. Near the South Pole, they are called aurora australis, or southern lights. In an aurora, gas molecules behave like the gas in a fluorescent lamp, glowing as they are struck by fast-moving charged particles in the solar wind.

◄ This house uses solar energy in three ways. Panels in the middle of the roof heat water for washing and heating. The black panels at the edge of the roof turn light into electrical current. Sunlight also warms air in the glass conservatory. The hot air then rises and is carried through the rest of the house by convection.

USING SOLAR RADIATION

When the sun is directly overhead and the sky is clear, one square kilometer (0.62 sq. mi.) of the Earth's surface receives about 1,000 megawatts of solar energy—enough to power a small city. It is becoming more important to use this kind of energy to produce heat and power.

Photovoltaic solar cells generate an electrical current when light shines on them. Panels of these cells are used to power space satellites and electrical equipment in regions that are far from power lines. Photovoltaic cells are typically made from thin slices of silicon. They are expensive because the silicon must be absolutely pure, except for carefully controlled amounts of other elements. Scientists are trying to develop cheaper solar cells using other materials.

A different type of solar panel heats water. Each panel contains pipes that are painted black to absorb heat from the sun's rays. Water flows through the pipes and is warmed by the absorbed heat. The water is not usually hot enough for use, so a boiler uses electricity or a fossil fuel to raise the temperature further.

Solar furnaces use hundreds of mirrors to concentrate the sun's rays onto one point. The mirrors move to follow the sun across the sky. Solar furnaces can develop temperatures greater than 5,000°C (9,000°F) and are used by research scientists. Similar set-ups use solar energy to produce steam for a turboalternator.

Some buildings are designed to capture the sun's rays to heat the air inside them and reduce heating costs in a way that does not require sophisticated technology.

▲ This solar power plant supplied electricity for the town of White Cliffs in New South Wales, Australia. The mirrors concentrated the sun's rays to turn water into high-pressure steam. This powered a converted diesel engine and generator set. The public electricity supply finally reached the town in 1993.

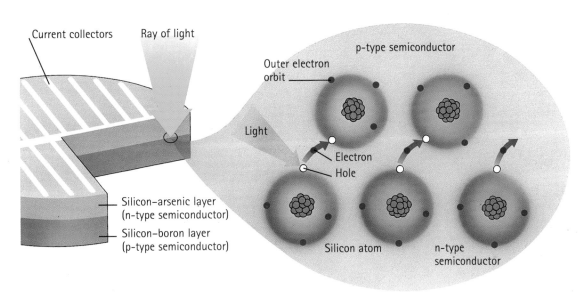

Current collectors

Ray of light

Outer electron orbit

p-type semiconductor

Light

Electron

Hole

Silicon atom

n-type semiconductor

Silicon–arsenic layer (n-type semiconductor)

Silicon–boron layer (p-type semiconductor)

◄ Photovoltaic cells are sandwiches of an n-type semiconductor, which has extra electrons, and a p-type that has electrons missing. Light energy makes electrons move from the n-type to fill the holes in the p-type. The electrons then flow as an electric current through an external circuit.

SEE ALSO PAGES:

THE ELECTROMAGNETIC SPECTRUM

The electromagnetic spectrum is the full range of electromagnetic radiation and includes radio waves, heat and light rays, X rays, and gamma rays.

Cellular telephones send and receive very-high-frequency radio signals.

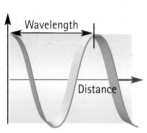

Wavelength is the distance between two neighboring peaks of an electromagnetic wave.

Traveling ray of light

■ Magnetic wave
▥ Electric wave

▲ An electromagnetic wave is a combination of electric and magnetic fields that vibrate in planes at right angles to one another.

E lectromagnetic radiation is a form of energy that travels at the velocity of light, 186,000 mi./sec (300,000km/sec). As it travels, its energy switches back and forth between electric and magnetic fields. As one field increases in strength, the other decreases. The rate at which this exchange happens is called the frequency of the radiation. Different types of electromagnetic radiation have different frequencies. Radio waves have lower frequencies than light rays, for example, and blue light has a higher frequency than red. The frequency of electromagnetic radiation, measured in hertz (Hz), is the number of times in one second that the electrical field reaches its maximum value.

Scientists say that electromagnetic radiation travels in waves. This is because the strengths of the electric and magnetic fields vary continually as they travel through space. The wavelength is the distance the wave travels in the time it takes the electric field to fall from its maximum value to its minimum value and then rise back to its maximum value. Because of this, the wavelength is the speed of light divided by the frequency. The signal from a radio station whose broadcast frequency is 1,200 kilohertz, or 1,200,000 Hz, has a wavelength of around 250 meters (820 ft.), for example.

RADIO AND MICROWAVE
Radio stations broadcast using frequencies in a range from 150,000 Hz to around 20,000,000 Hz. Each station uses a particular frequency, so receivers tune to a given station by only accepting waves at the correct frequency for that station. Land-based

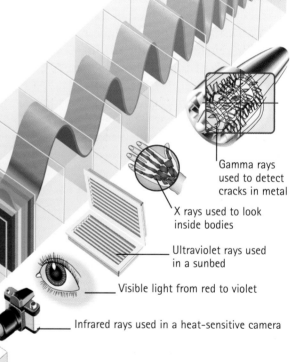

Gamma rays used to detect cracks in metal

X rays used to look inside bodies

Ultraviolet rays used in a sunbed

Visible light from red to violet

Infrared rays used in a heat-sensitive camera

High-frequency microwaves used to heat food in a microwave oven

Low-frequency microwaves used in radar

Ultrahigh-frequency (UHF) radio waves for TV transmissions

Radio waves used in radio broadcasts

The electromagnetic spectrum stretches from radio waves at the lowest frequencies to gamma rays at the highest frequencies. Visible light occupies a narrow range of frequencies in the middle of the electromagnetic spectrum. The wavelength variations in this artwork are not to scale.

television transmitters send signals between about 70 MHz and 800 MHz. (One megahertz is one million hertz.)

Satellite TV works at even higher frequencies. These electromagnetic waves are captured by dish-shaped antennae that point toward the satellite.

Radars bounce radio waves off planes, ships, and clouds to show their positions, which can be many miles away. They use wavelengths of a few centimeters (about 1 inch). Doppler radar measures the speed of moving objects from the minute change in the frequency of the reflected waves.

Microwave ovens use wavelengths of a few millimeters, which correspond to frequencies of billions of hertz. The radiation heats food by causing water molecules to vibrate.

INFRARED LIGHT AND BEYOND

Infrared radiation has frequencies just lower than those of visible light. Its wavelength ranges from 1 millimeter to 750 nanometers. A nanometer, or 1 nm, is one billionth of a meter, or $\frac{1}{25,000,000}$ of an inch. Hot objects give off infrared radiation, which is felt as heat. Visible light is the tiny part of the electromagnetic spectrum that human eyes can sense. The spectrum of colors stretches from red light at 770 nm to violet light at 400 nm.

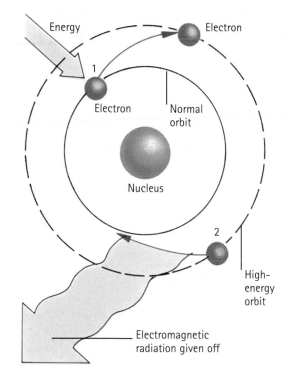

◀ The electrons of an atom move around its nucleus in orbits. The energy of each electron depends on its orbit. Energy can make an electron jump from its usual orbit (1) to an orbit with higher energy (2). When this happens, the atom takes in radiation of an energy that matches the energy gap between the two orbits. The atom gives off radiation if an electron falls from a high-energy orbit to a lower one.

Many aircraft radar systems bounce radio waves off clouds in the flight path ahead of the aircraft. A computer analyzes the echoes to reveal the size and distance of clouds. The computer can also identify potential hazards, such as icy hailstorms.

The energy of electromagnetic radiation increases as the wavelength becomes shorter. Invisible ultraviolet rays cause sunburn and have shorter wavelengths (100-400 nm) than visible light.

X rays have even shorter wavelengths, usually less than the diameter of an atom (0.1 nm). They penetrate flesh and bone.

Gamma rays have enormous energy and can be used to produce images of cracks deep inside pieces of metal.

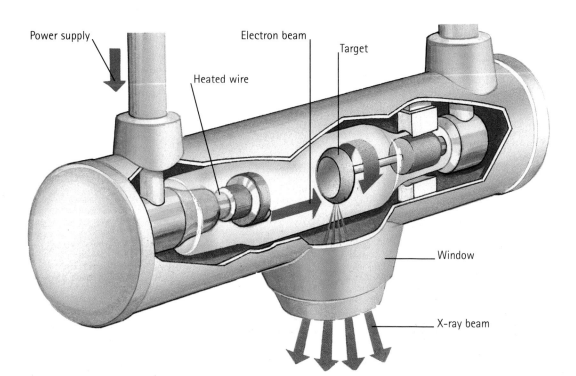

A hospital X-ray machine uses an X-ray tube to produce X rays. A heated wire emits electrons, which are accelerated by electric fields toward a metal target. The collision ejects electrons from the metal atoms. Further electrons fall into the spaces left by the ejected electrons. As they do this, the electrons lose energy in the form of X rays.

SEE ALSO PAGES:

142–3 Medical technology, 150–1 Atoms, 244–5 Radiation, 364–5 Electrical communication

TERRESTRIAL ENERGY SOURCES

Coal, oil, and natural gas are nonrenewable fuels that cause pollution and are becoming scarce. Solar power and hydroelectricity are unlimited and do not pollute.

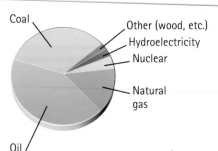

Most of our energy comes from the nonrenewable fossil fuels: coal, oil, and natural gas. Nuclear fuel is the nonfossil fuel that provides the most energy. Hydroelectric power is produced by falling water and is the largest source of renewable energy. Other energy sources include wood, wind power, solar power, and wave power.

Every day, the sun shines enormous amounts of energy onto the surface of the Earth. This energy is mostly in the form of heat and light. The heat keeps the planet at the correct temperature for life to exist. It also drives the winds and evaporates seawater that later falls as rain. Light from the sun allows us to see and also provides energy for growing plants and food for animals.

Developed societies depend on many different types of machines for use in communications, manufacturing, and transportation. Few of these machines are powered directly by the sun. Many use electricity that is produced by burning fossil fuels or by nuclear fission. Some, such as cars and trucks, burn fossil fuels in internal-combustion engines.

The fossil fuels—coal, oil, and natural gas—contain energy from sunlight that was trapped by organisms that lived millions of years ago. Fossil fuels store energy in the form of chemical energy.

COAL

This vast pile of coal is waiting to be burned at a power plant. Geologists estimate that there are enough coal reserves to last about 300 years. They also estimate that we have used about a fourth of all oil reserves.

Coal formed from fernlike plants that lived in swamps around 300 million years ago. Dead vegetation sank underwater to create peat bogs. Over time, layers of sand and clay sediment, sometimes

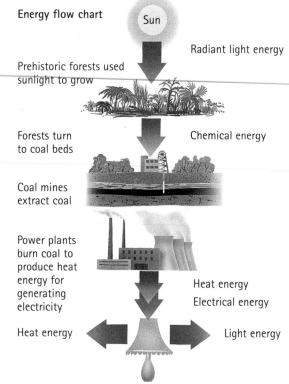

Energy flow chart

Radiant light energy

Prehistoric forests used sunlight to grow

Forests turn to coal beds

Chemical energy

Coal mines extract coal

Power plants burn coal to produce heat energy for generating electricity

Heat energy

Electrical energy

Heat energy

Light energy

Fossil fuels formed from plants that grew using energy from sunlight. When they burn, their chemical energy turns into heat that can be used to produce electricity.

thousands of feet thick, built up and buried the organic remains. The sediment solidified into rock. High pressure and temperatures broke down the plant remains to form coal. Coal consists of up to 90 percent carbon, with other carbon compounds containing hydrogen, nitrogen, and sulfur.

OIL AND GAS

Natural gas is mainly methane. The simplest hydrocarbon, methane, has the chemical formula CH_4. Crude oil is also called petroleum. It is a yellow, brown, or black liquid that is a mixture of hundreds of complex hydrocarbons.

Oil and gas formed from organisms that lived in the seas up to 180 million years ago. Dead organisms settled in deep layers on the seabed. Bacteria digested their remains and formed a hydrocarbon solid called kerogen. In a process similar to the formation of coal, sand and clay sediments gradually built up over the kerogen. The high pressure and temperature under the sediment layer decomposed the kerogen to form the simpler hydrocarbons that make up natural gas and oil. At the same time, the skeletons of the dead organisms turned into porous limestone.

As they formed, oil and natural gas seeped up through pores in the rock. Some escaped onto the Earth's surface, but much was trapped under layers of nonporous rock. Reservoirs of oil and gas then built up under this rock.

USING FOSSIL FUELS

Fossil fuels release heat energy when they burn in air. Coal, natural gas, and fuels made from crude oil are all used to provide heat for buildings. Gasoline and diesel oil burn in engines to provide mechanical energy for cars and other vehicles. The burning process produces hot gases that expand and force pistons in the engine to move. In this way, chemical energy in the fuel is converted to heat energy and then into mechanical energy. Steam engines use burning fuels to turn water into high-pressure steam that expands and forces pistons to move.

Fossil fuels are also used to generate electricity. Thermal power plants burn coal, gas, or fuel oil to boil water and produce steam. The steam drives turbines that make generator shafts rotate and produce electricity.

NUCLEAR ENERGY

About 10 percent of the world's electricity demand is generated from nuclear energy. In a nuclear fuel, atoms of uranium or plutonium produce heat energy as they split into smaller atoms. That heat is then used to boil water, as heat from furnaces is used in a conventional power station. The energy in nuclear fuels does not come from the sun. It is locked in the nuclei of atoms and released when those nuclei split. Nuclear fuels remain dangerously radioactive for thousands of years after they have been used in reactors. For this reason they must be stored carefully.

RENEWABLE ENERGY RESOURCES

Fossil fuels and nuclear fuels are not renewable energy resources. One day they will run out. These fuels also have other problems. Coal mining and oil and gas production can cause environmental problems. Burning fossil fuels produces carbon dioxide gas that contributes to global warming. Nuclear fuels produce highly dangerous waste.

In contrast, renewable energy resources will not run out. Solar cells generate electricity from sunlight, and solar panels heat water. Wood and other plants can be used to produce solid and liquid fuels. The wind, waves, and tides can be harnessed to generate electricity, as can the water in a dam. Geothermal energy systems use steam from hot rocks deep underground to generate electricity and provide heat.

▲ This windmill uses wind power to pump water. It produces no pollution and does not use up energy reserves. Although the windmill is large, it only produces enough power for a small electric motor.

▲ In some countries, hot rocks lie close to the surface. This Icelandic geyser spouts steam that comes from water boiled deep underground by geothermal energy. In some places, geothermal steam is used to drive electricity generators and to provide heat for homes and other buildings.

▶ The lights visible in this urban street use energy at a rate that is equivalent to burning approximately one ton of coal every minute. It will be difficult to fully replace fossil fuels with renewable fuels, so fuel will have to be used more economically in the future.

SEE ALSO PAGES:

210–11 Oil and refining, 213 Coal, 224–5 Gasoline and diesel engines, 338–9 Electricity, 357 Power cells, 458–9 Renewable energy

HEAT TRANSFER

Heat energy moves around by conduction, convection, and radiation. Transfer is from a region of higher temperature to a region of lower temperature.

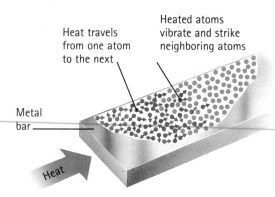

Heat travels from one atom to the next

Heated atoms vibrate and strike neighboring atoms

Metal bar

Heat

Heat flows from the hot part of a solid object to the cold part. Rapidly vibrating atoms in the hot part speed up the vibrations of their cooler and slower neighbors.

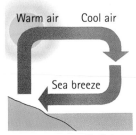

Warm air   Cool air

Sea breeze

Daytime: the land is warmer than the sea.

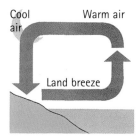

Cool air   Warm air

Land breeze

Nighttime: the sea is warmer than the land.

Sea breezes are caused by convection currents. Warm air rises and is replaced by heavier, cooler air.

The kettle absorbs heat directly from hot gases and radiant heat from the fire. The metal skin of the kettle conducts heat to the water inside it. Convection then spreads the heat through the water.

One of the properties of heat energy is that it flows from hotter objects to cooler objects. If a hot drink at 80°C (175°F) is placed in a room where the temperature is 25°C (75°F), the drink will gradually cool to 25°C. The temperature in the room will also increase slightly.

CONDUCTION OF HEAT
Conduction carries heat through an object until its temperature evens out. Dip a metal spoon into a hot drink, and the handle soon starts to feel warm. The hot liquid heats the part of the spoon that is in the drink. This increases the kinetic energy of its atoms and makes them vibrate with greater force. Heat travels up the spoon to the handle as vibrating atoms striking their neighbors and making them vibrate more vigorously.

CONVECTION OF HEAT
Convection carries heat through liquids and gases. Imagine heating a kettle of water on a stove. The heat source warms the water at the bottom of the kettle by conduction. As the water

gets hotter, it expands and becomes less dense. This makes the warm water rise, making room for cooler, denser water. The cooler water becomes warmer and less dense, and so the convection process continues.

RADIATION OF HEAT
Radiation is a process that carries heat in straight lines through empty space. It is how the heat of a radiator can be felt without touching the radiator. This form of energy flow is also called radiant energy transfer. It is carried by infrared radiation.

All objects give off radiant energy. The hotter an object is, the more radiant energy it gives off. An object that is cooler than its surroundings gets warmer as it takes in more infrared than it gives out. At

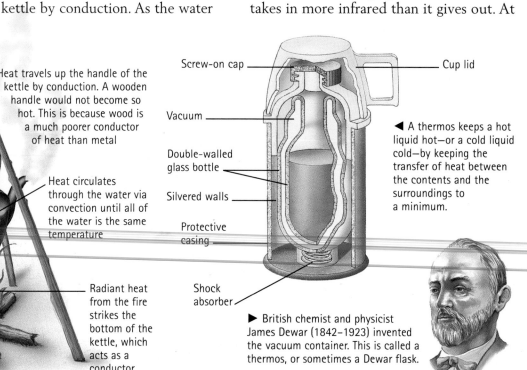

Heat travels up the handle of the kettle by conduction. A wooden handle would not become so hot. This is because wood is a much poorer conductor of heat than metal

Heat circulates through the water via convection until all of the water is the same temperature

Radiant heat from the fire strikes the bottom of the kettle, which acts as a conductor

Screw-on cap

Vacuum

Double-walled glass bottle

Silvered walls

Protective casing

Shock absorber

Cup lid

◄ A thermos keeps a hot liquid hot—or a cold liquid cold—by keeping the transfer of heat between the contents and the surroundings to a minimum.

► British chemist and physicist James Dewar (1842–1923) invented the vacuum container. This is called a thermos, or sometimes a Dewar flask.

higher temperatures, the frequency range of the radiation increases. The filament of a lightbulb glows white-hot at around 3,600°F, because some of its radiation is at frequencies higher than infrared.

HEAT TRANSFER EFFECTS

When the weather is hot and sunny, light-colored clothing helps people to keep cool by reflecting sunlight and absorbing smaller amounts of radiant energy than dark colors. Dark objects also give off more radiant energy than light objects at the same temperature. This is why car radiators and cooling panels on the backs of refrigerators are painted black: it helps them lose heat as rapidly as possible.

A cake taken from a refrigerator does not feel as cold as a bottle of milk at the same temperature. The reason is that heat flows from the hand into the bottle more rapidly than into the cake. The bottle is a better conductor of heat than the cake, and so the hand cools more quickly. The cake is full of tiny air bubbles. Air is a poor conductor of heat and so lowers the rate of heat transfer from the hand. Air acts as an insulator.

THERMAL INSULATION

Sometimes it is necessary to prevent heat from traveling from one place to another. Birds fluff up their feathers in the winter and people wear extra layers of clothing to trap an insulating layer of air next to their bodies. Cooks hold hot dishes with a cloth to insulate their hands. Metals are good conductors of heat; they contain freely moving electrons that can carry heat energy. Plastic, glass, and pottery are poor conductors of heat; they make good insulating containers for hot drinks and food.

Solar panels — Thick sod layer on roof

Thick wooden walls

Small windows

Wood is a renewable fuel for heating and cooking

This energy-efficient house has an insulated roof and walls, as well as small windows that reduce heat loss. It uses renewable solar energy and wood fuel.

MODERN MATERIALS

Vending-machine cups and fast-food containers are often made from expanded polystyrene. This material is a mass of tiny plastic bubbles. The gas in the bubbles acts as a heat insulator. Plastic foam may be used to insulate walls. This is because the foam prevents air convection in the space between the walls. People rescued from the sea are often wrapped in flexible foam blankets covered with a thin film of shiny aluminum. The foamed structure reduces heat loss, and the shiny surface on the inside reflects radiant energy back toward the person's body. The shiny outer surface loses little heat by radiation.

▲ Friction raises the skin temperature of NASA's space shuttle to 2,700°F during reentry. A layer of insulating ceramic tiles on the outside protects the cabin from overheating.

▲ This thermograph of a man's head shows small variations in temperature as differences in color. Blue areas are the coolest. This type of image can be used to show where heat leaks from buildings.

A computer's main board becomes hot as electrical signals pass through its processor. While many processors are fitted with cooling fans, some have heat sinks with metal fins that disperse heat from the processor. The fins provide a large surface area for contact with the surrounding air, which convects heat away.

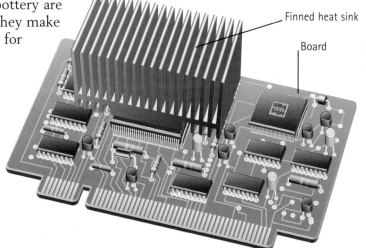

Finned heat sink

Board

HEATING AND COOLING SYSTEMS

Heating systems add heat to both objects and places in order to maintain a required temperature. Cooling systems function by removing excess heat.

Coal was the most widely used heat source for the Industrial Revolution of the 1800s. It was used to fuel the steam engines that drove machines and to provide heat for iron and steel manufacture. Coal smoke was a major cause of pollution in cities and industrial areas.

Humans feel most comfortable when the temperature is around 75°F (25°C). Depending on the time of day and the season, many parts of the world are hotter or colder than this temperature. Heating systems produce heat and raise the temperatures of cold objects and places. Cooling systems remove heat. They are often fitted to machines to remove waste heat that is produced while the machine is working and to prevent damage being caused by overheating. Industrial heating systems provide heat for manufacturing processes.

KEEPING WARM

One way to produce heat is to light a fire. The combustion of a fuel gives out heat energy. For thousands of years, people used wood fires to cook their food and to keep warm. About 300 years ago, coal became more available and started to take over from wood. Large houses had a fireplace and chimney in each room. Modern heating systems have just one source of heat. The heat is carried around the house to each room by pipes that contain hot water, steam, or hot air.

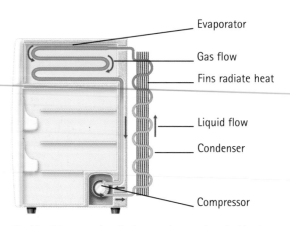

Liquid refrigerant absorbs heat as it vaporizes inside the evaporator coil of a refrigerator. The heat is released when a compressor turns the refrigerant back to liquid.

HEAT PUMPS FOR COOLING

The temperature of the surroundings is called the ambient temperature. An object will cool naturally if it is hotter than the ambient temperature. Refrigerators keep food at around 40°F (4°C), and freezers operate at about 5°F (−15°C). Both these types of devices keep their interiors cold by pumping heat from the inside to the surroundings. Pipes inside them contain a volatile liquid—a liquid that evaporates easily—called a refrigerant. This absorbs heat as it changes into a gas in an evaporator coil within the cooling cabinet. An electric pump then compresses the gas into another coil mounted on the outside of the cabinet. The pressure causes the refrigerant to become liquid and warm, so that it gives off heat to the surroundings.

▼ In this heating system, a furnace burns fuel to heat water in a boiler. A pump forces the hot water through pipes that connect to radiators in each room. Water from the boiler also heats the hot water cylinder. Cooled water returns to the boiler.

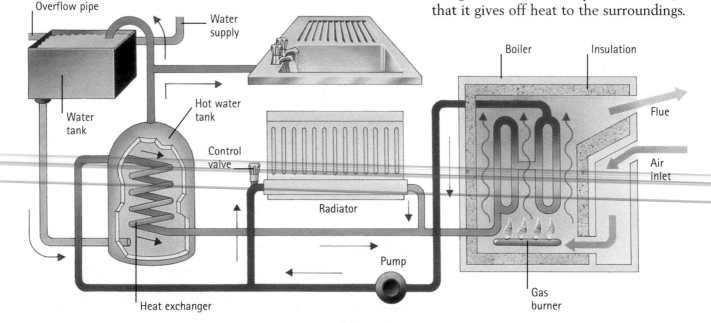

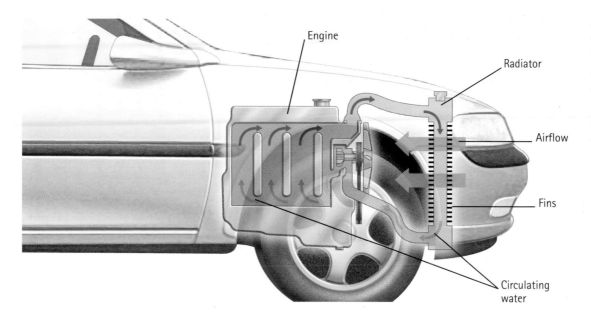

Engine

Radiator

Airflow

Fins

Circulating water

A car's cooling system keeps the main parts of its engine at around 175°F (80°C). A pump circulates water through the engine and then through the pipes of a radiator. Metal fins on the radiator pipes help conduct heat from the water inside the pipes.

HEAT PUMPS FOR HEATING
Some modern buildings are heated by heat pumps. They work in a similar way to the heat pumps in refrigerators. An evaporator coil is attached outside the building. This coil absorbs heat from the air or from the ground. The heat is released in condenser coils inside the building. For each unit of energy used to power the compressor, at least five units of heat energy are released into the building. Reversing the direction of pumping cools buildings in hot weather.

WASTE HEAT AND ENGINES
Engines are machines that change the chemical energy of a fuel into mechanical energy. Common examples are the gasoline and diesel engines that propel vehicles. These engines convert about one third of the fuel's energy into useful mechanical energy. Two thirds of the energy is produced as waste heat. This heat must be removed to prevent the temperature of the engine from becoming dangerously high. At temperatures higher than the normal running temperature, lubricating oils can break down. The moving parts of the engine then grind against each other and become damaged.

AIR AND WATER COOLING
Motorcycle engines are usually air-cooled. They are covered with metal fins that have a large surface area. Air rushes past the fins and cools them so that they conduct more heat away from inside the

engine. Larger engines have to be water-cooled to remove the heat that they generate. A pump forces water through a system of channels that surround the cylinders where the fuel burns. Waste heat warms the water, which then passes through thin pipes in a radiator. A fan blows air between the pipes in the radiator. This cools the water before it flows back into the engine.

USING WASTE HEAT
Most cars have a heater to keep the driver and passengers warm in cold weather. Hot water from the engine's cooling system passes through the tubes of a small radiator. A fan forces air around these and into the passenger compartment.

CHPs, or combined heat and power plants, are thermal power plants whose surplus heat from generating is supplied to homes and businesses.

The pipework in this combined heat and power plant carries waste steam and hot water from electricity generation to provide heat for houses and other buildings nearby. Other power plants lose this heat to the environment through cooling towers.

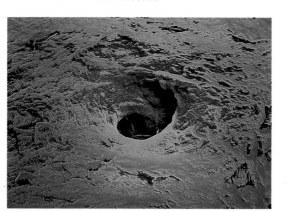

Thousands of human sweat pores release sweat onto the skin when the body gets too hot. As the sweat evaporates, it removes heat and cools the blood circulating under the skin.

SEE ALSO PAGES:
100–1 Skin, hair, and nails, 250–1 Heat transfer

COMBUSTION

Combustion is another name for burning. It is a chemical reaction between a fuel and oxygen that releases energy as heat and, sometimes, light.

Mixture of gas and air

Airhole

Gas

Air

The blue inner cone of a Bunsen-burner flame is a mixture of gas and air. Closing the airhole gives a bright yellow flame.

Candle wax melts easily to form a pool of liquid wax around the wick. Capillary action draws the wax up through the wick. The heat of the flame vaporizes the wax, which then burns as it mixes with air. Glowing particles of carbon make the flame bright yellow.

When a fuel burns, its molecules split into atoms that combine with oxygen to form other molecules. This process is called combustion. Most fuels are hydrocarbons, such as methane (CH_4). Hydrocarbons can burn in air, which is around 21 percent oxygen. When they burn completely, the products are carbon dioxide gas (CO_2) and water vapor, (H_2O).

If the supply of oxygen is limited, the products of combustion include toxic carbon monoxide gas (CO) and soot, which is a form of carbon.

Fuels burn extremely fiercely in pure oxygen. A mixture of acetylene gas, (C_2H_2), and oxygen burns at 6,000°F (3,300°C), which is hot enough to melt and weld steel.

THE BURNING PROCESS

A mixture of fuel and air must be heated to a certain temperature before it ignites. The minimum temperature for burning depends on the type of fuel. When a spark lights a gas burner, the heat of the spark breaks fuel and oxygen molecules into atoms. These atoms then recombine to form the products of combustion. As they do, the heat released by the reaction allows other fuel and oxygen molecules to break up and react together. This releases more heat, so the combustion process keeps itself going.

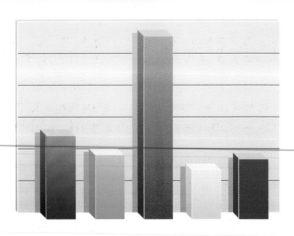

Different fuels release different amounts of energy during combustion. Comparisons are made by listing the amount of energy released by burning .04 ounces of fuel.

GAS, LIQUID, AND SOLID FUELS

Various types of burners are used to burn fuel gases such as methane and propane. Most burners work in the same way as a laboratory Bunsen burner. The fuel gas enters the burner through a small hole called a jet. The stream of gas draws in air and forms a flammable mixture. The mixture combusts at one or more holes at the top of the burner.

Liquid fuels, such as kerosene, must vaporize before they can burn. Diesel engines, jet engines, and oil-fired furnaces spray oil from tiny holes. The spray then vaporizes in the heat of combustion.

Solid fuels, such as coal and wood, burn by giving off flammable gases when they are heated. Chipped or powdered solid fuels burn faster than lumps.

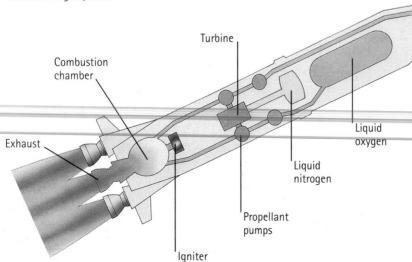

Turbine

Combustion chamber

Exhaust

Igniter

Propellant pumps

Liquid nitrogen

Liquid oxygen

Liquid fuel

There is no air in space, so rockets have to take their own supply of oxygen for combustion. The oxygen is stored at low temperatures as a liquid, which takes up much less space than gas. Slowly evaporating liquid nitrogen keeps the oxygen in liquid form. Burning a mixture of fuel and oxygen in the combustion chamber gives the rocket thrust.

SEE ALSO PAGES:

171 Nitrogen and oxygen,
420–1 Rockets and the space shuttle

EXPANSION AND CONTRACTION

Substances expand when they are heated; their volume increases as the temperature rises. The reverse is also true—substances contract when they are cold.

Thermometers use the expansion of a liquid to measure temperature. The liquid is kept in a bulb. A thread of the liquid moves up and down a fine tube that is marked with a temperature scale. The liquid is usually mercury or dyed ethanol.

— Bulb

— Mercury

At a constant pressure, doubling the absolute temperature of a gas doubles its volume.

The particles in a substance have more kinetic energy when the substance is hot than when it is cold. This means that the atoms, ions, or molecules that make up the substance move faster as temperature rises. This motion tends to push the particles farther apart and increase the volume of the substance. At the same time, the density of the substance decreases, because the mass occupies a greater volume.

SOLIDS
A three-foot-long iron bar expands by around ¹/₁₀₀ of a millimeter (¹/₂,₅₀₀ in.) for each 1°C temperature rise. When a hot day follows a frosty night, one kilometer (0.62 mi) of railroad expands almost 50 centimeters (20 in.) This is why railroads have occasional sliding joints to stop the rails buckling. Rapid heating can make glass dishes crack as they expand unevenly.

LIQUIDS
For a given change in temperature, most liquids expand or contract around one thousand times more than solids. Water is unusual—it contracts as the temperature rises from 32°F to 40°F. This is due to a change in the structure of water.

This blacksmith is cooling a newly fitted iron tire with water. When hot, the tire fits easily around the wooden wheel. As the iron cools, it shrinks to form a tight fit.

GASES
Gases compress more easily than liquids and solids. This is because there is more space between their particles. For this reason, the volume of a gas is measured at a fixed pressure, usually the average pressure of the Earth's atmosphere at sea level. When this is done, most gases expand by the same amount for each degree rise in temperature. In fact, the volume of a gas at constant pressure increases in proportion to its temperature above absolute zero (0K).

As day and night alternate, the Earth's atmosphere heats and then cools. Hot air rises because it is less dense than cold air. Moving air makes the winds blow and controls the Earth's weather patterns.

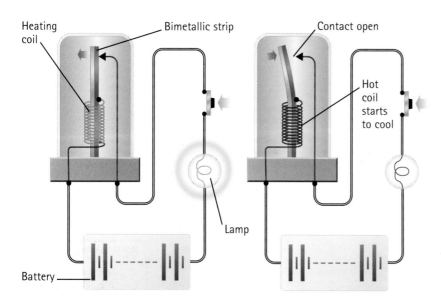

Heating coil

Bimetallic strip

Contact open

Hot coil starts to cool

Lamp

Battery

▶ For a 1° change in temperature, solids expand or contract by different amounts. For this reason, engineers must make a careful choice of materials when they design a building or a machine.

◀ Flashing lights in cars use bimetallic strips made of two metals that expand at different rates. When the light is on, the strip gets hot and bends. This breaks the circuit that heats it. The strip then cools, closes the circuit, and lights the bulb again.

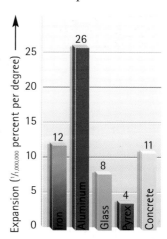

Expansion (¹/₁,₀₀₀,₀₀₀ percent per degree)

Iron	Aluminum	Glass	Pyrex	Concrete
12	26	8	4	11

SEE ALSO PAGES:
156–7 States of matter,
256 Kinetic theory,
257 Changes of state

KINETIC THEORY

The three states of matter are solid, liquid, and gas. Kinetic theory explains the properties of these three states in terms of particles and their movement.

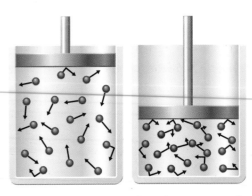

Compressing a gas into a smaller volume squeezes the particles closer together. The rate of collisions with the walls increases, so the pressure increases.

Chemists discovered that substances consisted of atoms, molecules, and other particles about 150 years ago. They already knew many of the properties of solids, liquids, and gases. They developed the kinetic theory to explain these properties in terms of moving particles.

A drop of dye spreads rapidly through hot water.

The dye diffuses more slowly in cold water.

Water molecules move slower in cold water than in hot water. The rate of diffusion of dye particles shows how the rate of diffusion, or spreading, depends on temperature.

SOLIDS

Solids have fixed volumes and shapes. They are also hard and almost impossible to compress. The particles that make up solids are very close together, and there are strong forces of attraction between them. These particles cannot move past each other but vibrate back and forth around fixed positions in the solid structure.

LIQUIDS

Like solids, liquids have fixed volumes; unlike solids, they have no fixed shape. A liquid flows to the lowest part of its container. Each substance has almost the same density when it is a liquid or a solid. The particles in a liquid are almost as close as in solids, but they have more energy and are free to move around each other.

GASES

Gases are easier to compress than liquids and solids. Decreasing the volume of a gas increases its pressure. Kinetic theory explains this observation by saying that the particles are widely spaced. The particles in a gas occupy only a tiny fraction of the whole volume of the gas. For example, a single cubic centimeter of water boils to make 1,700 cm^3 of steam at 100°C and atmospheric pressure. The molecules in steam are moving so fast and are so widely spaced that the attraction between particles has almost no effect compared to the solid or the liquid state.

Gases diffuse, which means that they spread out in all directions and completely fill their containers. This is how the smell of a strong perfume eventually fills a sealed room. Kinetic theory states that the particles of a gas are in continuous motion, traveling in zigzags as they collide with each other and the walls of their container. No energy is lost by the molecules during collisions because they are perfectly elastic.

The pressure of a gas is the result of the collisions of its particles with the walls of its container. Increasing the temperature of a gas increases the average kinetic energy of the particles. Their speed increases, with the result that they strike the container walls more often and with greater force, so they exert a greater pressure on the walls.

BROWNIAN MOTION

The first evidence for the movement of particles was recorded by British botanist Robert Brown (1773–1858) in 1827. He was looking through a microscope at pollen grains in a drop of water and noticed that they were moving in jerks around the microscope slide. The motion is caused by water molecules striking the pollen grains. If the experiment is done using smoke particles, which are lighter than pollen grains, the motion is greater. Each smoke particle scatters light into the microscope and is seen as a bright point.

Smoke particles from a fire reflect sunlight.

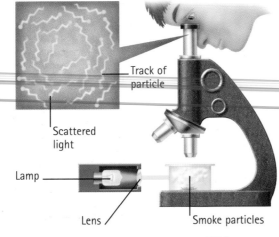

Track of particle

Scattered light

Lamp

Lens

Smoke particles

Smoke particles are seen as points of light that move as air molecules strike them.

SEE ALSO PAGES:

257 Changes of state, 292–3 Potential and kinetic energy

CHANGES OF STATE

Melting, freezing, boiling, and condensation are examples of changes of state. They are processes that change substances from one state of matter to another.

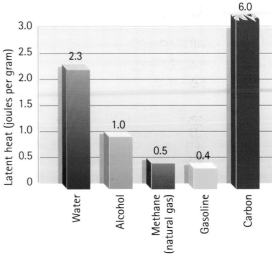

The amount of energy needed to change a known amount of a substance into a gas at its boiling point is called its latent heat of vaporization. The value indicates the strength of the forces of attraction between particles.

When a substance changes its state, it takes in or releases energy as its particles rearrange themselves. The particles in a gas, for example, are much more widely spaced than the particles in a liquid. This means that the process of boiling requires an input of energy for the particles to escape the attractive forces that hold them together in a liquid. The same amount of energy is returned if the gas condenses.

When an overheated dog pants, water evaporates from its tongue. This change of state removes heat from the tongue and so cools the animal.

▼ In a solid, strong forces of attraction hold particles in fixed positions. Heat increases the energy of the particles and raises the temperature of the solid until it melts.

MELTING

Heating a solid below its melting point makes the temperature of the solid rise. The energy of its particles increases as the temperature approaches the melting point. Once melting starts, the temperature does not rise, even though heat continues to flow into the melting solid. Each pure substance has its own particular melting point. The energy provides the particles with sufficient kinetic energy to break free from the solid structure. A high melting point is a sign that the forces that hold the solid together are particularly strong.

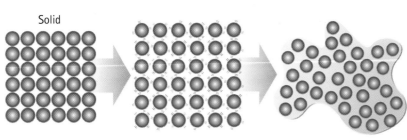

Solid

Particles in solids are arranged in fixed positions.

Heating a solid makes its particles vibrate more vigorously.

A solid melts as its structure breaks down.

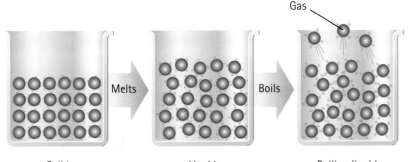

Gas

Solid — Melts → Liquid — Boils → Boiling liquid

EVAPORATION AND BOILING

All liquids evaporate, regardless of the temperature. Some particles in the liquid surface have enough energy to escape into the space above the liquid. Increasing the temperature increases the proportion of particles that have enough energy to escape, so liquids evaporate faster at higher temperatures.

The particles that escape from a liquid cause a pressure above that liquid. This is called the vapor pressure. It increases as the temperature increases. A liquid starts to boil when its vapor pressure equals the pressure of its surroundings. When this happens, bubbles of vapor form in the liquid and rise to the surface.

IMPURE SUBSTANCES

The presence of other substances alters the melting and boiling points of a pure substance. Salt, for example, causes ice to melt by lowering its melting point from 0° C (32°F) to –20°C (–4°F). But, adding salt also makes the boiling point of water higher than 100°C (212°F).

◄ When a solid melts, its particles remain close together, but the ordered structure of the solid breaks down. When a liquid boils, its particles become free to drift away from each other and fill the available space.

SEE ALSO PAGES:

156–7 States of matter, 194–5 Properties of solids, 256 Kinetic theory

THERMODYNAMICS

Thermodynamics is the study of the laws that control the direction in which heat will flow and how energy changes from one form to another.

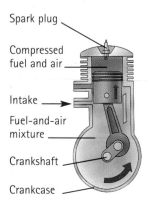

- Spark plug
- Compressed fuel and air
- Intake
- Fuel-and-air mixture
- Crankshaft
- Crankcase

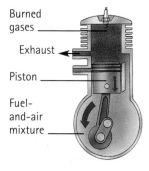

- Burned gases
- Exhaust
- Piston
- Fuel-and-air mixture

Two-stroke engines turn a fuel's chemical energy into mechanical energy and heat. The first stroke compresses and ignites the mixture. In the second stroke, burning gases push the piston down before more fuel and air blow them through the exhaust.

The study of thermodynamics began in the 1800s. Scientists used the results of experiments to draw up laws that describe how heat and energy behave in nature. These laws helped engineers to improve the design of machines such as steam engines, which change the chemical energy trapped in fuels into heat energy and then mechanical energy. As time went by, scientists realized that the same laws of thermodynamics apply to all processes, from the workings of diesel engines to the biological processes in living organisms.

THE FIRST LAW

The first law of thermodynamics states that energy can neither be created nor destroyed. One result of this law is that the amount of energy that flows into a device is matched by the amount of energy that flows out of it. Take the case of an electric lamp. Energy flows into the lamp in the form of electricity. The lamp produces heat and light as an electrical current flows through it, and the sum of the heat and light energy that the lamp gives out is equal to the amount of electrical energy that the lamp consumes. In other words, the amount of energy does not alter as the lamp glows, the energy simply changes from one form to another.

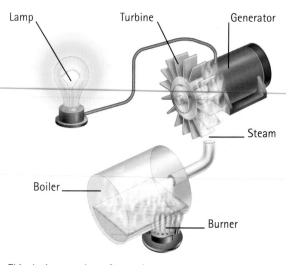

- Lamp
- Turbine
- Generator
- Steam
- Boiler
- Burner

This device uses heat from a burner to produce steam that drives a simple turbine and generator. Only a small proportion of the heat is converted to electrical energy.

THE SECOND LAW

The second law of thermodynamics states that all natural processes increase entropy. Entropy is a measure of the disorder of the universe—in other words, the random nature or chaos of the universe. One consequence of the second law is that heat flows from a hot place to a cooler place. The heat that was concentrated in a hot object becomes spread out and less ordered, so the process increases entropy.

Entropy also plays a part in chemical reactions. Many reactions cause entropy to increase by turning chemical energy into heat that spreads into the surroundings. Some reactions release gases, which are less ordered than liquids or solids.

▼ Only a small part of the heat from burning fuel in an engine turns into mechanical energy. The rest is lost in hot exhaust gases, through the radiator, and to the air that flows around the engine. As a car moves, its tires flex and become hot. Also, friction warms the air that passes over the car. When the brakes stop the car, they become hot and convert all the car's kinetic energy into heat.

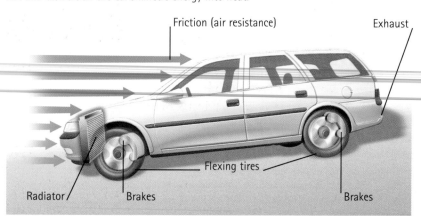

- Friction (air resistance)
- Exhaust
- Flexing tires
- Radiator
- Brakes
- Brakes

THE THIRD LAW

The third law of thermodynamics states that there is a minimum temperature, called absolute zero. At this temperature, matter has its minimum possible heat energy and cannot become colder.

It is impossible to reach absolute zero, because any object at absolute zero would immediately absorb heat from any object around it. Nevertheless, calculations show that absolute zero is –273.15°C (0K). Many thermodynamic calculations use temperatures on the thermodynamic scale, which sets absolute zero as 0K (zero Kelvin). The equations that describe the properties of gases are an example of the use of thermodynamic temperatures. The volume of a gas at constant pressure varies in proportion to its temperature above absolute zero. Also, if the gas is kept in a fixed volume, its pressure increases in proportion to its thermodynamic temperature.

WORK AND ENERGY

Fuels such as gasoline and diesel oil are called high-grade energy sources. They have this name because a small volume of fuel contains a large amount of useful chemical energy. If a driver races a car around a track and returns to exactly the same place, all the chemical energy released by burning the fuel will have turned into heat. The engine wastes over 70 percent of the fuel's energy as heat from the radiator and the exhaust. As the car travels down the road, friction converts kinetic energy into heat that warms the air and the tires. Brakes change kinetic energy into heat energy. At the end of a journey, all the energy in the fuel has spread out into the surroundings and imperceptibly warmed up the world. This heat energy is called low-grade energy because it is spread out and cannot do useful work.

EFFICIENCY

The efficiency of a machine is the proportion of the energy input that it turns into useful work. The energy input to a car engine is the chemical energy released by its fuel, for example, and its useful work output is the kinetic energy that drives the car's wheels.

Thermodynamic calculations show that the maximum efficiency of an internal-combustion engine cannot be greater than around 40 percent. Electric engines are much more efficient: some convert over 90 percent of their electrical energy input into work. However, no more than 45 percent of the heat produced in fossil-fuel or nuclear power plants is turned into electrical energy.

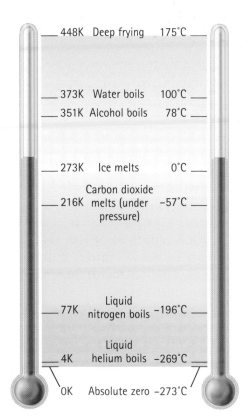

448K	Deep frying	175°C	
373K	Water boils	100°C	
351K	Alcohol boils	78°C	
273K	Ice melts	0°C	
216K	Carbon dioxide melts (under pressure)	–57°C	
77K	Liquid nitrogen boils	–196°C	
4K	Liquid helium boils	–269°C	
0K	Absolute zero	–273°C	

▲ In 1742, Swedish astronomer Anders Celsius (1701–1744) devised a temperature scale in which ice melts at zero degrees and water boils at one hundred degrees.

The thermodynamic scale of temperature starts at 0K (zero Kelvin), which is –273.15°C. This scale was devised by Lord Kelvin, the physicist who established the second law of thermodynamics.

People become hot when they exercise. This is because the processes that cause muscles to move also produce heat.

Growing plants take part of the energy in sunlight and store it as chemical energy in their tissues.

The hull of a speedboat and the body of a dolphin are both streamlined. Their smooth lines help them to pass through water with little energy being wasted.

SEE ALSO PAGES:

106–7 Muscles and movement, 224–5 Gasoline and diesel engines, 294–5 Work and energy

LIGHT

Light is a form of electromagnetic radiation that can be detected by cells in the eyes of animals. Light can be scattered, reflected, refracted, and diffracted.

Dutch physicist and mathematician Christian Huygens (1629–1695) developed techniques for making glass lenses for telescopes. He was the first person to describe light as a wave motion.

Visible light forms a spectrum of colors that range from red at longer wavelengths to violet at shorter wavelengths. The wavelength of infrared radiation is longer than visible light, and the wavelength of ultraviolet is shorter. The human eye cannot detect infrared or ultraviolet radiation.

Light is a form of electromagnetic radiation. The wavelengths of visible light are shorter than those of radio waves and infrared radiation, but longer than those of ultraviolet radiation and X rays. Each color of light has its own special wavelength. Visible light affects chemicals in the nerve endings in the backs of human eyes. These nerve endings then send signals to the brain, which interprets the signals as light. Nothing travels faster than light. Its speed in a vacuum is about 186,000 mi./sec (300,000km/sec). Light travels slightly slower through materials such as air, glass, or water.

BEAMS AND RAYS

Light travels from its source as a series of electromagnetic waves. Scientists find it convenient to draw arrow-shaped lines, called rays, that show the direction in which these light waves travel.

A beam of light consists of groups of light waves that all travel in roughly the same direction. The beam of light from a flashlight spreads slightly as it travels. The light appears fainter as distance increases, since its light waves are spread more thinly over a wider area.

The beam of light from a laser has almost parallel sides. This means that the light waves hardly spread out at all as they travel. This is why the beam from a laser can travel enormous distances before it becomes too weak to be seen.

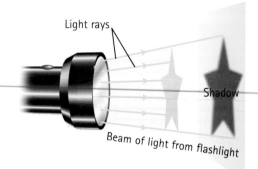

When an object is placed in a beam of light, the object casts a shadow that matches its own shape. This is because light travels in straight lines through space.

SCATTERING

We see light only when it travels into our eyes. We cannot see a beam of light that travels past us through clear air. Light beams become visible when air is foggy. This is because the tiny water droplets in fog reflect some light out of the path of the beam. The light scattered to the side of the beam enters our eyes and makes the beam visible. The microscopic particles in smoke can also scatter light.

Solid substances that scatter light are said to be translucent. Waxed paper lets light pass through it, for example, but scattering disorganizes the light rays and prevents a clear image from being seen. Transparent materials, such as glass, allow light to pass through them without scattering, so a clear image can be seen.

Car headlights appear blurred in fog. This is because water droplets in the fog scatter light rays, so some light appears to come from around the headlights.

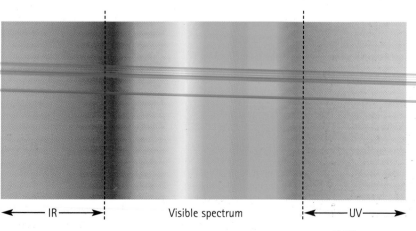

IR ← → | Visible spectrum | ← UV →

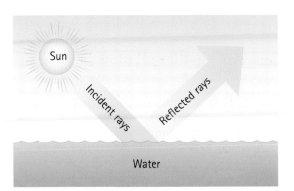

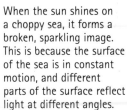

When the sun shines on a choppy sea, it forms a broken, sparkling image. This is because the surface of the sea is in constant motion, and different parts of the surface reflect light at different angles.

When we look in a mirror, the image that we see is a true match of our appearance, but with left and right reversed. The proportions and color of the reflection are accurate.

REFLECTION

Few visible objects produce light; most are visible because they reflect some of the light that falls on them. Some objects appear bright or shiny because they reflect most of the light that falls on them. Objects that are bright but matte scatter the light that they reflect. Mirrors produce clear images because they do not disturb the arrangement of the rays as they reflect. Dull objects absorb most of the light that falls on them and change it into heat.

REFRACTION

Light waves slow down when they move from air into a denser substance such as glass or water. The speed of light in water is three fourths of its speed in air. If a ray of light enters water or glass at an angle, it changes direction slightly. This effect, called refraction, causes lenses and other transparent objects to alter the appearance of things seen through them.

DIFFRACTION

When light waves pass through a hole or slit that has a similar width to their wavelength, they spread in all directions as they emerge. This effect is called diffraction. Waves that spread from separate openings can interfere with one another. Depending on the direction, some of the waves cancel each other out, and some reinforce each other to produce patterns of light.

INFRARED AND ULTRAVIOLET

Over 200 years ago, scientists performed a simple experiment to show that light is a form of energy. They used a glass prism to split sunlight into a spectrum of colors ranging from red through green to violet. They then shone each color in turn onto the bulb of a thermometer. The thermometer showed an increase in temperature as it absorbed energy from the light. The thermometer showed the presence of invisible infrared heat rays outside the spectrum in the dark space next to red light. Later, photographic film showed the existence of invisible ultraviolet radiation in the dark space next to violet light.

Dutch physicist Hendrik Lorentz (1853–1928) used mathematics rather than experiments to investigate light. He developed an electromagnetic theory of light to explain reflection and refraction effects.

A compact disc stores information as tiny pits in a sheet of aluminum. In a compact-disc player, these pits reflect laser light of a single frequency onto a detector that converts the reflected pulses of light into an electrical signal. In normal light, reflected light rays interfere with one another. This makes some frequencies appear more strongly than others. This is why the surface of a compact disc sparkles with color in white light.

Lighting effects create an exciting atmosphere. Ultraviolet lamps produce a light that cannot be seen directly, but that makes a dye in clothing glow blue. The dye emits light at a lower frequency than the ultraviolet light that illuminates it. This is an example of an effect called fluorescence.

SEE ALSO PAGES:

262–3 Reflection and absorption, 264–5 Refraction, 344–5 Electromagnetism, 380–1 Information technology

REFLECTION AND ABSORPTION

Light is reflected when it simply bounces off a surface. Absorption is when light changes into heat or some other form of energy when it strikes a surface.

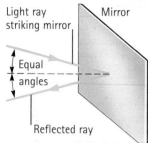

Light ray striking mirror — Mirror — Equal angles — Reflected ray

Light reflects off a mirror at the same angle at which the incoming ray strikes it.

The image that a mirror reflects is the opposite way around to the object, so this right-handed woman appears to be left-handed. This reversal is called lateral inversion.

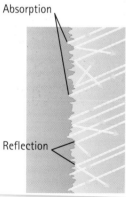

Absorption — Reflection

A light-colored object reflects more light than it absorbs. Dark-colored objects absorb more light.

▶ Soldiers use dull, dark clothing and paint lines on their faces to make themselves less visible on the battlefield.

A good mirror typically reflects around 98 percent of the light that strikes its surface. The mirror absorbs the rest of the light energy and changes it into heat that slightly warms the surface. A dull black object absorbs almost all the light that falls on it. Most of the light energy changes to heat, and very little reflects. A deep cave with soot-covered walls would be an almost perfect absorber: practically none of the light that entered the cave would come out again.

The sun, stars, and lamps are visible because they are hot and produce light. Most other objects are visible because they reflect some of the light that falls on them. White surfaces reflect light better than darker surfaces. Smooth, polished surfaces are the best reflectors. Rough surfaces tend to be poorer reflectors because they reflect light rays in all directions, and some light is absorbed in tiny cavities in the surface.

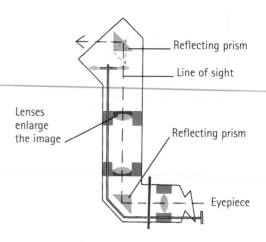

Reflecting prism — Line of sight — Lenses enlarge the image — Reflecting prism — Eyepiece

A simple periscope makes it possible to see over an obstruction. One type of periscope is used to see over protective lead walls in nuclear power plants.

MIRRORS

Ancient mirrors were made from sheets of polished metal, usually copper or brass. It was difficult to see a clear image in these mirrors because they were not perfectly flat, and they absorbed much of the light that fell on them. Modern mirrors are made from flat sheets of glass with a thin reflective coating of silver or aluminum on the back. The glass protects the coating and makes sure that it is perfectly flat.

A ray of light that strikes a flat mirror behaves like a ball when it strikes a wall: the light bounces off at the same angle at which it made contact. The incoming ray is called the incident ray. The angle at which it strikes is called the incident angle. This is measured against an imaginary line sticking out from the surface at 90 degrees. The outgoing ray is called the reflected ray. The angle at which it leaves the mirror is measured in the same way and is called the angle of reflection.

REFLECTED IMAGES

Mirrors produce reflected images of objects that are placed before them. Plane mirrors, which are flat, form undistorted images of the objects they reflect. When a person looks into a mirror, they see their own image. The image seems to be as far behind the mirror as the person is in front. The brain supposes that rays travel in straight lines and sees the image at the place the rays appear to come from.

FIBER OPTICS

Fiber-optics is a technology that uses strands of glass, called optical fibers, to channel light. Total internal reflection holds light within a glass fiber no matter how much the fiber is bent, and pulses of light can be used to carry telephone and data signals many miles through fiber-optic cables.

Surgeons use fiber optics to look inside lungs and other body cavities. Tools called endoscopes have one bundle of optical fibers that leads light to the tip of the endoscope; a second bundle carries an image back.

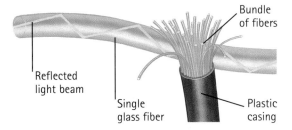

Bundle of fibers

Reflected light beam

Single glass fiber

Plastic casing

TOTAL INTERNAL REFLECTION

Reflection can happen at the surface between two transparent substances, such as air and glass. This is how windows can reflect images of their surroundings. This type of reflection happens only with rays that travel at a shallow angle to the surface. Think about the surface of a swimming pool. When light from an underwater object hits the surface at right angles, or an angle of incidence of zero degrees, it passes straight through without changing direction. If a ray strikes the underside of the surface at an angle of 45 degrees, when it emerges into the air, the ray makes an angle of just 20 degrees to the surface. This is because an optical effect called refraction bends the ray closer to the surface. If a light ray hits the surface at an angle of incidence of 49 degrees, or 41 degrees to the surface, refraction bends it so much that the ray does not emerge

into the air. Rays that strike at angles less than 41 degrees to the surface do not pass into the air. Instead, they reflect down from the surface. This is called total internal reflection.

The minimum angle of incidence at which all light is reflected internally is called the critical angle. It is determined by the two materials that meet at the surface. For light passing from water into air, the critical angle is 48.8 degrees. From glass into air, the angle is 41.1 degrees.

An important feature of total internal reflection is that practically no light is absorbed by the reflecting surface. Fiber optics uses this property to carry light over great distances through optical glass fibers. As light passes through a fiber, total internal reflection can bounce it off the inside of the fiber's surface many millions of times without it becoming too weak to carry a signal or an image.

▲ This lamp uses fiber optics to produce a decorative effect. The optical fibers are bundled together at one end. Light passes through a colored filter into the bundled end and emerges as pinpoints of brightness at the loose ends of the fibers.

▲ The dark marks at the bottom of this photograph are reflections of markings under the surface of the water. From above, the surface sparkles as it reflects sunlight.

The moon shines because it reflects sunlight. The birds and tree appear as black silhouettes because they block the path of the rays of moonlight.

SEE ALSO PAGES:

260–1 Light, 264–5 Refraction, 366–7 Telecommunications

REFRACTION

Refraction is the change of direction of light rays that can occur when the speed of light changes as it passes from one transparent substance into another.

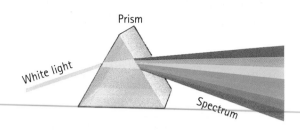

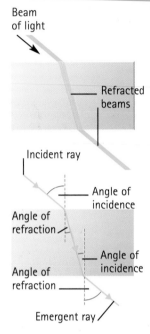

Beam of light

Refracted beams

Incident ray

Angle of incidence

Angle of refraction

Angle of incidence

Angle of refraction

Emergent ray

This ray diagram shows how refraction changes the path of light as it passes through a sheet of glass. When light passes from air into glass, the angle of incidence is greater than the angle of refraction. The direction changes again when the ray leaves the block, so the path of the emergent ray is parallel to the path of the incident ray.

Light rays travel in straight lines through any transparent substance, or medium. However, the speed of light depends on the medium. If light strikes the surface between two transparent media at right angles, it continues in the same direction. If it strikes at any other angle, the different speeds of light in the two media cause the light rays to change direction. This change of direction is called refraction.

REFRACTION AND WATER

When an underwater object is seen from outside the water, its appearance becomes distorted. This is because refraction changes the direction of the light rays that come from the object. When these rays enter the eyes of an observer, nerves in the eyes send signals to the observer's brain. The brain then constructs a picture based on where the rays appear to have come from. It does this without accounting for the effects of refraction, so the object's appearance is distorted. Looking at a straw in a glass of water, light rays from the part of the straw that is underwater refract at the surfaces between the water and glass and between the glass and the air. The rays appear to come from closer to the surface than they are, and the straw looks bent. If the straw were viewed from underwater, the part above water would be distorted.

White light is a mixture of all colors, including red, orange, yellow, green, blue, indigo, and violet. Dispersion of white light through a prism reveals this spectrum.

DISPERSION AND PRISMS

Different colors of light have different wavelengths. The extent of refraction of light depends on its wavelength. Shorter wavelengths are refracted through greater angles than longer wavelengths. Because of this variation, violet light refracts more than green light, which refracts more than red light. The separation of wavelengths by refraction is called dispersion. Using a prism, a triangular block of glass or plastic, maximizes the effect of dispersion. When white light enters a prism at the correct angle, dispersion splits it into a spectrum of different colors.

DISPERSION AND RAINBOWS

Rainbows appear when raindrops refract and reflect strong sunlight. Light passes into the raindrops, reflects off the back of them, and passes out of them. Each wavelength of light is refracted through a slightly different angle on the way into the drop and then on the way out. Each raindrop reflects all the wavelengths of light, but an observer sees colors only from drops that are in the correct position to refract light into the observer's eyes. This is why the rainbow that each observer sees depends on their position.

DISPERSION IN LENSES

Refraction alters the appearance and position of objects. The images we see are not the same as the objects that cause them. Lenses use this effect to produce magnified images. Lenses are usually made from glass or transparent plastic.

More than 300 years ago, scientists discovered how to make telescopes and microscopes by fitting several glass lenses together inside tubes. They soon found

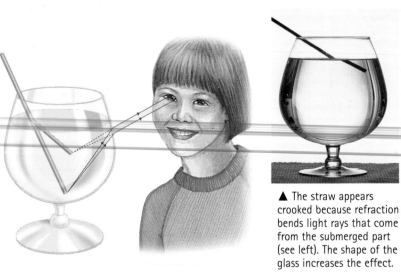

▲ The straw appears crooked because refraction bends light rays that come from the submerged part (see left). The shape of the glass increases the effect.

that dispersion limited the power of their lenses. The problem arose because lenses use refraction to produce magnified images. Each wavelength of light refracts differently, so the image that is seen is a combination of different-colored images, each of a slightly different size. Because of this, early microscopes and telescopes produced images that were surrounded by fuzzy, colored fringes. This effect is called chromatic aberration.

The greater the power of magnification, the more extreme the effects of chromatic aberration. The point is reached where magnified images become meaningless jumbles of overlapping colored shapes. Modern optical instruments reduce the problem of chromatic aberration by using combinations of lenses made from different types of glass. One part of the lens combination produces a magnified image with chromatic aberration; the other part corrects the aberration. Some lenses are made from pieces of different glass to fit snugly together.

THE REFRACTIVE INDEX
Refraction happens because light travels at different speeds in different media. The greater the difference in the speed of light in two media, the greater the effect of refraction at the boundary between them. Scientists use a number called a refractive index to measure the refracting power of a

Medium	Refractive index
Acetone	1.36
Air	1.00
Benzene	1.50
Crown glass	1.52
Diamond	2.42
Ethanol	1.36
Flint glass	1.66
Polystyrene	1.59
Quartz	1.46
Sodium chloride	1.53
Water	1.33

substance. The refractive index of a given substance is the speed of light in a vacuum divided by the speed of light in that substance. Refractive indexes are normally quoted for yellow light, which is in the middle of the visible spectrum. But the exact value of a refractive index depends on wavelength.

Light travels fastest through a vacuum, so the refractive index of a material is always greater than one. The refractive index of glass, for example, is 1.52, and the value for diamond is 2.42. The refractive index of air is only slightly greater than one.

Refractive indexes are important in the design of optical equipment. This is because a lens made from a material with a large refractive index will magnify more than a lens of the same shape but of a lesser refractive index.

The refractive index of a medium, or transparent material, is the speed of light in a vacuum divided by the speed of light in that medium. Refraction happens when light passes between two media with different refractive indexes.

Under certain weather conditions, ice crystals in the upper atmosphere refract and disperse light from the moon, causing a spectacular halo effect.

Refraction bends light rays from underwater objects as they pass through the water's surface. In this picture, refraction of light through ripples in the pool gives a distorted appearance to the parts of these people's bodies that are under the surface of the water.

▲ The speed of light in a diamond is less than half its speed in air. Strong refraction and dispersion of white light through the angled faces of a cut diamond cause it to sparkle with color as it moves.

SEE ALSO PAGES:
266–7 Lenses and curved mirrors, 268–9 Microscopes, 270–1 Telescopes, 284 The speed of light

LENSES AND CURVED MIRRORS

Lenses are curved pieces of transparent material. Like curved mirrors, they produce images that are larger or smaller than the object placed in front of them.

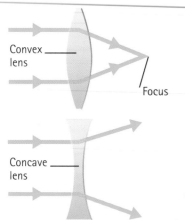

These ray diagrams show the path of light through lenses. A convex lens forms an image that is magnified by making light rays converge at a focus. A concave lens produces a diminished image by making light rays diverge from the lens's centerline.

▼ The centerline of a mirror or lens is called its principal axis. Any ray that strikes a concave mirror parallel to its principal axis reflects through a point called the principal focus of the mirror.

Lenses and curved mirrors produce images that are larger or smaller than the object on which they are focused. Ray diagrams help to visualize this by showing the paths of a few light rays, particularly those that strike a mirror or lens parallel to its principal axis, or centerline.

CONCAVE MIRRORS

A concave mirror curves inward and reflects light toward the inside of the curve. Rays that strike the mirror parallel to its principal axis all reflect through a single spot called the focal point. The distance of the focal point from the mirror is called the focal length. The shorter the focal length, the greater the magnification. The focal length depends on the curvature of the mirror. A tightly curved mirror has a short focal length and strong magnification.

CONVEX MIRRORS

Convex mirrors are curved like concave mirrors, but they reflect on the outside of the curve. When parallel rays of light strike a convex mirror, they are reflected outward. The focal point of a convex mirror is at the point behind the mirror that the reflected rays appear to come from. The shorter the focal length, the smaller the reflected image.

A concave mirror produces a magnified image of an object. The area of the actual image seen is smaller than would be seen in a flat mirror.

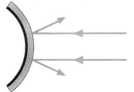

The reflective antiglare coating on the lenses of these sunglasses make them act as convex mirrors. Parallel rays reflect outward, forming a shrunken image.

MAGNIFICATION AND VIEW

Flat mirrors, or plane mirrors, form undistorted, unmagnified reflections. A concave mirror of the same size gives a magnified view of a smaller area—it is said to have a smaller angle of view. The magnification of a concave mirror is the number of times larger an image appears than the original object that is reflected. Concave mirrors are useful when a detailed view of a small area is required. This is why concave bathroom mirrors are helpful when shaving or applying makeup.

Convex mirrors have a wider angle of view than flat mirrors, but they produce smaller images. A convex mirror reflects more of the scene in front of it, but with less detail. Many stores have large, convex security mirrors fitted on the walls high above the customers. They give wide-angle downward views that include parts usually hidden from sight. They are often used in combination with video cameras, allowing a wider angle of view to fit in frame. Rear- and side-view car mirrors are slightly convex, so that the driver can see more of the scene behind the car.

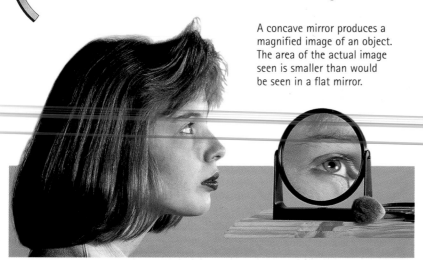

LENSES

Lenses work in a similar way to mirrors, but a lens affects the view of an object behind it, and a mirror affects the view of an object in front of it.

Lenses work by refracting light at their surfaces. Refraction causes the rays to bend as they enter a lens from the air. The rays bend again as they pass out through the opposite side of the lens. Lenses are usually circular in shape and are made from glass or clear plastic. Convex lenses are thicker in the middle than at the outer edge. Concave lenses are thinner in the middle than at the outer edge.

CONCAVE LENSES

Concave lenses are also called diverging lenses because they bend parallel rays away from each other. The focal point of a concave lens is at the point behind the lens that light rays appear to come from. Objects appear smaller through a concave lens, just as they do in a convex mirror. Increasing the steepness of the curvature decreases the focal length of concave lenses and makes the image even smaller.

The most common use for concave lenses is in glasses for nearsighted people. Concave lenses are also used in compound lenses for cameras, telescopes, and microscopes. They fit snugly against the

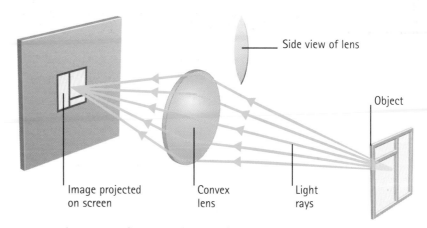

Image projected on screen — Convex lens — Light rays — Object — Side view of lens

▲ A convex lens can be used to focus light from an object onto a screen. The image is upside down and inverted from left to right.

outward curves of convex lenses that are made from other materials. Compound lenses reduce chromatic aberration, the blurring of images caused by different wavelengths of light being magnified to slightly different extents.

CONVEX LENSES

Convex lenses, or converging lenses, bend rays of light toward each other. They bend parallel rays toward a single point, called the principal focus. The focal length is the distance from the principal focus to the lens. Convex lenses are used in magnifying glasses and glasses for farsighted people. By concentrating sunlight at its focal point, a convex lens can be used to ignite paper and other flammable materials.

▼ The convex lens of a magnifying glass focuses light rays onto a point to form a magnified image. The image is said to be a virtual image because it cannot be projected onto a screen.

Convex lens

Object

Image

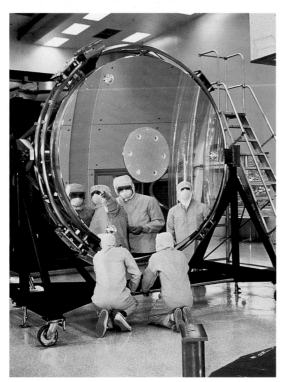

The main mirror of the Hubble space telescope has a diameter of 2.4 meters (7.9 ft). It is designed to collect as much light as possible from distant stars and galaxies.

▲ A magnifying glass uses a convex lens to reveal details that would be difficult to see with the naked eye.

SEE ALSO PAGES:

262–3 Reflection and absorption, 270–1 Telescopes

MICROSCOPES

Microscopes produce magnified images of objects that are too small to see with the naked eye. Electron microscopes can magnify an image up to 200,000 times.

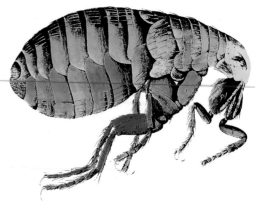

In 1665, British scientist Robert Hooke (1635–1703) published this drawing of a flea in his book *Micrographia*. He drew the flea as viewed through his microscope.

Dutch naturalist Antonie van Leeuwenhoek (1632–1723) was the first person to use magnifying lenses to study bacteria, yeast, and blood cells.

The human eye can see objects as small as one tenth of a millimeter (¹⁄₂₅₀ in.) in diameter. Large bacteria and other single-celled organisms are one hundred times smaller than this, and viruses are tens of thousands of times smaller. During the past 350 years, microscopes have made it possible to see such small objects, and some modern microscopes are powerful enough to show individual atoms.

OPTICAL MICROSCOPES

Optical microscopes use lenses to produce magnified images by refracting light. The first microscopes were probably the compound microscopes made in the 1590s by Dutch instrument maker Zacharias Janssen (1580–1638). Compound microscopes are so called because they use a combination of lenses to form images.

In the late 1600s, Robert Hooke (1635–1703) used a compound microscope to make detailed drawings of cells and tiny animals. Magnification was limited by distortion until 1830, when low-distortion lenses were invented. In 1865, microscopes helped French chemist Louis Pasteur (1822–1895) to show that infectious diseases are caused by tiny organisms.

THE LIMIT OF RESOLUTION

Even using distortion-free lenses, optical microscopes would only be able to resolve, or see details of, objects larger than the wavelength of visible light: around 500 nanometers, or 2,000-times magnification.

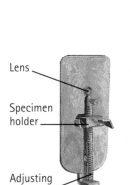

Lens

Specimen holder

Adjusting screw

Van Leeuwenhoek's microscope had a single lens, which he held close to his eye to view specimens.

MODERN OPTICAL MICROSCOPES

Modern optical microscopes look very different from earlier microscopes but work by the same principles. Small objective lenses are positioned close to the specimen, and lenses in the eyepiece form the image. There are usually three or more sets of objective lenses mounted on a rotatable turret that can rotate. Each set clicks into place to give different powers of magnification. Specimens must be thin enough for light to shine through them. Specimens may be stained with dyes and mounted on glass slides that fit on the platform. An electric lamp shines light up through the specimen. Combinations of light-polarizing filters can reveal extra detail.

Eyepiece lens

Objective lens

This compound microscope was made around 1675. It is similar to the one used by Robert Hooke.

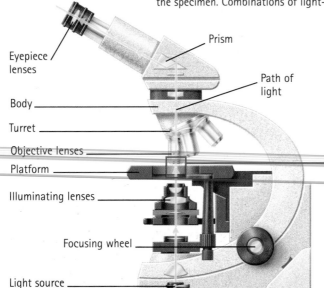

Eyepiece lenses

Body

Turret

Objective lenses

Platform

Illuminating lenses

Focusing wheel

Light source

Prism

Path of light

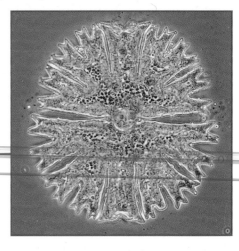

This image, viewed through an optical microscope, is magnified 200 times. It shows a single cell of the *Micrasterias* alga.

TRANSMISSION ELECTRON MICROSCOPES

The electron gun of an electron microscope contains a tungsten filament heated to 4,500°F. It emits electrons that are accelerated by high-voltage electric fields. The electron beam passes through circular electromagnets that act as lenses to focus the beam at the point where it passes through the specimen. The electrons form an image as they strike a fluorescent screen below the sample. The image is viewed through eyepiece lenses similar to those in optical microscopes. A pump removes air from the microscope to prevent gas molecules from scattering electrons.

▲ Russian-born U.S. physicist and engineer Vladimir Zworykin (1889–1982) developed the first electron microscopes during the 1930s.

▶ This image shows a *Salmonella* bacterium magnified 13,000 times by a transmission electron microscope. Bacteria such as this can cause a type of food poisoning.

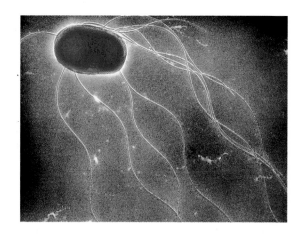

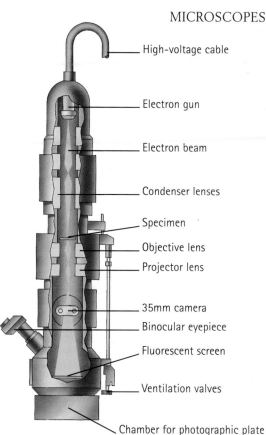

High-voltage cable
Electron gun
Electron beam
Condenser lenses
Specimen
Objective lens
Projector lens
35mm camera
Binocular eyepiece
Fluorescent screen
Ventilation valves
Chamber for photographic plate

ELECTRON MICROSCOPES

Electron microscopes can achieve up to 200,000-times magnification. This is because they form images using electrons instead of light. Electrons are particles that can behave like waves with extremely short wavelengths. The faster they travel, the shorter their wavelengths and the greater the possible magnification. Electron beams are focused using magnetic fields rather than glass lenses.

The two main types of electron microscope are the transmission electron microscope, or TEM, and the scanning electron microscope, or SEM. TEMs were developed in the 1930s. They shoot an electron beam through a thin sample and can show details of cells and viruses. SEMs, developed in the 1960s, scan a beam of electrons across the surface of the sample. This beam ejects electrons from the sample and generates a signal that produces a three-dimensional image on a monitor screen.

OTHER MICROSCOPES

Specialist microscopes use a number of methods to magnify by factors of one million or more. For example, field-ion microscopes use strong electric fields to

tear electrons from metal samples. These electrons form an image as they strike a screen that curves around the sample.

Atomic-force microscopes (AFMs) and scanning-tunneling microscopes (STMs) move tiny probes across the surfaces of samples. A computer analyzes signals from the probe to form an image on a monitor screen. Both microscopes show how atoms are arranged in substances. STMs work only with samples that can conduct electricity; AFMs can image nonconducting molecules, such as DNA.

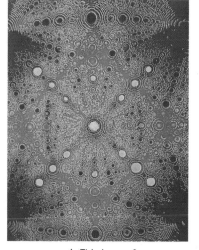

▲ This image from a field-ion microscope shows the arrangement of atoms (orange) at the tip of a platinum needle. This image is magnified 200,000 times.

◀ This scanning electron micrograph shows *Treponema* bacteria (blue) attached to the human intestine (pink). The image is magnified by a factor of 8,000.

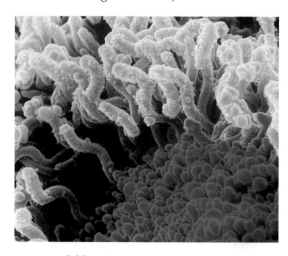

SEE ALSO PAGES:

142–3 Medical technology, 266–7 Lenses and curved mirrors

TELESCOPES

Telescopes produce magnified images of distant objects. Astronomical telescopes collect light or other forms of electromagnetic radiation from space.

The first telescope was made in 1608 by Dutch instrument maker Hans Lippershey (1570–1619). It consisted of two lenses fitted at opposite ends of a tube. In the following year, Italian physicist and astronomer Galileo Galilei (1564–1642) became the first person to use an optical telescope to study the sky.

OPTICAL TELESCOPES

Optical telescopes collect light from distant objects and produce magnified images. There are two main types: refracting telescopes have a large lens at the front to collect light; reflecting telescopes use a concave mirror. Both types use eyepiece lenses to form images.

The lenses of early refracting telescopes were made from poor-quality glass. They produced images that were blurred and surrounded by fuzzy, colored halos. The reflecting telescope, developed in 1668 by Isaac Newton (1642–1727), largely overcame these problems but introduced others. The main drawback was that Newton's metal mirror reflected only 16 percent of the light that fell on it.

The Arecibo radio telescope sits in a natural hollow in the mountains of Puerto Rico. The 305 meter (1000 ft) bowl reflects signals onto a 90-ton antenna 130 meters (427ft) above it.

Most modern astronomical researchers use reflecting telescopes. This is because refracting telescopes suffer from chromatic aberration, a blurring caused by each wavelength of light focusing slightly differently through a lens. Also, the detection of faint objects would require lenses so large that they would sag and form distorted images. Unlike lenses, mirrors can be supported from behind, so their size is less limited by sagging. Glass mirrors can be up to 5m (16 ft) across. They are coated with a layer of aluminum that reflects over 95 percent of light.

Galileo Galilei's refracting telescope magnified by only 20 times. In 1609, he used it to observe Venus and to discover the four principal moons of Jupiter.

In 1668, Isaac Newton built the first reflecting telescope. Instead of lenses, this type of telescope uses mirrors to gather and focus light.

In 1789, German-born British astronomer William Herschel (1738–1822) built a 12-meter (39-ft.) reflecting telescope with a 1.2-meter-wide (4-ft.) mirror.

In 1929, U.S. astronomer Edwin Hubble (1889–1953) used the 8-foot Hooker reflecting telescope, built in 1917, to prove that the universe is expanding.

A pair of binoculars is the equivalent of a pair of small telescopes. Prisms double back the path of light so that the optics fit in a compact case.

Eyepiece lenses

Prism

Prism

Objective lens

Path of light

BEYOND THE VISIBLE

Infrared and ultraviolet radiation lie either side of the visible spectrum. Studying these wavelengths gives information about the stars and clouds of dust in space that cannot be obtained from visible images.

Infrared telescopes can be blinded by infrared radiation from warm objects, so they must be operated at low temperature and work best on satellites. Ultraviolet telescopes must also be mounted on satellites, since the Earth's atmosphere filters out many ultraviolet wavelengths.

Ultraviolet telescopes are particularly useful for studying hot stars and clouds of glowing gases. Infrared telescopes locate cooler clouds of dust that emit no light.

RADIO TELESCOPES

In the 1930s, engineers developed beam antennae that could detect radio signals from precise locations. Pointing these antennae toward the sky, astronomers detected ultrashort radio signals coming from the locations of stars and galaxies.

Modern radio telescopes scan the sky with huge, bowl-shaped dishes that reflect radio signals onto small horn antennae. This arrangement can identify the position of each radio source with great accuracy. Sensitive radio receivers amplify the signals, and computers generate visual images and data for astronomers to study.

Information from radio telescopes has

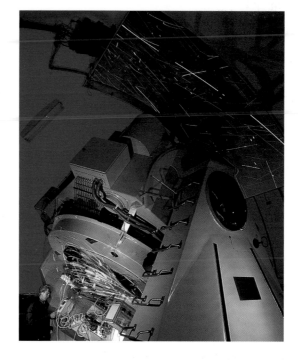

revealed many sources that are invisible through optical telescopes. Among them are quasars, extremely distant bodies that emit powerful radio signals.

X RAYS AND GAMMA RAYS

X rays and gamma rays are high-energy forms of radiation that are emitted when stars collide or explode, or when matter falls into a black hole. Space telescopes detect this radiation using tapered metal cylinders to focus the radiation onto detectors. Computers on Earth use data from the detectors to generate pictures.

◄ Operating since 1988, the 2.6-meter (9-ft.) Nordic Optical Telescope (NOT) is on a mountain on the Canary island, La Palma. At an altitude of 2,382m (7,818 ft.), it is above the dusty lower atmosphere and city lights that could interfere with observations at night.

British radio astronomer Martin Ryle (1918–1984) devised a way of using computers to combine the outputs of several normal radio telescopes to give the effect of a very large telescope. His team discovered many new objects, including quasars.

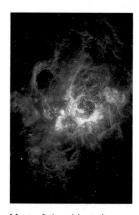

Most of the objects in space are known only by catalog numbers. Nebula NGC 604, shown here, is a cloud of dust and gas in the galaxy M33. The nebula is 1,500 light-years across, and its radiation takes 2,700,000 years to reach the Earth.

A group of amateur astronomers prepare their telescopes for an evening of viewing in the Arizona desert. Even a small, 15cm (6-in.) telescope has a resolving power that is equivalent to being able to see a human being from a distance of 250 mi. (400km). Amateurs such as these provide scientists with important information about meteor showers and other astronomical events.

SEE ALSO PAGES:

244–5 Radiation, 266–7 Lenses and curved mirrors, 416–17 Astronomical telescopes

COLOR

The sensation of sight is the result of light stimulating receptors in our eyes. The color that is seen depends on the mixture of wavelengths present in light.

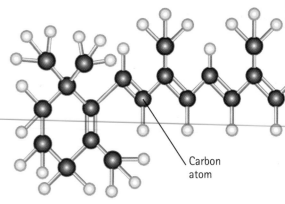

A beta-carotene molecule has a chain of alternating single and double bonds between carbon atoms. This makes beta-carotene absorb blue light and reflect orange.

Carbon atom

Visible light is electromagnetic radiation that has wavelengths in the 390–740-nanometer range. Receptors in the retina of the human eye detect the overall strength of light and the balance of frequencies in light. These receptors produce nerve impulses that the brain interprets as brightness and color. Light at 575 nanometers, for example, gives the sensation of greenish-yellow.

WHITE LIGHT
The light that comes from the sun and from electric lamps is called white light because it does not appear to be colored. When a beam of white light shines onto a prism, it emerges as bands of colored light. These bands make up a spectrum of colors that are arranged in the order red, orange, yellow, green, blue, indigo, and violet. The wavelengths of the colors decrease from red to violet. Mixing these colors of light together gives white light.

DESCRIBING COLORS
Colors are described in terms of three qualities: hue, saturation, and luminosity. Hue refers to the wavelengths present in colored light. Saturation indicates the strength of a color. Red, for example, is a more saturated version of pink. The third quality—luminosity—is the amount of energy in electromagnetic radiation. If the strength of the light falling on this page increases, for example, the luminosity of all the colors on the page will increase.

SOURCES OF COLOR
A few light sources produce colored light directly. The low-pressure sodium lamps that light some roads are an example. An electrical discharge causes the sodium vapor in the lamp to glow orange.

Sunlight and electric light appear white because they contain the full range of visible wavelengths in approximately equal proportions. Most sources of colored light work by removing certain ranges of wavelengths from white light. A stoplight glows red because it has a filter that absorbs all the wavelengths of light from a white lamp except red.

Colored objects absorb certain ranges of frequencies from white light and reflect others. The reflected wavelengths cause the color that is seen. A red tomato, for example, absorbs all the colors in white light except red. Some tomatoes are deep red, and others are red-orange. These differences in hue result from variations in the mixtures of wavelengths reflected by each tomato. A white piece of paper reflects all wavelengths. A black object absorbs all the light that falls on it.

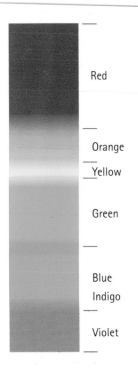

Red

Orange

Yellow

Green

Blue

Indigo

Violet

The visible spectrum is a continuous gradation of colors ranging from red through orange, yellow, green, indigo, and blue to violet.

▼ When viewed in white light, a white object reflects all wavelengths equally. A green object absorbs red, orange, yellow, blue, indigo, and violet light; it reflects green light. A red object absorbs orange, yellow, green, blue, indigo, and violet light; it reflects red light. A black object absorbs all wavelengths equally.

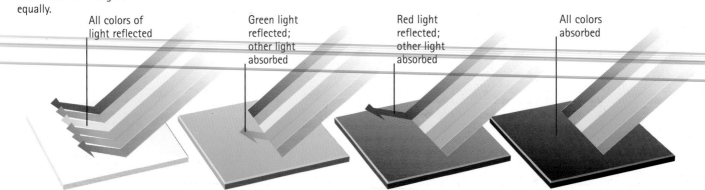

All colors of light reflected

Green light reflected; other light absorbed

Red light reflected; other light absorbed

All colors absorbed

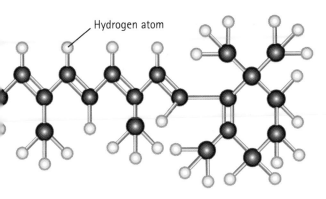

Hydrogen atom

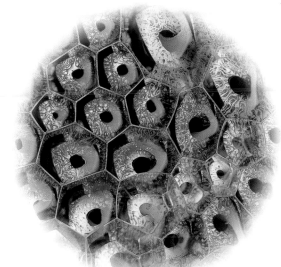

The film of a soap bubble may be thinner than the wavelength of visible light. Some wavelengths of light cancel out when white light reflected from the back of the film interferes with white light reflected from the front of the film. The color of the light depends on the thickness of the film and the angle from which it is viewed.

COLOR AND ELECTRONS

The electrons in atoms and molecules move in orbits that each have a different energy. Light has an energy that depends on its wavelength. When an object absorbs light, electrons jump directly from lower energy levels to higher energy levels. These excited electrons then fall back down to lower energy levels in a series of smaller steps, releasing heat as they do so.

DYES AND PIGMENTS

Many living things contain colored substances. The orange color of carrots, for example, is caused by a natural chemical called beta-carotene. Molecules of such substances often contain chains of carbon atoms that are joined by alternating single and double bonds. The electrons in these bonds absorb visible light as they move between energy levels. Chemists use their knowledge of natural colored substances to produce artificial dyes and pigments for dyeing textiles and for the manufacture of colored plastic, paint, and ink.

OPTICAL EFFECTS

When sunlight falls onto oil on a wet road, the colors of the rainbow are reflected by a thin layer of oil floating on the water. White light reflects from the upper and lower surfaces of the oil layer at the same time. When the reflected rays meet, some of their wavelengths add together and become stronger; others cancel each other out. This results in colored light. The color depends on the thickness of the oil layer and the angle at which it is viewed, so the colors swirl as the oil layer moves around. The same effect causes the coloration of soap bubbles and some insects' wings.

Theater lighting helps create an atmosphere. A typical stage might be equipped with dozens of lights, each with a powerful electric lamp that shines white light through a colored filter and a set of lenses.

A rainbow appears when strong sunlight shines from behind an observer onto rain falling in front of the observer. Raindrops act as prisms and split white light into its component colors. The full spectrum of colors is usually seen, with red on the outside of the bow and violet on the inside. The exact position of a rainbow varies with the position of the observer.

SEE ALSO PAGES:

219 Pigments and dyes, 246–7 The electromagnetic spectrum, 262–3 Reflection and absorption, 264–5 Refraction, 274–5 Color mixing

COLOR MIXING

Mixing colors together produces other colors. There are two different processes: one for mixing colored light and one for mixing colored substances.

Red, green, and blue are the primary colors of light. Mixing those colors together gives white light.

Magenta, yellow, and cyan are the primary colors of substances. Mixing them together gives black.

When a beam of light falls on a white screen, the color that appears depends on the wavelengths of light in the beam. If a beam of light of another color shines on the same spot, the color that appears results from the combination of the colors of light in the two beams. This process is called additive mixing, since two colors of light form a third color by adding their combinations of wavelengths together.

A different process occurs when two colored substances mix together. White light is a combination of all the visible wavelengths of light. When white light falls on a colored powder, for example, the powder absorbs certain wavelengths of light. The color that appears depends on the wavelengths that are reflected. If a second powder of a different color is mixed with the first, the second powder will absorb some of the wavelengths that are not absorbed by the first. The color that results depends on what is left of the white light after both powders have absorbed light. This process is called subtractive mixing, because the mixed color is formed by each colored substance in a mixture taking away a selection of wavelengths from white light.

PRIMARY COLORS

There are two sets of primary colors that can be mixed to make any other color. The primary colors for the additive mixing of light are red, green, and blue. Mixing these three colors in equal amounts gives white light. Mixing pairs of these colors in equal amounts yields the secondary colors: red and green give yellow light; green and blue give cyan light, which is a shade similar to turquoise; and red and blue give magenta light. Any color can be produced by the correct mixture of the three primary colors.

The primary colors for the subtractive mixing of paints and other colored substances are magenta, yellow, and cyan. The secondary colors for subtractive mixing are red, green, and blue.

MAKING PAINT

Paints are coatings that are used to decorate and protect surfaces. A typical gloss paint is made by first mixing natural oils and resins called alkyds. These are the binder materials that gradually harden in air after the paint has been applied. Thinner is added to make the mixture easier to pump through a filter, which removes any solid particles from the blended liquids. Pigment is mixed into the binder blend in a powerful mixer called a disperser. More thinner is added before the blend is pumped through a bead mill. Bead mills have rotating disks and glass beads that grind together and crush pigment particles between them. The final adjustments are made in a holding tank before the paint is packaged in cans or drums.

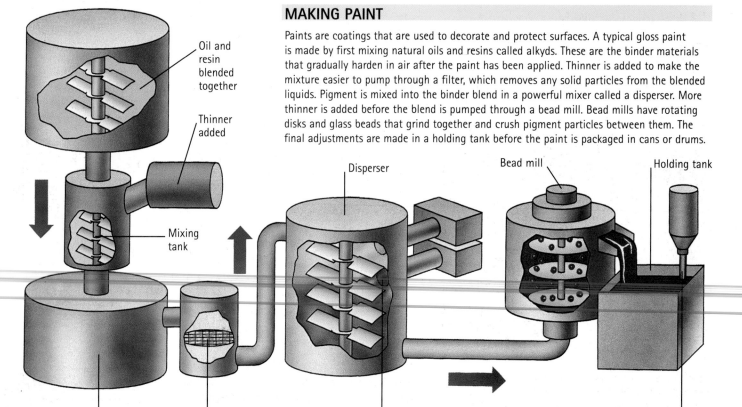

Oil and resin blended together

Thinner added

Mixing tank

Disperser

Bead mill

Holding tank

Settling tank

Filter tank

Pigment and paint thinner added

Final adjustments made

PAINTS AND PIGMENTS

Paints consist of white and colored solid particles, called pigments, mixed into a sticky liquid called a binder. The binder hardens as the paint dries and acts as a protective layer that holds the pigments.

Most pigments are metal compounds. The most widely used pigment is titanium dioxide (TiO_2) which is a white powder. Titanium dioxide is used to make paints, toothpaste, and many other products. Other pigments are strongly colored because they absorb specific wavelengths of light. Yellow and red pigments are often compounds of iron, for example, while blue pigments are compounds of cobalt. An enormous range of colors can be made by combining just a few pigments.

DYES

Dyes are strongly colored, complex organic compounds that are used to give color to products such as textiles and inks. Unlike pigments, dyes dissolve in water and other solvents.

Textiles are colored by dipping them into vats that contain dye solutions. The solutions soak into the fibers, forming chemical bonds with them. Chemicals called mordants are often added to help the dyes to attach firmly to the fibers.

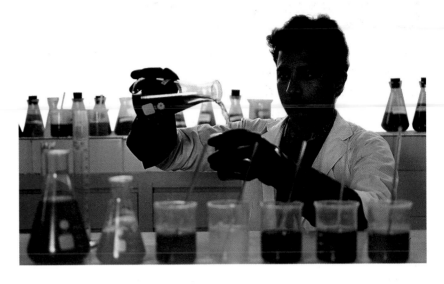

People have used natural dyes for thousands of years. In traditional leather dyeing, as seen here in Morocco, animal hides are soaked with dye solutions in pits in the ground. The hides may be soaked for many days.

COLOR PRINTING

Color pictures printed in books and newspapers seem to contain every color imaginable. However, most printing machines use just three colors—magenta, cyan, and yellow—and black. Magenta absorbs green light, cyan absorbs red, and yellow absorbs blue. Black absorbs all wavelengths. Together, these three colors can produce any other color.

A printed color picture consists of millions of tiny dots of the three colors together with black. Varying the sizes of these dots creates different shades. Seen from a distance, the dots blend together to give the patches of different colors that make up the whole picture.

TELEVISION SCREENS

The picture on a television screen or computer monitor is made up of tiny points of red, green, and blue light. The light comes from phosphors, which are chemicals that glow when they are hit by electrons. Three electron guns at the back of the tube fire beams of electrons at the phosphors. The beams scan across the screen from side to side and from top to bottom. Each beam scans one color of phosphors and varies in strength as it goes. The variations make the phosphors glow more or less strongly, depending on how much of each primary color is needed at each point. From a distance, the viewer's eye blurs the light from the individual phosphors, so the viewer sees the color that results by mixing the light from the three colors of phosphor.

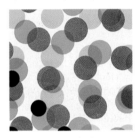

▲ Factories that use dyes often make their own dye mixtures from a standard range of colors. Quality-control testing ensures that the correct shade is achieved every time.

Color printers use groups of magenta, cyan, yellow, and black dots. From the normal reading distance, these dots appear as a blended shade of color.

A Trinitron television screen produces colors by blending light from red, green, and blue phosphor strips. Other types of screens use phosphor dots instead of oblong strips.

SEE ALSO PAGES:

219 Pigments and dyes,
272–3 Color, 370–1
Television and videotape

VISION

Vision is a process by which the brain takes signals from the eyes and converts them into images. Different animals have evolved with different types of vision.

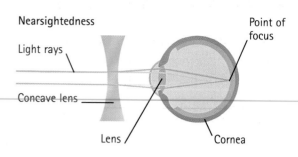

Nearsightedness · Point of focus · Light rays · Concave lens · Lens · Cornea

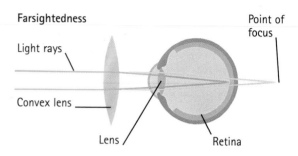

Farsightedness · Point of focus · Light rays · Convex lens · Lens · Retina

Eye defects prevent light from focusing on the retina (yellow rays). Glasses correct vision by helping the eyes' lenses to focus images onto the retina (brown rays).

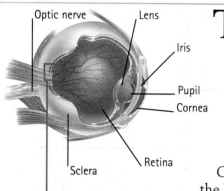

Optic nerve · Lens · Iris · Pupil · Cornea · Retina · Sclera

The human eye works in a similar way to a camera. Behind the transparent cornea is the iris, a ring of muscle that controls the amount of light that enters the eye through the pupil. A lens focuses this light onto the retina at the rear of the eye, adjusting focus for near and distant objects. Cells in the retina send impulses to the brain through the optic nerve.

THE HUMAN RETINA

The retina has millions of light-sensitive cells that are shaped like rods and cones. Rod cells function in dim light, but do not respond to color. Cone cells detect color, but only function in bright light. For this reason, humans cannot see color in dim light. Many other species, including cats and dogs, lack cones. They see the world in black-and-white images.

Cone · Rod · Nerve

Rod and cone cells in the retina send electrical signals through the optic nerve to the brain.

BINOCULAR VISION

Animals that have two eyes are capable of binocular vision. One eye sends slightly different information to the brain than the other eye. By comparing the information, the brain can build up a three-dimensional picture that allows the animal to judge the distance of objects.

EYE DEFECTS

Nearsighted people cannot focus clearly on objects that are far away. Their corneas and lenses focus light rays in front of the retina. One remedy is to wear glasses with concave lenses. An alternative is to use a laser to remove part of the cornea, which alters the focal length of the eye.

Farsighted people cannot focus well on nearby objects. Their corneas and lenses cannot bend the light rays enough to focus them on the retina. The remedy is to wear glasses with convex lenses that assist the cornea and lens.

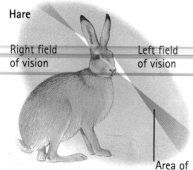

▲ The eyes of flies and many other insects consist of hundreds of separate, simple light receptors.

▼ The field of vision (light blue) shows the zone each eye can see. The zone of binocular vision (dark blue) is where the two fields of vision overlap.

Black and white · Ultraviolet · Visible spectrum · Infrared

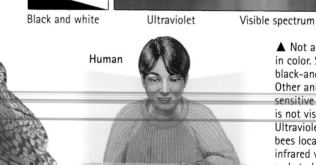

Hare · Right field of vision · Left field of vision · Area of binocular vision

Owl

Human

Hares have two tiny areas of binocular vision.

Owls have a wide area of binocular vision but can only look forward.

Humans have an intermediate area of binocular vision.

▲ Not all animals see in color. Some have only black-and-white vision. Other animals are sensitive to light that is not visible to humans. Ultraviolet vision helps bees locate flowers; infrared vision helps owls to hunt at night.

SEE ALSO PAGES:
114–15 Eyes and seeing,
266–7 Lenses and curved mirrors, 272–3 Color

OPTICAL ILLUSIONS

The brain and the eyes work together to create vision. Optical illusions happen when information from the eyes tricks the brain into seeing an unreal image.

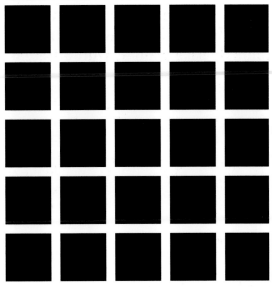

This pattern is known as Herman's grid. The contrast between the black squares and the white lines tricks the brain into seeing fuzzy gray shapes where the lines cross.

The lithograph *Belvedere* was created in 1958 by Dutch artist Maurits Escher (1898–1972). He specialized in producing optical illusions as works of art. For example, the top floor of the building has a totally different perspective from the bottom half, and the two parts are linked by columns that could not exist in a real building.

When the brain processes nerve impulses from the eyes, it often has to jump to conclusions to make sensible images from the information it receives. When a person looks into a mirror, for example, their brain forms an image of their face that appears to be behind the mirror. An optical illusion happens when the brain jumps to the wrong conclusion and builds a false image.

VISUAL ILLUSIONS

If you stare at an orange patch for a while and then look at a white sheet of paper, you will see a blue patch where the orange one had been. Blue and orange are complementary colors. This means that orange light contains all the wavelengths of white light except blue. By staring at the orange patch, cone cells in part of the retina slowly become used to orange light. When white light falls on that part of the retina again, the cone cells in that area are more sensitive to wavelengths that are not in orange light. This makes white light seem blue.

In another effect, a row of lamps that light in sequence give the impression of a single lit bulb moving along the row. This effect is used to display moving text in advertisements and digital newscasts.

PUZZLING IMAGES

Artists use perspective to create the illusion of solid objects in flat images. They draw lines in the shape of an upside-down V, for example, to represent a railroad track stretching into the distance, or paint a small mountain next to a large house to make the mountain seem farther away. Some artists use these techniques to make the brain see false perspectives.

Optical illusions can also happen when the brain misinterprets two-dimensional images. When a picture shows squares of different sizes, the brain sees smaller squares as being farther away than larger ones, even though they are not.

MIRAGES

Mirages are optical illusions that form in hot weather. They happen when sunlight heats the ground strongly. The layer of air directly above the ground becomes hot and less dense. This makes its refractive index less than that of the cooler air above it. The change in refractive index with height creates a lens effect. Light rays refract up, so the layer of air near the ground behaves like a mirror. An observer sees a reflection of the sky that resembles water. As the observer moves toward the water, the reflection also moves, so the observer never reaches the mirage.

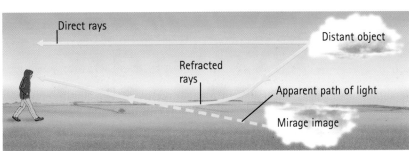

▲ In this mirage, the sky and distant mountains reflect to give an illusion of islands in a lake. In fact, the lake is hot sand.

SEE ALSO PAGES:
108–9 The brain and nervous system, 114–15 Eyes and seeing

277

PHOTOGRAPHY AND FILM

Photography records images. Conventional cameras record images on light-sensitive, or photosensitive, film. Digital cameras store image data in computers.

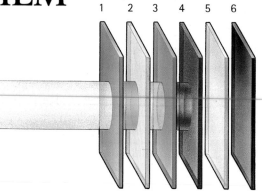

The six layers of color film: layer 1 records blue light; 2 absorbs excess blue light; 3 records green light; 4 records red light; 5 is the plastic base; 6 is an opaque coating.

In 1826, French physicist Joseph Niépce (1765–1833) used bitumen-coated pewter plates to take the first-ever photographs.

British physicist William Fox Talbot (1800–1877) invented the negative-and-positive process that is still in use today.

In the early 1880s, U.S. inventor George Eastman (1854–1932) developed flexible-roll films to replace the glass plates that had been used earlier.

As early as 1515, Italian artist, engineer, and scientist Leonardo da Vinci (1452–1519) described how an image could be made on the wall of a darkened room by letting light through a tiny hole in the opposite wall. This arrangement was called a camera obscura, meaning "dark chamber" in Latin. The image could be recorded by sketching over it by hand.

THE FIRST PHOTOGRAPHS

During the 1820s, Joseph Niépce took the first photographs by placing flat, bitumen-coated pewter plates on the wall of a camera obscura. Although he would expose the plates to light for eight hours or more, the images were not clear.

In 1837, French painter Louis Daguerre (1789–1851) recorded images on metal sheets coated with silver iodide, a photosensitive chemical. He would then treat these images, called daguerreotypes, with mercury vapor and common salt. Although mercury helped to prevent them from darkening in light, daguerreotypes had to be kept behind glass and viewed from a certain angle to see a clear image.

NEGATIVES AND POSITIVES

In 1841, William Talbot patented a process that steadily replaced Daguerre's method. Talbot's method used paper coated with silver iodide, and a basic form of camera. The photographer exposed the paper to light for around 30 seconds. The paper was developed by washing it with chemical solutions. Silver iodide crystals that had been exposed to light turned black, and unexposed crystals washed away. The image is called a negative because bright parts of the original scene appeared dark. Several positive prints of each photograph could be made by shining light through the negative onto photosensitive paper.

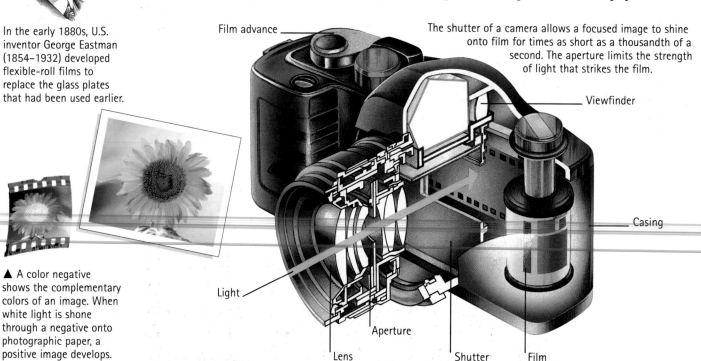

Film advance

The shutter of a camera allows a focused image to shine onto film for times as short as a thousandth of a second. The aperture limits the strength of light that strikes the film.

Viewfinder

Casing

▲ A color negative shows the complementary colors of an image. When white light is shone through a negative onto photographic paper, a positive image develops.

Light

Aperture

Lens

Shutter

Film

MODERN PHOTOGRAPHY

In 1889, the American George Eastman introduced roll film for use in small, hand-held cameras. Eastman's film consisted of a flexible strip of celluloid coated with a mixture of gelatin and silver bromide crystals. Winding the strip through the camera allowed several images to fit onto one roll. Enlarged positive images could be produced on specially treated, stiff paper.

By the early 1900s, there were many professional photographers; by the 1920s, amateur photography was also becoming popular. Flashbulbs and films for color transparencies were introduced in the 1930s. The first films for making color prints were launched in 1941. By the 1980s, cameras could automatically focus the lens and expose the film to the correct amount of light. Photographic laboratories now use machines that develop film and print color photographs of any size.

MOTION PICTURES

Motion pictures, or movies, for projection in theaters are recorded on cinefilm. A cinecamera takes 24 separate pictures every second on a long strip of film. The film is developed to produce transparent positive images. At the theater, the film passes through a projector, stopping at each image for ¼ of a second. A powerful light shines through the film, and lenses focus a large image onto the screen.

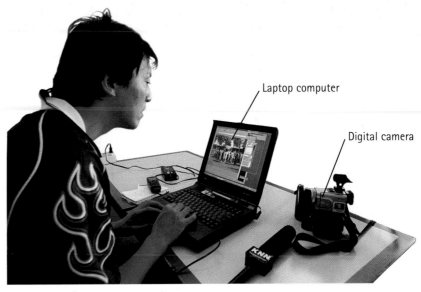

Laptop computer

Digital camera

DIGITAL CAMERAS

Digital cameras have a lens system and aperture just like ordinary cameras. Instead of film, they use a photosensitive plate made of semiconducting materials to detect images. Electronic circuits scan the plate and convert the information into a binary digital code. A computer memory chip records the data. This can then be passed to a larger computer that has software to adjust the colors and contrast of each image. Some can even move parts of an image around and add special effects, such as distortion and coloring. A printer can reproduce the image on any material— from paper to T-shirts.

Toshi Kaqnda created a TV station that broadcasts on the Internet. He uses a laptop computer to edit images from a digital camera before sending them to his file server in Japan for inclusion in the latest program. This technique provides news that is just a few minutes old when broadcast.

▲ A digital camera looks similar to a conventional camera. The number of separate photos it can take depends on the size of its memory chip.

▲ The film for a typical feature movie is around 1.6 mi. (2.5km) long. Each frame stays on the screen for only ¹⁄₂₄ of a second. The human eye blurs these frames into a smoothly moving image.

▶ The Futurescope at Poitiers, France, has a screen that surrounds the audience. Movies can be shown as separate scenes side by side or as one gigantic image.

SEE ALSO PAGES:

260–1 Light, 266–7 Lenses and curved mirrors, 360–1 Conductors, 376–7 Computers

SOURCES OF LIGHT

Light sources convert various forms of energy into light energy. The most common energy sources are electricity and heat from burning fuel.

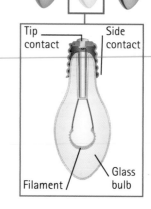

▲ Each bulb in a string of festive lights is a small version of a filament lamp.

◄ A modern filament lamp contains a coil of fine tungsten wire called a filament that glows when it carries a current. The first usable filament lamp was made by inventor Thomas Edison in 1879. It had a carbon filament.

This painting shows a group of diners in the early 1900s, illuminated by an oil lamp and candles.

If an object is heated to around 650°C (1,200°F) and does not burn, it will give off a dull, red light. As the temperature rises, the light becomes brighter and changes color from red to orange and to yellow. Above 1,250°C (2,300°F), objects give off white, incandescent, light. Many types of lamps produce light by heating something until it becomes incandescent.

CANDLES, OIL, AND GAS LAMPS

Candles use burning wax as a source of heat energy. In addition to heat, wax produces water, oxides of carbon, and carbon soot as it burns. The heat of the flame makes the carbon soot glow bright yellow. Oil lamps and gas lamps also produce a yellowish light from a luminous flame.

More efficient gas lamps burn premixed gas and air. The flame is hotter than in a simple gas lamp but contains no soot, so it does not glow. Instead, the flame heats a mantle. Mantles are hollow mesh thimbles made from cerium and thorium salts. They emit brilliant white light when heated.

Energy-efficient bulbs use one fifth the electricity used by a filament lamp to produce as much light.

FILAMENT LAMPS

Ordinary lightbulbs contain a fine, coiled wire, called a filament, that is made from tungsten. An electric current passes through the filament and heats it to over 1,800°C (3,200°F). At this temperature, it emits white light. Tungsten is used because it does not melt below 3,410°C (6,170°F) It has the highest melting point of all the elements. Tungsten would burn in air at 1,800°C, so the filament has to be enclosed in a glass bulb with a gas that will not react with tungsten. This gas is usually argon. Less than one fifth of the electricity used by a filament lamp is turned into light. The rest is lost as heat.

DISCHARGE TUBES

Discharge tubes contain low-pressure gas in a glass tube. When an electrical current passes through the gas, its atoms split into ions and electrons. They produce light as the current flows. Because they produce little heat, discharge tubes are much more

HOW STROBOSCOPIC LIGHTS WORK

Stroboscopic lamps produce rapid flashes of brilliant light. These lamps work in the same way as photographic flashguns. An electric power supply produces high-voltage energy that is stored in a capacitor. A trigger discharges the energy into a gas-filled flashtube, which emits an intense pulse of light that lasts only a few thousandths of a second.

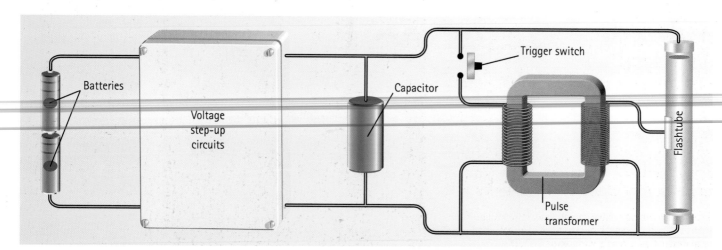

efficient light sources than filament lamps. Some discharge tubes use sodium vapor as the filler gas. Low-pressure sodium lamps produce an intense orange light that is used for lighting roads. Mercury-vapor lamps emit a purple-green light, and the coiled lights of advertising signs are filled with neon gas that emits a red glow.

Fluorescent tubes are discharge tubes that contain a mixture of argon gas and mercury vapor. When an electrical current passes through this mixture, it gives off ultraviolet light. A coating on the inside of the tube absorbs this light and gives off a white light similar to daylight.

ARC LAMPS AND FLASHLAMPS

The arc light, one of the most powerful light sources known, was invented in the 1800s before the filament lamp. It consists of two carbon rods connected to an electricity supply. A continuous spark, called an arc, flashes between the ends of the two rods. The temperature is over 5,000°F (9,000°F), enough to vaporize some of the carbon. Carbon atoms in the arc emit a dazzling white light.

Arc lamps were once used in movie projectors and searchlights. They have now been replaced by high-pressure discharge tubes that contain xenon or krypton gas and are extremely efficient. Smaller versions of this type of lamp are used in camera flash units.

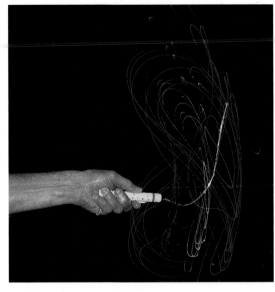

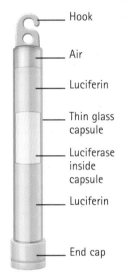

◄ A light wand consists of a battery and a small bulb attached to a bunch of optical fibers. Light reflects along the inside walls of the fibers and emerges from their ends.

- Hook
- Air
- Luciferin
- Thin glass capsule
- Luciferase inside capsule
- Luciferin
- End cap

▲ The chemicals inside a light stick mix when the plastic stick is bent and a glass capsule inside it breaks. The chemicals glow as they react.

CHEMICAL LIGHTS

Some plants and animals emit light by a process called bioluminescence. When the enzyme luciferase is present, a substance called luciferin reacts with oxygen, emitting light in the process. Different organisms have different types of luciferin that can glow pale red, yellow, green, or blue. Deep-sea anglerfish attract prey with a glowing bait that hangs over their mouths. Fireflies emit a yellowish light to attract mates. Chemists have now made synthetic luciferin-type compounds for use with luciferase in chemiluminescent light sticks.

▼ Flashlight fish live in dark ocean depths. They use bioluminescence to attract and dazzle prey.

Sparks flash out as molten metal pours into a mold. Each spark consists of a speck of hot metal that becomes incandescent as it reacts with oxygen in the air.

SEE ALSO PAGES:

180 Noble gases, 260–1 Light, 340–1 Electrical circuits

LIGHT ENERGY

Light energy is a form of electromagnetic radiation. Depending on circumstances, light can behave like a wave or like a stream of particles.

When artists and scientists want to describe an object, many of them start with its appearance. What they see depends on how the object reflects light and how their eyes detect that light. Obviously, it is impossible to look at light in the same way. Instead, artists take note of the way that light illuminates objects, and scientists look at how light affects the substances that come into contact with it. When they do this, they find that light sometimes behaves in a similar way to waves on a pond. On other occasions, light affects matter as if it were a stream of particles.

▲ A solar cell consists of two wafers of silicon semiconductor that are sandwiched between two electrical contacts. The layers have slightly different compositions, and sunlight makes electrons jump from one layer into the other. These electrons flow out of the cell through one electrical contact. Other electrons flow into the cell through the other contact and a current starts to flow.

THE PHOTOELECTRIC EFFECT
Photovoltaic cells, or solar cells, use the photoelectric effect to generate electricity from sunlight. The photoelectric effect occurs when visible light or ultraviolet radiation falls on the surface of certain materials. The light or radiation ejects electrons from the material, and can be measured by an electrical meter.

A curious detail of the photoelectric effect is that it only works with light that has a frequency above a certain value. Below that value, no electrons are emitted, no matter how strong the light that shines on the material. The minimum frequency for the photoelectric effect to happen depends on the type of material.

A single solar cell develops around 0.5 volts. The current available depends on the area of the cell. A solar cell 10 cm (4 in.) in diameter can supply a current of about 1.5 amps in bright sunlight. The solar cells in the panels pictured here are wired in series to provide greater voltage, and in parallel to give a stronger current.

Light energy spreads out from its source like the water ripples that spread out when a stone falls into a pond. This is an example of the wave-like behavior of light.

PHOTONS—LIGHT AS PARTICLES
In 1905, German-born U.S. physicist Albert Einstein (1879–1955) suggested an explanation for the photoelectric effect. His explanation was based on light behaving as if it were a stream of particles.

Electrons are held within any substance by their attraction to the nuclei within that substance. They need a shot of energy to break free from that attraction, just as a ball needs a kick to get up a hill. In the photoelectric effect, that kick of energy comes from light. Einstein proposed that light is a stream of packages of energy, called photons. The energy of each photon depends on its frequency. If the frequency of light is too low, the kick that a photon can give an electron is too weak, so the electrons cannot escape. Above a certain frequency, each photon has enough energy to eject electrons, as happens in the photoelectric effect.

LIGHT AS WAVES
Until Einstein suggested that light was made up of packages of energy, physicists had described light as being a type of wave motion. They came to this conclusion because of experiments that showed light behaving like sound waves or water waves.

In 1873, British physicist James Clerk Maxwell (1831–1879) drew up equations that described light as a combination of electric and magnetic fields that vibrate at right angles to each other, and also at right angles to the direction of travel of light.

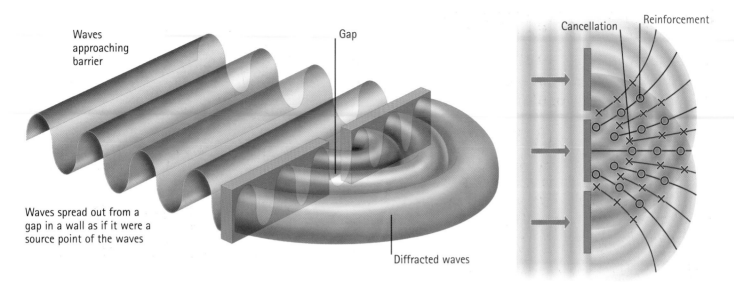

Waves approaching barrier

Gap

Waves spread out from a gap in a wall as if it were a source point of the waves

Diffracted waves

Cancellation   Reinforcement

DIFFRACTION

When water waves hit a wall with a small gap, waves spread out from that gap in a series of ever-widening circles, just as if the gap itself were a source of waves. This spreading from a gap is called diffraction. Sound waves also diffract. If a person walks past a house where music is playing through an open window, the bass notes are heard first as the person approaches the window. The highest treble notes can only be heard near the window because their high-frequency sound waves diffract less well. When light shines through a slit, it will not spread out unless the slit's width is similar to the light's wavelength.

INTERFERENCE

When water waves diffract through two side-by-side gaps, the gaps act as separate wave sources that are in step with each other. As the waves from these separate sources spread out, they interfere with each other. Where the crest of one wave meets the trough of another, the two waves cancel each other out, and the surface of the water remains calm. When two crests or two troughs meet, the result is an even larger crest or trough.

When light of a single wavelength shines through two tiny slits in a screen, it spreads out from the two slits and forms an interference pattern. Placing a screen in this pattern shows a series of light and dark lines where light waves reinforce each other in some places and cancel each other out in others. This is an example of light's wave-like behavior.

PARTICLES AS WAVES

Shortly after Einstein proposed that light could behave as a particle, French physicist Louis de Broglie (1892–1987) suggested that the opposite could be true: that particles could behave like waves. He calculated that only the lightest particles would have wavelengths that could be tested in experiments. In 1924, he fired a beam of electrons at a crystal. The electrons diffracted through gaps between the atoms in the crystal, and left an interference pattern on a photographic plate. The electrons had behaved as waves.

Gaps in a barrier act as new sources of waves. The waves from different gaps interfere with each other as they meet. This diagram shows how the wave peaks reinforce each other.

▲ This solar-powered lighthouse buoy has four solar panels covered with photovoltaic cells. The cells charge a battery that powers the light at night.

◄ It is possible that future spaceships will have enormous sails. Photons from nearby stars will hit the sails and drive the ships forward.

SEE ALSO PAGES:

244–5 Radiation, 344–5 Electromagnetism, 458–9 Renewable energy

THE SPEED OF LIGHT

Light travels through a vacuum in straight lines at a constant speed of around 186,000 miles (300,000km) per second. Nothing can travel faster than this speed.

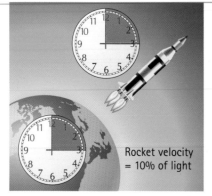
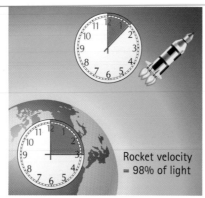

Rocket velocity = 10% of light

Rocket velocity = 98% of light

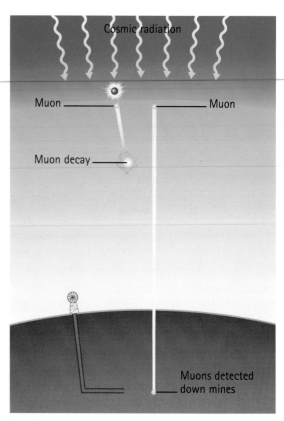

Strange things happen close to the speed of light. To an observer on the Earth, a rocket traveling at nearly the speed of light would appear to have shrunk in the direction of flight, and a clock on the craft would seem to move slowly. A passenger on the rocket would not be aware of these changes.

The mass of an object increases rapidly as its speed approaches that of light. Einstein's equations predict that the mass of any object would become infinitely large at the speed of light. This makes it impossible to reach the speed of light, so faster-than-light craft will probably only ever exist in science fiction.

Light travels 186,281 mi. (299,792km) in one second through a vacuum. This speed has the symbol c. At this speed, light takes about eight minutes to travel the 93 million mi. (150 million km) from the sun to the Earth, and 4.3 years from the nearest star, Proxima Centauri.

EINSTEIN AND RELATIVITY

Einstein produced theories of relativity that predict strange effects near the speed of light. He did this by considering what he called "inertial frames of reference."

Imagine a fly buzzing forward along a train at 2 meters per second. If the train were traveling at 100 meters per second, trackside observers would measure the fly's speed as 102 meters per second in their inertial frame of reference, while observers on the train would measure its speed as 2 meters per second in the inertial frame of reference of the train. At these speeds, the frames of reference tally.

Cosmic rays produce unstable particles, called muons, that travel near the speed of light. They would decay after only about 600 meters (1,900 ft.), but, in fact, they reach deep underground because relativity slows their decay.

Things would change if the train could travel at 1 meter per second slower than the speed of light. Observers in the frame of reference of the train would still see the fly moving forward at 2 meters per second. Observers by the track, however, would not see the fly moving at 1 meter per second faster than the speed of light. In fact, many things would seem strange. The fly and the train would appear squashed to a fraction of their length, and the fly would be moving only fractionally faster than the train—certainly slower than the speed of light.

Even at half the speed of light, a 100-meter-long train with a mass of 1,000 tons would seem to trackside observers to be only 87 meters long but 150 tons heavier. They would also say that the clocks on the train were running slow. The effects of relativity are bizarre, but they have all been seen for small particles.

SEE ALSO PAGE:

260–1 Light, 426–7 Time, 430–1 Space, time, and relativity

POLARIZATION

Polarized light consists of photons whose electric fields vibrate in one direction only. It is produced by passing normal, unpolarized light through a polarizing filter.

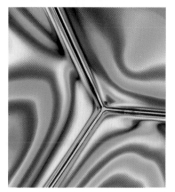

Areas of weakness in a plastic dish show up as colored stress patterns when viewed through crossed polarizers.

▲ Polarizing sunglasses cut glare by blocking the polarized light reflected by the water's surface.

Light consists of photons, packages of electromagnetic energy. They have electric and magnetic fields that vibrate at right angles to the direction of travel of light. In normal light, the electric fields of the photons vibrate in all possible directions around the direction of travel. In polarized light, more photons have fields that vibrate in one particular direction than in any other.

POLARIZING LIGHT

Ordinary sunlight and the light from lamps is unpolarized. It can be polarized by passing it through a polarizing filter. These filters are usually thin sheets of plastic that have been stretched in one direction so that crystals in the film are aligned in the direction of the stretch. The film lets past only photons whose electric fields vibrate in the direction set by the crystals. They absorb all other photons.

Light can also become polarized by reflection. Sunlight that reflects off water is partly polarized. This is because water reflects horizontally polarized photons much more efficiently than it reflects others. Polarizing sunglasses cut glare by blocking photons that are horizontally polarized and letting other photons pass.

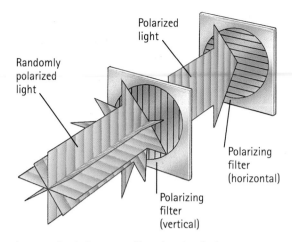

In crossed polarizers, one filter absorbs all photons apart from those whose electric fields vibrate in one direction. The second filter blocks those photons, so no light passes.

USES OF POLARIZED LIGHT

Polarized light can reveal details that are invisible in ordinary light. In most cases, two polarizing filters are used. Light is polarized in one direction by the first filter. The second filter is then turned until no light passes through it. This is when the filters polarize at right angles to each other and are said to be crossed polarizers.

Certain transparent objects twist the direction of polarization of light that passes through them. When this happens, the light is no longer completely blocked by the filter closer to the eye. Stressed or damaged areas of plastic and glass twist light in this way, so crossed polarizers can highlight where damage has occurred. Since many natural substances rotate the polarization of light, crossed polarizers attached to microscopes can show extra detail in microscopic organisms.

▲ Researchers have tested these goggles by heating them. They appear unaffected in normal light. But when placed between crossed polarizers (right), it becomes clear that the goggles have become severely weakened by the formation of bubbles inside the plastic. Although white light was used to illuminate the sample, colors appear because the stressed plastic rotates the light's polarization by different amounts according to frequency.

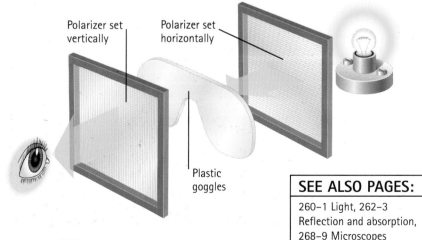

Polarizer set vertically

Polarizer set horizontally

Plastic goggles

SEE ALSO PAGES:

260-1 Light, 262-3 Reflection and absorption, 268-9 Microscopes

LASERS AND HOLOGRAMS

Lasers are devices that produce intense beams of light. The electromagnetic radiation in laser light has a single wavelength, and the waves all vibrate in step.

In 1960, U.S. physicist Theodore Maiman (1927–) built the first working laser from a cylinder of artificial ruby.

Laser light

Ordinary light

Unlike ordinary light, photons of laser light all have the same frequency and are synchronized.

The letters that make up the word "laser" stand for light amplification by stimulated emission of radiation. An atom gives out a photon of light if an electron in the atom falls from a higher energy level, or excited state, to a lower one. In most cases, excited electrons give off light in this way of their own accord. This is called spontaneous emission. In a few cases, the properties of the excited state prevent electrons from giving off light unless they are triggered by another photon of light. This process is called stimulated emission. A stimulated photon has the same wavelength as the photon that triggered its emission, and the two photons vibrate in step. Photons that have the same wavelength and vibrate in step are said to be coherent. It is the coherency of laser light that prevents a laser beam from spreading and makes it so intense.

TYPES OF LASERS

All lasers have two things in common. They contain a material that can be pumped to an excited state but that does not emit light spontaneously. They also have a source of light or electrical energy to pump that material to an excited state.

A computer-controlled laser moves across a stack of fabric. The beam fires downward and cuts out the shapes that are later stitched together to make garments.

The first laser, built in 1960, was a ruby laser. This type of laser contains a rod of synthetic ruby with mirrored ends. Bursts of white light from a coiled flashtube around the rod excite atoms in the ruby. Once one of the excited atoms manages to emit a photon spontaneously, that photon stimulates other excited atoms to emit light as it reflects back and forth between mirrors mounted at the ends of the rod. One of the end mirrors is half-silvered so the laser beam can undergo multiple reflections inside the tube and escape.

Other lasers use gas mixtures and dye solutions instead of ruby. In gas lasers, an electrical discharge provides energy to excite the gas atoms and start the laser action.

▶ The first laser produced light from a synthetic ruby. The ruby takes in ordinary light from a flashtube and emits it as laser light.

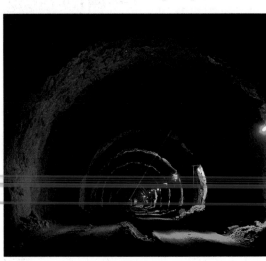

▲ Laser beams are extremely thin and straight. Here a laser beam is being used to check the accuracy of the direction of a long tunnel during its construction.

Laser beam

Totally reflecting mirror

Artificial ruby rod

Coiled flashtube provides the energy

Semisilvered mirror

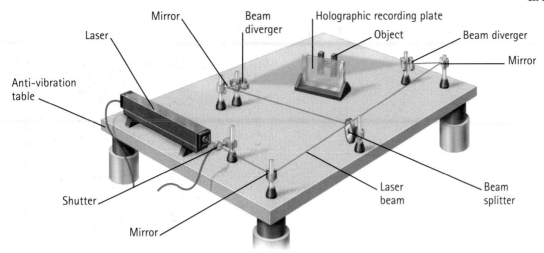

Mirror • Beam diverger • Holographic recording plate • Object • Beam diverger • Mirror • Laser • Anti-vibration table • Shutter • Mirror • Laser beam • Beam splitter

A hologram is usually recorded in a completely dark room. A gas laser emits a continuous beam of pure light. Mirrors split the beam, and diverging lenses form cones of light from each beam. The reference beam shines onto a holographic plate, while the object beam illuminates the object. The object scatters light onto the plate, which interferes with the reference beam and produces a hologram.

Helium–neon gas lasers produce red light, and argon laser light is green. Carbon-dioxide lasers produce infrared radiation. Dye lasers can be tuned to different frequencies by changing the dye mixture. The latest developments are lasers made from layers of semiconducting materials.

USES OF LASERS

A laser beam can travel many miles without spreading and becoming weaker. For this reason, range-finding machines use lasers to measure great distances by timing reflected pulses of light. Guidance systems use lasers to keep missiles and tunneling machinery on course.

Laser light is so concentrated that its energy can cut through paper, cloth, wood, and even metal. Surgeons use lasers to cut through tissue with great accuracy. The beam seals small blood vessels around the wound and limits bleeding.

Bar-code readers and CD players use laser beams to carry information as they scan across objects. Lasers send pulses of information down optical fibers in telecommunications systems.

HOLOGRAMS

Holography uses interference between laser beams to record three-dimensional images of solid objects on photographic film. To record a hologram, a laser beam is first split into two beams. One beam illuminates the object; this scatters light onto the film. The second beam goes directly to the film. The two beams of light interfere where they meet at the photosensitive layer in the film.

When developed and then viewed in daylight, a holographic plate looks like a window through which an object can be seen. This type of hologram is used on credit cards and some banknotes. When illuminated with laser light, a holographic plate produces a fully three-dimensional image. It is possible to walk around some holograms and view them from all angles.

Holography can be used to store vast quantities of information conveniently in pages. The pages of the image are turned by changing the angle at which the reading laser shines onto the holographic plate.

Hungarian-born physicist Dennis Gabor (1906–1979) developed the theory of holography in Britain in the 1940s. He had to wait for the invention of lasers to make his idea work.

This three-dimensional hologram is viewed by shining laser light onto a flat holographic plate.

This photograph shows the equipment needed to produce a hologram. Compare it to the drawing at the top of the page. You will see the laser, the diverging lenses, the rays of light, and the holographic plate.

SEE ALSO PAGES:

282–3 Light energy, 366–7 Telecommunications, 380–1 Information technology

FACTS AND FIGURES

THE SUN

Distance from Earth	149,503,000 km
Diameter	1,400,000 km (110 x Earth)
Mass	1.99 x 10³⁰ kg (330,000 x Earth)
Surface gravity	38 x Earth
Composition	H 71%, He 27%, minute traces of other elements.

The **core** is within one fourth of the sun's total radius. Its temperature of nearly 16 million K results from the thermonuclear reactions that convert hydrogen into helium.

The **photosphere** is the sun's visible surface, which emits heat and light. Its temperature is 5,500 K.

The **chromosphere** lies outside the photosphere and is 10,000 km thick. Its temperature range is 4,000–50,000 K.

The **corona** is the outer part of the sun's atmosphere. It is 70,000 km thick, and its temperature is around 200,000 K.

The **solar wind**, consisting mostly of protons and electrons, flows into space from the upper part of the corona.

ELECTROMAGNETIC RADIATION

Broadcast radio		*low frequency*
Television		
Microwaves		
Radar		
Infrared radiation		
Visible light	Red	
	Orange	
	Yellow	
	Green	
	Blue	
	Indigo	
	Violet	
Ultraviolet radiation		
X rays		
Gamma rays		*high frequency*

WAVE–PARTICLE DUALITY

Electromagnetic radiation has properties of both waves and particles. Particles also have wave properties—high-speed electrons have shorter wavelengths than light. Electron microscopes have greater magnifications than optical microscopes.

LIGHT AND MEDIA

Light can travel through a vacuum or through media such as air, glass, and water. A clear image of an object can be seen through a **transparent** medium. Light passes through a **translucent** medium, but a clear image of an object cannot be seen due to scattering. Light cannot pass through **opaque** substances.

OPTICS

Light waves travel in straight lines unless forced to deviate:

Diffraction is the spreading of waves as they pass through a narrow gap.

Dispersion causes white light to split into different colors during refraction.

Interference is the interaction of separate waves to give regions of high and low amplitude through mutual reinforcement and cancellation.

Reflection is the rebounding of light from a shiny surface or the boundary between two transparent media.

Refraction is the bending of the path of light as it moves across the boundary between two transparent media.

HEAT TRANSFER

Heat moves spontaneously from regions of higher temperature to regions of lower temperature. There are three mechanisms of heat transfer:

Conduction passes heat through a solid as vibrating particles bump into their neighbors. The solid itself does not move.

Convection moves heat through a fluid as changes in the fluid's density cause it to circulate in currents.

Radiation carries heat through a vacuum in the form of infrared light.

HEAT CAPACITY

The specific heat capacity of a substance is the energy required to increase the temperature of one kilogram of the substance by one kelvin.

Water	4,200 $(Jkg^{-1}K^{-1})$
Aluminum	880
Iron	460
Lead	130
Glass	600

MELTING AND BOILING POINTS

The **melting point** (mp) of a substance is the temperature at which it changes from the solid to the liquid state. It is the same as the freezing point of the substance.

The **boiling point** (bp) of a substance is the upper fixed temperature at which it changes from liquid to gas. This phase change happens more slowly at lower temperatures by evaporation.

	mp (°C)	bp (°C)
Water	0	100
Aluminum	660	2,450
Lead	327	1,750
Oxygen	–219	–183
Helium	–270	–269
Ethanol	–114	78

KEY INVENTIONS

A.D.	
350	Gas lighting using marsh gas
1000	Camera obscura
1010	Optical lens
1550	Glass lens for a camera obscura
1590	Compound microscope
1608	Refracting telescope
1641	Liquid-in-glass thermometer
1663	Reflecting telescope
1714	Mercury thermometer and the Fahrenheit temperature scale
1758	Achromatic lenses
1784	Bifocal spectacles
1792	Gas lighting using coal gas
1808	Practical arc lamp
1821	Modern hot-air central heating
1826	First photograph taken
1839	Calotype photography
1848	Kelvin temperature scale and the concept of absolute zero
1850	Photomicroscopy
1851	Mechanical refrigerator
1857	Silvered-glass mirror
1859	Battery-powered electric lamp
1878	Arc lamp for street lighting
1885	Incandescent gas mantle
1890	Telephoto camera lens
1892	Mercury-vapor lamp
1898	Osmium lamp filament
1899	Focusing camera lens
1900	Gas-fired room heater
1906	Color film for movies
1906	Tungsten filament lightbulb
1912	Ultraviolet microscope
1912	Modern color film
1915	Gas-filled tungsten-filament lamp
1919	Flash photography
1920	Neon lighting
1932	Radio astronomy
1935	Fluorescent lighting
1935	Sodium-vapor lamp
1935	Color transparency film
1936	Single-lens reflex camera
1938	Electron microscope
1945	Microwave oven
1951	Field ion microscope
1954	Solar-powered battery
1955	Fiber optics
1960	First practical laser
1966	Fiber-optic telephone cable
1974	Holographic electron microscope
1978	Scanning electron microscope
1981	Scanning tunneling microscope
1984	X-ray laser
1985	Atomic force microscope
1986	Disposable camera
1990	Hubble Space Telescope placed in Earth orbit
1991	Nuclear fusion briefly achieved
1995	X-ray telescope in Earth orbit

Possible future developments will focus on using hydrogen as a pollution-free fuel and developing nuclear fusion as a clean nuclear power source.

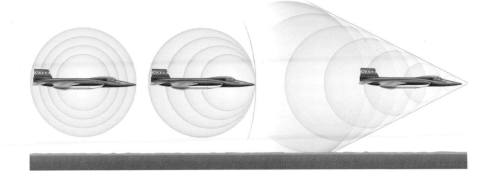

CHAPTER 7

FORCES AND MOVEMENT

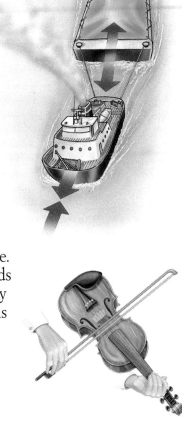

Forces are the pushes, pulls, and twists that make things move faster or slower, change direction, or change shape. Bicyclists push on pedals to make their bikes move; birds pull worms out of the ground, and cooks roll lumps of pastry into flat sheets. The force from a car's engine turns its wheels and makes the car accelerate; to slow down, friction in the brakes provides a force that decelerates the car.

The force of gravity makes objects fall toward the ground. Centripetal force makes the planets and satellites move in orbits and helps washing machines spin water out of wet clothes. Turning forces spin the shafts of motors and engines. They also twist doorknobs and tighten screws. Forces are often present even when nothing seems to be happening. A balanced seesaw does not move because there are two equal turning forces acting against one another.

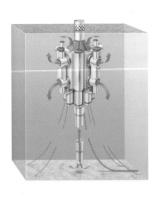

When forces move, work is done as energy changes from one form to another. Muscles do work when a person lifts a box onto a shelf. The body converts chemical energy from food into potential energy as the box is lifted. The greater the rate of work, the greater the power. Forces, work, and energy are what make things happen in the universe.

FORCE

A force is a push or a pull that causes an object to accelerate, slow down, or change shape. Forces can work in the same direction or against each other.

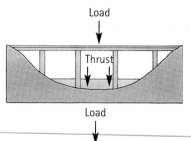

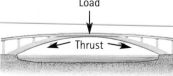

The load on a beam bridge is supported by vertical columns.

The load on an arch is carried by foundations on the riverbanks.

Cheetahs are the fastest ground animals, capable of bursts of speed estimated at around 70 mph (110kph) when hunting. The cheetah's legs muscles provide the force that accelerates them forward.

Distance

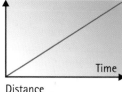

Time

Distance

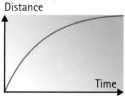

Time

▲ The upper plot shows the distance covered against time for an object moving at constant speed. The speed is the gradient of the line. The lower plot is for an object that is decelerating. An upward curve would indicate an accelerating object.

The tension in stretched elastic, the pull of gravity on a raindrop, and the thrust of a jet engine are all examples of force. A force is an influence that can make an object start to move, slow down, change direction, or change shape.

FORCE AND ACCELERATION

Acceleration is the most obvious effect of force. Drop a ball from a height and the force of gravity will make it move faster and faster toward the ground. The ball accelerates because the force is acting downward in the same direction as its motion. Throw a ball straight up into the air and the same force of gravity will make it move slower and slower. This effect is called deceleration, which is negative acceleration. The ball decelerates because the force of gravity acts in the opposite direction to its motion.

Increasing the force on an object will increase its acceleration. The relationship between acceleration, force, and mass is: *force = mass x acceleration.*

Forces can cancel one another out. A stone falling through water will reach a speed where the downward force of its weight is equal to the upward force caused by friction between the stone and water. The two forces cancel, so there is no acceleration. The speed remains constant.

PAIRS OF FORCES

Forces always occur in pairs. When a skier pushes backward with ski poles, for example, the backward force on the poles produces a force that pushes the skier forward. The forces are equal in size, but they act in opposite directions.

Sometimes, one force is less obvious than the other. The force that pulls a ball toward the ground is caused by gravity. Just as the Earth attracts the ball, so the ball attracts the Earth toward it. Because the Earth's mass is so great, however, its motion toward the ball is negligible.

STATIC FORCES

There are situations where forces act without causing motion. If this book is lying on a table, the force of gravity is acting downward on it. Forces can make objects accelerate. The book, however, is not moving because there is an equal and opposite force acting upward on it. As the book presses down on the table, the table presses upward on the book. The two forces are balanced, and so the book does not move. The upward force on the book is called the reaction force—it arises as a reaction to the weight of the book.

Backward thrust

Forward thrust

The miner's legs push back and downward along the ground as they support his weight and produce a force that moves the wagon forward.

▶ This man's legs push along the ground as he pulls the truck with his teeth. He sinks lower as the pulling force increases.

FORCE, WORK, AND ENERGY

A force does work when it causes a mass to move. Work is the conversion of one form of energy into another. When a person walks, for example, the leg muscles use chemical energy from substances in the blood to provide a force. The force does work as it makes the person move and increases his or her kinetic energy.

THE UNIT OF FORCE

The International System of Units, or metric system, is used for explaining the science of forces and motion. The unit of force is the newton, symbol N. Gravity exerts a force of 9.8 N on each kilogram of mass. A typical car engine can produce up to 4,500 N and the four jet engines of a Boeing 747 Jumbo jet develop a total thrust of more than 1,000,000 N when they are at full throttle for takeoff.

MEASURING FORCE

Forces are measured by their effects on things. A spring gauge is a simple force-measuring device. It has a spring attached to a pointer and a hook. As a force on the hook stretches the spring, the pointer moves along a scale marked in newtons. The pointer stays still on the scale when the tension force in the stretched spring matches the force applied at the hook. The stronger the spring, the greater the range of forces this type of gauge can measure.

◀ A potter's hands squeeze clay as it spins on a wheel. The force causes the clay to change shape.

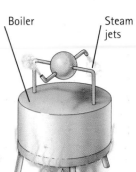

Boiler   Steam jets

Fire

▲ In this simple turbine of around A.D. 50, the force of the escaping steam made the turbine rotate.

COMBINED FORCES

In most cases, several different forces act at the same time to produce what appears to be the result of a single force. Imagine a rower sitting still in a boat on a river. The boat floats because its weight is balanced by its buoyancy. The weight of the rower is matched by the reaction force of the seat. If nothing is moving, then none of these forces does any work.

When the rower grasps the oars and pulls them, the blades of the oars push against the water. This action creates a reaction force that pushes the boat forward. At the same time, friction acts against the direction of travel. The acceleration or deceleration of the boat results from the difference between the push of the oars and the frictional force.

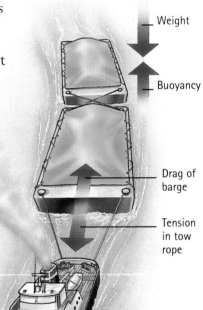

Weight

Buoyancy

Drag of barge

Tension in tow rope

Force of propulsion

Drag of tug

▲ These vessels float because their weights match their buoyancies. At constant speed, the tug's propulsive force matches the total drag on the tug and the two barges. Tension in the tow ropes pulls the barges forward.

◀ The pointer of this spring gauge shows the tension in the hook as the brick is pulled. When the brick moves at a constant speed, the spring gauge indicates the force of friction between the brick and the surface.

POTENTIAL AND KINETIC ENERGY

Potential energy is energy that is stored in an object as a result of its position or state. Kinetic energy is the energy that an object has due to its speed.

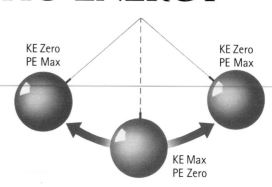

During a dive, divers gain speed and lose height, so their potential energy becomes kinetic energy.

Any moving object has kinetic energy. Moving cars, swinging hammers, and spinning wheels are examples of objects that have kinetic energy.

Stationary objects also have a form of energy due to their height or state. The water in a mountain lake has potential energy, since it could flow to a lower level.

A hydroelectric power plant uses the potential energy of high-level water to generate electricity. The potential energy first turns into kinetic energy as the water falls through pipes. Some of this kinetic energy transfers to turbogenerators that produce electrical energy as they turn.

KINETIC ENERGY

The kinetic energy of an object depends on its speed and its mass. A parked car has no kinetic energy at all. It has kinetic energy when it travels along a road because it is moving. A train traveling at the same speed as a car has more kinetic energy because of its greater mass.

Doubling the mass of a moving object doubles its kinetic energy; doubling the speed increases the kinetic energy by a factor of four.

A pendulum has maximum kinetic energy and minimum potential energy at the lowest point of its swing. Its kinetic energy falls to zero as its potential energy rises to a maximum at either extreme of the swing.

The standard unit of energy is the joule, symbol J. The kinetic energy (KE) in joules of an object is calculated using the expression $KE = \frac{1}{2}mv^2$, where m is the object's mass in kilograms and v is its speed in meters per second.

If a 40-kilogram child travels on roller blades at 5 meters per second, the kinetic energy is $\frac{1}{2} \times 40 \times 5^2 = 500$ joules. By comparison, a 4-gram bullet traveling through the air at 500 meters per second has $\frac{1}{2} \times 0.004 \times 500^2 = 500$ joules of kinetic energy. Although the child's mass is 10,000 times the mass of the bullet, the bullet need only travel 100 times faster than the child to have the same kinetic energy. This is because kinetic energy depends on the square of speed.

▼ A bullet has a large amount of kinetic energy because of its high speed. On impact, this energy causes damage as it transfers to the target, here a chocolate bar.

Spring   Plunger

Pulling back the plunger on a pinball machine compresses a spring. The force of the pull does work to store potential energy in the spring. When the plunger is released, the coiled spring expands and loses potential energy. It shoots a pinball and provides it with kinetic energy.

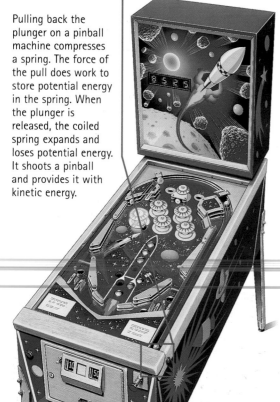

POTENTIAL ENERGY

Potential energy is the energy that an object has because of its position or state. Objects that can fall down possess potential energy. Compressed, stretched, or coiled springs also have potential energy.

One way to store energy as potential energy is to lift a brick up from the floor and place it on a table. The person or device that lifts the brick does work against the force of gravity to lift the brick up. Once on the table, the brick has gained potential energy equal to the amount of work done. If the brick were tied to a piece of string wound around the shaft of an electrical generator and then allowed to fall, its potential energy would turn into electrical energy during its fall.

When an object is lifted, the work done is equal to the downward force of gravity multiplied by the increase in height. Since the work done equals the increase in potential energy (PE), the expression for calculating the increase in potential energy in joules is $PE = mgh$, where m is the mass of the object in kilograms and h is the change of height. The constant g converts the mass of an object in kilograms into its weight in newtons. Its value is 9.8.

A one-kilogram bag of sugar on a two-meter-high shelf has a potential energy of $1 \times 9.8 \times 2 = 19.6$ joules more than it would have if it were on the floor. A five-kilogram bag of potatoes on the same shelf would lose $5 \times 9.8 \times 2 = 98$ joules of potential energy if it fell to the ground. It would have 98 joules of kinetic energy by the time it hit the floor.

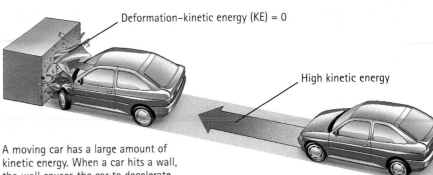

Deformation–kinetic energy (KE) = 0

High kinetic energy

A moving car has a large amount of kinetic energy. When a car hits a wall, the wall causes the car to decelerate rapidly. As a result, the wall exerts an enormous force on the car, which makes its body buckle at the point of impact.

ENERGY CONVERSIONS

A 1,000-kilogram car moving at a speed of 67 mph (108kph), or 30 meters per second, has 450,000 joules of kinetic energy. This energy has come from the chemical energy of the fuel that is released during combustion in the engine. Without friction and air resistance, the car would be able to coast to the top of a hill almost 150 ft. (46m) high. In reality, some of the energy would be used in overcoming friction and air resistance. The brakes of a car work by changing kinetic energy into heat energy—450,000 joules is enough to boil nearly five buckets of cold water.

During a crash, a car stops quickly, but its occupants and any loose objects continue moving forward.

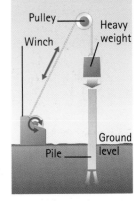

▲ A pile driver is a machine that rams steel girders, called piles, into the ground. A simple pile driver has a winch that hauls a heavy mass to the top of a frame. When the mass falls, it gathers speed and kinetic energy. The mass delivers more than one million joules of energy to the pile with each blow.

◄ The three pile drivers in this picture are preparing foundations. The piles will carry the weight of the final construction.

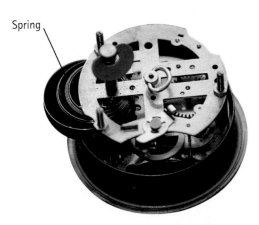

A mechanical clock is driven by the potential energy of a wound spring. An escapement mechanism releases this energy in precisely timed bursts that turn the hands.

SEE ALSO PAGES:
256 Kinetic theory,
294–5 Work and energy,
296–7 Momentum

WORK AND ENERGY

Work is done when a force moves through a distance. Energy is the ability to do work. Power is the rate at which work is done by converting energy.

A shot-putter's throw does work on a heavy iron ball to give it kinetic energy. The energy to do that work comes from the chemical energy of substances in the blood that come from food.

Machines do work as they change energy from one form into another. For example, an electric fan does work as it changes electrical energy into the kinetic energy of moving air. The electric motor in the fan uses electrical energy to provide a turning force that spins the fan. The fan blades apply a force to the air that makes it move. At each stage, energy produces a force that moves and does work.

HUMAN MACHINES
When people climb stairs, they change food energy into potential energy and heat. It takes less energy to descend stairs because the force of gravity assists the descent. Some energy is still required to move forward and keep the body upright.

Pulling a worm from the ground requires work. The exact amount of work depends on the friction between the worm and the soil, and the distance of the pull.

FIRST LAW OF THERMODYNAMICS
Thermodynamics is the study of energy and the ways that it converts from one form to another. The first law of thermodynamics states that the total energy content of the universe is fixed. Energy cannot be created or destroyed: it can only be changed from one form to another. Machines are energy converters, so the first law of thermodynamics helps engineers to design effective machines.

WASTE HEAT
One of the problems with all machines is that they produce waste heat. Machines such as car engines have radiators that remove waste heat to prevent the engine from becoming too hot. Electric motors contain small fans that blow cold air across the hot coils of wire inside.

Machines take in one form of energy and do work as they produce another form of energy. The waste heat does no useful work and represents wasted energy.

DOING WORK AND USING FUEL
When a digger does 20,000 joules (20 kJ) of work on a load, it uses fuel that provides around four times as much heat energy when it burns in the digger's engine. To release 80 kJ of chemical energy as heat, the engine burns approximately 0.1 in.^{3} (2 cm^3)—almost half a teaspoon—of diesel oil. Only 38 kJ of that heat is converted into mechanical energy. The rest is lost as heat in the exhaust and engine block. As the engine drives a hydraulic pump, the hydraulic fluid warms, and more energy is lost as heat. Heat is also lost in the hydraulic rams, leaving only 20 kJ is to do work.

Diesel fuel
80 kJ

Engine → Waste heat 52 kJ

Hydraulic pump → Waste heat 6 kJ

Hydraulic ram → Waste heat 2 kJ

Work lifting load 20 kJ

■ Machine
● Energy

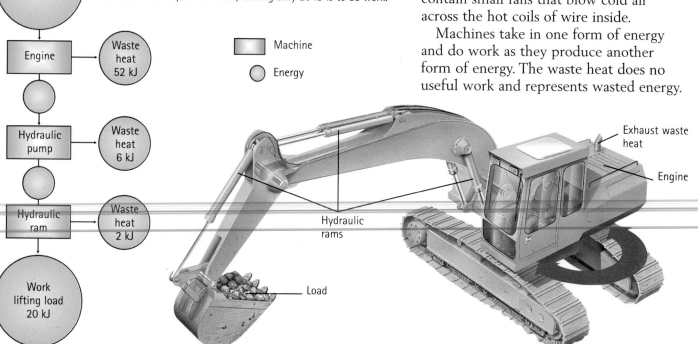

Exhaust waste heat

Engine

Hydraulic rams

Load

294

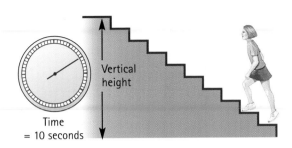

Time = 10 seconds

Vertical height

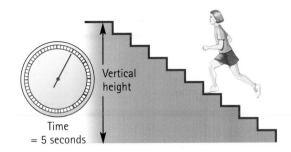

Time = 5 seconds

Vertical height

By walking upstairs, this girl uses half the power that she would use by running upstairs in half the time. The increase in potential energy is the same in both cases.

British mathematician and physicist William Thomson, Lord Kelvin (1824–1907), formulated the second law of thermodynamics in 1866. He also proposed the concept of absolute zero and devised the Kelvin temperature scale.

WORK AND ENERGY UNITS

Energy is measured in joules, symbol J. One thousand joules is one kilojoule (1 kJ), and one million joules is a megajoule (1 MJ). One kilojoule of heat energy can bring a teaspoonful of cold water to boil or run a flashlight for about 15 minutes.

A one-kilogram bag of sugar contains 21 megajoules of chemical energy. This amount of energy is the same as the increase in potential energy when three 70-kilogram (155-lb) people climb from sea level to the top of Mount Everest. In fact, each person eats the equivalent of more than one third of a bag of sugar to do this work because most of the chemical energy in food is converted into heat.

FORCE AND WORK

Work is done when a force acts on an object. One joule of work is done when a force of one newton moves a distance of one meter. If a force of 100 newtons is needed to push a pile of books across a table two meters long, the amount of work done is 100 x 2 = 200 joules. In this example, work is done to overcome the force of friction between the books and the surface of the table.

POWER

Sometimes people walk up flights of stairs; sometimes they run. In either case, the gain in a person's potential energy depends only on their mass and the vertical rise of the staircase. Climbing faster requires more effort: work is being done at a greater rate. Power is the rate of doing work or the rate of converting energy. It is measured in watts, symbol W. One watt is equivalent to doing one joule of work or converting one joule of energy in one second.

Power is energy divided by time. If a person who weighs 40 kilograms (88 lb) climbs a three-meter-high staircase, the increase in potential energy is just under 1,200 joules. If the person makes this climb in five seconds, their power is 240 watts. By dashing up the steps in one second, the same person's power is 1,200 watts—the same as a lawnmower engine. However, engines can develop power continuously. Human beings can only work at this level of power in short bursts.

Power is a useful measurement for comparing energy converters. For example, a 60-watt lightbulb takes in 60 joules of electrical energy every second. Its total output of heat and light is also 60 joules per second. A 120-watt television set converts energy at twice the rate of the bulb and will cost twice as much to run for the same time.

Car 40,000 watts (40 kilowatts)

Television 120 watts

Human 400 watts

A typical car engine is capable of producing around 40,000 watts of useful mechanical power. A television consumes around 120 watts of electrical power, and an average human being uses around 400 watts to run.

Work out

Heat out

Heat out

Food energy in

Heat out

Even bees obey the first law of thermodynamics. The total of the heat energy they produce and work they do is equal to the amount of energy they take in from food.

SEE ALSO PAGES:

106–7 Muscles and movement, 126–7 Food and nutrition, 292–3 Potential and kinetic energy

MOMENTUM

Momentum is the mass of a body in kilograms multiplied by its velocity in meters per second. It features in Newton's three laws of motion.

British mathematician and physicist Isaac Newton (1642–1727) devised three laws to describe the motion of objects.

More than 300 years ago, Isaac Newton used the ideas of momentum and inertia to formulate his three laws of motion. These laws describe and predict the effects of forces on objects. They give accurate predictions for most situations, but Einstein's relativity theory gives more accurate results for objects whose speeds approach the speed of light.

NEWTON'S FIRST LAW

The momentum of an object is equal to its mass multiplied by its velocity. If someone who weighs 50 kilograms (111 lb) runs at 10 meters per second, their momentum is 50 kg x 10 m/s = 500 kg m/s. In this case, the units of momentum are kilogram meters per second. When standing still, the person's momentum is zero.

Newton's first law of motion states that the momentum of an object stays constant until a force acts on it. For example, this page stays still until you turn it or the wind blows it. In both cases, a force makes it move and changes its momentum.

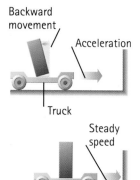

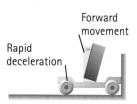

▲ A load standing upright in a truck will be pulled forward by its base if the truck accelerates. This can make a tall load tilt back or fall over. If the truck stops suddenly, the force of deceleration again acts through the base of the load, which can fall over.

▶ This car's engine develops enormous power to make it accelerate as quickly as possible. A vehicle's rate of change of momentum depends on its acceleration, which depends on the force the engine can apply to the road through the wheels.

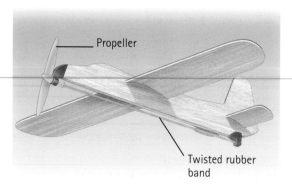

The second law predicts that maximum acceleration results when the plane has the smallest possible mass and the propeller develops the greatest possible thrust.

SPEED AND VELOCITY

Momentum is defined in terms of velocity, not in terms of speed. It is important not to confuse the velocity of an object and its speed. Velocity joins together two pieces of information: the speeds at which an object is moving and the direction in which it is moving. Velocity changes if either speed or direction change.

If two cars travel side by side in a straight line at 30 mph (50kph), they have identical velocities. If they travel at the same speed but in different directions, their velocities are not equal. If a third car travels in a circle at a constant speed, its velocity is constantly changing because it constantly changes direction away from a straight line.

NEWTON'S SECOND LAW

When a single force acts on an object, it makes it accelerate in the direction of the force. When throwing a ball, for example, force from the thrower's arm muscles accelerates the ball and increases its momentum. The greater the mass of the ball, the more difficult it is to accelerate.

Newton's second law of motion states that the rate of change of momentum of an object is proportional to the force that acts on the object. Since acceleration is the rate of change of velocity, mass times acceleration is the rate of change of momentum. Newton's second law is often written $F = ma$, where F is the force in newtons, m is mass in kilograms, and a is acceleration in meters per second squared.

NEWTON'S THIRD LAW

Newton's third law of motion states that whenever a force acts on one body, an equal and opposite force acts on some other body. The equal and opposite force is often called the reaction force.

When a spacecraft fires its rocket motor, the burning process in the combustion chamber causes hot gases to escape from the rocket's nozzle at high speed. Because the fuel and oxidant that feed the rocket have almost no momentum, the burning process must cause a backward force on the gas molecules to drive them out of the nozzle. The reaction force of the gases in the combustion chamber drives the craft forward. The mass of the spacecraft is much greater than that of the gases, so the craft accelerates much less than the gases at the same rate of change of momentum.

MOMENTUM AND INERTIA

Inertia is the tendency of an object to stay still or to move steadily in a straight line. Changing the momentum of an object requires that work is done against its inertia. It takes more effort to start bicycling from a standstill than it does to keep moving at steady speed in a straight line. This is because bicyclists must overcome their own inertia and that of the bicycle to start moving. At constant speed, the bicyclist need only overcome air resistance. Isaac Newton was the first person to realize that a force is needed to overcome inertia and make objects accelerate or decelerate.

Skiers depend on Newton's third law to be able to move: a backward push with the ski poles produces an equal and opposite reaction force that pushes them forward over snow.

CONSERVING MOMENTUM

When a gun fires a bullet, the force that acts on the bullet is equal and opposite to the recoil that acts on the gun. According to the second law, the rate of change of momentum must also be equal and opposite for the bullet and the gun. This means that the changes of momentum of the bullet and the gun must be equal and opposite, since both the firing force and the recoil force act for the same amount of time. In mechanics, opposite is shown by a minus sign, so the sum of the equal and opposite momentum values for the bullet and gun is zero before and after firing. This is an example of the conservation of momentum.

When two balls collide and rebound from each other, their combined momentum before collision is equal to their momentum after collision.

THE THREE LAWS OF MOTION

Far away from the Earth's gravity and its frictional forces, a spacecraft shows Newton's three laws of motion at work. The rocket motor fires gases backward to produce a force that propels the craft forward (3rd law). The spacecraft's acceleration is inversely proportional to the force from the motor and inversely proportional to its mass (2nd law). When the rocket switches off, the spacecraft continues at a constant velocity (1st law), flying in a straight line at a constant speed.

Acceleration proportional to thrust

Exhaust jet (backward)

Acceleration proportional to mass

297

SEE ALSO PAGES:

290–1 Force, 292–3 Potential and kinetic energy, 420–1 Rockets and the space shuttle

RELATIVITY AND GRAVITY

Newton explained gravity as the force of attraction between masses. Einstein's theories state that masses distort the geometry of the space around them.

The theories of relativity developed by German-born, U.S. physicist Albert Einstein (1879–1955) explain observations of astronomy and physics that defy Newton's laws.

The Earth's gravitational field attracts this falling car downward. The car also attracts the Earth upward, but the effect is too small to be measured.

Acceleration because of the Earth's gravity is 9.8 meters per second squared (9.8 m/sec^2). During one second, the speed of any free-falling object will increase by 9.8 meters per second. Acceleration because of gravity does not depend on mass: without air resistance, half a brick would accelerate just as quickly as a whole brick.

All masses attract each other. This attraction is called the gravitational force or the force of gravity. The strength of this force between two objects depends on their masses: doubling either mass will double the force between the objects; doubling both masses quadruples the force. The force between two objects decreases in proportion to the square of the distance between them: doubling the distance between two objects reduces the force to a fourth of its original strength.

The force of gravity between two objects only becomes readily apparent when one or both of the objects has great mass. The force between two people at a distance of 1 meter from one another is only about one millionth of a newton. Both people feel the gravitational pull of the Earth, which has a mass of 6 x 10^{24} (six million-billion-billion) kilograms.

GRAVITY, MASS, AND WEIGHT
At sea level, an object that has a mass of one kilogram is attracted to the Earth by a force of 9.8 newtons. This attraction is the object's weight. The mass of the moon is approximately one sixth the mass of the Earth, so a mass of one kilogram weighs one sixth of its weight on the Earth.

It is important to be aware of the difference between mass and weight. Mass is a measure of the amount of matter. It does not change from place to place. Weight is the force experienced by matter in a gravitational field. It varies with the strength of the gravitational field.

- The Earth has a mass of six million-billion-billion kilograms. The gravitational pull of this mass is such that an object in free fall accelerates at 9.8 m/sec^2 toward it.
- The moon has a mass one sixth the size of the Earth's mass, so its gravitational pull is one sixth as great.
- Jupiter is three hundred times as massive as the Earth. Its pull is three hundred times stronger, so free-fall acceleration near Jupiter is an enormous 3 km/sec^2.

The gravitational pull of a planet varies in proportion to its mass. Consequently, the rate of free-fall acceleration varies in direct proportion to the mass of a planet.

ACCELERATION AND FREE FALL
The force of gravity on a mass of one kilogram is 9.8 newtons; the force of gravity on a mass of two kilograms is 19.6 newtons. By Newton's second law, either mass would accelerate at a rate of 9.8 meters per second squared if gravity were the only force acting. In fact, any mass would accelerate at this rate, since the force of gravity increases in proportion to mass. The constant g has the value of 9.8 meters per second squared. It is used to calculate the effects of gravity.

Free fall is when an object drops under the force of gravity alone. Free fall is rare on the Earth, because air resistance opposes the pull of gravity on a falling object. This is why a feather falls slower than a stone in the Earth's atmosphere.

9.8 m/sec^2

Half a brick accelerates towards the ground at the same rate as a whole brick.

WEIGHTLESSNESS

An object is weightless only when it is in a zero gravitational field. There is a point between the Earth and the moon where the Earth's gravitational field cancels out the moon's, and objects are weightless.

An orbiting spacecraft is accelerating toward the center of its orbit under the force of gravity. This is why its occupants feel weightless—they are in free fall. This sensation can be felt closer to the Earth in a plane that flies in a parabolic curve with downward-acceleration *g*. A milder version of the same effect happens when a roller-coaster accelerates into a dip.

NEWTON AND GRAVITATION

In 1687, Isaac Newton published a law of gravitation that connected the force of gravity between two objects to their masses and the distance between them. It included a constant G, called the universal constant of gravitation. Newton's law is still used to predict the effect of gravity on objects, but it fails to explain how gravity works and why G has its value.

EINSTEIN AND RELATIVITY

In his Special Theory of Relativity of 1905, Albert Einstein stated that nothing —not even information—can travel faster than the speed of light. This created a problem with Newton's view of gravity, which required objects to exchange some sort of information at infinite speed in order to attract one another.

Ten years later, Einstein resolved this problem with his General Theory of Relativity. In this theory, Einstein

proposed that matter creates a distortion of the space that surrounds it. This is similar to the dip caused by placing a marble on a stretched sheet of rubber. In this distorted space, the shortest distance between two points is a curve. This is why a planet can bend the path of a passing object or even hold it in orbit—the object is simply following a straight line through space distorted by the planet.

Proof for the General Theory came from a total eclipse of the sun in 1919. Astronomers observed stars that should have been obscured by the sun. This proved that light from those stars had followed the curvature of space caused by the sun's mass. Since light has no mass, Newton's law would not have predicted the path of light to be affected by gravity.

◀ A spacecraft orbiting the Earth constantly accelerates toward the Earth under the pull of gravity. The craft's occupants feel weightless because they are in a type of free fall.

An astronaut, whose muscles are accustomed to the much stronger pull of the Earth's gravity, finds that it takes relatively little effort to jump high above the moon's surface.

◀ Skydivers experience the full acceleration of gravity for only a few seconds after they jump from an aircraft. As their descent becomes faster, the upward force of air resistance increases until it is equal but opposite to the downward pull of gravity. The speed of descent then remains constant at approximately 60 meters per second.

▲ Relativity describes gravity as a distortion of space, shown here as dips in a net. Although much heavier than the Earth, the sun (left) creates only a minor dip when compared with a smaller but more massive neutron star (center), or an immensely massive black hole (right).

SEE ALSO PAGES:

156–7 States of matter, 430–1 Space, time, and relativity

RAMPS AND WEDGES

Machines are devices that make it easier to do work against a force. Ramps and wedges are examples of simple machines based on inclined planes.

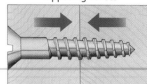

Opposing forces

When a screw holds two pieces of wood together, they are forced together as the screw tightens.

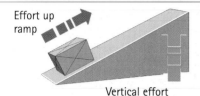

Effort up ramp

Vertical effort

It takes less force to push a load up a sloping ramp than to lift the same load straight up to the same vertical height.

▲ A wedge converts the downward force of a hammer blow into opposing sideways forces that can be used to split logs and rocks.

Machines do work as they move loads. The load moves when a force, called the effort, is applied to one part of a machine. It takes less effort to move a load with the help of a machine than without. The total amount of work done is the same, whether a machine is used or not.

RAMPS

Ramps are the simplest of all machines. They consist of a flat surface lifted up at one end to make an inclined plane. An example is a plank of wood with one end on the floor and the other end resting on a chair. It takes less effort to push a load up a ramp than to lift it straight up.

WEDGES

Wedges have two back-to-back sloping surfaces. The narrowest part of a wedge is where the two surfaces meet. Wedges are used for splitting objects made of wood or stone. A large hammer applies effort to the flat end of the wedge. The wedge directs this force out at right angles to its two sloping sides. The narrow end of the wedge drives its way into the object and the force from each sloping face splits the object apart. An ax is a hammer and a wedge combined in a single tool.

SCREWS

Screws are simple machines that hold things together. A screw consists of an inclined plane, called a thread, wrapped around a pointed cylinder. Effort is applied to a screw by using a screwdriver to turn its head. Rotating the head through a large angle moves the point of the screw forward by a short distance.

Bolts are similar to screws, but they are not pointed. The thread on the outside of a bolt fits into the inside thread of a nut. Some bolts multiply the turning force up to 40 times as they tighten with their nut.

MECHANICAL ADVANTAGE

When an effort is applied to one part of a machine, another part of the machine applies a force to a load. Most machines change a small effort into a large force that is applied to a load.

A number called the mechanical advantage of a machine is the ratio of the force on a load to the force of effort. The greater the mechanical advantage, the better the machine is at multiplying effort. The total amount of heat and work that comes out of a machine is equal to the total work put into the machine.

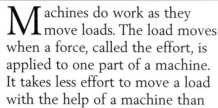

The hairpin bends in this road allow it to climb the hill at a gentler gradient than if the road were straight. The course of the road is considerably longer than if it were straight, but it can be climbed much more easily by cars and trucks.

Downward force

Sideways force

SEE ALSO PAGES:

290–1 Force, 294–5
Work and energy, 304–5
Complex machines

LEVERS AND PULLEYS

Levers and pulleys are simple machines. A lever is a combination of a bar and a fulcrum, or pivot. A pulley has a rope that passes over one or more wheels.

First-class lever

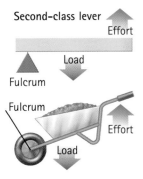

Pliers are pairs of first-class levers. The fulcrum is the pivot between the load in the jaws and the handles, where effort is applied.

Second-class lever

A wheelbarrow is an example of a second-class lever. The load is between effort and fulcrum.

Third-class lever

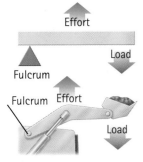

▲ The arm on the front of a mechnical digger is an example of a third-class lever. Effort from a hydraulic ram acts between the fulcrum and the load.

Effort applied to one part of a lever produces a force on a load at another part. Levers can act as force multipliers: the force that moves the load can be much greater than the effort applied to the lever. For example, a long thin metal crowbar can act as a lever and move enormous boulders that are too heavy to pick up unaided.

Two or more pulleys can also work together to multiply the force of the effort. Multiple pulleys not only multiply force, they also change the direction of the effort applied to one end of the rope.

LEVERS

A lever moves around a fixed point called the fulcrum. The distances of the load and the effort from the fulcrum affect how well the lever multiplies the force. A coin can be used as a lever to remove the lid of a can of paint. One edge of the coin fits under the lid and the rim of the can acts as a fulcrum. Pushing down on the free edge of the coin usually opens the lid. If the lid is too tight to open with a coin, the handle of a spoon will usually work. The effort acts farther from the fulcrum, so the free end of the spoon moves a greater distance and applies a greater force at the end of the spoon under the lip of the lid.

SINGLE PULLEYS

A pulley is a wheel that turns on an axle. There is a groove around the rim of the pulley wheel that holds a rope. Pulling on one end of the rope moves a load attached to the other end. When one pulley wheel is used, the force at the load is the same as the effort pulling on the rope. A single pulley does not multiply the effort, so there is no mechanical advantage. The direction of the force moving the load is different to the direction of the effort.

MULTIPLE PULLEYS

When two pulleys work together, one is attached to a high fixed support, such as a beam, and the other is attached to the load. One end of the rope is attached to the fixed pulley. The rope passes under the load pulley and over the fixed pulley. Pulling on the free end of the rope supplies the effort to lift the load.

Using two pulleys halves the effort required to lift a load, so an effort of 100 newtons can lift a load of 200 newtons, so the mechanical advantage of a two-pulley system is two. As the load moves one meter, the effort moves two meters. Since the work done is force times distance, the work put into the pulley—100 x 2 = 200 joules—is the same as the work done on the load: 200 x 1 = 200 joules.

In general, the mechanical advantage of a pulley system is equal to the number of pulleys the rope passes over.

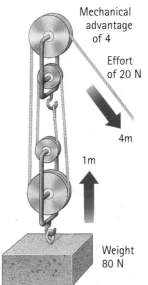

Mechanical advantage of 4

Effort of 20 N

4m

1m

Weight 80 N

Four pulleys working together multiply the force of the effort by four times. The distance moved by the effort is four times the distance moved by the load. Cranes and other machines use systems of pulleys and cables or chains to lift extremely heavy loads.

SEE ALSO PAGES:

290–1 Force, 292–3 Potential and kinetic energy, 304–5 Complex machines

WHEELS AND AXLES

Wheels are simple machines. A wheel is a load-bearing cylinder that revolves on a rod-shaped axle at right angles to the center of its circular face.

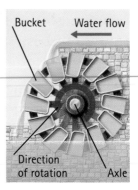

A wheel and axle act together as a rotating lever. The force of water falling on the rim of a water wheel is magnified to give a greater rotating force at the axle.

The wheel is possibly the single most important invention in the history of transportation. Before its invention nearly 6,000 years ago, loads were dragged over ground on heavy sleds. There are large forces of friction between sled runners and the ground. Wheels rotate on their axles, and the friction is much smaller, so less force is required to move a load.

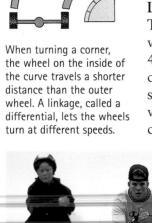

Modern car wheels fitted with pneumatic tires are descended from tree-trunk rollers that were used thousands of years ago.

THE FIRST WHEELS

The first step toward the invention of the wheel was the use of log rollers to shift heavy loads. Rollers reduce friction by turning as the load on them moves. Simple rollers have to be collected from behind the load and placed in front of it as it moves along.

The earliest wheel was probably sliced from the end of a round log. A straight, round branch would serve as an axle. Each end of the axle would fit into a hole cut into the center of two wooden disks. Carts using pairs of wheels on axles developed from the potter's wheel around 5,500 years ago in Mesopotamia, now Iraq. The soft clay pot rotated on the top wheel.

When turning a corner, the wheel on the inside of the curve travels a shorter distance than the outer wheel. A linkage, called a differential, lets the wheels turn at different speeds.

LATER DEVELOPMENTS

The first wagons for carrying heavy loads were fitted with solid wheels. Around 4,000 years ago, iron tools allowed carpenters in Mesopotamia and Egypt to shape pieces of wood to make spoked wheels. This type of wheel consists of a circular wooden rim attached to a central hub by rodlike spokes. Spoked wheels are lighter than solid wheels, so fast horse-drawn chariots became possible. From Roman times, wheels were often fitted with an iron band, called a tire. Tires helped to reduce wear but did not improve the ride. The pneumatic tires now used on cars and bicycles help to cushion bumps and provide a smoother ride. They were first patented in 1845.

WHEELS AS ROTARY LEVERS

A wheel-and-axle combination is a form of rotary lever. If a wheel is turned by a force at its edge, the force at the edge of the axle will be much greater.

Torque, or turning force, is force times the distance from the point where the force acts to the center of the wheel. This is how a large steering wheel helps make steering a car easier: the force to turn the wheel is applied at a great distance from the center of the wheel. Old ships had even larger wheels to turn their rudders against the force of moving water. Some valves are operated by turning a large wheel on a threaded shaft that controls the flow of a gas or liquid.

◀ Roller blades have several single wheels fitted in a row. The wheels are made of high-strength plastic. Moving requires an action similar to that of ice-skaters.

▶ The large diameter of a screwdriver's handle allows it to develop enough torque to shift even tight-fitting screws.

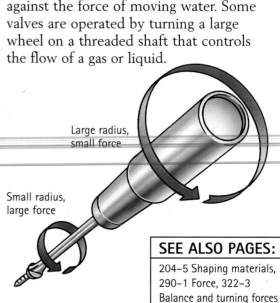

Large radius, small force

Small radius, large force

SEE ALSO PAGES:
204–5 Shaping materials,
290–1 Force, 322–3
Balance and turning forces

GEARS

When two or more gears mesh together, they transmit torque from one place to another and can change the speed of rotation.

A gear has toothlike cogs that protrude from its surface. A gear train consists of two or more meshing gears. A train of gears can alter the direction, speed, and torque of rotation from an input shaft to an output shaft.

ROTATIONAL SPEED
Two gears meshed together rotate in opposite directions. The speed of rotation is usually measured in revolutions per minute, abbreviated to r.p.m. A gear that makes one complete turn in a second, has a speed of rotation of 60 r.p.m.

The relative speed of two meshed gears depends on the ratio of cogs on the wheels. They rotate at the same speeds only if both of the gears have the same numbers of cogs. If the numbers of cogs are different, the gear with fewer cogs rotates faster than the gear with the greater number of cogs. If the numbers of cogs is 8 and 16, then the gear ratio is 1:2. The speed of the gears is 2:1. If the small gear rotates at 50 r.p.m. then the larger will rotate at 25 r.p.m.

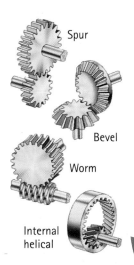

An 8-cog gear meshes with a 16-cog gear. Turning the smaller gear causes the larger gear to rotate with twice the turning force and half the speed.

Spur

Bevel

Worm

Internal helical

▲ Meshing gears can change the direction, speed, or force of rotation. Different gear trains change the axis of rotation in different ways.

► A car's transmission uses gears to match the speed and torque of an engine to the load. Climbing hills requires a high torque at low speed. High-speed cruising requires faster rotation and less torque.

A flexible chain connects the gears on a bicycle. The chain moves between different-sized gears to change the ratios of the gears to suit the road gradient.

ROTATIONAL FORCE
A gear is a combination of a wheel and levers. Each cog acts as if it were a lever attached to the center of the gear. In a train, the cogs on the gear attached to the input shaft exert leverage on another gear. When a small gear turns a larger one, there is a mechanical advantage. The larger gear turns with more torque than the smaller one, but more slowly.

GEARS AND CHAINS
Some machines have gears that are joined by a chain. Bicycles are an example. The cogs of the gears fit into slots on the chain. The gears rotate in the same direction. As with gears that mesh together, the change in speed and turning effort depend on the number of cogs on each gear.

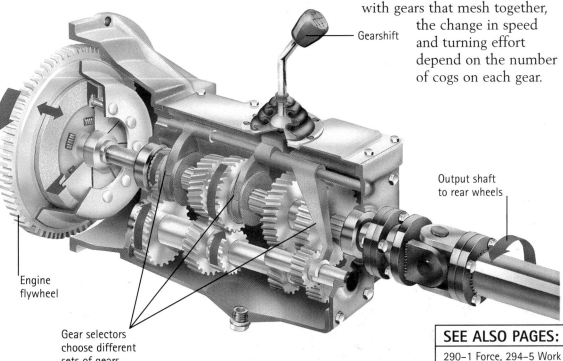

Gearshift

Output shaft to rear wheels

Engine flywheel

Gear selectors choose different sets of gears.

SEE ALSO PAGES:

290–1 Force, 294–5 Work and energy, 304–5 Complex machines

COMPLEX MACHINES

Complex machines are a combination of simple machines. They include ramps, wedges, gears, wheels and axles, and pulleys.

The shaft of a corkscrew is an inclined plane that spirals around a cylinder. Turning the screw drives it into the cork. The two lever arms then pull the cork out of the bottle.

Scissors consist of two levers attached together by a screw, which is the fixed point, or fulcrum, of the levers. The cutting edges are inclined planes.

▲ The cutter of a can opener works as a circular wedge mounted on a wheel and axle. The axle is turned by a lever. The handles are double levers that grip the can as the cutter bites into the lid.

▶ A winch consists of a wheel and axle mounted on a stand. The handle on the wheel acts as a lever that turns the axle. A rope or cable attached to the axle pulls the load.

The three classes of simple machines, also called primary machines, are inclined planes, including ramps, screws, and wedges; levers and wheels, including wheel-and-axle combinations; and pulleys.

Complex machines are combinations of two or more simple machines working together. A pair of scissors combines two levers that share a pivot with two inclined planes—the blades.

THE MACHINE AGE

Until almost 2,000 years ago, the main source of energy for operating machines was human or animal power. The Romans developed waterwheels to power saws and mills for grinding grain. Later, in the A.D. 600s, the Persians developed windmills to grind grain.

The development of the steam engine in the mid-1700s led to the industrial revolution and the machine age. Factories were built to house machines for weaving cloth, shaping metals, and manufacturing items for people to buy in stores. Each machine was connected to the steam engine by a system of rotating shafts, pulleys, belts, and gears. Most modern factory machines are powered by their own electric motors.

However complex, all machines are combinations of different types of inclined planes, levers, and wheels.

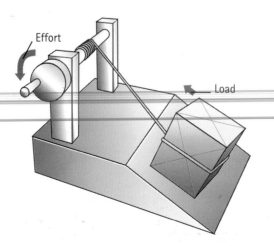

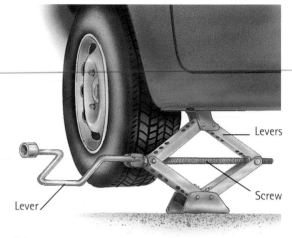

This type of jack consists of four levers pivoted at their ends. A handle and rotating screw works the levers to produce a large mechanical advantage.

COMPLEX MACHINES IN THE HOME

Almost anything in the home that has a moving part can be classed as a machine. A door handle, for example, acts as a lever that rotates an axle inside the door. This axle moves another lever that pulls back a type of bolt to release the door.

One type of jack works like a pair of scissors. It has a handle that works as a lever to rotate an axle. The axle has a screw thread along part of its length. As the axle rotates, the screw pulls a nut toward the handle and forces the arms of the jack closer together, and raises the load on the jack. It takes several turns of the handle to raise the load through a small distance, but the effort is small.

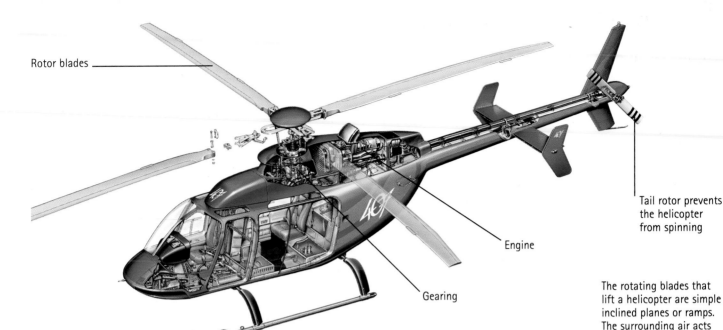

Rotor blades

Tail rotor prevents the helicopter from spinning

Engine

Gearing

The rotating blades that lift a helicopter are simple inclined planes or ramps. The surrounding air acts as a load that the ramps force downward. Air accelerating downward produces an upward reaction force that lifts the helicopter upward.

PISTON ENGINES AND VEHICLES

Machines that move around need portable power sources. Cars and trucks use piston engines that burn fuels like gasoline and diesel oil. The burning fuel-and-air mixture expands against pistons inside cylinders. The pistons drive a crankshaft around and around, just as a bicyclist's feet move the pedals of a bicycle. The crankshaft is simply a set of levers that turn an axle. The gear trains of a transmission work together in different combinations to alter the speed and turning effort of the engine output to match the load.

▼ A bucket dredge is a machine that bites into the ground with toothed buckets. The buckets are fixed around the rim of a huge wheel driven by a motor.

TURBINE ENGINES AND AIRCRAFT

Turbine engines have hundreds of angled blades attached to a central shaft or axle. High-pressure gases from burning fuels strike the blades, which work as levers as they cause the shaft to rotate.

In a turboprop engine, the turbine shaft drives a propeller, which is a set of wedges that force air backward. The reaction force drives the aircraft forward. In a turbofan engine, the turbine drives a compressor that may have hundreds of blades. Some of the air from the compressor feeds the combustion that drives the turbine. The majority bypasses the turbine and escapes from the back of the engine, driving the aircraft forward.

A train of gears in a watch drive the hands that show the time. There are 60 seconds in a minute, so the gears that connect the second hand to the minute hand have a gear ratio of 60:1. Since there are 60 minutes in an hour, the gears that connect the minute and hour hands also have a gear ratio of 60:1.

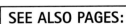

SEE ALSO PAGES:

224–5 Gasoline and diesel engines, 226–7 Jet engines and gas turbines, 300 Ramps and wedges, 301 Levers and pulleys, 303 Gears

SECOND LAW OF THERMODYNAMICS

Thermodynamics is the study of the conversion of energy from one form into another. The second law concerns entropy. This is a measure of disorder.

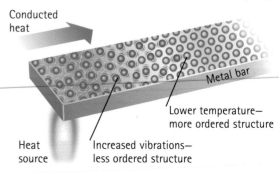

Entropy increases with the spread of heat. As heat spreads through a metal bar, its atoms become more disordered as they start to vibrate more vigorously.

The second law of thermodynamics starts from the common everyday observation that hot objects cool down. In other words, heat flows spontaneously, or naturally, from hot objects to cooler objects. Heat never flows spontaneously from a cold object to a warmer object. The second law then goes on to explain that heat flows because energy tends to spread out.

Heat flows from a hot body to a cooler one, so hot coffee always cools as it loses its heat to the surroundings. Coffee never spontaneously gets hotter by extracting heat from cooler surroundings.

HEAT FLOW

What makes heat flow from a hot place to a cooler place? Kinetic theory states that heat energy raises the temperature of a substance and increases the kinetic energy of its particles: particles move more quickly when they are hot than when they are cold. Heat travels through solids by conduction. For example, suppose two blocks of metal at different temperatures are placed in contact with one another. The fast-moving particles of the hot bar bump into slower particles of the cooler bar. These collisions transfer energy, so the slower particles speed up and the faster particles slow down. Eventually, the total heat content of the two blocks becomes evenly spread between them, and their temperatures become equal.

HEAT FLOW AND DISORDER

The second law of thermodynamics looks on heat flow as the spread of disorder. Think about solids again: their particles are arranged in fixed positions. In crystals, they are set in a regular ordered pattern called a lattice. When a solid is cold, its particles vibrate more slowly than when the temperature is higher. The structure is therefore more ordered at lower temperatures. Disorder increases as temperature increases. When a substance takes in heat, disorder increases.

The particles in liquids are free to move past each other. They are more disordered than solids. Gases are even more disordered than liquids, because their particles are even farther apart.

Compressed gases expand spontaneously if they are released. They take up more space, so the organization of their particles becomes less ordered and more chaotic.

▼ A gas becomes less disordered if it is compressed. This is because its particles occupy a smaller space and there are fewer possible combinations for the positions of its particles. As the gas becomes less disordered, there must be an increase in disorder elsewhere in the system. With a dry-cell-powered compressor, the increase in disorder takes the form of waste heat and chemical disorder in the dry cell.

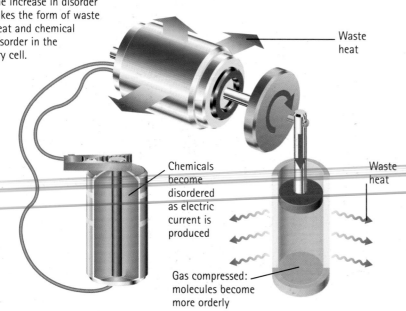

Chemicals become disordered as electric current is produced

Gas compressed: molecules become more orderly

Waste heat

Waste heat

FREEZING AND MELTING

When heat flows from a hot place to a cold place, the flow is accompanied by a spread of disorder. Everything in nature tends to become more disorganized, unless energy is used to do work to create organized structures. Ice starts to melt when it is taken from a freezer and placed in a warm room. Disorder increases as the solid melts to form a liquid. Freezing the water uses electrical energy in the freezer to pump heat out of the water and lower its temperature below 0°C (32°F). Water does not spontaneously freeze in a warm room because this change would involve a spontaneous decrease in disorder.

ENTROPY

The particles in substances would be most ordered, or least disordered, at −273.15°C. This temperature, called absolute zero, is 0K (zero Kelvin) on the Kelvin scale of temperature. The particles have the minimum possible energy of motion.

Scientists invented a quantity called entropy to measure the amount of disorder in substances. They say that entropy is zero at absolute zero and increases by different amounts for each substance as the temperature increases.

At a given temperature, large molecules have lower entropy than small molecules because they have more complex and ordered structures. Entropy increases greatly when a solid melts to form a liquid or a liquid boils to form a gas.

The state of this young child's playroom shows that the room's entropy has increased from when it was neat. Whoever straightens up the room will create more entropy in the form of waste heat and as exhaled moisture and carbon dioxide gas from the breakdown of complex molecules in the blood.

ENTROPY CHANGES

The second law of thermodynamics states that all energy changes are accompanied by increases in entropy. Most fuels and nutrients are complex organic molecules. They react with oxygen to release energy and produce smaller molecules such as carbon dioxide and water. Breaking large structures into smaller ones increases entropy. The production of heat also increases entropy.

Machines and living things produce waste heat as they change energy from one form to another. This waste heat spreads through the surroundings and increases entropy. It represents energy that does not perform useful work. As time goes by, the entropy of the universe increases as energy changes produce more and more waste heat. The universe will stop changing when all matter and all energy is uniformly spread.

At the end of time, all the energy in the universe will be in the form of heat that has uniformly spread out. When absolutely everywhere is at the same temperature, heat will not flow, so no work will be done—nothing will happen. Entropy will have reached its maximum value, and the universe will be dead and unchanging.

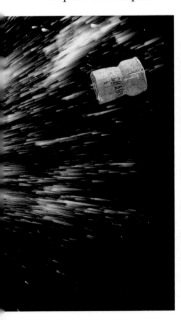

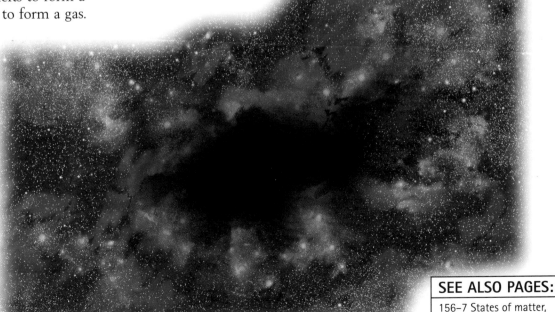

SEE ALSO PAGES:

156-7 States of matter, 250-1 Heat transfer, 256 Kinetic theory

FRICTION

Friction is a force that acts against the movement of surfaces that are in contact. Friction changes kinetic energy into heat energy as it resists motion.

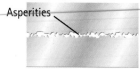

Asperities

Even a polished metal surface is covered with microscopic rough points called asperities. These points lock into one another and cause friction when the surfaces move.

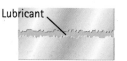

Lubricant

A film of lubricating oil holds the two metal surfaces apart. They slide past each other without making contact. Friction is reduced and movement creates far less heat.

When NASA's space shuttle enters the Earth's atmosphere at over 15,500 mph (25,000kph), friction with air molecules brakes the craft and raises its skin temperature to around 1,500°C. Friction is at work everywhere. Some of its effects are unwanted; others are useful.

USEFUL EFFECTS OF FRICTION

Humans walk forward by pushing backward with feet. Without friction, floors, roads, and sidewalks would be more slippery than an ice rink. People would fall as they tried to walk or run. It would also be impossible to pick up objects with completely slippery surfaces.

STATIC FRICTION

If a person tries to push a loaded crate along the floor, the force that resists the motion of the crate is friction. As the strength of the push increases, there comes a point when the crate starts to move. The force just before the crate moves is the limit of static friction. It depends on the combined weight of the crate and its contents. If the weight doubles, the limit of static friction also doubles.

The limit of static friction also depends on the materials of the surfaces in contact, in this case the crate and the floor.

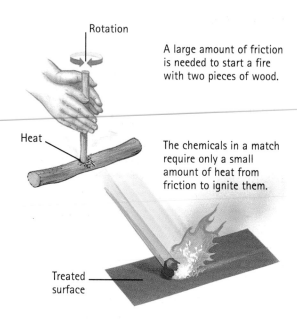

Rotation

A large amount of friction is needed to start a fire with two pieces of wood.

Heat

The chemicals in a match require only a small amount of heat from friction to ignite them.

Treated surface

MAKING FIRE

The simplest equipment for making fire depends on friction and consists of two dry wooden sticks. One stick is rapidly rotated against another until friction raises the temperature to around 570°F (300°C), and the wood starts to smolder.

Matches also use friction. When the head of a match is rubbed against the rough strip on the matchbox, friction makes the temperature rise. The heat causes chemicals in the match head and the strip to react together. As the temperature increases further, the head of the match burns in air and finally ignites the wood.

SLIDING AND ROLLING

Friction is a problem when moving loads. Early humans dragged loads on heavy sleds, or wooden sledges. The sled runners helped to support the loads, but there was still a great deal of friction between the moving runners and the ground.

Humans later discovered that rollers made it much easier to move heavy objects such as blocks of stone. Rollers rotate and reduce friction because the load does not slide in contact with the ground as it travels. The drawback of rollers is that the load leaves them behind as it travels along. Around 5,500 years ago, this problem was overcome by the invention of the wheel-and-axle combination.

Heavy parcels move easily down a gentle slope on this roller conveyer. Each roller is fixed in position and rotates with little friction as a load travels over it.

BEARINGS

Bearings are devices that support moving parts and allow them to move with less friction. Bearings are used in most types of machines, including cars, bicycles, electric motors, and roller skates. One type of bearing connects a moving shaft to a static support. Other bearings connect rotating objects to static shafts. Without bearings, friction between the two parts would slow the machine, waste energy as lost heat, and rapidly wear the surfaces in contact.

A typical bearing consists of an inner and an outer metal ring. In ball bearings, steel balls run in grooves between the two rings. In roller bearings, steel cylinders roll between the inner and outer rings. High-quality bearings can run so smoothly that friction wastes less than one percent of the energy consumption of a machine.

LUBRICANTS

Lubricants are fluids that hold sliding surfaces slightly apart to reduce friction. Mineral oils are the most common machine lubricants. Internal-combustion engines contain pumps that supply oil to lubricate the pistons as they slide inside cylinders. Oil is also continuously supplied to the bearings inside these engines.

Some machines use high-pressure air to lubricate air bearings that support shafts that rotate at extremely high speeds; others use graphite as a solid lubricant.

▼ Friction between the bobsled's metal runners and the ice is low because the downward pressure melts the ice to form a thin lubricating layer of water.

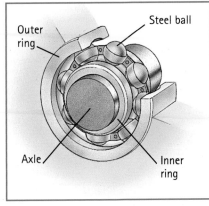

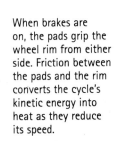

Each wheel of a roller skate is supported by a bearing. Steel balls roll inside grooves cut into the inner and outer rings.

SLOWING DOWN

Vehicles use bearings to reduce friction and help them move with the minimum amount of effort. Brakes cause deceleration by increasing the force of friction on wheels. Applying the brakes presses a hard pad of heat-resistant material against a steel drum or disk attached to each wheel. Friction between the material and the revolving part changes kinetic energy into heat and reduces the vehicle's speed. Heat is quickly lost to the surrounding air.

▼ Bicycle brakes usually consist of a pair of hard rubber pads mounted at the ends of curved levers. These levers are attached to the bicycle frame by a pivot. Applying the brakes causes the pads to move in until they press on the rim of the wheel.

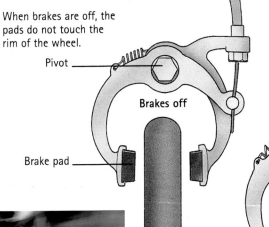

When brakes are off, the pads do not touch the rim of the wheel.

Pivot

Brakes off

Brake pad

Brake cable pull

Brakes on

Pads grip wheel rim

When brakes are on, the pads grip the wheel rim from either side. Friction between the pads and the rim converts the cycle's kinetic energy into heat as they reduce its speed.

SEE ALSO PAGES:

FLUIDS

Liquids and gases are classed as fluids because they are able to flow from one place to another. Finely powdered solids can also sometimes act as fluids.

There are three common states of matter—solid, liquid, and gas. Liquids and gases are classed as fluids. Fluids are able to flow because the forces of attraction between their particles are weak. As a result, gases and liquids can easily change shape. Solids cannot flow under normal conditions because there are strong forces of attraction between their particles, and their shapes are fixed.

The temperature at the top of this waterfall is slightly lower than the temperature at the bottom. Frictional forces in flowing liquids cause them to slow down and become slightly warmer.

GASES

Gases flow from places of high pressure to places of lower pressure. For example, air flows from a bicycle pump into a tire because the pressure inside the pump is greater than the pressure in the tire. Weather patterns are caused by flowing air. Winds blow across the Earth's surface because heat from the sun causes differences in air pressure.

LIQUIDS

Liquids are denser than gases, so the force of gravity makes them flow down. Water, gasoline, oil, and molasses are all liquids, but they flow at different rates. There are stronger forces of attraction between the particles in molasses than in water. As a result, water flows more easily and quickly than molasses. Liquids that flow with difficulty are said to be viscous. Viscosity varies from one liquid to another and decreases with increasing temperature.

Fine powders can be made to behave like fluids by floating them on an upward air current. This arrangement is called a fluidized bed. A fluidized powder flows like a liquid.

Honey is a viscous fluid. Charged parts on the molecules in honey attract them to each other. They cling together as the liquid flows, and slow its motion.

FLUIDIZATION OF SOLIDS

Solids such as cement and flour are fine powders. Each powder particle is millions of times larger than the molecules in liquids and gases, but it is possible to make these powders flow and act like fluids. Blowing air up through a fine powder lifts its particles and lowers the friction between them. This is why cement and flour can be loaded into tankers and unloaded by fluidizing them with air.

Power plants burn powdered coal in fluidized bed furnaces. The pulverized coal flows into a layer of sand that is kept fluid by high-pressure air. The air helps the coal burn and keeps the bed at the optimum temperature for efficient combustion.

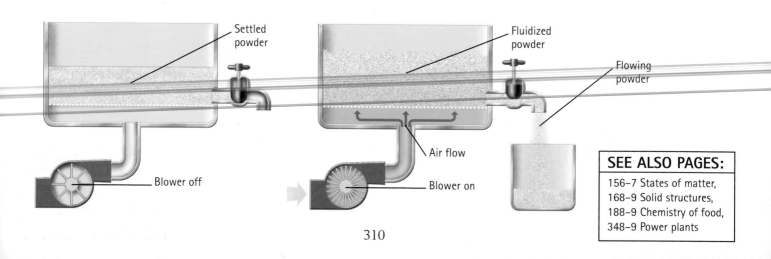

Settled powder

Blower off

Fluidized powder

Air flow

Blower on

Flowing powder

SEE ALSO PAGES:

156–7 States of matter,
168–9 Solid structures,
188–9 Chemistry of food,
348–9 Power plants

PRESSURE

Pressure is the result of a force pushing on a surface. Unlike solids and liquids, gases are easily compressed; their pressure increases as volume decreases.

At a depth of 3,000 ft. (1,000m) an armored suit protects the diver from being crushed by pressures more than 100 times atmospheric.

Divers feel the pressure of the water on their bodies. It pushes equally from all directions. The deeper the dive, the greater the pressure. Water pressure is the result of gravity pulling down on the water above the diver. On dry land, air pressure is the result of gravity pulling down on the gases in the Earth's atmosphere.

MEASURING PRESSURE

The unit of pressure is the pascal, symbol *Pa*. One pascal is equivalent to a force of one newton acting over an area of one square meter. Atmospheric pressure at sea level is approximately 101,000 Pa.

Pressure increases as area decreases. A 154-pound (70-kg) person in high heels exerts a higher pressure on the floor than a three-ton elephant on four large feet.

PUSHING WITH FLUIDS

Applying a force to the surface of a liquid increases the pressure at all points inside it. Hydraulic machines use this effect to move heavy loads. In a mechanical digger, the engine drives a pump that forces oil along pipes into cylinders. The pressure of the oil forces a piston to move along inside the cylinder. Oil can push on either side of the piston to make it move with immense force in either direction.

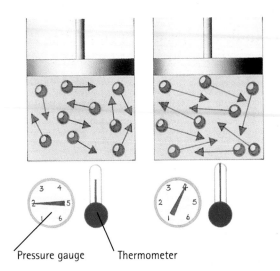

Pressure gauge   Thermometer

The pressure of a gas results from its molecules colliding with the walls of its container. As temperature increases, the collisions get more violent and the pressure increases.

PRESSURE AND COMPRESSIBILITY

Although gases fill the container in which they are placed, only a small proportion of that space is filled by molecules. The atoms or molecules of a gas are in constant motion; they exert pressure on their container as a result of their collisions with the container walls.

When a gas is compressed, its particles are contained in a smaller volume. They collide more frequently with the walls of the container, so the pressure increases. Liquids and solids have hardly any space between particles, so they do not compress as easily as gases do.

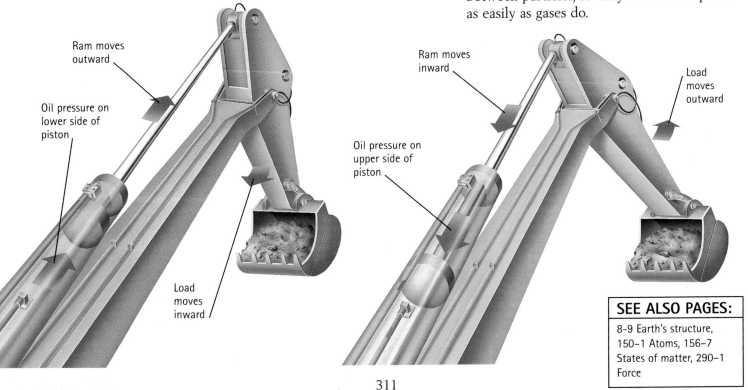

Ram moves outward

Oil pressure on lower side of piston

Load moves inward

Ram moves inward

Oil pressure on upper side of piston

Load moves outward

SEE ALSO PAGES:

8-9 Earth's structure, 150-1 Atoms, 156-7 States of matter, 290-1 Force

SOUND AS CHANGES OF PRESSURE

Sound consists of vibrations that travel through a medium, such as air or water. These vibrations can be detected by the ears of animals.

Prongs move out

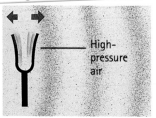

High-pressure air

When the prongs move out, they compress nearby air.

Prongs move in

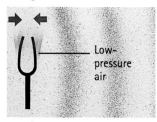

Low-pressure air

When the prongs move in, they create a region of low pressure.

▲ The prongs of a tuning fork vibrate at a steady rate. They create regions of high and low pressure in the air that radiate away from the fork at the speed of sound.

When people speak, the vocal cords in their throats vibrate back and forth. As they vibrate, they produce sound waves that travel at over 1,000 feet (340m) per second. These waves are changes in air pressure of around one ten thousandth the normal air pressure. The air does not move with a sound wave: it simply vibrates around an average position.

SOUND IN AIR

Sounds travel through air as a back-and-forth movement of air molecules. A vibrating surface makes sounds by alternately pushing and pulling at the layer of air surrounding it. This layer of air then pushes and pulls at the layer of air next to it, and so on. This is how vibrations travel through air.

SOUND IN OTHER MEDIA

Sound can travel through solids, liquids, or gases. It cannot travel through a vacuum because there are no particles to vibrate and carry sound waves. This is how the vacuum between the panes of a window provide sound insulation.

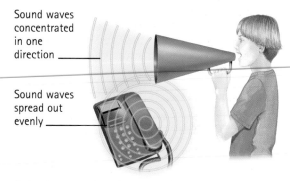

Sound waves concentrated in one direction

Sound waves spread out evenly

A simple cone makes the sound of a voice travel farther by concentrating it in one direction. A telephone ringer spreads sound so that it can be heard from any direction.

A substance that carries sound is called a medium, and the speed of sound depends on the density of the medium. Sound travels five times faster in water than it does in air, for example, and more than three times faster in glass than in water. This is because the particles in a dense medium, such as glass, are closer together than in a less dense medium, such as air. The closeness of particles in a dense medium helps vibrations pass more quickly from one particle to the next.

Compressing a gas increases its density, so the speed of sound in a gas increases as the pressure of the gas increases.

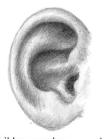

Children can hear sounds up to 20 kHz.

The ears of bats are sensitive up to 120 kHz.

▶ Dolphins and whales use high-frequency sound to communicate and to locate food. These sounds travel farther in water than they would in air.

Crickets can hear sound frequencies up to 100 kHz.

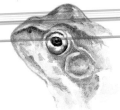

Some frogs can detect sounds up to 50 kHz.

◀ Different animals can hear sounds within different ranges of frequencies. The range of human hearing is from around 25 Hz to around 15,000 Hz (15 kHz). The upper limit falls with increasing age.

SONAR

Sonar was developed in 1915 by French physicist Paul Langevin (1872–1946). Its invention was inspired by the disaster of the White Star liner *Titanic*, which was sunk by an iceberg in 1912. Sonar provides information about underwater objects by the echoes that return from them. Vertical echoes give information about the seabed; angled echoes can help locate submarines and schools of fish.

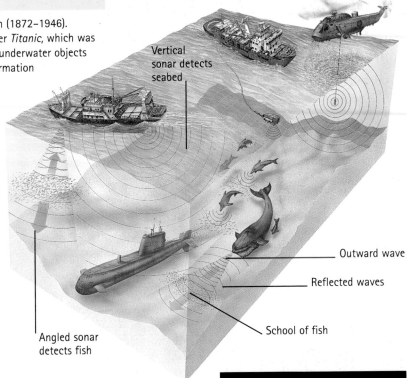

Vertical sonar detects seabed

Outward wave

Reflected waves

School of fish

Angled sonar detects fish

USING SOUND

Some animals have ears that detect sound as they travel through air or water. The ears convert vibrations into nerve impulses that travel to the brain. Other animals, such as snakes, sense ground vibrations.

Animals use sounds to communicate and to gather information about their surroundings. Sounds such as the noises of falling rocks or moving predators can provide warnings of imminent danger.

ECHOLOCATION

Some animals, such as bats, dolphins, and whales, use sound to navigate and locate food. They send out short bursts of high-frequency sound and analyze the returning echoes. This is called echolocation; it helps these animals to detect prey and estimate its speed and direction of motion. Ships use sonar—**s**ound **n**avigation **a**nd **r**anging—to form images of underwater objects and landscapes. A device similar to a loudspeaker emits intense pulses of sound. A computer analyzes the timing and direction of returning echoes to calculate the positions and sizes of objects.

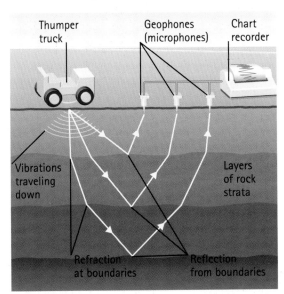

Thumper truck

Geophones (microphones)

Chart recorder

Vibrations traveling down

Layers of rock strata

Refraction at boundaries

Reflection from boundaries

Sound waves are refracted and reflected as they pass from one medium into another. Geologists analyze returning sound waves to build up pictures of rock layers.

INFRASOUND

Infrasound consists of sound waves that vibrate at frequencies below around 25 hertz, which is the lower limit of human hearing. Sounds in this range are said to be subsonic. Earthquakes send subsonic waves through the ground; explosions send them through the air. Although infrasound cannot be heard, its pressure waves can sometimes be felt.

ULTRASOUND

Ultrasound consists of sound waves that vibrate at frequencies greater than around 15 kilohertz, the upper limit of human hearing for most adults.

Ultrasonic waves penetrate liquids and solids better than lower-frequency sounds. This is why ultrasound is used in some types of sonar equipment and in body scanners that give images of internal organs and growing babies. Ultrasound echoes can also detect flaws inside welded metal objects, such as steel pipeline.

The energetic vibrations of ultrasound can be used to break kidney stones into pieces that are small enough to pass out of the kidney in urine. Water-filled ultrasonic baths are used to dislodge encrusted dirt from laboratory equipment.

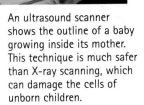

An ultrasound scanner shows the outline of a baby growing inside its mother. This technique is much safer than X-ray scanning, which can damage the cells of unborn children.

The speed of sound in air at sea level is 340 mi./sec. At an altitude of 6 mi. (10km), where the air is less dense, the speed is only 300 mi./sec. In water, the speed is 1,500 mi./sec., and in glass it is 5,000 mi./sec.

SEE ALSO PAGES:

20–1 Earthquakes, 111 Communication, 116–17 Ears, hearing, and balance

WAVE MOTION

A wave motion is a regularly repeating back-and-forth or side-to-side displacement. It describes how a form of energy moves through space.

Time   Float

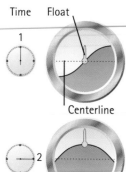

1

Centerline

2

3

4

5

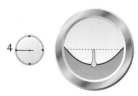

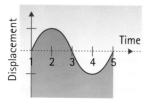

Displacement

Time

1 2 3 4 5

▲ As sea waves travel past the porthole of a ship, the water level goes up and down. The level at any time is measured as the displacement of the wave above or below the average water level. The wave can be represented by a graph that plots the variation of water level against time.

Examples of wave motions include sound, ripples on a pond, radio signals, and light. In each of these motions, a form of energy is carried by regularly alternating changes, or oscillations. Sound waves travel through the air as minute changes in air pressure. Water ripples as its surface moves vertically up and down.

With light and radio signals, unlike sound or water waves, no material moves as the wave passes. Both are forms of electromagnetic radiation where energy is transmitted by oscillations in electrical or magnetic fields.

TRANSVERSE OR LONGITUDINAL?

When a bottle floats in the sea, it bobs up and down with passing waves. It does not move along if there is no water current or breeze to propel it. This is because water waves are examples of transverse waves: the motion of the water is at right angles to the direction in which the waves travel. Electromagnetic waves are transverse: the electric and magnetic fields oscillate at right angles to the direction of travel. They also vibrate at right angles to one another.

Sound waves are longitudinal waves. Air oscillates back and forth along the line of travel of the waves. Some of the seismic waves from earthquakes are longitudinal pressure waves that make the ground vibrate back and forth as they pass.

AMPLITUDE AND FREQUENCY

The amplitude of a wave is the strength or intensity of the oscillation. Waves oscillate around an average position, called zero amplitude, just as water waves have peaks and troughs above and below the level of

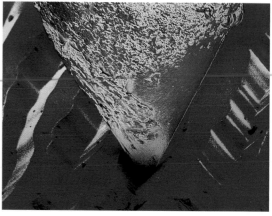

A diamond stylus follows the groove in a vinyl record. As the record turns, the side-to-side movement of the needle mimics the oscillations of the original sound wave.

calm water. Increasing the amplitude of sound makes it louder, and increasing the amplitude of light makes it brighter.

The frequency of a wave motion is the number of oscillations that are completed by the wave in one second. High-frequency sound has a higher pitch than low-frequency sound, so a higher note is heard. Increasing the frequency of light waves moves the color from the red end of the spectrum to the violet end.

Increasing the frequency of a wave motion decreases the wavelength, the distance between neighboring points of maximum amplitude on the wave.

Pitch of sound

Sound amplitude

High frequency—
short wavelength

Smaller amplitude

Low frequency—
long wavelength

Larger amplitude

◀ Waves are often drawn as plots of amplitude against time. The greater the frequency, the more oscillations there are per second and the shorter the wavelength.

▲ In the sound wave of a single, steady frequency, pressure variation takes the form of a sine wave. A short wavelength or high frequency represents a high-pitched note. A large-amplitude wave indicates a loud sound.

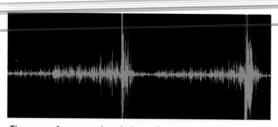

The wave from two hand claps plotted against time.

WAVE FRONTS AND RAYS

Wave fronts and rays are two ways of representing the direction of travel of waves. They give information about wave motion that cannot be represented in simple graphs of amplitude against time.

One way of showing wave fronts is to mark the positions at which the waves have their maximum displacement. When seen from above, the wave fronts of sea waves appear as rows of lines that each mark the crest of a wave.

Wave fronts move out from a point source as a series of ever-widening circles centered on the source. At large distances from the source, the wave fronts appear as parallel lines.

Rays are lines drawn at right angles to the wave fronts. They show the direction of travel of waves. The path of light waves is often represented as rays that travel in straight lines from the source.

WAVE BEHAVIOR

The path of a ray of light changes if it strikes a glass surface at an angle. This effect, called refraction, happens because light travels faster through air than through glass. Seismic waves from earthquakes and explosive charges refract in a similar way at rock boundaries. Geologists use seismic refraction to study underground rocks.

Reflection is when waves bounce off a surface at the same angle as they arrived. Examples include light reflecting from a mirror and sound echoing off a cliff face.

Diffraction happens when waves pass through a gap in a barrier. If the width of the gap is similar to, or smaller than, the wavelength, the gap acts as a new source and produces waves with semicircular wave fronts.

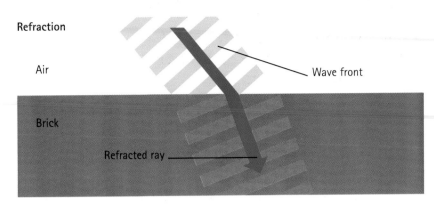

Refraction

Air

Brick

Wave front

Refracted ray

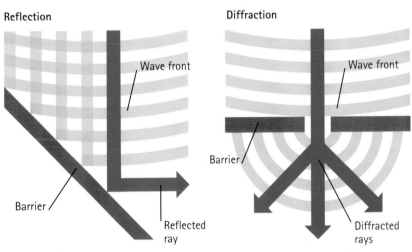

Reflection

Wave front

Barrier

Reflected ray

Diffraction

Wave front

Barrier

Diffracted rays

THE DOPPLER EFFECT

The waves in front of a moving source are closer together, so a stationary observer detects a higher frequency from an approaching source. As the source retreats, the apparent frequency is lower. This phenomenon, called the Doppler effect, is why the horn of a train seems to drop in pitch as it passes an observer.

The Doppler effect causes the light from distant stars to appear redder than the light from nearby stars. This indicates that distant stars are moving away faster than closer stars as the universe expands.

Refraction is the bending of a wave's path as it passes from one medium to another. Reflection is when a wave bounces off the boundary between two media. Diffraction is the spreading of a wave through a gap in a barrier.

◀ The wave fronts of the sound from a moving motorcycle are bunched up in front and stretched out behind. The closer the wave fronts, the higher the frequency, so the pitch of the engine noise falls as the motorcycle passes.

SEE ALSO PAGES:

262–3 Reflection and absorption, 264–5 Refraction, 370–1 Television and videotape

VIBRATIONS

Something vibrates when it changes its position or state in a regularly repeating pattern. Vibrations are described by their frequency and amplitude.

Sound	Level
Rocket takeoff	150
Pain threshold	140
Jet aircraft	130
Thunder	110
Heavy traffic	80–90
Orchestra	60–70
Conversation	40–50
Whispering	30
Leaves falling	20

Sound level is measured in decibels (dB). Each increase of 3dB represents a doubling of the loudness of a sound.

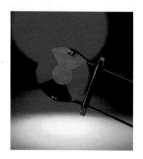

A thin slice of quartz crystal connected to two electrodes. When the crystal is placed in an electrical circuit, it causes a current in the circuit to vibrate at a precisely known frequency. That frequency is used in the timing mechanisms of quartz clocks and watches.

Vibrations are regularly repeating movements. The number of repetitions per second is called the frequency of the vibration. One cycle per second is one hertz, symbol Hz. A flying bee's wings vibrate up and down around 150 times each second, so the frequency of this vibration is 150 hertz, which is heard as a hum.

AMPLITUDE

Many sorts of vibrations happen around a position of rest. For example, a guitar string is in the rest position when it is still and stretched straight. When plucked, the string moves up and down by equal amounts either side of the rest position. The maximum distance the string travels away from the rest position is called the amplitude of the vibration.

Other types of vibrations also have amplitudes. The amplitude of an electrical signal, for example, can be the maximum voltage or current in each cycle.

The sound of a plucked guitar string slowly dies away. The vigor of the vibration steadily becomes less as air friction works against the string. In such cases, the amplitude is the first and largest deflection of the vibration.

The amplitude of a vibration is related to its energy. Large-amplitude sounds are loud, large-amplitude light is bright, and large-amplitude earthquakes can be strong enough to devastate cities.

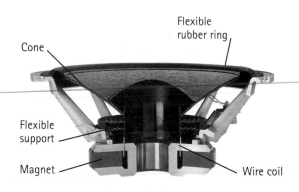

A flexible rubber ring supports the rim of a loudspeaker cone. The voice coil at the point of the cone moves the cone back and forth to produce sound waves.

VIBRATIONS AND OSCILLATIONS

The word "vibration" generally refers to something that moves very fast. "Oscillation" can refer to fast movements, but can also apply to slow repetitive motions, such as the up-and-down motion of the sea as waves go by.

EARTHQUAKES

The Earth's crust consists of giant slabs, called tectonic plates, that are slowly moving. Sometimes, forces build up when two plates meet and neither gives way. After a time, the plates tear apart at a point called the hypocenter, or focus, as much as 310 mi. (500km) below the Earth's surface. Stored energy is suddenly released and spreads intense vibrations in all directions. Vibrations that reach the surface are called earthquakes if their amplitudes are strong enough to be detected by humans. The position on the surface directly above the hypocenter is called the epicenter of an earthquake.

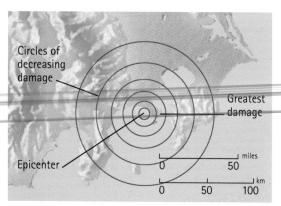

The effect pattern of the 1995 earthquake at Kobe, Japan.

▶ A seismograph plots the amplitude of ground vibrations. An amplitude increase of ten units is equal to an increase of one on the Richter scale.

◀ In around 20 seconds, the Kobe earthquake of 1995 toppled buildings and ripped roads apart. Tremors were felt as far as 60 mi. (100km) from the epicenter.

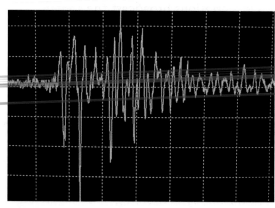

A seismic trace of the Kobe earthquake.

COMMUNICATION

Humans use sounds to communicate, but sound vibrations do not travel far in air. The amplitude of sound waves falls in proportion to the square of the distance of the sound source, so it is already difficult to hear someone shouting from a distance of a hundred meters.

Telephone systems can carry the sound of a voice over enormous distances. A microphone in a telephone converts sound waves into an electrical signal. A speaker in the telephone at the receiving end converts this signal back into sound.

VIBRATING ELECTRICAL CURRENTS

The electric current from a flashlight battery is a steady flow of electrons in one direction only. This type of current is called a direct current. The electric currents in telephone wires do not flow in one direction only. They repeatedly reverse their direction of flow back and forth, in step with a vibrating diaphragm in the microphone. The electrical signal from a microphone vibrates at frequencies between 40 Hz and 15,000 Hz (15 kHz).

Vibrating electric currents steadily fade as they travel along wires, but they travel much farther than sound waves moving through air. Electrical circuits called amplifiers boost the signals every few kilometers (miles) along the wire.

VIBRATING RADIO WAVES

Radio waves are vibrations of electric and magnetic fields that travel through space. They can be produced by transmitters that use electric circuits to generate currents that vibrate at between 1,000,000 Hz (1 MHz) and 1,000,000,000 Hz (1 GHz).

Radio stations broadcast the sounds of voices and music using circuits that combine a low-frequency sound signal and a high-frequency carrier signal. The signal then passes to a metal rod or wire called an antenna. Electrons in the antenna move back and forth in step with the vibrating current. Their movement produces electromagnetic radiation that vibrates in step with the currents in the antenna.

Television images and data can also be transmitted by combining an information signal with a carrier signal.

◄ Human throats contain a pair of membranes called vocal cords. They vibrate when air from the lungs passes between them. The lips, palate, and tongue modify these raw sounds to make the complex vibrations required for speech.

RECEIVING RADIO WAVES

Radio and TV receivers use antennae to receive radio waves. Radio waves make electrons in the antennae vibrate as they pass by. These tiny vibrating electric currents flow into the receiver where circuits extract the sound, vision, or other information that was fed into the transmitter. These signals are then boosted by amplifier circuits. In the case of sound, vibrating electrical signals pass through a spiral of wire, sometimes called a voice coil, in a loudspeaker. This coil is in a powerful magnetic field and is attached to a cone in the loudspeaker. The vibrating current makes the voice coil move in and out of the field. These vibrations move the loudspeaker cone, which makes the air vibrate to reproduce the original sound.

DAMPING

If a person hums a steady note, the air around that person vibrates at a steady amplitude. Its strength remains constant. Vibrations that have a steady strength are called undamped oscillations. They include notes played on wind instruments, like clarinets, and notes bowed on string instruments, such as violins and cellos.

When a guitar string is plucked or a note is played on a piano, the vibrations steadily die away. The amplitude of the vibration becomes less as the vibration loses its energy to air resistance, just as a rubber ball bouncing on a hard surface bounces less and less high as it loses energy on each bounce. These types of vibration are called damped oscillations.

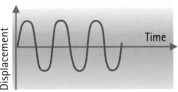

Undamped oscillations

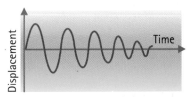

Damped oscillations

Each bounce of a bungee jump has a smaller amplitude than the one before. The energy of the bounce is gradually lost to the surroundings as heat. This is an example of a damped oscillation.

SEE ALSO PAGES:

RESONANCE

Resonance is the oscillation of an object at its natural frequency of vibration. A small repeated driving force causes an oscillation of larger amplitude.

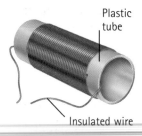

Wet finger moves in minute jerks

A wineglass emits a ringing note as a wet finger skids around its rim. The finger slips in a series of tiny jerks that supply the energy that allows the glass to vibrate at its natural frequency.

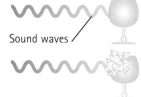

Sound waves

The sides of a glass will oscillate when struck by sound that matches its resonant frequency. The glass can break if the amplitude of vibration becomes too great.

The swing of a pendulum is an example of a regularly alternating motion called an oscillation. Whether a pendulum swings violently or gently back and forth, each complete swing takes the same amount of time. The frequency of the oscillation depends only on the length of the cord or wire that supports the swinging mass of the pendulum.

NATURAL FREQUENCIES

Any system that can oscillate will tend to do so at one particular frequency. That frequency depends on the system and is called the natural frequency or resonant frequency of the system.

Blowing across the neck of an empty bottle will produce a sound with a single note. That note is the natural frequency of the air in the bottle. Pouring some water into the bottle causes the note to rise. The volume of air in the bottle has changed, and so has its natural frequency.

RESONANCE AND ENERGY

If a person pushes a playground swing at the top of each stroke, the amplitude of the swing's motion increases rapidly. The energy of the oscillations also increases. A similar effect is noticed by people who sing in tiled bathrooms. The singer's voice supplies energy to the room and the sound waves bounce around easily between the walls. Certain notes sound louder and resound for a longer time than other notes.

In 1940, the Tacoma Narrows Bridge at Puget Sound, Washington, was destroyed by gusts of wind that caused it to twist at its natural frequency until it fell apart.

This is because the frequencies of the louder notes correspond to resonant frequencies of the air in the bathroom.

In the case of the playground swing, the pusher is the driving force for the system; in the case of the bathroom singer, his or her voice is the driving force. In both cases, the amplitude and energy of the oscillations increase rapidly when the frequency of the driving force matches the natural frequency of the system.

ELECTRICAL RESONANCE

Electrical resonance can happen when an electrical circuit favors one particular frequency of oscillating current. This type of circuit is called a tuned circuit. A typical tuned circuit has two electronic components: a capacitor and an inductor.

Capacitors have two closely spaced sets of metal plates that do not touch. They can store energy in an electrical field between the plates. Inductors are coils of wire. They can store energy in a magnetic field that surrounds the wire.

When an inductor and a capacitor are connected together to form a tuned circuit, electrons can oscillate back and forth between them. The driving force for the resonance comes from an input signal. Those parts of the signal that do not match the resonant frequency of the circuit cancel themselves out, so they are removed from the signal. The part that matches the tuned frequency resonates. The resonant frequency of such a circuit changes if either the inductance or the capacitance of the circuit changes.

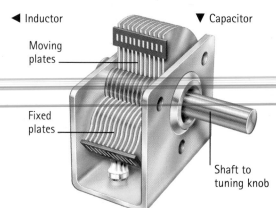

Plastic tube

Insulated wire

◀ Inductor

Moving plates

Fixed plates

▼ Capacitor

Shaft to tuning knob

A radio tuner contains an inductor and a capacitor in a circuit that oscillates at a resonant frequency. Turning the tuning knob alters this frequency by changing the overlap between two sets of plates in the capacitor.

TUNING IN

Radio and television receivers make use of electrical resonance to tune to one frequency at a time. As radio waves pass through the antenna of a receiver, they cause tiny oscillating currents to flow. If these currents passed straight through to the receiver's amplifier, a mixture of all the detectable radio and television stations would result. A resonant circuit filters out all frequencies apart from its resonant frequency. This is then boosted by the amplifier. The circuit is tuned by adjusting the capacitor until a station is found.

NUCLEAR MAGNETIC RESONANCE

The nuclei of certain atoms behave like tiny magnets. When placed in a powerful magnetic field, such nuclei align their fields with the main field. A pulse of radio waves can disturb the nuclei as they absorb energy from it. After the pulse, the nuclei realign themselves with the magnetic field. Nuclei absorb energy from the radio waves at particular frequencies that depend on the atoms around them. The nuclei resonate with the oscillating electromagnetic field as they flip around in step with it. Scientists use this effect, called nuclear magnetic resonance (NMR), to gather information about how atoms link together in complex molecules.

Magnetic resonance imaging (MRI) scanners in hospitals use NMR to produce images of patients' internal organs.

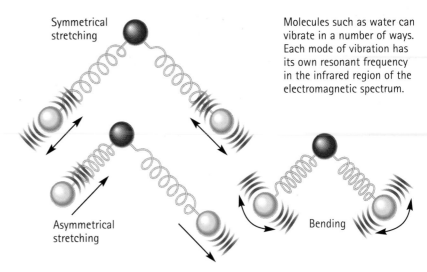

Molecules such as water can vibrate in a number of ways. Each mode of vibration has its own resonant frequency in the infrared region of the electromagnetic spectrum.

Symmetrical stretching

Asymmetrical stretching

Bending

In the symmetrical stretch, the two hydrogen–oxygen bonds in water expand and contract at the same time.

In the asymmetrical stretching mode, one of the bonds expands and the other contracts.

In the bending mode, the angle between the two bonds varies, but the bond length stays constant.

IR SPECTROSCOPY

The bonds between the atoms in a molecule are not rigid: they can each bend and stretch.

The vibration of a molecule has certain resonant frequencies that correspond to different combinations of bond vibrations. Some of these vibrations are stimulated by infrared, or IR, electromagnetic radiation.

Infrared spectroscopy shines a range of IR frequencies through a sample. The sample absorbs frequencies that match its vibrations, helping to identify the material.

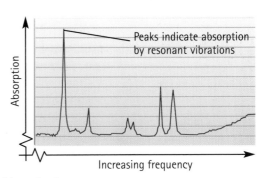

Peaks indicate absorption by resonant vibrations

Increasing frequency

Molecules absorb infrared radiation at frequencies that correspond to their vibrations. A plot of IR absorption can help to identify a compound.

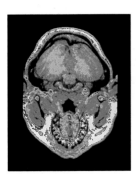

This magnetic-resonance-imaging (MRI) picture shows a slice through a human head. MRI is less dangerous than X-ray scanning and shows soft tissues in more detail.

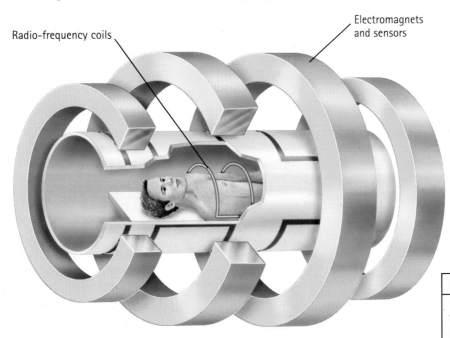

Radio-frequency coils

Electromagnets and sensors

In an MRI scanner, huge coils of wire produce a magnetic field. Radio waves make hydrogen atoms flip when their frequency matches the resonant frequency of the nuclei. Sensors send signals to a computer that constructs images from the incoming data.

SEE ALSO PAGES:

150-1 Atoms, 316-17 Vibrations, 340-1 Electrical circuits

VIBRATIONS OF STRINGS

A stretched string vibrates at a natural frequency that depends on its length and its tension. Strings vibrate when they are plucked, struck, or bowed.

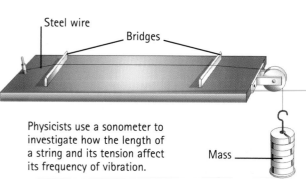

Physicists use a sonometer to investigate how the length of a string and its tension affect its frequency of vibration.

The sitar is a stringed instrument from northern India. The performer plucks seven strings with one hand while pressing four of them against the neck to alter the length that can vibrate. This alters their pitch. Twelve other strings and the large, hollow wooden body resonate with these vibrations and enrich the sound of the instrument.

Many musical instruments have taut strings that make sounds as they vibrate. The strings of guitars are plucked with fingers or with a small plastic pick called a plectrum. The strings of violins and cellos vibrate when a bow is drawn across them. Piano strings vibrate when struck by hammers connected to the keys.

TIMBRE AND OVERTONES

A note played on a guitar sounds different from the same note on a piano. The guitar string and the piano string vibrate at the same frequency, called the fundamental frequency. They also vibrate less strongly at frequencies that are multiples of the fundamental frequency. These frequencies are called overtones or harmonics. If the fundamental frequency, or first harmonic, is 200 Hz, then the first overtone, or second harmonic, is 400 Hz, and so on. Resonances in the instruments influence the balance of harmonics and modify the timbre, or quality, of the note.

TENSION, LENGTH, AND PITCH

The strings in guitars, pianos, and violins are anchored at each end so they have a fixed length. These instruments are tuned by tightening each string around a peg. The tauter the string, the higher the note.

Pianos have separate strings for each of the 88 notes on the keyboard. Pressing a key causes a hammer to strike the string and start it vibrating.

Performers change the notes of stringed instruments, such as guitars and violins, by using the fingers of one hand to press the strings and alter the length that can vibrate. Shortening a string increases its natural frequency of vibration. They pluck, strum, or bow with the other hand.

THE SOUND OF A VIOLIN

A violin bow consists of horsehairs stretched across a light wooden frame. The hairs are coated with a sticky, but dry, substance called rosin. Moving the bow hairs across a violin string pulls the string to one side. The string becomes tighter and then suddenly slips away from the bow hairs and springs back toward its original position. The string then sticks again to the bow hairs and is pulled to one side again. This process of pulling and slipping repeats very rapidly, causing the string to oscillate back and forth at its natural frequency of vibration (its resonant frequency).

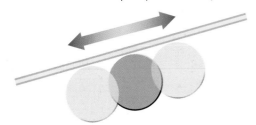

The rasping action of the bow causes a string to vibrate

Bow

Strings

Fingerboard

Tuning pegs

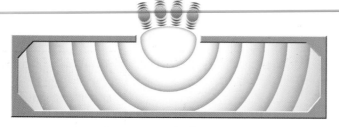

The body of a violin resonates when the strings are played. This increases the amplitude of the sound waves. The tone of a violin depends on its shape and the quality of the wood and the varnish that coats it.

SEE ALSO PAGES:

312–13 Sound as changes of pressure,
318–19 Resonance

VIBRATIONS IN TUBES

Wind instruments use columns of air that vibrate in tubes to produce sound. The frequency of the sound depends mainly on the length of the tube.

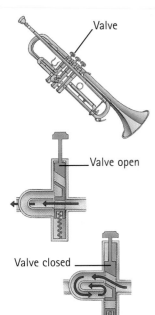

A trumpet has three valves. When the player pushes a valve's plunger, the air column is diverted through a loop of pipe. The valve changes the length of the air column, changing the note.

Wind instruments usually feature a long tube that contains a column of air. The performer blows down one end to cause vibrations, and the sound usually comes out the other end.

Brass instruments, such as trumpets and trombones, produce notes when the player's lips vibrate inside a mouthpiece. Clarinets, oboes, saxophones, and bassoons have reeds in their mouthpieces that vibrate when blown. Other wind instruments, such as flutes and recorders, produce vibrations from a stream of air that oscillates across the edge of a hole.

Vibrations from the mouthpiece include a range of frequencies. The frequency that resonates depends on the length of the column of vibrating air. The player selects a note by adjusting this length.

Trombones have a slide that changes the length of pipe; trumpets have valves that divert the sound through loops of pipe. Many wind instruments have holes along their lengths that can be covered by fingers or pads. Uncovering one or more holes has the effect of shortening the pipe and raising its resonant frequency.

The Australian didgeridoo is a single, long wooden pipe. The player's lips vibrate at the resonant frequency of the pipe. Sound comes out of the far end.

NODES AND ANTINODES

When a wind instrument is played, air molecules inside it vibrate back and forth. They do not all move at the same speed. At some places, called nodes, they do not move at all. At other places, called antinodes, they are moving at their fastest.

A simple tube instrument, such as a didgeridoo, has one antinode at the player's mouth and one at the end where the sound comes out. Resonance causes a node half way along the tube. Players can produce higher notes, or harmonics, by tightening their lips to increase the number of nodes along the pipe.

THE SOUND OF A RECORDER

The mouthpiece of a recorder sends a jet of air toward a wedge. The wedge causes eddies in the air. This makes the jet blow alternately above and below the wedge. The frequency of this oscillation is controlled by the resonant frequency of the column of air inside the recorder. Nodes and antinodes are illustrated here as loops that fit inside the tube.

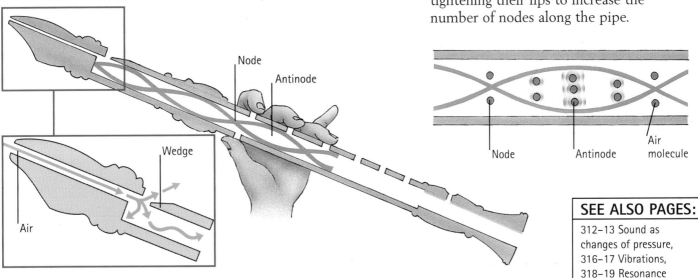

Node

Antinode

Node   Antinode   Air molecule

Wedge

Air

SEE ALSO PAGES:

312–13 Sound as changes of pressure,
316–17 Vibrations,
318–19 Resonance

BALANCE AND TURNING FORCES

Turning forces can make an object rotate. An object is balanced when turning forces operate equally against each other so that rotation does not happen.

The effectiveness of a wrench depends on its length. For the same force, doubling the length of the wrench doubles the torque.

Newton's third law of motion states that whenever a force acts on an object, an equal and opposite force matches it. A door opens when a person pulls its handle. The pulling force is matched by an equal force that acts through its hinges. This force points in the opposite direction to the force on the handle, but it acts along a different line. The result is a turning force, or torque, that makes the door turn on its hinges.

When a person sits on one side of a seesaw, the body weight is matched by an upward force that acts through the pivot. This results in a torque that drives that side of the seesaw to the ground. If someone of equal weight sits at the same distance on the other side of the pivot, he or she produces an equal and opposite torque, so the seesaw comes into balance.

CALCULATING TORQUE

A long-handled wrench will sometimes loosen a tight nut that will not respond to a smaller wrench. This is because a given force produces more torque when it acts farther from a pivot, in this case the nut. It is pointless to try to loosen a nut by pushing or pulling along the handle of a wrench. This is because torque only arises from force that acts at right angles to the

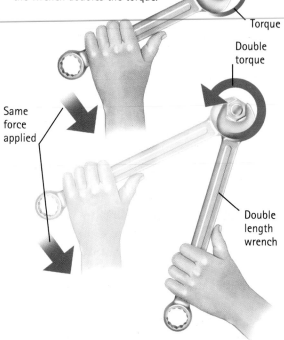

Force

Force

Force

Doorknobs, wrenches, and faucet handles all increase the turning effect of a hand. In each case, a force that acts at a distance from a pivot point produces a twisting force.

Same force applied

Torque

Double torque

Double length wrench

line between the pivot and the point where the force acts. At any other angle, at least part of the force will be resisted by a reaction force that acts along the wrench and has no turning effect.

Torque is calculated by multiplying the length of the line between the pivot and the point of action of the force by the part of the force that acts at right angles to that line. The mathematical expression is *torque = force x distance*. The usual unit of torque is the newton meter, symbol *Nm*, so the value of force in newtons must be multiplied by the distance in meters.

A torque of one newton meter is equivalent to a force of one newton pulling or pushing at right angles at the end of a one-meter-long lever. The motor of a food mixer produces a torque of around 1 Nm, the motor of an electric drill produces 2 Nm, and the engine of a car generates up to 150 Nm.

The weight of a 40-kilogram (88-lb) bicyclist is 40 x 9.8 = 392 Nm—their mass times the constant *g*. If they stand on a pedal attached to a 0.2-meter-long crank, the torque on the sprocket, or chainwheel, is 398 x 0.2 = 78.4 Nm— just over half the torque of a car engine.

► Pushing the pedals of a bicycle produces a torque in the sprocket, or chainwheel. The chain transfers torque to a gear attached to the hub of the rear wheel. The torque at the rear wheel can be increased for hill climbing by changing to a lower gear ratio.

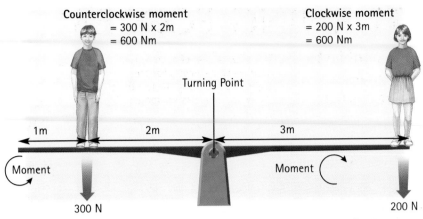

Counterclockwise moment
= 300 N x 2m
= 600 Nm

Clockwise moment
= 200 N x 3m
= 600 Nm

Turning Point

1m   2m   3m

Moment   Moment

300 N   200 N

A seesaw is balanced when the clockwise moment equals the counterclockwise moment. The boy's weight is 300 newtons (300 N) and he stands 2 meters (2m) from the pivot. He causes the

counterclockwise moment of 600 newton-meters (Nm). The girl is lighter (200 N), but she stands farther from the pivot (3m). She causes a clockwise moment of 600 Nm, so the seesaw is balanced.

BALANCE AND MOMENTS

A seesaw is a lever that pivots on a central fulcrum. Two people sitting on opposite ends of a seesaw will not move if the seesaw is exactly balanced. Gravity produces a downward force as it pulls on the mass of each person. The person on the right produces a torque that tries to rotate the seesaw clockwise. This torque is called a clockwise moment. The person on the left produces a turning force that attempts to rotate the seesaw counterclockwise: a counterclockwise moment.

Moments are calculated in the same way as torque: by multiplying force and distance. If the people on the seesaw cause equal but opposite moments, there is no overall torque: the seesaw is in balance. The masses of the two people do not have to be identical to balance. The heavier person can reduce his or her moment by moving closer to the pivot.

EQUILIBRIUM

An object is in equilibrium if all the forces and moments that act on it are in balance. An object that is in equilibrium will not accelerate or start to rotate.

A can of beans that stands on a flat surface is in equilibrium. The force of gravity acts on every particle in a can. These separate forces act together as if they were a single force pulling downward at one point. That force is the weight of the can; the point where it seems to act is called the center of gravity or center of mass. The reaction force to the weight of the can acts through its base.

If the can is tilted through a small angle, its center of mass will still be over its base. The reaction force acts at the rim of the can, producing a torque that tends to set the can upright. If it is tilted so that the center of mass is no longer over the base, the torque reverses and pulls the can over.

Standard weights are added to one side of the scales until they balance the objects on the other side. If the two arms of the scale are equal in length, the masses in the two pans are then equal.

This gymnast stays in balance while her center of gravity is directly above the beam. If she leans to one side, she will topple.

Stable equilibrium

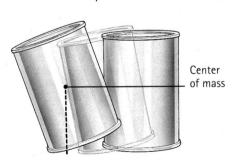

Center of mass

An object in stable equilibrium can be tilted through a moderate angle without its center of mass moving outside the footprint of its base. If tilted and then released, it will right itself.

Unstable equilibrium

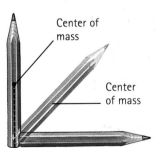

Center of mass

Center of mass

An object is in unstable equilibrium if a small angle of tilt takes its center of mass outside the footprint of its base. If tilted, it will topple until it reaches a more stable equilibrium.

Neutral equilibrium

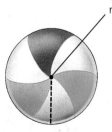

Center of mass

An object is in neutral equilibrium if it can roll without its center of mass straying outside the footprint of its base.

SEE ALSO PAGES:

290–1 Force, 296–7 Momentum, 298–9 Relativity and gravity, 303 Gears

CIRCULAR MOTION

An object in circular motion either spins or moves on a curved path around a fixed point. Different types of forces drive the two types of motion.

There are two types of circular motion. Wheels spin, for example, and the Earth orbits the sun. Different forces produce these two sorts of motion. Gyroscopic forces act on spinning objects; centripetal forces act on objects that move in a circle.

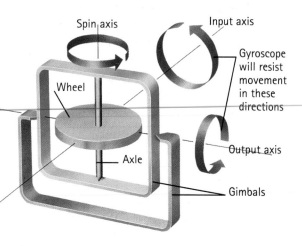

A gyroscope consists of a heavy wheel that spins on an axle. The frame that supports the axle can twist around the spin axis but not in any other direction.

GYROSCOPES

A gyroscope is a heavy wheel that can spin on its axis. When spinning, a gyroscope resists attempts to tilt it. This property is called gyroscopic inertia. Toy gyroscopes consist of a metal wheel whose axle is supported in a metal frame. The wheel is set spinning by pulling a piece of string wrapped around the axle. A toy gyroscope can balance on the tip of a pencil or finger. While the wheel spins, gyroscopic inertia prevents the axis of the gyroscope from changing its direction. This effect is used in gyrocompasses and gyrostabilizers.

Gyrocompasses contain gyroscope wheels that are spun continuously by electric motors. The gyroscope's axle is supported inside two linked rings called gimbals. Twisting the outer ring in any direction has no effect on the gyroscope that is spinning inside the inner ring.

Gyrocompasses are fitted to ships, aircraft, and rockets. Unlike magnetic compasses, they are not affected by rapid motion, magnetic objects, or electrical wiring. When the wheel in a gyrocompass starts spinning, its axle is set to point in a known direction. As the vehicle moves and changes course, the axle continues to point in the original direction.

Gyrostabilizers are complex machines that help ships to keep steady in rolling seas. Gyroscopes mounted inside gimbals

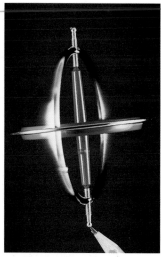

A toy gyroscope balances on the point of a pencil. The heavy metal wheel spins some 20 times every second. Gyroscopic inertia holds the gyroscope at a fixed angle and prevents it from tilting farther and falling from the pencil.

The dial of a gyrocompass looks similar to that of a magnetic compass. The position of the indicator is controlled by a gyroscope, not by magnets.

▶ The outer part of a gimbal frame can twist around in any direction. The spinning gyroscope wheel inside stays pointing constantly in one direction.

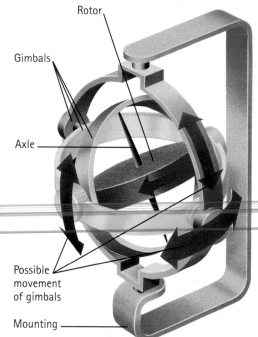

detect how the ship is tilting as it moves through waves. Sensors attached to the gimbals send signals to a computer that controls stabilizer fins attached to the hull of the ship. These fins act like wings. They force the ship to roll in the opposite direction to the force of the waves. Continuous adjustments to the fins makes the ship stay almost upright.

CENTRIPETAL FORCE

Objects that travel in circular paths behave in a different way from spinning gyroscopes. They experience centripetal force. Imagine a cat sitting in the middle of a field and a person trying to walk a dog around the edge of the field. If the dog is strong enough and wants to chase the cat, it will pull the leash toward the center of the field. While the owner attempts to travel in a straight line, the dog constantly pulls toward the cat. As a result, the dog and owner walk in a circular path around the cat. The dog provides a centripetal force that produces the circular motion.

The planets of the solar system move around the sun along paths that are approximately circular. The gravitational force between the sun and the planets provides the centripetal force that makes the planets move along curved paths in their orbits. In the same way, the Earth's gravity keeps the moon in its orbit.

CENTRIFUGAL EFFECTS

When a person sits in a moving car that enters a curve, he or she has the sensation of being pushed toward the outside of the curve. In fact, the sensation comes from the person's body wanting to keep moving in a straight line as the car steers into the curve. Although commonly called centrifugal force, this is simply an effect of inertia—the tendency of matter to keep moving at constant speed in a straight line.

Extractors use the centrifugal effect to remove water from clothes. Wet clothes are placed in a perforated metal drum. As it spins, water is flung out through the holes in its sides. This is because water droplets that form on the outside of the drum are not pulled toward the center of the drum with enough force to keep them in circular motion. Once the droplets detach themselves from the drum, they keep moving in a straight line.

Centrifuges work in a similar way to extractors. They are used to separate substances. When a mixture is spun, denser components of the mixture tend to drift away from the center of the spin more than the less dense components, which float toward the center of the spin. Food manufacturers use centrifuges to separate sugar crystals from syrup and cream from milk. In hospitals, centrifuges separate the different cells in blood and other body fluids. Ultracentrifuges spin at 200,000 revolutions per minute or more. They can separate molecules that have different masses. Very large centrifuges help astronauts to prepare themselves for the forces of taking off into space.

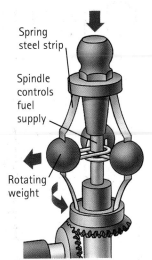

Spring steel strip

Spindle controls fuel supply

Rotating weight

A governor controls engine speed. As it rotates, the weights swing outward, pulling down a spindle that reduces the fuel supply at high speed.

An astronaut trains in a centrifuge. The centripetal force reproduces the massive acceleration of a rocket-powered launch as it moves toward escape velocity, the speed necessary to break free of the forces of gravity.

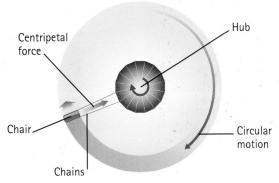

Centripetal force

Hub

Chair

Chains

Circular motion

◀ The chairs on this ride hang from a central hub by chains. The tension in the chains makes the chairs move in a circular path around the hub.

◀ Newton's first law of motion states that an object travels in a straight line unless a force acts on it. An object moving in a circle is constantly accelerating toward the center point under the influence of the centripetal force.

SEE ALSO PAGES:

FLOATING AND SINKING

A body floats in a fluid if the upward force from the fluid matches the downward force of gravity on its mass. This effect is called buoyancy.

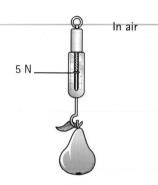

In air

5 N

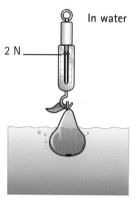

In water

2 N

The mass of the pear is the same whether it is surrounded by air or by water. It appears to weigh less in water due to the upthrust it experiences by displacing water.

▼ A floating object, such as a boat, displaces water from the space that it occupies. The weight of the displaced water is the same as the weight of the boat. Buoyancy is the result of water pressure.

Wood and oil float on water, so do steel ships. Balloons full of hot air or helium float up into the sky. Submarines rise to the surface from the depths of the sea. All these floating effects are caused by buoyancy, which is the name given to the upward force experienced by objects that are immersed in liquids or gases.

UPTHRUST
The weight of an object is the result of gravity acting on its mass. Weight always acts downward. When an object is immersed in a fluid, it experiences an upward force called upthrust. This force acts in the opposite direction to weight.

Upthrust is equal to the weight of the volume of fluid the object displaces, or pushes out of the way. This effect is called Archimedes' principle.

SINKING
Suppose that a concrete block has a volume of 1 m³ and a mass of 3,000 kilograms. Its weight is almost 30,000 N. Immersed in water, the block displaces 1 m³ of water, which has a mass of 1,000 kilograms and a weight of almost 10,000 N. As a result, there is an upthrust of 10,000 N on the block that acts against its weight of 30,000 N. The apparent weight of the block when submerged is 20,000 N. This concrete block will sink in water because the resultant force acting on it is 20,000 N downward. However, it will be easier to lift underwater because its weight is one third less than on dry land.

THE CAUSE OF UPTHRUST
When an object is immersed in a fluid, the upthrust is the result of the pressure of the fluid on the object. Pressure in a fluid acts in all directions and increases with depth. As a result, the pressure acting downward on the top of an object is less than the pressure acting upward on the bottom of the object. The result of these two forces acting against each other is an overall upward force—the upthrust.

Imagine a one meter cube in water with its top face one meter below the surface. The forces on the sides cancel each other out. The force from pressure of the water above is 10,000 N. The force from below is 20,000 N. The net force is an upthrust of 20,000 N–10,000 N = 10,000 N.

▼ Upthrust is the result of pressure increasing with depth. The pressure on the lower surface is greater than the pressure on the upper surface.

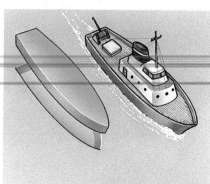

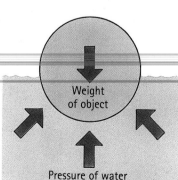

Weight of object

Pressure of water

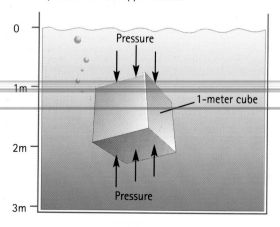

0

Pressure

1m

1-meter cube

2m

Pressure

3m

▶ The canopy of a hot-air balloon is made from synthetic materials that are light but tough. A wicker basket hangs underneath, and carries passengers and cylinders of liquefied butane gas for use in burners that heat the air in the canopy.

◀ A hot-air balloon holds around 1,500 cubic meters of hot air, which has a mass of 1,500kg. A balloon displaces 1,500 cubic meters of the surrounding cold air, which has a mass of about 2,000kg. Buoyancy gives an upthrust of 500kg.

Vent opens to allow hot air to escape for final descent

Opening in balloon

Gas burner

Flame

Butane gas in cylinders

FLOATING

Most types of wood float on water. Suppose that 1 m^3 of wood has a mass of 500 kg. Its weight in air is 5,000 N. When totally immersed it displaces 1 m^3 of water, which has a mass of 1,000 kg and a weight of 10,000 N. The upthrust on the wood is greater than its weight in air, so it floats to the surface. Floating objects are partly submerged so that the upward and downward forces are balanced. There is just enough of the object underwater to give an upthrust that is equal to the weight of the object in air. Placing weights on an object floating in water makes it sink lower into the water. It then displaces more water and the upthrust increases to match the greater downward force.

DENSITY AND FLOATING

The density of a substance is its mass per unit volume. The density of water is 1,000 kg/m^3. The value for concrete is around 3,000 kg/m^3, wood is around 500 kg/m^3, and steel around 7,800 kg/m^3. An object will float if its density is less than the density of water; it will sink if its density is greater. A steel ship floats because it is hollow. The average density of the steel hull and the air and fittings inside it is less than the density of water.

Hot-air balloons float because hot air is less dense than the cold air that surrounds them. Helium-filled balloons float because helium is less dense than air at the same pressure. As a helium balloon rises, it expands as the air pressure decreases.

Stem
Scale
Liquid
Glass bulb
Air
Weight

A hydrometer is a floating device that measures the density of liquids. The more dense the liquid, the greater the upthrust and the higher the hydrometer floats.

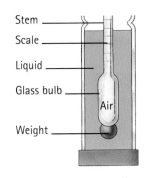

▶ Submarines consist of an airtight compartment surrounded by ballast tanks. The submarine dives by filling these tanks with water. Submerged, its neutral buoyancy makes sure that it neither floats nor sinks. It surfaces by using compressed air to force out the water.

Submarine dives
Air out
Ballast tanks full of water
Air pump
Air in
Water out
Water in

▲ The load line on the side of a ship shows how much load it can carry safely. How well a ship floats depends on the density of the water around it.

SEE ALSO PAGES:
290–1 Force, 310 Fluids, 311 Pressure, 332–3 Principles of flight

HARNESSING SEA POWER

Sea power is a renewable energy resource. Some devices use the energy of waves and tides to generate electricity; another uses temperature differences.

Oceans cover 70 percent of the Earth's surface. They absorb and store heat from the sun. This heat also drives winds across the surface of the oceans that cause waves to build up. The gravitational pulls of the sun and the moon cause tides that ebb and flow each day. The motions of the sea and the heat it contains are huge and inexhaustible energy resources. The challenge is to develop machines that can extract this energy and change it into a convenient form, such as electricity.

Osprey—for ocean-swell-powered renewable energy—was built in 1995. It has a mass of 8,000 tons, is 65 ft. (20m) tall and stands in 50 ft. (15m) of water 350 ft. (100m) off the shore of Scotland. Osprey was the world's first commercial power plant driven by waves. It produces two megawatts of electric power, enough for 400 homes.

▼ This oscillating water column device is at Islay, Scotland. It is pounded by ocean waves throughout the year, and provides a reliable source of energy.

WAVE POWER
When a wave one meter high and 25 meters wide crashes onto a beach, it loses about 125,000 joules of potential energy. If this were changed into electrical energy, it would be enough to run a desk lamp for around one hour. The wave power on a five-kilometer beach is around ten billion joules per hour, or 2.5 megawatts. This would be enough to run about 500 homes.

HARNESSING WAVE POWER
Waves are caused by wind, but are present even when the wind is not blowing. There are two ways of harnessing the energy in waves and converting it into electricity. Both change the up-and-down motion of waves into a rotational motion that can drive electric generators.

NODDING FLOATS
Some wave-energy converters consist of a series of flat floats arranged like hinges. As waves pass, the floats move up and down on the surface and pump oil through hydraulic motors that drive generators. They are anchored 350 ft. (100m) to 1-2 mi. (1.5-3km) offshore, behind the point where waves start to break.

OSCILLATING WATER COLUMNS
Most modern wave-energy converters use a form of oscillating water column, or OWC. Water moves up and down inside a vertical pipe as waves pass. This motion acts like a piston inside a cylinder. It pushes and pulls air through a turbine connected to a generator.

OWC generators can be anchored out at sea in the ocean swell, or built on shore in narrow, tapered channels that concentrate waves and amplify them.

The column of water forces air back and forth through a turbine with each passing wave.

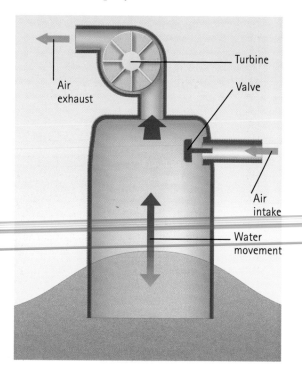

Turbine

Valve

Air exhaust

Air intake

Water movement

WAVES ON THE SHORE

Where large waves regularly pound the shore, tapered channels can be used to fill elevated reservoirs. The swell amplitude increases as a wave surges along the channel. At the narrowest point, water from the top of the wave breaks over a wall and falls into a tank. The water then turns a turbine and generator as it runs back into the sea through a pipe. This system is similar to that of a hydroelectric generator that uses water from a lake.

TIDAL POWER

Tidal power was first used over 900 years ago on the Spanish, French, and British coasts. The incoming tide filled storage ponds. At low tide, the water drained out of the ponds and turned waterwheels as it flowed back into the sea. Modern tidal schemes use a dam or barrage built across a river estuary. The estuary must be wide and tapered, so that there is a large difference between high and low water levels. Seawater flows through turbines as the tide rises and falls, providing power for about ten hours per day.

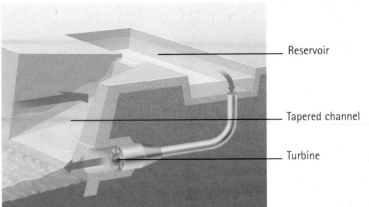

Reservoir

Tapered channel

Turbine

Surge devices channel waves into high reservoirs. The water drives a turbine as it flows back down from the reservoir. A 350-kilowatt power plant of this type has operated on the North Sea coast of Norway since 1986.

ENVIRONMENTAL IMPACT

While sea power is a free and renewable energy resource, the installations that harness it are expensive to build and maintain. They also affect the environment. Tidal barrages disturb wildlife and the balance of local ecosystems. Wave-energy converters out at sea can have beneficial effects, providing sheltered underwater habitats and protecting the shore from wave damage.

The tidal barrage at La Rance, France, is fitted with 24 turbines. There are similar tidal barrages in the Bay of Fundy in Canada and at Murmansk, in northwestern Russia.

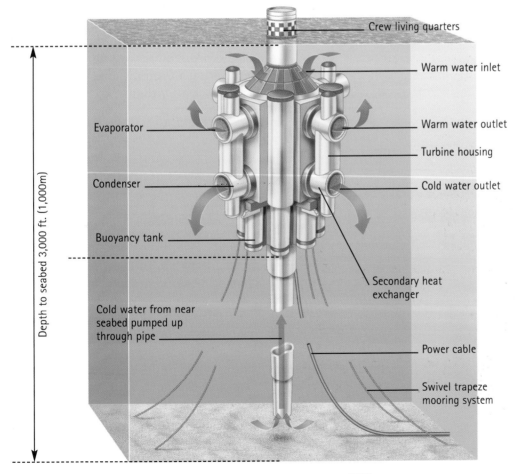

Crew living quarters

Warm water inlet

Evaporator

Warm water outlet

Turbine housing

Condenser

Cold water outlet

Buoyancy tank

Depth to seabed 3,000 ft. (1,000m)

Cold water from near seabed pumped up through pipe

Secondary heat exchanger

Power cable

Swivel trapeze mooring system

◀ An OTEC converter (ocean thermal energy converter) uses differences in temperature between warm surface water and cold water from 0.6 mi. (1km) lower. Warm surface water vaporizes a low-boiling-point fluid. The vapor drives a turbine and is condensed back to a liquid by cold water pumped up from the depths. Efficiency is low because pumping cold water uses much of the energy produced. Although OTEC devices are still experimental, the first working system was built in Cuba in 1930.

SEE ALSO PAGES:
248–9 Terrestrial energy sources, 310 Fluids, 348–9 Power plants, 458–9 Renewable energy

HARNESSING WIND POWER

Wind power is a renewable resource that comes from the energy of moving air. It can be used to propel ships, generate electricity, and move machinery.

Humans have harnessed and used the power of wind for thousands of years. Sailboats were common on the rivers and lakes of Egypt 5,500 years ago. In the 1340s, wind-driven pumps were first used to drain land in the Netherlands. A century later, windmills for grinding corn became common throughout Europe.

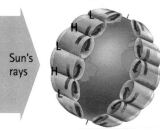

North Pole (high pressure)

Sun's rays

South Pole (high pressure)

Wind is the flow of air from high pressure areas (H) to low pressure areas (L). This flow creates six bands of airflow around the world, including the southwesterly winds that blow across the Atlantic and Pacific oceans.

MODERN DEVELOPMENTS
The fossil fuels used to provide most of our heat and power are not renewable. As their reserves fall, there is increasing interest in harnessing wind power. A few large ships have computer-controlled sails that assist the engines and save fuel. At the moment, scientists are most interested in harnessing wind power to generate electricity.

POWERED BY THE WIND

Wind has momentum as a result of its mass and velocity. When wind bounces off a sail, it creates a reaction force as required by Newton's third law of motion. By changing the angle of its sails, a boat or ship can move in any direction except directly toward the wind. A moderate wind of 10 meters per second (18.6 mph/30kph) exerts 130 newtons on each square meter of the sail's area.

ORIGINS OF THE WINDS
Winds are currents of air that move from areas of high pressure to areas of lower pressure. Low-pressure regions arise near the equator, where heat from the sun warms the air, making it less dense so that it rises up. At the same time, colder and denser air sinks. This downward motion creates areas of high pressure near the North and South poles.

The heating effect of the sun's energy causes air to circulate in north-south and south-north directions. At the same time, the spin of the Earth from west to east causes a sideways drift in the air. These two effects cause six bands of winds that blow across the world from northwest to southeast and northeast to southwest.

SAILS
Each cubic yard (meter) of air has a mass of about 3 lb (1.3kg) . This mass gives moving air its momentum. Air currents produce a pushing force against anything they strike. Sails are sheets of tough fabric that harness the force of the wind to drive sailboats and ships along the water.

The first windmills were developed by attaching triangular ships' sails to a central shaft. Instead of driving a ship along, the force of the blowing wind causes the sails to rotate the shaft. This rotation was used to drive pumps and mills to grind grain.

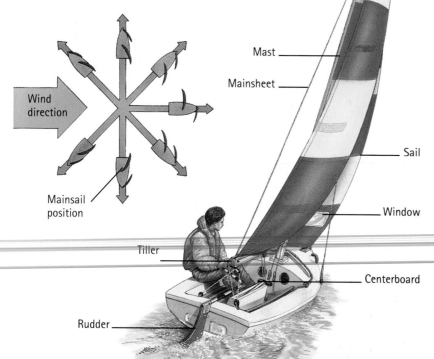

Wind direction

Mainsail position

Tiller

Rudder

Mast

Mainsheet

Sail

Window

Centerboard

Two sails reduce the fuel consumption of this ship by 10 percent. A computer controls motors that open, close, and turn the sails to the wind.

Canvas

Steel frame

Turnable mast

Close — Close

Open — Open

Fixed mast

WIND TURBINES

The sails attached to early windmills were inefficient because they extracted only a small part of the energy of passing air. Using propeller-shaped blades leads to greater efficiency. Modern machines have two or three blades up to 165 ft. (50m) long, called wind turbines. They drive electric generators standing on towers over 350 ft. (100m) high. Computer-controlled motors alter the angle of the blades and the direction they face in order to suit the speed and direction of the wind. In a moderate wind, a turbine of this size generates around 300 kilowatts of power, less than one thousandth of the power output of a coal-fired power plant.

WIND FARMS

Wind farms are groups of wind turbines that produce electrical energy for local communities. The Wintec Wind Farm near Palm Springs, California, has more than 4,000 turbines generating enough energy to power a city the size of San Francisco. This wind farm is situated in a natural dip in the ground that acts as an enormous solar energy collector. It fills with hot air that rises, drawing cooler air in from the Pacific Coast. This airflow picks up speed as it is channeled through a valley leading to the wind farm, creating the high winds that power the turbines.

THE FUTURE

A problem of wind power is that winds do not blow all the time. Most turbines need a minimum wind speed of about 12.5 mph (20kph) to start turning. This problem is largely overcome by connecting wind farms to a grid system of cables that links all the producers and all the consumers of electrical energy over a large area. In this way, the lack of wind in one place is made up for by wind blowing elsewhere. Although wind power supplies only a small part of the world's energy demand, its contribution will increase as stocks of fossil fuels continue to dwindle.

▲ Sartorius wind turbines rotate around a vertical axis. They spin in wind from any direction. The name is taken from a muscle that allows legs to cross with knees apart.

▲ Some wind turbines are located on platforms out at sea. Winds in these locations are more stable than on the land.

◄ This vertical-axis turbine is more efficient than a Sartorius turbine because the full length of each blade develops torque from the wind.

SEE ALSO PAGES:

10–11 Earth's atmosphere, 458–9 Renewable energy

PRINCIPLES OF FLIGHT

Machines fly by producing an upward force that overcomes their weight. They also generate thrust that drives them forward and helps them to steer.

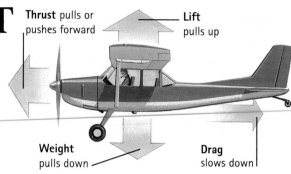

Thrust pulls or pushes forward — Lift pulls up

Weight pulls down — Drag slows down

Four forces act on an aircraft in flight. An aircraft will fly only when the lift, created by air flowing over the wings, is greater than its weight, and when the thrust of its engines is greater than the drag of the air.

Streamlined flow

Streamlining cuts down drag, or air resistance, by helping to create a smooth airflow. Teardrop-shaped objects are streamlined.

Flight is the movement of insects, birds, and aircraft through the air. Forces act on these objects to hold them up in the air. The principles of flight are the rules that govern the movement of objects as they fly through the air. They concentrate on the four forces—lift, thrust, drag, and weight—that act on all flying objects.

LIFT
The top surface of an aircraft's wing is curved, and the bottom is flatter. This shape is called an airfoil. Air that flows over the top of a moving wing has to travel a greater distance than the air flowing underneath. The air travels faster over the top than underneath. The pressure of air decreases when its speed increases. The pressure on the top surface of the wing is less than the pressure pushing up on the bottom surface. The overall force of lift pushes the wing up.

Turbulent flow

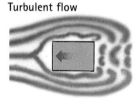

Square objects are not streamlined. They have sharply angled edges that create the turbulent flow that results in drag.

DRAG
Aircraft are held back by air resistance. This force is called drag. The faster an aircraft flies, the greater the drag.

Drag is a particular problem when designing high-speed planes, since its effect increases greatly with small increases in speed. To reduce drag, all external surfaces must be streamlined.

STEERING AN AIRCRAFT

Aircraft have movable parts on the wings and tail that are used to turn or tilt the aircraft in flight. Known as control surfaces, the ailerons, elevators, and rudder produce vertical or horizontal forces by diverting the air that flows around them. Two or three control surfaces have to be moved at the same time to make even a simple turn. In larger aircraft, the control surfaces are moved by hydraulic rams. In fly-by-wire aircraft, such as the Airbus A320, the control surfaces are operated by a computer system.

Aileron

Propellers
All airplanes had propellers until the 1940s. The shape of a propeller is an airfoil, similar to the wing. As the propeller is spun by the engine, it bites into the air to produce thrust.

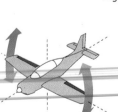

Rolling
Moving one aileron up and the other down makes the aircraft bank, or roll, to one side or the other.

Pitching
Lowering the elevators makes the nose dip and the tail rise. Raising the elevators makes the tail dip and the nose rise.

Yawing
Moving the rudder to the right turns the aircraft's nose to the right. Moving it to the left turns the nose to the left.

Rudder
Pushing the right rudder pedal moves the rudder to the right. Pushing the left rudder pedal moves the rudder to the left.

Control column
Pushing this column back and forth moves the elevators. Pushing it from side to side moves the ailerons.

THRUST AND PROPELLERS

All early airplanes were powered by gasoline-driven piston engines that spun propellers. Each blade of a propeller has an airfoil shape. As it moves through the air, it creates a forward force called thrust, just as the wing creates the upward force called lift. Many modern planes are fitted with variable pitch propellers that can alter the angle at which they bite into the air. The pilot changes engine speed and pitch in the same way that a bicyclist changes gear and pedals faster or slower.

THRUST AND JETS

Many modern planes are powered by jet engines. These gas turbine engines burn kerosene fuel to produce a stream of exhaust gases that thrust the airplane forward. The exhaust gases also spin a turbine at the rear of the engine that drives a compressor at the front. Turboprop engines use some of this power to drive a propeller. Turbofan engines have enormous compressors that shoot air around the engine to produce most of the engine's thrust.

Elevator

Rudder

Ailerons
The ailerons are joined by wires so that when one goes up, the other goes down. Moving them makes one wing rise and the other one drop.

HELICOPTERS

Helicopters use rotating blades to provide both lift and thrust. Two or more long rotor blades are attached to a shaft that sticks out of the top of the helicopter. Each blade is shaped like a long narrow wing that produces a downward force as it spins. This vertical force lifts the helicopter into the air. A smaller tail rotor provides a sideways force that prevents the helicopter from spinning. A helicopter can move in any direction by tilting the main rotors so that they are no longer parallel to the ground.

A glider's wings generate lift from the air that flows over them. A glider can rise in currents of warm air then dive gently to increase the airflow over the wings and provide lift.

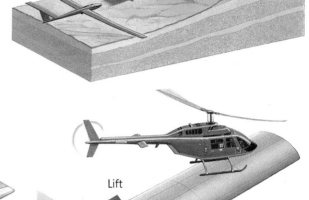

Rising currents of warm air

Lift

Thrust

▲ A helicopter's rotor blades provide both lift and thrust. The rotor blade has the same airfoil shape as a plane's fixed wing. As it spins, air flows over the blade, and produces lift. Tilting the whole rotor provides thrust.

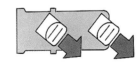

Nozzles point backward for normal forward flight

Nozzles rotate for lift and forward flight

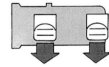

Nozzles point down for vertical takeoff or landing

Vertical Flight
The Harrier is one of the few fixed-wing planes able to rise vertically into the air and hover. It has four nozzles that direct thrust from the jet engines. When the nozzles point down, the plane moves vertically or hovers. When they point forward, it flies conventionally.

SEE ALSO PAGES:

75–7 Insects, 84–5 Birds, 226–7 Jet engines and gas turbines, 290–1 Force, 311 Pressure

SUPERSONIC FLIGHT

Supersonic aircraft can fly at speeds greater than the speed of sound Their design, with swept-back delta wings, differs from those of subsonic aircraft.

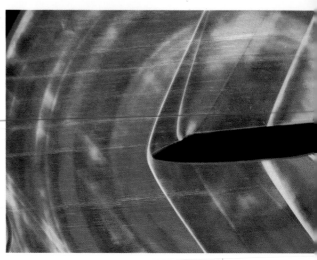

A model of NASA's space shuttle in a supersonic wind-tunnel test. A technique called schlieric photography reveals where shock waves form.

Spitfire, 1941
350 mph
Mach 0.53

Messerschmitt ME 262, 1944
550 mph
Mach 0.83

Bell XS-1, 1957
670 mph
Mach 1.02

Concorde, 1966
1,550 mph
Mach 2.03

Lockheed SR-71 1971
2,193 mph
Mach 3.30

Aircraft speed increased rapidly between the 1940s and the 1970s. Lift and drag increase with speed, so wings became smaller, thinner, and more swept-back to reduce drag.

In the early 1940s, propeller-engined fighter planes reached speeds of over 620 mph (1,000kph) in steep dives. The pilots observed severe buffeting that threatened to tear the wings off their aircraft. Scientists realized that these effects were caused by the aircraft approaching the speed of sound.

THE SOUND BARRIER

A moving aircraft disturbs the air and sends out noise and pressure waves that travel away from it in all directions at the speed of sound. When a plane reaches the speed of sound, the pressure waves cannot outrun it. The sound waves build up in front of the aircraft as a layer of densely compressed air called a shock wave.

To travel faster than the speed of sound, the pilot must fly the plane through this barrier and overtake it. There is a jolt as an aircraft breaks through the sound barrier because drag increases and lift suddenly decreases. Once through, the plane leaves the shock wave behind and flight is smooth again.

A plane flying at supersonic speeds leaves a trail of shock waves in its wake. When these waves of highly compressed air reach the ground, they are heard as a deep bang called a sonic boom.

MACH NUMBER

The speed of sound depends on the temperature, pressure, and humidity of air. Temperature can vary from 95°F (35°C) near the ground to –67°F (–55°C) high in the stratosphere, so the speed required for a plane to break through the sound barrier depends on the local conditions around it. This speed is given the value of Mach 1.0.

Speeds over Mach 1.0 are supersonic: from 770 mph (1,240kph) at sea level to around 660 mph (1,060kph) at 42,500 ft. (13,000m) altitude.

SUBSONIC AND HYPERSONIC

Subsonic speeds are below Mach 0.8, the approximate speed of a normal passenger jet. Transonic speeds range from Mach 0.8 to Mach 1.2. Hypersonic speeds are above Mach 5. The Concorde and fighter planes are supersonic aircraft; NASA's space shuttle enters the Earth's atmosphere at hypersonic speeds around Mach 20.

When an aircraft flies, sound waves spread out from it at the speed of sound. When the aircraft itself reaches the speed of sound—Mach 1.0—these sound waves pile up in front of the aircraft. Above the speed of sound, these waves form a shock wave that reaches the ground. The shock wave is heard as a sonic boom that can be powerful enough to break windows.

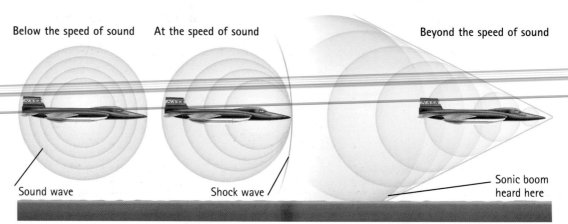

Below the speed of sound   At the speed of sound   Beyond the speed of sound

Sound wave   Shock wave   Sonic boom heard here

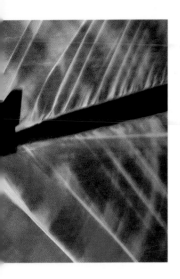

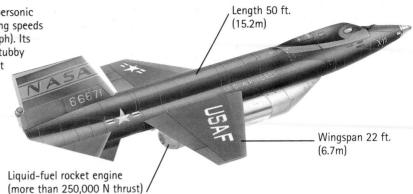

▶ In 1967, the U.S. X-15 supersonic aircraft flew at record-breaking speeds of around 4,520 mph (7,200kph). Its wedge-shaped tail and thin stubby wings were designed for flight at altitudes of around 62 mi. (100km).

Length 50 ft. (15.2m)

Wingspan 22 ft. (6.7m)

Liquid-fuel rocket engine (more than 250,000 N thrust)

SUPERSONIC WINGS

The top speeds of the world's fastest aircraft increased by more than six times between 1940 and 1999. The first plane to break the sound barrier was the Bell X-1 rocket plane in 1947. Scientists obtained information from early supersonic flights that helped them to design even faster aircraft.

In later designs, wings were swept back until they joined with the tail to form a single surface. This is called a delta wing; it helps make an aircraft more streamlined. The delta wing also fits snugly inside the supersonic shock wave, so the plane can pass through the sound barrier with minimum buffeting.

MOVABLE WINGS

Some supersonic fighter aircraft have wings that can move back and forth. Each wing is attached to a pivot in the plane's body. For takeoff and landing, the wings stick straight out from the fuselage to provide maximum lift. When flying at transonic and supersonic speeds, they move into a swept-back position to form a low-drag delta shape.

RECORD BREAKERS

The fastest winged aircraft is the rocket-propelled Bell X-15, built in 1959. It achieved a speed of Mach 6.72 in 1967. This record still stands because there is no longer any competition between countries to break the airspeed record. The fastest jet aircraft is the Lockheed SR-71, originally built as a spy plane. It achieved a speed of Mach 3.3 in 1971. Although no longer in military service, it is used for scientific studies in the upper atmosphere.

THE FUTURE

The Concorde is the only supersonic passenger aircraft. Profits from fares are small compared to the cost of designing and building this aircraft. There are plans for hypersonic passenger planes that can fly to the edge of space and travel across the Atlantic Ocean in under an hour.

HOTOL (horizontal takeoff and landing) aircraft could be hypersonic carriers in the future. Flying outside the atmosphere, HOTOL aircraft would use liquid oxygen to burn fuel in their engines.

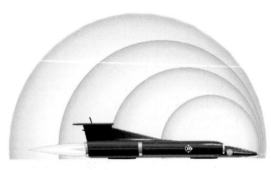

The Thrust supersonic car (SSC) is propelled by two jet-fighter engines. In 1998, it became the first land vehicle to break the sound barrier. Shock waves build up in front of the car as it approaches the speed of sound, the same way it happens in supersonic flight. A supersonic vehicle cannot be heard as it approaches because all the sound it makes is concentrated in the shock wave left behind it.

SEE ALSO PAGES:

84–5 Birds, 226–7 Jet engines and gas turbines, 290–1 Force, 298–9 Relativity and gravity

FACTS AND FIGURES

MOVEMENT

Speed

Speed is how quickly an object moves. An object that moves one meter (1 m) in one second (1 s) has a speed of one meter per second (1 m/s):

$$\text{Speed (m/s)} = \frac{\text{distance moved (m)}}{\text{time taken (s)}}$$

Velocity

Velocity is a measurement that describes both the speed of an object and its direction of travel. A car that turns a corner at a speed of 10 m/s does not have a fixed velocity because its direction changes at every instant.

Acceleration

Acceleration measures how quickly the velocity of an object changes. An object whose velocity increases by one meter per second in each second has an acceleration of one meter per second per second, or one meter per second squared (1 m/s^2):

$$\text{Acceleration (m/s}^2) = \frac{\text{change in velocity (m/s)}}{\text{time taken (s)}}$$

PROPERTIES OF MATTER

Inertia is a fundamental property of matter that causes it to resist efforts to change its velocity.

Momentum is calculated by multiplying the mass in kilograms of an object by its velocity in meters per second.

Momentum (kg m/s) = mass(kg) x velocity (m/s)

FORCE, ENERGY, WORK, AND POWER

Force

A force changes the momentum of an object. The unit of force is the newton (N). One newton (1 N) of force will accelerate a mass of one kilogram (1 kg) by one meter per second squared (1 m/s^2).

Force (N) = mass (kg) x acceleration (m/s^2)

Energy

The unit of energy is the joule (J). Ten joules (10 J) of energy will raise one kilogram (1 kg) of mass slightly more than one meter (1 m) vertically against the force of gravity.

Work

The unit of work is the joule (J). Work is done when energy converts from one form to another. One joule (1 J) of work is done when a force of one newton (1 N) moves a distance of one meter (1 m).

Work (J) = force (N) x distance (m)

Power

The unit of power is the watt (W). Power is the rate at which work is done or energy changes into another form. A machine that converts one joule (1 J) of energy in one second (1 s) has a power of one watt (1 W).

NEWTON'S LAWS OF MOTION

1st Law: An object will stay still or continue to move at a constant velocity unless a force pushes or pulls it.
2nd Law: The rate of change of the momentum of an object is proportional to the force that acts on it.
3rd Law: If one object exerts a force on another object, then the second object exerts an equal and opposite force (the reaction force) on the first.

SPEED

meters per second (m/s)	kilometers per hour (kph)	miles per hour (mph)
10	36	22
20	72	45
30	108	67
50	180	112
100	360	224
200	720	447
500	1,800	1,119
1,000	3,600	2,237

kilometers per hour	meters per second	miles per hour
10	2.8	6.2
20	5.6	12
30	8.3	19
50	14	31
100	28	62
500	139	311
1,000	278	621

AMOUNTS OF ENERGY

5 J = work done to shut a door
20 J = work done to throw a ball
1,000 J (1 kJ) = work done to climb a flight of stairs
4,000 J (4 kJ) = electrical energy in a typical fully charged AA battery
40,000 J (40 kJ) = heat energy required to boil a cup of water
120,000 J (120 kJ) = chemical energy in a teaspoon of sugar
300,000 J (300 kJ) = electrical energy in a car battery
34,000,000 J (34 MJ) = heat given out by burning a liter of gasoline

AMOUNTS OF FORCE

5 N = force (push) required to turn on a light switch
8 N = force to accelerate a 4 kg mass at a rate of 2 m/s^2
9.8 N = downward force of gravity pulling on a 1kg mass
20 N = force (pull) to open a soda can
2,000 N = force on a tennis ball struck hard by a racket
5,000 N = force from car engine
200,000 N = force from a jet engine

AMOUNTS OF POWER

1 W = flashlight bulb
60 W = electric lightbulb
250 W = washing-machine motor
300 W = running up stairs
1,000 W (1 kW) = cheetah running flat out
35,000 W (35 kW) = small car engine
250,000 W (250 kW) = large wind turbine
500,000,000 W (500 MW) = small power plant
2,000,000,000 W (2,000 MW) = typical coal-fired power plant
20,000,000,000 W (20,000 MW) = largest power plant in the world (Lower Tungusta River, Russia)

KEY DATES

1586 Dutch mathematician Stevinus demonstrates that different weights fall at the same speed in a vacuum.
1647 French scientist Blaise Pascal discovers that pressure at a depth underwater acts in all directions.
1668 Principle of conservation of momentum discovered by English mathematician John Wallace.
1684 Law of gravity described by English scientist Isaac Newton.
1842 Principle of conservation of energy—the basis for the first law of thermodynamics—discovered by German physicist Julius von Meyer (also independently by the British physicist James Joule).
1850 Second law of thermodynamics formulated by German physicist Rudolph Clausius.
1856 The term "kinetic energy" invented by British physicist William Thomson.
1905 Third law of thermodynamics formulated by German physical chemist Hermann Nernst.
1926 First flight of liquid-fueled rocket by U.S. engineer Robert Goddard.
1931 Gyrostabilizers for ships invented by U.S. engineer Elmer Sperry.
1947 Sound barrier broken by U.S. pilot Chuck Yeager.

CHAPTER 8

ELECTRICITY AND ELECTRONICS

E lectricity is all around us, present in the electrical charges of minute subatomic particles called electrons. Under certain conditions, these electrons move from atom to atom in an electrical current. Although Greek philosophers were aware of the power of static electricity as long ago as 600 B.C., it was only in the 1700s and 1800s that scientists started to understand electricity. Through their studies, they learned how to generate and use electrical currents.

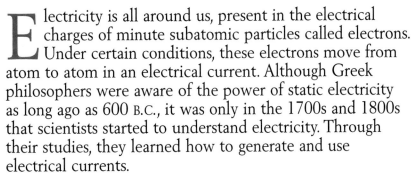

Such has been the success of the pioneers of electricity that it is now difficult to envisage a world without electricity. Much of the world's heating, lighting, and power depends on electricity. Without electricity, there could be no computers, radio, television, or spacecraft. Even the motor car, propelled by a nonelectrical internal-combustion engine, relies on electricity to fire its spark plugs and to power its lights and many of its controls. It is fair to say that electricity powers the modern world. It will continue to do so long into the future. But we can still look forward to modifications and improvements in the way in which electricity is generated and transmitted.

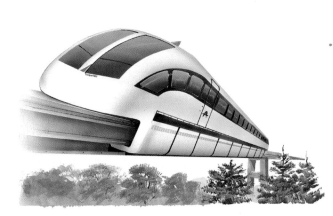

ELECTRICITY

Electricity is a form of energy created by the movement of minute charged particles called electrons. It is a vital source of power in the modern developed world.

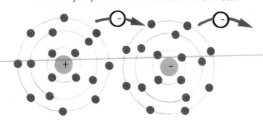

Electrons jump from atom to atom in a metal

When an electrical current flows through a metal, some electrons jump from atom to atom. The others orbit around the atomic nuclei, which are in fixed positions.

Italian scientist Alessandro Volta (1745–1827) was one of electricity's pioneers. By 1800, Volta had invented the first battery capable of holding an electric charge. It was called a voltaic pile.

U.S. physicist Robert Millikan (1868–1953) won the Nobel Prize for physics in 1923 for being the first person to measure the charge of an electron.

All matter—from the paper this book is printed on to the air that we breathe—is made up of tiny particles called atoms. Each atom has a positively charged center called a nucleus. Nuclei contain positively charged particles called protons and uncharged (neutral) particles called neutrons. Much smaller, negatively charged particles called electrons whizz around the nuclei at high speed.

The number of electrons in an object usually exactly matches the number of protons. The negative charges of the electrons balance the positive charges of the protons, and the object is neutral. An object that has fewer electrons than protons has a positive charge and will attract electrons. A negatively charged object has more electrons than protons. It will easily pass its surplus electrons to a positively charged object.

STATIC ELECTRICITY
Static electricity has intrigued people for many centuries. Around 2,500 years ago, the Greek philosopher Thales (625–547 B.C.) observed that rubbing a silk cloth over a piece of fossilized tree sap, called amber, caused not only the

cloth, but other lightweight objects, such as feathers, to be attracted to the amber. It is now known that this attraction occurs because rubbing drags electrons from the surface of the silk to the surface of the amber. The negatively charged amber attracts objects as it tries to lose its surplus

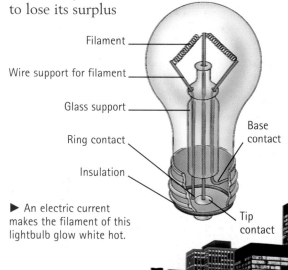

▶ An electric current makes the filament of this lightbulb glow white hot.

Filament
Wire support for filament
Glass support
Ring contact
Insulation
Base contact
Tip contact

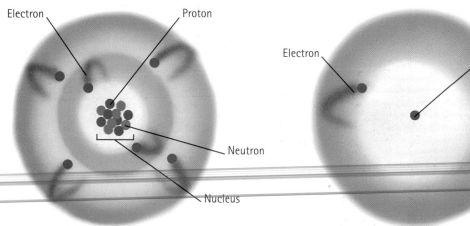

Carbon atom

The nuclei of atoms consist of positively charged protons and uncharged neutrons. Electrons are negatively charged, and travel around a nucleus at great speed. This carbon atom has six electrons, six neutrons, and six protons.

Electron
Proton
Neutron
Nucleus

Hydrogen atom

The positive charge of the proton in this hydrogen atom attracts the negatively charged electron toward the nucleus. In all atoms, the electrons travel around the nucleus in energy levels, sometimes called shells.

Electron
Nucleus
Energy level or shell

electrons to those objects. A similar effect is produced by running a comb repeatedly through dry hair or by a person shuffling along on a nylon carpet. This type of electricity is called static because the charge remains fixed (static) on the charged object—the amber, the comb, or the person—until it finds some way to escape or be discharged.

Lightning is a spectacular example of a natural discharge. As they rise and fall, currents of air produce friction inside a thundercloud. The friction causes charges to build up within the cloud. From time to time, the charge becomes large enough to cause a discharge to the ground in an enormous spark—lightning. Much smaller sparks cause the crackling sound that is sometimes heard when folding woolen or nylon clothing.

CURRENT ELECTRICITY

An electric current is a flow of electrons from a point with too many electrons to a point with too few, just as a current of water flows from higher to lower ground. Lightning is an enormous

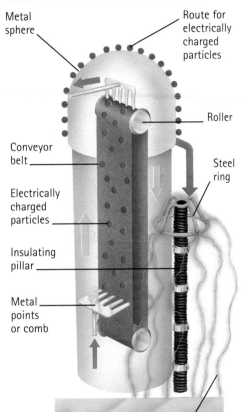

Metal sphere

Route for electrically charged particles

Roller

Conveyor belt

Steel ring

Electrically charged particles

Insulating pillar

Metal points or comb

Discharged particles

The rubber conveyor belt in a Van de Graaff generator carries electrons from a high-voltage supply to a metal sphere. As more electrons collect in the sphere, the voltage of the sphere increases. Large machines can produce 13 million volts of charge before the electrons in the sphere jump to a steel ring and flash to the ground like lightning. Small machines collect enough charge to make people's hair stand on end if they touch the sphere, because electrons travel to the tips of the hair and repel each other.

burst of charge. But the electric current that provides heat, light, and power for homes and industry is a regular flow that passes through cables to where it is needed. The cables are conductors—materials comprised of atoms containing electrons that can easily jump from one atom to the next.

Most current electricity is produced by generators in power plants. Some comes from chemical reactions in batteries, or from the action of light on photocells.

Electricity is useful because it can be converted into other forms of energy. Electric engines, or motors, convert electrical energy into mechanical energy. This can be used to create movement. Electric heaters produce heat energy when a current flows through their heating elements. Electric lamps produce light energy in a similar way—a current flows through a fine wire, which glows white hot.

The nighttime skyline of central Toronto shows just how much people rely on electricity to provide illumination.

SEE ALSO PAGES:

44 Winds, storms, and floods, 280–1 Sources of light, 354–5 Storage of electricity, 361–1 Conductors

ELECTRICAL CIRCUITS

Electrical circuits are collections of electrical components, such as resistors and diodes, that are linked by conducting wires and cables.

André-Marie Ampère (1775–1836), a French physicist, studied electrical circuits. The unit of electric current is called the ampere, or amp, and is named after him.

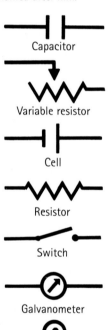

Capacitor

Variable resistor

Cell

Resistor

Switch

Galvanometer

Lamp

Electrical components each have their own unique symbol so that drawings of circuits, called circuit diagrams, can be understood worldwide.

Electrical circuits can be thought of as plumbing systems inside devices such as toasters and computers. Current flows through the conducting wires between components, and each component has an effect on the current that flows through it.

A material that conducts well, such as a metal, contains a large supply of free electrons. These are electrons that can move easily from atom to atom. Plastics and rubber have no free electrons. Materials like these are good insulators—they cannot conduct a current.

In an unconnected piece of conducting wire, the free electrons move around randomly. No current flows because there is no overall movement of the electrons from one end of the wire to the other. However, this changes if the two ends of the wire are connected to a cell, which is commonly called a battery.

The chemical reaction that occurs in a cell produces an excess of electrons at one terminal of the cell—the negative terminal—and a shortage at the other—the positive terminal. When the two ends of a wire are connected to the cell, the negative terminal starts to feed electrons into the wire. Because like charges repel, free electrons in the wire move along the wire toward the end that is connected to the

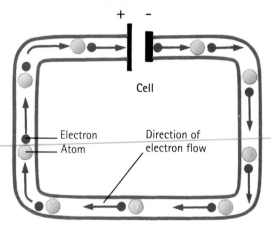

A cell drives the flow of electrons from atom to atom. The atoms stay in the same place; only some of the electrons move. Conventional current flows in the opposite direction to the electron flow.

Transistors can act as switches or amplifiers in circuits

positive terminal. There, the electrons drain back into the cell through the positive terminal. A current starts to flow.

Cells act as pumps that create a high pressure of electrons at one terminal and a low pressure at the other. This is a potential difference and is measured in volts.

The ability of a power source to push electrons around a circuit is called its electromotive force (emf).

Before the discovery of the electron, scientists thought that positive charges moved around circuits. The conventional current of the positive charges flows

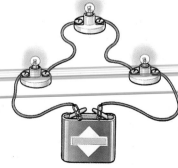

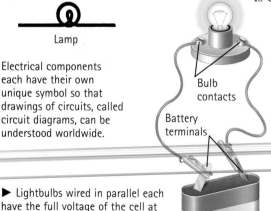

Bulb contacts

Battery terminals

► Lightbulbs wired in parallel each have the full voltage of the cell at their contacts. Each bulb shines as brightly as a single bulb in a simple circuit. Bulbs wired in series share the cell's voltage between them, so they shine less brightly.

Cell

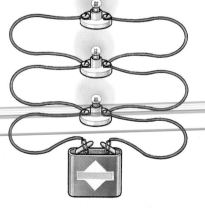

In a parallel circuit, each bulb is connected to the terminals of the cell. All the bulbs shine brightly.

Lightbulbs in a series circuit share the same current. They glow less brightly than in a parallel circuit.

Electronic components are often fitted to printed circuit boards to form electric circuits. Each component has two or more wire leads, which are its electrical contacts. The wires fit into holes in the circuit board and are connected electrically by tracks of metal on the surface of the board.

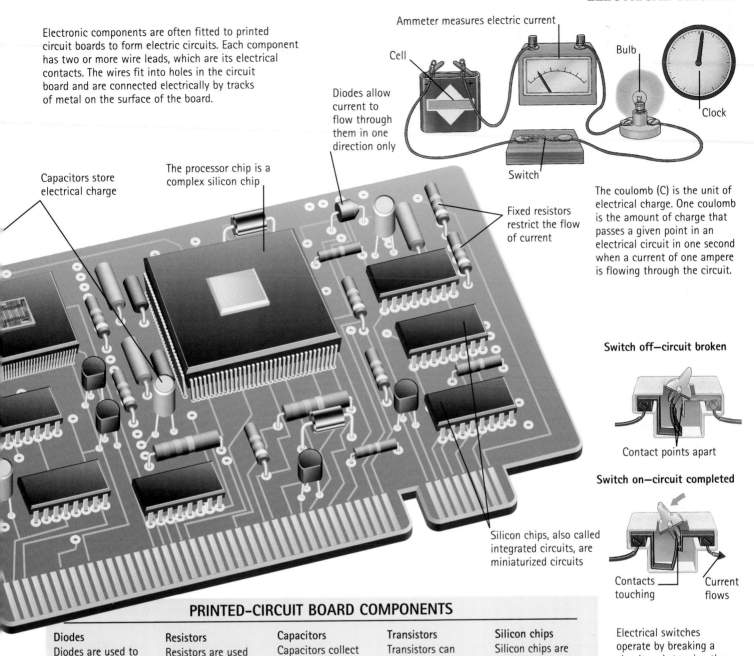

Ammeter measures electric current

Cell

Bulb

Clock

Diodes allow current to flow through them in one direction only

Switch

Capacitors store electrical charge

The processor chip is a complex silicon chip

Fixed resistors restrict the flow of current

The coulomb (C) is the unit of electrical charge. One coulomb is the amount of charge that passes a given point in an electrical circuit in one second when a current of one ampere is flowing through the circuit.

Switch off—circuit broken

Contact points apart

Switch on—circuit completed

Silicon chips, also called integrated circuits, are miniaturized circuits

Contacts touching

Current flows

Electrical switches operate by breaking a circuit and stopping the flow of current through a wire. When a switch is turned on, it completes the circuit and allows electrical current to flow around it.

PRINTED-CIRCUIT BOARD COMPONENTS

Diodes	Resistors	Capacitors	Transistors	Silicon chips
Diodes are used to change alternating current into direct current in a process called rectification.	Resistors are used to add a fixed or variable amount of resistance to an electrical circuit.	Capacitors collect and store charge. They can be used to smooth the flow of a variable current.	Transistors can amplify current, or switch a current on or off in response to a controlling signal.	Silicon chips are miniaturized electronic circuits. They are etched onto minute wafers of silicon.

from the positive terminal to the negative terminal. This is the opposite direction to the flow of electrons.

A cell drives a current in one direction only. This is a direct current, or DC. The current from power plants changes direction many times per second and is called an alternating current, or AC.

The amount of current that flows increases with the voltage, or potential difference, of the circuit. If the voltage doubles, so does the current.

RESISTANCE

The amount of current that flows through a wire depends on the metal from which it is made. Some metals contain fewer free electrons than others. In some cases the "free" electrons are less free to move.

The reluctance to allow electrons to flow freely is called resistance. Circuit components called resistors are designed to increase the resistance of a circuit. They can be connected in series—one after the other; or in parallel—side by side.

SEE ALSO PAGES:

356 Electrochemistry, 360–1 Conductors, 374–5 Microprocessors, 376–7 Computers

MAGNETS AND MAGNETISM

Magnets can attract and repel each other over a distance through space because of their magnetic fields. The effect is called magnetism.

Physician William Gilbert (1544–1603), doctor to English monarchs Elizabeth I and James I, introduced the term "magnetic pole."

The north and south poles of a horseshoe magnet point in the same direction.

A bar magnet has a pole at each end. When it hangs on a string, it turns to point its north pole to Earth's magnetic north.

Some ring magnets have one pole on the outside of the ring and one on the inside. Others have one pole on each face.

The lines of force of a magnet's field can be "seen" by sprinkling iron filings onto paper around the magnet. The iron filings follow the lines of force, which are concentrated at the magnet's poles. The attractive and repulsive fields between two magnets can also be seen.

Magnetism is named after Magnesian stone, from Magnesia, northern Turkey. Over 2,000 years ago, the ancient Greeks found that pieces of Magnesian stone attracted some metals. The stone was magnetite, a form of iron ore. A magnet is an object that behaves in the same way as magnetite.

Some metals, such as chromium, become weakly magnetic when a magnet is placed nearby. This magnetism, which disappears when the magnet is removed, is called paramagnetism.

Only three metals—cobalt, iron, and nickel—have the ability to become permanently magnetized when a magnet is placed near them and then removed. This property is called ferromagnetism.

A bar magnet can attract, pick up, and support nails, paper clips, and other small objects made of iron, nickel, or steel. (Steel is a mixture of iron with small amounts of carbon and other materials.) Any piece of iron or steel can be turned into a magnet by stroking it several times in one direction with one end of a permanent bar magnet.

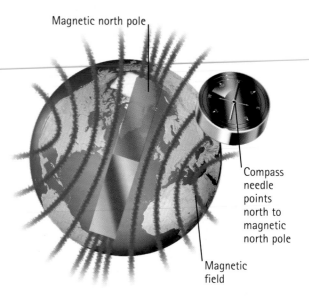

Earth acts like a huge magnet with magnetic north and south poles, both of which are close to the geographic north and south poles.

Magnetic north pole

Compass needle points north to magnetic north pole

Magnetic field

When an object is attracted to a bar magnet, it sticks to its ends, or poles, where the magnetic field is strongest. One pole of a magnet is north-seeking and the other is south-seeking. The north and south poles of two magnets will attract each other. Similar poles—north and north or south and south—will repel, forcing each other away.

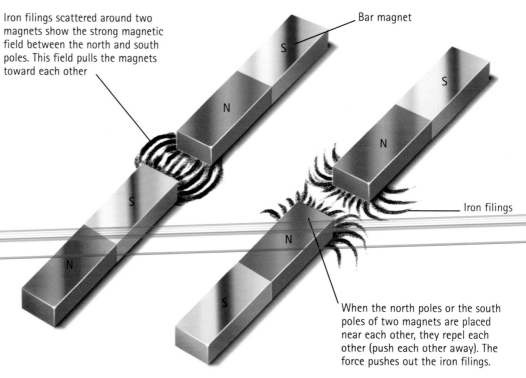

Iron filings scattered around two magnets show the strong magnetic field between the north and south poles. This field pulls the magnets toward each other

Bar magnet

Iron filings

When the north poles or the south poles of two magnets are placed near each other, they repel each other (push each other away). The force pushes out the iron filings.

Apart from enormous amounts of heat and light energy, the sun also pours subatomic particles into space, most of which are electrons. This invisible solar wind is electrically charged and affects Earth's magnetic field. The solar wind makes Earth's magnetic field lopsided—it extends much farther into space on the side of Earth farthest from the sun.

Aurora

Earth's magnetic field

Earth

Earth's magnetic field extends out into space on the side farthest away from the sun

Solar wind

MAGNETIC FIELDS

A magnetic field is the region around a magnet in which other magnetic objects can be affected by its magnetism. A magnetic object will always try to align itself with another object's magnetic field. The stronger the magnet, the larger its magnetic field.

Earth has its own magnetic field, which is strongest at its magnetic north and south poles. The magnetized pointer of a magnetic compass aligns itself north to south and is a handy aid to navigation.

Magnetism is a force that, although it is not fully understood, is put to use in numerous ways. Many machines, from car ignition systems to electric motors, make use of the properties of magnets. Video and audio tapes are coated with a thin layer of magnetic material. It is this material that allows them to be used for recording and playback.

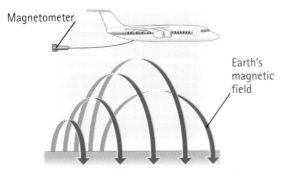

Magnetometer

Earth's magnetic field

Magnetometers are devices that measure the strength of a magnetic field. Towed behind aircraft, they can detect changes in Earth's magnetic field.

▼ Homing pigeons orient themselves to Earth's magnetic field. Migrating birds, such as terns, use the magnetic field to find their way accurately over thousands of miles.

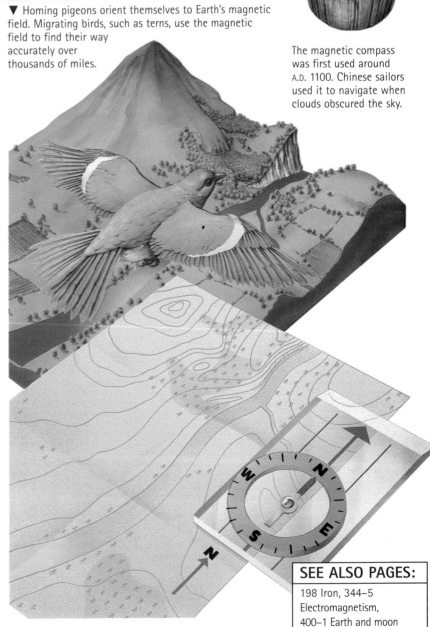

The magnetic compass was first used around A.D. 1100. Chinese sailors used it to navigate when clouds obscured the sky.

SEE ALSO PAGES:

198 Iron, 344–5 Electromagnetism, 400–1 Earth and moon

ELECTROMAGNETISM

Electromagnetism connects the current that flows through a wire to the magnetic field around that wire. It is used to drive motors and to generate electricity.

Danish physicist Hans Christian Ørsted (1777–1851) was the first person to study the link between electric current and magnetism.

Horseshoe, bar, and ring magnets are examples of permanent magnets. Their magnetism cannot be turned on and off. Electromagnets are not permanent magnets. They produce magnetism because of the flow of electrical current through a wire or a coil.

Danish physicist Hans Ørsted first noted the magnetic field produced by a current when, during one of his public lectures, he placed a compass near a wire through which a current was flowing. The magnetic needle of the compass moved, indicating the presence of the magnetic field around the wire.

Electromagnets usually contain a piece of wire that is coiled many times to increase the magnetic field. This coil is called a solenoid. In most cases, the solenoid is wrapped around a core of a magnetic material such as iron. When a current flows through the coil, the iron core becomes temporarily magnetized. This increases the power of the magnet by adding to the field of the coil.

It is possible to make a simple electromagnet by winding a coil of insulated wire many times around an iron nail and connecting the ends of the wire to the terminals of a battery.

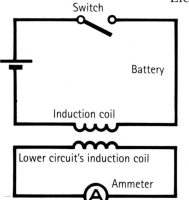

When the switch in the top circuit is closed, a brief pulse of current is registered by the ammeter in the lower circuit.

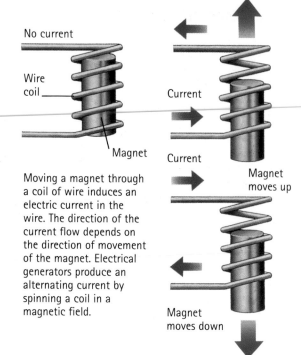

No current

Wire coil

Magnet

Current

Current

Magnet moves up

Magnet moves down

Moving a magnet through a coil of wire induces an electric current in the wire. The direction of the current flow depends on the direction of movement of the magnet. Electrical generators produce an alternating current by spinning a coil in a magnetic field.

Electromagnets are useful because their magnetic field can be controlled by changing the current that passes through the solenoid. Sometimes the current is simply switched on or off, as in the case of a junkyard crane's electromagnet.

In a loudspeaker, a variable current passes through a coil in the back of the loudspeaker cone. The varying magnetic field causes the cone to vibrate in the constant field of a permanent magnet. This produces air vibrations, or sound.

Maglev (magnetic levitation) trains and their tracks contain electromagnets. Magnetic repulsion makes the trains hover over the track, as well as driving them forward and stopping them.

U.S. physicist and Princeton professor Joseph Henry (1797–1878) discovered electromagnetic inductance. He built the first electromagnetic motor in 1829, two years before Faraday's discovery of induction.

The ignition circuit of a car's engine uses electromagnetic induction to produce a high-voltage spark using the current from a low-voltage battery. While the switch is open, charge collects in the capacitor. When the switch closes, this charge flows through the primary coil as a pulse of current. This pulse induces a voltage in the secondary coil that is great enough to produce a spark at the spark gap. It is this spark that ignites the fuel and air mixture in the cylinder.

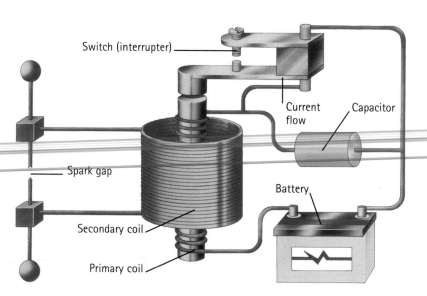

Switch (interrupter)

Current flow

Capacitor

Battery

Spark gap

Secondary coil

Primary coil

ELECTROMAGNETIC FIELD

When current passes through an electromagnet, a magnetic field is generated. The strength of this magnetic field depends on the number of turns in the coil of wire and the size of the electric current. Doubling either the number of turns or the size of the current produces a magnetic field that is twice as strong. The magnetic field drops to zero when the current is switched off.

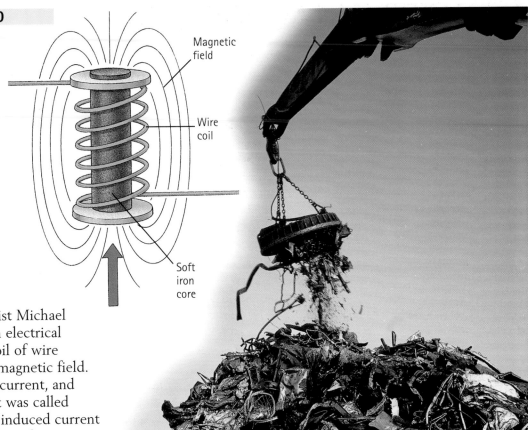

Magnetic field

Wire coil

Soft iron core

INDUCTION

In 1831, the British scientist Michael Faraday discovered that an electrical current flows through a coil of wire when it moves through a magnetic field. He called this an induced current, and the effect that produced it was called induction. The size of the induced current doubles if either the number of turns in the coil or the strength of the magnetic field doubles.

Electricity generators produce electrical current by making a coil rotate between two poles of a magnet. The movement in the field induces a current in the coil.

Induction coils use pulses of electric current in one coil to produce pulses in a second coil without either coil moving.

The pulse of magnetic field from the first coil affects the second coil as if it had been swept through a magnetic field. If the second coil has many more turns of wire than the first coil, a small current in the first coil will produce a much larger current in the second coil. Transformers use the same effect to change the voltage of an AC supply. This works with an alternating current because its direction of flow is constantly changing.

A large, disk-shaped electromagnet hangs from the arm of this junkyard crane. Steel and iron objects fly toward the magnet when the current is switched on. In this way, iron and steel can be separated for recycling.

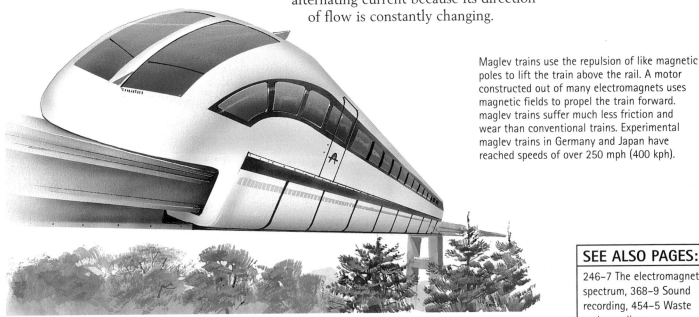

Maglev trains use the repulsion of like magnetic poles to lift the train above the rail. A motor constructed out of many electromagnets uses magnetic fields to propel the train forward. maglev trains suffer much less friction and wear than conventional trains. Experimental maglev trains in Germany and Japan have reached speeds of over 250 mph (400 kph).

SEE ALSO PAGES:

246–7 The electromagnetic spectrum, 368–9 Sound recording, 454–5 Waste and recycling

GENERATORS AND MOTORS

Generators produce electricity by a magnetic field acting on a moving coil. Motors produce motion by a magnetic field acting on a current-carrying coil.

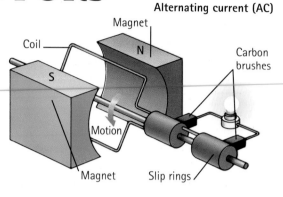

Alternating current (AC)

The current from the coil in this generator is almost zero, and will start to reverse as the top arm of the coil gets closer to the south pole of the magnet.

Electricity generators use electromagnetic induction to convert mechanical energy into electrical energy. In an electric motor, the current that flows through a coil produces a magnetic field that makes the coil rotate between two fixed magnets.

GENERATORS

One type of generator has coils of wire that can be spun in a magnetic field by a turbine-driven shaft. As the shaft rotates, the magnetic field points first in one direction through the coils, and then in the other.

The motion of the coil creates an electrical current that is strongest when the wires of the coil are closest to the two magnets. As the shaft rotates further, the current drops to zero at the point where the wires of the coil are directly between the magnets. The current then starts to increase in the opposite direction as the magnetic field reverses.

The same generator can be used to produce either AC or DC electricity, depending on how it is connected.

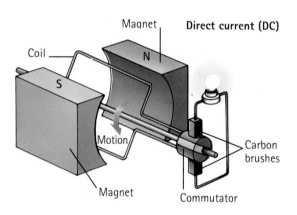

Direct current (DC)

The commutator in a DC generator reverses the connections of the coil at every half-turn. The output current flows in one direction only.

If the two ends of the coil are connected to the output cables through slip rings, the output cables are always connected to the same end of the coil, and the current switches back and forth as the coil spins. Generators that produce an alternating current are sometimes called alternators.

The same coil can produce DC electricity by connecting its two ends to the output cables through a device called a commutator, which reverses the output connections every time the current starts to reverse. A DC generator is sometimes called a dynamo.

Power plants use steam, water, or burning gas to drive the turbine that turns the generator. The turbine and generator are connected to the same shaft and the whole unit is called a turbogenerator.

In road vehicles and diesel locomotives, the main engine drives a generator that provides the electricity supply.

A bicycle dynamo is a simple electrical generator. As the bicycle wheel turns, it spins a coil between two fixed magnets.

A DC generator has several coils wound around the armature. As the armature rotates, carbon brushes tap current from whichever coil is in the strongest magnetic field. In this way, the generator produces an almost constant amount of electricity.

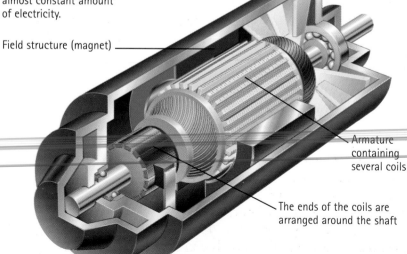

ELECTRIC MOTORS

An electric motor converts electrical energy into movement. Millions of electric motors, large and small, are used throughout the world. They power a vast range of things, from VCRs and toys to ventilation fans and electric vehicles.

In most motors, the magnet stands still while the coil of wire carrying the electric current turns inside it. When a current flows through the coil, the coil becomes magnetized. Since unlike poles attract and like poles repel, the coil rotates between the two poles of the fixed magnet until the north pole of the coil is facing the south pole of the fixed magnet.

The direction of the current then reverses; this reverses the poles of the coil. The coil's North Pole is now facing the North Pole of the magnet. Since like poles repel, the coil swings around another half a turn to line up its poles again. As long as the current in the coil reverses at every half-turn, the coil keeps turning around.

This is a close-up photo (magnified x 200) of a micromotor's gear cogs. Micromotors have been developed for use in space missions and microsurgery.

Battery
Carbon brushes
Magnet
Current
S
Motion
N
Coil

In this DC motor, current from a battery flows through a coil of wire. The magnetized coil then rotates in the magnetic field between the poles of a magnet.

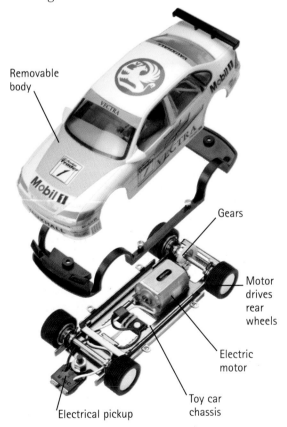

Removable body
Gears
Motor drives rear wheels
Electric motor
Toy car chassis
Electrical pickup

Some toy cars are driven by electric motors. The car connects to a direct-current (DC) supply through a pickup that fits into slots in an electrified track.

A DC motor uses a commutator to reverse the current at each half turn. An AC motor is more complex, because the supply current reverses many times a second. Instead of a permanent magnet, some AC motors have an electromagnet that runs from the same supply as the coil. In this way, the magnetic field of the coil and the fixed magnet both reverse when the supply current reverses.

FLEMING'S LEFT-HAND RULE

Fleming's left-hand rule predicts the direction in which a motor will turn by holding the thumb, forefinger, and middle finger of the left hand at right angles to each other. By lining up the forefinger with the magnetic field (south to north) and the middle finger with the current (positive to negative) the thumb indicates which way the coil will move.

SEE ALSO PAGES:

344–5 Electromagnetism,
348–9 Power plants,
350–1 Renewable energy sources

POWER PLANTS

Electricity is generated in power plants all over the world. Many burn fossil fuels to provide heat; others harness nuclear energy or renewable resources.

Natural petroleum can be refined to provide fuel oil for burning in power plant furnaces.

Natural gas produces less pollution than fuel oil when it burns. It is often burned in gas turbines.

Coal is more plentiful than natural gas. However, burning coal produces more pollution than burning natural gas. Many modern power plants filter and remove this pollution from the furnace gases.

Most electricity is generated in thermal power plants. These are factories that turn heat into electrical energy. In many power plants heat is provided by burning fossil fuels. Other power plants use the heat that is given off during a nuclear reaction to generate electricity.

FOSSIL FUELS
Fossil fuels are the remains of animals and plants that lived millions of years ago. The remains were covered by sediment and, over a period of millions of years, became underground fuel reserves.

Fossil fuels include oil, coal, and natural gas. They are all compounds of carbon and hydrogen. Most power plants that use fossil fuels burn vast quantities of them to produce steam from water. The steam then drives turbines, which, in turn, provide mechanical power for generators.

Gas-turbine power plants use the hot gases, created by burning natural gas, or fuel oil, to drive turbines without making steam.

Fossil fuels are used in the vast majority of power plants around the world, but they

The hot water from the condensers of this coal-fired power plant cools off in eight cooling towers. Some water is lost as steam, but most is reused.

do have drawbacks. The gases formed by burning fossil fuels include carbon dioxide, which causes global warming, and gases that form acid rain. Fossil fuels are also a nonrenewable resource.

NUCLEAR POWER
Nuclear power plants use nuclear fission (the splitting of atoms) to release huge quantities of heat from small amounts of

This generator (the plain blue cylinder to the right) shares a shaft with the turbine that drives it. A second turbogenerator is shown in the background.

NUCLEAR POWER PLANTS

In principle, the only difference between a nuclear power plant and a coal-fired or oil-fired power plant is the heat source—the rest of the generating process is similar for both types. A coolant takes heat from the reactor to a boiler, where the heat turns water into steam. The steam drives the turbine that turns the generator. Later the steam turns back to water in the condenser before returning to the boiler. Cooling water from the condenser loses its extra heat through cooling towers.

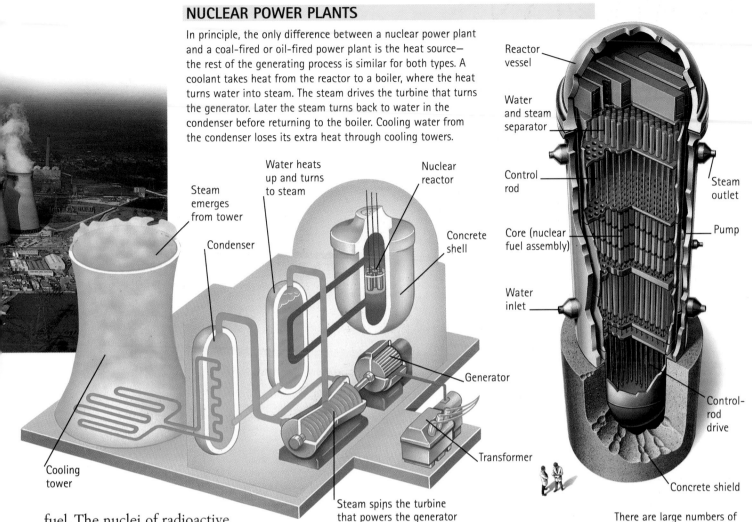

Steam emerges from tower

Water heats up and turns to steam

Nuclear reactor

Condenser

Concrete shell

Steam
Steam outlet

Reactor vessel

Water and steam separator

Control rod

Core (nuclear fuel assembly)

Pump

Water inlet

Generator

Transformer

Control-rod drive

Concrete shield

Cooling tower

Steam spins the turbine that powers the generator

There are large numbers of fuel rods and control rods inside a nuclear reactor. In the reactor above, they are immersed in water. This is the moderator and also the coolant.

fuel. The nuclei of radioactive elements, such as uranium, sometimes split. When they do, they release heat energy and tiny particles called neutrons. When these neutrons hit other radioactive nuclei, they can make them split, too. This starts what is called a chain reaction. Materials called moderators help the chain reaction occur. They slow down the neutrons, which improves their chances of causing fission. Control rods slow or stop the chain reaction by absorbing neutrons and preventing them from causing fission.

In the 1950s, nuclear power was seen as the solution to the world's energy needs. A little over two pounds of uranium fuel can provide as much energy as over 2,000 tons of coal without producing any carbon dioxide or acid-rain gases.

The neutrons released by fission reactions in the fuel rods are slowed by a moderator to improve their chances of causing other atoms to split. Control rods can stop or slow the chain reaction by absorbing neutrons.

Unfortunately, the high cost of handling and using nuclear fuel safely makes nuclear electricity expensive. Also, unsafe handling can be disastrous, as was shown by the 1986 explosion in the Ukraine at the nuclear power plant in Chernobyl.

Released neutrons

Control rod absorbs some neutrons

Fuel rod

Fuel rod

Moderator slows neutrons down

Fission

In 1942, Italian-born U.S. physicist Enrico Fermi (1901–1954) built the first nuclear reactor in a squash court at the University of Chicago.

SEE ALSO PAGES:

RENEWABLE ENERGY SOURCES

Unlike fossil fuels, renewable energy sources will never run out. They include sunlight, wind, tides, and rainwater in the form of hydroelectric power.

A vertical-axis wind turbine spins around an upright shaft. It can catch wind from any direction.

Three fourths of the world's electricity is generated by thermal power plants that run on fossil fuels or nuclear power. Fossil fuels produce pollution and are in limited supply. Nuclear fuels are expensive to use safely, and their waste is dangerous and difficult to store.

There are several other ways of driving electricity generators without creating pollution or the risk of nuclear accidents. Many of these alternatives use natural resources that will not run out. They are known as renewable energy sources.

WIND TURBINES

For many centuries, windmills have been used to grind grain and to pump water. They convert the power of the wind into useful mechanical power. Today, more sophisticated windmills, called wind turbines, use wind power to drive electricity generators.

The blades of a wind turbine can turn around a horizontal or a vertical shaft. Those that turn around a horizontal axis, similar to a windmill's, have a mechanism that points them into the wind if the wind direction changes. Vertical-axis turbines catch the wind from any direction.

A single wind turbine with 82-foot-long blades can provide enough electricity for a small community. They are most useful for remote villages and islands.

Most wind turbines are built in groups called wind farms. The largest wind farms are currently found in Denmark and the United States. A typical farm produces over 1,000 megawatts in windy weather.

Wind farms are often located on flat coasts or offshore, where the wind is stronger and less gusty than it is inland.

▶ Horizontal wind turbines look like propellers. The amount of power that they can generate depends on the speed and angle of the wind across their blades. An electronic control mechanism turns the turbine head to point into the wind direction at all times, thereby collecting the most power from the wind. A transmission system connects the turbine blades through a shaft to a generator in the turbine head.

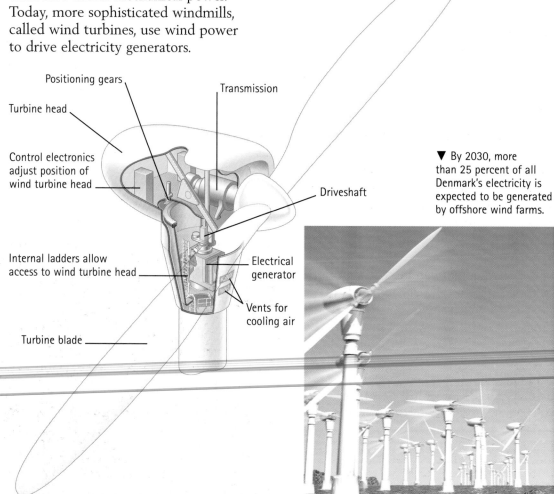

Positioning gears

Transmission

Turbine head

Control electronics adjust position of wind turbine head

Driveshaft

Internal ladders allow access to wind turbine head

Electrical generator

Vents for cooling air

Turbine blade

▼ By 2030, more than 25 percent of all Denmark's electricity is expected to be generated by offshore wind farms.

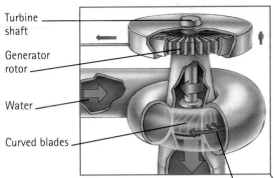

Turbine shaft
Generator rotor
Water
Curved blades
Water
Water

▲ Water enters the turbine through a curved pipe around its edge. Water passes through the turbine blades and leaves through the middle.

HYDROELECTRIC POWER (HEP)

Hydroelectric power (HEP) plants are often built in mountainous areas. There, rainfall is plentiful, and natural valleys can be dammed to provide a reservoir—a store of water. The largest single scheme is at Itaipu, on the Brazil–Paraguay border. This plant can generate over 12,000 megawatts of power. A scheme in China will soon generate 20,000 megawatts. HEP generates almost 20 percent of the world's electricity. Some hydroelectric power plants use a system called pumped storage. During the day, water flows from an upper reservoir down through the hydroelectric plant, turning turbines, before being collected in a lower reservoir. At night, when electricity demand is low, surplus power from other power plants pumps water up to the top reservoir.

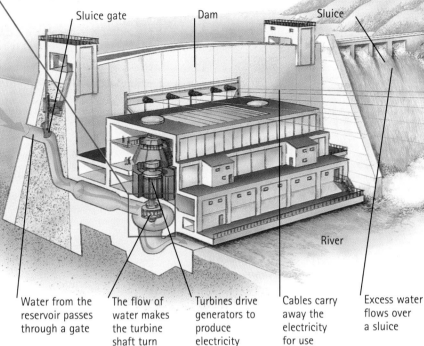

Sluice gate
Dam
Sluice

Water from the reservoir passes through a gate

The flow of water makes the turbine shaft turn

Turbines drive generators to produce electricity

Cables carry away the electricity for use

Excess water flows over a sluice

River

WATER POWER

There are three forms of water power: hydroelectric power, tidal power, and wave power. Hydroelectric power, or HEP, uses the force of water flowing out of a reservoir and through a dam to move turbines and generate electricity.

Tidal power harnesses the power of water as it flows into and out of a river estuary. A low-level dam, or barrage, is built across the estuary, and the tidal water turns turbines in the barrage as the tide rises and falls. The tidal power plant at La Rance, France, produces enough power for the needs of 300,000 people.

Wave-power devices use the up-and-down movement of waves to drive electricity generators. One such device is called a duck. Ducks are teardrop-shaped plastic floats (see page 459). They contain devices that pump water as they bob up and down in waves. Water from a string of ducks can pump enough water to drive a small turbine and generator.

SUNLIGHT

Heat from sunlight can be focused onto a boiler in the middle of thousands of mirrors in a field. Steam from the boiler drives turbogenerators similar to those found in a coal-fired power plant. Devices called photovoltaic cells produce a current whenever light shines on them. They are used to provide current for spacecraft and for some calculators and radios.

▶ At this geothermal power plant in Iceland, wells are drilled to tap into the heat lying beneath the Earth's surface. Water is pumped into the hot rocks where it turns to steam. This steam can be used to power electricity generators or to heat homes and offices.

GEOTHERMAL

The rocks beneath the Earth's surface are often hot. Geothermal power plants use the heat in these rocks to turn water into steam. The steam can be used to generate electricity or for heating.

SEE ALSO PAGES:
328–9 Harnessing wave power, 330–1 Harnessing wind power, 456 Resources

ELECTRICAL POWER DISTRIBUTION

Electricity distribution systems take electricity from the power plants where it is generated to the homes and businesses where it is used.

The network of power lines and cables that distributes electricity around a nation or a region is called a grid. A typical grid might receive electricity from coal-fired power plants near coal mines, from nuclear power plants on isolated beaches, and from hydroelectric plants in high mountains. The grid then supplies electricity to customers, who are often far from the electricity source.

REDUCING POWER LOSSES

When a current passes through a wire, the wire becomes hotter, and some of the electrical energy is lost as heat energy. This heating effect increases rapidly with the size of the current. If the current doubles, for example, four times as much heat is produced, so four times as much energy is wasted. Since electricity often flows hundreds of miles through the cables of a grid, wasting energy all the way, it makes sense to use the smallest possible current to keep energy losses low.

Fortunately, the amount of power transmitted by a cable can be increased by raising either the current or the voltage of the supply. Long-distance cables use extremely high voltages and low currents to reduce energy loss.

Step-up transformer

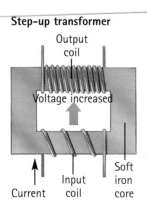

Step-down transformer

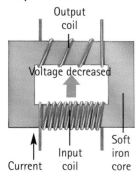

The ratios of input and output voltages of step-up and step-down transformers are the same as the ratios of the numbers of turns in their input and output coils.

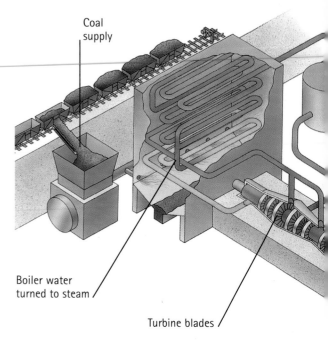

Transformers increase a power plant's output voltage to reduce power loss in long-distance cables. Substations near customers reduce the voltage for household use.

TRANSFORMERS AND SUBSTATIONS

Transformers convert AC electrical power from one voltage to another. They only work with alternating currents.

Transformers consist of two coils wrapped around a soft iron core, which often looks like a square doughnut. The AC supply is connected to one coil, called the primary coil, and the alternating current produces a magnetic field that switches back and forth with the current.

The core concentrates the magnetic field, which passes through another coil called the secondary coil. The alternating magnetic field induces an alternating voltage in the secondary coil, which is connected to the output terminals.

The output voltage depends on the input voltage and the number of turns in the two coils. If there are twice as many turns on the secondary coil than the primary coil, the voltage is doubled.

Transformers in power plants "step up" the generator output from a few thousand volts to between 100,000 and 400,000 volts—or even more—for the grid.

Near towns and cities, step-down transformers in substations typically

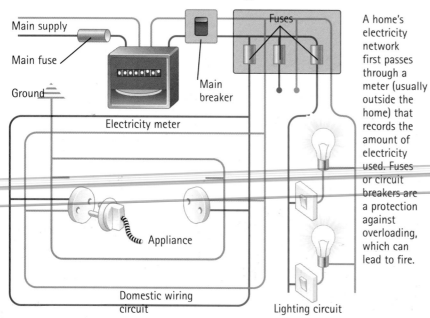

A home's electricity network first passes through a meter (usually outside the home) that records the amount of electricity used. Fuses or circuit breakers are a protection against overloading, which can lead to fire.

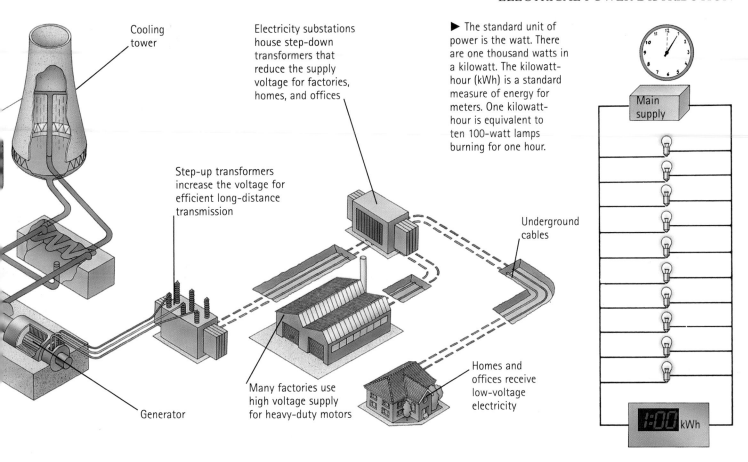

Cooling tower

Electricity substations house step-down transformers that reduce the supply voltage for factories, homes, and offices

Step-up transformers increase the voltage for efficient long-distance transmission

► The standard unit of power is the watt. There are one thousand watts in a kilowatt. The kilowatt-hour (kWh) is a standard measure of energy for meters. One kilowatt-hour is equivalent to ten 100-watt lamps burning for one hour.

Underground cables

Homes and offices receive low-voltage electricity

Many factories use high voltage supply for heavy-duty motors

Generator

Main supply

1:00 kWh

reduce the voltage to 33,000 or 11,000 volts for distribution. Some factories use power at this voltage for heavy-duty equipment. The rest is further stepped down to domestic supply voltage in local substations. In the United States ordinary household voltage is 110 volts. In Europe and the Middle East it is 220-240 volts.

ELECTRICITY IN THE HOME

Electricity from the local network first passes through a meter when it enters a household system. The meter records how much energy is used. Cables lead from the meter to a main switch, which can be used to disconnect the supply to the whole house when the household wiring system has to be examined or repaired by an electrician.

The power then passes to a fuse box that contains fuses or circuit breakers. Fuses are wires that burn and break the circuit if the current gets too large. Circuit breakers are switches that disconnect the circuit if the current gets too large. Both are safety devices, since a large current could potentially cause an electrical fire.

At the fuse box, the wires divide into separate circuits. Each circuit has a fuse or circuit breaker that is suited to the current that would normally pass through it. Lighting circuits draw the least current, and for safety reasons their fuses blow if the current is greater than a few amps. Wall-outlet circuits normally draw moderate currents. Air conditioners and electric stoves draw a lot of current. They often have their own circuits.

Electric streetcars, such as this one in Amsterdam, in the Netherlands, run on rails in the road. A pick-up on the roof of the streetcar collects current for the streetcar's motors.

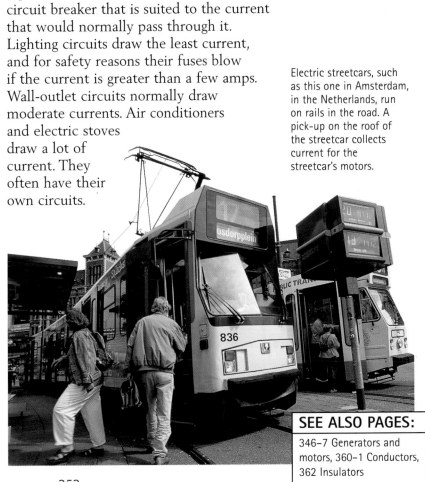

SEE ALSO PAGES:

346-7 Generators and motors, 360-1 Conductors, 362 Insulators

STORAGE OF ELECTRICITY

Electrochemical cells and batteries are self-contained and often mobile sources of energy. Capacitors are used to store electrical charge.

Stopper — Brass rod

Outer foil — Inner foil

A Leyden jar is a type of capacitor. Sheets of foil cover half the jar inside and out. The electric charge, applied through the brass rod, collects on the inner foil.

Electricity can be stored as charge in devices called capacitors, or as chemical energy in cells. Batteries are collections of cells linked together. A variety of chemical reactions can be used to store electricity. In primary cells the electricity runs out when the chemical reaction is complete, after which the cell must be discarded. In rechargeable cells, which are also called secondary cells or accumulators, the reaction can be reversed by pumping electricity into the cell. The recharged cell can then be used again.

CAPACITORS
A capacitor is a device that stores electrical charge. Capacitors consist of two charged metal plates that are separated by an insulator. Charges of opposite signs collect on each plate when a potential difference, or voltage, is applied across the plates. The amount of charge increases as the voltage increases. The ability of a capacitor to store charge is called its capacitance. Capacitors are used to help regulate the current in electrical circuits.

BATTERIES
The first cell was built by Italian physicist Alessandro Volta (1745–1827) in 1800. Volta's cell, also called a voltaic pile, was a stack of alternating plates of copper and zinc. Sheets of card kept the metal

This fruit cell consists of a steel paper clip and a brass thumbtack stuck into a lemon. The juice of the lemon starts the electrochemical reaction.

plates apart, and the whole assembly was soaked in a solution of acid. The solution started the chemical reaction that produced electricity.

The chemical reactions that run cells occur in two parts, or half reactions. One half reaction produces electrons at the negative electrode, or anode. The other half reaction consumes electrons at the positive electrode, or cathode. A solution called an electrolyte is in contact with the electrodes and provides the materials for the reactions. In Volta's cell, the copper sheets were the cathode, and the zinc sheets the anode. The acid solution was the electrolyte of the cell.

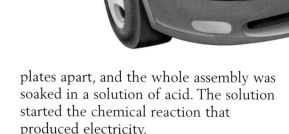

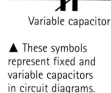

Fixed capacitor

Variable capacitor

▲ These symbols represent fixed and variable capacitors in circuit diagrams.

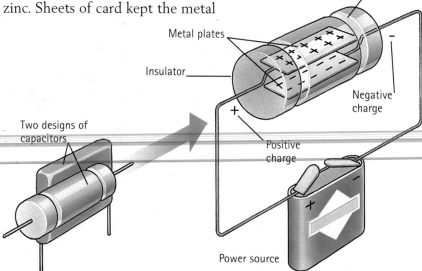

Two designs of capacitors

Metal plates

Insulator

Capacitor

Negative charge

Positive charge

Power source

A capacitor consists of two metal plates that are separated by an electrical insulator. Positive charge is stored on one plate, and negative charge on the other. The amount of charge stored at a given voltage depends on the size of the plates and the distance between them.

The rechargeable battery found in most motor vehicles is a collection of cells, in which lead plates are immersed in concentrated sulphuric acid and contained within a plastic casing. There are usually six cells, each consisting of one set of lead plates that is connected to the negative terminal and another set connected to the positive. A small dynamo, driven by the vehicle's engine, charges the battery whenever the engine is running.

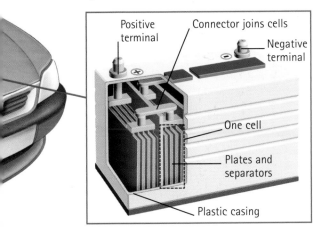

Positive terminal

Connector joins cells

Negative terminal

One cell

Plates and separators

Plastic casing

PRIMARY CELLS

The most commonly used type of primary cell is the zinc-carbon battery or dry cell, which was invented in the 1860s by French engineer Georges Leclanché (1839–1882). This type of battery is the standard battery for use in equipment such as flashlights, toys, and radios.

The steel casing of a dry cell covers a zinc cup, which is the anode. The cathode is a carbon rod that fits inside the zinc cup. The cathode is connected to a metal stud in the top of the battery. The space between the carbon rod and the zinc case contains a paste of ammonium chloride and zinc chloride.

Alkaline batteries are an improvement on zinc-carbon cells. They are made in the same shapes, sizes, and voltages as zinc-carbon cells. When used in the same equipment, however, an alkaline cell will last about six or seven times longer than a regular zinc-carbon cell. This is because the combination of chemicals in an alkaline cell produces so much more energy before the chemicals are depleted by the electrochemical reaction.

SECONDARY CELLS

Although primary cells can be made to last longer by using more efficient chemical reactions, they can only be used once. In some cases, attempting

to recharge a primary cell will make it explode. A secondary cell, on the other hand, can be recharged and reused a number of times before it stops working. Secondary cells are recharged by passing a small electrical current into the cell, often over a number of hours.

The lead-acid batteries used in many road vehicles contain secondary cells. The energy stored in the battery is used to power a vehicle's electrical systems. While the vehicle is running, its engine drives a small generator that charges the battery.

Nicads—cells with nickel and cadmium electrodes—are another type of secondary cell. Nicad cells can usually be recharged between 500 and 900 times before they have to be replaced. These rechargeable cells are often used to power portable electrical goods, including personal stereos and electric shavers.

BATTERY IMPROVEMENTS

Research work has already created new types of primary cells that produce more power for longer periods. Much work is being done to develop secondary cells that can store enough energy to power electric cars for long distances. Batteries of these cells must also be able to be recharged quickly at roadside recharging stations.

Positive terminal

Carbon rod

Zinc casing

Chemical paste

Negative terminal

This standard zinc-carbon cell has a carbon rod surrounded by a paste of ammonium chloride and zinc chloride. The paste causes a reaction between the carbon and the zinc. This generates a voltage.

This small disc-shaped cell is a zinc-mercuric-oxide cell. It is used to power hearing aids and watches, and also as a power source in digital cameras and portable electronic personal organizers.

The batteries of this French Citroën AX electric car may be charged overnight at home, then topped up during the day at rapid charge points in service stations, such as this one in La Rochelle, France. The batteries store enough charge to drive about 45 mi. (75km).

SEE ALSO PAGES:
162–3 Chemical reactions, 340–1 Electrical circuits, 356 Electrochemistry

ELECTROCHEMISTRY

Electrochemistry is the science of chemical reactions and electrical currents. It describes the conversion of energy between chemical and electrical forms.

Englishman Michael Faraday (1791–1867) had little formal education, but he went on to become a renowned scientist and the pioneer of electrochemistry. Faraday invented the first electric generator and investigated electrolysis.

Some electrochemical reactions occur spontaneously when two electrodes, dipped in a liquid, are connected to an electrical circuit. This is what happens in a battery. Other reactions occur when an electrical current passes through a liquid.

One type of electrochemical process is electrolysis, which is the chemical breakdown of a compound by an electrical current. Some liquids, called electrolytes, contain particles called ions, which are atoms or fragments of molecules that carry a positive or negative charge.

If two electrodes are connected to the terminals of a battery and placed in the electrolyte, positive ions, called cations, will be attracted to the negative electrode, or cathode. At the same time, negative ions, called anions, will be attracted to the positive electrode, or anode.

When an ion reaches an electrode, it loses its charge and changes chemically. When acidified water is electrolyzed, for example, positive hydrogen ions are attracted to the cathode. There, they pick up electrons and form hydrogen gas.

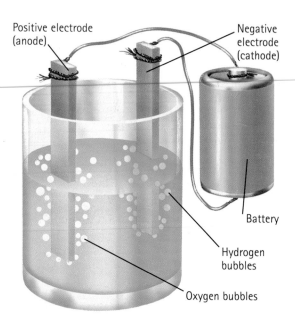

The current from a battery can split acidified water into hydrogen and oxygen. Bubbles of hydrogen form at the cathode, and bubbles of oxygen form at the anode.

Objects can be electroplated with a thin layer of certain metals in a cell where the object is the cathode, the plating metal is the anode, and the electrolyte contains cations of the plating metal. The metal cations become atoms at the cathode and form a surface layer of pure metal. Copper, gold, silver, and zinc are all used to plate objects in this way.

Many decorative objects, such as candlesticks, are made from a cheaper base metal and then electroplated with silver. The thin coating of silver provides an attractive finish and protection from corrosion.

These sheets have been coated with copper in an electroplating bath. They will be used to manufacture flexible printed-circuit boards.

SEE ALSO PAGES:
166–7 Bonding and valency, 178 Oxidation and reduction, 354–5 Storage of electricity

POWER CELLS

Different types of power cells generate electricity from chemical reactions, sunlight, and the action of pressure on crystals.

Power cells are used to provide electrical power for a variety of applications. The type of cell used depends on where and how it will be used.

Panels of solar cells

This Intelsat-V satellite orbiting Earth has two arrays of photovoltaic cells, commonly called solar cells, that are capable of generating electricity from sunlight.

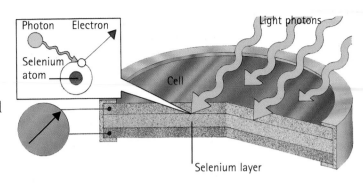

One type of photoelectric cell uses selenium as its cathode. It releases electrons when photons of light shine on it. The flow of electrons forms an electric current.

FUEL CELLS

Like batteries, fuel cells use chemical reactions to produce electricity. Unlike batteries, they continue to operate as long as they receive fuel and oxygen. The fuel may be hydrogen or a substance, such as natural gas, or petroleum, that contains hydrogen. The fuel and oxygen combine in the fuel cell to produce electricity and water.

Fuel cells are efficient and do not cause pollution. They are used in spacecraft, where the water they produce can be used for drinking, washing and cooking. Fuel cells are also used to power some types of electric road vehicles.

PHOTOELECTRIC CELLS

Photoelectric cells, or solar cells, produce electrical current from light. The cells contain a material that releases electrons when light shines on the cells. These electrons are then caught by a conductor, which is the negative terminal of the cell. The material itself is the positive terminal, since it becomes positively charged when the electrons jump out of it.

PIEZOELECTRICITY

Certain crystals, including quartz, develop a voltage when squashed or stretched slightly. This is the piezoelectric effect which may be used to power cells in the future. Some digital watches use the effect the other way round, passing an electric current through a crystal to obtain a very accurate vibration as a reference for time.

In a quartz watch, a voltage from the watch's battery makes a quartz crystal vibrate. The speed of these vibrations can be used to measure hours, minutes, and seconds.

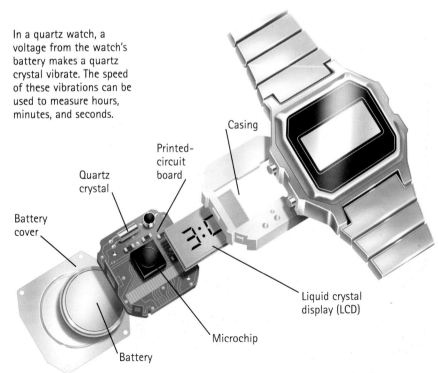

Battery cover

Battery

Quartz crystal

Printed-circuit board

Casing

Microchip

Liquid crystal display (LCD)

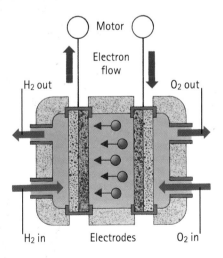

▲ Hydrogen and oxygen are pumped into a fuel cell, where a catalyst in the electrodes makes them react. The reaction produces electricity and water.

SEE ALSO PAGES:

ELECTRICITY THROUGH GASES

When an electrical current passes through a gas, it makes the gas glow and produces heat. These effects are seen in lightning and in artificial lighting.

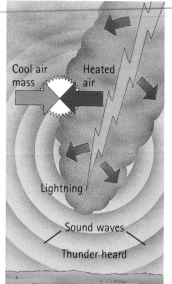

Lightning is a giant spark that jumps between opposite charges within clouds or between a cloud and the ground.

Gases such as air do not normally conduct electricity. This is because they consist of uncharged atoms and molecules, and so have nothing to carry an electrical current. However, this can change when a gas is heated or exposed to a strong electrical field. In these cases, electrons can be ripped from neutral atoms and molecules. The result is a plasma—a hot mixture of uncharged particles, electrons, and positive ions. The charged particles in a plasma can conduct electricity.

LIGHTNING

Lightning is a massive discharge of static electricity from one cloud to another or from a cloud to the ground. It occurs when air currents within storm clouds create pockets of electrical charge. Also, the negative charge in the base of the cloud repels electrons from the ground beneath it and causes an area of positive charge. The potential difference between these areas of opposite charge can reach hundreds of millions of volts.

In 1752, scientist and statesman Benjamin Franklin (1706–1790) risked his life by flying a kite on a metal wire in a storm to prove that lightning was electricity.

Eventually, the voltage becomes so great that a channel of air becomes ionized and current starts to flow between areas of opposite charges. The current heats the air and creates a path of plasma. Several strong surges of current, called strokes, then pass

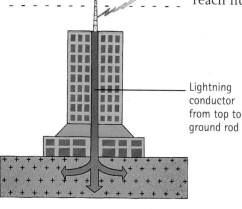

▲ The lightning rod was invented by Benjamin Franklin. It prevents damage to the top of high buildings and structures by attracting and absorbing lightning, which it transfers safely to a rod buried in the ground.

► Lightning comes in a number of forms. In sheet lightning, the charge leaps from one part of the cloud to another. In forked lightning, the charge leaps from the cloud to the ground, as shown in this view of a lightning storm in New Mexico.

This workshop gives an indication of the range of decorative designs and shapes that discharge tubes can be made into. Although commonly called "neon" tubes, gas-discharge tubes can contain argon, krypton, neon, or xenon.

St. Elmo's fire, or St. Elmo's light, is the glow that can be seen around tall buildings, aircraft propellers, and ships' masts during a storm. It occurs when the pointed ends of objects become highly charged and start to pull electrons from molecules in the air. The name came from sailors who thought the glow around the masts of ships was a sign that their patron saint St. Elmo (St. Erasmus) was looking after them.

through this path, heating the air to over 59,400°F. This rapid heating of the air causes both the flash of lightning and the bang of thunder. Since sound travels more slowly than light, a distant observer hears the noise of the thunder some time after seeing the flash of light.

Lightning can kill people and cause damage to buildings. Many tall structures are fitted with lightning rods, or conductors. These metal rods and cables connect the top of a building to a rod in the ground, which carries lightning away.

DISCHARGE TUBES

A controlled form of lightning is produced in the discharge tubes used for lighting and displays. These tubes contain a noble gas—neon, argon, krypton, or xenon—or mercury vapor, sealed in the tube at low pressure. When the current is turned on, it boosts electrons in the gas into a high-energy, or excited, state. The noble gases glow when this happens, as in the "neon" lights of advertising displays. Mercury glows with an invisible ultraviolet (UV) light. This light hits a coating on the tube and makes it glow, or fluoresce, white. This is how fluorescent tubes work.

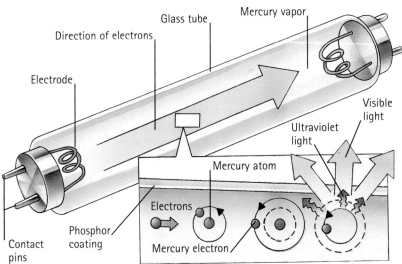

When current flows through a fluorescent tube, it boosts electrons in the mercury atoms to an excited state. These electrons emit UV light when they return to their normal state. The UV light makes the tube's coating glow.

SEE ALSO PAGES:

44–5 Winds, storms, and floods, 250–1 Heat transfer, 338–9 Electricity

CONDUCTORS

Electrical conductors will carry an electric current. Insulators normally will not conduct. Semiconductors can act either as conductors or insulators.

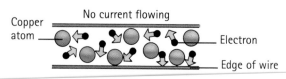

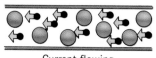

Current moves through materials that conduct electricity. When current flows through a copper wire, for example, the electrons all move in the same direction.

Metals are good electrical conductors because they contain plenty of free electrons that can move from atom to atom, carrying the current. The journey is not completely smooth, however, and interference along the way can hinder the flow of current. This phenomenon, called resistance, also causes the material through which the current is flowing to become warm. Good conductors, such as silver and copper, have low resistance.

Insulators, such as plastics and nonmetals, are substances whose electrons are not normally free to move between the atoms, or molecules. Under most conditions, the resistance of an insulator is high. If a large enough voltage is used, however, some of the electrons can be ripped out of their atoms or molecules. When this breakdown happens, those electrons are free to move and the resistance of the material drops.

A great amount of heat is generated when current flows through an insulator. The heat produced by a current, or arc, passing through air is used to melt metals in arc welding.

German physicist Gustav Kirchhoff (1824–1887) drew up a set of laws for calculating the amount of current flowing in a conductor. Working with German chemist Robert Bunsen (1811–1899), Kirchhoff also discovered the chemical elements cesium and rubidium.

An electric arc produces intense heat where it contacts electrodes. This heat can be used to weld pieces of metal together.

SUPERCONDUCTORS

Even good conductors, such as metals, offer some electrical resistance under normal conditions. There are, however, materials called superconductors. These offer almost no resistance. They are useful because they save a lot of energy when a strong current is necessary, as in a powerful electromagnet.

Some metals, such as aluminum and lead, can superconduct when they are cooled to incredibly low temperatures—just a few degrees above absolute zero (0°K). Liquid helium—expensive and difficult to handle—is used for cooling.

▶ A magnet hovers over a ceramic superconductor made of yttrium, barium, and copper oxides. This material only superconducts at very low temperatures.

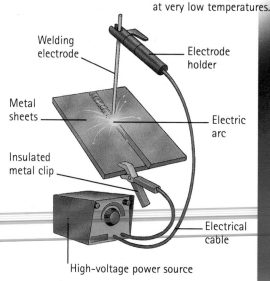

▲ In arc welding, an electrical current flows between a welding electrode and the metal objects that are to be welded. Heat from the electric arc melts the metal around the joint. A strongly welded joint forms once the metals have cooled and solidified.

360

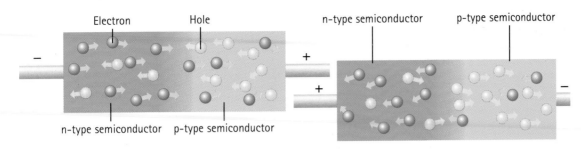

Electron   Hole

n-type semiconductor   p-type semiconductor

−   +

n-type semiconductor   p-type semiconductor

+   −

◀ Electrons move easily from n-type to p-type silicon, but much less easily in the opposite direction. In the left-hand diagram, current flows in the preferred direction. In the right-hand diagram, the voltage is reversed and very little current flows.

Some superconductors function when cooled to −320°F using liquid nitrogen. This is less expensive and easier than using liquid helium. Scientists have made materials that superconduct when cooled to −173°F using dry ice (solid carbon dioxide). In the future there will be superconductors that function well at close to room temperature.

SEMICONDUCTORS

Semiconductors have a much higher resistance than a normal conductor, but much lower than an insulator.

Like other semiconductors, silicon conducts better when it contains traces of impurities than when it is pure. The addition of an impurity is called doping.

If silicon is doped with phosphorus, which has one more electron per atom than silicon, the extra electrons can carry negative charge through the silicon. This is called n-type silicon.

A boron atom has one fewer electron than a silicon atom, so boron-doped silicon is a few electrons short. These gaps, called holes, carry positive charges. This is called p-type silicon.

Silicon transistors work as switches because electrons will not flow from p-type to n-type silicon.

An n-p-n transistor has a layer of p-type silicon between two n-type layers. Electrons will not flow between the two outer layers, the emitter and the collector, because they would have to pass from p-type to n-type silicon.

However, if electrons are fed into the middle layer, or base, they fill the holes in that layer, and a current can flow from the emitter to the collector.

Nobel Prize-winning U.S. physicist William Shockley (1910–1989) was a key member of the team that developed the first transistor in 1948.

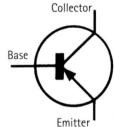

Collector

Base

Emitter

This is the electrical symbol for a transistor, showing its three component layers: the emitter, base, and collector.

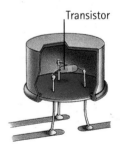

Transistor

A small current flowing into the base of an n-p-n transistor allows a larger current to flow between its emitter and collector.

SEE ALSO PAGES:

196–7 Properties of metals, 209 Ceramics, 217 New materials, 344–5 Electromagnetism

INSULATORS

Electrical insulators do not conduct electricity. They perform many tasks in electric circuits, as well as ensuring that the transmission of electricity is safe.

Single-core wire

Insulated multistranded wire

Pair of wires with insulation

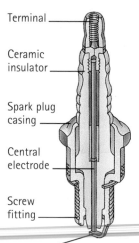

Electrical cable with three layers of insulation

▲ By placing a rubber or plastic insulator as a casing around a good conductor, such as a copper wire, electricity can flow along the wire without causing harm.

A good insulator is an extremely poor conductor. It has no mobile electrons, or at least not enough to carry an electric current if a voltage is applied across a piece of the material. This means that insulators act as barriers to the flow of electricity.

Rubber is one of the most effective natural insulators. Glass and plastics are also good insulators, as are porcelain and many other ceramics. Air and other gases insulate well, as does a vacuum. Many liquids—water being an exception—also insulate efficiently.

In an ordinary piece of electrical cord, the current-carrying cables are insulated in plastic to prevent them from forming a short circuit that could start a fire. Another insulating layer is wrapped around these wires to give extra protection against potentially harmful electric shocks.

This worker at a hydroelectric power plant is carrying out routine maintenance on a high-voltage insulator made from a ceramic material.

The wires used to form coils for solenoids and transformers are coated with a thin layer of insulating varnish that allows them to be wound together without forming short circuits.

Heavy-duty glass and ceramic insulators are used to isolate high-voltage power-transmission lines from the structures that hold them in place.

Terminal

Ceramic insulator

Spark plug casing

Central electrode

Screw fitting

Earth electrode

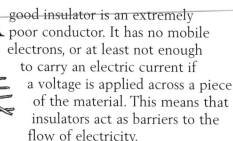

◄ Ceramic materials are excellent electrical insulators. They are used in many places. Here, a ceramic insulator prevents high-voltage charge from causing a short circuit inside a spark plug.

▶ The transformers at this electricity substation have heavy-duty ceramic insulators to keep the high-voltage cables from touching each other and to prevent electricity from leaking to the ground.

SEE ALSO PAGES:

208 Glass, 209 Ceramics, 215 Polymers, 352–3 Electrical power distribution

RESISTANCE

Resistance is the ability of a substance to resist the flow of an electrical current. Resistors are components in a circuit that provide a known amount of resistance.

German physicist Georg Ohm (1789–1854) discovered how the resistance of a material depends on its length, thickness, and the material from which it is made. Ohm's Law was published in 1827.

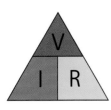

Ohm's triangle is used as a memory aid to calculate the current (I), voltage (V), or resistance (R) of a circuit using Ohm's Law: V = I x R.

Resistance is a measure of how much a circuit, or a component of a circuit, restricts the flow of electrons. Atoms collide with the electrons, slowing them down and causing some electrical energy to be converted into heat energy and sometimes light.

The length and thickness of a conductor both have an effect on its electrical resistance. The thicker a wire, the easier the current flows. This is because a wider cross-section contains more free electrons to carry the current.

The longer a wire, the greater its resistance. This is because there are more atoms in the path of the free electrons. This is why circuit designers try to use as little wire as possible to cut down on energy losses caused by resistance.

Resistors are components that are designed to reduce the amount of current that travels through a particular part of a circuit. They are often used to protect delicate components from carrying too great a current.

Thermistors are resistors whose resistance depends on temperature. They are often used in circuits that measure temperature. Light-dependent resistors are used to measure light intensity.

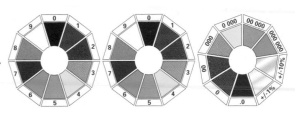

The value of a fixed resistor is encoded in three colored bands. A fourth band shows the possible variation of resistance between individual resistors of the given type.

Band 1   Band 2   Band 3

55Ω   24,000,000Ω

The left-hand resistor has a value of 55 ohms; the right-hand resistor is 24 million ohms. The silver bands show that these values are correct to within 10 percent.

Manually variable resistances can be adjusted by turning a knob or by moving a slider. They are used in the volume and tone controls of stereo equipment.

MEASURING RESISTANCE

The standard unit of resistance is the ohm (Ω), named after German physicist Georg Ohm. The resistance of a circuit is one ohm when a voltage of one volt makes a current of one amp flow.

Ohm's Law states that the resistance in a circuit is the voltage divided by the current. A voltage of two volts would make a current of two amps flow in a circuit that has a resistance of one ohm. But two volts would produce a current of only one amp in a circuit of two ohms. In other words, voltage is current multiplied by resistance; or current is equal to voltage divided by resistance.

The resistance of a thermistor (top) changes with temperature. Some variable resistors are adjusted by hand (middle). Others change when light strikes them (bottom).

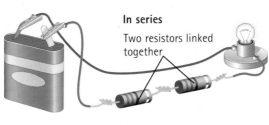

In series
Two resistors linked together

In parallel
Two paths for current

When resistors are wired in series, their resistances add together and the bulb glows dimly. When in parallel, there are two paths for the current to flow along, each with only one resistance, and the bulb glows brightly.

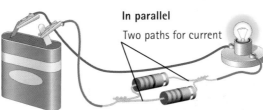

Fuses are safety devices that limit the size of the current that can pass through a circuit. If the circuit develops a fault, a surge of current is sent through the fuse. The resistance of the fuse wire makes it very hot, and it melts. The fuse then blows, breaking the circuit before further damage can occur.

Fuse wire

SEE ALSO PAGES:

340–1 Electrical circuits, 352–3 Electrical power distribution, 360–1 Conductors

ELECTRICAL COMMUNICATION

Electrical communication sends messages through a wire as an electrical signal or through the air as electromagnetic waves.

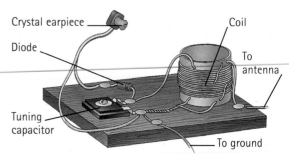

▲ This simple radio is called a crystal set. The radio signals pass to a coil and tuning capacitor that can be tuned to the frequency of a radio station.

In 1837, British inventor Charles Wheatstone (1802–1875) helped build the first electric telegraph.

U.S. inventor Samuel Morse (1791–1872) invented a code for sending messages by telegraph.

Electrical communication carries information from place to place in the form of electrical signals. The information might be a television signal, the sound of a radio presenter's voice, or computer data. The information is encoded as variations in an electrical signal.

The telegraph was the first electrical communications device. In 1774, George Lesage showed that balls of pith (vegetable fiber) in a device called an electroscope could be made to jump when a wire connected the electroscope to a source of electrical charge. Although this device showed that electrical signals could travel through a wire, it was not a practical system for sending messages.

The next step toward a practical telegraph system came in 1810, when André-Marie Ampère invented the ammeter. This device had a pointer that moved when a current passed through a wire.

In fact, it took until 1837 for British inventors William Cooke and Charles Wheatstone to invent a telegraph system that used five wires and five moving needles to encode letters and numbers.

Also in 1837, Samuel Morse patented a simpler telegraph system that used only one wire and a key that sent a

Telegraph keys were used to send messages in Morse code. At first, a machine at the receiving end of the telegraph wire registered the message as dots and dashes on paper tape. Later, operators recognized the sounds as letters.

RADIO TRANSMISSION

When a radio presenter is broadcasting, a microphone picks up the air vibrations, or sound waves, from the presenter's voice and turns them into an electric signal. This signal is an alternating current whose vibrations match those of the presenter's voice. The sound signal is sent to a broadcasting transmitter, where it is mixed with a second signal, called a carrier wave. The carrier wave vibrates thousands or even millions of times a second. Once they are mixed together, the two signals are turned into a radio wave. This can be beamed out through the air from the transmitting antenna. A radio that is tuned in to the correct radio station frequency will pick up the waves and convert them back into an electric signal. An amplifier then boosts that signal so that it can drive speakers to produce sound waves.

1 In a studio at the radio station a disk jockey or program presenter talks into a microphone.

2 The microphone turns sound waves into a vibrating electrical signal.

3 This signal is combined with another signal that vibrates very rapidly.

4 The combined signals are turned into radio waves for transmission from an antenna.

Crystal earpiece
Coil
Diode
To antenna
Tuning capacitor
To ground

x

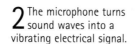

364

The Baygen Freeplay radio, created by the English inventor Trevor Baylis (1937–), needs no batteries. It uses power from a small generator driven by a windup spring mechanism. Winding up this Classic model for 25 seconds provides enough energy for 30 minutes of playing time. Later models hold enough power for one hour after only a few seconds of winding.

current down a wire when it was pressed. An operator used groups of short and long strokes to signal letters and numbers.

At the receiving end, a device pressed a pen onto a moving strip of paper when current flowed through the wire. Short keystrokes produced dots on the paper, longer strokes produced dashes. Later devices turned the dots and dashes into sounds that a trained operator would listen to through headphones.

Morse's system and his code of dots and dashes became the standard telegraphy system in the mid-1800s. It was widely used to send international messages until international telephone lines started to replace telegraph lines in the 1950s.

RADIO WAVES

Around 1886, German physicist Heinrich Hertz (1857–1894) discovered what came to be called electromagnetic waves. He found that when he used a high-frequency alternating current to produce a spark between two electrodes, a much fainter spark jumped across a gap in a separate loop of wire. Hertz realized that some invisible form of energy was traveling through the air between the two circuits. He had discovered radio waves.

In 1895, Italian electrical engineer Guglielmo Marconi (1874–1937) made a device that combined a circuit like Hertz's with a key similar to the one used in the Morse system. This combination could send pulses of radio waves over a radius of several miles. A receiver circuit could detect these pulses anywhere inside that radius. Because there was no need for the sender (transmitter) or the receiver to be connected by a wire, this was called wireless telegraphy. Marconi's invention was particularly useful for ship-to-shore and ship-to-ship communication.

Modern radio communication uses the fact that radio waves vibrate at a certain rate, or frequency, which is measured in thousands or millions of hertz (Hz). Each transmitter uses its own frequencies, called carrier frequencies. Filters in the receivers tune in to pick up one station at a time. Frequency modulation, or FM, encodes information such as sound waves or pictures as variations in the frequency of the carrier signal. Amplitude modulation, or AM, uses variations in signal strength.

Signal strength

Frequency

Electronic filters select a range of frequencies, which then pass to other circuit components. Frequencies outside that range are blocked out.

Signal strength

Frequency

A high-pass filter blocks frequencies below a certain level, called the cutoff frequency. A low-pass filter lets only low frequencies through.

Signal strength

Frequency

A band of frequencies can be selected by using a low-pass filter together with a high-pass filter. The upper and lower limits of the band are the cutoff frequencies of the high-pass and low-pass filters.

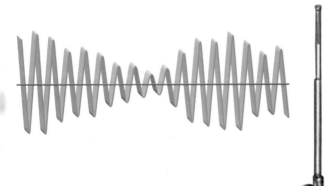

8 An amplifier boosts the sound signal for loudspeakers, which turns the signal back into sound.

5 The radio signal travels through the air and is detected by all radio antennas within the range of the transmitter.

6 A tuning circuit selects the radio signal for decoding.

7 The sound signal is decoded from the combined signal.

SEE ALSO PAGES:
366–7 Telecommunications,
368–9 Sound recording,
370–1 Television and videotape

TELECOMMUNICATIONS

Telecommunication is the transmission of electronic or electromagnetic signals to carry words, sounds, images, and other data over long distances.

Scottish-born inventor and teacher Alexander Graham Bell (1847–1922) built the first working telephone in 1875 in the U.S. and patented it one year later.

Bell's telephone used a coil and electromagnet to turn sounds into an electrical signal.

This telephone, dating from 1919, had a body with a mouthpiece and rotary number dial, and a separate earpiece.

People have needed to communicate over long distances for thousands of years. At first, the fastest way to send news and other information was by runners, then messengers on horseback or on boats.

Later, visible signals were passed through chains of observers and signalers who used smoke, reflected sunlight, and devices such as flags. These methods conveyed simple messages much more quickly than a messenger could.

The telegraph offered the first electrical communication system that could carry detailed messages over long distances in the form of coded electrical pulses.

In 1875, while working to improve the telegraph, Alexander Graham Bell invented the telephone. He did this by discovering a way to send the human voice along wires as electrical signals. Bell had no idea how successful the telephone would become—he believed that just a handful of his devices would ever be needed. Today, there are over a billion telephones in use worldwide.

Telephone systems advanced rapidly following Bell's invention. At first, human operators connected callers' lines manually by plugging the two ends of a cable into a socket, or outlet, for each caller. The first mechanical switchboard, or exchange, was patented in 1891. Most modern exchanges are now computerized. This allows callers to dial direct from their telephones to almost every country in the world.

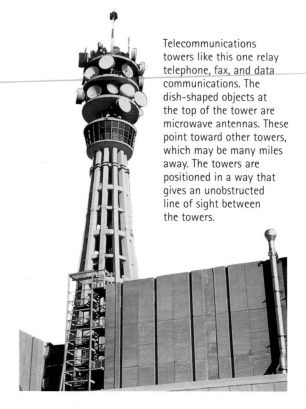

Telecommunications towers like this one relay telephone, fax, and data communications. The dish-shaped objects at the top of the tower are microwave antennas. These point toward other towers, which may be many miles away. The towers are positioned in a way that gives an unobstructed line of sight between the towers.

CABLES AND WIRES

Telephones rely on a network of cables and wires to carry electric signals for at least part of the distance between callers and receivers. Telephone lines can be strung between poles, buried underground, or laid on the ocean floor. The electric signal in a telephone wire travels thousands of times faster than sound travels through the air. Electric signals also travel much farther than the human voice, and amplifiers along the

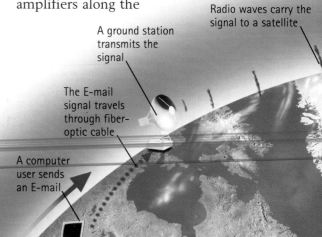

Radio waves carry the signal to a satellite

A ground station transmits the signal

The E-mail signal travels through fiber-optic cable

A computer user sends an E-mail

SATELLITE COMMUNICATIONS

Geostationary satellites orbit the Earth at a height of approximately 22,300 mi. (35,900 km). At this altitude, they orbit at the same speed as the planet rotates, so they stay above a fixed location on Earth's surface. In 1945, science-fiction writer Arthur C. Clarke suggested the use of geostationary satellites to relay phone calls, television images, and other signals between ground stations separated by thousands of miles. The first geostationary communications satellite, called *Syncom 2*, was launched in 1963. Since then, hundreds of communications satellites have been put into stationary orbits. These satellites receive signals from transmitter antennas on Earth's surface, amplify them, and then transmit them to receivers on the ground.

THE TELEPHONE

A telephone handset has a mouthpiece and an earpiece. When a caller speaks, the sound waves hit a thin metal diaphragm and cause it to vibrate. This vibration repeatedly compresses carbon granules in a cylinder behind the diaphragm. This makes their electrical resistance vary so that the current that flows between two electrodes in the mouthpiece mimics the sound waves of the speaker's voice. The incoming signal makes an electromagnet and diaphragm in the earpiece vibrate to reproduce the sound of the other caller's voice.

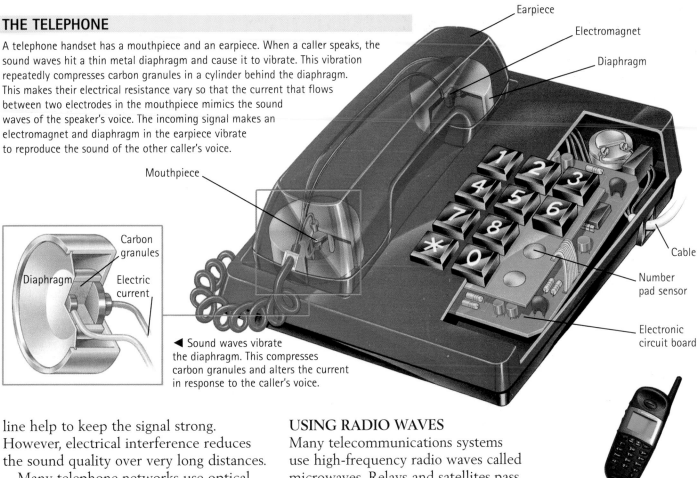

Earpiece

Electromagnet

Diaphragm

Mouthpiece

Cable

Number pad sensor

Electronic circuit board

Carbon granules

Diaphragm

Electric current

◄ Sound waves vibrate the diaphragm. This compresses carbon granules and alters the current in response to the caller's voice.

line help to keep the signal strong. However, electrical interference reduces the sound quality over very long distances.

Many telephone networks use optical fibers to connect exchanges. Optical fibers are thin threads of glass. Exchanges turn electrical signals into light signals. These travel through optical fibers without interference. A pair of optical fibers can carry up to 6,000 calls at one time.

USING RADIO WAVES

Many telecommunications systems use high-frequency radio waves called microwaves. Relays and satellites pass the signals around the world.

Cellular telephone networks use numerous antennas to transmit and receive signals within small areas called cells. When a caller uses a cellular phone, a microwave signal is sent to the nearest antenna, which connects the caller to the network. Regular signals from each cellular telephone let a central computer know where to direct incoming calls for that telephone.

A satellite relays the radio signal

A ground station transmits and receives signals

Message received

Cellular telephones provide portable communication for people on the go.

Pagers are small radio receivers that monitor a specific radio frequency. When a message is sent, a signal that is unique to the pager switches the pager on. The pager then collects and displays the message.

SEE ALSO PAGES:

364–5 Electrical communication, 380–1 Information technology

SOUND RECORDING

Sound recording stores electric signals that represent sound waves in a way that can be played back to reproduce the original sound.

U.S. inventor and physicist Thomas Alva Edison (1847–1931) was responsible for over 1,000 inventions. These included the first practical lightbulb and the first moving pictures player, called the kinetoscope. He made major improvements to early telephone systems. In 1877, he invented the sound-recording system called the phonograph.

Sound is a form of energy. When sound travels through air, it takes the form of waves of high and low air pressure. When these waves hit a human eardrum, the fluctuating pressure causes the eardrum to vibrate and send a signal to the brain.

Modern sound-recording methods detect sound vibrations and convert them into an electrical signal that can be stored and replayed later.

PHONOGRAPHIC RECORDING

The first practical method of recording sound was Edison's phonograph of 1877. Sounds were captured by a horn and used to vibrate a needle against a rotating cylinder. The needle cut a bumpy groove on the cylinder. When the cylinder was played, a needle tracing through the groove reproduced the original sound.

During the early 1900s, the quality of sound recordings improved with the invention of microphones. Microphones turn sound into an electric signal that can drive a groove-cutting machine. The quality of the replayed sound, called the reproduction, was also improved by using electric loudspeakers instead of a mechanical horn.

Sound waves

Diaphragm vibrates

Piezoelectric crystal

A microphone changes sounds into electrical signals. Sound waves cause a diaphragm to vibrate, producing a varying electrical current that resembles the vibrations of the original sound waves. In this microphone, a piezoelectric crystal converts sound waves into a current.

Microphone

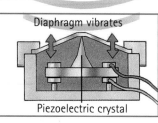

1 Thomas Edison's phonograph used a rotating cylinder and a needle to play recorded sounds. The needle produced vibrations by tracing a bumpy groove in a tinfoil sleeve on the cylinder. A horn turned these vibrations into sound.

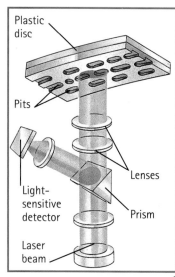

Plastic disc

Pits

Lenses

Light-sensitive detector

Prism

Laser beam

4 Since the early 1980s, compact discs have become a popular way to record sound and data. The information is stored as a sequence of pits on a film in the disc. As the disc spins in a laser beam inside a CD player, the pits reflect pulses of light onto a light-sensitive detector. This converts them into an electric signal.

3 Long-playing records, or LPs, turn at 33⅓ rpm. They started to replace 78-rpm records in 1948. Singles, which turn at 45 rpm, came later. The first stereophonic records were made in 1958.

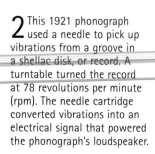

2 This 1921 phonograph used a needle to pick up vibrations from a groove in a shellac disk, or record. A turntable turned the record at 78 revolutions per minute (rpm). The needle cartridge converted vibrations into an electrical signal that powered the phonograph's loudspeaker.

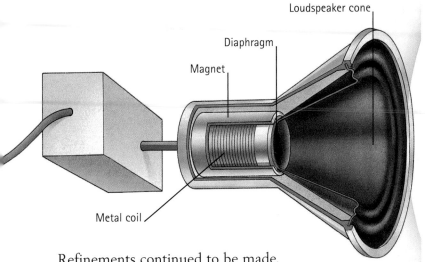

Loudspeaker cone

Diaphragm

Magnet

Metal coil

SYNTHESIZED SOUND

When an electric signal is played through a speaker, the type of sound produced depends on the shape, or waveform, of the signal. Synthesizers use circuits, called oscillators, to produce simple waveforms. Filtering and mixing these basic waveforms produces more complex signals. Some synthesizers modify recordings of musical instruments or sound effects to produce an output.

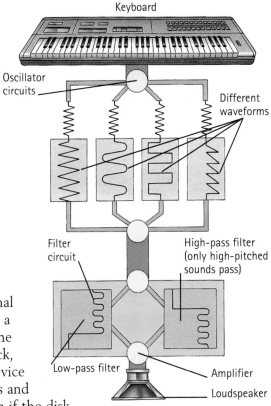

Keyboard

Oscillator circuits

Different waveforms

Filter circuit

High-pass filter (only high-pitched sounds pass)

Low-pass filter

Amplifier

Loudspeaker

Refinements continued to be made. Disks, or records, replaced cylinders; this increased the amount of music that could be recorded. Better groove-cutting machines and playback needles and more stable turntable speeds improved sound quality. Stereophonic sound, introduced in 1958, uses at least two microphones. The resulting separation of sounds gives the listener the impression that they are hearing a live performance.

▲ When an electric signal passes through the coil at the back of a loudspeaker cone, it produces a fluctuating magnetic field. The varying attraction and repulsion to a magnet behind the cone make the cone vibrate and produce sound waves.

MAGNETIC RECORDING

Magnetic recording became popular in the 1950s. Magnetic recorders store sounds using an electromagnet and magnetic tape.

When recording, the electric signal produces a fluctuating magnetic field in a coiled-wire device, called a head. Magnetic iron oxide particles in a tape line up with the field as the tape passes the head. This forms a magnetic pattern.

When the tape is played, the varying magnetic field induces a current in the head. That current can be amplified to reproduce the original sound.

Digital recording encodes the sound signal as a series of pulses on a disk or a tape. When the recording is played back, or read, the reading device recognizes these pulses and can decode them. Even if the disk or tape is damaged, the exact signal can still be read.

Compact discs (CDs) contain the pulses as holes in an aluminized film that can be read by a laser. Minidiscs, digital audio tapes, and computer discs store the signal as magnetized pulses that are read by a coil that is similar to a tape-playback head.

DIGITAL RECORDING

Phonography and basic magnetic recording both store sound signals as waves. Dirt in a record groove or slight changes in the magnetic field can drastically change the sound reproduction.

▲ Digital compact cassettes (DCCs) store sound information in digital form. Digital recording gives more accurate sound reproduction than recording on regular audiocassettes.

▶ The record head of a cassette-tape system magnetizes particles of iron oxide in a pattern that mimics the sound signal. On playback, this pattern produces an electric signal that can be amplified to reproduce sounds.

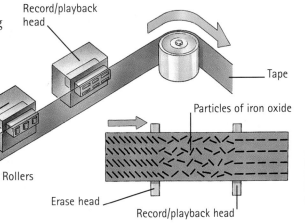

Record/playback head

Tape

Erase head

Rollers

Particles of iron oxide

Erase head

Record/playback head

SEE ALSO PAGES:

342–3 Magnets and magnetism, 357 Power cells, 364–5 Electrical communication

TELEVISION AND VIDEOTAPE

Television captures and transmits images and sounds to millions of television receivers all over the world. Videotape records images and their soundtracks.

Scottish electrical engineer and inventor John Logie Baird (1888–1946) was the first person to transmit a television picture by radio waves. He applied for patents as early as 1923, and worked almost until his death on new methods of transmission.

Television broadcasts began in Britain in 1936 and in the United States in 1939.

At first, few people owned television sets, and the cameras, transmitters, and receivers could process images only in black and white. Since then, the popularity of television has grown enormously, especially since the introduction of color television in 1953.

One of the pioneers of television was John Logie Baird. In 1926, Baird demonstrated a system called the Baird Televisor. It used a rotating disk with a spiral of lenses, called a Nipkow disk, to divide an image into horizontal lines. Each lens would focus a horizontal line from the image onto a photoelectric cell. The cell produced an electrical current that varied with the amount of light that fell on it. This process, called mechanical scanning, converted the image into a series of signals that could be transmitted as radio waves. The receiver turned the signal into a light of varying intensity. When this light passed through another Nipkow disk, it reproduced the image on a screen.

Modern television sets use electron guns to produce beams of electrons, which "paint" television images in lines on a screen. The beams are deflected by electrically charged plates that steer the beams from side to side and from top to bottom. Chemicals called phosphors glow when the beam hits them.

Standard U.S. and Japanese systems use 525 lines per frame, or image, and 30 frames per second. European television systems use 625 lines per frame and 25 frames per second. High-definition television, or HDTV, uses 1,125 lines to give sharper, more detailed images.

HOW TELEVISION WORKS

Light detectors in a TV camera convert light into electric signals, which are processed before being transmitted as radio waves. The screen of a television is the front of a funnel-shaped glass tube. The inside of the screen is coated with strips of phosphors—chemicals that glow three different colors when electrons hit them. Three electron guns at the back of the television tube fire beams of electrons at the three sets of phosphors behind the screen, which illuminate to create the picture.

Electron beams

Mask

Phosphor strips

Microphone boom

Viewfinder

Microphone

Electron guns

Lens

Deflector plates

Light detectors (blue, green, and red)

Cable carries signal from camera

Movable base

Picture on glass screen

VIDEOTAPE RECORDING

The tape in a videocassette has one broad track on which the picture information is recorded, a narrow control track, and another narrow track on which sound is recorded. The recording head magnetizes the tape in a similar way to an audiocassette recorder. The difference with a videocassette recorder is that the recording head rotates while the tape passes over it at an angle. This leaves diagonal stripes of recorded information on the tape.

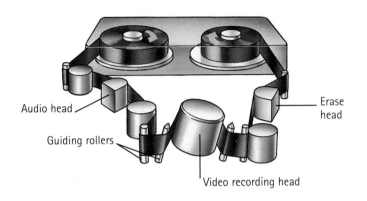

Audio head

Erase head

Guiding rollers

Video recording head

TRANSMISSION AND RECEPTION

Television cameras and sound-recording equipment collect pictures and sounds in television studios and from outside-broadcast locations.

The lens in a camera focuses incoming light onto filters that divide the image into its blue, green, and red components. These components shine onto light sensors called charge-coupled devices, or CCDs. There are three CCDs, one for each color. The CCDs convert light into electrical signals.

Often, several television cameras film at the same time. Editors select the best image at any one time and sometimes process the images with special effects.

Television transmitters broadcast television signals as radio waves. Relay stations receive the signals, amplify them, and retransmit them to cover audiences over large geographical areas. Relay stations can be on Earth or on geostationary satellites.

Television receivers normally use antennas to collect signals from the transmitter or from a relay on Earth. Some use small satellite dishes to receive signals from transmitters on satellites. Others receive signals through underground cables. These are supplied with signals by local TV stations or from a community antenna.

VIDEOCASSETTE RECORDING

The first videocassette recorder, or VCR, was made by Sony in 1969. VCRs record TV and sound signals onto magnetic tape.

A video camera-recorder, or camcorder, combines a video camera with a VCR machine. The VCR records the image and sound signals as they are produced. The recording can be replayed on the camera's liquid-crystal display (LCD) or through a normal television set.

Camcorders store video footage on tape. Some are small enough to fit in the palm of a hand.

Outside-broadcast television cameras are linked by radio signals to a transmitter that sends signals representing images and sound to the television studio.

SEE ALSO PAGES:
272–3 Color, 274–5
Color mixing, 366–7
Telecommunications

ANALOG AND DIGITAL SYSTEMS

Analog signals represent information as a continuous range of values. Digital signals use stepped, or discrete, values.

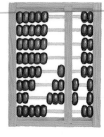

The abacus is an early form of calculator. It was used in China from about 5000 B.C. Each row of beads represents a set of numbers. For instance, the bottom row represents the numbers 1-10.

Pocket calculators use digital electronics to do calculations. They have been on sale since the early 1970s. Modern calculators can be as thin as a credit card.

Analog quantities have a continuous range of values. The measurement of temperature is analog because it can have any of an infinite number of values.

Digital quantities only have a fixed set of values within a range. An abacus is a basic form of digital system, since it can only represent whole numbers.

An electrical signal can be analog or digital. Its current can rise and fall in a smooth, analog way, or abruptly in stepped digital pulses.

The size, or amplitude, of a pulse of current can be used to represent a number. A series of pulses can be used to encode various types of data, such as sound, pictures, or text.

BITS AND BYTES

Computers store and process data in the form of bits. The word *bit* is formed from *b*inary dig*it*.

Each individual bit can have a value of 1 or 0. The 1 and 0 can represent true and false, yes and no, or they can be part of a larger binary number.

A byte consists of eight bits. It can represent any number from 0 to 255 in the form of binary notation.

The hands of a clock face can be in any of an infinite number of positions. They display time in analog form. The figures in an LCD display show a fixed range of values. They display time in digital form.

Bits can be processed by electronic switches called logic gates. These gates determine their value according to certain conditions and logical tests.

The 256 values of a single byte can, for example, represent all of the keys on a keyboard according to a code called ASCII. They can also represent any of 256 colors in a defined selection.

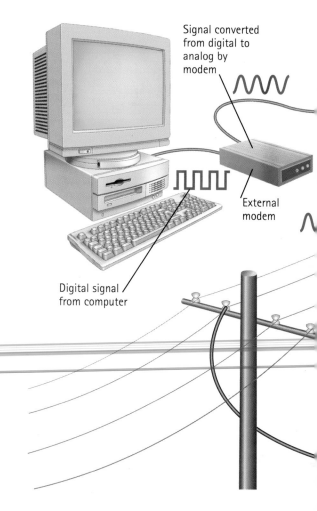

Signal converted from digital to analog by modem

External modem

Digital signal from computer

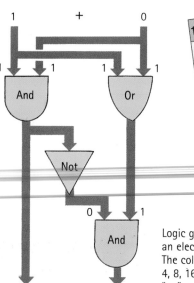

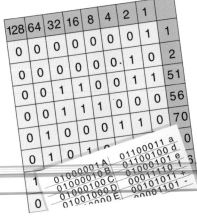

128	64	32	16	8	4	2	1	
0	0	0	0	0	0	0	1	1
0	0	0	0	0	0	1	0	2
0	0	1	1	0	0	1	1	51
0	0	1	1	1	0	0	0	56
0	1	0	0	0	1	1	0	70
0	1	0	1					0
1								
0								

01000001 A   01100011 a
01000010 B   01100100 d
01000100 C   01000101 e
01000100 D   00011110 +
01001000 E   00101011 +
              00001101 -

Logic gates use switches that control the flow of an electrical current. "1" is "true" and "0" is "false." The columns in the binary system have the values 1, 2, 4, 8, 16, 32, and so on. The binary number 111 equals an "on" value in each of the 1, 2, and 4 columns. Adding these together (1+2+4) gives 7 in the decimal system.

A sum of 1024 bytes is a kilobyte (KB); 1024 KB are a megabyte (MB). A gigabyte (GB) represents 1024 MB.

CONVERTING BETWEEN SYSTEMS

Devices called ADCs, or analog-to-digital converters, are used to digitize analog signals.

An ADC measures the value of an analog signal at a fixed rate, which is called the sampling rate. The numerical value of each sample is then expressed in a digital form that might, for example, be a number of pulses. The stream of digital values from the ADC can be processed by the logic circuits of a computer.

Digital signals carry information very accurately, since their pulses can still be decoded if the signal is slightly distorted.

Digital-to-analog converters, or DACs, perform the opposite task to ADCs. They decode digital data and produce a smooth analog signal.

One use of DACs is in compact-disc players, where they convert digital information into a sound signal.

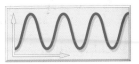

An analog electrical signal is a continuous wave with smooth fluctuations. A digital signal consists of individual, or discrete, steps or pulses.

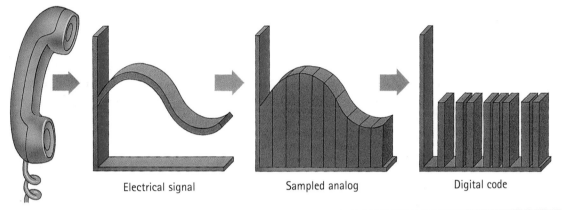

Electrical signal   Sampled analog   Digital code

Analog signals from a telephone can be changed into a series of digital pulses. In this form, signals are less likely to become distorted or noisy. To hear the sounds, the digital signals are changed back to analog signals at the receiver.

HOW A MODEM WORKS

The term modem is an abbreviation of *modulator–demodulator*. A modem modulates, or converts, the digital signal from a computer into an analog signal that can pass through a normal telephone line. The same device can demodulate the analog telephone signal from another computer's modem to reproduce the original digital signal.

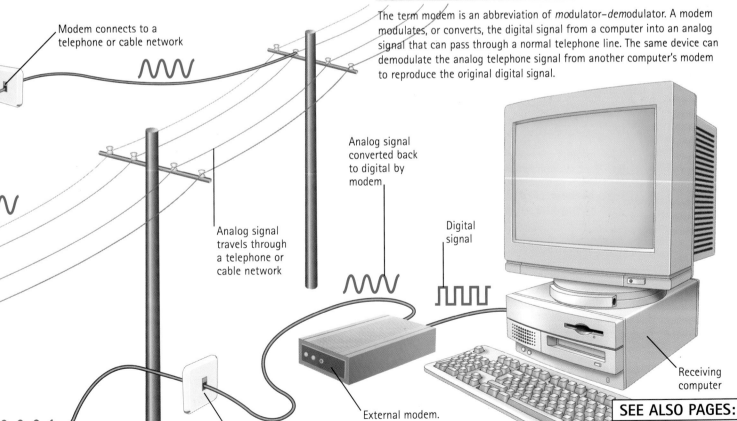

Modem connects to a telephone or cable network

Analog signal converted back to digital by modem

Analog signal travels through a telephone or cable network

Digital signal

Receiving computer

Telephone socket

External modem. Many modems are internal, which means that they are fitted inside a computer

SEE ALSO PAGES:
364–5 Electrical communication, 376–7 Computers, 380–1 Information technology

MICROPROCESSORS

Microprocessors consist of thousands of electronic circuits etched on silicon chips. They are used to control electric and electronic devices.

Modern electronic devices use vast arrays of circuits and switches to perform logic tests, modifications, and calculations on electrical signals. Input signals come from sensors within the device, such as the temperature sensor in a washing machine. Output signals are instructions that control devices such as motors, displays, and audible alarms.

Until the 1940s, vacuum tubes were the only electronic switches available. They were large and often unreliable. In 1948, however, a team at Bell Telephone Laboratories developed semiconducting transistors that could replace much larger vacuum tubes in many applications.

By the 1960s, transistors were replacing vacuum tubes in many electrical goods, most notably in portable radios.

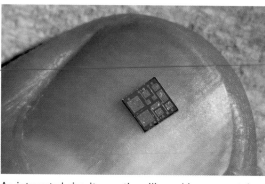

An integrated circuit on a tiny silicon chip may contain thousands of switches and other components.

SILICON CHIPS

In the 1960s, the miniaturization of circuits, which had started with the change from vacuum tubes to transistors, took another great step forward with the

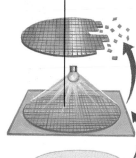

Photoengraving and chemical processes etch circuits on a silicon wafer

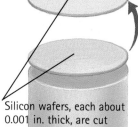

Silicon wafers, each about 0.001 in. thick, are cut from a cylinder of extremely pure silicon

▲ The manufacture of silicon chips starts with a rod of pure silicon that may be several inches in diameter. The rod is cut into round slices, called wafers, usually no more than 0.001 in. thick. Hundreds of integrated circuits are etched into the surface of each wafer. The wafers are then broken up into hundreds of chips, each of which carries a complete integrated circuit.

The control unit instructs other parts of the execution unit to collect data, perform calculations, and store results. It also gives instructions to send information through the bus interface unit to the random-access memory (RAM)

The bus interface unit controls the links between the microprocessor and other components. In a computer, it also manages the movement of information between the components of the microprocessor and memory-storage devices such as RAM chips. The RAM is not part of the microprocessor

Circuitry in the arithmetic logic unit (ALU) performs the microprocessor's calculations. Many processors are built with integral math coprocessors, which can handle complex mathematics quickly

The paging and segment units help the bus interface unit locate information

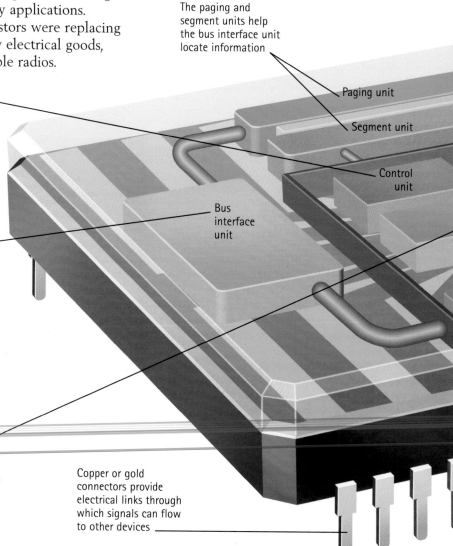

Paging unit

Segment unit

Control unit

Bus interface unit

Copper or gold connectors provide electrical links through which signals can flow to other devices

invention of integrated circuits. Integrated circuits contain all the conductors and transistors on the surface of a silicon chip.

Integrated circuits are produced by creating conducting paths of n-type and p-type silicon. The conducting paths are surrounded by channels of insulating silicon dioxide, which prevent short circuits between conductors.

With advances in technology, integrated circuits can now be made with thousands of transistors in little more than a half a square inch of silicon.

IMPACT OF MICROPROCESSORS

Microprocessors are collections of silicon chips that perform calculations and make decisions in electronic devices.

Simple microprocessors control the functions of digital watches, as well as washing machines and other appliances.

More complicated microprocessors are at the hearts of laptop computers and control systems for satellites and aircraft. If these technologies used vacuum tubes rather than microprocessors, a laptop computer would fill a swimming pool, and fly-by-wire aircraft would be too heavy to get off the ground.

Microprocessors are the controlling devices of computer games. These players are engaged in a two-person boxing simulation in an amusement arcade.

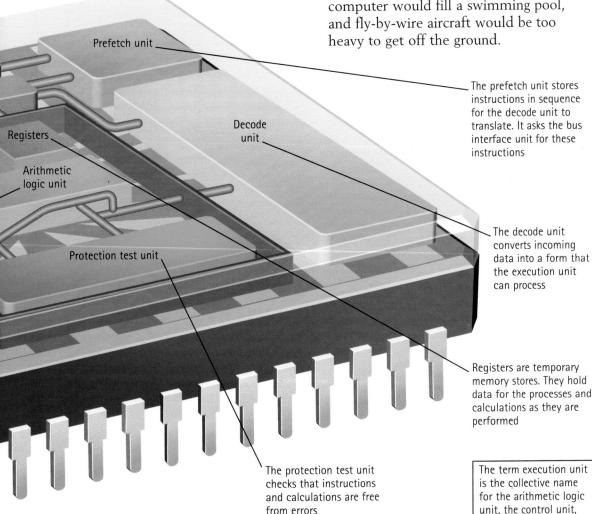

Prefetch unit

Decode unit

Registers

Arithmetic logic unit

Protection test unit

The prefetch unit stores instructions in sequence for the decode unit to translate. It asks the bus interface unit for these instructions

The decode unit converts incoming data into a form that the execution unit can process

Registers are temporary memory stores. They hold data for the processes and calculations as they are performed

The protection test unit checks that instructions and calculations are free from errors

The physical layout of a microprocessor is called its architecture. Even though many different types of architecture exist, all microprocessors work in a similar way. Microprocessors take instructions and data from memory. Units in the microprocessor handle, store, and control the incoming information in sequence. An execution unit checks what it should do, performs its tasks, and then passes on the results and instructions. Microprocessors are often linked to RAM chips; these store data. Microprocessors are also linked to interface chips. These control other parts of a machine, such as keyboards, monitors, motors, or robot arms.

The term execution unit is the collective name for the arithmetic logic unit, the control unit, the registers, and the protection test unit.

SEE ALSO PAGES:

COMPUTERS

Computers use microprocessors to process information according to sets of instructions. They are used for many tasks in education, leisure, and work.

The Electronic Numeric Integrator And Calculator (ENIAC), completed in 1946 at the University of Pennsylvania, used 18,000 vacuum tubes as switches.

In the 1960s, computers that were the size of a large room used circuit boards of transistors to perform operations.

Early home computers, such as the Sinclair ZX81, were very basic computers by modern standards. The ZX81 stored programs slowly and unreliably on audiocassette tape and had just one kilobyte of internal memory.

A modern computer can perform millions of calculations every second. Instructions from a user tell the computer the operations it should perform. The computer then carries out these instructions according to the rules of software programs. Computers process information in the form of electrical signals. The results are often presented on the screen or as a printed document.

The first electronic computer was built in Britain in 1943. It was the first of ten Colossus machines, which used vacuum tubes as electronic switches. A machine called ENIAC was completed in 1946 in the United States. These early computers were used for scientific calculations.

Since the 1970s, computers have used integrated circuits to perform calculations and to store information. Vastly powerful microprocessors and compact memory devices have been made possible by advances in integrated circuits. Due to these improvements, a modern home computer can handle animation and 3D design tasks that were once only possible using enormous computers.

Devices such as image scanners, color printers, digital cameras, and sound cards have created new uses for computers. These include desktop publishing, image editing, and speech synthesis.

INSIDE A COMPUTER

The part of a computer that performs calculations is called the central processing unit (CPU). Programs and information are stored in one or more hard drives and in random-access memory, or RAM. Data can be read from compact discs (CDs) and digital-versatile discs (DVDs). Data can also be stored on removable disks.

Input devices such as a keyboard, mouse, and joystick are used to enter instructions. Output devices, such as a monitor and a printer, are used to display information on a screen or in printed form (hard copy).

Network devices, modems, and ISDN cards allow computers to communicate with each other through network cables or through the telephone. Telephone cables are used to gain access to the Internet through the computer of an internet service provider, or ISP.

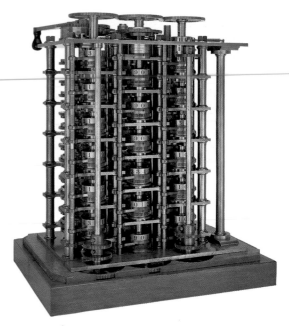

British mathematician Charles Babbage (1792–1871) completed his prototype Difference Engine No.1 in the 1830s. It was designed to calculate mathematical tables mechanically.

COMPUTER COMPONENTS

A computer's base unit contains a number of printed-circuit boards. The main board, called the motherboard, holds the central processing unit (CPU), the computer's clock, and the system memory. The random-access memory, or RAM, holds data that is being processed. Switching off the computer clears the data from the RAM.

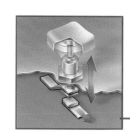

KEYBOARD
Pressing a key on the keyboard sends an electrical signal to the computer

MICROPHONE
Sounds can be recorded through a microphone and stored in digital form

JOYSTICK
Joysticks are used for easy control when playing computer games

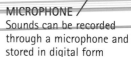

Read-only memory, or ROM, does not clear when the computer is switched off. The ROM includes instructions for the computer to start up when the power is switched on. Most of the information in a computer is stored on magnetic disks in the computer's hard drive. The base unit has slots where circuit boards called cards are fitted. These cards control the sound, graphics, and other functions of the computer. Spare slots, called expansion slots, allow further cards to be added to extend the capabilities of a computer. Modem cards allow computers to communicate through telephone lines. They can be fitted in the base unit or in their own separate housing.

The monitor screen, keyboard, and mouse plug into the base unit, as do printers, scanners, and other devices. These devices are called peripherals.

Laptop computers cram much of the computing power of a desktop machine into a small, portable case.

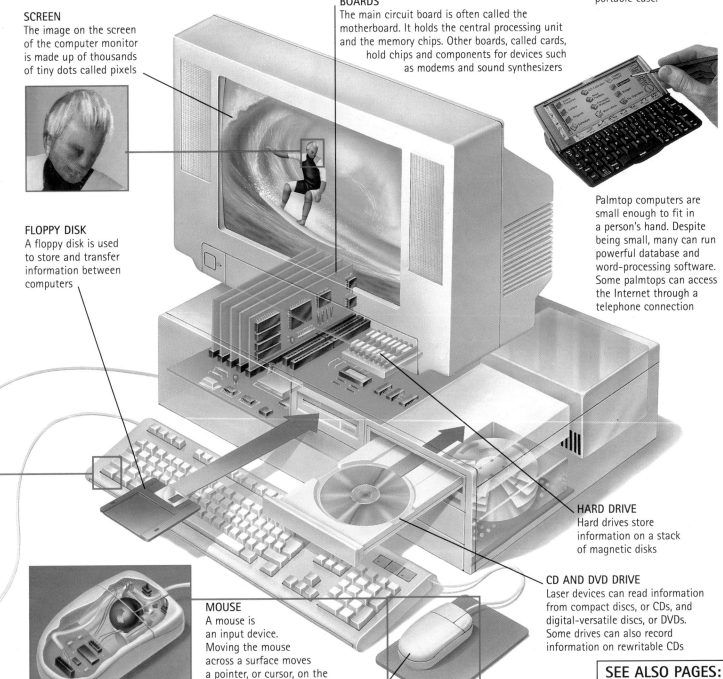

SCREEN
The image on the screen of the computer monitor is made up of thousands of tiny dots called pixels

BOARDS
The main circuit board is often called the motherboard. It holds the central processing unit and the memory chips. Other boards, called cards, hold chips and components for devices such as modems and sound synthesizers

Palmtop computers are small enough to fit in a person's hand. Despite being small, many can run powerful database and word-processing software. Some palmtops can access the Internet through a telephone connection

FLOPPY DISK
A floppy disk is used to store and transfer information between computers

HARD DRIVE
Hard drives store information on a stack of magnetic disks

MOUSE
A mouse is an input device. Moving the mouse across a surface moves a pointer, or cursor, on the screen. Instructions can be given by pressing areas on top of the mouse

CD AND DVD DRIVE
Laser devices can read information from compact discs, or CDs, and digital-versatile discs, or DVDs. Some drives can also record information on rewritable CDs

SEE ALSO PAGES:

378–9 Computer software programs, 380–1 Information technology

COMPUTER SOFTWARE PROGRAMS

Computer software programs are sets of instructions that allow computers to perform tasks. Some software programs also control peripheral devices.

A scanner detects the light that is reflected by an image. Software converts the signals from a scanner into a digital image.

The software in this laser printer provides the instructions that make a printer convert a digital image into a printed version of that image.

The lens of a digital camera focuses light onto charge-coupled devices, or CCDs, that detect light intensity. Software interprets the signals from CCDs to reproduce the image in digital form.

The components of a computer system fall into two classes: hardware and software. Computer hardware is the machinery of a system. The term "computer software" covers the programs that make hardware function.

The first software starts running when a computer is switched on. These programs, called boot files, tell the computer how to start functioning and take control of its component parts. The process is called booting up, or initializing, the computer. A computer's boot programs are stored in its read-only memory, or ROM.

A computer's operating system, or OS, is the software that controls and organizes the computer and the way other programs use it. DOS, Linux, Mac OS, Windows, and UNIX are examples of operating systems. Operating systems run the whole time that a computer is switched on.

The part of a computer system that lets an operator give instructions and see results is called the user interface, or UI. The UI normally consists of a range of screens. Each screen shows a list of options called a menu. An option can be selected by typing in a number or letter that represents that option. Once an option is selected, the computer might perform a function or the display might show another menu or request an input.

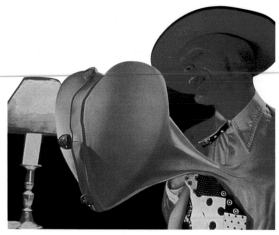

Powerful animation programs allow actors to be mixed with computer-generated effects. This technique was used in the film *The Mask*, starring Jim Carrey.

Graphical user interfaces, or GUIs, use small pictures to represent options. These pictures, called icons, are often chosen to give a visual indication of what an option does. An icon that starts a word-processing program, for example, might show a piece of paper and a pen.

Options in GUIs are chosen by moving a computer mouse on a mat. This causes a pointer, called the cursor, to move around the screen. Once the cursor is placed over an option, a click on the mouse makes the selection. Some computers use a trackball—a rolling ball in a socket—to move the cursor; others respond to voice commands, or a touch screen.

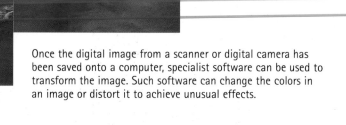

Once the digital image from a scanner or digital camera has been saved onto a computer, specialist software can be used to transform the image. Such software can change the colors in an image or distort it to achieve unusual effects.

COMMON APPLICATIONS

Applications are programs that allow a user to make a computer perform a specific task. A group of programs that are designed to be used together is called a suite of applications. A typical application suite might combine a word-processing program with a database program that organizes information and a graphics program that produces images.

The files that make a program work are normally saved onto a computer's hard drive from a CD-ROM or other disc format. Programs can sometimes be downloaded, or saved, from websites on the Internet.

Word processing is the single most common application for personal computers. Using a word-processing program, an operator can produce letters, reports, and other documents. Sections can be cut or copied from one part of a document and then pasted, or inserted, into another part of the same document or into a different document. Many word-processing programs also have features that can check spelling and basic grammar in a document.

UPDATES AND UTILITIES

Software producers regularly produce new versions of old programs. These are called updates. Installing an update normally adds new features and sometimes corrects problems and errors in the old version.

Utility programs are used to keep a computer running well. They can be used to check for parts of the memory that record information inaccurately. The software then makes sure that those locations are not used to save information, which could otherwise become damaged when it is stored. Utilities can also check for viruses—instructions that make a computer run abnormally. Many utilities fix stored files by removing viruses.

Desktop publishing (DTP) software allows images and text to be arranged on a computer screen. The DTP file that results can then be used to print the pages of a book, magazine, or newspaper.

Voice-activated command center

Lightweight folding robot arm

Tracked base

Automated machines and robots require software to make decisions and to tell them how to react. In the future, robotic personal assistants might be used to perform household tasks following spoken instructions.

Two small screens in a virtual-reality headset provide a view of the wearer's virtual surroundings. The dataglove simulates the feel of objects in those surroundings.

SEE ALSO PAGES:

374–5 Microprocessors, 376–7 Computers, 380–1 Information technology

INFORMATION TECHNOLOGY

Information technology is the storage, processing, and transmission of information by computers or computerized systems.

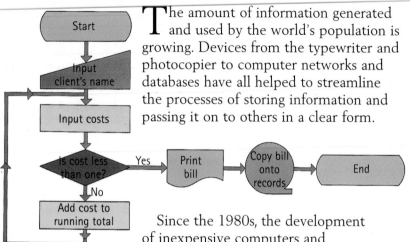

This flow diagram shows the sequence of steps performed by a typical computerized billing system. Programs like this are designed to reduce the work of a human operator by asking questions and making decisions based on the information the programs hold.

The amount of information generated and used by the world's population is growing. Devices from the typewriter and photocopier to computer networks and databases have all helped to streamline the processes of storing information and passing it on to others in a clear form.

Since the 1980s, the development of inexpensive computers and telecommunications systems has made access to information faster and easier. Whereas information used to be stored as written, typed, or printed documents, a large proportion of information is now stored in digital form on computers.

Database programs store vast amounts of information in an organized way. A database program can use this information to do calculations and produce reports in much less time than a person would require to do the same job.

Before the invention of computers and word processing, large organizations used large "pools" of typists to produce documents. This is a 1930s typing pool.

Many different kinds of information are kept in databases. A library might have a database that records the title, author, and publication date of each of its books. A more detailed database could be used to see how often each book is borrowed.

Companies use databases to manage lists of their customers and contacts. Databases are also used to keep track of a company's stock levels so that supplies can be ordered before stocks run out.

Keeping information in databases helps organizations to function efficiently. Information must often be kept securely, however, since rivals could cause damage to an organization if they had access to its databases. For this reason, most databases can only be entered using a password.

Photocopiers make quick, clear copies of documents. This photocopier works by shining light onto the original document. The reflected image is focused onto a drum charged with static electricity. The static charge remains on the drum where there are dark areas corresponding to a replica of the original document. Toner powder is attracted to the static charge on the drum, transferred to a sheet of copying paper and fixed by heat.

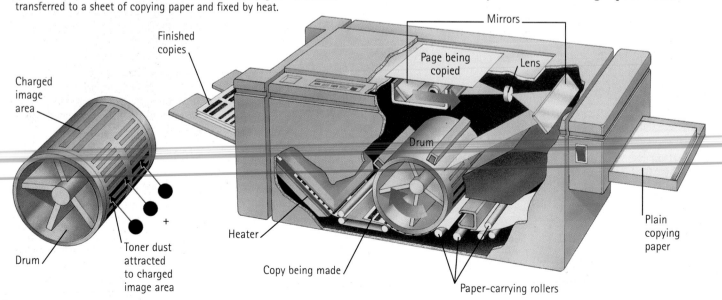

NETWORKS AND THE INTERNET

The information stored in a database is often used by many people on different machines. Users can share this information by connecting their computers to a network. A network might serve a room or a building. Telephone links can extend networks to cover several separate locations, sometimes in different countries.

The Internet is a special type of network. The development of the Internet started in the 1960s, when the United States government set up a network called ARPANET. This network was designed to withstand a nuclear attack because it can carry information even if one part of the network fails. A growing number of universities and institutions connected to the Internet during the 1970s and 1980s.

Since 1989, when the World Wide Web was created, Internet access has grown enormously. Hundreds of millions of people worldwide now access the Internet. Many use the Internet to send electronic messages, called E-mails, which can be sent rapidly between any two Internet connections. Other people search for information using Internet programs called search engines. Search engines look for collections of information, called websites, that are related to the search topic keyed in by the user.

Information such as images from a camera, computer files, or music can be sent by E-mail or viewed at websites.

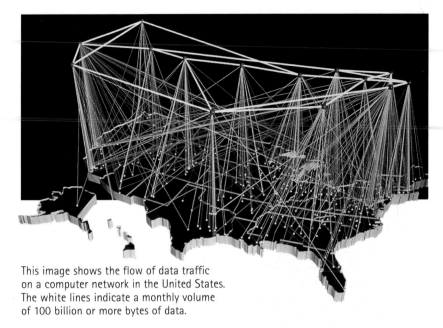

This image shows the flow of data traffic on a computer network in the United States. The white lines indicate a monthly volume of 100 billion or more bytes of data.

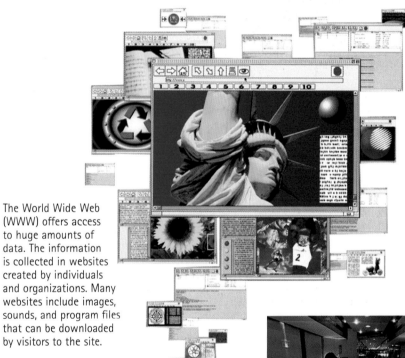

The World Wide Web (WWW) offers access to huge amounts of data. The information is collected in websites created by individuals and organizations. Many websites include images, sounds, and program files that can be downloaded by visitors to the site.

Video conferences save the time and expense of traveling to meetings by passing sounds and images between the two ends of a telephone connection.

▲ Internet cafés, such as this one in Bangalore, India, allow customers to hire a computer and surf the Internet.

SEE ALSO PAGES:

366–7 Telecommunications, 376–7 Computers, 378–9 Computer software programs

SMART TECHNOLOGY

Smart technology uses computer systems and microprocessors to help with everyday tasks and the exchange of information.

The term "smart technology" covers microprocessor-based technology and other devices that can gather and process information to make decisions or take actions based on that information.

Smart technology has made an enormous impact on everyday life. The importance of smart systems will continue to grow as computer technology develops.

The automatic teller machine, or ATM, was one of the first examples of smart technology made available to the public. Banks give their customers plastic cards to use in ATMs. The card has a magnetic strip encoded with customer account details. When a customer puts a card into the slot of an ATM, the machine reads the strip and asks for the customer's personal identification number, or PIN. The ATM then checks computer records. If the PIN is correct for the card, the customer can withdraw money, check the account balance, or make other inquiries.

Automatic teller machines, or ATMs, allow bank customers to obtain information about their accounts and perform money transactions. The ATM identifies customers by reading magnetic strips in their bankcards. Customers must confirm their identity by entering their secret personal identification number, or PIN.

Cardreader

Magnetic strip

Debit/credit card

Secure money storage

Data on balance and transactions stored and calculated on this computer

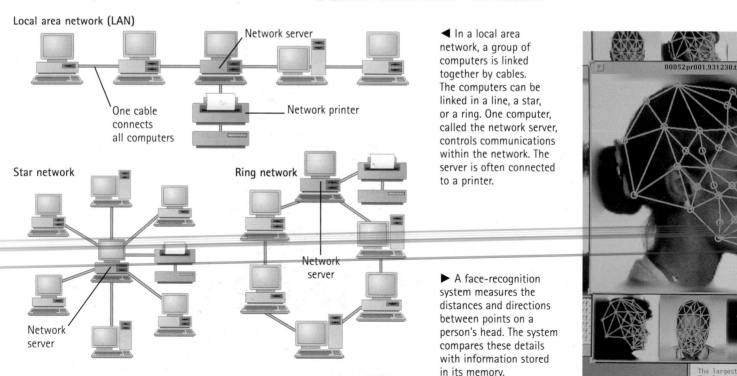

Local area network (LAN)

Network server

One cable connects all computers

Network printer

Star network

Ring network

Network server

Network server

◀ In a local area network, a group of computers is linked together by cables. The computers can be linked in a line, a star, or a ring. One computer, called the network server, controls communications within the network. The server is often connected to a printer.

▶ A face-recognition system measures the distances and directions between points on a person's head. The system compares these details with information stored in its memory.

00052pr001.931230.tiff

An ATM system is an example of a wide-area network, or WAN. Each ATM can contact a central computer, called a server, that stores account information. WANs normally use telephone links to carry signals between computers.

Schools and offices often have local area networks, or LANs. These normally use a network of cables to carry information between computers. Some systems use beams of infrared light to link computers over small distances.

BIOMETRICS

Biometrics is the measurement of a person's physical details. Fingerprinting is a biometric measurement, since it studies the details of skin patterns on fingertips.

Biometric security machines scan a part of a person's body and compare the scanned image with computer records to try to identify that person. The face, the hand, and the iris of the eye are particularly suitable for scanning.

MINIATURIZATION

One aspect of smart technology is the movement toward ever-smaller devices. Smart cards are small plastic cards that carry information in microchips. Wearable computers will soon have the power of a large computer but be small enough to be worn like glasses.

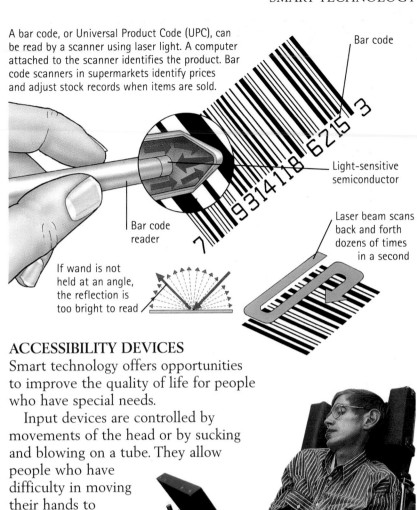

A bar code, or Universal Product Code (UPC), can be read by a scanner using laser light. A computer attached to the scanner identifies the product. Bar code scanners in supermarkets identify prices and adjust stock records when items are sold.

Bar code

Bar code reader

Light-sensitive semiconductor

Laser beam scans back and forth dozens of times in a second

If wand is not held at an angle, the reflection is too bright to read

ACCESSIBILITY DEVICES

Smart technology offers opportunities to improve the quality of life for people who have special needs.

Input devices are controlled by movements of the head or by sucking and blowing on a tube. They allow people who have difficulty in moving their hands to communicate with computers. A voice synthesizer can then turn their messages into spoken phrases.

▲ English physicist Stephen Hawking (1942–) uses a computerized speech synthesizer to speak to people.

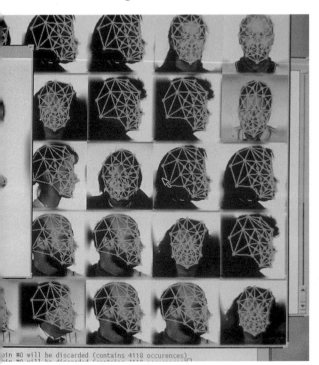

▲ This prototype of a wearable computer projects an image of a computer screen onto a panel in front of the eye. The wearer controls the computer by giving spoken commands and using the hand-held trackball.

SEE ALSO PAGES:

374–5 Microprocessors, 376–7 Computers, 378–9 Computer software programs

FACTS AND FIGURES

LAWS AND RULES OF ELECTRICITY

Electrical charge (measured in coulombs)

= current (amp) x time (second)

Potential difference (volts)

$$= \frac{\text{energy transferred (joule)}}{\text{charge (coulomb)}}$$

Resistance (ohms)

$$= \frac{\text{potential difference (volt)}}{\text{current (amp)}}$$

Domestic electrical energy consumption (kilowatt hours; kWh)

= power (kilowatt) x time (hour)

Current drawn by an electrical appliance in normal operation (amp)

$$= \frac{\text{power rating of appliance (watt)}}{\text{voltage (volt)}}$$

COMPUTER STORAGE TERMS

Bit	smallest unit of computer data
Byte	eight bits
Kilobyte	1,024 bytes
Megabyte	1,024 kilobytes
Gigabyte	1,024 megabytes

The word "bit" is shortened from *binary digit*. A digit of binary code can have one of two values: 0 or 1. These values can be stored as different magnetizations of specific locations on a computer hard drive, for example. Bits can be transmitted as pulses of current through cables, or as pulses of light through optical fibers.

ELECTRICAL CIRCUIT SYMBOLS

Electrical and electronic engineers and physicists use a number of symbols to enable them to draw complex circuit diagrams in limited spaces. Some of these symbols are shown in the table below.

KEY DATES

B.C.

c.600 Greek philosopher Thales of Miletus discovers that amber resin attracts light objects when rubbed.

A.D.

1600 British physician William Gilbert publishes the results of his experiments with electricity and magnetism.

1672 German physicist Otto von Guericke constructs the first electrostatic generator. It is a hand-cranked sulfur sphere.

1729–32 British physicist Stephen Gray discovers the principles of electrical conduction.

1745 Dutch physicist Petrus van Musschenbroek invents the Leyden jar, a simple capacitor.

1752 U.S. diplomat and scientist Benjamin Franklin invents the lightning rod after flying a kite in a storm.

1784-89 French physicist Charles Coulomb establishes laws of electrostatics.

1800 Italian physicist Alessandro Volta invents the voltaic pile, the first electric battery.

1827 German physicist Georg Simon Ohm devises a law that describes the relationship between current, resistance, and voltage in a circuit.

1831 British chemist and physicist Michael Faraday produces a current by turning a copper loop in a magnetic field.

1859 French physicist Gaston Planté invents the lead–acid storage battery.

1871 Belgian electrical engineer Zénobe Gramme begins manufacturing dynamos.

1873 British physicist James Clerk Maxwell publishes equations that describe the properties of electromagnetic waves.

1876 U.S. inventor Alexander Graham Bell invents the telephone.

1877 French engineer Georges Leclanché invents the zinc–carbon dry cell.

1882 French engineer Marcel Deprez achieves the first transmission of high-voltage electricity through cables over a distance of around 55 km.

1895 Italian electrical engineer Guglielmo Marconi makes first radio transmission over a distance of 2.4 km.

1910 French chemist and engineer Georges Claude invents the neon lighting tube.

1911 Dutch physicist Heike Kamerlingh Onnes discovers superconductivity of mercury cooled to 4.2 K (–268.7°C).

1914 U.S. inventor Thomas Alva Edison develops an alkaline storage battery.

1928 Swiss-born U.S. physicist Felix Bloch produces a complete theory of semiconductors.

1929 The BBC makes and transmits the world's first television shows.

1942 Italian-born U.S. physicist Enrico Fermi initiates the first controlled nuclear fission chain reaction.

1948 U.S. physicists John Bardeen, Walter Brattain, and William Shockley invent the transistor.

1951 The Experimental Breeder Reactor, EBR-1, at Idaho Falls, becomes the first nuclear reactor to produce electrical power.

1960 United States launch Echo 1, the first telecommunications satellite to orbit the Earth.

1961 Unimate becomes the first robot in service in a factory.

1969 U.S. Department of Defense establishes ARPANET, a data communications network that spawned the Internet.

1971 Intel Corporation launches the first microprocessor.

1981 IBM starts production of the first personal computer.

1985 Philips launch the CD-ROM as a computer data medium.

1989 British computer scientist Timothy Berners-Lee devises the World Wide Web to simplify Internet usage.

COMMON CIRCUIT SYMBOLS

Fixed resistor, Fixed capacitor, Triac, SCR, Transistors (NPN, PNP), Potentiometer or Adjustable resistor, Polarized capacitor, LED, Iron core transformer, Darlingtons, Variable resistor, Variable capacitor, Variable coil, Adjustable coil, MOSFETs, Variable resistor, Variable resistor, Variable resistor, Variable resistor, JFETs

CHAPTER 9

SPACE AND TIME

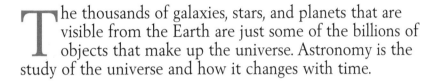

The thousands of galaxies, stars, and planets that are visible from the Earth are just some of the billions of objects that make up the universe. Astronomy is the study of the universe and how it changes with time.

Stars and planets have been studied since the first humans looked up at the night sky. They made sense of the bright dots they saw by grouping them into constellations. They followed the movements of the moon and planets, and developed a simple model of the universe. More recently, scientists have studied what stars are made of and how they form, evolve, and die. Most scientist believe the universe was born in a "big bang"—an instant when all matter was created and time began.

Almost all of the objects in the universe are too far away for missions from the Earth to visit. Astronomers use telescopes on the Earth and in orbit to gather information from the light, X rays, radio, and infrared radiation given out by distant objects. Space probes have visited some of the planets, comets, and asteroids, and twelve people have walked on the moon. Each year, astronomers and space scientists discover more objects in space and learn new details about those objects that have already been known for some time.

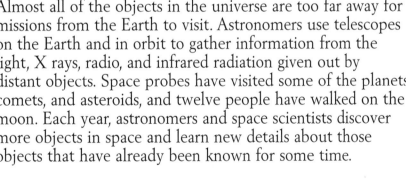

THE UNIVERSE

The universe consists of everything in space, and space itself. It is unimaginably vast, constantly changing, and it is expanding all the time.

The universe is everything that exists— from the smallest creature on the Earth to the largest, most distant structure in space. It is also dynamic. Everything in it follows a life cycle, whether it is a human who lives for 70-80 years, or a star for 10 billion years, each object in the universe is born, lives, and ultimately dies.

CONTENTS OF THE UNIVERSE

Our planet seems important and large compared to a human who lives upon it. Yet the Earth is a tiny speck when compared to the rest of the universe. The Earth is one of nine planets orbiting a star called the sun. There are more stars than anything else in the universe. It is impossible to count them, but we can estimate that there are at least a quintillion—100 billion billion.

The sun, like all other stars, is a glowing sphere of hot gas. It is a fairly average, medium-hot, yellow star that along with billions more, make up a galaxy. This vast spiral-shaped grouping of stars is our home

Quasars are a type of active galaxy that produce huge amounts of energy. They are some of the most powerful objects in the universe. In this false-color image of quasar 3C 272, the first quasar to be identified, the intensity of X rays emitted is shown by the different colors. The most intense are pale blue, green, and yellow.

galaxy, the Milky Way. With about 30 others it forms a cluster of galaxies in space. Together, they are called the Local Group. All over the universe are many more clusters of galaxies, which, in turn, are arranged in superclusters.

We see many galaxies from the Earth, but many more are beyond our vision. In all there are about 100 billion galaxies in the universe. We can see them in every direction. Some are so close, or so large, that we can make out their shapes and their individual stars. We see them through telescopes, either on land or in orbit around the Earth.

▼ The time light takes to travel is used for measuring distances in space. The light from the closest nighttime star takes 4.2 years to reach the Earth. The star is therefore 4.2 light-years away. The time for light to travel distances from more local places are shown as a comparison.

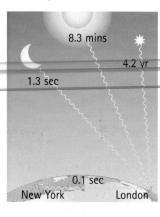

8.3 mins

4.2 yr

1.3 sec

0.1 sec

New York   London

1 Everything in the universe— the stars, the planets, and human life—consists of the same elements.
2 Humans are just one of billions of life-forms on the planet Earth. More than 6 billion people now live on its land.
3 Our planet, the Earth, is the only place in the universe known to support life.
4 The Earth is one of nine planets orbiting the star called the sun. Together the planets and the sun form the solar system.
5 The sun, and its system of planets, is just one of billions of stars in the Milky Way galaxy.
6 Countless galaxies we have never seen fill the universe. They are grouped in clusters.
7 Clusters of galaxies are strung together in superclusters that stretch across the universe. In between are huge, empty voids.

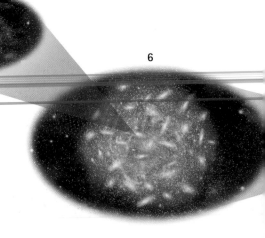

1 Swirling clouds of gas and dust, called nebulae, are the birthplace of stars. Often, they are themselves the remains of earlier generations, material blown out from short-lived, massive stars.

2 Spheres form in the gas as gravity pulls it together. As the gas compresses it begins to heat.

3 The young star—a protostar—continues to spin. Unused material is expelled.

4 Nuclear reaction begins in the hot core. Light and heat are produced.

5 The star shines steadily for billions of years.

MEASURING DISTANCES

It is easy to make measurements on the Earth. We use systems such as the SI, or metric, (kilometer, meter, centimeter) or U.S. Customary System, (mile, yard, foot, inch) to measure how large, or how long something is. These systems are used to measure some of the smaller things in space, such as a crater on the moon, or even the distance of Pluto from the sun.

Some things are so big, or so far away, that these measuring systems will not work because the numbers become too long to handle. Astronomers use different units. Within the solar system they use the Astronomical Unit (AU). One AU is the distance between the Earth and the sun, about 93 million mi. (150 million km). This unit is used to measure the distance to other objects. The sun to Mars is 1.5 AU, to Jupiter 5.2 AU, and so on.

When measuring outside the solar system, to stars and galaxies, or the size of a galaxy from side to side, astronomers use light-years (l.y.). Light travels faster than anything—186,281 mi. (299,792km) per second. A light-year is the distance that light travels in a year. That is 5.88 trillion miles (9.46 trillion km). The Milky Way galaxy is 100,000 l.y. across.

▲ Stars are born all the time. Spinning spheres of gas form inside large clouds of gas and dust. Once hot enough, the sphere's hydrogen is converted to helium. Light and heat are produced and the star is born. Through its life and, finally, death, it will shed material which will, in turn, be used to make new stars.

◄ New stars are born in the Eagle Nebula, 7,000 light-years away. At the tips of the huge columns of gas and dust are oval-shaped clumps. They look tiny compared to the columns, but they are new stars being born.

EXPANDING UNIVERSE

Everything in the universe is moving. The Earth spins on its axis once each day and we experience day and night alternately, as we bathe in sunlight, then face dark space. Every other planet and moon, each tiny piece of space rock, and each of the countless stars spins on its own axis.

Such objects also move through space as they spin. The Earth, for example, travels around the sun once every year; each complete trip is known as an orbit. At the same time, the sun, the Earth, and all the other bodies that make up the solar system, move as a whole. They orbit around the center of the Milky Way galaxy. From our place in the Milky Way, we look deep into space and see galaxies. The galaxies live in clusters that are rushing away both from our galaxy and each other. The farther away the cluster, the faster it recedes. The universe itself is expanding all the time, and has been doing so ever since it was created.

American astronomer, Edwin Hubble (1889–1953) sits in front of the telescope that he used to observe the universe. In 1924, he presented the first evidence to show that other galaxies existed outside our own. In 1929, he proved that the universe is expanding.

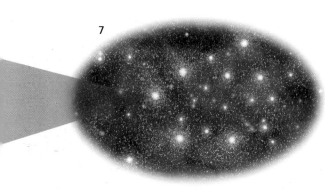

7

SEE ALSO PAGES:

242–3 Heat and light from the sun, 390–1 Galaxies, 392–3 Stars, 393 The sun, 398–9 The solar system

THE UNIVERSE: ORIGINS AND FUTURE

The universe was born in an explosion called the Big Bang about 13 billion years ago, and has been changing and growing ever since. It will exist for trillions of years.

Almost all astronomers believe that the universe was created about 13 billion years ago in a huge explosion called the Big Bang. In the tiniest fraction of time, too short to be measured, the universe was born. It was an enormous amount of energy packed into an unimaginably small space, but in a fraction of a second the universe inflated. It grew from smaller than a pinprick to larger than a galaxy. The universe has been expanding ever since.

The energy created in the Big Bang was transformed into atomic particles. Within three minutes, the temperature had dropped from 18 octillion°F (or 18 followed by 27 zeros) to 1.8 billion°F and continued to fall. By this time the universe consisted of 77 percent hydrogen and 23 percent helium. All the other elements and compounds were created from these two. After 300,000 years, the universe, which until this time had been like an opaque soup, became transparent. Its temperature dropped to 5,432°F. About one billion years after the Big Bang, gravity was pulling the hydrogen and helium into clouds. Spinning spheres of gas formed, and the first stars and galaxies were born.

▼ This cool, dense cloud of hydrogen in the constellation of Orion is producing stars. The colors indicate the different temperatures of the cloud and stars embedded in it. The dust of the cloud is yellow. A bright, newborn star (red) is at center right.

▲▶ Matter has been cooling, changing, and expanding out from the point of explosion ever since the Big Bang. For around the first quarter of a million years it was a soup of hydrogen and helium particles that slowly came together to form stars and galaxies.

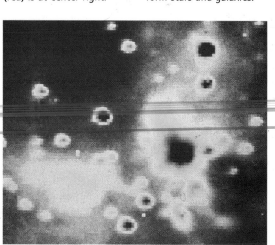

Big Bang

10 yr

100 yr

1,000 yr

10,000 yr

1 Nothing existed before the Big Bang. All we know is that within the tiniest fraction of a second, enough energy to make all the material in the universe had come into existence. As the universe cooled, this energy was transformed into atomic particles.

2 Just after the Big Bang, the universe was unimaginably small. It then began to expand suddenly, and inflated hugely in every direction. The universe was full of energy and its temperatures soared.

3 The universe had to cool down from a temperature of about 18 octillion to about 5,432°F, before atoms could form. Atoms are the minute units of matter. The atoms consisted mainly of hydrogen, the simplest and most plentiful substance found in the universe. The rest were more complex atoms of helium.

4 Hydrogen and helium filled the universe with a thin dark fog. The gas atoms in denser parts were pulled into separate, much smaller, clouds by gravity. (Gravity is the force by which objects attract one another.) The centers of the clouds, where the gas atoms were packed together, heated and gave birth to stars as the galaxies formed.

EVIDENCE FOR THE BIG BANG

Light from distant galaxies takes billions of years to reach us, and in this way we can see what galaxies were like years ago. Using very powerful telescopes we can look back to a time when galaxies were young and the universe was in its infancy. The most distant objects we can see are galaxies as they were ten billion years ago.

The galaxies are moving apart. This suggests that everything was once concentrated in a single place. Additional evidence for the Big Bang came in 1965 when scientists found heatwaves left from the vast explosion coming from every direction in space. In 1992, the COBE satellite detected the ripples in the heat caused by cooling after the Big Bang. Yet, astronomers realize that they still haven't found the majority of the universe's matter—the material of which it is made. They call this dark matter, and it makes up about 90 percent of the universe. Once found, it may help to fill some of the gaps in the universe's history.

THE FUTURE OF THE UNIVERSE

Cosmologists are astronomers who study the origin of the universe. They are also interested in the future of the universe. Some believe that the universe will continue to expand, growing larger and cooler. Eventually all the stars will die, and the universe will be cold and dark. We know that as the galaxies move apart, the gravity of one pulls on the other, and slows this expansion. Some cosmologists believe that, in trillions of years' time, gravity will have slowed the galaxies completely, until they are stationary.

Gravity will then pull the galaxies back toward each other. The universe will contract until it is all together in one point. As its material packs ever closer together it will heat up. Eventually, the universe will collapse violently inward in an implosion called the Big Crunch. Everything will be destroyed and it will be the end of the universe. But, this may be followed by another Big Bang and the creation of a new universe.

In 1992, it was announced that the satellite *Cosmic Background Explorer* (COBE) had traced the background radiation and ripples left over from the Big Bang, 13 billion years before.

We do not know exactly when the universe was created, but now believe it was around 13 billion years ago. All the matter in the universe, time, and space were created together in the Big Bang. The matter was, at first, atomic particles, then atoms and compounds. All the complex materials we know today, including our planet, our homes, and our own bodies, started in this way.

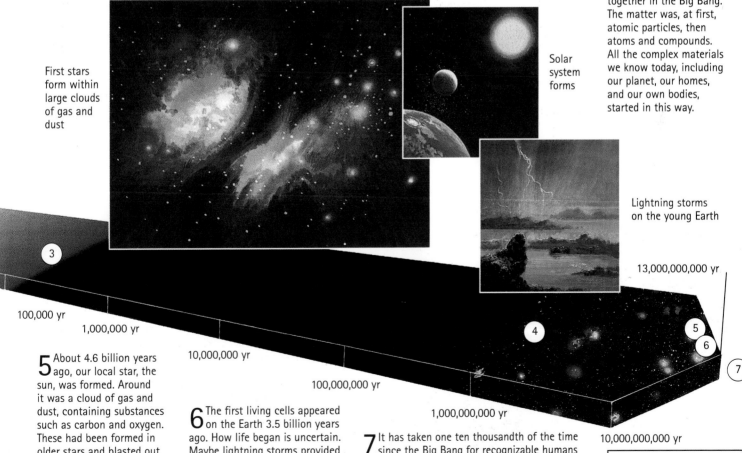

First stars form within large clouds of gas and dust

Solar system forms

Lightning storms on the young Earth

3

100,000 yr

1,000,000 yr

10,000,000 yr

100,000,000 yr

1,000,000,000 yr

4

5

6

7

13,000,000,000 yr

10,000,000,000 yr

5 About 4.6 billion years ago, our local star, the sun, was formed. Around it was a cloud of gas and dust, containing substances such as carbon and oxygen. These had been formed in older stars and blasted out into space when the stars died. This material came together to form the planets.

6 The first living cells appeared on the Earth 3.5 billion years ago. How life began is uncertain. Maybe lightning storms provided the energy to start chemical reactions in the soup of elements on the young planet.

7 It has taken one ten thousandth of the time since the Big Bang for recognizable humans to develop from apes. Today, scientists try to work out the story of the universe by sending out space satellites that look back across time.

SEE ALSO PAGES:

GALAXIES

Galaxies exist throughout the universe. They are enormous groups of stars held together by gravity. We live in a spiral arm of the Milky Way galaxy.

▼ Galaxies begin as huge masses of gas. As they shrink under the pressure of gravity, the gas at the center becomes dense enough to start forming stars. Some galaxies start spinning, forming a spiral or barred spiral galaxy.

1 A slowly spinning mass of gas collapses under the pressure of gravity, and the first stars are formed at the center. As the cloud shrinks, its turning speed increases.

2 Gas clouds meet in the swirling disk, and attract more clouds because of their extra gravity. Stars start to form here, too.

3 There is no gas left at the center to make new stars, but the arms are rich in raw star material. The galaxy is now in the prime of life.

Wherever you look in the universe there are galaxies. There are billions of them—vast collections of stars, gas, and dust. Each one can contain hundreds of thousands of stars or even many billions.

Galaxies are classified according to their shape. The three main types are elliptical, spiral, and barred. A fourth type, the irregular, is galaxies with no distinctive shape. More than half of all the galaxies we can see are ellipticals. They range from the smallest to the largest galaxies and contain little gas or dust, where new star formation could take place. About a third are either spirals or barred spirals. Their centers contain old stars, and their arms hold young stars and new ones being born from clouds of gas and dust. The young ones are very bright and the outshine the stars between the spirals.

THE MILKY WAY

The galaxy we live in is called the Milky Way. Viewed from the outside, we would see it as a barred spiral galaxy made up of over 200 billion stars. Our star, the sun, is located in one of the spiral arms. The arms are made up of stars, and nebulae of gas and dust where new stars are born. The center contains older stars. The sun takes about 220 million years to orbit the center. The galaxy is 100,000 l.y. across and 2,000 l.y. thick.

▶ **THE SUN'S NEIGHBORS IN THE MILKY WAY**
1 Cone Nebula   2 Rosette Nebula   3 Orion Nebula
4 Lagoon Nebula   5 Solar System   6 California Nebula
7 Trifid Nebula   8 Vela Supernova Remnant
9 North America Nebula

Astronomers do not know exactly why the galaxies have these shapes, but it could be because of the way they were formed. The amount of material in a galaxy, the speed of its spin, and the rate at which its stars form all help to determine its shape. Astronomers have also studied colliding galaxies and seen that two can join to form one new large galaxy. This can be the result of a direct hit or a glancing blow, and leads to a period of intense star formation in the new galaxy. It is thought that galaxies will continue to join in this way, so that in the future there may be fewer, but larger, galaxies.

ACTIVE GALAXIES

There are some galaxies known as active galaxies, and these are different from the others in their characteristics and appearance. A typical active galaxy has a luminous core that may vary in brightness, and from which two huge jets of material are emitted. In the very center,

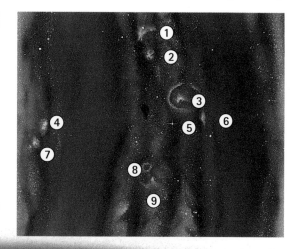

The Milky Way

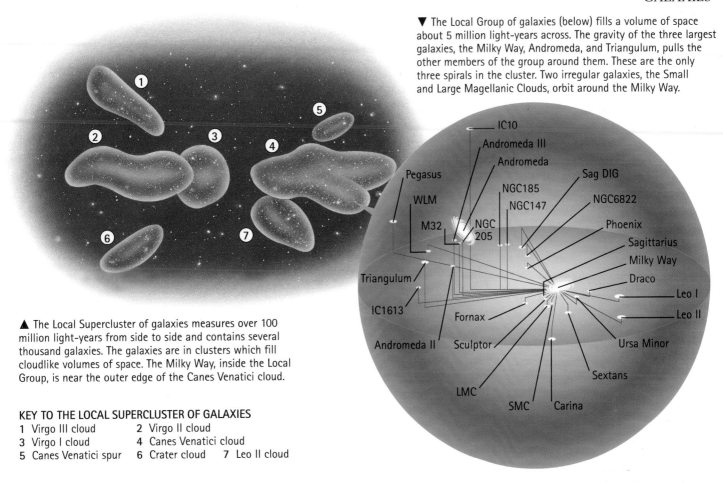

▼ The Local Group of galaxies (below) fills a volume of space about 5 million light-years across. The gravity of the three largest galaxies, the Milky Way, Andromeda, and Triangulum, pulls the other members of the group around them. These are the only three spirals in the cluster. Two irregular galaxies, the Small and Large Magellanic Clouds, orbit around the Milky Way.

▲ The Local Supercluster of galaxies measures over 100 million light-years from side to side and contains several thousand galaxies. The galaxies are in clusters which fill cloudlike volumes of space. The Milky Way, inside the Local Group, is near the outer edge of the Canes Venatici cloud.

KEY TO THE LOCAL SUPERCLUSTER OF GALAXIES

1 Virgo III cloud	2 Virgo II cloud
3 Virgo I cloud	4 Canes Venatici cloud
5 Canes Venatici spur	6 Crater cloud 7 Leo II cloud

a glowing ring of dust and gas surrounds a supermassive black hole. Quasars, blazars, Seyfert galaxies, and radio galaxies are all examples of active galaxies. Astronomers think that one model can account for the different types, but they have been classified into groups because of the angle at which they appear when we see them in our sky.

CLUSTERS AND SUPERCLUSTERS

Galaxies gather in groups called clusters. Our galaxy, the Milky Way, is one of about 30 galaxies that make a small cluster called the Local Group. Most of the group are small and faint. About half of them are elliptical, and around a third irregular in

shape. There are more massive and much brighter spiral galaxies. Several thousand galaxies make up the larger clusters. The Virgo Cluster, about 50 million light-years away, contains more than 2,000 galaxies with three giant ellipticals and many bright spirals.

Clusters are arranged into even larger groups called superclusters. These are the largest structures in the universe, and measure more than 100 million light-years across. A supercluster can contain dozens of clusters. The Local Group belongs to a supercluster that is centered on the Virgo Cluster. The supercluster consists of 11 main cloud-shaped clusters in a roughly oblong volume of space.

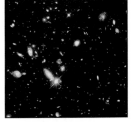

This view into space took ten days to make. All but one of the objects are galaxies, seen for the first time in this image. The faintest are about four billion times dimmer than we can see with our eyes. Because of the vast distances their light had to travel to reach the Earth, the galaxies are seen as they were around ten billion years ago.

Those galaxies without any particular shape are classified as irregular galaxies (Irr). They contain a lot of gas and dust.

Elliptical galaxies are ball-shaped, and range from roughly spherical (E0) to an elongated compressed-ball shape (E7).

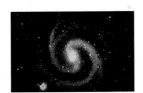

Spiral galaxies are disk-shaped. Arms radiate from a central nucleus. They range from tight arms (Sa) to loose arms (Sc).

Barred spirals have a bar-shaped nucleus from which arms radiate. They range from tight arms (SBa) to loose arms (SBc).

SEE ALSO PAGES:

392–3 Stars, 394–5 The sun, 414–15 Studying the universe

STARS

There are billions of stars in the universe. Each one is a ball of hot, glowing gas that changes size, temperature, and color over its long lifetime.

In 1906, Danish astronomer Ejnar Hertzsprung (1873–1967) observed that the temperature and luminosity of a star were linked. He found that stars could be arranged in a family, from hot, bright stars to cool, dim ones.

There are more stars than anything else in the universe. Our sun is the closest; the rest appear only as bright dots of light in the night sky. Astronomers study their light to find out what they consist of, and how big and how hot they are.

Stars come in different sizes and colors and, although all are hot, they come in a range of temperatures. Each one consists of a gas familiar to us on the Earth and held together by gravity. Inside the core, hydrogen is converted into helium. In this nuclear reaction, enormous amounts of energy are produced and then given off. We feel some of the sun's energy in the form of heat, and see it as light. But other forms of energy such as ultraviolet radiation and X rays are also emitted by the sun and stars.

THE LIFE OF A STAR

The stars that we see are at different stages of their lives. All stars start by converting hydrogen into helium in their core. After the hydrogen is used up, the helium is converted into new elements, such as carbon and oxygen. During this process, the stars change size, throw off material, and change temperature and color. The hottest are the bluest, the

The Pleiades star cluster was born about 78 million years ago from a nebula of gas and dust. About 100 stars are surrounded by remains of the nebula.

yellow ones cooler, and the red cooler still, although the red dwarfs still have a surface temperature of 5,432°F. Some stars convert their gas more quickly than others. A star's mass, the amount of material it consists of, influences how long it will live, the development stages it will go through, and how it will eventually die. Many stars, like the sun, shine for billions of years before they run out of fuel. Others, those that have a higher mass than the sun, use their fuel up more quickly and so have shorter lives. A star's mass also influences its luminosity, or brightness. The more massive the star, the greater its luminosity.

These strands of gas are the remnant of the Vela Nebula, a supernova that exploded about 12,000 years ago. The gas will eventually be used to form new stars.

▶ Stars like the sun follow a life cycle. Like all other stars they are born in a nebula of gas and dust. Once nuclear reaction starts, the star shines, or becomes luminous. The sun is a main-sequence star, and will shine steadily for several billion years until the hydrogen is used up and it matures into a red giant. Next, it will slowly shed its outer layers into space, until only the shrunken core is left. The star will then die. Its small, hot body will cool into a white dwarf, a cold, dark cinder in space.

▲ At first the star shines steadily as it converts hydrogen into helium.

▲ The core's hydrogen is nearly used up. The core collapses and becomes hotter.

▲ The helium starts to convert to carbon. The outer parts of the star move outward.

▲ The star gets larger and larger. The outer layers cool and turn from orange to red.

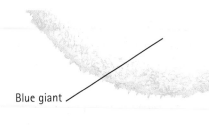

Blue giant

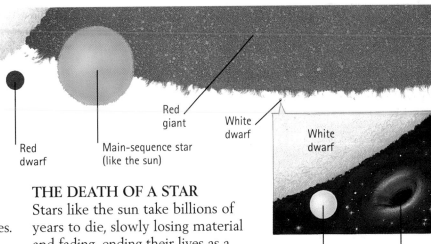

Red dwarf

Main-sequence star (like the sun)

Red giant

White dwarf

White dwarf

Neutron star

Black hole

All stars are born from clouds of gas and dust called nebulae. Small clouds form within a nebula and condense, spinning and pulling the material into the center by gravity. As the material in the center becomes compressed, its temperature rises. At about 18 million°F, a nuclear reaction starts, and the star is born.

Most stars are born in pairs, like twins. These pairs and other stars are born within a group of stars called a cluster. Some stars spend the rest of their lives as part of a cluster. The stars in other clusters drift apart. This is what happened to the sun and the brother and sister stars it was born with. There are two sorts of star clusters in the night sky. The open clusters are loose collections of young stars that will eventually disperse. Globular clusters are tightly knit groupings of older stars. These stars were born together, have spent their lives as part of a cluster, and will die in the cluster. Once a star has started shining, it is called a main-sequence star. The sun is a main-sequence star, and will remain so for billions of years. As the sun uses up its helium, it will mature into a red giant, before entering the final stage of its life cycle: its death.

THE DEATH OF A STAR

Stars like the sun take billions of years to die, slowly losing material and fading, ending their lives as a dwarf star. Stars with over eight times the mass of the sun end their lives in a much more dramatic way. Once nuclear reaction ceases, the star collapses and blows itself apart in a supernova explosion, leaving only a core behind.

The name supernova comes from the star's sudden change of appearance. The explosion looks like a super, new (*nova* is Latin for "new"), bright star in the sky. The future of the core-remains depends on the mass. Those stars with three times the mass of the sun continue collapsing until they produce a black hole. Those with less mass leave a tiny neutron star. They are so densely packed that a handful weighs billions of tons. A rapidly spinning neutron star is called a pulsar. It sends out beams of energy, like the rotating beam of a lighthouse. It spins many times a second, and if the Earth is in the path of the beam, the star's energy pulses can be detected.

Stars vary enormously in size. The largest are the supergiants which can be up to several hundred times larger than the diameter of the sun. Next in size are the giants, either blue or red, which measure up to 100 times the sun's diameter. Blue stars are the hottest and brightest. The smallest stars are the dwarfs, which are much smaller than the size of the sun.

▼ After an ordinary star collapses, it becomes a white dwarf, and finally cools to become a dead black dwarf.

▲ The star is a red giant. It is up to 100 times larger than the original star.

▲ The fuel in the core is used up, and nuclear reaction stops. The core collapses.

▲ The outer layers are pushed off into space. The core shrinks to the size of a small planet.

SEE ALSO PAGES:

THE SUN

Without the sun there would be no life on the Earth. It also helps us to understand other stars in the universe. Like them, it is a changing ball of hot gas.

The hot gas on the sun's surface is constantly moving. It gives the sun a mottled appearance. By looking at its edge we can see the jets, flares, and prominences that appear all over its surface.

The sun is the nearest star to the Earth. It is the only one that we can see in close-up. The sun is a globe of hot gas, mainly hydrogen, which is so large that 1,300,000 planet Earths would fit inside it, and 109 would fit across its face.

Inside its core it is very hot, around 27 million°F. Here, nuclear reactions are converting the hydrogen into helium. In the process, huge amounts of energy are produced that, after tens of thousands of years, eventually reach the sun's surface. Once there, the energy escapes into space as heat, light, and other types of radiation. The light and heat are essential to us on the Earth, but the other radiations, such as ultraviolet rays, can be harmful. The Earth's atmosphere shields us from much of it.

The surface of the sun is called the photosphere. It is cooler, around 9,932°F. The photosphere is not solid, but is the sun's visible outer edge. The sun spins, and its equatorial regions take about 25 days to go around once, while the polar regions take about ten days longer. We can also observe how the surface and the atmosphere change from week to week and year to year.

SURFACE FEATURES

Sunspots are darker, cooler areas on the sun's photosphere, and range from a few thousand to tens of thousands of miles across. The spots are caused by strong magnetic fields within the sun that slow down the flow of heat from inside. They are not permanent features. They follow a regular 11-year cycle of appearances and last for only weeks at a time. Sunspots form and disappear progressively closer to the equator before disappearing altogether as a new cycle starts at higher latitudes.

The sun's surface is a violent place and regularly releases short-lived bursts of energy, called flares, into space. Larger eruptions, or prominences, stretch for many thousands of miles into the sun's atmosphere and can last for months.

Short-lived flares of hot gas burst from the sun's surface. They only last a few minutes.

Spicule

Flare

Sunspots are cooler, darker areas on the sun's surface. Nearby are faculae, clouds of glowing hydrogen just above the surface.

Prominence

Sunspot

Facula

The corona, the outer atmosphere of the sun, is not normally visible—it is outshone by the sun's disk. However, the corona can be seen during a total eclipse.

A huge stream of glowing gas flows out from the sun's surface. The prominence has arched over to form a loop. It will last for several hours before collapsing back.

The photosphere is the sun's outer surface. It is a very active, 310-mile (500-km) thick layer of gas. All over the surface are circular granules formed by the ever-moving hot gas, and spicules, jets of gas stretching upward. Immediately above the surface is the inner atmosphere, called the chromosphere.

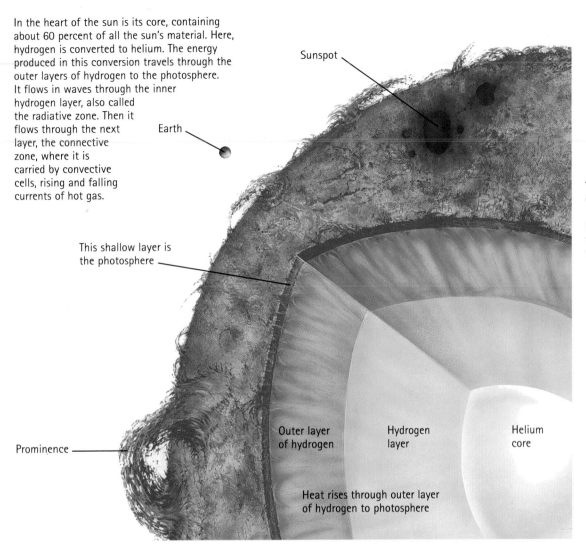

In the heart of the sun is its core, containing about 60 percent of all the sun's material. Here, hydrogen is converted to helium. The energy produced in this conversion travels through the outer layers of hydrogen to the photosphere. It flows in waves through the inner hydrogen layer, also called the radiative zone. Then it flows through the next layer, the connective zone, where it is carried by convective cells, rising and falling currents of hot gas.

Sunspot

Earth

This shallow layer is the photosphere

Prominence

Outer layer of hydrogen

Hydrogen layer

Helium core

Heat rises through outer layer of hydrogen to photosphere

The American astronomer George Ellery Hale (1868–1938) studied the sun and its spots. His work led him to discover magnetic fields within sunspots.

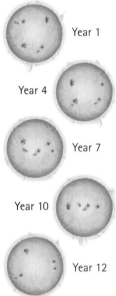

Year 1

Year 4

Year 7

Year 10

Year 12

At the start of each 11-year cycle, sunspots appear well to the north and south of the sun's equator. As time continues, they appear closer until, at the end of the cycle, they appear along the equator. Finally the spots in this cycle disappear, and a new cycle starts by producing spots well to the north and south.

THE SUN'S ATMOSPHERE

Immediately above the sun's surface is the chromosphere, a layer of hydrogen and helium, about 3,100 miles (5,000km) thick. At its farthest edge, where it merges into the outer layer of atmosphere, the corona, its temperature is about 900,000°F. The corona stretches for millions of miles into space and is very thin and hot, around 5.4 million°F. It gives off a constant stream of particles, called the solar wind, which travel through the solar system.

THE LIFE OF THE SUN

The sun was formed from a nebula, a cloud of gas and dust, about five billion years ago in the Milky Way galaxy. It has been shining steadily ever since, using up about seven million tons of material every second. It is presently about halfway through its life. In about five billion years' time, when the hydrogen in its core has been converted to helium, the core will collapse. The sun's outer layers will swell out, cool, and change

color. The sun will have moved from the main sequence stage of its life to become a red giant.

When the helium starts to form carbon, the sun will change color from red to yellow and enter another stage. It will lose its outer layers of material as it continually shrinks and expands. The inner layers will collapse, and what remains of the original sun will be packed together into a small star, a white dwarf. This will slowly fade and die as a black dwarf.

The sun will continue to shine for billions of years. But in about five billion years it will swell into a red giant. The Earth will grow hotter, water will boil away, and life will die out. The sun will engulf Mercury and Venus, and the Earth will be inside its atmosphere.

SEE ALSO PAGES:

170 Carbon, 180 Noble gases, 242–3 Heat and light from the sun

CONSTELLATIONS

A constellation is an area of the night sky. Its stars make a dot-to-dot picture. Astronomers use 88 of these pictures to help them find their way around the sky.

The Greek astronomer and geographer Ptolemy (A.D. 100–170), who lived in Alexandria, Egypt, listed the 48 constellations that had been used by ancient astronomers from around 2000 B.C. This list grew into the 88 constellations we use today.

The Big Dipper

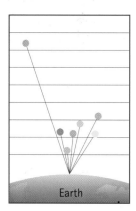

Earth

The seven stars in the Big Dipper appear to be the same distance away (top) when seen from the Earth. In fact, they are different distances from us. The star at the left is up to three times as far away as the others.

▶ Part of the figure of Orion, the hunter, has been drawn around the stars in the night sky. Two bright stars mark his shoulders. The three that mark his belt are the key stars to look for when identifying Orion. The line to the bottom left is his sword, hanging from the belt.

From anywhere on the Earth you can look into the sky and see thousands of pinpoints of light. They are all stars, and belong to our galaxy, the Milky Way. There are so many stars that, at first, it is difficult to tell them apart. But there are distinctive patterns in the sky, and astronomers use these to find their way around. They draw imaginary pictures around the star patterns to help to remember them. The very first pictures were created over four thousand years ago. We still use these as well as some more recently devised ones.

CELESTIAL SPHERE

Astronomers looking out from the Earth imagine a great star-studded sphere surrounding them. They look at the inside edge of this imaginary celestial sphere. The sphere is divided into 88 pieces, like an enormous jigsaw puzzle. Each piece is a constellation and has a star pattern with an imaginary picture. Astronomers around the world use this system of 88 constellations with their star patterns.

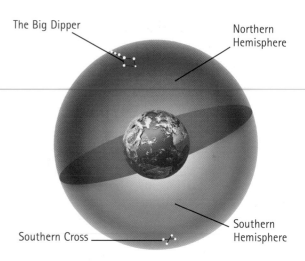

The Big Dipper

Northern Hemisphere

Southern Cross

Southern Hemisphere

The celestial sphere surrounds the Earth. It is divided into two domes, the Northern and Southern Hemispheres, which are made into flat maps (see right). The celestial equator is the dividing line between the two maps.

SKY PICTURES

The pictures in the sky include real and imaginary humans, animals, sea creatures, and tools of the artist and scientist. We do not know exactly who created the first pictures, or when, but a system of 48 was in use by around A.D. 150. This is when the Greek geographer and astronomer Ptolemy listed them in his book *Almagest*. These 48 constellations include figures from Greek mythology, such as the hunter, Orion, the flying horse, Pegasus, and the Centaur who is half-man and half-horse. The other 40 constellations were created in more recent times, and include some of the great inventions, such as the telescope and the clock.

THE ZODIAC

As we look toward the celestial sphere from the Earth, we see the sun, the moon, and all the plants (except Pluto) move across the sky in a regular procession. They do so within a band of sky that is about 20 degrees wide. The constellations in this band make up what we call the zodiac. The ancient astronomers identified twelve constellations in this band, today we recognize thirteen. Because of the Earth's rotation around the sun, the sun seems to spend about one month in each constellation.

LOOKING AT THE CONSTELLATIONS

It is impossible to see all 88 constellations from one point on the Earth. People living in the Northern Hemisphere see those in the Northern Hemisphere of the celestial sphere, as well as some from its southern half. People living in the Southern Hemisphere see the constellations in the celestial sphere's Southern Hemisphere, and some from its northern half. But even these stars are not seen at one time. The Earth rotates on its axis once a day, and follows a yearly path around the sun, within the celestial sphere. These movements mean that the portion of available sky seen from any one spot changes during the course of the year, and that portion of sky will appear to rotate during the course of a night.

SOUTHERN HEMISPHERE SKY

The Southern Cross is the smallest of all eighty-eight constellations, but it is bright and easy to find. It is a good place to start when exploring the southern sky. It is in the thick, starry band of the Milky Way. There are so many stars here that, as we look into the disk of our galaxy, they make a river of milky light across the sky.

NORTHERN HEMISPHERE SKY

The stars in the northern sky seem to move around the star Polaris, the bright star in the very center of the map. It is in the constellation of Ursa Minor, close to its companion Ursa Major. The seven stars in the tail and lower back of Ursa Major are called the Big Dipper. This is one of the easiest patterns to find, and it is a good starting point for finding your way around the northern sky.

Pegasus, the Flying Horse

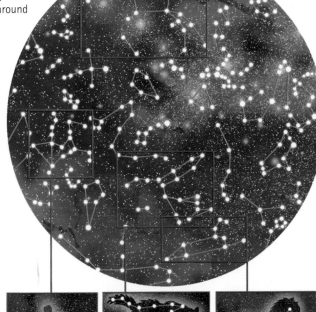

Ursa Major, the Big Dipper

Leo, the Lion

Phoenix, the Fire Bird

Hercules, the Giant

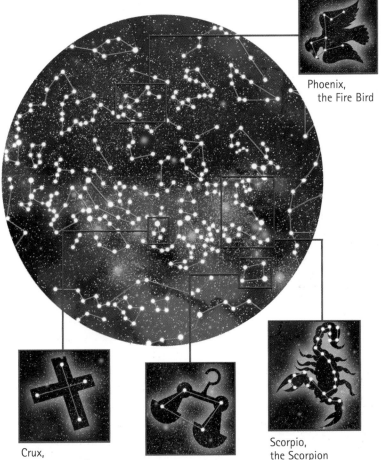

Crux, the Southern Cross

Libra, the Scales

Scorpio, the Scorpion

THE STAR MAPS

The maps show the major constellations of the sky. The stars in the center of the maps can usually be seen all year from the corresponding hemisphere on the Earth. It is those near the edge that are seen only during particular seasons, or at certain times of night. The brightest stars are those with the largest dots. Some appear bright only because they are close to us. Others are bright because they really are bright stars. All the stars are so far away they appear to be the same, equal distance from us. In fact, the stars in any constellation are unrelated and are vast distances from each other.

SEE ALSO PAGES:
390–1 Galaxies, 392–3 Stars, 414–15 Studying the universe

THE SOLAR SYSTEM

The solar system is the sun and the family of objects that orbit it. They were made from the same cloud, and stay together because of the sun's strong gravity.

The sun is the largest object in the solar system. Next comes Jupiter, the largest planet, followed by the other three gas giants, Saturn, Uranus, and Neptune. All four have rings and large families of moons. The Earth and the other planets are smaller.

The sun, our local star, dominates the solar system. It is the largest object in the system and the most massive. It contains over 95 percent of all the solar system material. The rest is used up in the objects that orbit the sun. These are nine planets, more than sixty moons, billions of asteroids, and billions of comets.

Because of the sun's great size, it has a powerful gravitational pull, and this pull keeps the solar system together and controls the movements of the planets.

THE BIRTH OF THE SOLAR SYSTEM

About five billion years ago, the material that now makes up the sun and planets was part of a great cloud of gas and dust, called the solar nebula. The cloud was mainly hydrogen and helium but included a tiny percentage of other elements. It spun around and its material was pulled toward the center. The solar nebula was now a ball of gas surrounded by a disk of gas and dust. The central ball became the sun and the disk material produced the planets and other bodies. Much more unused material was blown away into space.

Sun

Jupiter

Pluto

Neptune

Uranus

Saturn

Moon

Venus

Earth

Mars

Mercury

▼ Measurements in the solar system are measured in astronomical units (AU). One AU is 93 million mi. (149.6 million km), the average distance of the Earth from the sun.

| Mercury 0.39 AU | Venus 0.72 AU | Earth 1 AU | Mars 1.52 AU | Jupiter 5.20 AU | Saturn 9.54 AU | Uranus 19.19 AU |

0 1 2 3 4 5 6 7 8 9 10 11 12 13 14 15 16 17 18 19 20 21 22 23 24 25 26 27

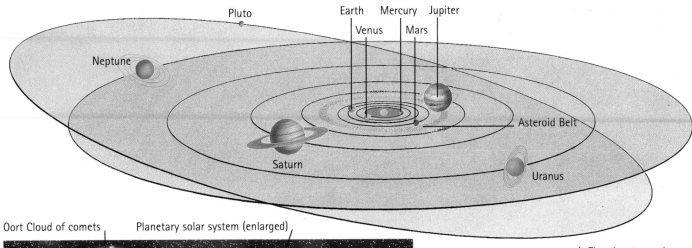

Pluto · Earth · Mercury · Jupiter · Venus · Mars · Neptune · Saturn · Asteroid Belt · Uranus

Oort Cloud of comets · Planetary solar system (enlarged)

◀ A spherical-shaped region of comets surrounds the planetary solar system. It contains billions of comets, each following its own orbit around the sun. The sphere is called the Oort Cloud and measures 100,000 AU from side to side. Beyond it is interstellar space.

▲ The planetary solar system is disk-shaped. The planets go around the sun in elliptical orbits, and in a counterclockwise direction. The length of orbit and the time taken to complete an orbit increases with successively distant planets.

PLANETS

The planets started to form about 4.6 billion years ago. The material closest to the sun made the four rocky worlds, Mercury, Venus, Earth, and Mars. Farther away in the outer disk where it is much colder, rocky bodies formed and then pulled large amounts of gas toward them. These were the large gas planets, Jupiter, Saturn, Uranus, and Neptune. Pluto was created from different material.

ASTEROIDS AND COMETS

Rocky material between Mars and Jupiter failed to form into a planet because Jupiter's strong gravity kept pulling it apart. This material became the Asteroid Belt, a doughnut-shaped ring of rocks. At the edge of the solar system, way beyond the planets were billions of chunks of dust, rock, and snow. Many were thrown out of the system, but many remained and formed the Oort Cloud of comets. Each asteroid and comet follows its own path around the sun.

OTHER SOLAR SYSTEMS

There are many more stars like the sun in the universe. Astronomers have always thought it was possible that one of these had a system of planets orbiting around it. The stars, however, are so distant and so bright that detecting a dull planet close to a star was, for a long time, impossible.

During the 1980s, astronomers discovered the first stars surrounded by disks of gas and dust. A decade later the first planets around stars other than the sun were discovered. The first was in 1995 around the star 51 Pegasi. The planet is at least 150 times more massive than the Earth, 20 times closer to its star than the Earth to the sun, and it orbits every 4.2 days. About 15 other stars with a planet have now been found. Astronomers cannot see the planets directly, but they can detect the small wobble in the star that is produced by the pull of the planet's gravity as it orbits around it. In the not-too-distant future new telescopes will give us our first views of these new worlds.

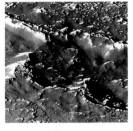

There are more than 60 moons in the solar system. The smallest moons are around 18 mi. (30km) across. The third largest, Callisto, whose surface is shown here, is about the same size as the planets Pluto and Mercury.

Most of the solar system material is found in the sun, planets, and moons. The small amount that remains is found in the billions of minor members of the system, such as this asteroid.

luto
9.60 AU
at its closest)

Neptune 30.10 AU

Pluto
49.50 AU
(at its farthest)

29   30   31   32   33   34   35   36   37   38   39   40   41   42   43   44   45   46   47   48   49   50

SEE ALSO PAGES:

EARTH AND THE MOON

The Earth is the largest of the rock planets and the third planet from the sun. The moon, a ball of rock about a fourth of the Earth's size, accompanies it in space.

Life is found everywhere on the Earth—in its oceans and on its land. It is home to millions of different species. Humans evolved on it about three million years ago.

The Earth and the moon move together through space. They are both spheres of rock, but are very different worlds. The Earth is unique in the solar system because it is a very wet place and full of life. It has also changed a lot since it was formed 4.6 billion years ago, and continues to change. In contrast, the moon is a dry and dead world where very little has happened in the past three billion years.

PLANET EARTH

About two thirds of the Earth is covered in water. Most of it is liquid, but in the polar regions, where it is much colder, it is solid ice. The rest of the surface is made of landmasses, the continents. The water and the land sit on top of the Earth's outer shell of rock, its crust. This is split into plates of rock: eight giant ones and several smaller ones. They, in turn, sit on top of a mantle of hot, molten rock.

The plates move around on the molten rock and produce changes in the Earth's landscape. When two plates push into each other, the crust can be forced up

The gravitational pull of the planets in our solar system changes the Earth's orbit from circular to elongated over a period of about 100,000 years.

and mountains result. Under the oceans when plates move apart, molten rock wells up between them and forms ridges. Molten rock also erupts from volcanoes and flows across the land.

Surrounding the Earth is an atmosphere of about 78 percent nitrogen and 21 percent oxygen. It provides the air we breathe and protects us from harmful radiation from the sun and space. It lets sunlight through and helps control temperature. Water is absorbed in the lower atmosphere, condenses into clouds, and falls back to the Earth as rain or snow. The water and winds also have a shaping effect on the landscape as they erode it.

ORBITS AND SPIN

The Earth takes 365.25 days to complete one orbit around the sun. As it moves along its orbit it also spins on its axis; one spin takes 23.9 hours. The moon accompanies the Earth as it travels around the sun, orbiting the Earth at an average distance of 238,600 miles (384,400km)—on average because the moon's orbit is elliptical, so the distance from the Earth varies. The moon takes 27.3 days to make one orbit around the Earth. As it travels, it spins on its axis. The time for one spin is also 27.3 days, the same amount of time as one orbit. As a result, the moon always has the same side facing the Earth.

From space our planet appears blue and white. The blue is from the water that covers two thirds of its surface. The white is from the clouds in the atmosphere surrounding it.

Atmosphere
Crust
Upper mantle
Rocky mantle
Molten metallic outer core
Solid metal core

▲ When the Earth was younger and hotter its heavy iron sank to its center to form a core. The lighter rocks floated above this. The Earth has cooled, but the mantle and part of the core material is still molten.

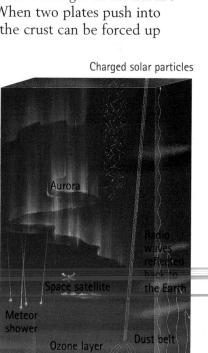

Charged solar particles

Aurora

Radio waves reflected back to the Earth

Space satellite

Meteor shower

Ozone layer

Dust belt

Cosmic rays

Aircraft

Clouds

Atmosphere

Exosphere

Thermosphere

Ionosphere

Mesosphere

Stratosphere

Troposphere

The Earth's atmosphere is divided into layers. Nearest to the planet is the troposphere which contains more than 75 percent of the atmosphere. The highest layer, the exosphere, around 310 mi. (500km) above the surface, contains very little air, and fades away into space.

EARTH'S MOON

The same side of the moon always faces the Earth. The dark maria, or seas, several hundred miles across are easily seen. Surrounding them are mountain ranges formed when the huge crater bowls were created. Smaller craters cover the surface.

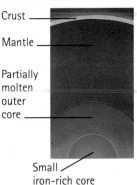

Crust

Mantle

Partially molten outer core

Small iron-rich core

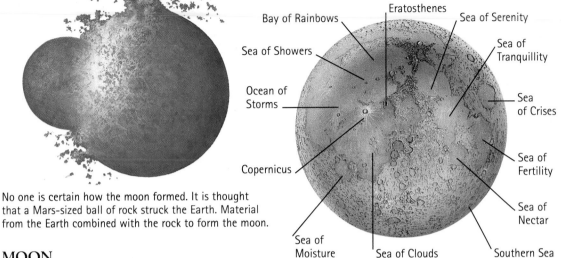

Eratosthenes
Bay of Rainbows
Sea of Serenity
Sea of Showers
Sea of Tranquillity
Ocean of Storms
Sea of Crises
Copernicus
Sea of Fertility
Sea of Nectar
Sea of Moisture
Sea of Clouds
Southern Sea

No one is certain how the moon formed. It is thought that a Mars-sized ball of rock struck the Earth. Material from the Earth combined with the rock to form the moon.

▲ The moon's crust is about 40-60 mi. (60-100km) thick. Above it is the regolith, a surface of dust and rock. Because of the moon's very weak gravity there is no atmosphere, wind, or weather.

MOON

The moon does not have any light of its own, but shines because sunlight is reflected off it. One half of the moon is always lit by the sun and the other half is in darkness. Similarly, the Earth always has one half in daylight and one in the darkness of night. As the moon travels around us, we see differing amounts of the sunlit half. In this way, the moon appears to change shape. These different shapes are the phases of the moon.

A complete cycle of the moon's phases takes 29.5 days. It goes from the new moon, when the side facing us is completely dark; to the full moon, when this side is completely lit; and back to the new moon, to start all over again. It is possible to see some of the moon's surface features by looking at it with the naked eye. The lighter areas are older, higher land, and the darker ones, younger, lower, and flatter land. Binoculars or a telescope reveal that the whole of the surface is covered in impact craters. Most of these were formed when the moon was bombarded by space rocks between three and four billion years ago. Over the next billion years lava seeped through cracks in the moon's crust and flooded the largest craters to form maria (*mare*, singular, is the Latin for "sea"). These are the dark regions visible to the naked eye. The first astronomers to observe them called them seas because that is what they thought they were.

Large areas of the Earth's surface have been changed by humans. As population increases, their buildings, farming, and communication systems will cover more of it.

There are about 850 active volcanoes on the Earth. Lava flows from them and changes the surrounding landscape. Occasionally it even forms a new island.

Half of the moon is always in sunlight. The phases of the moon depend on how much of the lit half we can see from the Earth. At the new moon, when the Earth, moon, and sun are roughly in line, we cannot see any of the lit half. About a week later, at the first quarter, we can see half of the part of the moon that is in sunlight. And at the full moon we can see all of it. By the last quarter we can again see only half of the lit part.

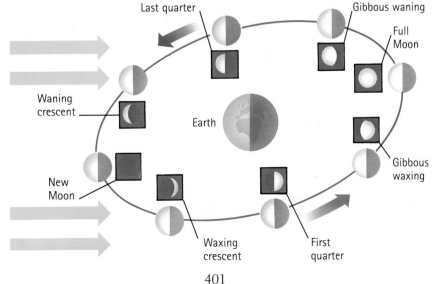

Last quarter

Gibbous waning

Full Moon

Waning crescent

Earth

New Moon

Gibbous waxing

Waxing crescent

First quarter

SEE ALSO PAGES:

2 Earth and the solar system, 8–9 Earth's structure, 10–11 Earth's atmosphere, 398–9 The solar system

ECLIPSES

When the moon is in the Earth's shadow, the moon is eclipsed. When the moon covers the sun and stops its light reaching the Earth, the sun is eclipsed.

In a total lunar eclipse the moon is completely covered by the Earth's shadow. Unlike a solar eclipse, no special equipment is needed to observe a lunar eclipse. As long as the moon is in the sky and there are no clouds covering it, the eclipse should be visible.

As the Earth orbits the sun, the moon orbits around the Earth. From the Earth, the moon is sometimes in the sky at the same time as the sun. Although the sun is four hundred times larger than the moon, they appear roughly the same size in our sky. This is because the moon is four hundred times closer to the Earth than the sun. If the moon is directly in line with the sun it will eclipse the sun. When the moon is on the opposite side of the Earth to the sun, it might pass through the Earth's shadow and be eclipsed itself.

LUNAR ECLIPSE

As the moon travels around the Earth it can move out of the sun's light and into the shadow cast by the Earth. But the moon's path does not take it through the Earth's shadow on each orbit. So the moon is not eclipsed every time it travels around the Earth, but only up to three times each

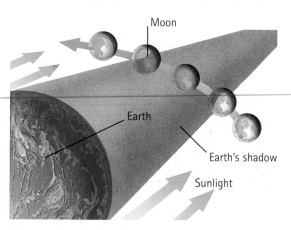

The moon is eclipsed as it passes through the Earth's shadow. It does not become invisible because a little sunlight is diffused into the shadow by the Earth's atmosphere.

year. When the moon is completely in the Earth's shadow, it is a total lunar eclipse. When the moon is only partially covered by shadow, it is a partial lunar eclipse.

SOLAR ECLIPSE

The moon passes between the Earth and the sun each time it orbits around the Earth. As it does so, the moon's phase is the new moon. The moon facing away from the Earth is lit, and the side facing the Earth is dark. When the moon lies directly between the sun and the Earth it blocks out the sun's light and casts a shadow onto the Earth. The sun is eclipsed. If the sun's disk has been completely covered by the moon's, the sun is totally eclipsed. When the moon partially covers the sun it is a partial eclipse. Eclipses do not happen at every new moon, since the Earth, moon, and sun are not usually directly aligned, and the moon does not cover the sun's disk. Solar eclipses happen only once or twice each year, and then are only visible from the parts of the Earth covered by the moon's shadow. During a total eclipse it is possible to see the sun's faint outer atmosphere, the corona, normally lost in the glare of the sun's disk.

Just before and after the sun's disk is totally eclipsed by the moon, a diamond-ring effect can be seen. For a few seconds, the sun's light is shining between mountains on the lunar surface to create an enormous sparkling diamond in the sky.

▼ The moon casts a shadow into space. When the shadow reaches the Earth, anyone standing in the darkest part, the umbra, will experience a total solar eclipse. The sun will be eclipsed for almost 7½ minutes.

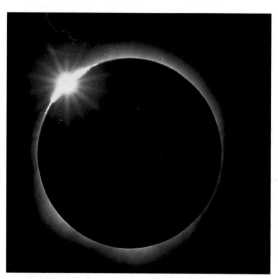

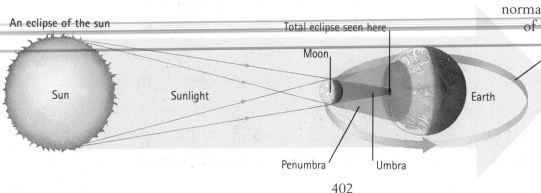

An eclipse of the sun

Sun
Sunlight
Total eclipse seen here
Moon
Moon's orbit
Earth
Penumbra
Umbra

SEE ALSO PAGES:
242–3 Heat and light from the sun, 394–5 The sun, 400–1 Earth and the moon

MERCURY

The closest planet to the sun is a small, rocky, airless world. Mercury's crater-covered surface faces extreme temperatures, but has not changed for billions of years.

Wherever you look on Mercury the view is of a crater-covered, rocky landscape. Above it is a black sky because of the lack of atmosphere to reflect sunlight.

Mercury is the second smallest of the planets. From the Earth we can see only faint markings on its rocky surface.

Extremely thin atmosphere

Crust

Rocky mantle

Huge iron-nickel core

Mercury is a rocky planet with a particularly large metal core. Surrounding this is rock, and above it an atmosphere so thin it barely exists. During sunrise to sunset the temperature on the surface reaches 842°F, but during the long night the temperature drops to about -274°F.

Mercury is difficult to see and study from the Earth because it is never far from the sun's glare in our sky. Much of what we know about Mercury comes from *Mariner 10*, the only space probe to visit it. It took photographs of nearly all of one side which, once radioed back to the Earth, were combined to give an overall picture of much of the planet's surface.

SURFACE

Mercury is covered with craters that were formed when it was bombarded by some meteorites about four billion years ago. The craters range from a few feet to hundreds of miles across. The largest, the Caloris Basin, is about 800 miles (1,300km) wide. Inside it are flat plains of solidified lava that once oozed from the planet's interior. Mercury's surface is also crossed by wrinkles and ridges a few miles high. These were formed as the hot, young Mercury cooled and shrank. The planet's outer mantle and crust wrinkled like the skin on a dried apple.

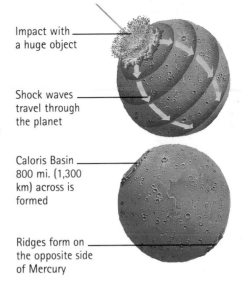

Impact with a huge object

Shock waves travel through the planet

Caloris Basin 800 mi. (1,300 km) across is formed

Ridges form on the opposite side of Mercury

The dominant feature on Mercury, the Caloris Basin, was formed when a 62-mi. (100-km)-wide body crashed into the planet. Shock waves traveled through the planet, creating hills and mountains.

ORBIT AND SPIN

Mercury's orbit is elongated. Its distance from the sun varies from 45 million miles (70 million km) when farthest away, to only 29 million miles (46 million km) when nearest. So the sun in Mercury's sky sometimes appears one and a half times the diameter, and feels twice as hot. Mercury orbits at 30 mi./sec. (48km/sec), making it the fastest moving planet. It takes only 88 days to complete one orbit. It spins as it travels, taking 59 days to make one spin. The combination of its fast orbit and slow spin means anyone standing on Mercury would have to wait 176 days between one sunrise and the next—a year (88 days) would be shorter than a day (176 days).

The *Mariner 10* space probe flew past Mercury three times from 1974 to 1975. Its cameras took sequences of overlapping photographs that were combined to give us a global view of this planet.

SEE ALSO PAGES:

394–5 The sun, 398–9 The solar system, 418–19 Exploring space

VENUS

The hottest planet in the solar system is a hostile world. A thick choking atmosphere surrounds a rock planet with a surface shaped by volcanic activity.

The sun is barely visible in the dull, orange sky. It is hidden by the thick clouds of Venus' atmosphere. At nighttime the stars are totally hidden from view.

Venus is a rock planet, second from the sun, and similar in size to the Earth. It appears as a bright star, either after sunset or before sunrise, so it is called "the morning star," or "the evening star." It shines brightly because sunlight is reflected off its cloud tops. But the rock world below is hidden from view. Venus spins slowly, taking 243 days to turn once, and it is the only planet to turn clockwise when viewed from its North Pole.

Maat Mons, at 5.5 mi. (9km) high, is one of the largest volcanoes on Venus. Lava flows, hundreds of miles wide, stretch across its base. Radar information recorded by *Magellan* was computer-processed to produce this image.

The surface of Venus is completely hidden by dense clouds. The clouds circle the planet every four days or so, forming Y- or V-shaped patterns.

VENUS' ATMOSPHERE

Venus' dense atmosphere consists mainly of carbon dioxide. It contains so much material that it would feel denser than water and the pressure is 90 times greater than that on the Earth. The atmosphere also contains sulfur dust, and droplets of sulfuric acid from erupting volcanoes from when the planet was young. Sunlight penetrates the atmosphere and warms the surface of the planet. The ground radiates heat, but the atmosphere traps the heat, warming the planet even more. The average surface temperature reaches 867°F.

SURFACE FEATURES

Space probes sent by the former Soviet Union have traveled through Venus' atmosphere to land on the surface. However, the planet's physical features have been mapped by probes using radar and working from above the thick clouds. The most recent and successful was the American probe *Magellan* in 1990–1994. Its probes revealed a surface about half a billion years old and formed by volcanic activity. Venus is a smooth planet; 85 percent of its surface is volcanic plain, dotted with hundreds of volcanic craters and lava flows. There are also over 900 impact craters that were formed when rocks collided with the planet.

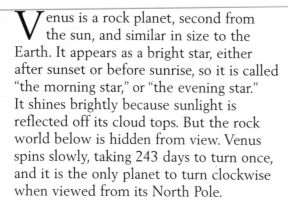

Atmosphere

Crust

Mantle

Partly molten metallic core

Venus is a typical rock planet, with a metal core, rocky mantle, and crust. But the atmosphere surrounding it makes it a hostile place for humans.

▶ Venus is not the closest planet to the sun, but it is the hottest because its thick atmosphere is very efficient at holding in the sun's heat. This is called the greenhouse effect, because it works like glass trapping heat in a greenhouse.

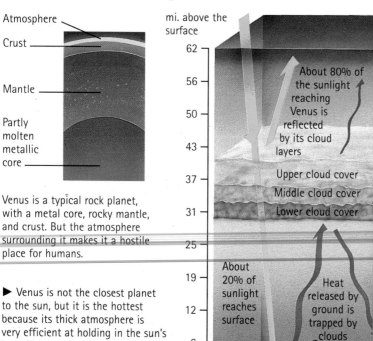

mi. above the surface

62
56
50
43
37
31
25
19
12
6
0

About 80% of the sunlight reaching Venus is reflected by its cloud layers

Some heat escapes

Upper cloud cover

Middle cloud cover

Lower cloud cover

About 20% of sunlight reaches surface

Heat released by ground is trapped by clouds

Carbon dioxide holds in heat

▲ The *Magellan* spacecraft mapped 98 percent of the Venusian surface between 1990–1994. It recorded features of the surface using radar to see through the cloud layers.

SEE ALSO PAGES:

394–5 The sun, 398–9
The solar system, 418–19
Exploring space

MARS

Mars is the planet most similar to the Earth. It is a dry, rocky, red world about half the size and much colder. Robot spacecraft have landed on it to search for life.

Mars is known as the Red Planet. It has not only a red surface, but also a red sky. The color comes from wind-borne dust blown from the reddish, iron-rich surface.

Mars has cold regions at its North and South Poles. These polar regions are covered with water ice, and carbon dioxide ice.

Atmosphere

Crust

Mantle

Iron core

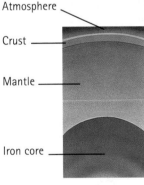

Mars is made of dense rock with a metal core. An atmosphere, about 100 times thinner than the Earth's, comprised mainly of carbon dioxide gas, surrounds Mars.

▶ The *Pathfinder* probe landed on Mars on July 4, 1997. It opened up to allow the *Sojourner* robotic vehicle to move down its ramp (at left) and explore the surface.

Mars is the fourth planet from the sun, about one and a half times farther from the sun than the Earth. Its distance makes it a much colder planet than the Earth and its average temperature is well below freezing. It does, however, appear fiery red and was named after the Roman god of war because of its bloodlike appearance. The coloring comes from the rock and soil strewn across its surface. The rock is rich in iron oxide, better known as rust.

SURFACE FEATURES

Volcanic activity, meteorite bombardment, and running water, all in Mars' distant past, have shaped its surface. Much of the surface is rock-strewn desert, with dusty dunes, and craters formed by meteorites. But giant features rise above it and cut into it. The volcano Olympus Mons, the highest mountain in the solar system, is 375 miles (600km) across and rises 15 miles (24km) above the surrounding plain. Equally spectacular is the Valles Marineris, a canyon system that runs around 2,800 miles (4,500km) across Mars and is, in parts, 5 miles (8km) deep. There are also valleys that look like dried-up riverbeds formed when Mars had running water over 3 billion years ago.

Mars has two tiny, dark, irregular-shaped moons. They are made of carbon-rich rock and are thought to be two asteroids caught by Mars' gravity.

Deimos

Phobos

Phobos is about 18 mi. (27km) long; it is the larger moon and closer to Mars. Deimos is about 9 mi. (15km) long.

SEARCH FOR LIFE

Less than a century ago people believed that martians, a form of intelligent life, lived on Mars. Today we know this is false, but primitive life may exist there. In the past Mars was warmer and wetter, and under these conditions life may have developed. Two American *Viking* space probes landed on Mars in 1976. Experiments on board tested for signs of life, but none were found.

More spacecraft were sent to investigate Mars in the 1990s. They orbited the planet, mapped it, studied its weather, and finally landed on it. *Pathfinder* landed after a 7-month journey in 1997. It carried a small six-wheeled robotic rover, named *Sojourner*, which explored the landing site. More craft are being prepared for missions to Mars.

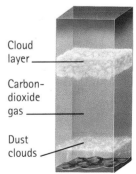

Cloud layer

Carbon-dioxide gas

Dust clouds

Strong winds raise huge dust clouds. At night the carbon dioxide freezes to form frost.

SEE ALSO PAGES:

398–9 The solar system, 400–1 The earth and the moon, 418–19 Exploring space

JUPITER

Jupiter is the largest and most massive of all the solar system planets. It is a gas giant with a surface of colorful clouds, 16 moons, and a thin ring system.

There is no solid surface on Jupiter. The outer edge that we can see is clouds at the top of layers of gas. Sixteen moons move across its sky as they orbit around the planet.

The Galileo probe reached Jupiter in 1995, and circled the planet for two years before it sent a probe into the atmosphere and investigated the moons.

Jupiter is so huge that 11 planet Earths would fit across its diameter, and 1,300 would fill it. It consists of almost 90 percent hydrogen, mostly as gas, with about 10 percent helium, and traces of other elements. The outer part of Jupiter is gas, below this liquid, and in the center is a solid core. It is the fifth planet from the sun, and takes twelve years for one orbit. Jupiter rotates fast on its axis, taking less than 10 hours for one turn.

JUPITER'S WEATHER

Jupiter's rapid spin, combined with heat rising from inside, creates and drives the planet's weather—different pressure systems and winds of up to 400 mph (650kph). The planet's striped appearance is caused by dark zones of falling gas and light zones of rising gas, which create storms where they meet. The largest of these are visible from the Earth, and space probes have detected giant bolts of lightning. A huge hurricane storm, the Great Red Spot, is an atmospheric whirlpool that rotates counterclockwise every six days.

Io is one of Jupiter's Galilean moons, named after the astronomer Galileo Galilei who studied them. Its rocky surface is red and yellow because of the sulfur that erupts from its many volcanoes.

JUPITER'S MOONS

Surrounding Jupiter is a thin ring system and a large, varied family of moons. There are 16 moons: four large and 12 small. The four largest ones, Io, Europa, Ganymede, and Callisto, are known as the Galilean moons. Ganymede is the largest moon in the solar system and is larger than the planets Pluto and Mercury. Io has the most active volcanoes on it.

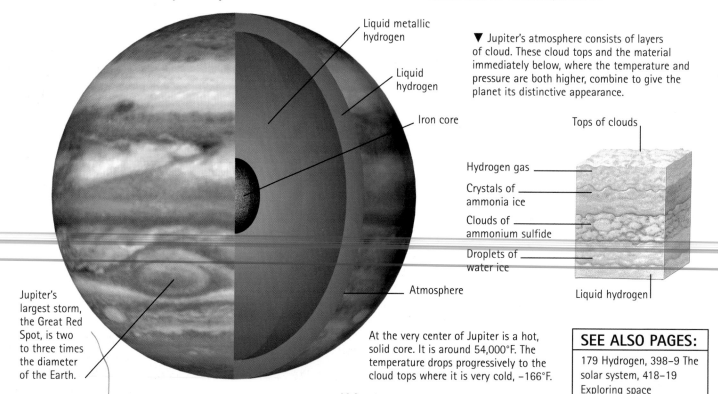

Jupiter's largest storm, the Great Red Spot, is two to three times the diameter of the Earth.

Liquid metallic hydrogen

Liquid hydrogen

Iron core

Atmosphere

At the very center of Jupiter is a hot, solid core. It is around 54,000°F. The temperature drops progressively to the cloud tops where it is very cold, −166°F.

▼ Jupiter's atmosphere consists of layers of cloud. These cloud tops and the material immediately below, where the temperature and pressure are both higher, combine to give the planet its distinctive appearance.

Tops of clouds

Hydrogen gas

Crystals of ammonia ice

Clouds of ammonium sulfide

Droplets of water ice

Liquid hydrogen

SEE ALSO PAGES:

179 Hydrogen, 398–9 The solar system, 418–19 Exploring space

SATURN

Saturn looks like a bright yellow star from the Earth. Space probes have revealed a colorful planet with an amazing system of rings and a large family of moons.

Saturn does not have a solid surface. Its outer layer, a haze of ammonia crystals, is difficult to see through. The ring system dominates the sky.

Because of its fast spin, Saturn is compressed in shape, with a bulging middle. A gap in the rings, the Cassini Division, contains ring pieces.

Atmosphere

Liquid hydrogen

Liquid metallic hydrogen

Iron core

Saturn consists mainly of hydrogen. This is in a gaseous form farthest from the surface, turning to liquid further in. Close to the iron core the liquid hydrogen becomes metallic in form.

▶ The small probe *Huygens*, carried to Saturn by the *Cassini* space probe, will use a parachute to slow its descent to Titan.

Saturn, the second largest planet and the sixth from the sun, is a gas giant that consists mainly of hydrogen. Its outer surface is not solid, but made of bands of clouds of ammonia, water, and methane, and colored by phosphorus and other elements. The bands are surrounded by a haze that hides the stormy weather below. Some weather disturbances can be seen from the Earth. About three times every century, violent storms disturb the surface. They are seen as large white spots near the planet's equator.

Three space probes sent to Saturn have taught us much about the planet. *Pioneer 11* was the first in 1979, then *Voyager 1* and *2* in 1980–1981. They not only revealed details of the planet, but observed its ring system, and discovered 12 of its moons. Another craft, *Cassini*, is on its way to explore it. On arrival in 2004, it will orbit and study Saturn for four years and will drop a small probe into Titan's atmosphere.

SATURN'S RINGS

All four gas giants are surrounded by a ring system, but Saturn's is the most extensive and spectacular. The broad, but thin, system appears to be divided into several

The *Huygens* probe will test Titan's thick, nitrogen atmosphere as it descends. No one yet knows what kind of surface it will find underneath.

wide rings, but each of these consists of thousands of separate narrow ringlets. Each ringlet is made of icy rock pieces ranging from tiny specks to chunks as big as a house. The system is only a few feet thick in parts but stretches out to almost 310,700 miles (500,000km).

The rings are not as old as the planet. They are thought to be only a few hundred million years old and are the remains of a moon or comet that was torn apart. Saturn is tilted on its axis as it orbits the sun, so we see the rings from different angles. Twice in each orbit they fully face the Earth, and twice only their edges face the Earth and disappear from view.

SATURN'S MOONS

Saturn has at least 18 moons and probably over 20. It is expected that *Cassini* will find more smaller ones. Saturn's largest, and the second largest in the solar system, Titan, is the only moon in the solar system known to have an atmosphere—consisting mainly of nitrogen and methane. The smallest, Pan, is only about 12.5 miles (20km) across. It is one of a handful that orbits Saturn within the outer ring system.

Saturn's rings consist of billions of particles in orbit around the planet, and range in size from tiny, ice-coated rock grains, to massive icy rocks. The largest fragments are found in the inner rings, and fine particles in the outer rings. The rings could be the remains of a small moon 62 mi. (100km) across.

SEE ALSO PAGES:

179 Hydrogen, 398–9 The solar system, 418–19 Exploring space

URANUS

Uranus is the seventh planet from the sun, and only just visible with the naked eye. It is a gas giant with a ring system and a large family of moons.

The sky above Uranus is black. The sun is only a distant, bright star. A thin system of rings surrounds Uranus. Each is made of dark chunks of rock.

Uranus' surface is almost featureless. It consists mainly of hydrogen and helium. Methane gas gives the planet its blue-green coloring.

Atmosphere of hydrogen, helium, and methane

Mantle of ammonia, water, and methane ice

Iron silicate core

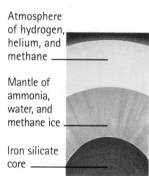

The only solid part of Uranus is its core. Above this is a cold layer of liquid and ice, and above that a layer of gas.

▶ An artist's view of Uranus from the smallest of its five main moons, Miranda. It is thought that Miranda was once smashed apart by an enormous impact, and then re-formed.

Uranus is the third largest planet in the solar system. It is four times larger than the Earth, but so distant that it is difficult to see. Uranus is 19 times farther from the sun than the Earth, so it receives little heat and light. It is a cold and dark place. The temperature at its cloud tops is around –328°F, and even when the sun is in Uranus' sky, the sky remains black.

Uranus travels around the sun on its side. Its axis is tilted from the vertical by 98 degrees, so its North Pole is pointing slightly south. Its rings and moons orbit around its middle.

DISCOVERY

Its remote position in the solar system meant that Uranus was not known in ancient times. The planet was only discovered in 1781 when the astronomer William Herschel (1738–1822) observed it through his telescope. From that time telescopes have been used to investigate the distant planet, but even the most powerful reveal little. It was only in 1986, when the space probe *Voyager 2* reached Uranus, that we got our first good look. *Voyager 2* took images of the planet, its rings, and moons, and transformed our knowledge of the Uranian system.

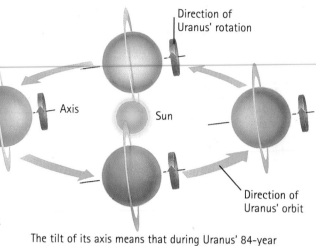

Direction of Uranus' rotation

Axis

Sun

Direction of Uranus' orbit

The tilt of its axis means that during Uranus' 84-year orbit each pole has a 40-year summer when the sun shines constantly, followed by a 40-year winter period.

MOONS AND RINGS

The five largest of Uranus' moons were known before *Voyager 2* reached Uranus. Ten more, each less than 62 miles (100km) across, were discovered by the probe. Since then, more have been found. By the start of the year 2000, 18 were known, and three more potential moons were being monitored. Most of the moons are named after Shakespearean characters. The main moons are Titania, Miranda, Oberon, and Ariel.

Uranus' ring system, with at least 11 major rings, seems to be almost upright around the planet. This is because Uranus is tilted on its side. The rings consist of pieces of rock roughly three feet across.

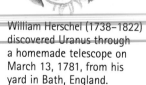

William Herschel (1738–1822) discovered Uranus through a homemade telescope on March 13, 1781, from his yard in Bath, England.

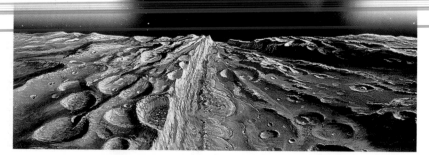

SEE ALSO PAGES:

398–9 The solar system, 416–17 Astronomical telescopes, 418–19 Exploring space

NEPTUNE

Neptune is the most distant of the four giant gas planets. It is a blue, windy, and cold world, with a ring system and a family of eight moons.

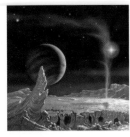

Neptune, and the distant sun, are seen in Triton's sky. The planet's cloud tops and the methane in its atmosphere give it a blue, banded appearance.

This bright blue gas world is the fourth largest planet in the solar system and eighth from the sun. But, for 20 out of every 248 years, it becomes the most distant planet when Pluto comes closer to the sun than Neptune. Neptune is difficult to see from the the earth, and like Uranus, the first clear view of it was from the *Voyager 2* space probe. It reached Neptune in 1989, after its successful trip to Uranus in 1986.

NEPTUNE'S APPEARANCE

Neptune's atmosphere is mainly hydrogen and helium. Like Uranus, it also contains methane, which gives the planet its brilliant blue color. Neptune is bluer than Uranus because there is more methane in Neptune's upper clouds.

White and dark features appear on Neptune's surface. The Great Dark Spot was seen by *Voyager 2*, but had disappeared by 1994 when the Hubble Space Telescope looked at the planet. The dark spots and white clouds are forced around Neptune by high winds. Neptune spins in a counterclockwise direction (when viewed from the north) but the winds blow in the opposite direction, from east to west. Speeds of 1,400 mph (2,200kph) make them the fiercest in the solar system.

The Great Dark Spot is at center left. It may have been a storm area and was large enough to contain the Earth. Nearby are white clouds are methane ice.

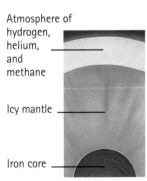

Atmosphere of hydrogen, helium, and methane

Icy mantle

Iron core

▲ Neptune's solid core is surrounded by a mantle of icy water, methane, and ammonia. Above is the gas layer made of about 80 percent hydrogen.

▶ Neptune is very large in Triton's sky. The moon's surface is frozen nitrogen and methane, and at −391°F, is the coldest surface in the solar system.

DISCOVERY

Neptune was not known to ancient astronomers. It is not visible to the naked eye and was discovered after astronomers had been observing Uranus. They noticed that Uranus' path was affected by the gravitational pull of an unknown body. In 1845, John Couch Adams (1819–1892) in England, and Urbain Le Verrier, in France, worked out the position of an unknown planet whose gravity pulled on Uranus. In 1846, Neptune was discovered, as predicted, by German astronomer Johann Galle (1812–1910).

MOONS AND RINGS

Neptune's largest moon, Triton, was also discovered in 1846, and a second moon, Nereid in 1949. A further six moons were discovered by *Voyager 2* in 1989. Triton is a rock body, larger than Pluto, that orbits in the opposite direction to the other moons. It may not have started life as a moon but was captured by Neptune's gravity. *Voyager 2* also found four faint and narrow rings around Neptune.

▶ Urbain Le Verrier (1811–1877), a French astronomer, calculated the position of an unknown planet that affected the orbit of Uranus. He gave his predictions to Johann Galle who, in 1846, found the planet Neptune.

SEE ALSO PAGES:
398–9 The solar system,
416–17 Astronomical telescopes

PLUTO AND THE MINOR PLANETS

Pluto is the smallest, coldest, and most distant planet. We know little about it, but what we do know suggests that Pluto is only a minor member of the solar system.

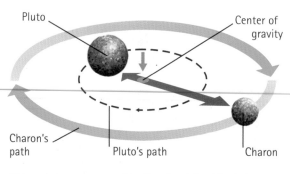

Charon is large compared to the planet it orbits, being about one fourth of Pluto's mass. This affects how they move. They both revolve around their center of gravity, so that Pluto, as well as Charon, moves in a circle.

Charon and the sun are seen in Pluto's sky. Pluto s so far from the sun that it is a cold and dark world. The sun appears a thousand times fainter than it does from the Earth.

Pluto is a ball of rock with a frozen nitrogen and methane surface. It is thought to have impact craters on it.

Thin atmosphere of methane and nitrogen

Icy mantle

Large rocky core

Pluto is always cold, about -364°F. When its orbit takes it closest to the sun it warms up, and some of its ice turns to gas and forms an atmosphere.

Pluto is the ninth and final planet in the solar system. Some astronomers think that it is not a planet at all, but is one of the minor members of the solar system. There are vast numbers of these, and they form three main groups.

The asteroids are rocky bodies in the planetary part of the solar system. Most are in the asteroid belt between the planets Mars and Jupiter. Farther out are the Kuiper Belt objects, which form a belt stretching from Neptune's orbit to the outer solar system. The outer edge is occupied by the spherical Oort Cloud made up of the third group, the comets.

PLUTO

Pluto is a small ball of icy rock, which probably became captured into a planetlike orbit. Its orbit is different from those of the other planets—it is much less circular, and is also tilted by 17 degrees to the Earth's orbit. This means that Pluto's distance from the sun varies from 2.7–4.6 billion miles (4.45–7.38 billion km). At its closest distance, Pluto is closer to the sun than Neptune. This happens once during each of Pluto's 248-year orbits when it remains the second most distant planet for about 20 years.

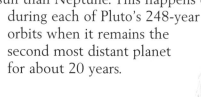

No one has seen either Pluto or Charon in detail, but this artist's impression shows what astronomers think they are like. Pluto is shown in Charon's sky, above a frozen sea of methane.

Pluto was discovered in 1930 by U.S. astronomer Clyde Tombaugh (1906–1997). Its moon, Charon, was discovered in 1978. It is about half the size of Pluto and also made of rock and ice. They follow paths around each other like a double planet. As they circle, they spin and keep the same sides facing toward each other.

As a small, rocky body, Pluto seems out of place when compared with the gas giants, its four nearest planets. Pluto is so far from the Earth (2.7 billion mi./4.3 billion km at its nearest) that it has not yet been investigated by a space probe.

But the *Pluto-Kuiper Express* will start its journey to Pluto in December 2004, and then go on to investigate the Kuiper Belt.

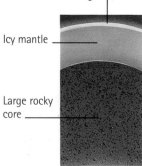

Kuiper
Belt

A

B C

Asteroid Belt

ASTEROIDS

Billions of asteroids orbit the sun. Over
90 percent make up the asteroid (or main)
belt, a doughnut-shaped ring between
Mars and Jupiter. They are sometimes
called the minor planets, as they are
each rocky bodies orbiting the sun. They
are the remnants of a planet that did not
form when the solar system was young,
4.6 billion years ago.

Ceres, the first to be discovered, in
1801, is also the largest. It is spherical
and about 579 miles (932km) wide. Most
asteroids are smaller, about a billion are
more than half a mile wide, but many
more are only a few feet across. Asteroids
are made of rock, metal, or a combination
of the two.

Over ten thousand individual asteroids
have been discovered and had their orbits
recorded. Each has been given a name.
Our only close-up views have been
provided by two space probes. The first to
be seen was Gaspra, by the *Galileo* probe
in October 1991. The *NEAR* (Near Earth
Asteroid Rendezvous) probe showed us
Mathilde in 1997 and Eros in 1998.

KUIPER BELT

The Kuiper Belt is named after the
Dutch-born, U.S. astronomer Gerard Kuiper
(1905–1973). It is a ring of cometlike
objects, thought to be made of ice, snow,
rock, and dust. There are estimated to be
at least 70,000 of them larger than 62
miles (100km) across. They are so distant
that we can only see the closest of them.
The first were discovered
in the last years
of the 1900s.

The asteroid belt, between
Mars and Jupiter, consists
of billions of asteroids. The
largest, Ceres, has a face
pitted with impact craters
and a width of 620 mi.
(1000km). Other asteroids
follow paths (A, B, and C)
within the inner solar
system. The Kuiper Belt,
which consists of tens of
thousands of icy rock
bodies, lies beyond
Neptune's orbit.

▲ The asteroid Ida, imaged by the *Galileo* space probe, is
about 32 mi. (52km) long. Its surface is pitted where other
asteroids have collided with it. A tiny asteroid, Dactyl,
thought to have broken off Ida, orbits it like a moon.

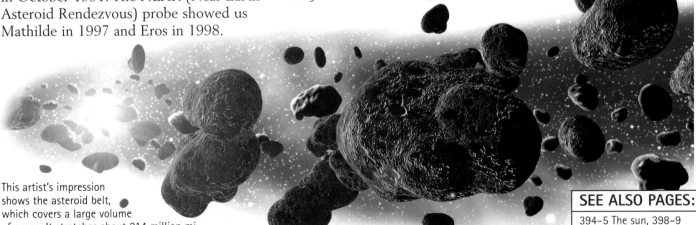

This artist's impression
shows the asteroid belt,
which covers a large volume
of space. It stretches about 214 million mi.
(344 million km) from its inner to outer edge.

SEE ALSO PAGES:

394–5 The sun, 398–9
The solar system, 418–19
Exploring space

COMETS

Comets are dirty snowballs. Vast numbers of them live at the very edge of the solar system. When one travels close to the sun it grows a giant head and two tails.

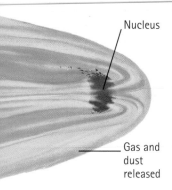

Nucleus

Gas and dust released

A cometary nucleus is heated up when close to the sun. The gas and dust released forms a coma, many times the diameter of the Earth, and tails that can be 62 million mi. (100 million km) in length.

A comet forms a new coma and tails on each return to the sun. The tails are longest after the closest approach, and they always point away from the sun. A comet will average about 100 returns before its gas and dust are used up.

Astronomers have estimated that about 10 trillion comets make up the Oort Cloud, the enormous spherical cloud that surrounds our solar system. The cloud is about 4.7 trillion miles (7.6 trillion km) across. Each comet follows its own orbit around the sun. They are all potato-shaped balls of snow and rocky dust, only miles across.

HEAD AND TAILS

Occasionally a comet leaves the Oort Cloud and travels into the inner solar system toward the sun. Close to the sun the comet grows in size and brightness. The sun's heat turns the snow on the surface of the snowball nucleus to gas, and some dust is released. The gas and dust form a bright head around the nucleus, the coma. More gas and dust is blown away and forms two tails. The dust tail is yellowish-white, the gas tail, bluish.

PERIODIC COMETS

When a comet is close to the sun and has a head and tails, it can be seen in the Earth's sky. Some comets return regularly to our sky. The time between returns is a comet's period. Encke's Comet has the shortest period of all, just 3.3 years. Halley's Comet returns about every 76 years. These are just two of the estimated 135 comets with periods of less than 200 years. They are known as short-period comets. Other comets that return, but not for thousands of years, are known as long-period comets.

The regular return of Halley's Comet has meant it has been seen by thousands of people throughout history. Space probes were sent to it on its last return in 1986. The most successful, *Giotto*, traveled inside its coma, and people saw a cometary nucleus for the first time. Another probe, *Stardust*, will visit Comet Wild 2 in 2004. This probe will return to the Earth, carrying dust and gas from Wild 2.

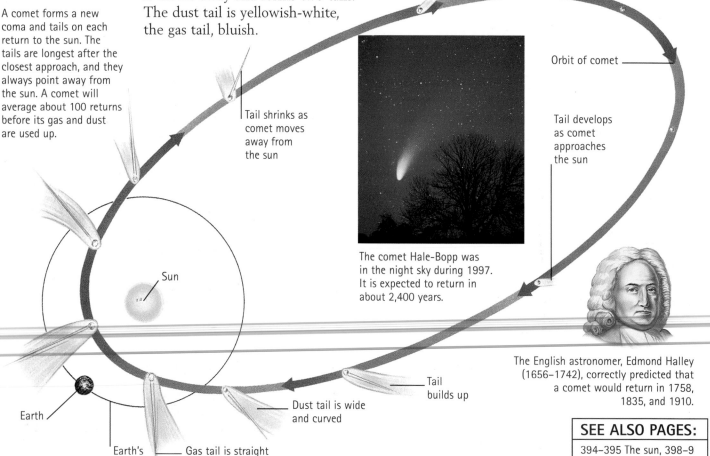

Tail shrinks as comet moves away from the sun

Orbit of comet

Tail develops as comet approaches the sun

Sun

The comet Hale-Bopp was in the night sky during 1997. It is expected to return in about 2,400 years.

Earth

Earth's orbit

Gas tail is straight and narrow

Dust tail is wide and curved

Tail builds up

The English astronomer, Edmond Halley (1656–1742), correctly predicted that a comet would return in 1758, 1835, and 1910.

SEE ALSO PAGES:

394–395 The sun, 398–9 The solar system, 418–19 Exploring space

METEORS AND METEORITES

Tiny pieces of solar system space rock burn up in the Earth's atmosphere. Larger chunks that land on the Earth's surface are called meteorites.

This iron and nickel meteorite, discovered in California in 1976, is the second largest found in the U.S. It is nicknamed "The Old Woman."

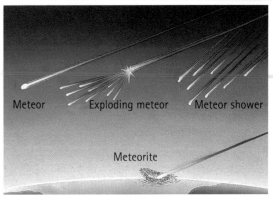

Meteors occur 50-75 mi. (80-120km) above the Earth's surface. Meteors in a shower all seem to start at the same point in the sky. A meteorite, a space rock that reaches the surface, can produce a crater.

Pieces of space rock and dust, called meteoroids, exist throughout the solar system. As the Earth moves through space it collides with many of them. Over 200,000 tons of space rock enters the Earth's atmosphere each year. Most pieces are tiny and burn up in the atmosphere. Larger ones survive and land on the Earth.

METEORS AND METEOR SHOWERS

Dust pieces, no larger than a grain of sand, speed through the atmosphere toward the Earth faster than a bullet. The dust is heated and parts of it burn off, producing a column of light known as a meteor. Meteors are about three feet across and 12.5 miles (20km) long and last less than a second. Because a meteor viewed from the Earth looks like a streak of starlight shooting across the sky, they are also called shooting stars. About ten an hour can be detected in a moonless, cloudfree sky.

A meteor shower consists of related meteors from the same region of the sky, at the same time every year. Showers are caused by the Earth traveling through a stream of meteoroids. The stream forms from dust that is shed by comets.

A meteor is a column of light produced by a tiny piece of space dust burning in the Earth's atmosphere.

METEORITES AND CRATERS

Large space rocks that do not burn up in the atmosphere and crash on the Earth's surface are known as meteorites. They start life as part of a comet or an asteroid. More than 3,000 of them, weighing half a pound or more, land each year. Most are made of rock, some are iron, others are a mixture of the two. Craters form when large meteorites collide with the land; they can range in size from several feet to 87 miles (140km) across. Most were formed over 50 million years ago. The 124 miles (200km) wide Chicxulub Crater, under the Gulf of Mexico, was formed when a huge rock impacted with the Earth 65 million years ago.

The Barringer Crater, in Arizona, was formed about 52,000 years ago when a large meteorite struck the Earth. The iron meteorite, thought to be about 100 feet wide blasted the surface material away on impact and formed this 0.8 mi. (1.2km)-wide crater.

SEE ALSO PAGES:

10–11 Earth's atmosphere,
398–9 The solar system,
400–1 Earth and the moon

STUDYING THE UNIVERSE

For thousands of years, astronomers have studied the universe. With the aid of modern technology, they can now learn about its past and predict its future.

Nicolaus Copernicus (1473–1543), a Polish astronomer, published his theory that the sun and not the Earth is the center of the universe.

Italian astronomer, Galileo Galilei (1564–1642), used the telescope to support the idea that the Earth and other planets move around the sun.

English scientist, Sir Isaac Newton (1643–1727), built the first reflecting telescope in 1668. He showed that the gravity we have on the Earth is also in the universe. It, for example, allows the moon to orbit the Earth.

Early civilizations watched the stars and planets to predict the coming of the seasons. But it was the ancient Egyptians and Greeks who first studied them as a science. The word astronomy comes from two Greek words meaning "star laws."

These early astronomers used what they saw as a basis for their timekeeping and navigation. They formed the stars into constellations, watched the changing face of the moon and the slow passage of the planets across the sky. In the daytime, they watched the sun climb high and then fall out of view. To them everything seemed to revolve around the Earth. Our planet was the center of a universe that included the moon and just five other planets— Mercury, Venus, Mars, Jupiter, and Saturn— with a sphere of stars surrounding it all.

This idea of the universe, called the Ptolemaic theory, was held for many hundreds of years. However, some of the observations did not fit in with this idea of the universe, but no other theory suited their religious beliefs so well. The work of European astronomers in the 1500s and 1600s changed all that.

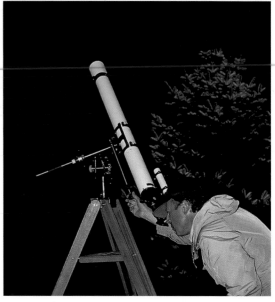

Amateur astronomers use small optical telescopes to study the universe. Details of familiar objects, such as the moon, can be seen in close-up.

MODERN ASTRONOMY

Modern astronomy began in the 1500s when Nicolaus Copernicus suggested that the planets orbit the sun. Proof for this came from Galileo Galilei when he made discoveries about the moon and planets, using the newly-invented telescope during 1609 and 1610. In the 1680s, Isaac Newton described how gravity affects objects in space.

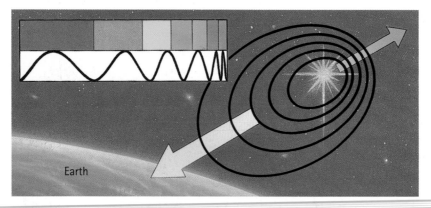

Earth

We can learn about the temperature and composition of a star or galaxy by studying its light. It can also tell us if an object is moving away or toward us. The length of the light wave is directly related to its color. Waves from an object going away are stretched apart, and redder. Those approaching are pushed together, and bluer.

Light is only one form of energy wave collected from space. The longer radio waves through to the shorter gamma rays are all collected. Only visible light and part of the radio spectrum penetrate far through the Earth's protective atmosphere.

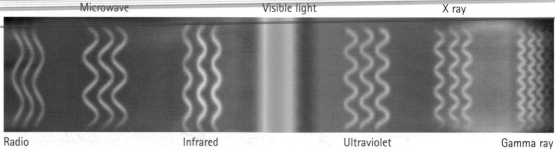

Microwave Visible light X ray

Radio Infrared Ultraviolet Gamma ray

DIFFERENT VIEWS OF THE ORION NEBULA

Every object in the universe gives out a range of radiation, but our eyes can see only the visible light waves. This means that we only see part of an object when we look at it. For example, we can only see the light that is emitted from the center of a galaxy. An X-ray image would show that it extends far beyond the center. These six images are all of the Orion Nebula, but at different wavelengths. The infrared images on the right show different temperatures. Clockwise from top left: new stars forming, hydrogen heated by newborn stars, a cold cloud of hydrogen, and dust clouds heated by newborn stars.

Optical image of Orion Nebula.

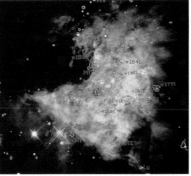

X-ray and optical images combined.

Infrared images taken at four different wavelengths.

During the following years, astronomers continued to concern themselves with the positions and movements of objects in the night sky. At the same time, they were making new discoveries with increasingly powerful telescopes. The planet Uranus was discovered in 1781, and the first asteroid in 1801. Instruments such as the camera and the spectroscope were fitted to telescopes. Cameras could record details that the human eye could not see. The spectroscope split the light of stars to reveal their composition.

CHANGES IN THE 20TH CENTURY

During the late 1800s and the early 1900s, astronomers turned their attention to the nature of objects in the universe, rather than how they moved. From this time on, practical astronomy (making observations) worked hand in hand with theoretical astronomy (developing ideas using the laws of science).

Astronomers went on to find out, and prove, many more things about our universe: there are many galaxies beyond our own, the universe is expanding, how elements are created inside stars, and how it all started in a Big Bang.

New methods and new tools of investigation helped them in their work. Light is just one of the forms of radiation that objects give off. They also emit radio waves, microwaves, infrared, ultraviolet, X rays, and gamma rays. Each of these can be collected by special telescopes, and the information can be combined to give a more complete view of the universe. Telescopes collecting different radiations are based on land, in orbit around the Earth, and on space probes.

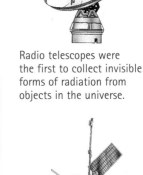

English astronomer Fred Hoyle (1915-) showed how elements such as carbon and oxygen are created inside stars.

Radio telescopes were the first to collect invisible forms of radiation from objects in the universe.

Since the 1970s, spaceprobes such as *Mariner 10* have been sent to investigate objects within the solar system.

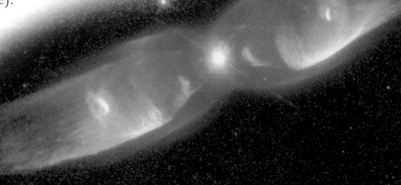

The image of this planetary nebula, a dying star, was made by the Hubble Space Telescope. The Hubble is one of the satellite telescopes in orbit around the Earth. Unobstructed by the atmosphere, they have a clear view deep into space and are able to operate throughout the day and night.

SEE ALSO PAGES:

246-7 The electromagnetic spectrum, 416-17 Astronomical telescopes

ASTRONOMICAL TELESCOPES

Telescopes are astronomers' most important tool. They provide information by collecting light, radio, and other energy waves from space.

Refracting telescope

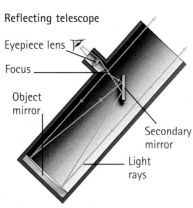

- Object lens
- Focus
- Light rays
- Eyepiece lens

Reflecting telescope

- Eyepiece lens
- Focus
- Object mirror
- Secondary mirror
- Light rays

These are the two simplest designs of optical (light-gathering) telescopes used by astronomers. In a refractor, the light enters and is bent to form an image at the focus. This is then magnified by the eyepiece lenses. Reflectors use a main object mirror, and then a smaller secondary mirror to direct the light to the eyepiece.

▶ The Earth's spin means that stars, caught on a long-exposure photograph, appear as trails of light in the sky. Telescopes inside these domes on Hawaii are attached to mounts with a countermovement so they stay focused on a star as the Earth rotates.

Telescopes have been used by astronomers since the early 1600s. One of the first astronomers to use one was the Italian, Galileo Galilei. His telescope allowed him to see craters on the moon's surface, observe the stars in the Milky Way, and study four of Jupiter's moons. The telescope was then a new invention, used mainly on land. Galileo published his discoveries, encouraging others to turn the telescope to the night sky.

HOW A TELESCOPE WORKS

The first telescopes used lenses to collect light from a distant object. This was then focused to form an image of the object. Another lens then magnified the image for the astronomer. The result was that a faint, distant object became larger, brighter, and clearer.

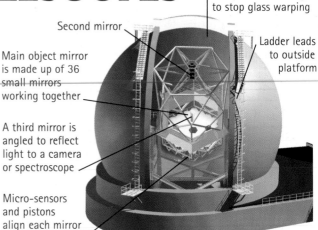

- Temperature of dome is kept near freezing to stop glass warping
- Second mirror
- Main object mirror is made up of 36 small mirrors working together
- A third mirror is angled to reflect light to a camera or spectroscope
- Micro-sensors and pistons align each mirror as dome rotates
- Ladder leads to outside platform

Keck I, the first telescope to use a segmented mirror, was completed in 1992. It is housed next to an identical telescope, Keck II, 4,200 meters above sea level, at the top of Mauna Kea, an extinct volcano in Hawaii.

A telescope using a lens for collecting light is called a refractor. Most telescopes today use a mirror and are known as reflectors. The first reflector was designed in 1668 by the English scientist, Isaac Newton. Both types were equally used until the 1900s when the reflector rose in popularity. By the end of the 1900s, astronomers wanted telescopes with light-gathering power beyond the capability of a single mirror. So, many of today's most powerful telescopes use more than one mirror to collect light. The two Keck telescopes in Hawaii, for example, each have 36 six-sided mirrors joined together to make one large mirror, 33 feet wide.

USING THE TELESCOPE

In modern astronomy, the astronomers' eyes have been replaced at the telescope's eyepiece by sensitive electronic cameras using CCDs (charged-coupled devices). These build up an image over minutes or hours and pick up information the human eye could never see. A second instrument, a spectroscope, which splits the light into its spectrum of colors, may also be attached to the telescope. The study of lines in the spectrum can reveal the elements inside a star and its temperature. The computer is vital to astronomers. They use it to control the telescope, record the information it collects, and help him analyze that data.

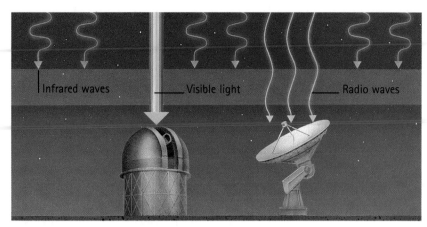

Infrared waves — Visible light — Radio waves

Only some of the radiation emitted by stars reaches the Earth's surface. Much of it is blocked by the Earth's atmosphere. Light and shortwave radio, as well as some infrared radiation, gets through and can be collected by telescopes on the surface of the planet.

▶ Radio telescopes collect radio waves from space in a large dish. They are reflected to a receiver and collected. They can then be processed by a computer to turn them into images.

Reflector dish

Tilt

Receiver

Revolving base

TELESCOPES ON THE EARTH

The Earth's atmosphere blocks our best view of the universe. It makes the stars twinkle and blurs the images of galaxies. Sites on mountaintops are chosen for telescopes because the air is clear and thin. These telescopes are so powerful that the data collected in just a few nights can keep astronomers busy for months or years.

Modern telescopes are large, but sensitive instruments, and they need protection from the environment. They are housed inside domes with an opening panel that reveals the night sky above. The dome revolves, thus allowing the telescope to point in any direction. The astronomers and technicians using the telescope are in a separate control room.

TELESCOPES IN SPACE

Some observations of objects in space are totally impossible from the Earth. The atmosphere absorbs some forms of energy, such as X rays, and reflects others back into space. The only place to collect these forms of radiation is above the Earth's atmosphere. Telescopes have been used in space for about thirty years and are launched by rocket or space shuttle. Once in orbit around the Earth they can make continuous, uninterrupted observations of the universe. They collect a range of energy waves, including light, in the same way as conventional telescopes. Data collected is sent to a ground-control station on the Earth where it is stored in

a computer. The satellites work for a few years, then they are replaced by newer instruments. At present, the Chandra X-ray Observatory is searching the universe for X rays; SOHO (Solar and Heliospheric Observatory), an ultraviolet telescope, has been looking at the sun since 1995; and the Hubble Space Telescope, which collects lightwaves, can see objects fainter than those seen by ground-based telescopes.

▼ This view into deep space, made by the Hubble Space Telescope, combines 342 separate images. The telescope looked at a tiny area of the sky, the size of a grain of sand at arm's length. It kept looking for 10 days, all the time collecting light from distant space. This view contains 1,500 galaxies never seen before.

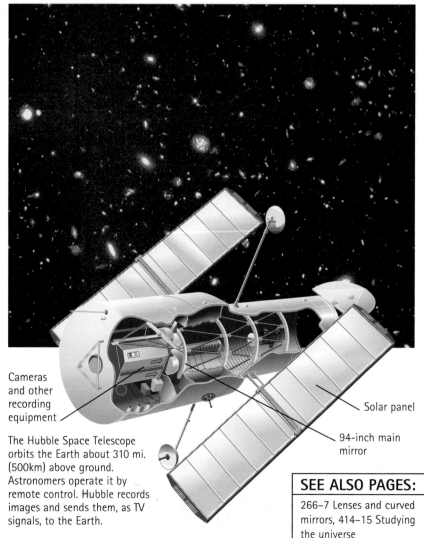

Cameras and other recording equipment

The Hubble Space Telescope orbits the Earth about 310 mi. (500km) above ground. Astronomers operate it by remote control. Hubble records images and sends them, as TV signals, to the Earth.

Solar panel

94-inch main mirror

SEE ALSO PAGES:
266–7 Lenses and curved mirrors, 414–15 Studying the universe

EXPLORING SPACE

Astronomers send robot spacecraft to explore space. These send back to the Earth stunning images and data about the planets, moons, asteroids, and comets.

Robot space explorers have been working in the solar system for over thirty years. They are called space probes, and are about the size of a family car. They have shown us the rocky deserts of Mars, an active volcano on Io, and the snowball heart of a comet; returned rock from the moon; and dropped through poisonous atmospheres. They have been outstandingly successful at making investigations and discoveries. We have learned much about the solar system by using them and will continue to do so from new missions already journeying to their targets, and others being planned.

Most space probes are launched into space by a rocket, but a few are taken there aboard a space shuttle. Once released into space, a probe starts its journey toward its target. It may not

arrive for years, but on arrival its real work begins. Scientific equipment on board is switched on, and the probe starts its investigations for the astronomers back on the Earth. When its work is over the probe is switched off and left in space.

SPACE PROBE FIRSTS

Luna 2 was the first successful space probe to reach another world. It crash-landed on the moon in 1959 and was the first of a series of Soviet *Luna* probes that studied the moon for almost 20 years.

Mariner 10 successfully visited Mercury and Venus in 1973, and was the first probe to visit two planets. Venus, Mars, Jupiter, and Saturn have each been investigated by a number of probes. Uranus (1986) and Neptune (1989) were the last planets to be visited. They were studied by the same probe—*Voyager 2*. Pluto remains the only planet still not visited.

The sun and some of the solar system's smaller members have also been explored by space probes. Craft visiting planets such as Jupiter and Saturn have looked

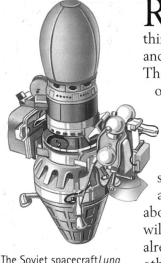

The Soviet spacecraft *Luna 9* was the first to make a soft (controlled) landing on another world. It landed on the moon in February 1966, and transmitted the first close-up photographs of the lunar surface.

Two identical Soviet robot vehicles, both called *Lunokhod*, explored the moon, one in 1970, the second in 1973. They were driven by remote control from the Earth. Together they covered nearly 30 mi. (48km) on the moon's surface.

LANDING ON COMET WIRTANEN

The *Rosetta* space probe is now being prepared for an encounter with Comet Wirtanen in 2012. The probe is in two parts, a lander craft will land on the comet's surface as an orbiter circles at a distance. Together they will investigate the comet's material, which dates from the time of the formation of the solar system.

▶ The space probe *Cassini*, launched in 1997, will reach Saturn in 2004. On arrival it will orbit the planet and its moons for four years. *Cassini* will release the miniprobe *Huygens* to investigate Titan, Saturn's largest moon, and the only one in the solar system that has an atmosphere.

▼ Before launch, technicians fitted a heat shield to the miniprobe *Huygens*. Its 160 insulating silica tiles will protect the craft against temperatures of up to 3,632°F as it drops through Titan's upper atmosphere. The heat shield will then be ejected and *Huygens'* instruments will test Titan's lower atmosphere.

closely at their moons, many of them far too small to be seen from the Earth. The *Giotto* space probe gave us our first close-up of a comet when it visited Halley's Comet in 1986. Our first view of an asteroid was obtained in 1991 by the *Galileo* space probe on its way to Jupiter.

WORKING ROBOT

A space probe carries everything that it will need for its mission. This includes not only scientific experiments to carry out its work, but also power sources, small thruster rockets for changing direction, and equipment for recording and transmitting the data it has collected.

The task a probe has to carry out, as well as the way it will do it, influences its design. There are three basic ways in which probes complete their tasks. A flyby probe studies its target as it flys past it. The probes *Voyager 1* and *2* have been the most successful of this type so far. Between 1979 and 1989, they flew past Jupiter, Saturn, Uranus, and Neptune.

Alternatively, a probe can be an orbiter; this type reaches its target and goes into orbit around it. The probe *Magellan* orbited Venus from 1990 to 1994 and gathered data to produce maps of 98 percent of Venus' surface. The third way is for a probe to land on its target.

Landers work alone, or journey to their target with an orbiter. They then split to carry out their individual tasks. Landers have already successfully worked on the moon, Venus, and Mars.

A similar sort of probe to the lander is the miniprobe; this splits from a larger probe once at the target. The *Galileo* space probe released a miniprobe into Jupiter's atmosphere in this way in 1996. The probe *Cassini* will release a miniprobe called *Huygens* when it reaches Saturn in 2004. It will descend through the thick atmosphere of Titan, Saturn's largest moon.

▼ Planning, building, and testing spacecraft takes many years. Here, four identical *Cluster* satellites are being tested by technicians in Germany in 1994. But their launch a year later was not a success. Four new satellites with identical experiment packages were built to be launched in 2000. Orbiting the Earth in formation, they will study the interaction between the solar wind and the Earth's atmosphere.

SEE ALSO PAGES:

398–9 The solar system, 420–1 Rockets and the space shuttle

ROCKETS AND THE SPACE SHUTTLE

A rocket can carry space probes, satellites, astronauts, and scientists. To break free from the Earth's gravity, it must travel at escape velocity: 7 mi./sec. (11km/sec).

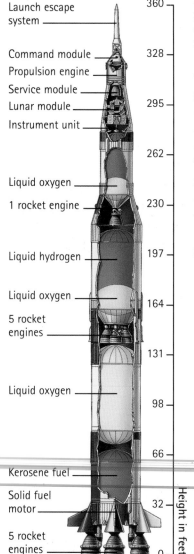

U.S. rocket pioneer Robert Goddard (1882–1945) carried out rocket-based experiments and launched the first liquid-fuel rocket in 1926.

The knowledge necessary for space travel was developed in the late 1800s, when the first rockets were designed. A significant step in space-rocket technology came in 1926 with the launch of the first liquid-fuel rocket. Designed and launched by the rocket scientist, Robert Goddard, its flight lasted just two and a half seconds and it reached a height of 41 feet. His work, and that of other rocket scientists, led to the launch of the first space rockets in the 1940s and 1950s.

An *Ariane 44LP* rocket lifts off from the European Space Agency's launch site at Kourou in French Guiana. The main rocket has four boosters—two solid- and two liquid-fuel.

ROCKET TECHNOLOGY

Most of a rocket is taken up by the fuel needed to power it into space. Only a small part of it is set aside for the cargo, which travels in the nose. The rocket's fuel needs an oxidizer, a chemical that contains oxygen. At liftoff, the fuel and the oxidizer are mixed and burned. This expands the fuel and converts it into hot gas. The gas is forced out of nozzles at the bottom of the rocket, powering the rocket and its cargo off the ground and into space. The heavier the cargo,

the more fuel is needed, but the addition of fuel also increases the weight of the rocket. Discardable booster rockets, attached to the outside of the lower body of large rockets, help to give extra thrust at the launch. The main rocket is also designed to work in stages. Each has its own fuel supply and engines, and is used in turn and then discarded as the rocket climbs farther from the Earth. Only the final stage of the rocket will make the

Launch escape system

Command module

Propulsion engine

Service module

Lunar module

Instrument unit

Liquid oxygen

1 rocket engine

Liquid hydrogen

Liquid oxygen

5 rocket engines

Liquid oxygen

Kerosene fuel

Solid fuel motor

5 rocket engines

Height in feet

360
328
295
262
230
197
164
131
98
66
32
0

Saturn V rockets launched astronauts from Cape Canaveral to the moon between 1969 and 1972.

Titan III launched *Viking* space probes to Mars in 1974.

The European rocket, *Ariane V*, first flew in 1997.

Chinese *Long March* rockets launch satellites.

Since 1967, *Soyuz* has launched Soviet cosmonauts.

The Japanese *H-IIA* rocket launches satellites into orbit.

journey into space where it will release its cargo. Hundreds of rockets have lifted off for space in the past 50 years, mostly carrying satellites, and space probes, but also astronauts. However, rockets are very short-lived and expensive and each one can be used only once. Within about ten minutes of a launch a rocket has lifted its cargo into space and its work is over.

SPACE SHUTTLE

A new type of space vehicle, the space shuttle, was launched in 1981. The shuttle's main difference from the conventional rocket is that it is a reusable system. It uses rocket technology to launch into space, but then returns to the Earth like a glider plane. Two of its three main parts can be reused many times. The three main parts of the shuttle are

the orbiter, the fuel tank, and the two booster rockets. The crew and cargo fly inside the orbiter, the space plane. This is the part of the shuttle that is launched into space. It acts as a workshop for the astronauts while in space, and then brings them safely home.

There are four different orbiters, *Columbia*, *Discovery*, *Atlantis*, and *Endeavour*. Only one orbiter is in space at any given time. They are used as space laboratories where astronauts and scientists carry out experiments and test equipment. They are also used for launching, retrieving, and repairing satellites, launching space probes, and for building the International Space Station (ISS).

A Japanese *N-II* rocket lifts off from the launch center on Tanegashima Island, in southern Japan. The launch center includes spacecraft assembly and testing sites, and a satellite-tracking site.

THE SPACE SHUTTLE

A typical shuttle trip into space lasts a week. The actual launch is operated by onboard computers controlled by the launch control team. Once in space, the mission control team takes over. The orbiter is about the size of a small airplane. The large red-orange fuel tank supplying the main engines contains about one third liquid oxygen and two thirds liquid hydrogen. It is the only part of the shuttle not reused. The booster rockets are later recovered by ship for reuse.

1 The shuttle is ready for liftoff. This is the only time all its components are together. It is lifted off the ground by two boosters and the three engines on the orbiter.

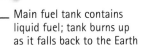

Main fuel tank contains liquid fuel; tank burns up as it falls back to the Earth

Nose-cone protects against heat of 2,300°F on reentry

Heat insulation felt and tiles are fixed to the outside of the orbiter

Two side reusable rocket boosters of solid fuel provide a thrust of 3 million pounds at takeoff

Two engines either side of the tail move the orbiter into (and during) orbit

Three main rocket engines

2 About two minutes after leaving the ground, explosive bolts release the two booster rockets. The main fuel tank is ejected six minutes later.

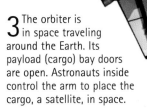

3 The orbiter is in space traveling around the Earth. Its payload (cargo) bay doors are open. Astronauts inside control the arm to place the cargo, a satellite, in space.

4 On its return to the Earth, the orbiter descends through the atmosphere, returning to land like a glider. Its rudder, movable edges on the wings, and a drag chute bring it to a stop on the runway.

SEE ALSO PAGES:

178 Oxidation and reduction, 418–19 Exploring space, 422–3 Humans in space

HUMANS IN SPACE

Nearly 400 men and women have traveled into space since 1961. Twenty-six of them have left the Earth's orbit and visited the moon.

On April 12, 1961, Soviet cosmonaut Yuri Gagarin, aboard *Vostok 1*, became the first human to travel into space.

On June 16, 1963, the Soviet cosmonaut Valentina Tereshkova, aboard *Vostok 6*, became the first woman to travel into space.

American astronaut Neil Armstrong became the first human to step onto another world, the moon, on July 20, 1969.

In July 1975, American *Apollo 18* and Soviet *Soyuz 19* spacecrafts docked together in space for the first time.

The first travelers in space were not humans. Dogs, chimpanzees, and monkeys were among the first creatures to test spaceflight. Their trips paved the way for flights by humans. The Soviet Union and the United States both prepared to launch a human into space in 1961. The first flight, lasting 108 minutes, was by Yuri Gagarin and started a race between the two nations. This continued for almost a decade, and culminated in an American landing on the moon.

Today, these two countries still offer the only way that humans can travel into space, either aboard the Soviet *Soyuz* rocket or the American space shuttle. They each take space travelers from other countries, so now people from many nations have been into space. These travelers are called astronauts, although those on Soviet spacecraft are called cosmonauts. Each undertakes about two years of training before a first flight.

DRESSED FOR SPACE

An EMU (Extravehicular Mobility Unit) spacesuit protects the astronaut from radiation and the temperature extremes of space. The suit consists of up to 15 separate layers of material. Heated or cooled water is pumped through tubes in the suit to keep the body's temperature constant. A backpack includes a radio and enough oxygen for several hours' supply. Each astronaut carries an instrument to measure his or her exposure to radiation. This restricts the amount of time an astronaut can spend working in space.

American astronauts perform an experiment in the shuttle *Atlantis*. They are observing the growth of ice crystals in the weightless conditions of space.

SURVIVING IN SPACE

The human body is not built for living in space. Not only do space travelers have to take everything needed for survival, including air to breathe, but once in space they have to cope with a weightless environment. Gravity is not felt in space, so neither the astronaut, nor anything in the spacecraft, has any weight. Normal activities, such as eating, sleeping, and working, have to continue, but all in weightlessness. Astronauts and anything else float effortlessly around the craft.

Inside a spacecraft there is air for breathing, bunks for sleeping, a small area for eating and relaxing, and a bathroom. Astronauts work in a separate indoor area, or can go outside the craft to carry out work. They may need to work outside for several hours if, for example, they are repairing a satellite. This involves catching, fixing, and then releasing it back into space. Any trip outside requires a protective spacesuit. Once in space, astronauts are secured to the craft to stop them floating away. Alternatively they wear a manned maneuvering unit (MMU), a backpack with rocket thrusters to control movement and direction.

The *Kvant 2* service module was added in December 1987

Antenna for sending messages to the Earth

HUMANS IN SPACE

The American space shuttle, *Atlantis*, docked with the Soviet space station, *Mir*, in June 1995. They stayed linked together for about 100 hours. Three cosmonauts already on board *Mir* were joined by two cosmonauts and five astronauts from *Atlantis*. The three on *Mir*, who had been in space for over three months, subsequently returned home on the shuttle.

Kvant 1 was added in April 1987. It is for science and astronomy work

Progress M is an unmanned spacecraft for transporting supplies to *Mir*

The central *Mir* module was the first into space in 1986. The astronauts live here

The space shuttle *Atlantis* docked with *Mir* in June 1995 for about 100 hours

The solar panels convert sunlight to electricity for powering *Mir*

SPACE STATIONS

Astronauts spend a few days at a time in space aboard the space shuttle. Longer periods—weeks, months, or over a year—have been spent on the *Mir* space station. A space station is a craft permanently in orbit around the Earth. It is both a home and a workplace for astronauts. Russian cosmonauts have lived on seven different space stations since 1971, sometimes with astronauts from other countries. The first were all called *Salyut*, but *Mir* was the last and most successful one. *Mir* was too large to launch all at once. Parts were transported separately and assembled in space. *Mir* was continuously inhabited by cosmonauts from February 1987 to mid-1999.

The International Space Station (ISS) is now being assembled in orbit around the Earth. It will take about 70 flights by Russian *Proton* rockets and American shuttles to carry all the parts into space for assembly. The first arrived in 1998, and the station should be fully completed by 2004. A cooperative effort by sixteen nations, the ISS will provide living quarters and science laboratories for up to seven astronauts.

▲ This artist's impression shows how the International Space Station (ISS) will look when complete. When built it will be about the size of a football field. The living and working modules are in the center.

In the future, this hotel could be the destination of the first space tourists. It is one of a number that have been designed to go into orbit around the Earth. The moon is also being considered as a potential destination for tourists.

SEE ALSO PAGES:

418–19 Exploring space,
420–1 Rockets and the
space shuttle

ARTIFICIAL SATELLITES

Hundreds of artificial satellites have been put into orbit around the Earth. They monitor the planet, help us navigate, aid communications, and look into space.

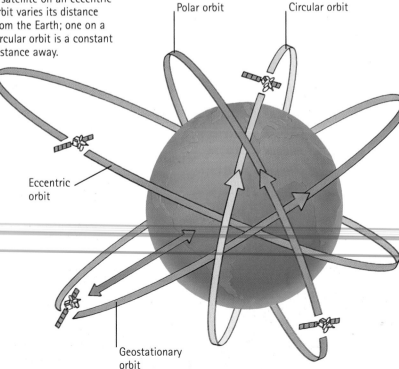

Sputnik 1 was the first satellite put into orbit around the Earth. The 23-in. diameter aluminum sphere was launched by the Soviets on October 4, 1957. It contained a battery, a radio transmitter, and instruments to test the Earth's upper atmosphere.

▼ Satellites occupy one of four main types of orbit. Polar orbits take satellites over the Earth's poles. Geostationary orbits keep a satellite in a fixed position above the Earth. A satellite on an eccentric orbit varies its distance from the Earth; one on a circular orbit is a constant distance away.

A satellite is an object that orbits a planet. The moon is the Earth's natural satellite and all the planets except Mercury and Venus have them. Natural satellites, however, are usually referred to as moons, and man-made satellites, often called artificial satellites, are what is usually meant by the word "satellite."

There are about 1,000 of them working in space right now. Each one is a scientific package designed to carry out a particular job. They orbit from about 185-620 miles (300-1,000km) above the Earth's surface and are launched into orbit by a rocket or occasionally by a space shuttle.

Once in orbit the satellite is activated and will continue to work for several years. All eventually stop, perhaps through the failure of a part or of the power supply. The dead satellite will, in time, fall out of its orbit and burn up as it drops through the Earth's atmosphere.

Satellites are placed in particular orbits, depending on the job they have to do. Some satellites need to stay above the

same part of the Earth all the time. These are placed in a geostationary orbit about 22,400 miles (36,000km) above the Earth's equator. This orbit allows the satellite to remain over the same point on the Earth's surface at all times. Many communication satellites are positioned like this and work together as a global network. Other satellites, such as weather satellites, work in polar orbit, watching the whole of the Earth's surface as it turns below.

A satellite's power is supplied by solar cells. The cells are either in panels, which look like wings coming from the sides of the satellite, or are wrapped around the satellite's body. They convert the sunlight that falls onto them into electricity. Panels of cells are folded for launch, and opened once in space. The panels are positioned so that they always face the sun.

A satellite control center monitors a satellite during its lifetime, tracking it, receiving its signals, and sending it commands. Stick- or dish-shaped antennae on the satellite are kept pointing toward the Earth to send and receive data. Tiny rocket thrusters on board can be fired to keep the satellite in the correct position and facing the right way.

▶ A geostationary communications satellite passes telephone calls, TV shows, and computer data between different countries across the world.

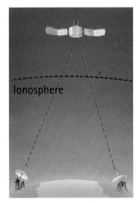

Ionosphere

▼ These satellite dishes on an apartment building in Germany are all pointing toward a communications satellite so that they can receive TV signals.

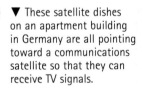

Polar orbit

Circular orbit

Eccentric orbit

Geostationary orbit

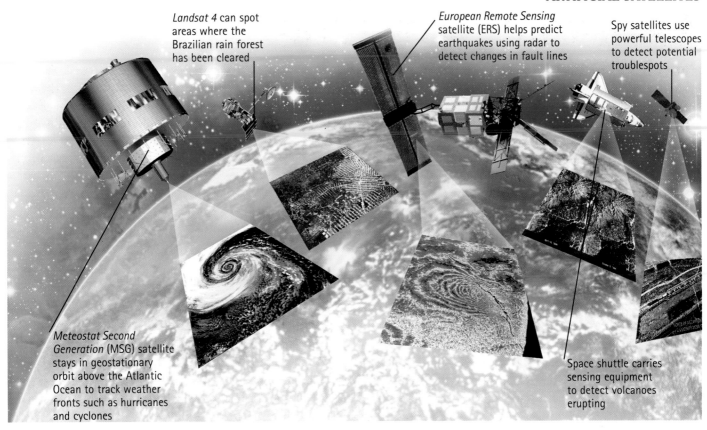

Landsat 4 can spot areas where the Brazilian rain forest has been cleared

European Remote Sensing satellite (ERS) helps predict earthquakes using radar to detect changes in fault lines

Spy satellites use powerful telescopes to detect potential troublespots

Meteostat Second Generation (MSG) satellite stays in geostationary orbit above the Atlantic Ocean to track weather fronts such as hurricanes and cyclones

Space shuttle carries sensing equipment to detect volcanoes erupting

SATELLITES AT WORK

Most satellites are made and operated by commercial companies. There are a number of different types: navigation, communication, scientific, military, and Earth-monitoring. The first started working over 40 years ago.

Communication satellites are such a part of everyday life, that we use them without realizing it. A sports event or concert happening at one place can be seen by people on the other side of the world at the same time. Cameras film the action, the TV signal is beamed to a satellite above the event, and the signal is relayed around the Earth by satellites until it reaches one above the opposite side of the planet. The signal is sent down to the Earth where it is received and the event is watched. Millions of telephone conversations and Internet connections, are also handled this way.

Our daily weather forecasts use information from weather satellites that are positioned around the globe. They observe the cloud patterns, monitor the Earth's atmosphere, record its temperature range, and look out for storms. All of the Earth's surface has been imaged many times by satellites studying the planet's natural resources including its forests, icecaps, and

oceans. They reveal short- and long-term changes to the planet.

Military satellites can be used for spying on other countries, guiding missiles, or being a weapon themselves. Navigation satellites pinpoint any position on the Earth and are an invaluable aid to navigators on land, sea, and in the air. Astronomical satellites, such as the Hubble Space Telescope, look into space and give us spectacular views of the stars and galaxies.

Many of the satellites surrounding the Earth are studying our planet. They provide information about the state of the Earth now, and information that forecasts future events, as well as monitoring long-term changes on its surface.

A geologist checks his location using a handheld GPS (Global Positioning System) receiver. Signals are sent between the handset and up to half of a network of 24 GPS satellites in orbit around the world. Signals from the satellites are used to calculate the geologist's position, which is displayed on the handset.

SEE ALSO PAGES:

10–11 Earth's atmosphere, 42–3 Weather forecasting, 400–1 Earth and the moon, 420–1 Rockets and the space shuttle

TIME

From the earliest times humans have used the seasons, the movement of the Earth, and the passage of the sun and the moon across the sky to measure time.

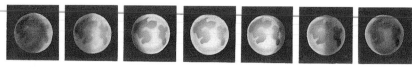

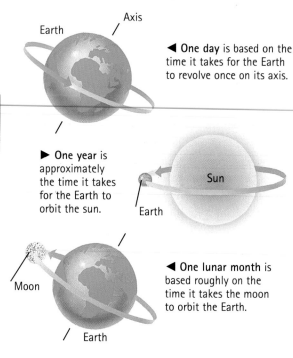

Earth / Axis

◀ **One day** is based on the time it takes for the Earth to revolve once on its axis.

▶ **One year** is approximately the time it takes for the Earth to orbit the sun.

Sun

Earth

Moon

◀ **One lunar month** is based roughly on the time it takes the moon to orbit the Earth.

Earth

The Earth's two movements in space, its spin and its orbit around the sun, give us our day and year. The moon orbits the Earth as it follows its path around the sun. It takes 27.3 days for one orbit, but a little longer—29.5 days—to complete its cycle of phases, the basis of our month.

One complete cycle of the moon's phases lasts 29.5 days and is the basis for our mo(o)nth.

The time system we use is based on the movement of the Earth. One spin of the planet on its axis is a day, and one orbit around the sun is a year. As the Earth spins, the sun is seen to rise in the sky, climb to its highest point, and then descend until it disappears from view.

The sun is at its highest point in the sky when a place on the Earth faces the sun directly. This happens day after day, as the Earth continually spins. Part of the day it is lit by the sun, the rest of the time the sun is out of view and it is nighttime. The starting- and finishing-point for the day is midnight, and halfway through the day is noon, the hour closest to the time when the sun is at its highest in the sky.

We no longer look at the sun and moon to tell the time. Instead we rely on public clocks.

The Aztecs of Central America developed an accurate calendar over 500 years ago. The face of the Aztec sun god was carved in the center, and signs for the 20 days of each month were carved around the edges.

CALENDARS

Ancient civilizations used these movements to regulate their lives. The Babylonians had, by 2400 B.C., divided the year into 12 equal parts, and the

day into 24 hours. They and, independently, the Egyptians, calculated the year's length as 365 days and 6 hours. This is very close to the real figure of 365 days, 6 hours, 41 minutes, and 59 seconds.

Calendars were devised to keep track of days, months, and years. They were used to mark holidays and festivals, and to plan work, such as planting seeds and harvesting crops. The Julian calendar, authorized by the Roman leader, Julius Caesar, was introduced in 46 B.C.

By the 1500s, the Julian calendar was no longer in step with the Earth's movements. To compensate, the Gregorian calendar was introduced in 1582. Decreed by Pope Gregory XIII, it is the one that we use today. When it was finally adopted by Great Britain and its colonies in 1752, 11 days had to be skipped. The day after September 2 became September 14 to get the calendar back on track. Other nations developed their own calendars, and some of them are still in use. The Chinese, for example, have a calendar based on the movements of the moon, with a 60-year cycle. However, the Gregorian calendar is internationally recognized.

THE FOUR SEASONS

Spring, summer, fall, and winter occur annually as the tilted Earth orbits the sun. The tilt of the Earth's axis causes progressive changes in the length of the day and the temperature on the Earth. These are the seasonal changes experienced as the Northern and Southern Hemispheres of the Earth are tilted alternatively toward, and then away from, the sun. Early farmers recorded these changing seasons and in this way made the first calendars.

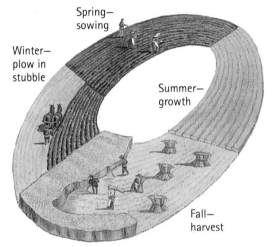

Spring—sowing

Winter—plow in stubble

Summer—growth

Fall—harvest

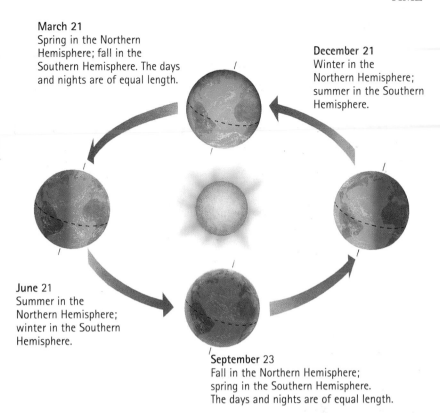

March 21
Spring in the Northern Hemisphere; fall in the Southern Hemisphere. The days and nights are of equal length.

December 21
Winter in the Northern Hemisphere; summer in the Southern Hemisphere.

June 21
Summer in the Northern Hemisphere; winter in the Southern Hemisphere.

September 23
Fall in the Northern Hemisphere; spring in the Southern Hemisphere. The days and nights are of equal length.

SEASONS

The Earth is tilted at an angle of 23.5 degrees as it spins on its axis, always pointing to the same spot in space. This means the North Pole tilts toward the sun for part of the yearly orbit and away for the rest of the time. When the Earth is facing the sun, the sun is high in the sky and it is summer in the Northern Hemisphere. Six months later, as the North Pole points away from the sun, it is winter in the Northern Hemisphere. In the Southern Hemisphere this is reversed.

DAY LENGTH

Although all days are the same length, the hours of daylight in the course of a day differ throughout the year. This is true for most of the world. The exceptions are the equator, where there are about 12 hours of daylight every day, and the regions around the North and South Poles.

The day with the maximum daylight hours, called the summer solstice or the longest day, is June 21 in the Northern Hemisphere, and December 21 or 22 for the Southern Hemisphere. The shortest day, the winter solstice, when we have the maximum nighttime hours, is December 21 or 22 in the Northern Hemisphere, and June 21 in the Southern Hemisphere.

This is because the axis of the Earth is tilted. People in the hemisphere tilted toward the sun see the sun pass higher across the sky, so it is in the sky longer between sunrise and sunset. Twice a year, halfway between the solstices, are the fall and spring equinoxes. Everywhere in the world around March 21 and September 23, there are an equal number of daylight and nighttime hours.

People living in the Arctic and Antarctic regions see the sun continuously in the sky for six months, followed by six months of darkness. The sun travels around the sky each day, reaching its highest point at midday, its lowest at midnight. This happens because, for example, in the northern summer the North Pole is tilted toward the sun, and the sun is high in the sky, so high that it does not rise or set.

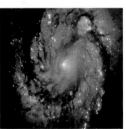

Time moves forward, not back. Yet we can look back in time by looking into the universe. The light from this spiral galaxy takes so long to reach us, that we see it as it was about 50 million years ago.

Birds and animals, moving with the seasons, instinctively know when it is time to move from one place to another. These geese are flying south for the winter after spending summer in the north.

SEE ALSO PAGES:

3 Earth's rotation, 93 Migration, 430–1 Space, time, and relativity

427

MEASURING TIME

The movement of the Earth and the moon around the sun has always been the basis of time measurement. We have also invented other ways to measure it.

In the Middle Ages, candle clocks measured off equal units of time as the flames melted the wax.

Water clocks were used in ancient Egypt. The amount of water dripping from one bowl to another marked the time passed.

Sundials, used for centuries, show the time by plotting the changing position of the sun's shadow during the day.

Sandglasses, popular in the Middle Ages, were used to measure short periods of time.

Ancient civilizations developed calendars to keep account of the passage of large portions of time such as days, months, and years. The smaller portions of time, the hours and the minutes, were marked by timepieces. They either used the sun to directly indicate the time, or they measured the passing of an interval of time.

The earliest time-measuring instruments were those used by the ancient Egyptians. During the day they used a simple form of sundial, called a shadow clock. It was made of two wooden rods, one cast a shadow onto the other, which had a dial to indicate the hour. At night they observed the position of stars in the sky, and also used a water clock. Water was allowed to flow from one vessel to another. Inside the lower vessel was a scale indicating the passing of the hours as the water flowed. Sundials and water clocks were later used in Greece and Rome, and then in Europe. The sandglass, measuring the passage of time by the flow of sand between two bulbs of glass, was also used. Some people still use sandglasses (as egg timers) and hourglasses.

MECHANICAL TIMEKEEPING

The first mechanical clocks were made during the late 1200s. They were clocks intended for general use and placed in a church or other public place where many people could see them. A clock is set in motion by one of two ways—by winding up a spring or by raising a weight. Gears with teeth, or cogs, move the hour, minute, and second hands over the face and indicate the time.

Small domestic clocks and the first watches were developed in the 1500s. Cheap, factory-made wristwatches made time available to everyone by the beginning of the 1900s.

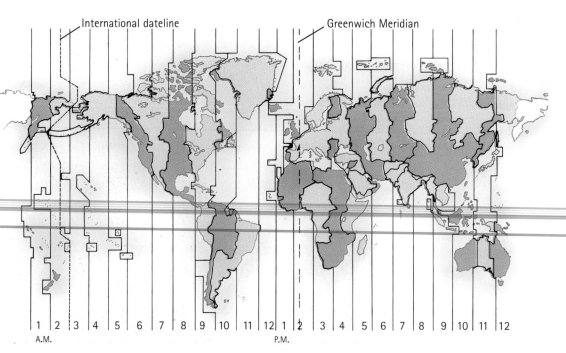

International dateline

Greenwich Meridian

► The world is divided into 24 time zones, starting at the prime meridian (0° longitude) at Greenwich, England. Each zone west of the meridian is an hour earlier than the last; each zone to the east is one hour later.

1 2 3 4 5 6 7 8 9 10 11 12 1 2 3 4 5 6 7 8 9 10 11 12
A.M.   P.M.

428

Timekeeping is needed in every aspect of our lives. However, extremely precise timekeeping is often needed in work and leisure activities. In this sports stadium, accurate time is displayed on an electronic timing board. The split-second timing of track and field events often determines the winner.

on the Greenwich meridian (0° longitude) was devised and soon became accepted across the world. Time zones to the east are progressively ahead of Greenwich, those to the west, increasingly behind. Tokyo, Japan is nine hours ahead of GMT, so when it is 2:00 A.M. in Greenwich, it is 11:00 A.M. in Tokyo. On the opposite side of the world from Greenwich, in the Pacific Ocean, is the international date line, where one day ends and the next begins.

PRECISION TIMEKEEPING

The precise measurement of time has always been important. In the 1700s, astronomers could determine precise time by their observations of the sun and stars. Navigators wanted to carry that time to sea in a clock so that they could calculate their longitude. The clockmaker John Harrison (1693–1776) developed the marine chronometer for this purpose. Precision timekeeping is still important to navigators, and it is used in many other activities.

The most accurate clocks are atomic clocks. In fact, they keep time more accurately than the spinning Earth. The time used by everyone today is based on the average rates of a number of atomic clocks around the world. The clocks work by counting the vibrations of light given off by atoms. The most recent, an atomic clock using cesium atoms, is accurate to within one second in 15 million years.

Mechanical clocks, such as this Italian monastery clock from the 1400s, sound the hours and indicate them on a dial.

Chronometers were developed in the 1700s for navigation at sea. They were set in motion by a slowly unwinding spring.

Wristwatches became a popular way of telling the time in the 1900s. They were originally powered by a small spring. More recent quartz watches tell the time by recording the vibrations of a quartz crystal. Many types are available for the astronaut, the deep-sea diver, the schoolchild, or the fashion conscious.

INTERNATIONAL TIME

Because the Earth is spinning, different places face the sun at different times of day. When it is midday in London, it is dawn in New York, and in Adelaide, in Australia, it is still night. If people were to read the time directly from the sun's position, clocks worldwide would be set to thousands of different times. Chaos would result; for example, it would be impossible to run trains to an accurate timetable.

In 1880, England adopted the time of the Royal Observatory at Greenwich as its standard time, known as Greenwich Mean Time (GMT). By 1884, GMT was adopted as the basis of standard time for the whole world. A system of 24 time zones centered

The most accurate clocks are cesium-beam atomic clocks. Here, a scientist uses an infrared detector to look at the laser beam of an atomic clock. Several lasers are used in the clock to measure an atom's vibration. This particular clock has an accuracy of one billionth of a second per day—one second in three million years.

SEE ALSO PAGES:

3 Earth's rotation, 400–1 Earth and the moon, 426–7 Time

SPACE, TIME, AND RELATIVITY

Space, time, and gravity are interlinked. Gravity affects everything in space. The gravity of a black hole is so strong it can even change the pace of time.

The famous scientist Albert Einstein (1879–1955) published his theory of General Relativity, concerning gravity, in 1915. His work led to such ideas as black holes and the Big Bang.

Today, as in the past, scientists seek to understand how the universe works. As we find out more, our ideas improve, or even replace, old ones. This happened in the early years of the 1900s. Isaac Newton's theory of gravity was improved and in part replaced, by a new theory. In 1915, the German-born, U.S. physicist Albert Einstein developed a theory that he called General Relativity which related space and gravity.

In Einstein's theory, the gravity of an object distorts space. This is difficult to imagine, but start by thinking of a rubber sheet. An object like a marble placed on the sheet will dent it. Now imagine the marble is a massive star and the rubber sheet is space. The star dents the space near it. Other similar massive objects will make a dent, or gravitational well, in space near them.

Astronomers tested this idea during a total solar eclipse in 1919. The light of the sun was eclipsed and the starlight from a much more distant star could be seen. The starlight traveled close to the sun on its way to the Earth and bent by a predicted amount as it passed the sun, thus proving that gravity bends space.

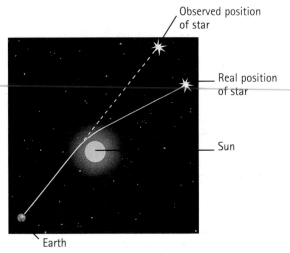

The gravity of the sun bends space near it. As the light from a distant star passes the sun on its way to the Earth, it, too, is bent. So astronomers on the Earth observe the star away from its true position (continuous line).

BLACK HOLES

An object such as a black hole makes more than a dent in the space around it. A black hole is what is left over from a massive star that has collapsed at the end of its life. The original star has been supercompressed and now has gravity so strong that it has formed a deep, steep-sided, gravitational well. Light cannot escape, so it is black. Because nothing at all can escape from the well, we think of it as a hole in space. A hole's gravity distorts not only space around it, but also time itself. The flow of time is so disturbed that it runs slower and slower the nearer it is to the hole.

A black hole is the remains of a giant star that has blown up. The core that is left after the explosion creates such a powerful gravitational field that any object passing close enough will be pulled into it.

TIMELINE OF SPACE EXPLORATION

A system of constellations helps people understand the night sky.

The first discoveries are made with the newly invented telescope.

It is proved ours is not the only galaxy—there are millions more in the universe.

Astronomers start to use radio, and later, X-ray and infrared telescopes.

The Space Age begins with the launch of *Sputnik*, the first satellite.

Soviet cosmonaut Yuri Gagarin becomes the first person in space on April 12, 1961.

| 2000 B.C. | A.D. 1609–10 | 1924 | 1930s–40s | 1957 | 1961 |

WORMHOLE THROUGH SPACE AND TIME

A wormhole is a theoretical tunnel that offers a shortcut to a distant place in space. This theory is based on our present understanding of space, time, and gravity. The wormhole has two mouths, one at each end of a tunnel. Entry and exit is possible at both ends. One end is at the starting-point of the journey, the other at the destination. Space can be curved, so a distant destination can be brought much closer. Traveling through a wormhole would be considerably quicker than taking the long route through space.

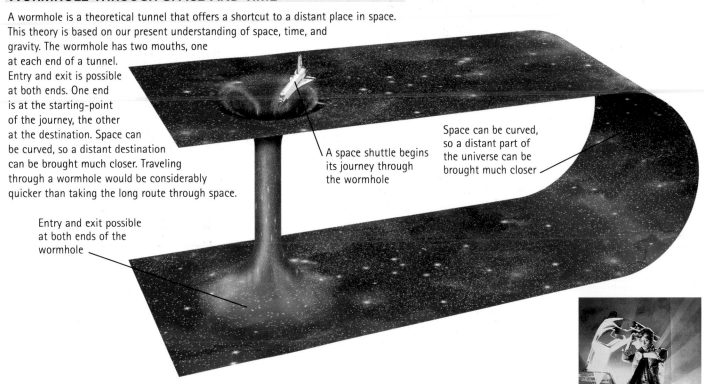

A space shuttle begins its journey through the wormhole

Space can be curved, so a distant part of the universe can be brought much closer

Entry and exit possible at both ends of the wormhole

TIME TRAVEL

All objects, including space, have three dimensions: length, height, and width. Scientists believe that objects also have a fourth dimension: time. Each day we move through the four dimensions, called space-time. We can move in all directions through space—up and down, side to side, back and forth. But we can only move forward through time.

Scientists once suggested that black holes could offer a way of traveling to very distant places quickly. Perhaps to another part of our universe, or even to a different universe. They now know this isn't possible. But a wormhole, a black hole that could be controlled, might offer the chance of superfast, time-beating travel. Anything traveling through a wormhole would move faster than the speed of light. Einstein's theory of relativity states that something traveling faster than light will move backward through time. But wormholes are only a theory, and they cannot be built. So time travel remains science fiction.

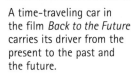

A time-traveling car in the film *Back to the Future* carries its driver from the present to the past and the future.

SEE ALSO PAGES:
284 The speed of light, 298–9 Relativity and gravity

Astronauts walk on the moon. For the first time exploring a world other than the Earth.

1969

Robotic spacecraft explore other planets. *Viking* landers look for life on Mars.

1976

The giant outer planets are investigated by the two *Voyager* space probes.

1980s

Telescopes in orbit around the Earth make many discoveries and look farther into space.

1980s–90s

The space shuttle carries parts to build the International Space Station.

1999

The world's largest and most powerful telescope, the Very Large Telescope, is built in Chile.

2000

FACTS AND FIGURES

SOLAR SYSTEM

Sun
Diameter at equator: 1,400,000 km
Spin period at equator: 27 days
Mass (Earth = 1): 330,000
Average surface temperature: 5,500°C

Mercury
Radius at equator (Earth = 1): 0.38
Distance from sun (Earth = 1): 0.39
Spin period: 58.7 days
Orbit period: 87.9 days (0.24 years)
Mass (Earth = 1): 0.06
Surface temperature: –180°C to 430°C
Moons: 0
Surface gravity (Earth = 1): 0.38

Venus
Radius at equator (Earth = 1): 0.95
Distance from sun (Earth = 1): 0.72
Spin period: 243 days
Orbit period: 224.7 days (0.62 years)
Mass (Earth = 1): 0.82
Average surface temperature: 460°C
Moons: 0
Surface gravity (Earth = 1): 0.90

Earth
Radius at equator: 6,378 km
Mean distance from sun: 149,600,000 km
Spin period: 23.93 hours
Orbit period: 365.26 days
Mass (Earth = 1): 1
Average surface temperature: 15°C
Moons: 1
Surface gravity: 9.8 ms^{-2}

Mars
Radius at equator (Earth = 1): 0.53
Distance from sun (Earth = 1): 1.52
Spin period: 24.6 hours
Orbit period: 686.9 days (1.88 years)
Mass (Earth = 1): 0.11
Surface temperature: –87°C to 17°C
Moons: 2
Surface gravity (Earth = 1): 0.38

Jupiter
Radius at equator (Earth = 1): 11.2
Distance from sun (Earth = 1): 5.2
Spin period: 9.9 hours
Orbit period: 11.9 years
Mass (Earth = 1): 318
Cloud-top temperature: –125°C
Moons: 16
Gravity at cloud tops (Earth = 1): 2.34

Saturn
Radius at equator (Earth = 1): 9.42
Distance from sun (Earth = 1): 9.54
Spin period: 10.6 hours
Orbit period: 29.5 years
Mass (Earth = 1): 95
Average cloud-top temperature: –140°C
Moons: at least 18
Gravity at cloud tops (Earth = 1): 0.93

Uranus
Radius at equator (Earth = 1): 4.01
Distance from sun (Earth = 1): 19.2
Spin period: 17.2 hours
Orbit period: 84.0 years
Mass (Earth = 1): 14.5
Average cloud-top temperature: –200°C
Moons: at least 18
Gravity at cloud tops (Earth = 1): 0.90

Neptune
Radius at equator (Earth = 1): 3.88
Distance from sun (Earth = 1): 30.1
Spin period: 16.1 days
Orbit period: 164.8 years
Mass (Earth = 1): 17.2
Average cloud-top temperature: –200°C
Moons: 8
Gravity at cloud tops (Earth = 1): 1.13

Pluto
Radius (Earth = 1): about 0.18
Distance from sun (Earth = 1): 29.4
Spin period: 6.4 days
Orbit period: 247.7 years
Mass (Earth = 1): around 0.002
Average surface temperature: –220°C
Moons: 1
Surface gravity (Earth = 1): around 0.07

THE EARTH'S MOON

Radius at equator: 1,738 km
Average distance from Earth: 384,400 km
Spin period: 27.3 days
Orbit period: 27.3 days
Mass (Earth = 1): 0.012
Surface temperature: –173°C to 127°C
Surface gravity (Earth = 1): 0.17
New moon to new moon: 29.5 days

On July 20, 1969, U.S. astronauts Neil Armstrong and Edwin Aldrin became the first humans to walk on the moon.

LARGEST MOONS

Moon	Planet	Radius (km)
Ganymede	Jupiter	2,630
Titan	Saturn	2,575
Callisto	Jupiter	2,400
Io	Jupiter	1,815
Moon	Earth	1,738
Europa	Jupiter	1,570

YEARLY METEOR SHOWERS

Quadrantids	January 1–6
Lyrids	April 19–25
Eta Aquarids	April 24–May 20
Delta Aquarids	July 15–August 20
Perseids	July 23–August 20
Orionids	October 16–27
Taurids	Oct. 20–November 30
Leonids	November 15–20
Geminids	December 7–16

STARS AND GALAXIES

The ten brightest stars:
Sirius—Dog Star
Canopus
Alpha Centauri
Arcturus
Vega
Capella
Rigel
Procyon
Achernar
Betelgeuse

CONSTELLATIONS OF THE ZODIAC

Aries—the ram
Taurus—the bull
Gemini—the twins
Cancer—the crab
Leo—the lion
Virgo—the virgin
Libra—the scales
Scorpius—the scorpion
Sagittarius—the archer
Capricornus—the goat
Aquarius—the water carrier
Pisces—the fishes

MILKY WAY

Diameter: 100,000 light years
Disk thickness: 2,000 light years
Center thickness: 6,000 light years
Mass: 1 trillion solar masses

LOCAL GROUP: THE TEN NEAREST GALAXIES

Galaxy	Type
Milky Way	Spiral
Sagittarius	Elliptical
Large Magellanic Cloud	Irregular
Small Magellanic Cloud	Irregular
Ursa Minor	Elliptical
Draco	Elliptical
Sculptor	Elliptical
Carina	Elliptical
Sextans	Elliptical
Fornax	Elliptical

TECHNOLOGY

Most powerful telescopes on the Earth
Very Large Telescope, 4 x 8 m, Chile
Large Binocular Telescope, 2 x 8.4 m, Arizona
Hobby–Eberly, 11 m, Texas
Keck I, 10 m, Hawaii
Keck II, 10 m, Hawaii

Key space telescopes

Name	Frequency	Launch date
Oao	UV	1962
Explorer 42	X-ray	1970
Hubble	Visible–UV	1990

CHAPTER 10
CONSERVATION AND THE ENVIRONMENT

Conservation means "keeping safe." Conservation of the environment means not only looking after natural wild places and wildlife, but also maintaining historical treasures, such as buildings and objects from the past.

Natural resources include all the things that help to maintain life, including sunlight, water, air, soil, oil, minerals, plants, and animals. There are more than six billion people on the Earth today, and they all need land to live on, food to eat, and fuel for power. The challenge for human beings is to find a balance between what is needed and how to care for the environment.

Global awareness is a new phenomenon. Some conservation issues are local, such as when local woodland is threatened with clearing to make way for a new road. Other issues are important to people everywhere. These include recycling, saving energy, avoiding pollution, and feeding the hungry.

New schemes are being developed to encourage conservation. For example, the "debt for nature" idea means that a poor country has some of its international debt canceled in exchange for setting aside areas for conservation. If local people see that looking after plants and animals helps them live better lives, there is a much better chance for conservation to work.

THE NATURAL BALANCE

From the tiniest bacterium to the largest mammal, all living things share the planet. These organisms form communities that live together in a balanced state.

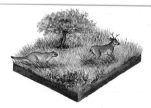

The Kaibab example shows how humans can destroy the natural balance. Pumas and coyotes kept the deer population stable.

When humans shot the pumas and coyotes, the deer population exploded. The result was too many deer and too little food. Many animals starved.

A community of organisms that lives in a particular area, along with the soil and other nonliving material, forms what scientists call an ecosytem. Ecosystems can be as small as a water-filled hole in a forest tree, or as large as the forest itself. In a perfect ecosystem, all the components are balanced. For example, plants provide food and oxygen needed by animals, and their waste products are recycled in the soil to be used by new plants as they grow.

ECOLOGY

Ecology is the study of animals and plants in their natural environment. Ecologists try to find out why animals and plants live in some places but not in others. They also study the conditions needed for survival.

Most organisms are well-adapted to the place where they live—their habitat—and to their relationships with other plants and animals. But, outside interference may affect this. Many of the world's natural ecosytems have taken thousands of years to reach a balanced state. If the climate does not change suddenly, an ecosystem can stay balanced for thousands of years to come. But humans often upset these balanced environments.

THE KAIBAB EXAMPLE

An example of how humans can disrupt a balanced environment comes from the Kaibab Plateau, located mostly in northern

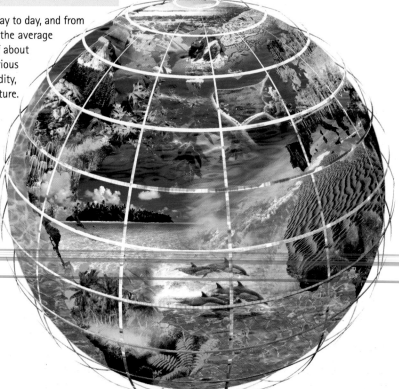

THE CLIMATE

▼ Climate shapes our planet and determines the landscape, vegetation, and wildlife of each region. This map shows the Earth's main climate zones.

The weather in a region varies from day to day, and from season to season. Climate describes the average weather of a region over a period of about 50 years. Climate is the result of various factors, including air pressure, humidity, precipitation, sunshine, and temperature.

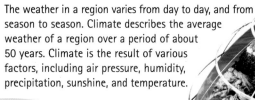

The world's nine main climate zones are: Polar (mauve), Subpolar (light blue), Temperate (light green), Subtropical (orange), Desert (yellow), Tropical (dark green), Equatorial (dark blue), Subpolar (pink), and Mediterranean (red).

Sparrowhawk preys
on birds

Sunlight

Birds eat caterpillars

Caterpillars feed
on leaves

Fungi help to decompose
leaf litter

Falling leaves decompose
(break down) and the
nutrients pass into soil

Root tip and
root hairs take
nutrients from
the soil

Bacteria
break down
nutrients

Elephants drink alongside
springbok antelope and
zebra at a waterhole in
Etosha National Park,
Namibia, southern Africa.

This diagram shows
the natural balance in a
temperate woodland. The
sun is the primary source
of energy. This energy is
passed from the tree (the
producer) to other living
things (the consumers)
that depend on it.

Arizona. The deer population was kept
in check by coyotes and pumas. When
people hunted these predators, the natural
balance was upset. With fewer predators
to control their numbers, there were soon
too many deer for the available food. As a
result, many deer and other animals were
forced to compete for the same food
sources and died of starvation.

FOOD CHAINS

Ecologists study what animals, plants,
and other organisms eat in order to
learn about how they are linked together
in food chains. In a food chain, there are
usually several levels. At the first level
are the producers—green plants. They use
energy from the sun to make new growth.
Plants are eaten by consumers—animals
called herbivores (plant-eaters). These
consumers are in turn eaten by animals
called carnivores (meat-eaters).

Each member in the food chain feeds
on, and obtains energy from, the previous
level. In this way, energy is transferred
from level to level. When living things
die, their bodies break down and release
nutrients into the ground, and the
process begins all over again.

LIVING TOGETHER

Species play different roles in their
habitats. Herds of grazing animals on the
African grasslands all appear to be eating
the same food—grass and leaves. In fact,
each species feeds on different plants or
different parts of a particular plant. For
example, the giraffe's long neck allows
it to feed on leaves out of reach of other
animals. Each species has its own place,
or niche, in nature. All can live together,
as long as there is no outside interference.

HUMAN INTERFERENCE

Human interference is a serious problem
in today's world. At Etosha National Park
in Namibia, for example, people began
digging gravel to build roads. Gravel pits
filled with stagnant water, in which deadly
anthrax germs thrived. Wildebeests and
zebras drank the infected water, became
ill, and were easy prey for lions. The lion
population grew, but their prey died out.
So the lions began hunting eland antelope,
which were resistant to anthrax, until the
lions again faced starvation. Nature keeps
a balance between predator and prey.
Unless people learn lessons from nature,
the balance will continue to be disrupted.

Destruction of the rain
forest in Costa Rica means
that a once rich and varied
natural ecosystem has
been replaced by a human-
designed monoculture of
nothing but cattle.

SEE ALSO PAGES:

442 Why species die out,
444 Endangered species,
462 Conservation action

ACTION ZONES

Each of the world's landscapes offers living space for a variety of plants and animals. Each habitat is an action zone where change can bring damage or destruction.

In Mali, in Western Africa, on the fringe of the Sahara Desert, plants cannot survive overgrazing by flocks of domestic animals, such as goats. As plants and their roots are nibbled away, the sand dunes take over.

Climate, soil, and living things create habitats. A habitat is the home of a particular species of plant or animal, providing the plant or animal with food, shelter, and the conditions that allow them to survive. Each habitat is a complex, well-balanced system. The plants and animals within the habitat are suited to, and dependent on, their environment and on one another.

BIOMES AND MICROHABITATS

The various types of habitats classified by scientists include woodland, forest, desert, mountainside, pond, river, marsh, and ocean. A specific area of grassland, such as the pampas of Argentina, is a habitat. A large general habitat, such as a grassland or rain forest, is called a biome. Each biome contains thousands of small and specialized living spaces—just as a huge building contains many rooms. These spaces can be as small as a pool of water or a patch of grass. They are known as microhabitats, and they support their own community of plants and animals.

The largest of all the Earth's biomes are the oceans. Oceans cover an amazing 71 percent of the planet's surface. The oceanic biome is arranged in layers, according to how warm or salty the water is, and how far down the sunlight reaches. There are wide variations in temperature, from the warm seas of the tropical Indian Ocean to the icy waters of Antarctica. Within the oceans are also special habitats. They include coral reefs, sandy shores, and river mouths or estuaries.

A CAREFUL BALANCE

Human activity can interfere with the mechanisms of the world's biomes. Conservationists were alarmed when, in 1974, oil companies began building a pipeline in Alaska, south from Prudhoe Bay to Valdez. It was feared that the

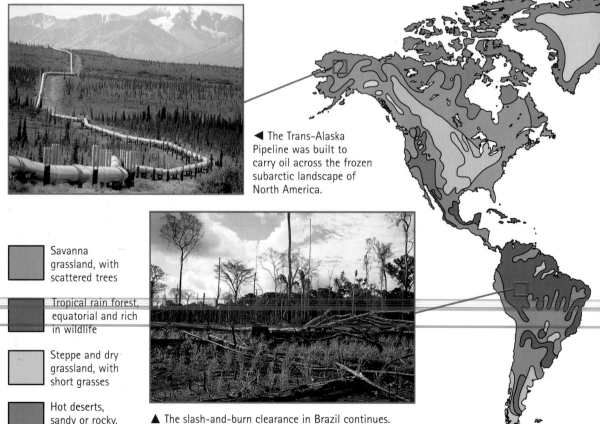

▼▶ This map shows the world's main conservation action zones. The colors on the map show the main type of vegetation found in each region.

◀ The Trans-Alaska Pipeline was built to carry oil across the frozen subarctic landscape of North America.

KEY TO MAP

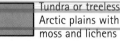 Cold desert, with low temperatures and little rain

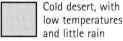 Tundra or treeless Arctic plains with moss and lichens

Temperate woodland with deciduous trees

 Coniferous forest of cool northern regions

Savanna grassland, with scattered trees

Tropical rain forest, equatorial and rich in wildlife

Steppe and dry grassland, with short grasses

Hot deserts, sandy or rocky, with little rain

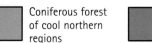

▲ The slash-and-burn clearance in Brazil continues. When a rain forest dies, a rich habitat is lost forever.

436

pipeline crossing the tundra might damage the permafrost (soil that is frozen all year round) and interfere with the annual migration of caribou herds. Fortunately, the damage was less than was at first feared. But in South America, damage to the Amazon rain forest from highway construction, logging, and ranching has been far more serious. Vast areas of forest have disappeared in the past 20 years.

In northern Africa, people keep flocks of sheep and goats—far more than the scant vegetation can support. The hungry animals nibble the shoots and roots of the plants, killing the plants. Along the southern fringe of the Sahara Desert, precious grass, shrubs, and trees have been lost in this way. Without the protection of the plants, whose roots help bind the thin soil, the land quickly becomes desert. In places, the Sahara is advancing by more than 25 miles (40km) a year.

CLIMATE CHANGE

Each of the world's habitats depend on climate. A change in climate can bring a disastrous change in a habitat and affect

animals, plants, and people. Weather records going back to the 1600s show that the world is gradually getting warmer. The 1990s broke records for high temperatures worldwide, with four of the ten hottest years ever recorded.

In the future, climate change may cause polar icecaps to melt, releasing huge amounts of water into the oceans. Sea levels will rise, and floods could become more frequent in low-lying countries.

Volunteers dig ponds to restore lost habitats for plants and wildlife. Many old ponds have been drained and filled in. Creating new ponds helps frogs, newts, and other creatures to survive, even in urban environments.

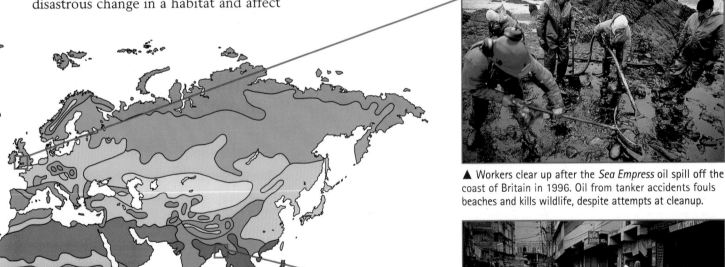

▲ Workers clear up after the *Sea Empress* oil spill off the coast of Britain in 1996. Oil from tanker accidents fouls beaches and kills wildlife, despite attempts at cleanup.

▲ Climate change can bring disaster to whole communities. Flooding in Bangladesh is just one example of many.

SEE ALSO PAGES:

36–7 Climate, 460–1
Climate change, 462–3
Conservation action

SAVING THE RAIN FORESTS

Rain forests are the world's richest biomes. These forests grow mainly near the equator. Rich in wildlife, they are under threat from humans.

Rain forests contain more species of plants and animals than any other habitat on the Earth. The largest rain forests are the tropical forests of South America, Africa, and Southeast Asia. The tropical climate is always warm and wet, with no winter, and plants grow all year long. The result is a thick growth of trees, ferns, vines, and other plants. These, in turn, support an extraordinarily rich variety of animal life, particularly insects and birds.

Emergent tree

Leafy canopy

MULTISTORY FOREST

Plants grow rapidly in a rain forest, and to reach the sunlight, trees grow very tall. The rain forest has three distinct layers: the forest floor, the understory, and the canopy. Most of the trees have shallow roots, and get their nutrients from the upper layers of soil. Many

Closely grouped tree trunks of understory

Lianas twine around the tree trunks

This red-breasted toucan lives in Itataia National Park, in Brazil. In much of the Amazon forest, wildlife is threatened by loss of habitat.

Rafflesia on the forest floor

Forest monkeys like the bearded saki of South America live in the treetops. If their forest is cleared by people, these animals have only a slim chance of survival. Forest animals need large areas where they can live undisturbed.

support themselves with roots that grow outward, acting like props or buttresses. Smaller trees, seedlings, and shrubs form the lower layers nearer to the ground.

The main canopy is usually between 100 and 164 feet above ground, where the slender trunks break into a cluster of branches. The tallest trees reach even higher—around 197 feet.

The canopy shades the understory from sunlight, and here it is much darker. The understory consists of tree trunks that are covered with lianas (climbing plants) and laced together by creepers. The forest floor is surprisingly free of clutter. Leaves, fruit, animal droppings, and the bodies of dead forest animals decompose quickly when they fall to the ground. Their remains are absorbed as nutrients by plant roots and are used to make new growth.

A RICH HABITAT

Although they cover only six percent of the Earth's surface, tropical rain forests contain about three fourths of all known species of animals and plants. There are

Rain-forest trees have massive trunks to support them. Only the tallest trees emerge through the canopy formed by the leafy branches. Most of the animals and many plants live in the trees.

DEFORESTATION

As rain forests are cleared to provide timber, the soil becomes exposed. Some of the forest land is quickly replanted with crops, but the soil usually supports only a few harvests before farmers have to move to a new area. Land is also used for farming and cattle ranching. Clearing plants from high ground may cause flooding. Soil is washed into rivers, causing them to silt up. Without tree roots to bind the soil, topsoil is eroded and washed away. In the hot sun of the dry season, exposed soils bake hard and crack, making them useless for wildlife or agriculture.

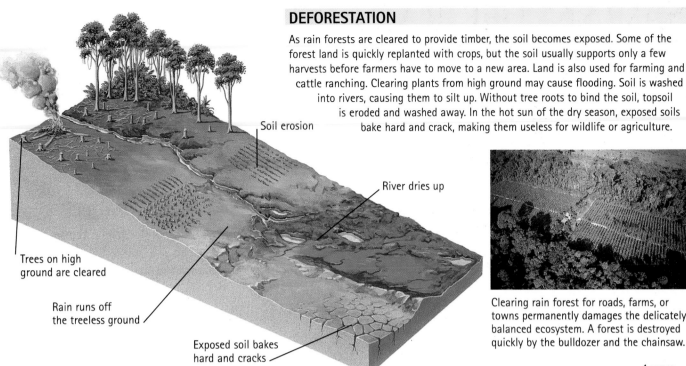

Soil erosion

River dries up

Trees on high ground are cleared

Rain runs off the treeless ground

Exposed soil bakes hard and cracks

Clearing rain forest for roads, farms, or towns permanently damages the delicately balanced ecosystem. A forest is destroyed quickly by the bulldozer and the chainsaw.

plants in flower or producing fruit everywhere and at every time of the year. These provide a constant food supply for birds, bats, insects, snakes, tree frogs, antelopes, monkeys, and other animals.

TEMPERATE RAIN FORESTS
Temperate rain forests are found in coastal regions where onshore winds carry constant rain. These are chiefly in northwestern North America, southern Chile, Tasmania, and New Zealand. Typical trees in these forests are redwoods and sitka spruce in the Northern Hemisphere, and eucalyptus and Antarctic beech in the Southern Hemisphere. Plant and animal life is less abundant than that in tropical rain forests.

THREATS TO RAIN FORESTS
The trees of the rain forests are prized as timber, and large areas of rain forest in the Amazon (South America), Malaysia and Indonesia (Southeast Asia), and the Congo (Africa) have been destroyed by logging. Forests have also been cleared to make way for plantations of rubber, coffee, bananas, and sugarcane, or to provide pasture for cattle. Often this is done by cutting trees and burning scrub—this is the slash-and-burn method. Highways have been cut through the forest, mines dug, and new settlements built.

When trees are cleared from a hillside, the soil may be left exposed and is quickly washed away by heavy rain. Once-rich forest becomes lifeless wasteland.

RESCUING FORESTS
We need the rain forests. They act as the Earth's lungs, giving off oxygen into the atmosphere. They also contain many plants that are used in medicine. There are many species of plants and animals still waiting to be discovered. Others may have already become extinct, unnamed and unknown. International conservation organizations are trying to persuade governments to work together to protect the remaining rain forests.

Forests need managing. This researcher holds seedlings raised in a nursery. They will grow into new forest trees in a reforestation scheme in Sabah, in Borneo.

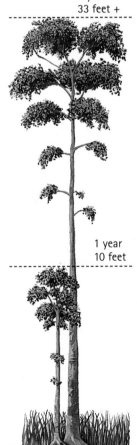

4 years
33 feet +

1 year
10 feet

Fast-growing trees planted for timber may grow to 82 feet in a few years.

SEE ALSO PAGES:

OCEAN LIFE

Oceans cover nearly three fourths of the surface of the Earth. They are home to countless living things, ranging in size from the microscopic to the gigantic.

The four oceans of the world are the Arctic (the smallest), the Indian, the Atlantic, and the Pacific. The Pacific is roughly as large as the other three oceans put together. It is also much deeper than any other ocean. These four oceans hold 97 percent of all the water on the planet. The oceans lose water constantly because water vapor is drawn into the air by the sun's heat. But most of this water returns as rain. Rainwater running off the land carries salts and other minerals into the oceans.

A catch is landed on the deck of a fishing boat. Fishing fleets competing for dwindling fish stocks are often forced to sail far from home waters to exploit the fish populations of other areas.

OCEAN ZONES

The ocean has two main zones, the ocean basin (the deepest part) and the shallow continental shelf at the edge of land. Along the coast, the seashore forms a constantly changing margin between sea and land. There are different types of shoreline. Where coastal rocks are soft, features such as cliffs change quickly. Hard rocks wear away more slowly.

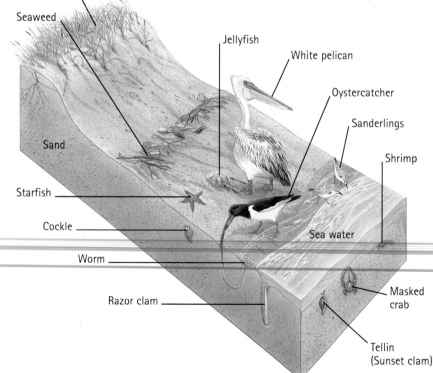

Dune grasses
Seaweed
Jellyfish
White pelican
Oystercatcher
Sanderlings
Sand
Shrimp
Starfish
Cockle
Sea water
Worm
Razor clam
Masked crab
Tellin (Sunset clam)

On this island beach in Okinawa, Japan, the incoming tide has left a rim of trash, much of it plastic. The sea cannot get rid of such material naturally, because plastic will not rot away, or biodegrade.

Even the everyday action of a relatively calm sea will erode the shoreline.

FISHING

Humans have made use of the oceans for thousands of years, as a means of transportation, as a dumping ground for waste, and as a source of food. Fishing is an ancient human activity, but until the 1800s, people did not catch enough fish to threaten fish stocks. This situation changed with the introduction of modern fishing vessels, larger nets, and devices, such as radar, for tracking schools of fish.

Of the almoset 20,000 fish species, only about 30 are caught in large amounts as food. Today valuable fish, such as cod and haddock, are becoming rare in areas where they once numbered millions. The reason is that modern fishing methods are overly efficient, and nets often trap immature fish that have not been able to breed yet. Commercial fishing catches have quadrupled since 1950. Quotas (methods of rationing numbers caught) and fishing limits are supposed to protect fish stocks from being wiped out, but they are often ignored. Many countries now have a 200 miles (320km) limit around their coasts to try to conserve their fish stock.

Many species of birds, mollusks, crustaceans, and plants live on the seashore. A sandy shore constantly changes shape as waves break on it, moving up and down the sand with the tides. The wildlife must be adaptable, able to live and search for food both in and out of the water.

Coral reefs are found in tropical seas. The largest is Australia's Great Barrier Reef, at over 1,250 mi. (2,000km) long. Teeming with wildlife, coral reefs are threatened by the demand for coral, and by the introduction of new species, which can upset the delicate natural balance.

Trade in coral has become a serious threat to the future of coral reefs. Tourist demand for coral is high, and this encourages coral dealers to raid the reefs. In some cases they destroy living reefs with explosives.

POLLUTION

The oceans have become a dumping ground for all kinds of waste. Every year over three million tons of oil is spilled into the sea. Much of this is washed out of the tanks of oil tankers before they reload. About half of the pollution of the oceans is caused by waste dumping—domestic waste being pumped into the sea. Other waste is thrown overboard from ships.

A walk along a beach at low tide will reveal trash washed up by the sea. Plastic bottles and discarded nylon fishnets cause special problems, because they will not decay naturally and remain a lasting danger to wildlife. Chemicals are often toxic to people, as well as to fish.

WHALING

Although whaling in Europe began over 1,300 years ago, it was the huge demand for whale oil and other products that encouraged hunters in the 1800s to seek out new kinds of whales. In the 1900s, fast whaling ships and explosive harpoons made killing more efficient. Whalers hunted the largest whales—the blue, sei, and fin. More than 1.5 million whales were killed between 1925 and 1975, and the giant whales came close to extinction. Whaling bans may save them, but only if all the whaling nations cooperate.

CORAL REEFS

The coral reefs are probably the Earth's oldest living communities. Most living reefs are between 5,000 and 10,000 years old, but they rest on dead reefs, which are millions of years old. The reefs are as rich in wildlife species as the rain forests. A single reef may contain 3,000 species of coral, mollusk, crustacean, and fish. The delicate balance of the reefs is damaged by pollution of the water, removal of coral for sale as souvenirs, and overhunting by spearfishers. The largest reef, Australia's Great Barrier Reef, is a protected national park, but reefs in other areas of the world are at risk.

Drift nets used by fishing boats may be 60 mi. (100km) long. These nets have been called floating walls of death because they trap not only fish, but also many hundreds of seabirds, sharks, turtles, and sea mammals, such as dolphins. Discarded nets left in the water remain floating death traps.

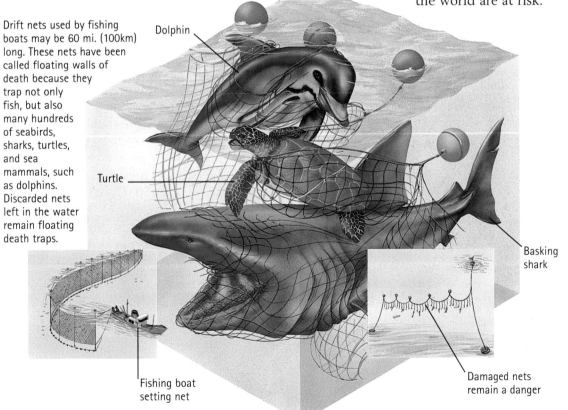

Dolphin

Turtle

Fishing boat setting net

Basking shark

Damaged nets remain a danger

Whaling has become a subject of international controversy. It continues despite protest action by the environmental organization Greenpeace. Norway and Japan are two of the countries that want to continue whaling. Whale meat is prized in both countries.

SEE ALSO PAGES:
444–5 Endangered species, 452 Water pollution, 462 Conservation action

WHY SPECIES DIE OUT

Animal species usually become extinct because they are unable to adapt to changing conditions. The rate of extinctions worldwide has accelerated since the 1600s.

The silversword plant of Hawaii is at risk from hungry sheep and goats, as well as from introduced insects, which compete with the local insects that pollinate the silversword plants.

There are two problems for wildlife today. The first is a lack of living space. The second is interference from humans. People compete with wild animals for space, and usually people win.

NATURAL EXTINCTIONS
Sometimes there are natural reasons for extinction. These include sudden changes in climate, dwindling food supplies, or competition from other species with similar ways of life. Any of these factors, or a combination of them, can lead to extinction. Scientists have found evidence of mass extinctions in the past. The most famous of these is the disappearance of the dinosaurs and giant sea reptiles 65 million years ago.

HUNTING TO EXTINCTION
The appearance of the first human beings about two million years ago introduced a new and powerful predator. Even the prehistoric hunters of the Stone Age wiped out animals in large numbers. They drove herds of bison and wild horses over cliffs, for example. But they usually hunted to meet only their basic needs and seldom killed more animals than they could eat. The arrival of humans on islands could be devastating—

the giant moa birds of New Zealand were hunted to extinction by the Maoris.

HUMANS AND ANIMALS
As humans became more numerous, they domesticated some animals and pursued others. They hunted some animals for food, for their skins, or for sport— European kings set aside forests as hunting parks in which to hunt deer and wild boar for the table. From the 1800s, guns, traps, and poisons took a heavier toll on wildlife, and animals were killed in ever greater numbers. As more land was taken over for farming or ranching, wild animals regarded as harmful or dangerous were exterminated as pests. Farmers waged war against any creature that they feared

Diatryma

Smilodon

Birds and mammals took over the dinosaurs' role as hunters on land. Diatryma was a formidable and large, flightless bird. Its remains have been found in New Mexico and Wyoming. Smilodon was a saber-toothed cat, about the same size as a lion. It roamed what is now the Western Hemisphere. Both animals died out, to be replaced by more efficient predators.

Dodo

Great auk

The dodo and great auk both fell victim to human hunters. The dodo was an island bird, and island species are vulnerable to any new arrivals. The great auk was a victim of fashion. Its feathers were used in bedding, replacing those of the eider duck, which itself had almost been wiped out. The eider survived. The auk did not.

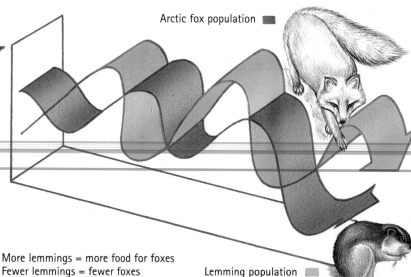

Arctic fox population

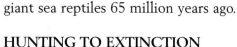

More lemmings = more food for foxes
Fewer lemmings = fewer foxes

Lemming population

Animal populations rise and fall in a natural cycle. As the population of a preyed-on species, such as lemmings, rises and falls, the numbers of their predators, such as foxes, may also increase and decrease, lagging slightly behind the prey. When food is plentiful, lemming numbers boom. More lemmings mean more food for arctic foxes. Too many lemmings mean they starve, and have to migrate to find new food.

DISTRIBUTION OF WOLVES

Wolves have survived centuries of persecution by people. These intelligent and adaptable predators were once widespread, but today their distribution is greatly reduced. Hunting and poisoning have driven several subspecies of wolves to extinction. There are now only small numbers of wild wolves in North America and even fewer in Europe.

Worldwide distribution of wolves

Past distribution of wolves
Present distribution of wolves

would prey on domesticated animals, and they shot, poisoned, or trapped eagles, hawks, wildcats, foxes, and wolves.

EXTINCT BIRDS

The dodo was a large, flightless bird of the island of Mauritius, in the Indian Ocean. Sailors who landed there in the 1500s found that the clumsy dodos were easy to catch for food. The ships brought cats and rats to the island, and these animals ate the dodo chicks and eggs. By 1860, all that remained were drawings, bones, and one stuffed specimen.

The same fate overtook the great auk, a flightless bird, which was the penguin of the northern seas. Auks had few enemies until people started killing them, first for food and oil, then for their feathers. Like many seabirds, the great auk nested in large colonies. Ships visited each nesting site in turn, and killed all the birds. By 1844, there were two birds and one egg left. Two Icelandic fishermen killed this last pair, and smashed their egg.

THE FATE OF THE WOLF

Farmers blame wolves for killing sheep and cattle. In Europe, there are now only scattered populations of wolves in Spain, the Balkans, and Italy. Gray wolves were once abundant in North America, but they were shot and poisoned so ruthlessly that by the 1880s there were none left on the Great Plains. Hunters used bait poisoned with strychnine, but the poison had a much wider effect. It killed any animal that ate the bait—coyotes, foxes, bears, wildcats, eagles, and crows. It also got into the water supply and tainted the grass, killing horses, bison, and antelope.

SAVE THE TIGER

There were once eight subspecies of tiger. The Bali, Caspian, and Javan tigers became extinct between the 1940s and 1980s. The Siberian, Sumatran, Indochinese, and South China tigers are all very rare, and today there are only about 5,000 Bengal tigers left in India.

The giant panda is at risk because of its specialized diet of bamboo shoots. If the bamboo dies, so do the pandas. Found in the wild only in China, giant pandas are among the most endangered species.

A Chinese pharmacy displays tiger bones and seahorses that are being sold as medicines, alongside plant-based remedies. Demand for traditional animal cures adds to the pressure on already endangered species.

Tigers, including this captive albino, breed very successfully in captivity. Their survival in the wild, however, is uncertain. They need large areas of wilderness in which to hunt, and their habitat is under threat. Even in game reserves, they are not safe from poachers who kill them for their skins, and for use in traditional Asian medicines.

SEE ALSO PAGES:

ENDANGERED SPECIES

Many species are in danger, either because of hunting or because their habitat is threatened. Plants and animals introduced by humans can also be a threat.

Habitat destruction is the major reason that an animal becomes endangered. Forest animals of the tropics are increasingly under threat from the chainsaws and the bulldozers used by people who are destroying the forest for farmland or timber. Animals such as great apes and monkeys, and carnivores such as the jaguar and tiger, cannot survive unless they have large areas in which to live and find food.

THE SKIN TRADE
Fashion and vanity have also contributed to the decline of many animal species. Birds such as the egret have been hunted for their feathers. Snakes and alligators have been killed for their skins, which are used to make bags and shoes. The spotted furs of cats such as the leopard and ocelot are still used to make coats, although the fur trade declined in the face of growing criticism from people who are opposed to what they see as the exploitation of defenseless animals.

COLLECTORS AND PETS
During the 1800s, collectors took large numbers of insects, such as butterflies, and birds' eggs for display in their homes. Big game hunters shot animals for trophies. Such activities are frowned on today, but people still raid the nests of rare birds for eggs to sell and buy exotic animals like parrots and tortoises. The pet trade takes thousands of animals from the wild, many of which die before they reach their intended owners.

WILDLIFE TRADE
Although millions of wild animals are trapped or killed each year for their skins, other body parts are also in demand. Rhinoceroses are shot by poachers so that their horns can be made into dagger handles, much prized in the Middle East. In spite of international agreements to protect the elephants and control the trade, elephants are hunted for their tusks and ivory ornaments are sold to tourists.

POLLUTION
Pollution is a threat to all animals, because like people, animals need clean water and clean food. River and lake animals, in particular, are very sensitive to changes in their environment. In the past 50 years, farm pesticides, fertilizers, and chemical waste have been washed into rivers. This has led to a fall in the numbers of many animals, such as the European otter, and also of some fish and invertebrates.

Birds of prey, such as the peregrine falcon, were badly hit in the 1950s by the use of chemical insecticides such as DDT. The poisons from the chemicals got into the food chain, and affected reproduction. Very few chicks hatched out of their eggs.

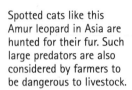

Spotted cats like this Amur leopard in Asia are hunted for their fur. Such large predators are also considered by farmers to be dangerous to livestock.

Red kites are useful scavengers. These birds of prey were once common, but were persecuted by farmers and gamekeepers. Today, their numbers are recovering.

The corncrake is a very rare grassland bird. It once thrived in wheat fields, but could not survive the introduction of combine harvesters and early harvests.

PLANTS IN DANGER

About ten percent of all plant species in the world are listed as endangered. Plants are a rich genetic resource. But wild plants are being allowed to die out, even though there are many ignored or unknown plants which could be important in the future for food or medicine. Both farmers and breeders are concentrating on growing fewer and fewer main species. Reserves and gene banks have been set aside to protect the wild relatives of crop species—for example, there are 12,000 types of wheat and corn. Some fear that genetically-engineered varieties of plants will cross-pollinate with organic crops.

◀ The lady's slipper orchid is admired for its beauty. Many such rare ornamental plants are raised by growers, but although they are protected, some are still taken from the wild.

In Africa, black and white rhinoceroses are endangered because they have been hunted for their horns. Asian rhinos are also rare, due to loss of their forest habitat.

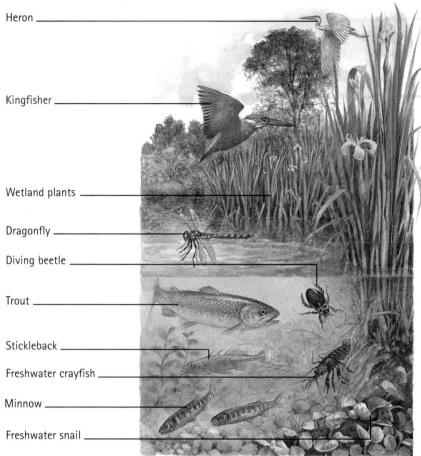

Heron

Kingfisher

Wetland plants

Dragonfly

Diving beetle

Trout

Stickleback

Freshwater crayfish

Minnow

Freshwater snail

During the 1800s, many birds of prey, such as hawks and eagles, were shot by farmers and gamekeepers to protect their chickens and pheasants. Now many birds of prey are protected, but they still face an uncertain future.

INTRODUCED SPECIES
The introduction of species into a new environment can have unexpected and destructive effects. In Australia, prickly pear cactus brought in from South America soon choked grazing lands. The rabbit, taken to Australia in the 1800s, quickly became a serious pest, as has the cane, or giant, toad. It was introduced from Central and South America in the 1930s to control beetles that were eating sugarcane. But they also ate native frogs,

These redheaded lovebirds are waiting to be sold to tourists in Sao Tomé, West Africa. Wild birds taken for the pet trade do not survive the shock of captivity for long.

lizards, birds, and other creatures. The cane toad is now a pest in its own right.

ZOOS
For many people, seeing a lion in a game reserve or a bear at the zoo is the closest they get to seeing an animal in the wild. Zoos have a role to play in conservation, through education and through breeding schemes to save rare species. Some animals have become so rare in the wild—down to less than 20 individuals—that captive breeding is often the only chance of saving the species from extinction.

NATIONAL PARKS
Parks and game reserves offer sanctuary for wild animals. Nature reserves were first set up on a large scale in the late 1800s, the first was Yellowstone National Park, in Wyoming. With protection, rare animals can increase in number. Arabian oryx in Arizona, for example, breed well. Once their numbers increase, some captive-bred animals can be returned to their native habitats to live free of human interference.

Rivers and lakes are affected both by pollution and recreational uses, like water-sports. So, too, are the carefully balanced wildlife communities that depend on clean water.

Chemical and industrial pollution can kill entire populations of fish. Contaminated water may take years to recover.

SEE ALSO PAGES:
434–5 The natural balance, 442–3 Why species die out, 452 Water pollution, 462–3 Conservation action

POPULATION EXPLOSION

Until the 1600s, the population of the world grew slowly. It rose from 150 million in A.D. 100 to around 500 million in 1600. Then the rate accelerated.

The Earth's 6 billion people occupy about 15 percent of the land area. Much of the planet is too hot or too cold to support permanent populations.

By 1850, when the Industrial Revolution was in full swing in Europe and North America, the population of the world had more than doubled to over one billion. Today, there are more than five times as many people on the planet.

Immigrants, like this Italian family arriving in New York in the early 1900s, had to settle in a strange country, learn a new language, and find work. Most did so quickly. They became new Americans but also kept their old cultural traditions. Today, millions of modern migrants seek new lives in other countries.

IMMIGRATION

Immigration, or the movement of people from one country or continent to another, affects population growth greatly. In the 1800s, millions of people left Europe for the United States and Canada in search of a better life. Others settled in Australia and New Zealand. During the 1900s, millions of migrants from Asia, Africa, and Central America moved to the United States and Europe to find better education and health care.

CAUSES OF GROWTH

The explosive rise in human numbers over 150 years was not caused by people having more children. It was caused by the fact that people lived longer. Though birth rates stayed much the same, death rates fell. More children survived to become adults, because food supplies increased and public health improved.

In today's developed countries, birth and death rates are roughly equivalent. Population growth is therefore slow, or nonexistent. In some prosperous countries, such as Germany and Sweden, the population is actually falling.

In the countries of the developing world, death rates have fallen steadily since the 1950s, owing to improvements in medicine and child welfare. Agricultural output has risen rapidly, but in some parts of the world the population is increasing so quickly that food production cannot keep up. At current rates, Kenya, in Africa, doubles its population every 17 years.

Population growth in millions
A.D. 1–1750

700, 470, 420, 255, 200

A.D. 1, 1000, 1500, 1600, 1750

The population of the world rose slowly in the first millennium. During the second, it began to grow faster. Experts expect the rise to slow during the third millennium.

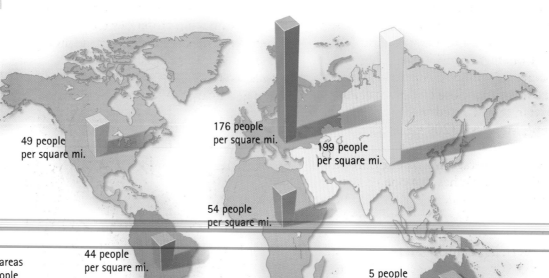

49 people per square mi.

176 people per square mi.

199 people per square mi.

54 people per square mi.

44 people per square mi.

5 people per square mi.

Population density by continent

▶ This map shows which areas of the world have most people per square mile. Europe and Asia are the most densely populated regions in the world (shown by the tallest blocks). Australia is the most sparsely populated region.

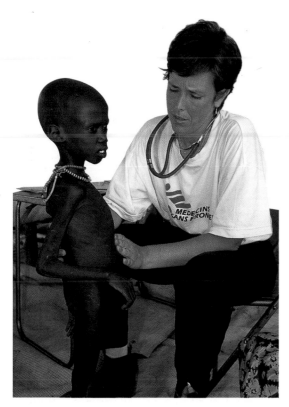

Thousands of children starve in famine-hit regions every year. Relief workers can help to some degree, but only well-financed, long-term projects will beat world hunger.

In much of Africa, children comprise 45 percent of the population. This is in contrast to Europe and North America, where the populations are steadily aging.

POPULATION DISTRIBUTION
Of the seven continents, Asia has by far the most people. Nearly six out of ten people in the world live in Asia. Between them, China and India have nearly 40 percent of all the world's people. China had about 1.3 billion people in the year 2000, with India close behind at 1 billion. Next come the United States (276 million), Indonesia (209 million), and Brazil (168 million).

While the average woman in Europe, Australia, or Japan has just one or two children, her equivalent in Africa and Asia has six or seven. The large family is still common in many poor countries because infant mortality is high and parents need children to do useful work and to help support them in old age.

Many women in poor countries still find it difficult to get contraceptive advice to help them limit the size of their families. Some governments have brought in drastic

programs to check population growth. China instituted a policy of one child per family. This strict family planning policy meant that China's population grew more slowly than India's, where 30 babies are born every minute. The United Nations estimates that, at its present rate of growth, India will overtake China's population by 2015, and become the country with the most people.

EDUCATION AND DEVELOPMENT
The education of women is a key factor in population growth. Well-educated women tend to have fewer children. In societies with a high standard of living, such as the United States, population growth is slow. In the future, population numbers will be controlled either through family planning and economic improvement—or as a result of famine and disease, as has happened many times throughout history.

Today, the world's growing population has greater opportunities to move around the planet. Tourism enriches the incomes of many countries. Immigration is easier. But it is also easier for infectious diseases to spread quickly to many parts of the world.

The message of this Chinese poster is simple: one child equals a better life. China imposed this population-control policy very strictly, but began to relax it in the late 1990s. Other countries have found it more difficult to persuade people to abandon the traditional large family.

A group of senior citizens, in Arizona, enjoy a session of pool aerobics. In prosperous countries, more people are living longer. Many retired people are active well into their eighties.

SEE ALSO PAGES:
230–1 Food production,
448–8 Food and farming,
450–1 City living

FOOD AND FARMING

Farmers produce most of our food and many of the materials in the products we use. Farmland is a limited resource and one that must be protected.

Crop dusting from the air is a fast way to get pest-control chemicals onto crops. If chemicals are used carelessly, they can affect wild plants and animals, sometimes with disastrous results.

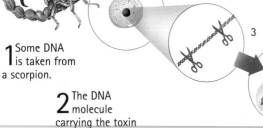

A scientist sprays a strawberry crop. New plants grown in research establishments may one day change the look and taste of the food we eat.

Important crops grown worldwide for domestic consumption include cereals (wheat, corn, and rice), root crops (potatoes and cassava), pulses (beans and peas), fruits and vegetables, oil crops such as soybeans, sugar from cane and beets, nuts, and crops such as tea and coffee. Farmers also raise livestock, such as cattle, sheep, pigs, goats, chickens, and fish.

However, fertile farmland and food resources are unevenly spread around the world. Europe, North America, and Australia produce more than enough food to feed their populations. But in less developed countries, where soils are poor and water scarce, farmers may be unable to feed even their own families.

CHANGING FARMING METHODS

Once all farmers were subsistence farmers. They grew just enough for their family, with some left over to sell in the local market. In poor countries, about half the people still live like this.

Today, in richer countries, fewer than 8 percent of people work on the land. Many farmers grow just one crop, such as wheat or bananas. This is called a cash

Many egg-laying chickens are kept in close, cramped conditions.

Free-range chickens are raised in more natural conditions outdoors.

crop. People who once had their own small farms now work on plantations. Modern, large-scale farming changes the environment forever. It makes people dependent on wages and trade. If the world price of one crop, such as coffee, falls, then coffee workers in many countries suffer.

A farmer today grows more food than a farmer a hundred years ago. Scientists have developed disease-resistant plants, and farmers use chemical fertilizers to replace nutrients in the soil, and chemical and biological pesticides to control pests.

But these gains come at a price. Modern farms can be food factories, with environments that are unfriendly to wild

GENETIC ENGINEERING

Scientists are beginning to decipher the chemical codes that control the characteristics of all living things. With this knowledge, they can exchange genes between bacteria, animals, and plants to create organisms with useful new characteristics—for example, a cabbage that caterpillars cannot eat. This diagram shows a method of genetic engineering that can add a toxin gene, from an animal such as a scorpion, to cabbages and other plants normally eaten by caterpillars. The added gene is carried by a bacterium that infects the plant cells. The new plants have leaves that are poisonous to caterpillars, but are safe for people to eat because humans destroy the toxin when they digest food.

1 Some DNA is taken from a scorpion.

2 The DNA molecule carrying the toxin gene is extracted.

3 Enzymes that cut DNA snip out the parts with the toxin gene.

4 The part of the DNA with the toxin gene is then transplanted into a bacterium.

5 The bacterium transfers its DNA to laboratory cabbage plants.

6 The toxin in the cabbage leaves kills insect pests.

plants and animals. Very few of the many varieties of food plants that were once grown have survived, so the countryside is a less rich and diverse place.

GREEN REVOLUTION

In the 1960s, food scientists introduced new varieties of wheat, rice, and other crops. These plants grew faster, were more resistant to disease, and produced larger harvests. They brought benefits to farmers in developing countries, like India, where harvests were often doubled.

This green revolution has helped feed the world's hungry people, but it has not solved the food shortage. The world's farmers grow in total enough food to feed everyone, but it is not distributed fairly. Europe and North America produce more food than they need, but the surplus is sometimes thrown away or fed to animals.

ORGANIC FARMING

In the developed world, supermarkets and their customers have a big say in what foods are grown. Today, many people are switching to organic foods—foods grown by traditional methods without chemicals. For example, they choose free-range eggs, not eggs that have been laid by hens that are kept in cramped conditions. Food scares, such as that over BSE (bovine spongiform encephalopathy), or mad cow disease, in Britain, have become more common. People are concerned about the quality and safety of the food they eat.

GENETIC MODIFICATION

Genetic engineering makes it possible for scientists to produce new kinds of plants and, one day, even animals. In many countries, there have been large plantings of genetically modified soybeans, and experiments with tomatoes and corn. No one can say yet whether the benefits of genetic modification—plants that are disease- and pest-free—will outweigh the possible effects on human health or on the environment in which these plants grow alongside wild plants.

An American farmer works in a field of organically grown onions. Organic produce grown by traditional methods is becoming more popular.

In Kenya, in Africa, fetching the water is usually the task of the women. This simple water pump makes the work of many women easier.

Rice planting is normally carried out by hand, but machines can now do the work, as shown here. These machines in Japan save people from backbreaking work in the rice fields.

Topsoil is rich in humus and nutrients

Water table

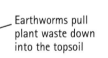

Earthworms pull plant waste down into the topsoil

Moles eat earthworms and dig tunnels that help circulate air

Rock fragments

Subsoil is a layer of fine material containing clay

Bedrock—the solid rock that forms the lowest layer under the soil and rock fragments

Tiny creatures such as beetles, centipedes, and woodlice in soil break down plant and animal matter into nutrients that, in turn, nourish growing plants

All agriculture is dependent on the soil. Creatures living in the soil break down plant and animal matter into nutrients that are, in turn, taken up by new plants. Farming methods must allow these creatures to survive, or the fertility of the soil will suffer. Most farmers care for their soil, but overly intensive farming can lead to soil erosion and crop failure.

SEE ALSO PAGES:

66–7 Plants and people,
126 Food and nutrition,
230–1 Food production,
232–3 Food processing

CITY LIVING

In 1800, no more than one in 20 people lived in a city. Today, 8 people in 20 are city-dwellers, and there are increasing problems with crowding and pollution.

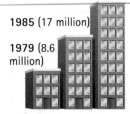

2000 (20-25 million)

1985 (17 million)

1979 (8.6 million)

Mexico City began to expand in the 1940s. Its population tripled between 1980 and 2000. It is now the joint largest city in the world, with Tokyo-Yokohama.

Cities have been getting larger and more populated since the 1800s, as people moved from the country into towns looking for work. Chicago grew from a town of 4,000 people in 1840 to a city with more than 1 million inhabitants in 1890. In 1900, there were only 19 cities in the world with over 1 million people. By the 1990s there were nearly 300.

MEGACITIES

The two largest city areas in the world are Tokyo-Yokohama, in Japan, and Mexico City, in Mexico. Both have populations of about 20 million people. Most of the world's 25 fastest-growing cities are in the developing world. India and China have a number of booming cities, as do countries in South America and Africa.

OVERCROWDING

As cities grow, there are acute housing shortages. Fast-growing cities such as São Paulo, in Brazil, are surrounded by slums.

Traffic jams, like this one in Bangkok, in Thailand, are common in cities everywhere. The car offers mobility but only at a very slow speed.

Millions of people move into these shanty towns in the hope of finding work and education in the city. Too often they are disappointed, and find no homes or schools, let alone clean water or sanitation.

Overcrowded cities cannot provide enough homes or jobs for people. This can lead to social problems, such as poverty, crime, drug abuse, and family breakdown. Rundown areas of inner cities can become

Pedestrian-only schemes, as here in Bordeaux, in southwestern France, make city streets more pleasant for pedestrians.

The Indian seaport city of Mumbai (Bombay) is home to over 12 million people. It has some of India's most elegant housing, but also some of its worst slums. This is Nariman Point, where slum dwellers make their own shelters. Mumbai's population quintupled, or grew by a factor of five, between 1941 and 1981, and it still draws in new settlers from all over western India.

slums. Those who can afford to move out settle in the suburbs, where there are larger houses with more land.

URBAN SPRAWL

Few cities have spread in a planned way. Sometimes people have tried to rebuild existing cities—this happened with Paris in the 1800s. Sometime, planners create a new city, like Brasilia, built in the 1960s as the new capital of Brazil. But most modern cities simply expand. As they grow, they swallow up farmland and countryside. Roads radiate out from the center, and suburbs are built along the roads. The effect on the environment is dramatic. Los Angeles, for example, was a small town in 1850. Today, it covers a staggering 466 square miles (1,207km^2).

TRAFFIC MANAGEMENT

As cities grow, people have to get around them. Public transportation can seldom cope, and cars jam roads. Suburbs become areas where commuters sleep, traveling to work every day. Traffic jams are not new. Jams were frequent in Victorian London where there were horse-drawn vehicles. But the car is a challenge. For the first half of the 1900s, the car offered many people freedom and mobility. In the second half, it brought pollution, noise, and gridlock.

City planners have tried to separate people and cars, by marking certain areas for pedestrians and bicyclists only. New or revived public transportation systems, like subways, are being encouraged. Public transportation is kinder to the environment. But getting people out of their cars has not been easy.

THE CHANGING CITY

Today, most city economies are based on banking, shopping, entertainment, and tourism. Central shopping areas are falling into disuse, with shoppers driving to huge shopping malls out of town. Financial districts or business areas, like Wall Street or Madison Avenue may also shrink as more people work from home. Bringing new life back into inner cities is one of the great challenges for the 21st century.

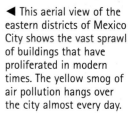

◄ This aerial view of the eastern districts of Mexico City shows the vast sprawl of buildings that have proliferated in modern times. The yellow smog of air pollution hangs over the city almost every day.

There is a clear dividing line between new housing and irrigated cotton fields in Phoenix, Arizona. As cities spread, the farmland vanishes beneath new homes and roads.

Special paths offer bicyclists some relief and protection from overcrowded roads.

◄ Even in cities, some wild animals find new niches. Foxes have become urban residents. Instead of hunting rabbits and other small animals, they raid the garbage for food. Their main enemy is the car, which kills many foxes every year.

SEE ALSO PAGES:

446–7 Population explosion, 453 Air pollution, 462–3 Conservation action

WATER POLLUTION

Water is vital to every living thing on our planet. However, too often it is polluted by sewage, animal waste, or dissolved chemicals and fertilizers.

Liquid waste from factories and farms pours into rivers and streams, making drinking water unsafe and killing wildlife.

Collecting water for the family is a daily chore in many countries. Here, girls pump water from a well in Burkina Faso, in West Africa. Indoor plumbing is still a luxury in countries where water is in short supply.

All the water in the world goes around and around in a great cycle called the hydrological cycle. Water that falls as rain soaks into the ground and is taken up by plants, or runs off and forms rivers.

HOW WATER IS POLLUTED

Water is described as polluted if the amounts or kinds of substances contained in it are likely to cause harm to people, animals, plants, or the environment. Clean water is a precious resource. Many countries lack regular rainfall, and water storage is often inadequate. In developing countries, wells and rivers often cannot meet the needs of growing populations. To make things worse, water supplies may be polluted by waste.

Water is a very good solvent. It is able to dissolve more solids than many other liquids. Water dissolves minerals when it passes through rocks as groundwater. Water in rivers, lakes, and streams almost always contains dissolved chemicals or debris suspended in it.

WASTE DISPOSAL

Rivers and seas have traditionally been used for the disposal of waste. Fast-flowing rivers carry sewage and other waste away from people's homes and into the oceans, where the natural processes of decay can usually cope. But in slow-flowing waters or in places where too much waste is put into the water, the natural decaying processes cannot deal with the waste. The water may then become polluted with disease-carrying sewage. Water also becomes polluted by oil and chemicals from factories, which natural decay processes cannot handle.

FERTILIZERS AND RIVERS

Water can also be polluted by becoming too rich in nourishment. Sewage, animal waste, and fertilizers can eventually kill the life in a river. Bacteria in the river water use oxygen to break down this organic waste into nutrients. The nutrients encourage the growth of certain plants, such as algae. As these plants die, they, too, add to the organic waste in the water. The bacteria can use so much oxygen to break down the waste that none is left for the fish. They will die if they can't swim to water that has more oxygen.

▼ Waste water entering rivers contains nutrients. Too many nutrients result in too many algae, too much new waste, and, finally, a dead river.

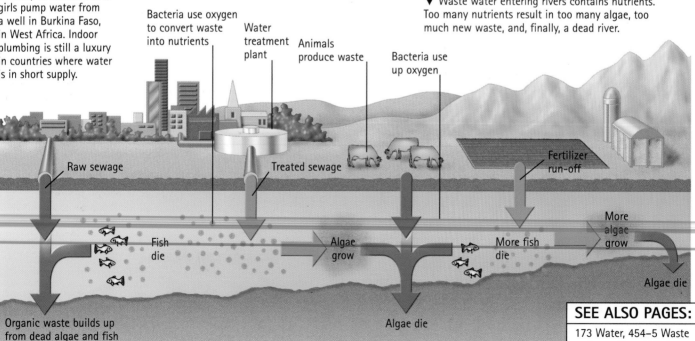

Bacteria use oxygen to convert waste into nutrients

Water treatment plant

Animals produce waste

Bacteria use up oxygen

Fertilizer run-off

Raw sewage

Treated sewage

Fish die

Algae grow

More fish die

More algae grow

Organic waste builds up from dead algae and fish

Algae die

Algae die

SEE ALSO PAGES:

173 Water, 454–5 Waste and recycling, 462–3 Conservation action

AIR POLLUTION

Air is a mixture of gases. Without air and the oxygen in it, most living things could not exist. Keeping the air free from pollution is vital for our health.

Sources of CO pollution

Industry 6.8%

Fuel burning 10.3%

Others (waste disposal, chemical spray, etc.) 12.3%

Transportation 70.6%

Carbon monoxide gas (CO) is pumped into the atmosphere by factories. It is the main pollutant in exhaust fumes from vehicles. In busy traffic, high levels of this gas are dangerous to health.

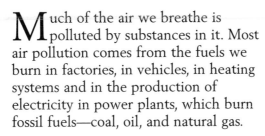

Much of the air we breathe is polluted by substances in it. Most air pollution comes from the fuels we burn in factories, in vehicles, in heating systems and in the production of electricity in power plants, which burn fossil fuels—coal, oil, and natural gas.

WHAT POLLUTES THE AIR?

Technology makes our lives easier. But this technology relies on power, and much of that power comes from burning fuel. When burned, fuels such as coal, oil, and gas release millions of tons of gases, such as carbon monoxide, carbon dioxide, sulfur dioxide, and nitrogen oxide, into the air, together with ash, dust, and soot. This not only damages people's health but also harms wildlife.

The fogs that enveloped many European cities in the 1800s were a mixture of fog and smoke from coal fires. Today, the problem is smog, caused by traffic fumes and waste gases from industry and homes. It is the result of chemical reactions caused by the action of sunlight on nitrogen oxides and unburned

A bicyclist wears a mask as protection against the harmful exhaust fumes of urban traffic. A reduction in the number of cars on the road would alleviate this problem.

fuel from car exhausts. Photochemical smog is an urban health hazard, especially in cities with high levels of sunshine.

ACID RAIN

Water droplets in clouds are naturally acidic, because the carbon dioxide in air dissolves in water to form a weak acid. Burning fossil fuels increases the chemistry in the air, and forms stronger acids. The result is acid rain. This kills trees in forests, and makes freshwater too acidic for fish and other water animals to live in. It can also damage the stonework of buildings.

Here, the Eiffel Tower, in Paris, is shrouded in a haze of smog—tiny particles of factory smoke, exhaust fumes, and other pollutants. Smog is worse on warm, sunny days. It can cause eye irritation and chest problems, especially for the elderly and babies.

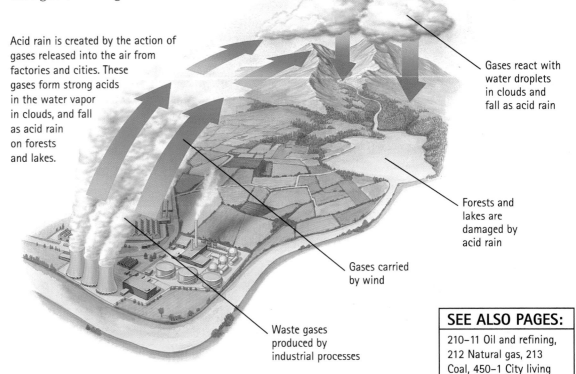

Acid rain is created by the action of gases released into the air from factories and cities. These gases form strong acids in the water vapor in clouds, and fall as acid rain on forests and lakes.

Gases react with water droplets in clouds and fall as acid rain

Gases carried by wind

Forests and lakes are damaged by acid rain

Waste gases produced by industrial processes

SEE ALSO PAGES:

210–11 Oil and refining, 212 Natural gas, 213 Coal, 450-1 City living

WASTE AND RECYCLING

The Earth has a limited amount of natural resources. Some of these—air, water, soil, fuels, and plants—can be reused if we recycle them.

Every week most of us throw away several bags full of garbage. Some of this garbage could be used again—it can be recycled. Recycling is the name given to the processes that allow materials to be used more than once. By recycling, we use fewer resources that cannot be replaced. They are called nonrenewable resources.

GETTING RID OF WASTE

People today use vast amounts of materials such as paper, glass, steel, and aluminum to make books, newspapers, packaging, bottles and jars, vehicles, cans, and much more. As soon as people have used a product, they throw it away. Every day, huge amounts of garbage have to be

disposed of safely. Much of it is burned. Much more is dumped into holes in the ground and buried—this is called landfill disposal. Too much trash is dumped into the ocean. None of these three methods is a good thing for the environment, although burning in modern incinerators can produce useful energy in the form of heat.

SAVING MATERIALS

It is vital to save as many of the Earth's materials as possible. A tree can be replaced with another tree. Once a lump of iron ore or a drum full of oil has been used, however, it is impossible to renew it.

About half our domestic waste is paper, which can be recycled if collected carefully. By recycling paper there is less pollution from burning. The process also

Millions of tons of waste are produced every year. Most of it is buried in landfill sites. Dangerous liquids may leak into the soil or into nearby water.

Radioactive waste is toxic, and has to be carried very carefully to treatment plants before it is stored deep underground. It remains dangerous for centuries.

▶ In a modern recycling plant, mixed material (but no organic matter) is passed along a conveyor belt and sorted into reusable materials—steel, aluminum, paper, and glass. Recycling plants are expensive, but will become essential as vital resources become scarce.

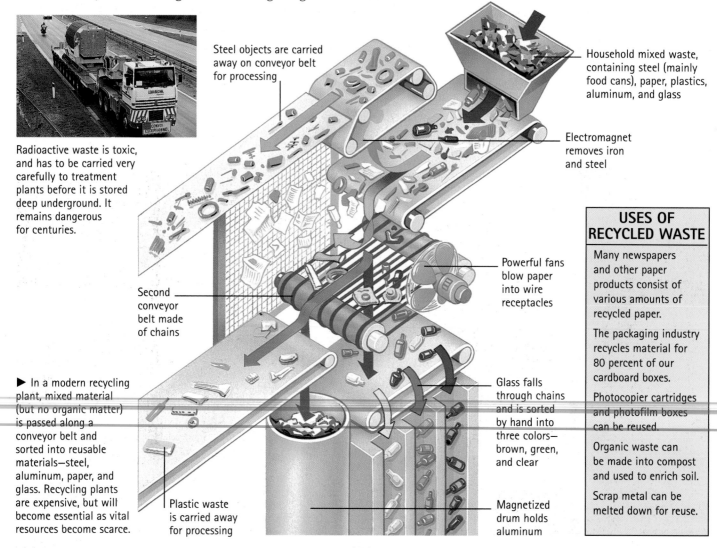

Steel objects are carried away on conveyor belt for processing

Household mixed waste, containing steel (mainly food cans), paper, plastics, aluminum, and glass

Electromagnet removes iron and steel

Second conveyor belt made of chains

Powerful fans blow paper into wire receptacles

Glass falls through chains and is sorted by hand into three colors—brown, green, and clear

Plastic waste is carried away for processing

Magnetized drum holds aluminum

USES OF RECYCLED WASTE

Many newspapers and other paper products consist of various amounts of recycled paper.

The packaging industry recycles material for 80 percent of our cardboard boxes.

Photocopier cartridges and photofilm boxes can be reused.

Organic waste can be made into compost and used to enrich soil.

Scrap metal can be melted down for reuse.

protects natural forest habitats that would otherwise be cleared to plant softwood trees to feed the ever-hungry paper mills. Many towns now have recycling points—with containers for different materials, or special collections for recyclable trash. Separating glass bottles by color (green, brown, and clear), makes recycling easier. It also helps if households sort their garbage into groups (metal, paper, plastic, etc.).

NEW FROM OLD

Old glass jars and bottles can be crushed and melted to make new glass objects. So can metals. It uses up a lot of energy to extract aluminum from its ore (the rock that contains the metal), so by recycling cans made of aluminum, energy is saved. It used to be expensive to recycle the cans because they also contained steel, which had to be separated from the aluminum. Today, cans are now made only from aluminum, so recycling them is easier.

It is important to recycle metals because they will not last long. Scientists estimate that aluminum will run out in the 2200s, and iron in about 2160. Lead, zinc, mercury, and tin will be used up much sooner, by about 2020. Aluminum and steel (made from iron) are relatively easy to recycle. About 30 percent of the aluminum and 50 percent of the steel made each year is recycled from scrap.

RECYCLING PLASTIC

Recycling plastic is possible, but not as simple. Plastic waste can be melted down to make new plastic, but first the different kinds of plastic are separated. Another method is to heat the plastic in an airless container to produce a mixture of hydrocarbons, which can be separated into useful liquid fuels, oil, and tar.

BURNING

Incineration, or burning, is the most common method of disposing of waste. When this is done in modern incinerators, waste can be changed into heat energy and used to generate electricity. Organic waste, like food remains, can be burned or made into compost to return to the soil. Organic waste acted on by special bacteria produces methane gas, which can be drawn off and burned as fuel.

This international symbol shows that a card, envelope, or packaging product is made from recycled paper.

Old newspapers can be recycled. The paper is pulped and mixed with wood pulp. The ink is removed so that the recycled paper is clean.

To recycle metal, mixed scrap metal is broken into fragments. A spinning magnetic drum (left) separates out the magnetic ferrous metal (iron). Garbage is picked out by hand and the clean fragments are melted down and made into new steel.

Polyethylene, a plastic widely used in packaging, is sorted and compressed into bales before being shredded and reused.

SEE ALSO PAGES:

204–5 Shaping materials, 434–5 The natural balance, 456–7 Resources

RESOURCES

Resources are the substances we use to make the things we need. There is a limited stock of many of them. Most cannot be replaced once they have been used.

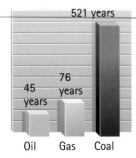

521 years

76 years

45 years

Oil Gas Coal

This graph shows how long the three main fossil fuels are expected to last at current usage.

Fiberglass is used to line and insulate roof spaces.

Foam is pumped into wall cavities to insulate.

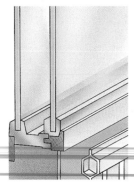

Storm windows prevent heat loss.

▲ Thermal insulation reduces heat loss from buildings and saves energy. Three methods of insulation are shown here.

To prepare a meal, we need food, water, pots and pans, cutlery, an oven, and fuel to provide heat. The food and water, the metals from which the oven and the utensils are made, and the fuel that is burned to produce heat are all resources. They are called natural resources because we obtain them from the Earth.

ENERGY

One of our most important resources is energy. We need energy to warm our houses, to run factories and vehicles, and to light streets and homes. Much of this energy comes from the burning of fuels such as coal, oil, and gas, which are present on the Earth in limited quantities.

The word fossil comes from a Latin word meaning "dug from the ground." Coal, oil, and natural gas are called fossil fuels because they are the remains of plants or animals. They were formed very slowly over millions of years and are nonrenewable. In other words, they cannot be replaced.

METALS

Metals are an extremely valuable resource. Many of the things we use every day are made from metal. People have been using some metals, such as copper and iron, for thousands of years. Most metals are found in minerals called ores, which are chemical compounds that contain a high proportion of the metal. Only a few, such as gold and

Farmers use irrigation to keep plants growing when rain is scarce. These sprinklers are watering apple trees in Provence, during a hot summer in southern France.

copper, are found in the Earth's crust in a pure form. Metals that are already becoming scarce include gold, tin, copper, silver, and platinum.

The metal produced in the greatest quantity is iron, and estimates of how long it will last vary from as little as 160 to over 400 years. New deposits of metals may be discovered, and new technology may mean that existing resources will be mined more efficiently. But the costs of mining will rise, and substitutes for some metals will be needed.

UNDERWATER RESOURCES

We get most of the minerals we use from quarries and mines on land, although oil and gas are also extracted from rocks beneath the oceans. In the future, robot machines will mine the deep ocean floor. The seabed and seawater itself are rich in minerals. Already manganese nodules can be sucked up from deep seabeds. Other minerals could be extracted chemically from the waters of the ocean.

Renewable resources include plants such as trees grown for timber. As long as we do not use these valuable resources faster than new trees can grow, we will have a constant supply of wood products.

Nonrenewable resources are gone forever once used. Fossil fuels such as coal, oil, and gas have been burned in huge amounts during the past 200 years. Unless they can be used more efficiently, they will soon be used up.

WILL THEY RUN OUT?

No one knows how long the Earth's nonrenewable resources will last. New reserves of coal, oil, and gas are still being found on land and in the oceans. However, some of these new reserves are difficult to reach, and extracting the fuel will be expensive. It is thought that there is enough uranium (the fuel used in nuclear power plants), and coal to last for several hundred years. Oil and natural gas are less abundant and may run out during this century. What is certain is that one day in the future, the fossil fuels will run out. So it is important to switch to other sources of energy which are renewable.

WATER AND ITS USES

With over 70 percent of the Earth's surface covered with water it might seem that water is plentiful. But only 3 percent is freshwater, and more than three fourths of that freshwater is frozen, most of it around the North and South poles. About a third of the world's people live in areas where rainfall is low or unreliable, and where water is a precious resource.

About 75 percent of the water we use is taken by farmers to water crops. The figure is highest in the poorer countries, where irrigation can account for as much as 90 percent of water use. Building dams to trap water in artificial lakes is one way to provide water for irrigation schemes. A second is to channel water from rivers. A third is to build desalination (salt-removing) plants to convert saltwater from the sea into freshwater.

Irrigation can transform land that was near-desert, allowing crops to grow where none grew before. But this can be a wasteful process. Only about a third of the water actually helps the plants to grow. The rest is wasted; it evaporates or soaks away. It is possible to use sprinklers that deliver water directly to the roots of the plants, making irrigation more efficient.

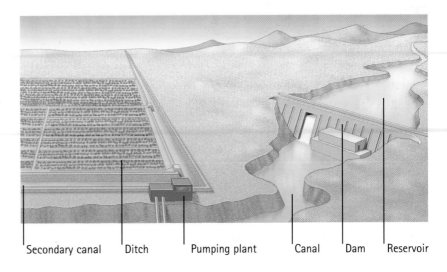

Secondary canal   Ditch   Pumping plant   Canal   Dam   Reservoir

Large irrigation schemes may rely on a dam holding back water to form a reservoir. Pumps send the water along secondary canals for distribution to the crops growing in the fields. The dam may also be used to provide water for power plants that generate electricity.

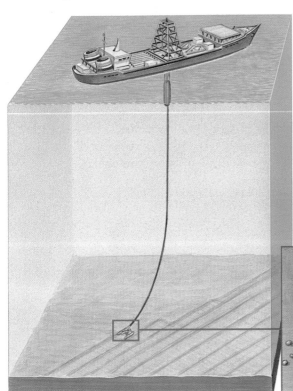

MINERALS FROM THE SEABED

The ocean floor contains huge amounts of manganese (a metal used in steel and industrial processes). The manganese is in the form of round lumps, called nodules, mixed with other elements, such as iron and nickel. The nodules are dredged up by ships fitted with hoses that scrape and suck at the ocean floor.

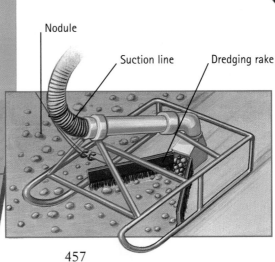

Nodule

Suction line   Dredging rake

Nodules look like hailstones. The minerals are washed into the sea by erosion of the land. About one fifth of the nodule is manganese.

SEE ALSO PAGES:

210–11 Oil and refining, 212 Natural gas, 213 Coal, 458–9 Renewable energy

RENEWABLE ENERGY

Materials and energy sources that can be used over and over, are called renewable resources. Using these resources helps us to preserve the planet.

Three-bladed wind turbines stand in rows on a wind farm in California. Wind power makes a useful and environmentally clean contribution to power supplies.

A container catches rainwater—a simple water-saving device used in Kenya.

Renewable resources include the wind, which blows more or less continuously. Wind power can be harnessed to drive machinery and generate electricity. Other renewable resources are the sun, the waters of the rivers and oceans, and energy produced by plants and animals.

WIND POWER

The first windmills were used to drive machinery for grinding flour and other tasks. Today, windmills pump water from underground sources and also drive turbine generators to make electricity without pollution.

A collection of modern windmills make up a wind farm. The most efficient wind machines have two or three blades, like the propeller of an aircraft. An electricity generator is located inside the head of the machine. The head can rotate to keep the blades pointed into the wind. There are also windmills with curved blades that spin on a vertical axis.

SOLAR ENERGY

The sun gives out vast amounts of energy from nuclear fusion within it. The Earth receives a tiny part of this energy, and this makes life possible on our planet. Solar power provides a very clean form of heat, with no environmental side effects. Solar

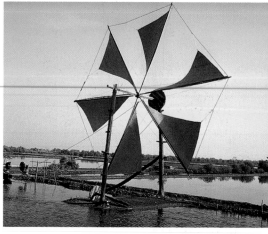

Wind power is good for continuous tasks. This windmill is driving a pump that, in turn, raises water from irrigation channels onto the fields where it is needed.

cells, like the ones used on spacecraft, convert sunlight directly into electricity. Solar panels attached to buildings can use energy from sunlight to heat water for heating systems. Solar furnaces use huge curved mirrors to focus the sun's rays.

PLANT POWER

Firewood can be a renewable resource, if enough new trees are planted, but burning wood causes pollution and adds to global warming. Plants are a potentially valuable source of fuel, chemicals, and other materials. Soybeans and olives are grown for their oils, used mainly in cooking. But less well-known plants such as the creosote plant contain oily chemicals that could one day provide an alternative to gasoline as a fuel. Cars have already been made to run on fuels made from sugarcane and other plants.

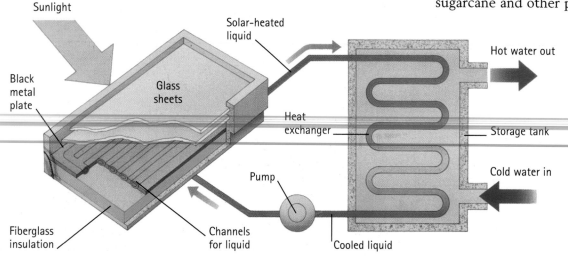

Sunlight

Solar-heated liquid

Hot water out

Black metal plate

Glass sheets

Heat exchanger

Storage tank

Cold water in

Pump

Fiberglass insulation

Channels for liquid

Cooled liquid

In a solar heating system, energy from sunlight is trapped inside a glass-topped panel by a black plate, which absorbs heat rays. The heat energy warms liquid, which flows through a heat exchanger to heat the water for domestic heating.

Animals are still a useful source of power. In Thailand's dense forests, trained elephants are used to move logs. They are cheaper than machines and do much less damage to the environment.

ANIMAL POWER
Working animals are one of humanity's oldest resources. Horses, donkeys, camels, oxen, and elephants still work in many parts of the world, carrying loads and pulling vehicles. For a small farmer, a horse can be cheaper than a tractor. It burns no fuel and causes no pollution. Sometimes animals can work in muddy places where machines would get stuck.

WATER POWER
Falling water provides enough force to drive turbines to generate electricity. In hydroelectric power plants, a dam is built to store water in a lake or reservoir. Valves allow a controlled amount of water to fall through turbines, which spin. A reservoir is usually refilled by rain or water from

rivers. In pumped storage power plants, there are two reservoirs at different levels. Water is pumped up the slope from the low reservoir to refill the high reservoir. This is done at night, when the demand for power is low, and the high reservoir is full by daybreak.

WAVE POWER
Electricity can be produced by using the motion of ocean waves. Water does not travel along with a wave; instead it moves up and down. This motion can be used to drive generators. Another way to use the ocean's power is in tidal power generators. These take advantage of the daily inward and outward flow of water into a river estuary to drive generators.

The Hoover Dam, built in the 1930s, is the highest concrete dam in the United States. Damming the Colorado River created Lake Mead, an artificial lake, 115 mi. (185km) long. The lake irrigates about 980,000 acres (400,000 hectares) of farmland. The dam's hydroelectric plant generates about 1.5 million kilowatts of electricity.

One method of generating power from ocean waves uses rows of floats called nodding ducks. As the floats bob up and down, the energy in their movement is used to generate electricity. The hub where each float pivots contains either a generator to produce electricity directly, or a water pump. The pump sends water through the float to a turbine that drives a generator.

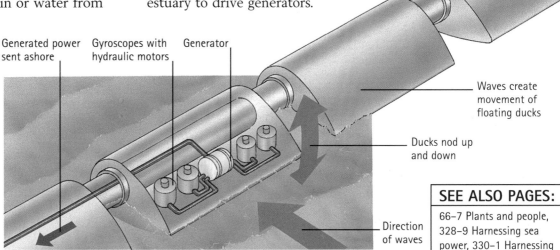

Generated power sent ashore — Gyroscopes with hydraulic motors — Generator

Waves create movement of floating ducks

Ducks nod up and down

Direction of waves

SEE ALSO PAGES:
66–7 Plants and people, 328–9 Harnessing sea power, 330–1 Harnessing wind power

CLIMATE CHANGE

Many scientists think the Earth is getting warmer. Such a change will alter landscapes, change the crops we grow, and affect existing natural communities.

Natural events, such as volcanic eruptions, affect climate. The large eruption of Mount Pinatubo in the Philippines, in 1991, sent huge clouds of material into the atmosphere. The smoke and ash reduced the amount of sunlight reaching the ground. This altered local weather, and affected climate around the globe.

In the past, the Earth's climate warmed and cooled over a period of millions of years. During the ice ages, the climate was cooler; then it warmed up again. Since the 1700s, however, more rapid climate changes have been taking place. Most scientists agree that this global warming is caused by people. Our factories, homes, and cars give out waste gases that rise into the atmosphere. These gases act like a blanket, warming the globe. If this global warming continues, it could change the world's climates and cause sea levels to rise.

OZONE LOSS

In the 1970s, scientists discovered that something was happening to the ozone layer over the South Pole. This layer shields us from harmful ultraviolet (UV) rays from the sun. Ultraviolet radiation can cause skin cancer. That is why it is essential to cover up and wear suntan lotion to protect yourself from sunburn.

The "Slip, Slap, Slop" campaign, in Australia, urged people to slip on a shirt, slap on a hat, and slop on suntan lotion to protect them from the ultraviolet rays of the sun.

The ozone layer has become thinner, and a hole appears every year above the Antarctic. A similar hole has also been observed above the Arctic. The ozone holes are caused by a group of gases called chlorofluorocarbons (CFCs), which have been used in aerosols, such as hairsprays, and in older-model refrigerators. Ozone is destroyed when CFCs drift up into the atmosphere and release chlorine atoms that then break down the ozone molecules. To preserve the protective ozone layer, CFCs are being gradually replaced by less harmful gases.

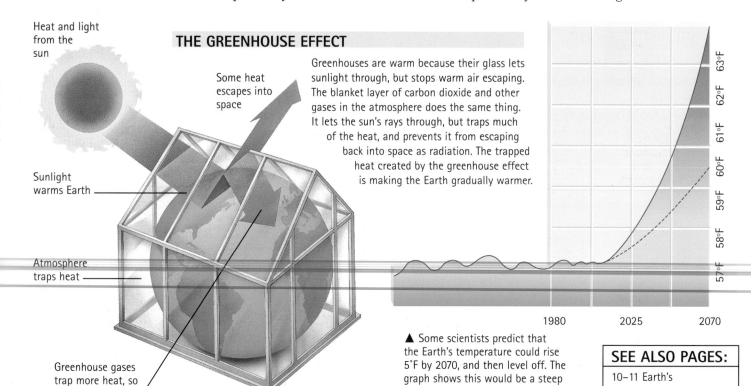

Heat and light from the sun

Some heat escapes into space

Sunlight warms Earth

Atmosphere traps heat

Greenhouse gases trap more heat, so Earth gets warmer

THE GREENHOUSE EFFECT

Greenhouses are warm because their glass lets sunlight through, but stops warm air escaping. The blanket layer of carbon dioxide and other gases in the atmosphere does the same thing. It lets the sun's rays through, but traps much of the heat, and prevents it from escaping back into space as radiation. The trapped heat created by the greenhouse effect is making the Earth gradually warmer.

63°F
62°F
61°F
60°F
59°F
58°F
57°F

1980   2025   2070

▲ Some scientists predict that the Earth's temperature could rise 5°F by 2070, and then level off. The graph shows this would be a steep rise from the levels of the 1900s.

SEE ALSO PAGES:
10–11 Earth's atmosphere, 36–7 Climate, 244–5 Radiation

TOURISM AND HERITAGE

Tourists can now travel almost anywhere, even to the South Pole. Mass travel and tourism puts pressure on wild places as well as on sites of historic importance.

Garbage litters the slopes of a mountain in the Annapurna Conservation Area, in the Himalayas. So many people now visit the Himalayas, the world's highest mountains, that the environment is under real threat.

I n the 1800s, only local people and a few intrepid travelers ever saw the wonders of remote places such as the Himalayan mountains. Today, climbers almost have to wait in line to climb Mount Everest, and backpackers wander on the mountain slopes. With the introduction of cheap travel by plane in the 1950s, mass tourism became possible. Today, it is a huge business with an enormous environmental impact. Every week, planes full of hundreds of tourists from Europe, North America, and Japan land in faraway places like Gambia, the Seychelles, or Thailand. People can now travel around the world in only a few hours. They can visit the South Pole to photograph the huts left by the first explorers, or watch African animals from a truck or a balloon.

PARKS AND HERITAGE SITES

Nature reserves and national parks have two main functions. They protect wild places and wildlife. They also allow people to see and enjoy these things. World heritage sites include natural wonders such as the Grand Canyon, and the Great Barrier Reef and Ayers Rock in Australia. There are also historic human sites, such as the Inca city of Machu Picchu in Peru, Stonehenge in England, the pyramids in Egypt, or the Parthenon in Greece.

CHANGING SITES

Many people who live in towns and cities enjoy the outdoors—hiking, climbing, visiting famous sites, or trying adventure sports, such as skiing, whitewater rafting, or rock climbing. As more people visit popular areas, new sites are constantly sought for exploitation and development. Often this means new roads, airports, hotels, and entertainment complexes.

Golf courses take the place of farmland. Beaches that were once quiet breeding grounds for turtles or seals sprout bright lights and noisy hotels. Tourists travel to see wild and beautiful places. Too often, they find those places have vanished.

Wild places and historic sites need protection from their own popularity. Old buildings are in need of conservation from the destructive effects of pollution. Wild animals and plants often need new homes within this changing landscape. Everyone today can make a contribution and preserve the planet for future generations.

▲ Hotels form a wall of concrete along this beach in Hawaii. Many tourist islands have suffered environmental damage and the loss of many rare plants and animals.

▶ The African plains are still rich in wildlife, and managed tourism is becoming a vital part of the continent's economy. Here, a hot air balloon floats above the Masai Mara National Reserve in Kenya, in Africa. Tourists now visit to shoot with cameras, not guns.

SEE ALSO PAGES:

438–9 Saving the rain forests, 446–7 Population explosion, 462–3 Conservation action

CONSERVATION ACTION

Conservation describes the actions taken to protect the Earth and its resources. It is vital to repair the damage done to the planet, particularly during the 1900s.

Conservation means caring for the Earth and using its resources wisely. In the past 30 years, more people have become aware of the damage caused to the environment by greedy and careless behavior. Ecologists and conservationists have shown how wildlife and wild places are being destroyed. Governments are now making laws to reduce the pollution released into the air and water. Recycling schemes are encouraging people to reuse things they used to throw away.

This male bighorn sheep lives high in the Rocky Mountains. These wild sheep are threatened by hunting, loss of habitat, and by diseases they catch from domestic sheep.

INTERNATIONAL ACTION

Conservation can be a local concern—for example, saving a tree from being cut down or creating a small wildlife reserve. But tackling world problems such as the destruction of the rain forests calls for action on a global scale. That is why international discussions are important. At the 1992 Earth Summit in Rio de Janeiro, in Brazil, many governments drew up a global action plan to save the planet. It is hoped that all countries will be persuaded to follow this plan.

A loggerhead turtle is released into the Mediterranean Sea. Tagging marine turtles allows scientists to monitor how far these rare animals travel and where they breed.

PROTECTING WILDLIFE

A good way to protect wildlife is to preserve an entire habitat in a national park. To succeed, this has to be done with the support of the local people. If they benefit from the park and its visitors, they are more likely to take an active part.

About 60 biosphere reserves have been set up by the United Nations so far. These form a network of areas that will include examples of all the world's major types of vegetation. The reserves contain undisturbed plants and farmland, and are managed for conservation.

Conservation also involves activities that anyone can do. These include fieldwork,

▲ A game warden in Kenya stands guard beside a pile of elephant tusks. The tusks will be burned as part of the campaign to deter poachers and the illegal trading in ivory.

▶ The Amazon rain forest is still being destroyed at a catastrophic rate by logging and burning, as well as forest fires like this one in Brazil. Less than half of the world's original rain forests remain, and most of them are in the Amazon river basin of South America. Some countries, such as the Philippines, have already lost more than 80 percent of their natural rain forest.

Water conservation is vital, especially in areas where rainfall is seasonal or erratic, and clean drinking water is in short supply. Village wells like this one in Burkina Faso, in West Africa, must be maintained and new wells dug. As populations increase, such traditional water sources can prove inadequate. Cross-border, water-sharing schemes help, with water-rich countries supplying water to thirstier neighbors.

Sharks are caught for food and killed for sport. Catching, marking, and releasing sharks helps scientists keep a check on their dwindling numbers.

Air pollution in cities is caused by cars. Regulating exhaust emissions will help make the air less dirty and dangerous.

which can range from setting up teams to combat poaching of African rhinos to digging ponds for frogs. Fundraising is an important part of conservation work. So is education, because by involving young people in the work, there is a better chance of making sensible choices in the future. Governments and multinational companies have to be advised, informed, and challenged about conservation issues.

VANISHING SPECIES
Natural environments most in danger include tropical forests, wetlands, and coral reefs. Some experts warn that by the year 2050 half the species alive today could have vanished unless action is taken quickly. The loss of a single plant species is a tragedy, because with each plant, as many as 30 species of animals may also face extinction, depending as they do on that plant for food or shelter.

Each species is a storehouse of genetic resources. The rosy periwinkle is a plant of the forests of Madagascar. Drugs made from this plant can help children suffering from leukemia (a form of cancer). If the periwinkle had died out, its medical value would never have been known.

SUCCESSES AND PROBLEMS
Conservation success often comes slowly. In 1983, there were only 350 rhinos left in Kenya. By 2000, this number had risen to over 450, thanks to antipoaching efforts made by the Worldwide Fund for Nature and the Kenyan Wildlife Service.

Parrots live for as long as 50 years, but in the wild, parrots are in serious trouble. About 90 of the 330 parrot species face extinction. The main causes are loss of forest habitat and the pet trade. For every parrot sold in a pet store, probably four die on the journey. So serious has the birds' plight become that only captive breeding programs may save some species.

CONCERNS FOR THE FUTURE
There are a number of pressing concerns for the future. They include: climate change and global warming; the protection of the ozone layer; the loss of tropical rain forests; the threat to farmland and fertile soils; the threat to wild plants and animals and the loss of biodiversity; the unchecked growth of human population resulting in building, traffic congestion, and pollution; and the need to conserve and recycle nonrenewable resources, such as fossil fuels and minerals.

People everywhere can take action and make conservation happen.

▲ It helps to raise rare breeds like these young parrots in captivity before releasing them into the wild.

◄ New trees mean new timber for the future and new homes for the native wildlife. Treecare is a vital part of conservation work. Here, children plant tree seedlings in Thailand, a country where wild forests have been depleted by the timber trade.

SEE ALSO PAGES:

FACTS AND FIGURES

ENDANGERED SPECIES

Species have always become extinct, but the rate at which species are dying out today is far greater than when the dinosaurs died out 65 million years ago. More than 5,000 species are officially declared to be in danger. The threats to these animals include hunting, trapping, fishing, loss of habitat, pollution, and competition from other species.

Endangered species are listed in the *Red Data Book* of the International Union for the Conservation of Nature and Natural Resources. Animals such as the tiger, snow leopard, and mountain gorilla may not exist in the wild by the time the next century dawns.

Animals close to extinction include:
Javan rhinoceros *c*.40–50 left
Kakapo bird of New Zealand *c*.40 left
Kouprey of Southeast Asia *c*.300 left
Siberian crane fewer than 30 left
Leatherback turtle *c*.500 left in the mid-1990s compared to 6,500 in the 1980s

MAKE A DIFFERENCE

We can all help reduce pollution and waste. Here are some suggestions for how you can promote a better environment:
• Choose products with the least amounts of wasteful packaging.
• Turn off heating, lights, and appliances when they are not needed.
• Bicycle, walk, or use public transportation wherever possible to reduce car usage and the pollution it creates.
• Recycle household waste, especially metal cans, glass bottles, and paper.
• Make sure all dangerous or poisonous materials are disposed of safely.
• Look after the plants and animals in your local environment.

GLOBAL ACTION

Rich and poor nations find it hard to agree on conservation measures that do not lower people's standard of living .
The 1992 United Nations Conference on Environment and Development (UNCED), known as the Earth Summit, took place in Rio de Janeiro, Brazil. A total of 178 countries sent delegates, including 100 government leaders.

A major agreement made at the meeting was the Convention on Protecting Species and Habitats, known as the biodiversity agreement. There were other agreements on sustainable development, climate change, and discussion of other problems such as deforestation and ocean fish stocks.

CONSERVATION BODIES

Many governments have departments with responsibilities for environmental issues. A world body called the Global Environment Facility, set up in 1991, is funded jointly by the World Bank, the United Nations (UN) Development Program, and the UN Environment Program. Nongovernment organizations such as Greenpeace and the World Wide Fund for Nature play a major role in highlighting issues of concern and funding programs to combat pollution and save vanishing wildlife.

KEY DATES

1705	British inventor Thomas Newcomen invents the steam engine. The Industrial Revolution and increased coal burning soon follow.
1700s	European cities grow, and their air and water become polluted.
1800s	Big game hunters from Europe shoot animals such as lions, elephants, and deer for trophies. In North America, hunters kill most of the bison on the North American plains.
1848	The U.K. government passes the Public Health Act to restrict smoke and ash emissions.
1889	First sewage treatment plant opens in London.
1896	Swedish chemist Svante Arrhenius proposes that carbon dioxide warms the atmosphere.
1932	Whipsnade Zoo in England is the first zoo to keep animals in large enclosures, not in cages.
1935	Whalers are prohibited from killing near-extinct right whales.
1952	A week of severe smog causes 4,000 deaths in London. This incident prompts the Clean Air Act of 1956.
1955	U.S. Congress passes the Air Pollution Control Act, granting $5 million per year to pollution research.
1957	A reactor fire at Windscale, England, releases radioactive material to the environment.
1961	Twelve nations sign a treaty to protect Antarctica's natural environment from damage.
1961	World Wildlife Fund founded as an independent fund-raising organization for conservation.
1962	U.S. marine biologist Rachel Carson publishes *Silent Spring*, in which she gives evidence of environmental damage caused by pesticides such as DDT.
1964	West German government bans nonbiodegradable soap powder.
1966	The world's first tidal power plant opens on the River Rance in France.
1971	Greenpeace formed in Canada by opponents of nuclear weapons testing.
1972	U.S. Landsat-1 becomes the first environmental-study satellite.
1974	Catalytic converters that reduce automotive emissions become available in the U.S.
1975	Convention on the International Trade of Endangered Species (CITES) bans trade in products from endangered animals.
1975	Unleaded gasoline becomes available in the U.S.
1975	Mediterranean countries agree on a UN regional sea program to clean up the Mediterranean.
1982	Japanese Antarctic station *Syowa* reports thinning of ozone layer since the mid-1960s.
1986	A reactor explosion and fire at Chernobyl, Ukraine, releases 1,000 times more radiation than the 1957 fire at Windscale.
1989	Signatories of the Montreal Protocol agree to phase out chlorofluorocarbons (CFCs).
1989	Oil tanker *Exxon Valdez* spills oil along 1,500 kilometers (900 mi.) of Alaskan coastline.
1991	Iraq releases oil into the Persian Gulf, causing the world's largest oil spill.
1992	A UN Earth Summit at Rio de Janeiro, Brazil, produces a global environmental action plan.
1994	Work starts on China's Three Gorges Dam. The 1.6-km-wide dam will flood almost 600 km of valley. Ecologists fear the impact of the reservoir on local wildlife will be enormous.
1996	A report by the International Union for the Conservation of Nature and Natural Resources (IUCN) lists 5,205 endangered species.
1997	Fires destroy large areas of forest in Indonesia and cause severe smoke and air pollution.
1998	A UN summit at Kyoto, Japan, targets a 5 percent cut in carbon dioxide emissions by 2012.
1999	Climatologists confirm the 1990s to have been the hottest decade ever recorded, probably because of global warming.
2000	The world tiger population is estimated at less than 10,000. There were 100,000 in 1900.

READY
REFERENCE

NUMBERS AND UNITS OF MEASUREMENT

S.I. UNITS

The International (Metric) System, or *Système International d'Unités* (S.I. units) came into being in October, 1960. S.I. units have been adopted by most countries. The system is based on seven principal units:

meter (m)
The meter is the S.I. unit of length. It is the distance light travels, in a vacuum, in 1/299,792,458 of a second.

kilogram (kg)
The kilogram is the S.I. unit of mass. It is the mass of an international prototype, which is a cylinder of platinum–iridium alloy kept at Sèvres in France.

second (s)
The second is the S.I. unit of time. It is the length of time for 9,192,631,770 microwave-frequency oscillations of the cesium-133 atom to occur.

ampere (A)
The ampere is the S.I. unit of electrical current. When a current flowing through each of a pair of wires, separated by one meter of vacuum, produces a force equal to 0.0000002 (2×10^{-7}) newton per meter, that current is one ampere.

Kelvin (K)
The Kelvin is the S.I. unit of temperature. It is 1/273.16 of the thermodynamic temperature of the triple point of water.

mole [mol]
The mole is the S.I. unit of substance. It is the amount of substance that contains as many elementary units as there are atoms in 0.012 kg of carbon–12.

candela [cd]
The candela is the basic unit of luminous intensity. It is the intensity of a source of light, of frequency 520 x 10^{12} Hz, that produces 1/683 watt per steradian (the steradian is a unit of solid angle).

METRIC SYSTEM OF MEASUREMENT

Length
10 mm (millimeters) = 1 cm (centimeter)
10 cm = 1 dm (decimeter)
10 dm = 1 m (meter)
10 m = 1 dam (decameter)
10 dam = 1 hm (hectometer)
10 hm = 1 km (kilometer)
1,000 m = 1 km

Area
100 mm^2 = 1 cm^2 (square centimeter)
10,000 cm^2 = 1 m^2
100 m^2 = 1 are
100 are = 1 hectare
10,000 m^2 = 1 hectare
100 hectare = 1 km^2
1,000,000 m^2 = 1 km^2

Volume
1,000 mm^3 = 1 cm^3 (cubic centimeter)
1,000 cm^3 = 1 dm^3
1,000 dm^3 = 1 m^3
1,000,000 cm^3 = 1 m^3

Capacity
10 ml (milliliter) = 1 cl (centiliter)
10 cl = 1 dl (deciliter)
10 dl = 1 l (liter)
1,000 ml = 1 l
100 cl = 1 l
1,000 liters = 1 cubic meter (m^3)

Mass
1,000 g (gram) = 1 kg (kilogram)
1,000 kg = 1 t (ton; metric ton)

NUMBER SYSTEMS

Decimal Base 10	Binary Base 2	Hexadecimal Base 16; Hex
1	1	1
2	10	2
3	11	3
4	100	4
5	101	5
6	110	6
7	111	7
8	1000	8
9	1001	9
10	1010	A
11	1011	B
12	1100	C
13	1101	D
14	1110	E
15	1111	F
16	1000	10
17	10001	11
18	10010	12
19	10011	13
20	10100	14
25	11001	19
30	11110	1E
40	101000	28
50	110010	32
100	1100100	64

NUMBER PREFIXES

Number	Prefix
1 trillionth	pico- (p-)
1 billionth	nano- (n-)
1 millionth	micro (μ-)
1 thousandth	milli- (m-)
1 hundredth	centi- (c-)
1 tenth	deci- (d-)
Ten	deca- (da-)
1 hundred	hecto- (h-)
1 thousand	kilo- (k-)
1 million	mega- (M-)
1 billion	giga- (G-)
1 trillion	tera- (T-)

FRACTIONS, DECIMALS, AND PERCENTAGES

Fraction	Percentage	Decimal
½	50.00%	0.500
⅓	33.33%	0.333
¼	25.00%	0.250
⅕	20.00%	0.200
⅙	16.67%	0.167
⅛	12.50%	0.125
⅒	10.00%	0.100
⅔	66.67%	0.667
¾	75.00%	0.750
⅜	37.50%	0.375
⅝	62.50%	0.625
⅞	87.50%	0.875

U.S. CUSTOMARY MEASUREMENTS

Length
12 inches = 1 foot
3 feet = 1 yard
22 yards = 1 chain
10 chains = 1 furlong
8 furlongs = 1 mile
5,280 feet = 1 mile
1,760 yards = 1 mile

Mass
437.5 grains = 1 ounce (1 oz.)
16 oz. = 1 pound (1 lb; 7,000 grains)
2,000 pounds = 1 short ton
2,240 pounds = 1 long ton

Area
144 square inches = 1 square foot
9 square feet = 1 square yard
4,840 square yards = 1 acre
640 acres = 1 square mile

Capacity (U.K. Imperial)
20 fluid ounces = 1 pint
4 gills = 1 pint
2 pints = 1 quart
4 quarts = 1 gallon

Volume
1,728 cubic inches = 1 cubic foot
27 cubic feet = 1 cubic yard

Capacity (U.S. Customary—dry)
2 pints = 1 quart
8 quarts = 1 peck
4 pecks = 1 bushel

Capacity (U.S. Customary—liquid)
16 fluid ounces = 1 pint
2 pints = 1 quart
4 quarts = 1 gallon (8 pints)
1 U.S. gallon = 0.8 U.K. gallon
31-42 gallons = 1 barrel

Mass (U.S. Customary)
2,000 lb = 1 ton (short ton)
1 short ton = 1.12 long ton

CONVERSION TABLES

MASS

grams (g)	ounces (oz.)
1	0.04
2	0.07
3	0.11
4	0.14
5	0.18
6	0.21
7	0.25
8	0.28
9	0.32
10	0.35
20	0.71
30	1.06
40	1.41
50	1.76
100	3.53
200	7.05
250	8.82
500	17.64
1,000	35.27

ounces (oz)	grams (g)
1	28.3
2	56.7
3	85.0
4	113.4
5	141.7
6	170.1
7	198.4
8	226.8
9	255.1
10	283.5
11	311.8
12	340.2
13	368.5
14	396.9
15	425.2
16 (1 lb)	453.6
17	481.9
18	510.3
19	538.6
20	566.9

kilograms (kg)	pounds (lb)
1	2.2
2	4.4
3	6.6
4	8.8
5	11.0
6	13.2
7	15.4
8	17.6
9	19.8
10	22.0
20	44.1
30	66.1
40	88.2
50	110.2
60	132.3
70	154.3
80	176.4
90	198.4
100	220.5
1,000	2,204.6

pounds (lbs)	kilograms (kg)
1	0.45
2	0.91
3	1.36
4	1.81
5	2.27
6	2.72
7	3.18
8	3.63
9	4.08
10	4.54
20	9.07
30	13.61
40	18.14
50	22.68
60	27.22
70	31.75
80	36.29
90	40.82
100	45.36
1,000	453.59

LENGTH

centimeters (cm)	inches (in.)
1	0.39
2	0.79
3	1.18
4	1.57
5	1.97
6	2.36
7	2.76
8	3.15
9	3.54
10	3.94
20	7.87
50	19.69
100	39.37

inches (in.)	centimeters (cm)
1/8	0.3
1/4	0.6
3/8	1.0
5/8	1.6
3/4	1.9
7/8	2.2
1	2.5
2	5.1
3	7.6
4	10.2
5	12.7
6	15.2
7	17.8
8	20.3
9	22.9
10	25.4

meters (m)	feet (ft)
1	3.28
2	6.56
3	9.80
4	13.10
5	16.40
6	19.70
7	23.00
8	26.20
9	29.50
10	32.80
20	65.60
25	82.00
50	164.00
100	328.10
500	1,640.40
1,000	3,280.80

feet (ft)	meters (m)
1	0.30
2	0.61
3 (1 yard)	0.91
4	1.22
5	1.52
6	1.83
7	2.13
8	2.44
9	2.74
10	3.05
20	6.10
25	7.62
50	15.24
100	30.48
300 (100 yards)	91.44
500	152.40
1,000	304.80

kilometers (km)	miles
1	0.62
2	1.24
3	1.86
4	2.49
5	3.11
6	3.73
7	4.35
8	4.97
9	5.59
10	6.21
20	12.40
25	15.50
50	31.10
75	46.60
100	62.10
500	310.70
1,000	621.40

miles	kilometers (km)
1	1.61
2	3.22
3	4.83
4	6.44
5	8.05
6	9.66
7	11.30
8	12.90
9	14.50
10	16.10
20	32.20
25	40.20
50	80.50
75	120.70
100	160.90
500	804.70
1,000	1,609.30

AREA

square centimeters (cm²)	square inches (sq. in.)
1	0.16
2	0.31
3	0.47
4	0.62
5	0.78
6	0.93
7	1.09
8	1.24
9	1.40
10	1.55
20	3.10
50	7.75
100	15.50

square inches (sq. in.)	square centimeters (cm²)
1	6.45
2	12.90
3	19.35
4	25.80
5	32.26
6	38.71
7	45.16
8	51.61
9	58.06
10	64.51
20	129.00
50	322.60
100	645.20

square kilometers (km²)	square miles (sq. mi.)
1	0.39
2	0.77
3	1.16
4	1.54
5	1.93
6	2.32
7	2.70
8	3.09
9	3.48
10	3.86
20	7.72
50	19.30
100	38.60
500	193.00

square miles (sq. mi.)	square kilometers (km²)
1	2.59
2	5.18
3	7.77
4	10.40
5	13.00
6	15.50
7	18.10
8	20.70
9	23.30
10	25.90
20	51.80
50	129.50
100	259.00
500	1,295.00

VOLUME

cubic centimeters (cm³)	cubic inches (cu. in.)
1	0.061
2	0.122
3	0.183
4	0.244
5	0.305
6	0.366
7	0.427
8	0.488
9	0.549
10	0.160
50	3.050
100	6.100

cubic inches (cu. in.)	cubic centimeters (cm³)
1	16.39
2	32.77
3	49.16
4	65.55
5	81.94
6	98.32
7	114.70
8	131.10
9	147.50
10	163.90
50	819.40
100	1,639.00

HOW TO CONVERT

Temperature

Celsius to Fahrenheit	multiply by 9, divide by 5 and add 32
Fahrenheit to Celsius	subtract 32, multiply by 5 and divide by 9
Celsius to Kelvin	add 273.15
Kelvin to Celsius	subtract 273.15

Length

millimeters to inches	multiply by 0.03937
inches to millimeters	multiply by 25.40
centimeters to inches	multiply by 0.3937
inches to centimeters	multiply by 2.54
meters to yards	multiply by 1.0936
yards to meters	multiply by 0.9144
kilometers to miles	multiply by 0.6214
miles to kilometers	multiply by 1.6093

Mass

grams to ounces	multiply by 0.03527
ounces to grams	multiply by 28.349
kilograms to pounds	multiply by 2.2046
pounds to kilograms	multiply by 0.4536

Area

cm² to square inches	multiply by 0.155
square inches to cm²	multiply by 6.4516
m² to square feet	multiply by 10.764
square feet to m²	multiply by 0.0929
hectares to acres	multiply by 2.471
acres to hectares	multiply by 0.4047
km² to square miles	multiply by 0.386
square miles to km²	multiply by 2.59

Volume

cm³ to cubic inches	multiply by 0.061
cubic inches to cm³	multiply by 16.3871
m³ to cubic feet	multiply by 35.315
cubic feet to m³	multiply by 0.0283

Energy

joules to calories	multiply by 0.238
calories to joules	multiply by 4.186
megajoules to kilowatt hours	multiply by 0.278
kilowatt hours to megajoules	multiply by 3.6

Power

kilowatts to horsepower	multiply by 1.341
horsepower to kilowatts	multiply by 0.7457

TEMPERATURE TABLES

Fahrenheit °F	Celsius °C	Kelvin °K
−459.67	−273.15	0
0	−32	241.15
32	0	273.15
212	100	373.15

Fahrenheit-to-Celsius Table

°F	°C	°F	°C
1	−17.2	60	15.6
2	−16.7	70	21.1
3	−16.1	80	26.7
4	−15.6	90	32.2
5	−15.0	100	37.8
10	−12.2	150	65.5
20	−6.7	175	79.4
30	−1.1	200	93.3
40	4.4	210	98.9
50	10.0	212	100.0

Celsius-to-Fahrenheit Table

°C	°F	°C	°F
1	33.8	21	69.8
2	35.6	22	71.6
3	37.4	23	73.4
4	39.2	24	75.2
5	41.0	25	77.0
6	42.8	26	78.8
7	44.6	27	80.6
8	46.4	28	82.4
9	48.2	29	84.2
10	50.0	30	86.0
11	51.8	50	122.0
12	53.6	60	140.0
13	55.4	70	158.0
14	57.2	80	176.0
15	59.0	90	194.0
16	60.8	95	203.0
17	62.6	96	204.8
18	64.4	97	206.6
19	66.2	98	208.4
20	68.0	99	210.2
		100	212.0

GEOMETRIC SHAPES

POLYGONS
A polygon is a flat shape with three or more straight sides.

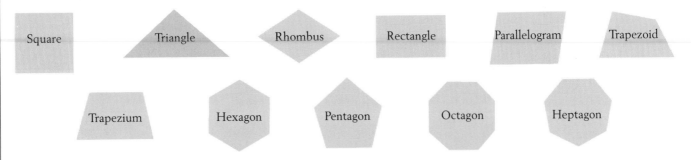

Square • Triangle • Rhombus • Rectangle • Parallelogram • Trapezoid

Trapezium • Hexagon • Pentagon • Octagon • Heptagon

SOLID SHAPES
Solid shapes have three dimensions: length, width, and height.

Sphere • Cube • Cuboid • Cone • Cylinder • Prism • Pyramid

PARTS OF A CIRCLE
A **circle** is a curved line on which all points are equally distant from the center. The **circumference** of a circle is the length around its outside. An **arc** is a part of the circumference. The **radius** of a circle is a straight line between a point on the circumference and the center of the circle. A **chord** is a straight line between two points on the circumference. The **diameter** is a chord that passes through the center of a circle; its length is twice the radius. A **sector** is an area bounded by two radii and an arc of the circumference. A **segment** is an area bounded by a chord and an arc of the circumference.

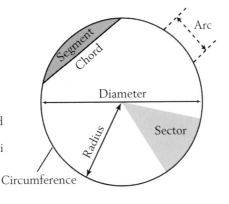

Segment • Chord • Arc • Diameter • Radius • Sector • Circumference

Key	
A	= area
a, b, c	= length
B	= base area
d	= diameter
h	= height
r	= radius
V	= volume
π	= 3.14159

AREAS OF SHAPES

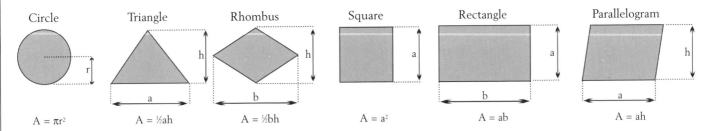

Circle	Triangle	Rhombus	Square	Rectangle	Parallelogram
$A = \pi r^2$	$A = \frac{1}{2}ah$	$A = \frac{1}{2}bh$	$A = a^2$	$A = ab$	$A = ah$

VOLUMES OF SOLIDS

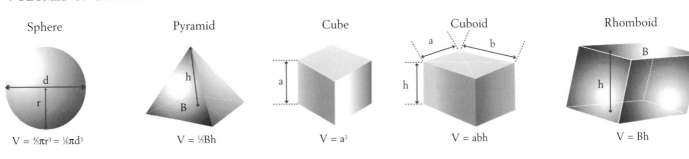

Sphere	Pyramid	Cube	Cuboid	Rhomboid
$V = \frac{4}{3}\pi r^3 = \frac{1}{6}\pi d^3$	$V = \frac{1}{3}Bh$	$V = a^3$	$V = abh$	$V = Bh$

FAMOUS SCIENTISTS

Archimedes (c.287–212 B.C.)
A Greek mathematician and inventor, Archimedes invented a spiral pump for raising water. The pump, called an Archimedes screw, is still used. He discovered differential calculus and the formula for the volume of a sphere. He is best known for his work on buoyancy, which he is said to have discovered when he noticed how his body displaced water in a bath. He was killed by a Roman soldier during an invasion of his home city of Syracuse, on the island of Sicily.

Nicolaus Copernicus (A.D. 1473–1543)
Born in Poland, Copernicus studied mathematics, church law, medicine, and astronomy. After 30 years of work, he put forward a theory that the Earth rotates daily on its own axis, and that the Earth and the other planets orbit the sun with years of different lengths. This challenged the accepted belief that the Earth was the center of the universe. Copernicus published his work only days before his death, but his theory was developed and expanded by other leading astronomers including Kepler, Galileo, and Newton.

Tycho Brahe (1546–1601)
Brahe was born in southern Sweden, which at the time was under Danish rule. Studying astronomy before the invention of the telescope, Brahe discovered serious errors in the astronomical tables of the time. He made it his life's work to correct those errors. He proved that comets were heavenly bodies and calculated the length of a year on the Earth to within one second. Brahe's assistant, Johannes Kepler, used his teacher's observations to calculate that Mars travels in an elliptical orbit.

Blaise Pascal (1623–1662)
Born in France, Pascal invented a calculating machine (1647), and later the barometer, the hydraulic press, and the syringe. He studied fluid pressure, showing that pressure in a liquid acts equally in all directions and that changes in pressure are transmitted instantly.

Galileo Galilei (1564–1642)
An Italian astronomer and mathematician, Galileo improved the refracting telescope. He observed the phases of Venus and was one of the first people to study sunspots. He found that a pendulum swings at a constant rate and discovered the laws of falling bodies. By supporting Copernicus's theory of the universe, he fell foul of the religious authorities and had to renounce his beliefs. Under house arrest in Florence, he continued his research until he died, even after becoming totally blind in 1637.

Robert Boyle (1627–1691)
An Irish-born scientist, Boyle performed experiments on air, vacuum, combustion, and respiration. In 1662, he observed that the pressure and volume of a gas at a fixed temperature are inversely proportional. This relationship is now called Boyle's law. Boyle also studied acids and alkalis, density, crystallography, and refraction.

Isaac Newton (1642–1727)
British physicist and mathematician Isaac Newton is well known for his work concerning gravity, but this was just part of a host of important laws and discoveries he made. He developed his three laws of motion and discovered that white light is made up of rays of light of different colors. He also built the first reflecting telescope (1868). Newton was involved in many disputes throughout his life, most notably a conflict with Gottried Leibniz over who first discovered calculus.

Benjamin Franklin (1706–1790)
Born in Boston, Massachusetts, Franklin was a printer, politician, statesman, prolific writer, and inventor. He encourged active communication between people in scientific research, and his work led to the establishment of the American Philosophical Society. He invented the fuel-efficient Franklin stove, the lightning rod, bifocal lenses for glasses, the first copying machine, and the harmonica. Franklin's most famous scientific work concerned electricity. He developed the fluid model of electrical current, understanding that it consists of the movement of charged microscopic particles. In a famous kite-flying experiment he proved that lightning was a form of electricity.

Joseph Priestley (1733–1804)
British chemist Joseph Priestley discovered oxygen in 1774. He also identified many other gases, including ammonia, carbon monoxide, nitrous oxide, and sulfur dioxide. He discovered that green plants give off oxygen and require sunlight. Priestley supported the French Revolution and opposed the slave trade. He emigrated to the United States in 1794.

Antoine Lavoisier (1743–1794)
Regarded as the founder of modern chemistry, French scientist Lavoisier showed air to be a mixture of gases, which he named oxygen and nitrogen. He also proved that water contains hydrogen and oxygen. He devised a method of naming chemical compounds and was on the commission that devised the metric system. A critic of the French Revolution, Lavoisier was guillotined in Paris in 1794.

John Dalton (1766–1844)

British chemist Dalton's scientific work started in the fields of color blindness and meteorology. From 1787 he kept a weather journal, recording some 200,000 observations. He advanced a theory of atoms in 1803, proposing that molecules are made from atoms combined in simple ratios. In 1808, Dalton published the first table of comparative atomic weights. He also researched the force of steam and expansion of gases by heat, and developed his law of partial pressures.

Michael Faraday (1791–1867)

This British physicist and chemist discovered benzene in 1825 and was the founder of electrochemistry. He discovered electromagnetic induction, which led to the dynamo and electric motor. His work contributed greatly to modern understanding of electricity, electrolysis, and the development of the battery. Faraday was the first person to use pressure to turn a gas into a liquid.

Charles Darwin (1809–1892)

Darwin studied first medicine and then biology before becoming the naturalist aboard H.M.S. *Beagle*, a scientific survey ship bound for South America in 1831. Returning to Britain in 1836, he wrote many works on plants and animals. He is most famous for his theories regarding evolution, particularly his works *On the Origin of Species by Means of Natural Selection* (1859) and *The Descent of Man* (1871). Darwin believed that species were not created individually, but evolved over a long period of time from other species in a struggle for existence in which only the fittest survived.

Gregor Mendel (1822–1884)

Born in Austria, Mendel was ordained as a priest in 1847. He trained as a science teacher while growing plants in a series of experiments. In researching inheritance in plants—especially edible peas—Mendel discovered and developed a number of the key principles that govern genetics. These include the law that traits are inherited independently of each other— the basis for recessive and dominant gene composition. The importance of his work was not recognized until it was rediscovered in the early 1900s.

Louis Pasteur (1822–1895)

A French chemist, Pasteur was the first person to show that microbes cause fermentation and disease. He developed the process of using heat to kill germs (pasteurization) and popularized the sterilization of medical equipment, which saved many lives. Pasteur discovered vaccines for rabies and anthrax. In 1888 he founded the Pasteur Institute in Paris for the treatment of contagious disease. He worked there until his death.

James Clerk Maxwell (1831–1879)

This British physicist was the first person to write down the laws of magnetism and electricity in mathematical form. In 1864 he proved that electromagnetic waves are combinations of oscillating electric and magnetic fields. Maxwell identified light to be a form of electromagnetic radiation, and he increased understanding of the movement of gases, showing that the velocity of molecules in a gas depends on their temperature.

Joseph John Thomson (1856–1940)

Thomson studied at Cambridge University in England, where he became Professor of Experimental Physics in 1884. His work led to the discovery of the electron. Thomson discovered that gases are able to conduct electricity and was a pioneer of nuclear physics. Thomson won the 1906 Nobel Prize in physics.

Marie Curie (1867–1934)

Polish-born Marie Curie and her husband, Pierre, worked in Paris. Along with Henri Becquerel, they were awarded the 1903 Nobel Prize in physics for their work in discovering radioactivity. In 1906 Marie Curie became Professor of Physics at the Sorbonne, Paris. There she isolated the elements polonium and radium, and discovered plutonium. Curie received the 1911 Nobel Prize in chemistry. She died of pernicious anemia caused by many years of exposure to radiation.

Ernest Rutherford (1871–1937)

This New Zealand-born physicist worked with J.J. Thomson at Cambridge University. Rutherford discovered the presence of nuclei in atoms. Along with Frederick Soddy, he proposed that radioactivity results from the disintegration of atoms and was the first person to split the atom. He won the 1908 Nobel Prize in chemistry for his studies of the different types of radiation.

Albert Einstein (1879–1955)

Born in Germany, Einstein is most famously associated with his 1905 Special Theory of Relativity, which related matter and energy in the equation $E = mc^2$. This and his 1915 General Theory of Relativity redefined the way scientists view the universe. His other achievements included a photoelectric theory, for which he was awarded the 1921 Nobel Prize in physics.

Dorothy Hodgkin (1910–1994)

Born in Egypt, Hodgkin studied at Oxford and Cambridge Universities. She was then a research fellow at Oxford. She was an early user of computers in her field of X-ray crystallography. In 1964, she was awarded the Nobel Prize for chemistry for her discovery of the structure of vitamin B_{12} and other complex molecules, including penicillin and insulin.

INVENTIONS AND DISCOVERIES

Aircraft
The first heavier-than-air craft was a glider built by British inventor George Cayley in 1808. The concept was developed further by German glider builder Otto Lilienthal, who invented an arched-wing glider in 1877. The first controlled, powered flight was in 1903, when U.S. brothers Orville and Wilbur Wright built and flew their Wright *Flyer 1* at Kitty Hawk, North Carolina. The Wrights continued to develop more controllable aircraft throughout the first decade of the 1900s and inspired many others to develop the potential of air transportation.

Antiseptic
In 1865 British surgeon Joseph Lister read French chemist Louis Pasteur's proposal that airborne microbes caused infection. Through his experiences with bone fractures, Lister devised a series of successful trials that used a solution of carbolic acid, or phenol, to protect wounds from microbes in the air. Today, antiseptics are widely used in surgery and health care, as well as to sterilize food preparation areas.

Deoxyribonucleic acid (DNA)
Nucleic acids were first discovered in 1869 by Swiss physiologist Friedrich Miescher. In 1944, a U.S. team led by Canadian-born Oswald T. Avery showed that DNA transmits genetic information. In 1953 DNA's structure was detailed as a double helix by James Watson and Francis Crick. Their findings were aided by the research of two crystallographers, Maurice Wilkins and Rosalind Franklin. The team won the 1962 Nobel Prize.

Dynamite
In the early 1860s Swedish chemist Alfred Nobel worked to develop a way to safely use the powerful but unstable explosive nitroglycerine. In 1867 he patented a mixture, based on nitroglycerine and a type of clay called kieselguhr, that was stable until it was ignited by a detonator. Nobel called this mixture dynamite. Dynamite soon became widely used for blasting tunnels and quarries.

Electron microscope
In 1932 German scientists Max Knoll and Ernst Ruska produced a microscope that used beams of electrons rather than light to produce images. Knoll and Ruska's microscope could magnify by 17 times. Modern electron microscopes magnify by up to 2 million times—much more than is possible with an optical microscope. They make it possible to investigate materials and organisms that could not be viewed through an optical microscope.

Helicopter
It took more than four centuries for Leonardo da Vinci's designs for a vertical-takeoff, heavier-than-air craft to become reality. The first fully controlled helicopter was the twin-rotored Focke–Wulf *Fw 61* helicopter, designed by German aircraft designer Heinrich Focke in 1936. By 1938 the *Fw 61* had established a number of records, including altitude and distance.

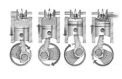

Internal-combustion engine
Etienne Lenoir is credited with producing the first internal-combustion engine to operate successfully. His two-stroke engine was built in 1860. In 1867 German engineers Nikolaus Otto and Eugene Langen developed a basic internal-combustion engine, and in 1876 Otto patented the first practical four-stroke internal-combustion engine—the forerunner of the engines that now power motor vehicles all over the world.

Jet engine
In 1930 a British Royal Air Force cadet, Frank Whittle, patented his design for a jet engine. Whittle tested a complete jet engine on the ground in 1937. Around the same time, German engineer Hans von Ohain built a similar engine that would power the first-ever jet aircraft, the Heinkel *He 178*, in 1939. The first sucessful jet aircraft was the Gloster *E28/39*, with a Whittle-designed *W-1* jet that gave a maximum thrust of 3,800 KN. The Gloster first flew on 15 May 1941.

Laser
The principle of laser action was detailed as early as 1917 by Albert Einstein. In the 1950s that theory was put into practice: U.S. physicists Gordon Gould, Theodore Maiman, Leonard Schawlow, and Charles Townes all developed lasers at this time, as did Soviet physicists Nikolay Basov and Aleksandr Prokhorov. In 1964 Maiman's ruby laser was used to treat lesions of the retina—the first practical application of a laser. Since then, many types of lasers have found uses in medicine, industry, and communications.

Lightbulb
In 1801 British chemist Humphry Davy demonstrated incandescence, which is the ability of substances to give off light when heated to high temperatures. In 1878 U.S. scientist Joseph Wilson Swan made the first lightbulb using an incandescent carbon filament in a glass bulb from which the air had been pumped. U.S. inventor Thomas Alva Edison produced a similar bulb one year later. Edison went on to develop the equipment needed to produce the first practical lighting systems.

Microchip

In 1947 U.S. physicists John Bardeen, Walter Brattain, and William Shockley invented the semiconducting transistor. By 1971 a microchip was launched that had 2,300 transistors etched on a single chip. Much more powerful microchips are now available. They are used as the processors of computers and the microprocessors that control the operations of household appliances such as washing machines.

Photography

In 1826 French inventor Joseph Niépce made the first permanent photographic image on bitumen-coated metal plates. From 1829 until his death in 1833, Niépce worked with French artist and inventor Louis Daguerre. By 1837 Daguerre had developed the first practical techniques for printing photographs. In 1841 British scientist William Talbot patented a process that used a negative image to make several copies, or prints, of a single image.

Printing

The Chinese used engraved blocks of wood to print on paper before A.D. 200; molded metal type may have been developed by the Koreans as early as the 1300s. The first European printing press to use movable type is credited to German printer Johann Gutenberg around 1447. William Caxton used a similar press in England from 1476, while Juan Pablos set up a press in Mexico City in 1539.

Radio

German physicist Heinrich Hertz was the first to demonstrate the existence of radio waves in 1888. His discovery was applied by Italian inventor Guglielmo Marconi, who built the first radio system in 1895. In 1901 Marconi transmitted a radio signal across the Atlantic Ocean. In 1906 the first voice broadcast was made by Canadian physicist Reginald Fessenden.

Satellite

The first artificial satellite, *Sputnik 1*, was built by the Soviet Union and launched on October 4, 1957. *Sputnik 1* carried a radio beacon and a thermometer. Since then hundreds of satellites have been launched for a variety of applications, including global surveying, communications, and military surveillance. *TIROS 1*, the first weather satellite, was launched in 1960.

Sound recording

In 1855 French inventor Leon Scott built a phonautograph that recorded sound vibrations on paper. In 1877 Thomas Edison developed the phonograph, which recorded sound as a groove in tinfoil and could then play back the sound. The first gramophone to use discs was invented by Emile Berliner in 1887. Dutch company Philips launched the first tape cassette in 1961 and, with Sony, the CD in 1980.

Space rocket

Russian physicist Konstantin Tsiolovsky first suggested the use of rockets for space research in the 1800s. U.S. engineer Robert Goddard launched the first liquid-fuel rocket in 1926. German-born rocket scientist Wernher von Braun developed the V-2 long-range rocket in the 1940s and went on to lead the development of NASA's Saturn V rocket, which launched the Apollo missions to the moon.

Spinning jenny

In 1764 British inventor James Hargreaves developed one of the first machines to increase the efficiency of the textiles industry. Named after his daughter, the hand-operated spinning jenny teased out a number of threads from a single bundle of fibers onto a number of individual spindles. This allowed yarn to be made faster.

Steam engine

The French physicist Denis Papin detailed the principles of steam power in 1679. In 1712 Thomas Newcomen and Thomas Savery built the first practical steam engine, which was widely used to pump water out of mines. In 1768 British engineer James Watt built a steam engine, patented the following year, which played a major role in the Industrial Revolution.

Telephone

Based on what he had learned from his work to improve the telegraph, Scottish-born inventor Alexander Graham Bell filed a patent application for his telephone device at noon on January 14, 1876—just two hours before U.S. inventor Elisha Gray did the same. In March 1876 Bell transmitted intelligible words over a prototype telephone for the first time.

Television

In 1884 German scientist Paul Nipkow invented a disc with a spiral of lenses that split an image into lines as it rotated. British inventor John Logie Baird used a Nipkow disc in his mechanical television system, which he first demonstrated in 1926. The BBC used Baird's system to broadcast news and shows from 1929. Electronic television was developed in the 1920s and 1930s by Russian scientist Vladimir Zworykin and U.S. inventors Philo Farnworth and Allen DuMont.

X rays

In November 1895 German physicist Wilhelm Conrad Roentgen was working in his laboratory with a cathode-ray tube and a fluorescent screen. He noticed that some form of radiation was lighting up a screen that was shielded from the cathode rays. He named the radiation "X rays." A month later he took the first X-ray photograph, or radiograph. It showed the bones in his wife's hand. Roentgen won the 1901 Nobel Prize in physics for his work.

GLOSSARY

acceleration The rate of change in the velocity of a moving object.

acid A chemical compound that usually includes hydrogen that dissolves in water to produce hydrogen ions.

airfoil A teardrop-shaped structure that produces force as it cuts through air. Aircraft wings and control surfaces are airfoils.

alkali A base that dissolves in water to form hydroxide ions, and forms salt with acids.

alloy A mixture of two or more metals, or a mixture of a metal and a nonmetal.

astronomical unit (AU) A unit of measure equal to the average distance between the Earth and the sun—93 million mi. (150 million km).

atom The smallest particle of matter that has the chemical properties of an element.

atmosphere The gases and clouds that surround a planet, star, or moon.

bacteria Microscopic living organisms, some of which can cause diseases.

base A substance that can react with an acid to form a salt and water.

biodegradable Able to decompose in the natural environment by biological means in a moderate amount of time.

biome A climatic region, made up of different habitats, inhabited by distinct forms of plant and animal life.

biotechnology The use of living organisms to generate useful products.

black hole A dark region of space that is so massive that not even light can escape its gravitational pull.

catalyst A substance that increases the rate of a chemical reaction but is unchanged at the end of the reaction.

cell The basic unit from which all living things—plants and animals—are composed.

cloning The creation of genetically identical organisms by natural or artificial means.

color spectrum The range of frequencies of visible light; the colors of the rainbow arranged in order of frequency.

combustion The scientific term used to describe all forms of burning.

compound A substance that consists of two or more elements chemically bonded together.

conductor A substance through which heat or an electrical current can flow.

constellation A pattern of stars in a region of the night sky. There are 88 constellations.

density Mass per unit volume; a measure of how tightly packed the mass is in a substance.

DNA Deoxyribonucleic acid. DNA is present in every cell and carries all the genetic information of an organism.

eclipse When one star, planet, or satellite passes in front of another, blocking the light from a celestial body such as the sun.

ecosystem A self-contained community of plants and animals and their environment. A rain forest is an example of an ecosystem.

electrochemistry A branch of chemistry that interrelates chemical reactions and electrical currents.

electromagnetic waves Waves of constantly changing electric and magnetic fields, such as light, radio, and X rays.

electron A subatomic particle that has a negative electrical charge and that usually orbits the nucleus of an atom.

element A substance that cannot be transformed into simpler substances by chemical reactions.

enzyme A chemical substance that occurs in living organisms and that acts as a catalyst for chemical reactions in those organisms.

equator An imaginary circle on the surface of a planet or star at and equal distance from each of its two poles.

erosion The process by which material is worn down and transported by water, wind, gravity, or ice.

escape velocity The velocity an object must reach to escape the gravity of an astronomical object such as a planet.

evolution Fundamental changes in the genetic makeup of a species over many generations.

fault A break or fracture in rocks along which movement has taken place; a joint between two tectonic plates—often a source of earthquakes.

force A form of pushing or pulling influence that can change the velocity of an object or modify its shape.

fossil fuel An energy-containing substance formed from the remains of prehistoric plants or animals; coal, oil, or gas.

friction A force that resists motion between surfaces that are in contact.

galaxies A collection of millions or billions of stars, planets, gas, and dust bound together by gravity.

gas A low-density form of matter that will fill a container of any size or shape.

gene A section of DNA that passes from parents to offspring and determines physical characteristics in an organism.

genetic engineering The science of altering or transplanting genes to create new organisms or to produce useful substances.

gestation In mammals, the time during which a fetus develops and is nourished inside its mother's body.

gravity A force of attraction between objects that is due to their mass.

greenhouse effect The retention of heat by the Earth's atmosphere as a result of gases such as methane and carbon dioxide.

habitat The place where an animal or plant lives or grows.

hormone A chemical substance produced by an organism to control processes of the body.

hydraulics The use of the pressure in a liquid to transfer power.

inertia The tendency of objects to resist a change in their velocity.

igneous rocks Rocks formed under the Earth's surface when molten material solidifies.

immunization A medical procedure that primes the body's immune system to fight specific infections.

infrared radiation Electromagnetic waves just beyond the low-frequency limit of the visible spectrum.

insulator A substance that does not conduct electricity or heat well.

invertebrate A creature that does not have a backbone.

isotopes Atoms of an element that have the same number of protons, but different numbers of neutrons in their nuclei.

kinetic energy The energy an object has because of its speed.

laser (light amplification by stimulated emission of radiation) A device that produces a narrow, intense beam of light of a single frequency. Lasers are used in medicine, communications, and industry.

lightning A flash of light caused by a large discharge of static electricity through gases in the atmosphere.

light year The distance light travels in one Earth year; 6 trillion mi. (9.5 trillion km).

liquid A fluid state of matter that collects at the bottom of its container.

luminous The term used to describe any object that gives off light.

magnet An object that attracts iron, nickel, and cobalt, and attracts or repels other magnets.

magnetic field A region of space in which a magnet experiences a force.

metamorphic rock Rock that has been modified by heat, pressure, or both.

mineral A naturally occurring substance that is usually found in rocks.

mixture Two or more substances that occupy the same volume but are not chemically bonded together.

molten A substance that has melted and is in a liquid state.

nanotechnology The science and engineering of nanometer-scale objects.

neutron A subatomic particle that has the mass of a proton but no electrical charge.

nucleus (*plural* nuclei) A mass of protons and neutrons at the core of an atom.

orbit The path of one body around another, such as the moon's path around the Earth.

ore A mineral from which useful products, such as metals, can be extracted.

oxidation The addition of oxygen to, or the removal of hydrogen from, a compound; the loss of electrons from a substance; the opposite of reduction.

oxide A compound of one or more elements bonded with oxygen.

ozone layer A layer of the atmosphere that contains a high concentration of ozone (O_3), a gas that absorbs harmful ultraviolet radiation from the sun's rays.

permafrost Soil or rock that is constantly below the freezing point of water.

planet A large sphere of matter that orbits around the sun or another star.

pneumatics The use of the pressure in a gas, usually air, to transfer power.

polymer A substance that consists of huge molecules made by a chemical reaction that links together many small molecules, called monomers, in a chain or network.

potential energy The energy that an object has as a result of its position or state.

pressure The force exerted over a specific area by a solid, liquid, or gas.

proton A subatomic particle that has the mass of a neutron and a positive electrical charge equal in size to the charge of an electron; the nucleus of a hydrogen atom.

radiation Electromagnetic energy that travels in waves; matter and energy released by the decay of a radioactive substance.

radioactivity The tendency of the unstable nuclei of certain isotopes to release radiation.

recycling The collection and reuse of materials to conserve energy and resources.

reduction The removal of oxygen from, or the addition of hydrogen to, a compound; the addition of electrons to a substance; the opposite of oxidation.

reflection A process in which a wave, often of light, bounces off of another medium.

refraction The bending of light waves as they cross the boundary between transparent substances of different densities.

renewable energy Sources of energy, such as wind or tides, that can be harnessed to generate power without being used up.

reproduction The process in which living things make more organisms similar to themselves in order for a species to survive.

resistance The ability of a substance to prevent or reduce the flow of an electrical current through it.

respiration The absorption of oxygen in order to release energy from food, and the emission of carbon dioxide and moisture.

satellite An object that orbits a larger object. The moon is a natural satellite of the Earth. Many artificial satellites orbit the Earth to provide telecommunications links and photographic images of its surface.

sedimentary rock A type of rock formed from the sediment—stones, sand, dead organisms, and mud—that gathers under a body of water and hardens over time.

semiconductor A substance that conducts electricity better than an insulator, but not as well as a conductor.

solid A state of matter that has a definite shape due to the forces that hold it together.

solution A mixture that consists of a solid or gas dissolved in a liquid.

species A group of similar organisms that can produce fertile offspring.

star A large sphere of gases, mostly hydrogen and helium, in which nuclear fusion produces heat and light. The sun is a star.

superconductivity The ability to conduct an electrical current without losses due to resistance. Certain materials become superconductors at very low temperatures.

synthetic Chemical compounds and other substances artificially made by chemical reactions in a factory or chemicals plant.

tectonics The study of the plate structures that form the Earth's crust, and the forces and processes that change it.

telecommunications The transmission of information over long distances by electrical, optical, or radio signals.

tissue The cells that make up a particular part of a plant or animal.

troposphere The lower 8 mi. (13.5km) of the Earth's atmosphere.

ultraviolet radiation Electromagnetic radiation beyond the high-frequency limit of the visible spectrum.

vacuum A space that contains no matter. A partial vacuum contains a greatly reduced concentration of matter at low pressure.

velocity The distance traveled by a moving object in a particular direction in a given amount of time, usually a second.

vertebrate A creature that has a backbone.

vibrations Regularly repeated movements that are described in terms of the frequency and the amplitude of the movement.

virus In biology, a microscopic organism—smaller than bacteria—that can carry or cause disease in another organism.

wavelength The distance between two similar points in a wave.

weight The strength of the pull of gravity on an object due to its mass.

X rays High-frequency radiation that can pass through some opaque objects.

Computer terms

algorithm A set of rules for calculations.

ASCII A system of codes used to represent letters, numbers, and other characters.

bug An error in the computer hardware or software that causes it to fail.

bit Binary digit; the smallest piece of data.

byte Eight bits.

CD-ROM A type of compact disc that holds computer programs and information.

data The general term for the information handled by a computer.

database An organized collection of data that can be sorted, added to, and retrieved.

disk A data-storage device. Hard disks are fixed in computers; removable disks are portable data stores.

file A collection of information, such as a document or an image, stored with a specific name.

hardware The physical equipment that makes up a computer system.

input device Equipment that puts information into a computer, such as a mouse, keyboard, or scanner.

Internet A communications network that links computers throughout the world.

mainframe A powerful computer that can be used by many people at the same time.

microprocessor The powerful set of miniature electronic circuits, etched on a silicon chip, that processes data in a device.

network A group of computers linked to share information and resources.

operating system The programs that run a computer and its many parts. The operating system starts up every time a computer is switched on.

peripheral A part of a computer system that is outside the computer itself, such as a keyboard or printer.

pixel A picture element. Pixels are the dots that can light up to form an image on a computer monitor or television screen.

program A set of instructions, in order, that are used carry out a particular job.

RAM (Random Access Memory) Memory where data is held as it waits to be processed. The contents of the RAM are lost when the computer is switched off.

ROM (Read Only Memory) Where essential programs and data are held. The ROM keeps its contents when the power is off.

software The name given to all the programs used to run a computer.

virus A program that is designed to cause damage such as deleting files.

Visual Display Unit (VDU) The display screen used with a computer.

word processor A program that allows users to store, edit, and print documents.

INDEX

ACKNOWLEDGMENTS

The publishers wish to thank the following for their contribution to the book:

Photographs *(t = top; b = bottom; m = middle; l = left; r = right)*
Page 2 *b* Photo Library International/ESA/Science Photo Library; 4/5 *t* Dr. B. Booth/GeoScience Features; 5 *tr* Dr B. Booth/GeoScience Features; *mr* John Reader/Science Photo Library; 6 *tl* John Reader/Science Photo Library; *l* John Reader/Science Photo Library; 7 *t* John Reader/Science Photo Library; *r* George Roos, Peter Arnold Inc./Science Photo Library; *br* John Reader/Science Photo Library; 8 *tl* Dr. B. Booth/GeoScience Features 9 *b* Pekka Parviainen/Science Photo Library; 10 *tl* Nils Jorgensen/Rex Features; 11 *bl* Simon Fraser/Mauna Loa Observatory/Science Photo Library; *br* DRA/Still Pictures; 13 *tl* Aaron Chang/The Stock Market; *br* PowerStock Photo Library; *bl* GSFC/Science Photo Library; 14 *tl* B. Murton/Southampton Oceanography Centre/Science Photo Library; 15 *bl* W. Haxby, Lamont-Doherty Earth Observatory/Science Photo Library; 16/17 *t* NASA/Science Photo Library; 17 *tr* David Parker/Science Photo Library; *mr* M. Hobbs/GeoScience Features; 18 *tr* D. Decobecq/Still Pictures; 19 *mr* Alan Watson/Still Pictures; *bl* Dr. B. Booth/GeoScience Features; *br* Prof. Stewart Lowther/Science Photo Library; 20/21 *b* Paul X. Scott/Sygma; 21 *mr* Rex Features; 22 *tl* Science Photo Library; *ml* Martin Bond/Science Photo Library; 23 *ml* Bill O'Connor/Still Pictures; 24 *tr* Dr. B. Booth/GeoScience Features; *br* Dr. B. Booth/GeoScience Features; 25 *tr* Dr. B. Booth/GeoScience Features; *mr* Dr. B. Booth/GeoScience Features; *br* Dr. B. Booth/GeoScience Features; *b* Alan Watson/Still Pictures; 26 *tl* Ben Johnson/Science Photo Library; *ml* Dr. B. Booth/GeoScience Features; *tr* Dr. B. Booth/GeoScience Features; 27 *t* Vaughan Fleming/Science Photo Library; *tr* Arnold Fisher/Science Photo Library; *mr* Vaughan Fleming/Science Photo Library; *br* Dr. B. Booth/GeoScience Features; *bl* Novosti/Science Photo Library; 28 *tl* James L. Amos, Peter Arnold Inc./Science Photo Library; *ml* Claude Nuridsany & Marie Perennou/Science Photo Library; *l* Adrienne Hart-Davis/Science Photo Library; *bl* Sinclair Stammers/Science Photo Library; *br* Tony Craddock/Science Photo Library; *tl* The Stock Market; 29 *ml* Dr. B. Booth/GeoScience Features; *bl* Dr. B. Booth/GeoScience Features; *tr* Mike Jackson/Still Pictures; 30 *tl* U.S. Dept. of Energy/Science Photo Library; *l* Dr. B. Booth/GeoScience Features; *tr* Dr. B. Booth/GeoScience Features; 30/31 *b* Sinclair Stammers/Science Photo Library; 31 *tr* Adam Jones/Science Photo Library; *r* Astrid & Hans-Frieder Michler/Science Photo Library; *br* Simon Fraser/Science Photo Library; 32 *tl* Rex Features; *ml* Martin Bond/Science Photo Library; *br* Farrell Grehan/Science Photo Library; 33 *tl* Martin Bond/Science Photo Library; *bl* Dr. B. Booth/GeoScience Features; 35 *r* Simon Fraser/Science Photo Library; *b* William Ervin/Science Photo Library; *ml* Gary Braasch/Tony Stone Images; *tl* Mehau Kulyk/Science Photo Library; 39 *bl* Dr. B. Booth/GeoScience Features; 40 *tl* Keith Kent/Still Pictures; 41 *tr* Stewart Cook/Rex Features; *r* Bob Evans/Still Pictures; 42 *bl* David Parker/Science Photo Library; *b* Crown Copyright/National Meteorological Library; 43 *tr* Peter Menzel/Science Photo Library; *r* David Parker/Science Photo Library; *b* The Stock Market; 45 *tr* NASA/Science Photo Library; *br* JHC Wilson/Robert Harding Picture Library; 46 *tl* Royal Geographical Society/The Bridgeman Art Library; *tr* Royal Geographical Society/The Bridgeman Art Library; *br* R. Maisonneuve, Publiphoto Diffusion/Science Photo Library; 47 *b* GeoScience Features/NASA; 51 *mr* Tom Pantages/Phototake NYC/Robert Harding; 52 *tl* P. Morris/Ardea; 54 *tr* Peter Parks/Oxford Scientific Films; *bl* Barry Dowsett/Science Photo Library; *br* Microfield Scientific Ltd/Science Photo Library; 55 *br* Klein/Hubert/Still Pictures; 57 *r* Peter O'Toole/Oxford Scientific Films; *b* John Brown/Oxford Scientific Films; 59 *br* E. A. Janes/NHPA; 60 *tl* Nigel Cattlin/Holt Studios; *b* Nigel Cattlin/Holt Studios; 62 *br* Kenneth W. Fink/Ardea; 63 *b* Scott Camazine/Oxford Scientific Films; 65 *br* John Mead/Science Photo Library; 67 *tl* Nick Gunderson/Tony Stone; 69 *br* Laurence Gould/Oxford Scientific Films; 70 *ml* Valerie Taylor/Ardea; *br* Peter Parks/Oxford Scientific Films; 71 *tr* A.N.T./NHPA; 72 *tr* Still Pictures; 73 *br* Zig Leszczynski/Oxford Scientific Films; 76 *br* Hans D. Dossenbach/Ardea; 77 *bl* P. Robert/Sygma; 79 *b* David B. Fleetham/Oxford Scientific Films; 80 *br* Stephen Dalton/NHPA; 83 *bl* Francois Gohier/Ardea; 84 *br* Hans & Judy Beste/Ardea; 86 *tl* Martyn Colbeck/Oxford Scientific Films; *b* Mark Carwardine/Still Pictures; 89 *mr* Matthew Polak/Sygma; 90 *br* Ferrero-Labat/Ardea; 92 *tr* Konrad Wothe/Oxford Scientific Films; 93 *tr* Roland Seitre/Still Pictures; 94 *tr* Regis Cavignaux/Still Pictures; *bl* Bill Wood/NHPA; 95 *b* C. Weaver/Ardea; 98 *tr* V Rocher, Jerrican/Science Photo Library; 99 *tr* BSIP Meulliemiestre/Science Photo Library; 100 *bl* Quest/Science Photo Library; 101 *tr* Richard Wehr/Custom Medical Stock Photo/Science Photo Library; 102 *tl* Jerry Young; *bl* Science Photo Library; 103 *br* CNRI/Science Photo Library; 104 *tl* Scott Camazine/Science Photo Library; 105 *tm* Philippe Plailly/Science Photo Library; *tr* Quest/Science Photo Library; 106 *tl* Laura Bosco/Sygma; 107 *bl* Don Fawcett/Science Photo Library; 109 *ml* CNRI/Science Photo Library; 110 *tl* Bridgeman Art Library; *br* Thomas Raupach/Still Pictures; 112 *tr* Larry Mulvehill/Science Photo Library; 113 *tr* Prof. P. Motta/G. Franchitto/University "La Sapienza", Rome/Science Photo Library; 114 *tl* Kingfisher; *tr* CNRI/Science Photo Library; 117 *tl* BSIP GEMS EUROPE/Science Photo Library; *tr* Prof. P. Motta/Dept. of Anatomy/University "La Sapienza", Rome/Science Photo Library; 119 *t* Rex Features; *b* Mark Clarke/Science Photo Library; 120 *ml* Quest/Science Photo Library; 121 *bl* CNRI/Science Photo Library; 122 *tr* National Cancer Institute/Science Photo Library; 124 *bl* Science Photo Library; 125 *br* CNRI/Science Photo Library; 126 *tl* Julian Holland; *tr* Julian Holland/Rainbows End Cafe, Glastonbury; *b* John

Kelly/Tony Stone; 127 *bl* David Scharf/Science Photo Library; 128 *bl* Dr. C. Liguory/CNRI/Science Photo Library; 129 *tl* David Scharf/Science Photo Library; *br* Eye of Science/Science Photo Library; 130 *tl* Kingfisher; 131 *tl* Simon Fraser, Royal Victoria Infirmary, Newcastle upon Tyne/Science Photo Library; 133 *t* Dept. of Clinical Radiology, Salisbury District Hospital/Science Photo Library; 133 *r* V. Clement, Jerrican/Science Photo Library; 134 *tr* Kingfisher; 135 *br* Biophoto Associates/Science Photo Library; 136 *tl* Alain Dex, Publiphoto Diffusion/Science Photo Library; 137 *b* Juergen Berger, Max-Planck Institute/Science Photo Library; 138 *tl* James King-Holmes/Science Photo Library; *tr* CNRI/Science Photo Library; 139 *tl* John Walmsley; *br* John Walmsley; 140 *tr* Jorgen Schytte/Still Pictures; 141 *tl* CC Studio/Science Photo Library; *br* Matt Meadows, Peter Arnold Inc./Science Photo Library; 142 *tr* Deep Light Productions/Science Photo Library; *ml* Chris Bjornberg/Science Photo Library; *br* John Greim/Science Photo Library; 143 *t* Montreal Neuro. Institute/McGill University/CNRI/Science Photo Library; *br* Wellcome Dept. of Cognitive Neurology/Science Photo Library; 146 *tl* Science Museum/Science Photo Library; *b* Bridgeman Art Library/Joseph Wright of Derby; 147 *tr* Mary Evans Picture Library; *bl* Mary Evans Picture Library; 148 *bl* Charles D. Winters/Science Photo Library; *b* Charles D. Winters/Science Photo Library; 149 *tl* Mary Evans Picture Library; *br* Photo Researchers/Science Photo Library; 151 *tr* Philippe Plailly/Science Photo Library; *tr* Philippe Plailly/Science Photo Library; 152 *tr* Martyn F. Chillmaid/Science Photo Library; 153 *tr* David Stewart-Smith/Katz Pictures; *mr* Dylan Garcia/Still Pictures; *br* Rex Features; 154 *bl* John Greim/Science Photo Library; 154/155 *b* James King-Holmes/Science Photo Library; 155 *tl* Tek Image/Science Photo Library; *tr* Peter Menzel/Science Photo Library; *br* James King-Holmes/Science Photo Library; 156/157 *t* Photo Library International/Science Photo Library; 158/159 *t* Pekka Parviainen/Science Photo Library; 158 *b* Nigel Cattlin/Holt Studios; 159 *br* Richard Megna/Fundamental/Science Photo Library; 160 *tr* P. Nieto, Jerrican/Science Photo Library; 161 *tr* Klaus Guldbrandsen/Science Photo Library; 162 *br* Patrick Barth/Rex Features; 163 *tr* John Mead/Science Photo Library; *bl* Mills Tandy/Oxford Scientific Films; 164 *tl* James Holmes/Zedcor/Science Photo Library; 165 *tr* David Taylor/Science Photo Library; *br* Sygma; 166 *b* Charles D. Winters/Science Photo Library; 167 *b* Rosenfeld Images Ltd/Science Photo Library; 169 *tl* Rex Features; *tr* Richard Folwell/Science Photo Library; 170 *tl* D. Giry/Sygma; *ml* Clive Freeman, The Royal Institution/Science Photo Library; 171 *tr* NASA/Science Photo Library; *l* Charles D. Winters/Science Photo Library; 172 *tl* Gianni Giansanti/Sygma; 173 *ml* J. P. Delobelle/Still Pictures; *tr* Stephen Dalton/NHPA; 174 *tl* Charles D. Winters/Science Photo Library; 175 *tr* Michael Freeman/Phototake NYC/Robert Harding; *r* Professor Max Perutz, MRC Laboratory of Mollecular Biology/Science Photo Library; 176 *tl* Ullstein Bilderdienst; 177 *bl* Stephen Dalton/NHPA; *br* Philip Moore/Rex Features; 178 *b* Milepost 92½; 179 *b* F. Pitchal/Sygma; 180 *b* David Parker/Science Photo Library; 181 *bl* Bernhard Edmaier/Science Photo Library; 182 *tl* Robert Harding; *tr* R. Bossu/Sygma; 183 *tr* Cornu, Publiphoto Diffusion/Science Photo Library; 184 *b* David Taylor/Science Photo Library; 185 *tr* Martin Bond/Science Photo Library; *b* Holt Studios/Willem Harinck; 186 *tr* Martin Bond/Science Photo Library; 188/189 *b* Holt Studios/Inga Spence; 189 *r* Nigel Cattlin/Holt Studios; 190 *tl* John Walmsley; 191 *tl* James King-Holmes/Science Photo Library; *b* Tony Stone; 194/195 *t* Jon Jones/Sygma: 194 *bl* David Parker/Science Photo Library; *br* Andrew Syred/Science Photo Library; 195 *b* Rover Group; 196/197 *t* Robert Harding; 197 *tr* U.S. Dept. of Energy/Science Photo Library; *bl* David Parker/Science Photo Library; *br* Rex Features; 198 *tr* Sygma; 199 *tr* Rex Features; *br* John Meek; 200 *tr* Alex Bartel/Science Photo Library; 201 *tr* P. Perrin/Sygma; 202 *bl* Klaus Guldbrandsen/Science Photo Library; 202/203 *b* National Railway Museum/Science & Society Picture Library; 204/205 *b* Philippe Plailly/Science Photo Library; 205 *tl* Nils Jorgensen/Rex Features; 207 *tr* Claude Nuridsany & Marie Perennou/Science Photo Library; 208 *bl* Robert Harding; 209 *bl* Bruce Frisch/Science Photo Library; 210 *tl* Alex Bartel/Science Photo Library; *tr* Harry Nor-Hansen/Science Photo Library; *tl* Pekka Parviainen/Science Photo Library; 211 *tr* Robert Harding; *b* Simon Fraser/Science Photo Library; 212 *tr* Fred Dott/Still Pictures; *b* Allen Green/Science Photo Library; 214 *tr* Peter Menzel/Science Photo Library; *l* Titleist; 215 *tr* Eye of Science/Science Photo Library; *br* I. Vanderharst/Robert Harding; 216 *tr* Craig Prentis/Allsport; 217 *tr* Manfred Kage/Science Photo Library; *ml* Science Museum/Science & Society Picture Library; *bl* Rex Features; *bl* Marchon UK Ltd; 218 *tl* Shout/Robert Harding; *tr* Astrid & Hanns-Frieder Michler/Science Photo Library; 219 *tr* Rosenfeld Images Ltd/Science Photo Library; *bl* Mark Edwards/Still Pictures; (219 Alex Bartel/Science Photo Library); 220 *tl* Still Pictures; *tr* A. Woolfitt/Robert Harding; *tl* Robert Harding; 223 *bl* David Drain/Still Pictures; 227 *b* Milepost 92½; 228 *ml* Rosenfeld Images Ltd/Science Photo Library; 230 *tr* Ed Young/Agstock/Science Photo Library; 232 *tl* U.S. Dept. of Energy/Science Photo Library; *tr* Maximilian Stock Ltd/Science Photo Library; 233 *br* Ed Young/Science Photo Library; 234 *l* Corbis; *b* Rosenfeld Images/Science Photo Library; 234/235 *t* Doug Martin/Science Photo Library; 235 *tr* Hartmut Schwarzbach/Still Pictures; *bl* Bernard Sidler/Sygma; *br* Bernard Sidler/Sygma; 236 *bl* Volker Steer, Peter Arnold Inc./Science Photo Library; 236/237 *t* NASA/Science Photo Library; 237 *br* Klaus Guldbrandsen/Science Photo Library; 242 *tl* Bluestone Productions/TCL Stock Directory; *bl* NASA/Science Photo Library; *tr* Bavaria-Bildagentur/Telegraph Colour Library; 243 *tl* V.C.L./Tipp Howell/TCL Stock Directory; *tr* Werner Gartung/Katz Pictures; *mr* Simon Fraser/Science Photo Library; *b* U.S. Dept. of Energy/Science Photo Library; 244 *tl* Pekka Parviainen/Science Photo Library; 244/245 *t* Jack Finch/Science Photo Library; 245 *tr* Fergus O'Brien/Telegraph Colour Library; *mr* John Mead/Science Photo Library; 246 Jeff Jacobson/Katz Pictures; 247 *mr* Dick Luria/Science Photo Library; 248 *bl* Mark Edwards/Still Pictures; *br* PowerStock Photo Library; 249 *tr* David Parker/Science Photo Library; *mr* Simon Fraser/Science Photo Library; *br* Hartmut Schwarzbach/Still Pictures; 251 *tr* David Woodfall/Still Pictures; *br* Dr. Arthur Tucker/Science Photo Library; 252 *tl* 'Dark Landscape in the Black Country' by Constantin Emile Meunier/Museé D'Orsay, Paris/The Bridgeman Art Libary; 253 *mr* Paul Shambroom/Science Photo Library; *br* Dr. Jeremy Burgess/Science Photo Library; 254 *ml* Conmet/Telegraph Colour Library; 255 *tr* Rural History Centre, University of Reading; 256 *bl* Jordi Cami/Environmental Images; 257 *tl* Klein/Hubert/Still Pictures; 258/259 *b* Gerard Soury/Oxford Scientific Films; 259 *mr* J. T. Turner/Telegraph Colour Library; *br* Schuster/Robert Harding; 260 *br* J. T. Turner/Telegraph Colour Library; 261 *br* Jamie Baker/Telegraph Colour Library; 262 *tl* Ralf Schultheiss/Tony Stone; *b* Clint Clemens/International Stock/Robert Harding; 263 *tr* Adam Hart-Davis/Science Photo Library; *mr* John Cocking/TCL Stock Directory; *b* David Nunuk/Science Photo Library; 264 *b* Jerome Wexler/Science Photo Library; 264/265 *b* Belinda Banks/Tony Stone; 265 *mr* Pekka Parviainen/Science Photo Library; *br* The Stock Market; 266 *tr* Tony Hopewell/Telegraph Colour Library; *bl* Martyn F. Chillmaid/Robert Harding; 267 *bl* NASA/Science Photo Library; 268 *tr* Dr. Jeremy Burgess/Science Photo Library; *br* Michael Abbey/Science Photo Library; 269 *tm* CAMR/A. B. Dowsett/Science Photo Library; *mr* Dr. Erwin Mueller/Science Photo Library; *br* Jackie Lewin, EM Unit, Royal Free Hospital/Science Photo Library; 270 *b* Frank Zullo/Science Photo Library; 271 *tr* David Parker/Science Photo Library; *br* Space Telescope Science Institute/NASA/Science Photo Library; *b* David Parker/Science Photo Library; 273 *tr* Dr. Jeremy Burgess/Science Photo Library; *r* Donald Cooper/Photostage; *b* J. Bright/Robert Harding; 274 *ml* Masterfile/Telegraph Colour Library; 275 *tr* Shehzad Nooran/Still Pictures; *bl* GeoScience Features; *br* Vaughan Fleming/Science Photo Library; 276 *l* Anthony Bannister/NHPA; 277 *tl* Cordon Art M.C. Escher's 'Belvedere' © 1999 Cordon Art B.V.-Baarn, Holland; *b* Damien Lovegrove/Science Photo Library; 279 *tr* Patrick Durand/Sygma; *mr* Fuji Photo Fil (UK) Ltd; *b* Yves Forestier/Sygma; 280 *tl* 'The Artist's Dinner Party' by Viggo Johansen/Nationalmuseum, Stockholm/The Bridgeman Art Library/©DACS 2000; *l* Martin Bond/Science Photo Library; 281 *tr* John Cleare/Mountain Camera; *bl* Arnulf Husmo/Tony Stone; *br* Ron and Valerie Taylor/Ardea; 282 *tl* Philippe Plailly/Science Photo Library; *bl* John McGrail/Telegraph Colour Library; *tr* Adam Hart-Davis/Science Photo Library; 283 *r* World View/Bert Blockhuis/Science Photo Library; *b* Julian Baum/Science Photo Library; 284 *bl* Space Frontiers/Telegraph Colour Library; 285 *tl* Tony Craddock/Science Photo Library; *ml* Bildagentur Schuster/Roth/Robert Harding; *bl* Crown Copyright/Health & Safety Laboratory/Science Photo Library; 286 *tr* Philippe Plailly/Science Photo Library; *bl* Bildagentur/Bramaz/Robert Harding; 287 *br* Philippe Plailly/Science Photo Library; *bl* G. Germany/Telegraph Colour Library; 290 *tl* Ferrero-Labat/Ardea; *br* John Massis/Rex Features; 291 *tr* Alan Abramowitz/Tony Stone; 292 *tl* Jerome Prevost/Tony Stone Images; *br* Dr. Gary S. Settles & Stephen S. McIntyre/Science Photo Library; 293 *tr* Rex Features; *br* Paul Van Riel/Robert Harding; *bl* John Meek; 294 *tl* Gray Mortimore/Allsport; *tr* Jean-Paul Ferrero/Ardea; 296 *b* Mark Thompson/Allsport; 297 *t* Shaun Botterill/Allsport U.S.A.; 298 *tl* AKG London/IMS; *l* The Kobal Collection; 298/299 *b* Ken Fisher/Tony Stone; 299 *t* NASA/Science Photo Library; *br* Julian Baum/Science Photo Library; 300 *b* Robert Harding; 301 *b* Stewart Cohen/Tony Stone; 302 *bl* David Madison/Tony Stone; 303 Royer PH./Explorer/Robert Harding; 304/305 *b* Leuchtges-UNEP/Still Pictures; 305 *br* David Parker/Science Photo Library; 306 *tl* Victoria Pearson/Tony Stone; 306/307 *b* Paul Dance/Tony Stone; 307 *tr* Alan Aspinall/Tony Stone; 308 *b* Nick Vedros/Tony Stone; 309 *b* Daikusan/Tony Stone; 310 *tl* Tom Till/Tony Stone; *tr* Oscar Burriel/Science Photo Library; 312 *br* Kevin Schafer/NHPA; 313 *mr* Yves Baulieu, Publiphoto Diffusion/Science Photo Library; 314 *tr* Dr. Jeremy Burgess/Science Photo Library; 316 *ml* Astrid & Hans-Frieder Michler/Science Photo Library; *tr* B&W Louspeakers; *br* Carlos Munoz-Yague/Eurelios/Science Photo Library; 317 *tr* Adam Woolfitt/Robert Harding; *r* Allsport/Vandystadt; 318 *tr* Hulton-Getty; 319 *bl* Wellcome Dept. of Cognitive Neurology/Science Photo Library; 320 Herbie Knott/Rex Features; 321 *tr* Rogan Coles/Redferns; 322 *b* Jed Jacobsohn/Allsport U.S.A.; 323 *tr* Nicholas DeVore/Tony Stone; *r* Tony Stone; 324 *tl* Adam Hart-Davis/Science Photo Library; *bl* Robert Harding; 324/325 *b* Martin Rogers/Tony Stone; 325 *r* Genesis Space Photo Library; 326/327 *t* Jean Becker-Sygma; 328 *tl* Graham Burns/Environmental Images; *bl* Martin Bond/Environmental Images; 329 *r* John Novis/Environmental Images; 330/331 *t* NKK Corporation; 331 *tr* David Hoffman/Environmental Images; *r* Martin Bond/Science Photo Library; *br* Martin Bond/Science Photo Library; 334/335 *t* Dr. Gary Settles/Science Photo Library; 335 *r* Tony Craddock/Science Photo Library; *b* Keith Kent/Science Photo Library; 338/339 *b* Martin Bond/Science Photo Library; 339 *r* Science Museum/Science & Society Picture Library; 345 *tr* Robert Harding; 347 *tr* Volker Steger/Sandia National Laboratory/Science Photo Library; *bl* Hornby Hobbies Ltd; 348/349 *t* Mark Edwards/Still Pictures; 348 *b* Collections/Nick Oakes; 350/351 *b* Pat & Tome Leeson/Science Photo Library; 351 *b* Massimo Lupidi/Still Pictures; 353 *br* Mark Edwards/Still Pictures; 355 *br* Catherine Poedras/Science Photo Library; 356 *b* Simon Fraser/Northumbria Circuits/Science Photo Library; 357 *tl* Comsat/Science Photo Library; 358/359 *b* Keith Kent/Science Photo Library; 359 *t* Tony Larkin/Rex Features; 360 *bl* Robert Harding; 360/361 *b* David Parker/IMI/University of Birmingham High TC Consortium/Science Photo Library; 362 *tr* U.S. Dept. of Energy/Science Photo Library; *b* Science Photo Library; 364 *bl* John Walmsley; 365 *tl* Science Museum/Science & Society Picture Library; 366 *tr* Conor Caffrey/Science Photo Library; 367 *r* Julian Holland; *br* Julian Holland; 369 *br* Damien Lovegrove/Science Photo Library; 370 *tl* Illustrated London News; 371 *tr* Digital Studio; 371 *mr* Jeremy Young/Rex Features; *br* J.L.Atlan/Sygma; 374 *tr* Charles Falco/Science Photo Library; 375 *tr* Peter Menzel/Science Photo Library; 376 *tl* Los Alamos National Laboratory/Science Photo Library; *tr* Science Museum/Science & Society Picture Library; 377 *tr* Rex Features; *mr* Psion; 378 *tr* The Ronald Grant Archive; *b* CorelDraw; 379 *tr* Kingfisher; *bl* James King-Holmes/W Industries/Science Photo Library; 380 *tr* Hulton Getty Picture Library; 381 *tr* NCSA, University of Illinois/Science Photo Library; *bl* Weiss, Jerrican/Science Photo Library; *br* Hartmut Schwarzbach/Still Pictures; 382 *tl* Jason Bell/Katz Pictures; 382/383 *b* Volker Steger, Peter Arnold Inc./Science Photo Library; 383 *mr* Jon Jones/Sygma; *br* Yves Forestier/Sygma; 386 *tr* X-ray Astronomy Group, Leicester University/Science Photo Library; 387 *mr* Space Telescope Science Institute/NASA/Science Photo Library; *br* Hale Observatories/Science Photo Library; 388 *bl* Royal Observatory, Edinburgh/Science Photo Library; 391 *mr* Space Telescope Science Institute/NASA/Science Photo Library; 392 *tr* Celestial Image Co./Science Photo Library; *ml* Royal Observatory, Edinburgh/AATB/Science Photo Library; 396 *b* David Nunuk/Science Photo Library; 398 Victor Habbick Visions/Science Photo Library; 399 *mr* NASA/Science Photo Library; *br* NASA/Science Photo Library; 401 *bl* Sipa-Press/Rex Features; *br* C. Simonpietri/Sygma; 402 *tl* Jason Ware/Science Photo Library; *m* David Nunuk/Science Photo Library; 404 *tr* David P. Anderson, SMU/NASA/Science Photo Library; 405 *b* NASA/Science Photo Library; 406 *tr* NASA/Science Photo Library; 408 *tr* Chris Butler/Science Photo Library; 411 *mr* NASA/Science Photo Library; 412 *m* Detlev Van Ravenswaay/Science Photo Library; 413 *b* David Parker/Science Photo Library; 414 *tr* John Bova/Science Photo Library; 415 *tl* Rev. Ronald Royer/Science Photo Library; *mt* Dr. William Hsin-Min Ku/Science Photo Library; *tr* K. Krisciunas, Royal Observatory, Edinburgh/Science Photo Library; *b* Space Telescope Science Institute/NASA/Science Photo Library; 416 *bl* Richard J. Wainscoat/Still Pictures; 417 *br* Space Telescope Science Institute/NASA/Science Photo Library; 419 *tl* European Space Agency/Science Photo Library; *br* Science Photo Library; 420 *tr* European Space Agency/Science Photo Library; 421 *tr* David Baker; 422 *tl* Novosti/Science Photo Library; *ml* Novosti/Science Photo Library; *b* NASA/Science Photo Library; 423 *t* John Frassanito, NASA/Science Photo Library; *mr* NASA/Science Photo Library; 424 *br* Michael Klinec/Environmental Images; 425 *b* Ken M. Johns/Science Photo Library; 426 *ml* Collections/Bill Wells; 427 *mr* Space Telescope Science Institute/NASA/Science Photo Library; *br* Christian Moullec/Rex Features; 428/429 *t* Mark Thompson/Allsport; 429 *br* Alexander Tsiaras/Science Photo Library; 431 *mr* The Ronald Grant Archive; 434/5 *t* C. Weaver/Ardea; 435 *br* William Ervin/Science Photo Library; 436 *tl* Romano Cagnoni/Still Pictures; *ml* Robert Harding; *br* Irene Lengui/Holt Studios; 437 *tr* Andy Burridge/Holt Studios; *r* Steve Morgan/Environmental Images; *br* K. McCullough-Christian Aid/Still Pictures; 438 *bl* Kevin Schafer/NHPA; 439 *tr* Martin Wendler/NHPA; *br* Jean-Paul Ferrero/Ardea; 440 *tl* John Hyde/Environmental Images; *tr* Jimmy Homes/Environmental Images; 441 *r* Sue Wells/ICCE; *br* Steve Morgan/Environmental Images; 442 *tr* Tim Davis/Science Photo Library; 443 *b* Andy Purcell/ICCE; *br* Mark de Fraeye/Science Photo Library; 444 *tl* T. Kitchin & V. Hurst/NHPA; *l* John Daniels/Ardea; *bl* Bobby Smith/Ardea; *b* GeoScience Features; 445 *br* Paul Glendell/Environmental Images; *bl* Mike Harrison/ICCE; 446 *tl* Hulton Getty; 447 *tl* Hartmut Schwarzbach/Still Pictures; *tr* Sally & Richard Greenhill; *br* Richard Smith/Sygma; *b* The Times/Rex Features; *l* David J. Cross/Still Pictures; *tr* Pete Addis/Environmental Images; *tr* Stephen Whitehorne/Environmental Images; 449 *tr* Jim Gipe/Agstock/Science Photo Library; *mr* Paul Harrison/Still Pictures; *br* Jimmy Holmes/Environmental Images; 450 *tr* Tim Lester/Science Photo Library; *l* A. Groom/ICCE; *b* Peter Menzel/Science Photo Library; 451 *t* Stuart Franklin/Magnum; *tr* GeoScience Features; *mr* Sustrans; *b* Ian Beanes/Ardea; 452 *l* Mark Edwards/Still Pictures; 453 *bl* F. Pitchal/Sygma; *tr* Joe Pasieka/Science Photo Library; 454 *l* Steve Morgan/Environmental Images; 455 *r* Mark Edwards/Still Pictures; *br* Hank Morgan/Science Photo Library; *b* James Holmes, Coopers Metals/Science Photo Library; 456 *tr* Patrick Bertrand/Still Pictures; 458 *tl* Poerterfield Chickering/Science Photo Library; *tr* Jack Fields/Science Photo Library; *ml* Paul Harrison/Still Pictures; 459 *tl* Serge Viallet/Sygma; *tr* David Parker/Science Photo Library; 460 *tr* Mark Edwards/Still Pictures; *tl* Porcher/Bijeon/Sipa Press; 461 *tl* David Woodfall/NHPA; *ml* D. Fineman/Sygma; *b* Martin Harvey/NHPA; 462 *tr* Lorette Dorreboom/Environmental Images; *tl* William Ervin/Science Photo Library; *ml* Rob Hadley/Environmental Images; *b* Herbert Girardet/Environmental Images; 463 *tr* John Isaac/Still Pictures; *mr* Trevor Perry/Environmental Images; *br* Kevin Schafer/Still Pictures; *b* Mark Edwards/Still Pictures

Additional artwork: Jonathan Adams, Marianne Appleton, N. Ardley, Mike Atkinson, Graham Austen, Craig Austin, Richard Berridge, Louise Bolton, Simone Boni, Richard Bonson, Peter Bull, Julian Burgess, Robin Carter, Jim Channell, Kuo Kang Chen, Jeanne Colville, Tom Connell, Richard Coombes, Sandra Doyle, Richard Draper, David Eddington, Brin Edwards, David Etchell, Jeff Farrow, D. Fletcher, Eugene Fleury, Chris Forsey, Mark Franklin, Garden Studio, Sally Goodman, Jeremy Gower, Ray Grinaway, Terence Gubby, Terry Hadler, Alan Hancocks, A. Hardcastle, Hardlines, Ron Hayward, G. Hinks, Karen Hiscock, Christa Hooke, Lisa Horstman, Ian Howatson, Industrial Artists, Ian Jackson, Bridgette James, John James, E. Jenner, Ron Jobson, Kevin Jones, Felicity Kayes, Roger Kent, Elly and Christopher King, Terence Lambert, Adrian Lascom, Steve Latibeaudiere, Ruth Lindsay, Rachel Lockwood, Bernard Long, Mike Long, Chris Lyon, Kevin Madison, Mainline Design – Guy Smith, Alan Male, Maltings Partnership, Janos Marffy, Shane Marsh, Josephine Martin, Eve Melavish, Simon Mendez, Carol Merryman, Ian Moores, Patrick Murey, William Oliver, R. Payne, Bruce Pearson, David Phipps, Jonathan Potter, Malcolm Porter, Sebastian Quigley, E. Rice, Paul Richardson, John Ridyard, Steve Roberts, B. Robinson, Eric Robson, Mike Rolfe, David Russell, Valerie Sangster, Mike Saunders, Nick Shewning, Chris Shields, Mike Stacey, Roger Stewart, Lucy Su, Mike Taylor, Simon Teg, George Thompson, Ian Thompson, Linda Thursby, Guy Troughton, Simon Turvey, T.K. Uayte, Ross Watton, Phil Wear, Paul Weare, David Webb, Steve Weston, Graham White, Peter Wilkinson, Ann Winterbotham, John Woodcock, David Wright.